The Legal Writing Handbook

The Legal Writing Handbook

Research, Analysis, and Writing

Laurel Currie Oates

Director, Legal Writing Program
University of Puget Sound School of Law

Anne Enquist

Writing Advisor,
University of Puget Sound School of Law

Kelly Kunsch

Reference Librarian,
University of Puget Sound School of Law

Little, Brown and Company
Boston   Toronto   London

Library of Congress Catalog Card No. 92-73824

ISBN 0-316-62194-3

Third Printing

MV-NY

Published simultaneously in Canada
by Little, Brown & Company (Canada) Limited

Printed in the United States of America

To my parents, Bill and Lucille Currie,
my husband, Terry, and my children, Julia and Michael.
Thank you.

To my family, Steve, Matt, and Jeff Enquist,
and my parents, Arthur and Agnes Meiering,
for their love, support, and patience.

To my parents, blame them.
— K^2

Summary of Contents

Part IV

A Guide to Citation   *481*

Part V

A Guide to Effective Writing   *505*

Part VI

A Guide to Correct Writing   *709*

Contents

Part I

A Foundation for Legal Writing   *1*

Chapter 1

An Overview of the United States Legal System   *3*

| | Part II | | |

The Legal Writing Process   *87*

| Chapter 5 | | |

The Objective Memorandum   *89*

Chapter 6

The Opinion Letter   *251*

Chapter 7

Trial and Appellate Briefs   *263*

Chapter 8

Oral Advocacy   *355*

Chapter 15

Computer-Assisted Legal Research   *447*

Chapter 16

How to Approach a Legal Research Problem: Sample Research Plans   *469*

Part IV

A Guide to Citation   **481**

Chapter 17

Legal Citation   **483**

Part V

A Guide to Effective Writing   **505**

Chapter 18

Effective Writing — The Whole Paper   **507**

Chapter 19

Connections Between Paragraphs   *527*

Chapter 20

Effective Paragraphs   *535*

Chapter 21

Connections Between Sentences   *567*

Chapter 22

Effective Sentences   *591*

Chapter 23		

Effective Words 629

Chapter 26

Punctuation 773

Chapter 27

Mechanics 843

Preface

Legal writing is both simple and complex. On the one hand, it is simply a matter of organizing information into well-established formats and following well-established patterns of analysis. It is being methodical about research and correct about citation, grammar, and punctuation when the document is written. That much is a big job, but a fairly simple job.

On the other hand, legal writing is complex. Part of the complexity is keeping all those simple tasks organized. Beyond that, however, legal writing is complex because it requires creativity, insight, and judgment.

Within the parameters of accepted formats and types of argumentation, for example, legal writers must create an organization where one did not previously exist and create arguments that have not been made before.

But that is not all. In addition, legal writers must have the insight and ability to cut to the heart of a matter. They must be able to see what is really at stake in a case; they must be able to look at the big picture and know where to focus their and their reader's attention.

And that is still not all. At all times, legal writers must exercise judgment: They must know what matters most and what matters least, what is effective, what is persuasive, what is extraneous, and what is just plain irrelevant.

This book, then, is about both the simple skills of legal writing and the complex art of legal writing. For the law student or the practicing lawyer, it brings together the three major components of legal writing — research, writing, and analysis — and discusses each from the most basic level to the more advanced, sophisticated levels.

Part I of the *Handbook* provides background information about the United States legal system and introduces legal analysis and argumentation. Part II uses a step-by-step approach to take the reader through the process of writing an objective office memorandum, an opinion letter, and a trial and an appellate brief. Throughout the process, it shows the integration of research, writing, and analysis.

Most important, all of this is done in context. That is, the points about research, analysis, and writing are presented within the structure of realistic cases. Further, each point is illustrated and reinforced by numerous examples from memoranda and briefs.

Parts III, IV, V, and VI are all resource materials. Parts III and IV provide more in-depth information about research and citation; Parts V and VI provide more in-depth information about writing. Parts III, V, and VI also include references to *The Practice Book for the Legal Writing Handbook.*

In short, *The Legal Writing Handbook* is three books in one: It is a complete book about research, a complete book about analysis, and a complete book about writing. Thus, just about everything a law student needs to know about legal writing is here, in one book.

Laurel Currie Oates
Anne Enquist
Kelly Kunsch

January 1993

Acknowledgments

This book has truly been a collaborative effort. It is the result of the work of many colleagues and students, all of whom deserve recognition.

First among those whom we wish to thank is Barbara Barker. Barbara wrote Chapter 17 and helped edit many other chapters, particularly in the book's early stages. Mary Beth Harney was also critical to the book's development in the early stages. She helped conceptualize the book and allowed us to use many examples of her own writing.

We are also indebted to our friend and colleague, Marilyn Berger, who introduced us to the people at Little, Brown and encouraged us to persevere. Former Dean Fred Tausend was also a significant supporter of this project in its early years. Thanks to him and our current dean, Jim Bond, we had the institutional support and their personal encouragement, both of which were necessary to complete this project.

We have been fortunate throughout this process to have had the critiques and counsel of numerous colleagues who have taught legal writing. A heartfelt thank you to Deborah Dowd, Margaret Morgan, Jill Ramsfield, Chris Rideout, Barry Shanks, Michael Charneski, Crystal Crawford, Bill Tuthill, John Nivala, Julie Monfils, Martha Schaeffer, Janet Dickson, Steve Bernheim, Nancy Bradburn-Johnson, Linda Dyckman, Irene Scharf, Tim Bakken, Jeff Ramsdell, David Walter, Marc Lampson, Nancy Soonpaa, Susan McClellan, Ed Raftis, Jennie Zavatsky, Bob Chang, and Jessie Grearson.

In addition, we have also benefited from the knowledge and advice of many other faculty members at the University of Puget Sound Law School: Janet Ainsworth, David Boerner, Melinda Branscomb, Annette Clark, Sid DeLong, John Mitchell, Mark Reutlinger, John Strait, and John Weaver. One other faculty member who deserves a special note of appreciation is our friend and favorite collaborator, Paula Lustbader.

Perhaps the most important collaborators in this project have been our students. Their writing appears throughout the book, and they were our first readers. So many made recommendations and allowed us to use their writing that we cannot mention them all, but we want them to know how much we appreciate their part in what we think of as "their book."

Some students made substantial contributions and deserve special recognition. Thank you to Susan McClellan, Annette Clark, Luanne Coachman, Mary Lobdell, Eileen Peterson, Lance Palmer, Edwina Martin-Arnold, Vonda Sargent, Melissa May, Kevin Dougherty, Cindy Burdue, Amy Blume, and Chris Fredrikson.

Finally, and undoubtedly most important, is our secretary, Lori Lamb. Besides her hard work and patience, we want to acknowledge her special contribution to this book: She kept us sane when we were going insane.

The Legal Writing Handbook

Part I

A Foundation for Legal Writing

All knowledge builds on prior knowledge. The ability to under-stand concept B depends on prior knowledge of concept A; the ability to understand concept C depends on prior knowledge of both A and B.

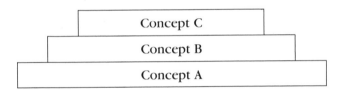

This is particularly true in legal writing. Before you[1] can do legal research, you must know what resources are available and the weight given to each; before you can write, you must possess not only basic writing skills but also an understanding of your audience, your purpose, and the conventional formats.

---

1. Throughout this book, the authors have deliberately used a somewhat more informal writing style than that which is recommended for legal writing itself. Writing a textbook, like writing anything else, is governed by who the reader is, what the writing's purpose is, what the conventions are for that type of writing, and what relationship the writer wants to have with the reader. Thus, a slightly more informal style seemed appropriate for this textbook. Notice, for example, that the authors use both first and second person, some contractions, some colloquial phraseology, and more dashes than they recommend for legal writing.

The primary danger in using a more informal style is that students may con-sciously or unconsciously emulate the authors' style in their legal writing. As a pre-caution against this possibility, the authors suggest that students read section 27.5 before beginning to write a legal memorandum or brief and, as always, consider the audience, purpose, and conventions of the type of writing they are doing.

Underlying this knowledge, though, must be an understanding of the system in which you are operating. You must understand the United States system of government and, within that larger system, the United States system of law. In addition, you must begin developing the ability to think like a lawyer. The four chapters in Part I lay the foundation for legal writing.

Chapter 4
An Introduction
to Analyzing
Statutes and Cases

Chapter 3
An Introduction to
Legal Analysis

Chapter 2
An Introduction to Common
and Enacted Law

Chapter 1
An Overview of the United States
Legal System

An Overview of the United States Legal System

The United States system of government. For some, it is the secret to democracy, the power to elect one's leaders and the right to speak freely. For others, it is a horrendous bureaucracy, a maze through which one must struggle to obtain a benefit, to change a law, or to get a day in court. For still others, it is more abstract, a chart in a ninth-grade civics book describing the three branches of government and explaining the system of checks and balances.

For lawyers, the United States system of government is all of these things and more. It is the foundation for their knowledge of the law, the stage on which they play out their professional roles, the arena for the very serious game of law.

No matter which metaphor you prefer — foundation, stage, arena — the point is the same. To be successful as a law student and a lawyer, you must understand the system. You must know the framework before you can work well within it.

Like most complex systems, the United States system of government can be analyzed in a number of different ways. You can focus on its three branches — the executive branch, the legislative branch, and the judicial branch — or you can focus on its two parts, the federal government and the state governments. See Exhibit 1.1.

In this chapter, we do both. We look first at the three branches, examining both their individual functions and their interrelationships. We then examine the relationship between state and federal government, again with an eye toward their individual functions and powers.

EXHIBIT 1.1	Two Perspectives on the United States System of Government

The Three Branches of Government	The Relationship Between Federal and State Governments
Executive branch Legislative branch Judicial branch	State governments Federal government

§1.1 THE THREE BRANCHES OF GOVERNMENT

Just as the medical student must understand both the various organs that make up the human body and their relationship to each other, the law student must understand both the three branches of government and the relationships among them.

§1.1.1 The Executive Branch

The first of the three branches is the executive branch. In the federal system, the executive power is vested in the President; in the states, it is vested in the governor. (See Article II, Section 1 of the United States Constitution and the constitutions of the various states.) In general, the executive branch has the power to implement and enforce laws. It oversees public projects, administers public benefit programs, and controls law enforcement agencies.

The executive branch also has powers that directly affect our system of law. For example, the President or a governor can control the lawmaking function of the legislative branch by exercising his or her power to convene and adjourn the Congress or by vetoing legislation. Similarly, the President or a governor can shape the decisions of the courts through his or her judicial nominations or by directing the attorney general to enforce or not to enforce certain laws.

§1.1.2 The Legislative Branch

The second branch is the legislative branch. Congress's powers are enumerated in Article I, Section 8, of the United States Constitution, which gives Congress, among other things, the power to lay and collect taxes, borrow money, regulate commerce with foreign nations and among the states, establish uniform naturalization and bankruptcy laws, promote the progress of science and the useful arts by creating copyright laws, and punish counterfeiting. Powers not granted Congress are given to the states or left to the people. (See the Tenth Amendment to the United States Constitution.) The state constitutions enumerate the powers given to the state legislatures.

Like the executive branch, the legislative branch exercises power over the other two branches. It can check the actions of the executive by enacting or refusing to enact legislation requested by the executive, by controlling the budget and, at least at the federal level, by consenting or refusing to consent to nominations made by the executive.

The legislative branch's power over the judicial branch is less obvious. At one level, it can control the judiciary through its power to establish courts (Article I, Section 8, grants Congress the power to establish inferior federal courts) and its power to consent to or reject the executive branch's judicial nominations. However, the most obvious control it has over the judiciary is its power to enact legislation that supersedes a common law or court-made doctrine or rule.

Note

The legislative branch also shares its lawmaking power with the executive branch. In enacting legislation, it sometimes gives the executive branch the power to promulgate the regulations needed to implement or enforce the legislation. For example, although Congress (the legislative branch) enacted the Internal Revenue Code, the Internal Revenue Service (part of the executive branch) promulgates the regulations needed to implement that code.

§1.1.3   The Judicial Branch

The third branch is the judicial branch. Article III, Section 1, of the United States Constitution vests the judicial power of the United States in one supreme court and in such inferior courts as Congress may establish. The state constitutions establish and grant power to the state courts.

a.   The Hierarchical Nature of the Court System

Both the federal and the state court systems are hierarchical. At the lowest level are the trial courts, which have fact-finding as their primary function. The judge or jury hears the evidence and enters a judgment.

At the next level are the intermediate courts of appeal. These courts hear the majority of appeals, deciding (1) whether the trial court applied the right law and (2) whether there is sufficient evidence to support the jury's verdict or the trial judge's findings of fact and conclusions of law. Unlike the trial courts, these courts do not conduct trials. There are no witnesses, and the only exhibits are the exhibits that were admitted during trial. The decisions of the appellate courts are based solely on the written record and the attorneys' arguments.

At the top level are the state supreme courts[1] and the Supreme Court of the United States. The primary function of these courts is to make law. They hear only those cases that involve issues of great public import or cases in which different divisions or circuits have adopted or applied conflicting rules of law. Like the intermediate courts of appeals, these courts do not hear evidence; they only review the trial court record. See Exhibit 1.2.

An example illustrates the role each court plays. In *State v. Patterson* (see Chapter 7), the defendant was charged with first-degree assault. At the trial court level, both the state and the defendant presented witnesses and physical evidence. On the basis of this evidence, the trial court decided the case on its merits, the trial judge deciding the issues of law (whether the eyewitness identifications should be suppressed), and the jury deciding the questions of fact (whether the state had proved all of the elements of assault beyond a reasonable doubt).

Both issues were decided against the defendant: The trial court judge ruled that the identification evidence was admissible, and the jury found that the state had met its burden of proof. Disagreeing with both determinations, the defendant filed an appeal with the intermediate court of appeals.

In deciding this appeal, the appellate court could consider only two issues: whether the trial court judge erred when he denied the defendant's motion to suppress the identification testimony and whether there was sufficient evidence to support the jury's verdict.

Because the first issue raised a question of law, the appellate court could review the issue *de novo.* It did not need to defer to the judgment of the trial court judge; instead, it could exercise its own independent judgment to decide the issue on its merits.

The appellate court had much less latitude with respect to the second issue. Because the second issue raised a question of fact and not law, the appellate court could not substitute its judgment for that of the jury. It could only review the jury's findings to make sure that they were supported by the evidence. When the question is one of fact, the appellate court can decide only (1) whether there is sufficient evidence to support the jury's verdict or (2) whether the jury's verdict is clearly erroneous — not whether it would have reached the same conclusion.

---

1. New York is a notable exception. In New York, the trial courts are called "supreme courts," the intermediate court of appeals is the "supreme court, appellate division," and the supreme, or highest, court is the "court of appeals."

EXHIBIT 1.2	The Roles of the Supreme, Intermediate, and Trial Courts

Supreme, or Highest, Court

- Like the intermediate court of appeals, it reviews the written record and exhibits from the trial court.
- Like the intermediate court of appeals, it has broad powers to review questions of law: It determines whether the trial court and intermediate court of appeals applied the right law correctly. Its power to review factual issues is, however, very limited. Like the intermediate court of appeals, it can determine only whether there is sufficient evidence to support the decision of the jury or, if there was no jury, the decision of the trial court judge.

Intermediate Court of Appeals

- The intermediate court of appeals reviews the written record and exhibits from the trial court.
- When an issue raises a question of law, the intermediate court of appeals may substitute its judgment for the judgment of the trial court judge; when an issue raises a question of fact, the appellate court must defer to the decision of the finder of fact (the jury or, if there was no jury, the trial judge).

Trial Court

- The trial court hears witnesses and views evidence.
- The trial court judge decides issues of law; the jury decides questions of fact. (When there is no jury, the trial court judge decides both the questions of law and the questions of fact.)

Regardless of the type of issue (law or fact), the appellate court must base its decision on the written trial court record and exhibits and the attorneys' arguments. Consequently, in *Patterson,* the intermediate court of appeals did not see or hear any of the witnesses. The only people present at the appeal were the judges and the attorneys. Not even the defendant, Patterson, was present.

If Patterson lost his first appeal, he could petition the state supreme court (through a writ of certiorari), asking it to hear his case. If the state supreme court granted the petition, its review, like that of the intermediate court of appeals, would be limited. Although the supreme court would review the issue of law *de novo,* it would have to defer to the jury on the question of fact.

Most of the cases that you will read in law school are appellate court decisions, decisions of the state or federal intermediate court of appeals or supreme court. These cases, however, represent only a small, and perhaps not representative, percentage of the disputes that lawyers see during the course of the year. See Exhibit 1.3.

Thus, as you read the cases in your casebooks, remember that you are seeing only the proverbial tip of the iceberg. For a case to reach the Supreme Court, the parties must have had the financial means to pursue it, and the Court must have found that the issue raised was significant enough to grant review.

b. The Federal Courts

In the federal system, most cases are heard initially in the federal district courts, the primary trial court in that system. These courts have original jurisdiction over most federal questions and have the power to review the decisions of some administrative agencies. Each state has at least one district court, and many have several. For example, Indiana has the District Court for Northern Indiana and the District Court for Southern Indiana. Cases that are not heard in the district court are usually heard in one of several specialized courts: the United States Tax Court, the United States Court of Claims, or the United States Court of International Trade.

EXHIBIT 1.3   Numbers of Cases That Move Through the Court System

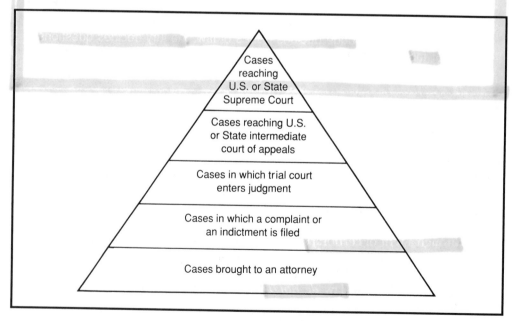

Cases reaching U.S. or State Supreme Court

Cases reaching U.S. or State intermediate court of appeals

Cases in which trial court enters judgment

Cases in which a complaint or an indictment is filed

Cases brought to an attorney

| EXHIBIT 1.4 | The Thirteen Federal Judicial Circuits* |

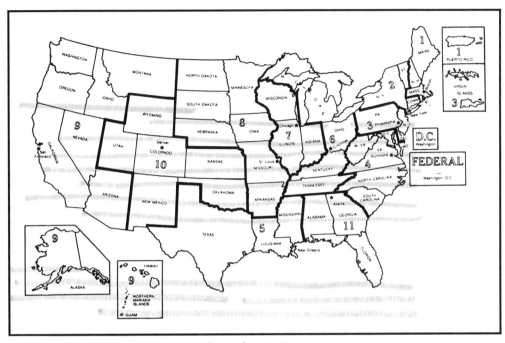

*Reprinted from *Federal Reporter* (West's National Reporter System) with permission of West Publishing Company.

| EXHIBIT 1.5 | The Roles of the U.S. Supreme Court |

United States Supreme Court

Role 1	Role 2
Highest court in the federal court system	Final arbiter of the United States Constitution
Reviews decisions of the United States Court of Appeals and other federal courts	Mediates disputes between the federal government and the states and various state governments; interprets the United States Constitution

The intermediate court of appeals is the United States Court of Appeals. There are currently thirteen circuits: eleven numbered circuits, the District of Columbia Circuit, and the Federal Circuit. (See Exhibit 1.4.) The Federal Circuit, which was created in 1982, reviews the decisions of the United States Claims Court and the United States Court of International Trade, as well as some district court and administrative decisions.

The highest federal court is the United States Supreme Court. Although many people believe that the Supreme Court is all-powerful, in fact it is not. As with other courts, there are limits on the Supreme Court's powers. It can play only one of two roles.

In its first role, the Supreme Court plays a role similar to that of the state supreme courts. In the federal system, it is the highest court, the court of last resort. In contrast, in its second role, it is the final arbiter of federal constitutional law, interpreting the United States Constitution and determining whether the federal government or a state has violated rights granted under the United States Constitution. See Exhibit 1.5.

Thus, although people often assert that they will take their case all the way to the Supreme Court, they may not be able to. The Supreme Court can hear the case only if it involves a question of federal constitutional law or a federal statute. The Supreme Court does not have the power to hear cases involving only questions of state law. For example, although the United States Supreme Court has the power to determine whether a state's marriage dissolution statutes are constitutional, it does not have the power to hear purely factual questions, such as whether it

---

EXHIBIT 1.6   The Federal Court System

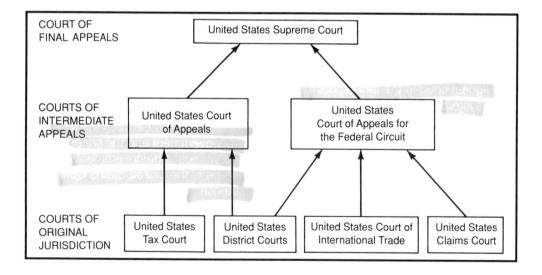

would be in the best interests of a child for custody to be granted to the father or whether child support should be set at $300.00 rather than $400.00 per month.

Each year the United States Supreme Court receives more than 5,000 requests for review (writs of certiorari). Of the approximately 160 cases that it actually hears, about two thirds are appeals from the United States Court of Appeals and one third are from the state courts.

Exhibit 1.6 illustrates the relationships among the various federal courts.

Note

Because the United States District Court and Court of Appeals hear so many cases, not all of their decisions are published. When they are published, district court opinions are published in either the *Federal Supplement* or *Federal Rules Decisions,* and current Court of Appeals decisions are published in *Federal Reporter, Second Series.* (Decisions from the specialized courts are published in specialized reporters.)

All United States Supreme Court decisions are published. The official reporter is *United States Reports,* and the two unofficial reporters are *West's Supreme Court Reporter* and *United States Supreme Court Reports, Lawyer's Edition* (see Chapter 12).

c.   State Courts

A number of courts operate within the states. At the lowest level are courts of limited jurisdiction. These courts can hear only certain types of cases or cases involving only limited amounts of money. Municipal or city courts are courts of limited jurisdiction, as are county or district courts and small claims courts.

At the next level are courts of general jurisdiction. These courts have the power to review the decisions of courts of limited jurisdiction and original jurisdiction over claims arising under state law, whether it be under the state constitution, state statutes, or state common law.

About half of the states now have an intermediate court of appeals. These courts hear appeals as of right from the state courts of general jurisdiction, and the bulk of their caseload is criminal appeals. Because of the size of their workload, many of these courts have several divisions or districts.

Every state has a state supreme court. These courts review the decisions of the state trial courts and courts of appeals and are the final arbiters of questions of state constitutional, statutory, and common law.

Decisions of state trial courts are not usually published. In addition, because of the volume, not all decisions of intermediate state courts of appeals are published. Those that are, and all decisions of the state su-

EXHIBIT 1.7   **The State Court System**

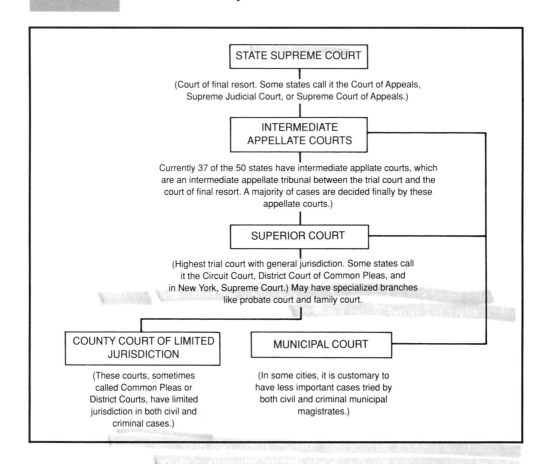

preme court, appear in one of West Publishing Company's regional reporters and the state's official reporter, if one exists.

Exhibit 1.7 illustrates the typical relationship among the various state courts.

d. Other Courts

There are also several other court systems. As sovereign entities, many native American tribes have their own judicial systems, as does the United States military.

§1.2   The Relationship Between the Federal and State Governments

It is not enough, however, to look at our system of government from only the perspective of its three branches. To understand the system, you must also understand the relationship between the federal and state governments.

§1.2.1   A Short History

Like most things, our system of government is the product of our history. From the early 1600s until 1781, the "United States" were not united. Instead, the "country" was composed of independent colonies, all operating under different charters and each having its own laws and legal system. Although the colonies traded with each other, the relationship among the colonies was no closer than the relationship among the European countries prior to 1992. It was not until the Articles of Confederation were adopted in 1781 that the "states" ceded any of their rights to a federal government.

Even though the states ceded more rights when the Constitution became effective in 1789, they preserved most of their own law. Each state retained its own executive, its own legislature and laws, and its own court system.

Thus, our system of government is really two systems, a federal system and the fifty state systems, with the United States Constitution brokering the relationship between the two. See Exhibit 1.8.

§1.2.2   The Relationship Between Laws Enacted by Congress and Those Enacted by the State Legislatures

As citizens of the United States, we are subject to two sets of laws: federal law and the law of the state in which we are citizens (or in which we act). Most of the time, there is no conflict between these two sets of laws: Federal law governs some conduct; state law, other conduct. For example, federal law governs bankruptcy proceedings, and state law governs divorce.

Occasionally, however, both Congress and a state legislature enact laws governing the same conduct. Sometimes these laws coexist. For example, both Congress and the states have enacted drug laws. Acting under the powers granted to it under the Commerce Clause, Congress has made it illegal to import controlled substances or to transport them across state lines; the states, acting consistently with the powers reserved to them, have made the possession or sale of controlled substances within the state illegal. In such instances, citizens are subject to both laws. A defendant can be charged under federal law with transporting a drug across state lines and under state law with possession.

There are times, however, when federal and state law do not complement each other and cannot coexist. An act can be legal under fed-

EXHIBIT 1.8 **The Relationship Between the Federal and State Systems**

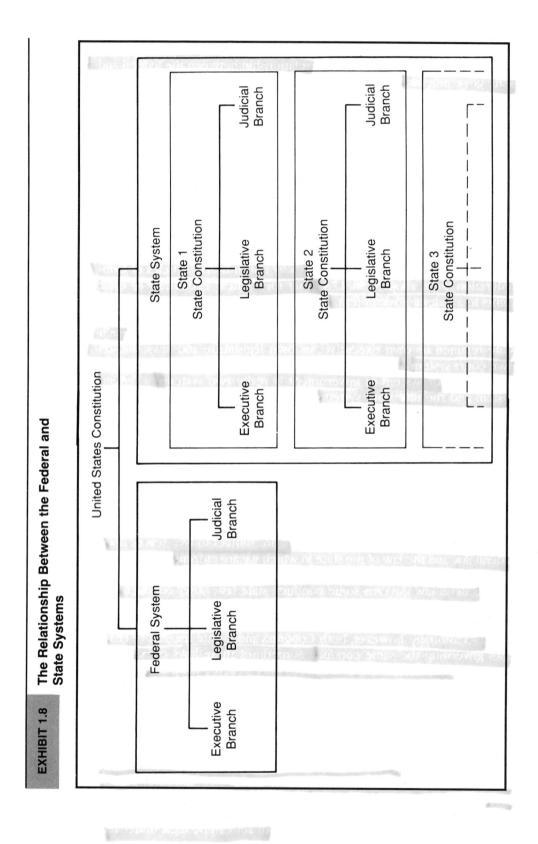

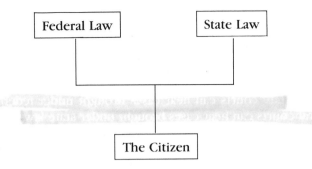

eral law but illegal under state law. In such instances, federal law supersedes state law, provided that the federal law is constitutional. As provided in the Supremacy Clause (Article VI, Clause 2), laws enacted by Congress under the powers granted to it under the Constitution are the "supreme Law of the Land; and the Judges in every State shall be bound thereby. . . ."

The answer is different when the conflicting laws are from different states. Although there are more and more uniform laws (the Uniform Child Custody Act, the Uniform Commercial Code), an activity that is legal in one state may be illegal in another state. For instance, although prostitution is legal in Nevada as a local option, it is illegal in other states.

Application 1.1

1. A federal statute makes it illegal to emit more than 15 parts per 10,000 of particulate X into the air. A state statute makes it illegal to emit more than 5 parts per 10,000 of particulate Y into the air. Which statute or statutes govern?

2. A federal statute makes it illegal to emit more than 15 parts per 10,000 of particulate X into the air. A state statute makes it illegal to emit more than 25 parts per 10,000 of particulate X. Which statute or statutes govern?

3. A federal statute makes it illegal to emit more than 15 parts per 10,000 of particulate X into the air. A state statute makes it illegal to emit more than 5 parts per 10,000. Which statute or statutes govern?

4. States A and B border each other. Although there is no federal law or law in State B making the emission of particulate X illegal, in State A it is illegal to emit more than 5 parts per 10,000. If the factory is in State A, is the emission of 10 parts per 10,000 of particulate X illegal? Is the result the same if the factory is in State B?

§1.2.3   The Relationship Between Federal and State Courts

The relationship between the federal and state court systems is complex. Although each system is autonomous, in certain circumstances the state courts can hear cases brought under federal law and the federal courts can hear cases brought under state law.

For example, although the majority of cases heard in state courts are brought under state law, state courts also have jurisdiction when a case is brought under a provision of the United States Constitution, a treaty, and certain federal statutes. Similarly, although the majority of cases heard in the federal courts involve questions of federal law, the federal courts have jurisdiction over cases involving questions of state law when the parties are from different states (diversity jurisdiction).

The appellate jurisdiction of the courts is somewhat simpler. In the state system, a state's supreme, or highest, court is usually the court of last resort. The United States Supreme Court can review a state court decision only when the case involves a federal question and when there has been a final decision by the state's supreme, or highest, court. If a state has an intermediate court of appeals, that court has the power to review the decisions of the lower courts within its geographic jurisdiction.

In the federal system, the United States Supreme Court is the court of last resort, having the power to review the decisions of the lower federal courts. The United States Court of Appeals has appellate jurisdic-

---

EXHIBIT 1.9   **Subject Matter Jurisdiction of the Federal and State Courts**

**Subject Matter Jurisdiction
of the Federal Courts**

Cases arising under the United States Constitution
Cases arising under a treaty
Cases arising under federal statutes
Cases in which the United States is itself a party
Cases involving state law if the dispute is between citizens of different
     states or a state and a citizen of a different state

**Subject Matter Jurisdiction
of the State Courts**

Cases arising under the United States Constitution and certain federal
     statutes
Cases arising under the state's own constitution, statutes, or common law

tion to review the decisions of the United States District Courts and certain administrative agencies. See Exhibit 1.9.

Application 1.2

1. Which courts have subject matter jurisdiction over cases arising under the Social Security Act (a federal statute)? The federal courts? The state courts?

2. Which courts have subject matter jurisdiction in a child custody case brought under your state's Marriage and Divorce Act? The federal courts? Your state's courts?

3. Defendant Smith believes that the sentence imposed by your state's trial court violates the Eighth Amendment's prohibition against cruel and unusual punishment. Which courts have subject matter jurisdiction? Your state's appellate courts? The United States Supreme Court?

4. State A has enacted a statute making all abortions illegal. Which courts have the power to determine whether the statute is constitutional? State A's courts? The United States Supreme Court?

---

§1.2.4   The Relationship Among Federal, State, and Local Prosecutors

The power to prosecute cases arising under the United States Constitution and federal statutes is vested in the Department of Justice, which is headed by the Attorney General of the United States, a presidential appointee. Assisting the United States Attorney General are the United States Attorneys for each federal judicial district. The individual United States Attorneys' offices have two divisions: a civil division and a criminal division. The civil division handles civil cases arising under federal law, and the criminal division handles cases involving alleged violations of federal criminal statutes.

At the state level, the system is slightly different. In most states, the attorney for the state is the state attorney general, usually an elected official. Working for the state attorney general are a number of assistant attorney generals. However, unlike the United States attorneys, most state attorney generals do not handle criminal cases. Their clients are the various state agencies. For example, an assistant attorney general may be assigned to the department of social and health services, the department of licensing, the consumer protection bureau, or the department of worker's compensation, providing advice to the agency and representing the agency in civil litigation.

Criminal prosecutions are handled by county and city prosecutors. Each county has its own prosecutor's office, which has both a civil and a criminal division. Attorneys working for the civil division play much the same role as state assistant attorney generals. They represent the

EXHIBIT 1.10   Federal, State, and Local Prosecutors

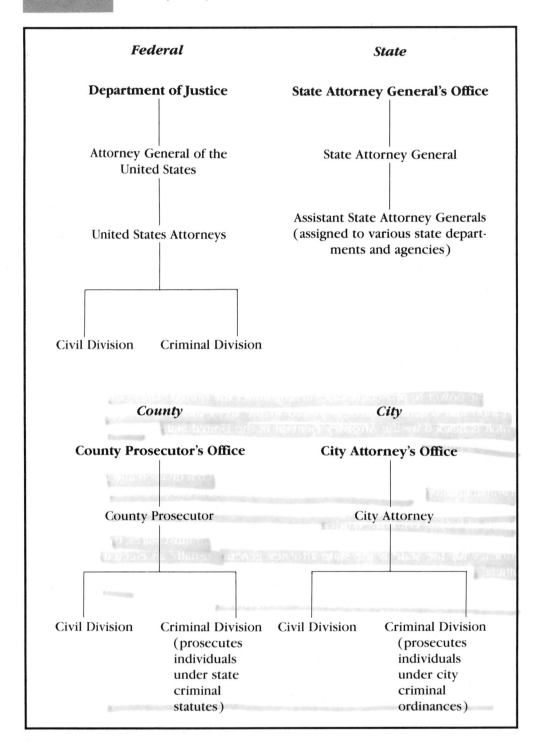

county and its agencies, providing both advice and representation. In contrast, the attorneys assigned to the criminal division are responsible for prosecutions under the state's criminal code. The county prosecutor's office decides whom to charge and then tries the cases.

Like the counties, cities have their own city attorney's office which, at least in large cities, has civil and criminal divisions. Attorneys working in the civil division advise city departments and agencies and represent the city in civil litigation; attorneys in the criminal division prosecute criminal cases brought under city ordinances. State, county, and city prosecutors do not represent federal departments or agencies, nor do they handle cases brought under federal law. See Exhibit 1.10.

§1.3   A Final Comment

Although there are numerous other ways of analyzing the United States system of government, these two perspectives — the three branches perspective and the federal-state perspective — are the foundation on which the rest of your study of law will be built. Without such a foundation, without a thorough understanding of the interrelationships among the parts of the system, many of the concepts that you will encounter in law school would be difficult to learn.

This is particularly true of legal writing. Without understanding both the role each branch plays and the relationship between state and federal government, you cannot be an effective researcher or an effective legal analyst. You must understand the United States system of government so that you can determine which sources to look at in the library. In addition, you must understand the United States system of government before you can tackle the topic of the next chapter, determining whether a particular case or statute is mandatory or persuasive authority.

Chapter 2

An Introduction to Common and Enacted Law

As you saw in Chapter 1, our system of government is complex. To some extent, each of the three branches has the power to create law. The legislative branch enacts statutes, the executive branch promulgates regulations, and the judicial branch both interprets the statutes and regulations and, in the absence of enacted law, creates its own common law rules.

In this chapter we explore further the relationship between the three branches and the law that they create.

§2.1 COMMON LAW

Historically, most of our law was common law, or law created by the courts. Rights to property (Property), the rights of parties to enter into and enforce contracts (Contracts), and the right of an individual to recover from another for civil wrongs (Torts) were all governed by common law doctrines developed originally in England and adopted in this country by the states.

This common law relies on a system of precedent. Each case is decided not in isolation, but in light of the cases that have preceded it. In other words, instead of creating new rules for each case, the courts apply the rules announced and developed in earlier cases. The system works as follows.

Assume for the moment a blank slate. You are in a state with no statutes and no common law rules.

In the first case to come before your state's courts, Case A, a mother asks the court to grant her custody of her two children, a 2-year-old son and a 4-year-old daughter. There are no statutes or earlier cases to which the court can look for guidance. The court must make its own law. Looking at the facts of the case before it, the court must decide whether the mother should be awarded custody.

Assume that the court grants the mother's request for custody because, given the ages of the children, the court believes that it is in the children's best interest to remain with their mother. The Tender Years Doctrine is born.

Not long after, another mother requests custody of her children, a 4-year-old son and a 14-year-old daughter.

Unlike Case A, in Case B the slate is not blank. In deciding Case B, the court will be guided by the court's decision in Case A. The reasoning in Case A (that given the ages of the children it is in the children's best interest to remain with their mother) now becomes the "rule" in Case B.

Applying this rule, the court grants the mother custody of her 4-year-old son: Given his age, it is appropriate that he remain with his mother. It also grants the mother custody of her 14-year-old daughter, relying on the daughter's gender. It is most appropriate, the court reasons, that a teenage daughter remain with her mother.

In deciding the next case, Case C, the court applies the rule announced in Case A (that it is in the best interest of young children to remain with their mother) and in Case B (that it is appropriate that teenage daughters remain with their mother), granting a mother custody of 5- and 10-year-old daughters even though the mother has a history of abusing alcohol. Because the mother is not currently drinking, the court holds that it is in the girls' best interest to remain with their mother.

Thus, each case builds on past cases, the reasoning in one case becoming the rule in the next.

Case A

The court's reasoning: It is in the best interest of young children to remain with their mother.

Case B

Rule that the court applies: It is in the best interest of young children to remain with their mother (cites Case A).

Additional reasoning: It is in the best interest of teenage daughters to remain with their mother.

Case C

Rules that the court applies: (1) It is in the best interest of young children to remain with their mother (cites Cases A and B).

(2) It is in the best interest of teenage daughters to remain with their mother (cites Case B).

Additional reasoning: It is appropriate to grant custody to mother despite her history of alcohol abuse because mother is not currently drinking.

Of course, not all of the rules announced in earlier cases are applied in subsequent cases. (If Case D involves the custody of a 1-year-old girl whose mother does not have a history of alcohol abuse, the court would apply only the rule announced in Case A; it would not need to consider the additional rules set out in Cases B and C.) Nor does each case add to the existing law. (The court could decide Case D without giving additional reasons to support its conclusion.)

In addition, in certain circumstances, the courts are not bound by rules from earlier cases. Because the law is court-made, a higher court can overrule the rules set out either in its own decisions or in the decisions of lower courts within its jurisdiction, substituting a new rule for the common law rule announced and applied in the earlier cases.

§2.2   ENACTED LAW

Although historically most of our law was common law, today much of it is enacted law. Acting under the authority granted to them, the legislative and executive branches have enacted and promulgated numerous statutes and regulations, some of which have superseded the common law. For example, state statutes have replaced common law rules governing the relationship between landlords and tenants, and the Uniform Commercial Code has replaced the common law rules governing commercial contracts.

Enacted law, however, seldom stands on its own. In the process of interpreting and applying statutes, the courts often announce new rules. Although these rules are not common law rules, they are rules nonetheless, and unless the legislature enacts legislation changing the rule, they will be followed by the courts in subsequent cases.

The relationship between common law, statutes, and cases interpreting and applying statutes becomes clearer if we look once again at the example begun in the preceding section.

This time presume that not long after the court decided Case D the state legislature enacted a statute rejecting the Tender Years Doctrine. Instead of giving preference to mothers, the statute now requires that the courts grant custody "in accordance with the best interest of the children." No longer is the mother to be given preference; instead, in determining custody, the court is to consider a number of factors including the parents' wishes; the children's wishes; the interaction and interrelationship of the child with parents and siblings; the child's adjustment to his or her home, school, and community; and the mental and physical health of all of the individuals involved.

This statute supersedes the common law doctrine set out in Cases A, B, C, and D. These cases are no longer good law, and the rules set out in them will not, at least to the extent that they are inconsistent with the statute, be followed in subsequent cases. Thus, when Case E comes before the court, the court applies the statute and not the common law doctrine.

The application of the statute is not, however, always clear. For example, in Case E the mother contends that she should be given custody not because the children are young but because she has always been their primary caretaker. Although the statute does not specifically address this argument, the court agrees with the mother, holding that

---

EXHIBIT 2.1   **The Types of Law**

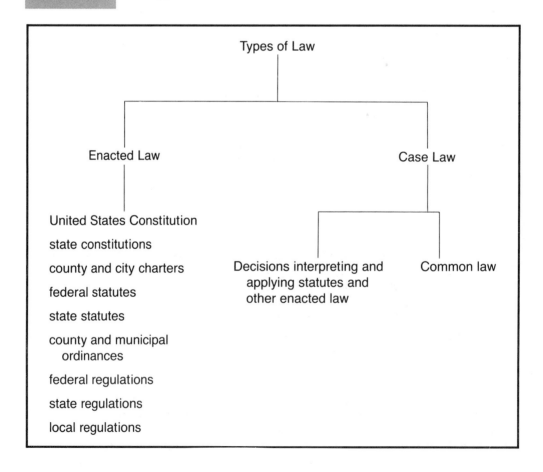

because the mother has always been the primary caretaker, it would be in the children's best interest to remain with her.

Because this "rule" (that the court can consider which parent has been the primary caretaker) is not inconsistent with the statute, it can be used by the courts in subsequent cases. In deciding Case F, the court will apply not just the statute but also the rule announced in Case E. Similarly, in deciding Case G the court will consider not only the statute but the rule in Case E and any rules announced in Case F. Just as the courts look to precedent in deciding a case involving a common law rule, they also look to precedent in deciding a case brought under a statute.

Thus, in our legal system, there are two types of law: enacted law and case law. Enacted law, when broadly defined, includes any law that has been adopted, enacted, or promulgated by either the people or a legislative body. The United States Constitution, the constitutions of each of the states, federal statutes, state statutes, city and county ordinances, and regulations promulgated by federal, state, and local agencies are all considered enacted law. In contrast, case law is law that has not been promulgated by the people or by a legislative body. It is law that has been created and announced by the courts in written opinions.

The trick is in knowing which law to apply.

Note

Although the terms "case law" and "common law" are sometimes used interchangeably, they are not synonyms. The term "common law" refers to law created by the courts in the absence of enacted law. For example, most of tort law and much of property law are based not on statutes, but on common law doctrines created by the courts. In contrast, the term "case law" is broader. It refers to the written decisions of the courts and encompasses not only decisions announcing and applying common law, but also decisions interpreting and applying enacted law.

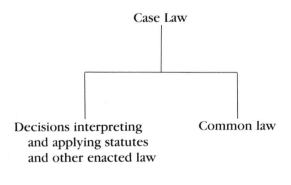

§2.3   Mandatory versus Persuasive Authority

Not all enacted and common law is given equal weight. In deciding which law to apply, courts distinguish between mandatory and persuasive authority.

Mandatory authority is law that is binding on the court deciding the case. The court must apply that law. In contrast, persuasive authority is law that is not binding. Although the court may look to that law for guidance, it need not apply it.

Determining whether a particular statute or case is mandatory or persuasive authority is a two-step process. You must first determine which jurisdiction's law applies (that is, whether federal or state law

---

EXHIBIT 2.2   **Ranking of Authorities**

United States Constitution

State Constitution
Cannot take away rights granted by the U.S. Constitution

Federal Statutes
Cannot take away rights granted by U.S. Constitution; in addition, Congress can only enact laws that are consistent with the grant of power given to Congress under the Constitution.

State Statutes
Cannot take away rights granted by the constitution; in addition, a state legislature can only enact laws that are consistent with the power granted to states by the U.S. Constitution and to that particular state legislature by that state's constitution.

United States Supreme Court
Bound by the United States Constitution and United States Code insofar as the code is constitutional. Not bound by its own prior decisions, decisions of state courts, or decisions of lower courts.

State Supreme Court
Bound by the United States' and the state's constitution, decisions of the U.S. Supreme Court interpreting the U.S. Constitution or relating to a dispute involving that state, and state statutes insofar as those statutes are constitutional. Not bound by its own prior decisions, decisions of federal courts not related to federal constitutional questions or involving the state, the decisions of other states, or decisions of lower courts within the same state.

applies and, if state law applies, which state's law applies); you must then determine which of that jurisdiction's statutes and cases are binding on the court that will be deciding the case.

§2.3.1   Which Jurisdiction's Law Applies?

Sometimes determining which jurisdiction's law applies is easy. For example, common knowledge (and common sense) tells you that federal law probably governs whether a federal PLUS loan constitutes income for federal income tax purposes. Similarly, you would probably guess that a will executed in California by a California resident would be governed by California state law. At other times, though, the determination is much more difficult. You probably would not know what jurisdiction's law governs a real estate contract between a resident of New York and a resident of Pennsylvania for a piece of property located in Florida.

EXHIBIT 2.2   *(continued)*

United States Court of Appeals	*State Court of Appeals*
(13 circuits) Bound by U.S. Constitution, United States Code, and United States Supreme Court decisions. Not bound by decisions issued by United States District courts, nor is any given circuit bound by its own prior decisions or the decisions of another circuit.	Bound by the U.S. and state constitution, decisions of the State Supreme Court and the U.S. Supreme Court relating to federal constitutional questions. Not bound by its own prior decisions, decisions by the courts of any other state, or by the decisions of any lower court within the same state.
United States District Courts	*State Trial Courts*
(These are the trial courts in the federal system.) Each court is bound by the U.S. Constitution, the United States Code and decisions of the United States Supreme Court, and the Court of Appeals for the circuit in which the district court is located. The opinions of the district court may or may not be published, and, although they have some persuasive authority, no court is bound by them.	Courts bound by the U.S. and state constitutions, state statutes, decisions of the United States Supreme Court relating to federal constitutional issues, and decisions of the state supreme court and state court of appeals for the geographic area in which the trial court is located. In most states decisions of the trial courts are not published. Whether or not such decisions are published, no court is bound by them.

Although the rules governing the determination of which jurisdiction's law applies are beyond the scope of this book (they are studied in Civil Procedure, Federal Courts, and Conflicts), keep two things in mind.

First, remember that in our legal system, federal law almost always preempts state law. Consequently, if there is both a federal and a state statute on the same topic, the federal statute will preempt the state statute to the extent that the two are inconsistent. For example, if a federal statute makes it illegal to discriminate in the renting of an apartment on the basis of familial status but under a state statute such discrimination is lawful, the federal statute governs — it is illegal to discriminate on the basis of familial status. There are a few instances, however, when a state constitutional provision or a state statute will govern: If the state constitution gives a criminal defendant more rights than does the federal constitution, the state constitution applies. States can grant an individual more protection. They cannot, however, take away or restrict rights granted by the federal constitution or a federal statute.

Second, although legal scholars still debate whether there is a federal common law, in the federal system there is not the same body of common law as there is in the states. Unlike the state systems, in the federal system, there are no common law rules governing adverse possession or intentional torts such as assault and battery, false imprisonment, or the intentional infliction of emotional distress. Thus, if the cause of action is based on a common law doctrine, the case is probably governed by state and not federal law.

§2.3.2   What "Law" Will Be Binding On the Court?

Within each jurisdiction, the authorities are ranked. The United States Constitution is the highest authority, binding both state and federal courts. Under the Constitution is other state and federal law.

In the federal system, the highest authority is the Constitution. Under the Constitution are the federal statutes and regulations, and under the federal statutes and regulations are the cases interpreting and applying them.

In the state system, the ranking is similar. The highest authority is the state constitution, followed by (1) state statutes and regulations and the cases interpreting and applying those statutes and regulations and (2) the state's common law.

In addition, the cases themselves are ranked. In both the federal and state systems, decisions of the supreme court carry the most weight: When deciding a case involving the same law and similar facts, both the court of appeals and the trial courts are bound by the decisions of the supreme or highest court. Decisions of intermediate courts of appeal come next; the trial courts under the jurisdiction of the intermediate court of appeals are bound by the court of appeal's decisions. At the bottom are the trial courts. Trial court decisions are binding only on the parties involved in the particular case.

Statutes and cases are also ranked by date. More recent statutes supersede earlier versions, and more recent common law rules supersede early rules by the same level court. Courts are bound by the highest court's most recent decision. For example, if there is a 1967 state intermediate court of appeals decision that makes an activity legal and a 1986 supreme court decision that makes it illegal, in the absence of a statute, the 1986 supreme court decision governs. The 1986 decision would be mandatory authority, and all of the courts within that jurisdiction would be bound by that decision.

Application 2.1

1. In 1930, in Case A, the supreme court of your state set out a common law rule. In 1956, in Case B, the supreme court of your state changed that rule. In your state, which case would be binding on a trial court: Case A or Case B?

| Case A | State Supreme Court | 1930 |
| Case B | State Supreme Court | 1956 |

2. Same facts as in #1 except that in 1971, in Case C, your state court of appeals modified the test set out in Case B, adding a requirement. In your state, what test would a trial court use: the test set out in Case A, the test set out in Case B, or the test set out in Case C?

Case A	State Supreme Court	1930
Case B	State Supreme Court	1956
Case C	State Court of Appeals	1971

3. Same facts as in #2 except that in 1976 your state legislature enacted a statute that completely changed the common law rule. What is now mandatory authority: the statute or the case(s)?

Case A	State Supreme Court	1930
Case B	State Supreme Court	1956
Case C	State Court of Appeals	1971
State Statute		1976

4. Same facts as in #3 except that in 1980, in Case D, a case involving the application of the 1976 statute, the court of appeals gives one of the words in the statute a broad interpretation. (The word was not defined in the statute itself.) In applying the statute, which courts are bound by the court of appeals's decision in Case D: A trial court within the court of appeals's geographic jurisdiction? A trial court out-

side the court of appeals's geographic jurisdiction? The division of the court of appeals that decided Case D? A division of the court of appeals other than the division that decided Case D? The state supreme court?

State Statute		1976
Case D	State Court of Appeals	1980

5. In 1985, in Case E, a different division of the court of appeals applies the 1976 statute. In reaching its decision, the court declines to follow the decision in Case D: Instead of interpreting the word broadly, the court interprets it narrowly. The losing party disagrees with this decision and files an appeal with the state supreme court. In deciding this appeal, is the state supreme court bound by the decision in Case D? The court of appeals decision in Case E?

Case D	State Court of Appeals	1980
Case E	State Court of Appeals	1985

6. Same facts as in #5 except that in 1989 the state legislature amends the statute, explicitly defining the word that was the subject of debate in Cases D and E. The legislature elects to give the word a very narrow meaning. In Case F, brought before a state trial court in 1990, what would be controlling: the 1976 version of the statute? the 1989 version of the statute? Case D? the court of appeals decision in Case E? the supreme court's decision in Case E? (In case E the Court of Appeals defined the word narrowly; the supreme court defined it broadly.)

State Statute		1976
Case D	State Court of Appeals	1980
Case E	State Court of Appeals	1985
Case E	State Supreme Court	1986
Amended version		1989
of statute		

Chapter 3

An Introduction to
Legal Analysis

"Think like a lawyer." By now, you have heard this phrase numerous times. During law school orientation, it was a mantra: "In law school, you will learn to think like a lawyer"; "Our job is to teach you how to think like a lawyer"; "Law school will change you. When you leave, you will think like a lawyer."

But what does it mean to think like a lawyer? Do lawyers think differently than accountants, doctors, and stockbrokers do? The answer is yes and no. Although each group must be able to think critically, it is only the lawyers who think dialectically. Accountants, doctors, and lawyers collect and use information; lawyers collect, use, and argue.

This chapter introduces you to the dialectical mode of thinking. In it, you will see in the context of a sample case how lawyers argue both the law and the application of that law to a particular set of facts.

§3.1 MEETING THE CLIENTS

Law is about people. Consequently, we begin this chapter with the parties to this dispute: Mr. and Mrs. Greenbaum.

Mr. Greenbaum

Four weeks ago, Mr. Greenbaum left his wife of twelve years and moved into an apartment. Today he is in the office of his attorney, Julia Michael, talking about divorce.

Mr. Greenbaum begins the interview by telling Ms. Michael that he has decided to file for divorce. On hearing this, Ms. Michael encourages

Mr. Greenbaum to talk. She asks Mr. Greenbaum how long he and Mrs. Greenbaum have been separated, whether Mr. Greenbaum is interested in talking to Mrs. Greenbaum about reconciliation, whether Mr. Greenbaum is interested in meeting with a counselor, and whether Mr. Greenbaum has talked to Mrs. Greenbaum about the custody of the children or the division of property.

In doing this, Ms. Michael has two goals. First, she wants to make sure that Mr. Greenbaum actually wants to file for divorce. Many people go to an attorney not because they want a divorce but because they want someone to talk to or because they want to put pressure on their spouse. Second, she wants to begin identifying the issues. Is there a dispute over the custody of the children? Over the division of the property? Over child or spousal support?

In this case, Mr. Greenbaum tells Ms. Michael that he does, in fact, want a divorce. He and his wife have gone through counseling, and reconciliation does not seem likely.

He also tells her that his primary goal is to get custody of the children.

Mrs. Greenbaum

At about the same time, Mrs. Greenbaum is in the office of her attorney, Matthew Jeffrey. Mrs. Greenbaum tells Mr. Jeffrey that her husband left home four weeks earlier without telling her that he was moving out and without making arrangements for the children or for the disposition of the property. The children are currently with Mrs. Greenbaum, and she wants to keep them and the couple's home.

§3.2   OBTAINING THE FACTS

What the attorney does at this point depends on how much he or she knows about custody actions. An attorney who practices family law will know what questions to ask; one who doesn't, may not. In the latter case, the attorney will be able to ask only general questions. Instead of getting all of the information, his or her goal is to get the information that is needed to find the applicable statute or common law doctrine.

For the purposes of this section, let's assume that the attorneys know very little about child custody. As a consequence, during this initial interview, they find out only that Mr. and Mrs. Greenbaum have two children, Tom, age 9, and Mary, age 7; that Mr. Greenbaum, the CEO of a small family business, thinks that he should have custody because his wife is inconsistent in her dealings with the children; and that Mrs. Greenbaum, a high school teacher, thinks that she should get custody because she has, since the birth of the children, been their primary caretaker.

§3.3   LOCATING THE APPLICABLE STATUTE

An attorney who practices family law will know, from memory, both the number of the applicable statute and its language. Our attorneys, however, know only that custody actions are governed by state statute. They do not know the number of the applicable statute, and it has been several years since either one has read it.

As a result, they must locate the applicable statute. They do this by looking in their state's code, using the subject or topic index to locate the number of the applicable section and then locating the text of that section in the main volumes.

For the purposes of this problem, let's assume that the attorneys locate the following statute.

UNIFORM MARRIAGE AND DIVORCE ACT*

Section 402: Best Interests of Child
> The court shall determine custody in accordance with the best interests of the child. The court shall consider all relevant factors including:
>> (1) the wishes of the child's parent or parents as to his custody;
>> (2) the wishes of the child as to his custodian;
>> (3) the interaction and interrelationship of the child with his parent or parents, his siblings, and any other person who may significantly affect the child's best interest;
>> (4) the child's adjustment to his home, school, and community; and
>> (5) the mental and physical health of all individuals involved.
>
> The court shall not consider conduct of a proposed custodian that does not affect his relationship to the child.

The next step is to determine whether this section is, in fact, the applicable section. Is section 402 the section that the court will use in determining which parent will be granted temporary and permanent custody?

The answer to this question is often in the title of the statute. In codifying a statute, the code revisor indicates the scope of the section in its title. Unfortunately, in this case, the title is of little help: It does not indicate whether the statute applies to temporary custody decisions, permanent custody decisions, or modification proceedings. The attorneys must look further.

The next place they look is the text of the statute. In the first sentence, the legislatures states that "[t]he court shall determine custody...." Although this phrase tells the attorneys that the statute governs child custody, it does not tell them whether it governs initial custody decisions.

---

*This Act has been reprinted through the permission of the National Conference of Commissioners on Uniform State Laws, and copies of the Act may be ordered from them at a nominal cost at 676 N. St. Clair St., Ste. 1700, Chicago, Ill. 60611, (302) 915-0195.

The next place that the attorneys look is the other sections in the same chapter or act. The table of contents is set out below.

Custody*

From this list, it appears that there are two other sections that potentially apply to child custody actions: section 403, Temporary Orders, and section 409, Modification.

When the attorneys examine these sections, they find that they do relate to child custody. Section 403 gives the court the power to award temporary custody.

Section 403: Temporary Orders*

(a) A party to a custody proceeding may move for a temporary custody order. The motion must be supported by an affidavit as provided in Section 410. The court may award temporary custody under the standards of Section 402 after a hearing or, if there is no objection, solely on the basis of the affidavits.

(b) If a proceeding for dissolution of marriage or legal separation is dismissed, any temporary custody order is vacated unless a parent or the child's custodian moves that the proceeding continue as a custody proceeding and the court finds, after a hearing, that the circumstances of the parents and the best interest of the child require that a custody decree be issued.

(c) If a custody proceeding commenced in the absence of a petition for dissolution of marriage or legal separation under subsection (1)(ii) or (2) of Section 401 is dismissed, any temporary custody order is vacated.

In contrast, Section 409 deals only with the modification of existing child custody orders.

Thus, although there is nothing in the Uniform Act that specifically states that section 402 governs temporary and permanent custody decisions, the attorneys determine that section 402 is the applicable sec-

---

*This Act has been reprinted through the permission of the National Conference of Commissioners on Uniform State Laws, and copies of the Act may be ordered from them at a nominal cost at 676 N. St. Clair St., Ste. 1700, Chicago, Ill. 60611, (302) 915-0195.

tion by reading the title, the language of section 402, and the other related statutes.

Question

Is section 402 mandatory or persuasive authority?

§3.4   ANALYZING THE STATUTE

Having determined that section 402 is the applicable section, the attorneys begin to analyze it, taking it apart and examining each part closely. Who determines which parent gets custody, and how is that decision made?

The answer to the first question is in the first sentence of the statute. The legislature states that it is the court that determines which parent gets custody: "The court shall determine . . . ." The statute does not say, however, who has the "burden of proof." Is it the father who has the burden? The mother? The parent with custody? The parent without custody?

Question

What does the phrase "burden of proof" mean? If you don't know, where can you find the answer?

The answer to the second question is also in the first sentence of the statute. The legislature states that "[t]he court shall determine custody in accordance with the best interests of the child."

At this point, the attorneys stop and think about what the legislature has done. In enacting this statute, has the legislature set out a list of elements, or has it created a standard?

Question

As a practical matter, what is the difference between a statute that sets out a list of elements, or requirements, and one that sets out a standard or a general principle? Why would the legislature select one approach in some instances and another approach in other instances?

After looking at the statute more carefully, the attorneys determine that the legislature has set out a standard. In determining which parent gets custody, the court will consider "the best interests" of the children. Although the five-item list looks like a list of elements, it is not. A parent does not have to prove each item in the list. Instead, the legislature has listed the factors that it wants the courts to consider in deciding what would be in the best interests of the children. Thus, in enacting section 402, not only has the legislature set out the standard, but it has also provided the court with instructions for applying it.

Note

In reading a statute, you need to look at every word in the statute. For example, note that in the second sentence the legislature has used the word "shall" rather than "may" or "can." Because the legislature has used "shall," the court has no discretion. It must do what the legislature says.

Also note that the legislature tells the court not to consider all factors but only those factors that are "relevant." Finally, look at the word "including." Through its use of this word, the legislature tells the court that it considers the five factors set out in the statute to be relevant. The courts must, therefore, consider each of them. The legislature does not, however, tell the court to look only at those five factors. If there are other relevant factors, the court must also consider them.

Question

Is each parent's occupation a relevant factor? Who would decide, and how would they make their decision?

Application 3.1

Write a one-page letter to your client in which you paraphrase and explain section 402.

§3.5   LOCATING AND ANALYZING THE CASES

The attorneys have identified and analyzed the applicable statute. Their search for the "law," however, is not over. Even though custody decisions are governed by statute and not common law, they still need to locate and read the applicable cases.

EXHIBIT 3.1   **Statute Codifies Common Law Rule**

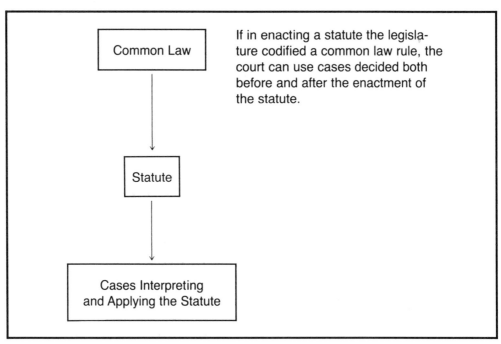

To understand why, you must understand the relationship between the common law, section 402, and the cases interpreting and applying section 402.

Historically, custody decisions were governed by common law. Because there was no statute, the courts were free to create their own common law rules. Although the rule was not the same in every state, in most states the courts adopted the Tender Years Doctrine, a rule that granted the custody of young children to the mother unless the court found her to be unfit.

The common law has, however, been superseded by statute. Acting under the authority granted to them by the federal and state constitutions, state legislatures have enacted statutes setting out the rules to be used in deciding child custody. In some instances, these statutes codified the common law rule. The legislature simply adopted and put into statutory form the common law rule. In other instances, the legislature abolished the common law rule, replacing it with a different rule or standard.

In those states in which the legislature simply codified the common law rule, the cases setting out or applying the common law rule are still "good law," and the courts can look to them to find the policy underlying the common law rule and statute or to see how the rule was applied in analogous cases. See Exhibit 3.1. This is not, however, the case in those states in which the legislature abolished the common law

---

EXHIBIT 3.2   Statute Changed Common Law Rule

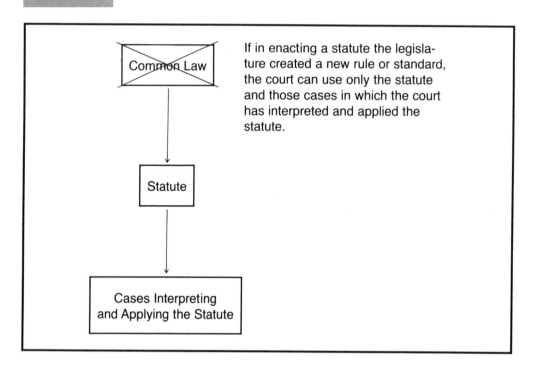

rule and enacted a new rule or standard. In these states, the cases decided before the enactment of the statute are not good law and should not, as a general rule, be used in interpreting or applying the statute. The courts can use only those cases decided after the enactment of the statute. See Exhibit 3.2.

The attorneys find cases interpreting and applying the statute using the annotations, or notes of decision, that follow the text of the statute in an annotated code. In this instance, assume that the attorneys locate only the following two hypothetical cases: *In re Marriage of Huen* and *In re Marriage of Nabrinski.*

In re Marriage of Huen
24 Official Rep. 9, 678 Reg. Rep. 68 (1986)

This is an appeal from an order granting the mother custody of her two sons. The facts are as follows.

Deana and Daniel Huen were married in 1979. Both worked until 1982, at which time Mrs. Huen quit work to care for the couple's twin sons. Since 1982, Mrs. Huen has assumed primary responsibility for the children. She takes care of their day-to-day needs, and she supervises their medical care, schooling, and religious training. Although Mr. Huen concedes that Mrs. Huen has been providing the children's primary care, he argues that he is equally able to provide such care, and, given the sex of the children, that it would be in their best interest to grant him custody.

The trial court granted custody to Mrs. Huen. In so doing, the court stated that the sex of the child was not a relevant factor. The court also stated that given the ages of the children, it would be in the best interests of the children to grant custody to their mother. Mr. Huen has appealed, arguing that the trial court erred in applying the Tender Years Doctrine.

We find that the trial court did err. The Tender Years Doctrine is no longer the law in this state. The legislature abolished it when it enacted section 402. The standard now applied is the "best interests of the child."

We do, however, uphold the decision of the trial court. If a child is too young to express his or her preference, the best interests of the child dictate that the trial court award custody of the child to the primary caretaker, absent a finding that the primary caretaker is unfit to have custody. In this case, Mrs. Huen was the primary caretaker; accordingly, the trial court did not err in granting her custody. Thus, although we might have reached a different result had the children been older, we hereby affirm the trial court's ruling.

In this case, the court does two things. First, it states that the statute supersedes the common law rule. There is no longer a presumption that the mother should be granted custody of young children. The courts must follow the statute and award custody in accordance with the best interests of the child. Second, it creates a new rule. The court states that when "the child is too young to express his or her preference, the best interests of the child dictate that the trial court award custody of the child to the primary caretaker absent a finding that the primary caretaker is unfit to have custody." The court then applies this new rule, holding that because the mother had been the primary caretaker, the trial court did not err in granting her custody.

Questions

1. Is the trial court's statement that "the sex of the child is not relevant" a rule, part of the court's holding, or dicta? (See Glossary of Terms.)

2. Is the trial court's statement that it might have reached a different result had the children been older a rule, part of the court's holding, or dicta?

Application 3.2

In one paragraph, summarize the rules set out in *In re Marriage of Huen.*

IN RE MARRIAGE OF NABRINSKI
38 Official Rep. 501, 489 Reg. Rep. 66 (1988)

This case arises as the result of a trial court order granting custody of a girl, age 7, and a boy, age 11, to their father.

In deciding which parent should be awarded custody, the court must consider the best interests of the children. Section 402, Uniform Marriage and Divorce Act. In deciding what would be in the best interests of the children, the court must consider the wishes of the parents and child as to custody; the interaction and interrelationship of the child with his or her parent or parents, siblings, and any other person who may significantly affect the child's best interest; the child's adjustment to home, school, and community; and the mental and physical health of all individuals involved. *Id.*

In addition, the court must look to see which parent has been the primary caregiver. *In re Marriage of Huen,* 24 Official Reporter 9, 678 Regional Reporter 68 (1986). Absent evidence that the primary caretaker is an unfit custodian, custody will be given to that parent. *Id.*

In determining which parent is the primary caregiver, the court will look to see who was the primary caregiver at the time the parents separated. The parent who provided for the daily needs of the children will be deemed to be the primary caregiver, and to ensure continuity in the lives of the children, except in exceptional circumstances, custody will be granted to him or her.

In this case, the mother was providing the primary care for both children. She took them to school and picked them up after school, and she supervised their after school activities and homework. She is also the one who maintained the home: she cleaned the house, did the laundry, did the shopping, and prepared the meals. We do, therefore, find that the trial court erred in granting custody of the children to their father. Consequently, even though we might have reached a different result if the mother were still involved with other men, because these indiscretions were in the past, this court finds that it would be in the best interests of the children to grant custody to the mother. We, therefore, reverse the holding of the trial court.

In this case, the court repeats the statute and the rule set out in *In re Marriage of Huen.* It also creates an additional rule. In determining which parent is the primary caregiver, the court will look to see which parent was the primary caregiver at the time the couple separated. The court also explains the rationale for this rule. The court states that by granting custody to the parent who was the primary caregiver at the time the couple separated, it is trying to ensure continuity in the children's lives.

Question

In *Nabrinski,* what is the court's holding? Are any of the court's statements dicta?

Application 3.3

In one paragraph, summarize the rules set out in *In re Marriage of Nabrinski.* In writing your paragraph, make clear the relationship between the factors set out in the statute and the rules set forth in the case.

Question

Are *Huen* and *Nabrinski* mandatory or persuasive authority?

----

§3.6   Synthesizing the Law

The attorneys now have before them both the text of the statute and the cases in which the courts have interpreted and applied the statute. The next step is to put the pieces together.

In many instances, this is done by a legal intern or an associate. The intern or associate researches the law and then prepares an in-house memorandum in which he or she summarizes and applies the law to the facts of the client's case. The beginning of one of these memos would look like this.

EXAMPLE

Discussion

Section 402 of the Uniform Marriage and Divorce Act sets out the standard that the trial court must use in awarding custody.

Section 402: Best Interests of Child

The court shall determine custody in accordance with the best interests of the child. The court shall consider all relevant factors including:

(1) the wishes of the child's parent or parents as to his custody;

(2) the wishes of the child as to his custodian;

(3) the interaction and interrelationship of the child with his parent or parents, his siblings, and any other person who may significantly affect the child's best interest;

(4) the child's adjustment to his home, school, and community; and

(5) the mental and physical health of all individuals involved.

The court shall not consider conduct of a proposed custodian that does not affect his relationship to the child.

The state supreme court has held that this statute supersedes the common law in effect at the time the statute was enacted. *In re Marriage of Huen,* 24 Official Reporter 9, 678 Regional Reporter 68 (1986). Consequently, there is no longer a presumption that the custody of young children should be awarded to the mother. *Id.* at 11, 678 Regional Reporter at 69. The supreme court has, however, held that if "the child is too young to express his or her preference, the best interests of the child dictate that the trial court award custody of the child to the primary caretaker absent a finding that the primary caretaker is unfit to have custody." *Id.*

In determining which parent is the primary caretaker, the courts look to see which parent was acting as the primary caretaker at the time the parents separated. *In re Marriage of Nabrinski,* 38 Official Reporter 501, 489 Regional Reporter 66 (1988). By awarding custody to the primary caretaker, the courts seek to ensure, to the extent possible, continuity of care. *Id.*

In reading this example, note several things. First, look at the organizational scheme. The writer has set out first the statute and then the rules from the cases. This is correct. Because child custody actions are governed by statute, the analysis must begin with the statute and not the cases. Second, note the focus of the discussion. Although the rules are presented in date order (the statute first, the rule from *Huen* second, and the rule from *Nabrinski* last), neither the dates nor the names of the cases are the focus. Instead, the writer has focused on the decision-making process:

1. In awarding child custody, the standard is best interests of the child;

2. If the child is young, it is usually in the best interests of the child to grant custody to the child's primary caretaker;

3. In determining which parent is the primary caretaker, the courts look to see which parent was the primary caretaker at the time the parents separated.

Finally, note that the writer has done more than just quote from the cases. He or she has summarized the rules, putting them into his or her own language.

There may, however, be a problem with the way in which the rules are presented. Has the writer accurately explained the relationship between the factors listed in the statute and the rules set out in the cases?

Application 3.4

Now that you have all of the law, rewrite the client letter from Application 3.1. In doing so, do not quote either the statute or cases verbatim.

_____

§3.7   GATHERING ADDITIONAL INFORMATION

After receiving the letters from their attorneys, Mr. and Mrs. Greenbaum decide to file for divorce. In his Petition for Dissolution of Marriage, Mr. Greenbaum requests sole custody of the children. In her Answer, Mrs. Greenbaum counters, also asking for sole custody. Because the parties do not agree on custody, a hearing is scheduled.

For both attorneys, the next step is to collect more information. Now that they know the law, they know what types of information they need to make their case to the court.

For purposes of this exercise, let's assume that the attorneys obtain the following information.

CITY
MEDICAL CENTER

PSYCHOLOGICAL EXAMINATION REPORT

Mr. Greenbaum	Mrs. Greenbaum
Date of Birth:	Date of Birth:
January 15, 1959	January 12, 1960

Examination Dates:	Examination Dates:
July 27 & 28, 1993	July 25 & 26, 1993

Examination Procedures:

Draw-a-Person Test, Wechsler Adult Intelligence Scale, Story Recall, Bender-Gestalt (five-second delay, copy, memory), Rorschach Test, Thematic Apperception Test, Word Association Test, Concept Sorting Test, Minnesota Multiphasic Personality Inventory, Sentence Completion Test, Diagnostic Interviews.

IDENTIFICATION AND REFERRAL: This examination is being completed at the request of Dr. Herbert Modlin, who was requested to do a comprehensive evaluation by Mrs. Greenbaum's attorney for the purpose of aiding and assisting in the determination of appropriate child custody. The parties have been married for 12 years and the children in question are a son Tom, age nine, and a daughter, Mary, age seven. Tom is in the fourth grade, and Mary is in the first grade. Mrs. Greenbaum is a school teacher. Mr. Greenbaum is a business executive. Both parties are seeking custody of their children, and both have alleged that they would be fit to have custody of the children.

Both parties are college graduates and married just prior to Mrs. Greenbaum's completing her education. She taught school after they married until her first child was born. They have been typically upwardly mobile with Mr. Greenbaum advancing in his business career. They report usual social and recreational activities, at least at the beginning and middle of their marriage. More recently, they have moved in separate directions with different interests, and this has contributed to and is part of the marital discord.

Each continues to relate to his or her parental family and both have living parents who are active and supportive. They have been financially stable, and both are responsible in terms of money management.

Neither reports intense quarreling but rather a drifting apart.

Mr. Greenbaum is seeking custody of his children and alleges that his relatively flexible schedule will facilitate parenting the children. Mrs. Greenbaum is also seeking custody, and because she teaches school, her schedule is compatible with the children's school on a daily basis as well as at vacation times. She would require childcare assistance on school mornings.

The children are presently residing with Mrs. Greenbaum. Appropriate arrangements for childcare have been maintained by Mrs. Greenbaum consistent with her employment schedule.

EXAMINATION PROCESS: Both parties cooperated fully and completely with the examination. Although the examination was requested by the wife and her attorney, the husband was more than willing to cooperate and believed that all parties would benefit from the examination. No unusual mannerisms or behaviors were noted in either of these individuals. Both were appropriate in affect, mood, and behavior during the examination. Both dressed appropriately for the examination. There are no indications of manipulative or other types of behavior that might tend to taint the results. There is every indication that the results of this examination are a valid and reliable estimate of both of their intellectual and emotional functioning. Neither of these parents was using any medication at the time of the examination on a regular basis. Both are right-handed and wear corrective glasses.

EXAMINATION FINDINGS: <u>Mrs. Greenbaum</u>: The patient's cognitive functioning is intact. Overall she functions within the Bright-Normal range of intellectual abilities. She does somewhat better on verbal as opposed to nonverbal tasks. Her memory is intact, and she shows good judgment. There are no indications of organic brain syndrome.

This examination does not reveal any gross dysfunction or indications of extreme, acute, or chronic psychopathology. The patient is sensitive to a wide range of feelings but somewhat emotionally liable. Although she is likely to become excited with little provocation, she is able to regain control of herself relatively quickly. She does integrate positive feelings into her life but occasionally has difficulty managing depression. She is the kind of person who would rely on chemicals and perhaps alcohol to relieve such depression. To some extent her use of alcohol is situational — her way of medicating herself. Her desire for custody may also be, at least at some level, motivated by her desire to punish her husband.

She is the kind of person who may be mildly inconsistent in discipline and likely to give in to demands that children make on her rather than dealing with some of the attending emotional stress. She can be flexible, however, and will not allow those tendencies to go too far before she is able to regroup and appropriately and consistently provide direction as well as discipline. Her discipline practices are lenient and rely on more abstract use of love and affection as opposed to structure. She is the kind of person who values individual differences and supports persons in achieving their potential as opposed to forcing persons to fit into preconceived roles. Her expectations, however, are high, and she expects a great deal from herself as well as others.

The patient is capable of forming and maintaining intimate and genuine relationships. She is slightly inconsistent in relationships as her mood shifts and she becomes somewhat emotionally liable; this causes her difficulties in maintaining relationships at a high level. This is much more likely to be a problem in her relationships with adults (and men in particular) as opposed to how she relates to young children.

Mr. Greenbaum: This patient is a hard-driving, achievement-oriented person. He manages his life and life circumstances in a relatively compulsive, routine, scheduled manner. His interactions with people are managed in the same way. He has the potential to be sensitive to feelings but in many instances will avoid or make an effort to disguise sensitive feelings. To some extent, he is a hyper-masculine person who bolsters himself with excessive displays of masculinity. He does have the potential to be a nurturing and sensitive person, but this is not the primary way that he ordinarily functions.

This man's parenting skills reflect his overall personality development and character traits. He is rigid in his discipline and overly consistent. He does not show a great deal of flexibility, and his expectations are that his desires, orders, and mandates will be carried forward without question and without compromise. This is not done by him in any harsh or brutal fashion, but rather calmly and with assertiveness. He adheres to very structured moral and ethical standards and expects people to fit into a mold that will satisfy societal and cultural expectations. His expectation, for example, would be that his children behave in ways that are normally expected for boys and girls, and it would be difficult for him to tolerate deviations.

To some extent this man expects more adultlike behavior from children than may be appropriate. He does not always attempt to put himself in the child's place to understand desires, motivations, and needs of the child. These last comments are subtle and not reflective of any gross misunderstanding he has of children and their behavior.

DIAGNOSTIC IMPRESSION: No formal psychiatric diagnosis is provided for either of these individuals at the present time. Neither shows symptomatology at the time of this examination. The personality characteristics described above can be encapsulated in summary fashion by viewing Mr. Greenbaum as a compulsive type of individual and Mrs. Greenbaum as a mildly hysterical and emotionally effervescent person. In both instances, however, these personality characteristics are not debilitating, nor do they in any way impair functional capacity.

EXPLANATORY FORMULATION: Both of these parents are fit to have custody of their children. Neither of them is harmful to the children, nor would they be damaging to the children in any way.

Certain predictable outcomes, however, are possible based on this psychological evaluation. If the children were placed with Mrs. Greenbaum, it is very likely that their life would be less structured but more emotionally exciting, and there would be more responsiveness, at least at their present ages, to their emotional needs and individual differences. Mrs. Greenbaum is less concerned with form and more interested in the substance of relationships. If the children were placed with Mr. Greenbaum, there would be more routine and regularity to their life, slightly less responsiveness to emotional and nurturing needs, and more concern with behavior fitting into well-defined and prescribed standards.

There are, of course, advantages and disadvantages to both modes of childrearing and understanding of the nurturing parenting process. Actually the styles of these two parents complement each other and in an intact family would provide the best of both dimensions. Where custody, however, is an issue, either of these parents can provide adequate and sufficient custodial parenting but with the differences suggested above.

R.E. Schulman, Ph.D.

R.E. Schulman, Ph.D.
Certified Psychologist

RES/vw

Date: August 2, 1993

M The Menninger Foundation

August 17, 1993

Dear Mr. Skoloff:

I have completed my clinical evaluation of the four members of the Greenbaum family. I assume you have received a report of the psychological test results from Doctor Schulman. As you know, I have utilized Doctor Schulman's findings in my evaluations.

I understand that the court will need to make a decision concerning child custody and, to the extent that it may be helpful, I have a contribution to make. In my opinion, Mrs. Greenbaum is the preferred parent for custody of the two children at the present time for the following reasons:

1. As a trained and experienced schoolteacher, Mrs. Greenbaum has above average knowledge of growth and development in children and age-appropriate management of children.
2. Mrs. Greenbaum is able to experience and react to the two children as separate individuals with different needs because of the age, sex, and personality characteristics.
3. Mrs. Greenbaum is warm, outgoing, and appropriately emotional.
4. Mrs. Greenbaum's motives in seeking custody are pure. She wants custody because she believes that only she can provide the loving and nurturing environment that young children need.
5. Mr. Greenbaum tends to some rigidity concerning standards of behavior and is a bit lacking in flexibility. He emphasizes efficiency and reason at the expense of feelings. He is uncomfortable with emotional expressions and may inadvertently discourage normal emotional development of the children.

I am strongly in favor of visitation rights for the noncustodial parent. Although under some circumstances such visitation can be destructive, in this case I do not find in the parents a degree of bitterness, vindictiveness, and desire to continue warfare which would make visitation a trying experience for the children. Both parents may well continue to express some disapproval of the other, but probably not to a degree which the children cannot handle.

I am strongly opposed to joint custody for children of this age. In our culture, the latency period (ages six to twelve) is a period for defining and consolidating basic personality traits which will determine significant coping devices of that individual for years to come. These traits are selected, tried out, modified, and developed into efficient, stress-handling techniques, chiefly within the family: security and safety notably influence psychological development of a child at this age. He needs a place to belong, and home should be a place of trust where there are predictable, trustworthy people with whom the child can interact meaningfully without unnecessary fear of disruption and unpredictability. If one has a home base that is secure and consistent, then one can venture into the wide, wide world without undue apprehension.

If I can be of further assistance in this case, please feel free to call upon me.

Sincerely yours,

Herbert C. Modlin, M.D.

Herbert C. Modlin, M.D.

HCM:gn

Enclosures

§3.8   IDENTIFYING THE LEGALLY AND EMOTIONALLY SIGNIFICANT FACTS

The next step is to go through the affidavits, identifying the legally and emotionally significant facts.

A fact is legally significant if the court would consider it in determining whether the legal requirements are, or are not, met. For example, in the *Greenbaum* case, any fact that the court would consider in determining the "best interests" of the children is legally significant. Other facts, and in particular those facts that relate to the behavior of the parent but do not affect the parent's relationship to the child, are not legally significant and will not (or should not) be argued by the attorneys or considered by the court.

Note

Notice the circular nature of legal analysis. The attorneys could not determine which statute applied until they had at least some of the facts. However, it wasn't until they knew which statute applied that they knew which facts were legally significant.

Question

Under section 402 of the Uniform Marriage and Divorce Act, which of the following facts are legally significant? Explain your answers.

     a.   the amount that each parent earns
     b.   a parent's tendency to gamble
     c.   a parent's sexual practices
     d.   a parent's relationship with his or her own parents
     e.   the child's academic, artistic, or athletic abilities

In our case, the attorneys determine which facts are legally significant by going through the affidavits, identifying the facts that the court would consider in evaluating each factor. Do the same in the following chart.

Legally Significant Facts	
Factor	*Legally Significant Facts*
1. Preference of parents	
2. Preference of children	
3. Interaction & interrelation-ship	
4. Adjustment to home, school, and community	
5. Physical and mental health	
6. Other factors	
7. Conduct that court will not consider	

Question

Are the facts that you listed next to number 7 legally significant? Why or why not?

_____

The attorneys also identify those facts that are emotionally significant.

An emotionally significant fact is a fact that, although not legally significant, may sway the court. For example, although in a criminal action the defendant's age and reasons for committing the crime are usually not legally significant, a judge may be more inclined to rule in favor of a 90-year-old widow who stole a loaf of bread because she was hungry than a 20-year-old junkie who stole to support a drug habit. Remember, judges are people, and they will find some cases more emotionally appealing than others.

Question

In a child custody action, which of the following facts would be emotionally significant?

    a. a grandparent's statements about how much one of the parents loves his or her children

    b. information indicating that in the past one of the parents had a drug or alcohol problem

    c. the fact that one of the parents is a well-known personality in the community

    d. the fact that one of the parents is well-educated and the other never graduated from high school

    e. the fact that one parent regularly attends church and the other attends church only on major religious holidays

_____

Application 3.5

In the *Greenbaum* case, which facts, if any, are emotionally significant?

Emotionally Significant Facts	
Facts That Favor Mr. Greenbaum	*Facts That Favor Mrs. Greenbaum*

§3.9   FORMULATING ARGUMENTS

The next step is to formulate the arguments. Given the law and the facts, what arguments can the attorneys make in trying to persuade the court to grant their client custody?

There are three types of cases: cases in which the law itself is in dispute; cases in which the application of the law is in dispute; and cases in which both the law and its application are disputed. In the first type, the parties argue the law itself. The plaintiff asks the court to apply Rule A, and the defendant asks the court to apply Rule B. In the second type, the parties agree that Rule C applies. What they disagree about is (1) what the facts are or (2) how Rule C should be applied to the facts. In the third type, the parties disagree both about the law and about how the law should be applied to the facts of the case.

The *Greenbaum* case falls into the third category. Although both sides agree that the standard is best interests of the children, they disagree about what test the court should apply. While Mrs. Greenbaum's attorney wants the court to apply the rules set out in *Huen* and *Nabrinski,* Mr. Greenbaum's attorney wants the court to disregard those rules. She thinks that because the rules are inconsistent with the statute, they should not be applied. In addition, both sides will argue the facts, arguing both about what the facts are and about how the law should be applied to them.

Question

How much latitude do the courts have in interpreting and applying a statute? Who decides whether a court has exceeded its power and changed the law instead of interpreting it?

§3.9.1   Arguing the Law

In the first type of case, the law itself is in dispute. The parties disagree about which statute or common law rule applies or about how the statute or rule should be interpreted.

As in the other types of cases, in this type of case it is not enough to simply state your position. You cannot just state that the court should interpret the statute in a manner that supports your client's position. You must make arguments.

In the *Greenbaum* case, the attorneys can make several types of arguments: They can support their position by arguing the plain language of the statute, legislative intent, or public policy.

a.   Plain Language Arguments

In arguing that the plain language of the statute supports the position being advocated, an attorney emphasizes what the statute does, and does not, say. For example, in the case that we are working on, Mr. Greenbaum's attorney would argue that rules set out in *Huen* and *Nabrinski* are inconsistent with the plain language of the statute. The statute does not tell the court to award custody to the parent who was the primary caregiver at the time the couple separated. It tells the court to consider all relevant factors.

Application 3.6

Write out what the father's attorney, Ms. Michael, would say in arguing that the rules set out in *Huen* and *Nabrinski* are inconsistent with the plain language of the statute. After you have written out the father's argument, think about how the mother's attorney would respond. Can Mr. Jeffrey also make an argument based on the plain language of the statute? If you think that he can, write out that argument.

b.   Legislative Intent

Attorneys also use legislative intent to support their interpretation of the law. In enacting the statute, did the legislature intend result A or did it intend result B? Before our attorneys can make an argument based on legislative intent, they need to do more research.

Evidence of the legislature's intent can be found in several different places. Sometimes the legislature explains its intent in the statutory section itself or in an introductory section that precedes the act. At other times, legislative intent can be found in the comments, if there are any, that accompany the statute or in the records of the legislature (the transcripts of legislative hearings on the statute or act, committee reports discussing the statute or act, or transcripts of floor debate).

In our problem case, the attorneys begin their search with the section of the Marriage and Divorce Act that explains the Act's purpose.

SECTION 102 PURPOSES: *RULES OF CONSTRUCTION**

This Act shall be liberally construed and applied to promote its underlying purposes, which are to:

(1) provide adequate procedures for the solemnization and registration of marriage;

(2) strengthen and preserve the integrity of marriage and safeguard family relationships;

(3) promote the amicable settlement of disputes that have arisen between parties to a marriage;

(4) mitigate the potential harm to the spouses and their children caused by the process of legal dissolution of marriage;

(5) make reasonable provision for spouse and minor children during and after litigation; and

(6) make the law of legal dissolution of marriage effective for dealing with the realities of matrimonial experience by making irretrievable breakdown of the marriage relationship the sole basis for its dissolution.

The phrases in this section that are potentially applicable are those stating (1) that the Act is to be liberally construed to promote its underlying purposes, (2) that in enacting the Act the legislature sought to mitigate the potential harm to the children caused by the process of legal dissolution of marriage; and (3) that the legislature sought to make reasonable provisions for spouses and minor children during and after litigation. These statements are, however, so broad that they are of little use to either side.

The next thing that the attorneys look for is a legislative history, that is, the records from legislative hearings, committee reports, and floor debate. Unfortunately, none are available: The hearings and floor debate have not been transcribed, and there was no written committee report.

In the absence of such information, the attorneys turn to the Uniform Act itself, locating and reading the Commissioners' Notes that follow section 402. Although these comments were written by the commissioners who drafted the Uniform Act and not the state legislature, they are of some value. If the state legislature had the comments before it when it adopted the Uniform Act, the attorneys can argue that the Commissioners' Notes reflect not only the intent of the commissioners but also the intent of the legislature.

---

*This Act has been reprinted through the permission of the National Conference of Commissioners on Uniform State Laws, and copies of the Act may be ordered from them at a nominal cost at 676 N. St. Clair St., Ste. 1700, Chicago, Ill. 60611, (302) 915-0195.

The following notes follow section 402 of the Uniform Act.

COMMISSIONERS' NOTES TO SECTION 402*

This section, excepting the last sentence, is designed to codify existing law in most jurisdictions. It simply states that the trial court must look to a variety of factors to determine what is the child's best interest. The five factors mentioned specifically are those most commonly relied upon in the appellate opinions; but the language of the section makes it clear that the judge need not be limited to the factors specified. Although none of the familiar presumptions developed by the case law are mentioned here, the language of the section is consistent with preserving such rules of thumb. The preference for the mother as custodian of young children when all things are equal, for example, is simply a shorthand method of expressing the best interest of children — and this section enjoins judges to decide custody cases according to that general standard. The same analysis is appropriate to the other common presumptions: a parent is usually preferred to a nonparent; the existing custodian is usually preferred to any new custodian because of the interest in assuring continuity for the child; preference is usually given to the custodian chosen by agreement of the parents. In the case of modification, there is also a specific provision designed to foster continuity of custodians and discourage change. See Section 409.

The last sentence of the section changes the law in those states which continue to use fault notions in custody adjudication. There is no reason to encourage parties to spy on each other in order to discover marital (most commonly, sexual) misconduct for use in a custody contest. This provision makes it clear that unless a contestant is able to prove that the parent's behavior in fact affects his relationship to the child (a standard which could seldom be met if the parent's behavior has been circumspect or unknown to the child), evidence of such behavior is irrelevant.

These notes seem to support the mother's request for custody. For, even though there is nothing in the statute itself that states that there is a presumption that it would be in the best interests of the children to give custody to the mother, the commissioners state that "the preference for the mother as custodian of young children when all things are equal . . . is simply a shorthand method of expressing the best interests of the children . . . ."

Application 3.7

Write out what Mrs. Greenbaum's attorney, Mr. Jeffrey, would say in arguing that the rules set out in *Huen* and *Nabrinski* accurately reflect the legislature's intent in enacting section 402. After you have written out Mrs. Greenbaum's argument, think about how Mr. Greenbaum's attorney might respond. Can Ms. Michael make an argument based on legislative intent? If you think that she can, write out her argument.

c. *Public Policy*

Closely related to arguments based on legislative intent are arguments based on public policy. When attorneys make this type of argument, they argue that Rule A is more consistent with public policy than is Rule B or that, as a matter of public policy, Rule A and not Rule B should be adopted.

The question, of course, is what is public policy? In general, policies reflect societal values. As a society, we want to protect the rights of the innocent, compensate those who have been injured, and conserve judicial resources.

In setting out the purposes of the Act (look once again at section 102 on page 54), the legislature listed some of the policies underlying the Uniform Child Custody Act. There may, however, be others. Can Mr. Greenbaum argue that, as a matter of public policy, the court should protect the rights of fathers, giving them an equal opportunity for custody?

Application 3.8

1. If you represent Mrs. Greenbaum, write out the arguments that her attorney might make in arguing that the rules set out in *Huen* and *Greenbaum* are consistent with public policy. If you represent Mr. Greenbaum, do the opposite. Write out the arguments that Mr. Greenbaum's attorney would make in arguing that the rules set out in those cases violate public policy.

2. Working with your group, prepare a five-minute oral argument. If you represent Mrs. Greenbaum, argue that the court should apply the rules set out in *Huen* and *Nabrinski;* if you represent Mr. Greenbaum, argue that the rules set out in those two cases are inconsistent with the statute and should not, therefore, be applied.

§3.9.2   Arguing the Application of the Law to the Facts

In addition to arguing the law, our attorneys can argue the application of the law to the facts. They can make factual arguments based on the plain language of the statute and rules; arguments based on analogous cases; and, once again, arguments based on policy.

a.   *Factual Arguments Based on the Plain Language of the Law*

The first type of argument, a factual argument based on the plain language of the law, is the most common. The attorney simply applies the law to the facts of the case.

Law	+	Facts	=	Legal Conclusion
Speed limit is 55 mph		Plaintiff was driving 65 mph		Plaintiff has violated the law

In our sample case, the attorneys can make a number of factual arguments. They can make arguments based on each of the factors, and they can apply the rules set out in the cases.

We begin with the first of the five factors. In this case, both parents want custody.

Law	+	Facts	=	Legal Conclusion
Parents' wishes as to custody		Father wants custody		Factor favors father
		Mother wants custody		Factor favors mother

Because both parents want custody, an evaluation of this factor results in a draw. Both parents can use this factor to support their arguments.

However, there may be a way in which Mr. Greenbaum's attorney, Ms. Michael, can use this factor to her client's advantage. Look carefully at the psychologist's report. In it, the psychologist states that he thinks that the mother's desire to get custody may be based, at least at some level, on her desire to "punish" the children's father. This is an opening, and, if the father wants it, an opportunity to make an argument.

EXAMPLE

MR. GREENBAUM'S ARGUMENT

It would not be in the best interests of the children to grant custody to Mrs. Greenbaum. Although Mrs. Greenbaum has requested custody of Tom and Mary, she wants custody not because she believes that such an award would be in the best interests of the children but because she wants to punish her husband. She feels rejected, and to counter this rejection, she has resorted to self-medication. Although Mrs. Greenbaum is a good parent, her desire for custody is motivated at least in part by her desire to punish Mr. Greenbaum.

EXAMPLE

MRS. GREENBAUM'S RESPONSE

The children's mother asks this court to grant her custody of her two children, Tom, age 9, and Mary, age 7. Both children have lived with their mother since Mr. Greenbaum moved out of the house without making arrangements for them.

Mrs. Greenbaum has not asked for custody to punish Mr. Greenbaum. She has requested custody because she wants to keep the children and because she believes that such a grant would be in the best interest of the children. As Dr. Modlin stated in his report.

> Mrs. Greenbaum's motives in seeking custody are pure. She wants custody because she believes that only she can provide the loving and nurturing environment that young children need.

Affidavit of Dr. Modlin.

As you read these two arguments, note several things. First, each side has applied law to fact. They have not talked about just the law, and they have not talked about just the facts. Instead, they have used both the law and the facts to support their requests for custody.

Second, in making arguments, each attorney has presented the facts in the light most favorable to his or her client. The attorneys have emphasized those facts that support their arguments and de-emphasized those that do not. Also note that Mrs. Greenbaum's attorney has included facts that do not directly relate to the first factor. For example, he has stated that it was the father who left the family home.

Questions

1. Why did the attorney include the statement that it was the father who left home? Is it, in the context of the first factor, legally significant? If not, is it an emotionally significant fact? What inference is Mrs. Greenbaum's attorney asking the court to make?

2. In addition to including the statement that it is the father who left the family home, the mother's attorney has also included the names and ages of the children. Why did Mr. Jeffrey include these facts? Are they legally significant? Emotionally significant?

———————

Finally, look at the language that each side uses. The packaging of an argument can be almost as important as the content. For example, note that while Mr. Greenbaum's attorney refers to Mrs. Greenbaum as "Mrs. Greenbaum," Mrs. Greenbaum's attorney refers to her as "the children's mother." This choice of labels was calculated. Although times are changing, many judges are still predisposed to grant the custody of young children to their mother. Consequently, while Mr. Greenbaum's attorney wants to de-emphasize the fact that Mrs. Greenbaum is the mother of young children, Mrs. Greenbaum's attorney wants to emphasize it.

Now let's look at the second factor. Neither child has stated a preference as to which parent he or she would like to live with, and there is nothing in the record that seems to support a finding that the children prefer, secretly or otherwise, one parent over the other.

Question

Because neither child has expressed a preference, how should the attorneys handle this factor? Should they discuss it, ignore it, or argue it?

———————

We now move to the third factor, "the interaction and interrelationship of the child with his parent or parents, his siblings, and any other person who may significantly affect the child's best interests." For the moment, assume that Mr. Greenbaum's attorney has prepared the following drafts of her argument relating to the third factor.

EXAMPLE   VERSION 1

Mr. Greenbaum's Argument

In deciding custody, the court must also consider "the child's interaction and interrelationship with his parent or parents, his siblings, and any other persons who may significantly affect the child's best interest." In this case, this factor weighs in favor of Mr. Greenbaum. It would, therefore, be in the best interests of the children to grant him custody.

> ### EXAMPLE   VERSION 2
>
> #### MR. GREENBAUM'S ARGUMENT
>
> As the head of his own business, Mr. Greenbaum is able to set his own schedule. He can, therefore, stay at home with the children until they leave for school, and he can take time off to stay with the children when they are ill or to take them to the doctor or dentist. If granted custody, he would hire a housekeeper to care for the children in the afternoon and to clean the house, do the laundry, and prepare the evening meal.
>
> Mr. Greenbaum sets high standards for both himself and his children. In addition, unlike Mrs. Greenbaum, he is consistent. He sets reasonable rules, and he enforces them calmly. Mr. Greenbaum also plays with the children on a regular basis, and he takes them camping and fishing.

In each of the versions set out above, Ms. Michael gives the judge only "half the package." In version 1, she sets out the law and her conclusion but does not give the judge the facts. In version 2, she sets out the facts but not the law or her conclusion.

Recognizing what she has done wrong, Ms. Michael writes another draft.

> ### EXAMPLE   VERSION 3
>
> #### MR. GREENBAUM'S ARGUMENT
>
> In deciding custody, the court must also consider "the child's interaction and interrelationship with his parent or parents, siblings, and any other person who may significantly affect the child's best interests." In this case, Mr. Greenbaum has an excellent relationship with his children. He interacts with both children: He frequently plays with both children, and he takes both children camping and fishing. He has also established a good parent-child relationship.
>
> He has also set high standards for both of his children, and he works to help them meet those standards. He is also a consistent disciplinarian. He has established fair rules and, unlike Mrs. Greenbaum, enforces those rules consistently and quietly.
>
> In addition, Mr. Greenbaum has a flexible work schedule. In the morning, he can stay at home until the children leave for

school, and when necessary, he can take time off to take them to the doctor or dentist. If granted custody, Mr. Greenbaum also plans to hire a housekeeper. The housekeeper would care for the children after school and, so that he could spend more time with the children, the housekeeper would also clean the house, do the laundry, and prepare the evening meal.

Because Mr. Greenbaum interacts well with his children and has a good parent-child relationship, this factor supports a finding that it would be in the best interests of the children to grant custody to Mr. Greenbaum.

This version is much better than the first two. Not only has Mr. Greenbaum's attorney set out the rules and facts, but she has also tied, or applied, specific parts of the rule to specific facts. For example, she has taken the word "interaction" from the statute and identified the facts that could be used to prove that Mr. Greenbaum interacts well with his children. "He interacts with both children: He frequently plays with both children, and he takes them camping and fishing." Similarly, she has taken the word "interrelationship" and identified the facts that could be used to prove that Mr. Greenbaum has a good relationship with his children.

Question

Mr. Greenbaum's attorney talks about the statute in terms of the parent-child relationship. Is this what the legislature meant when it instructed the court to look at the child's interrelationship with his parent or parents? If you were Mrs. Greenbaum's attorney, how would you argue this portion of the statute?

You should also note that in arguing this factor, Mr. Greenbaum's attorney discusses Mr. Greenbaum's ability to care for the children. Although the statute does not explicitly call for such information, most judges want it and, because it relates to and perhaps determines a parent's interaction and relationship to the children, Ms. Michael decided to put the information here.

Question

As an attorney, you will be required to make numerous tactical decisions. For example, in arguing the third factor, you would have to decide whether you wanted to discuss only Mr. Greenbaum's interaction and interrelationship with the children or whether you wanted to compare his interaction and interrelationship with that of Mrs. Greenbaum.

How would you have argued this factor? As Mr. Greenbaum's attorney, would you have discussed only Mr. Greenbaum's strengths? Only Mrs. Greenbaum's weaknesses? Both sides' strengths and weaknesses? What would you do if you were the attorney representing Mrs. Greenbaum?

_____

Application 3.9

We now turn to the rules set out in *Huen* and *Nabrinski.* What arguments would each side make? Are the ages of the children significant?

_____

b.   Arguments Based on Analogous Cases

Because our system is one based on precedent, cases can be used in two ways: as the source, or authority, for a rule and as an example of how that rule has been applied in similar cases. If the earlier case is favorable, supporting the client's position, the attorney will emphasize the similarities between the two cases, arguing that because the client's case is like the earlier case, the court should reach the same result. In contrast, if the earlier case is unfavorable, the attorney will try to distinguish the earlier case, arguing that because the facts are different, the court should reach the opposite conclusion. See Exhibit 3.3.

In our sample problem, the cases seem to support Mrs. Greenbaum's position. Accordingly, in comparing her case to *Huen* and *Na-*

EXHIBIT 3.3   Arguments Based on Analogous Cases

The court reached the result that you want the court to reach in your case:	*The court did not reach the result that you want the court to reach in your case:*
• Emphasize similarities • De-emphasize differences • Argue that because the cases are similar, the court should reach the same result	• De-emphasize similarities • Emphasize differences • Argue that because the differences are significant, the court need not reach the same result

brinski, her attorney emphasizes the similarities and de-emphasizes the differences.

EXAMPLE

MRS. GREENBAUM'S ARGUMENT

Our case is like *In re Marriage of Huen* and *In re Marriage of Nabrinski.* In both of these cases, the mother was the primary caregiver at the time of separation. In *Huen,* the mother took care of the children's day-to-day needs and supervised their medical care, schooling, and religious training. In *Nabrinski,* the mother supervised the children's after-school activities and homework and maintained the home, doing the cooking, cleaning, and shopping.

In our case, it is Mrs. Greenbaum, and not Mr. Greenbaum, who is the primary caregiver. Like the mothers in *Huen* and *Nabrinski,* Mrs. Greenbaum prepares the children for school and is with them after school and on school holidays. In addition, it is Mrs. Greenbaum who takes the children to the doctor and the dentist, attends school conferences, and shops for the children. Finally, it is Mrs. Greenbaum who maintains the home. Mrs. Greenbaum is the one who does the cleaning, the laundry, and the shopping.

In contrast, Mr. Greenbaum's attorney wants to distinguish the cases.

Application 3.10

Can Mr. Greenbaum use the analogous cases to his advantage? Write out the arguments that you think his attorney might make.

---

c. *Policy Arguments*

The final type of argument is a policy argument. In addition to using policy in arguing the law, attorneys use policy in arguing the application of the law to the facts. Given the facts of this case, and our values, who should get custody? As a matter of public policy, should custody be given to a father who left the home without making arrangements for the children?

Application 3.11

1. Write out the policy arguments that you could make on behalf of your client.

2. Working with your group, prepare a five-minute oral argument in which you apply the law to the facts of the sample case. If you are representing the mother, argue that, given the facts, she should get custody. If you represent the father, argue that he should get custody. Note: Some groups will also be asked to play the role of the judge, asking questions and issuing a decision.

A Final Note

You now have at least some idea of what it means to think like a lawyer. You have seen how lawyers analyze statutes and cases and what types of arguments they make in arguing on behalf of their clients. The following chapters will help you develop these skills, explaining in more detail how lawyers research, analyze, argue, and write about legal problems.

Chapter 4

An Introduction to Analyzing Statutes and Cases

With this chapter, we move from a general discussion of our system of government, types of law, and the legal process to two of the basic skills that you will need as an attorney: the ability to analyze statutes and the ability to analyze, or brief, cases.

A statute should not be read in the same way as a novel or even a textbook. A statute must be analyzed, that is, broken apart and applied to the facts of the client's case.

§4.1 THE STRUCTURE OF A STATUTE

Most statutes have three parts: the title, the text, and historical notes.

3 parts of statute

§ 2-201. **Formal Requirements: Statute of Frauds.*** (1) Except as otherwise provided in this section a contract for the sale of goods for the price of five hundred dollars or more is not enforceable by way of action or defense unless there is some writing sufficient to indicate that a contract for sale has been made between the parties and signed by the party against whom enforcement is sought or by his authorized agent or broker. A writing is not insufficient because it omits or incorrectly states a term agreed upon but the contract is not enforceable under this paragraph beyond the quantity of goods shown in such writing.

Title of statute

---

*Reprinted from *Massachusetts General Laws Annotated,* © 1990, with permission of West Publishing Company.

65

Text of statute

(2) Between merchants if within a reasonable time a writing in confirmation of the contract and sufficient against the sender is received and the party receiving it has reason to know its contents, it satisfies the requirements of subsection (1) against such party unless written notice of objection to its contents is given within ten days after it is received.

(3) A contract which does not satisfy the requirements of subsection (1) but which is valid in other respects is enforceable

(a) if the goods are to be specially manufactured for the buyer and are not suitable for sale to others in the ordinary course of the seller's business and the seller, before notice of repudiation is received and under circumstances which reasonably indicate that the goods are for the buyer, has made either a substantial beginning of their manufacture or commitments for their procurement; or

(b) if the party against whom enforcement is sought admits in his pleading, testimony or otherwise in court that a contract for sale was made, but the contract is not enforceable under this provision beyond the quantity of goods admitted; or

(c) with respect to goods for which payment has been made and accepted or which have been received and accepted

Historical notes

(section 2-606). St. 1957, c. 765, § 1, effective Oct. 1, 1958.

§4.2 Analyzing the Statute

Analyzing a statute is a four-step process. After (1) determining whether the statute is applicable, (2) read the statute carefully, (3) applying each part to the facts of the client's case and (4) interpreting the ambiguous language.

Step 1: Determine Whether the Statute Is Applicable

Determining whether a particular statute is applicable is itself a two-part process. You must determine the scope of the statute and the statute's effective date.

There are several places you can look to determine the scope of a particular statute. Sometimes there will be a section or paragraph explicitly defining the scope of the act or a particular statutory section. At other times, the scope can be inferred from the title or from the legislative history or official comments accompanying the act.

For example, to determine the scope of Article 2 of the Uniform Commercial Code, look first to the table of contents that precedes the Act.

ARTICLE 2.   Sales

PART 1.   SHORT TITLE, GENERAL CONSTRUCTION, AND SUBJECT MATTER*

Section

PART 2.   FORM, FORMATION, AND READJUSTMENT OF CONTRACT

Now look up section 2-102.

§4-2-102.   Scope — Certain Security and Other Transactions Excluded From This Article*

(1) Unless the context otherwise requires, this article applies to transactions in goods; it does not apply to:

(a) Any transaction which, although in the form of an unconditional contract to sell or present sale, is intended to operate only as a security transaction, nor does this article impair or repeal any statute regulating sales to consumers, farmers, or other specified classes of buyers; and

---

*Reprinted from *Massachusetts General Laws Annotated,* © 1990, with permission of West Publishing Company.

(b) The donation, whether for or without valuable consideration, acquisition, preparation, transplantation, injection, or transfusion of any human tissue, organ, or blood or component thereof for or to a human being. (Laws 1965, S.B.104, § 1. Repealed and reenacted Laws 1977, H.B.1400, § 5.)

Prior Compilations: C.R.S.1963, § 155-2-102.

Note that many of the terms used in this statutory section are defined in other sections. For example, the table of contents indicates that the term "goods" is defined in section 4-2-105. See page 67.

Thus, Article 2 applies only to transactions in goods. It does not apply to contracts for services or to contracts intended to operate only as security transactions. In addition, it does not supersede any statutes regulating sales to consumers, farmers, or other specified classes of buyers.

Determining the effective date of a statute is much easier. It is usually set out in the act itself, in the historical notes following the text of the particular statutory section, or in the notes or comments accompanying the act. For example, the effective date of the Uniform Commercial Code is set out in Article 10. See Exhibit 4.1.

Step 2: Read the Text of the Statute Carefully

The next step is to read the text of the statute carefully, asking yourself the relevant questions and looking at the language and punctuation that the legislature used.

Although your questions will vary depending on the statute and the reasons you have for reading it, the following are representative.

a. Does the statute describe the decisionmaking process? (For example, who has the burden of proof? Who is the decision-maker? What level of proof is required?)

b. Does the statute set out a rule or a standard? (Is there a list of requirements that must be met, or has the legislature simply set out factors that the decision-maker should consider?)

c. What is the relation of the parts to the whole? (Does the statute set out only one rule or test, alternative rules or tests, or a rule and exceptions to that rule?)

In addition, pay close attention to the way in which information is grouped and to the words and punctuation that the legislature selected. Different inferences will be drawn depending on whether information is in one sentence or paragraph or in different sentences or paragraphs. Similarly, a list in which the items are connected with an "and" will be treated very differently from a list in which the items are connected with an "or." For example, look again at section 2-201, pages 65-66.

EXHIBIT 4.1   **The Effective Date of a Statute***

EFFECTIVE DATE—REPEALS   **§ 4–10–101**

ARTICLE 10
Effective Date

PART 1
1966 CODE

Law Review Commentaries

U.C.C. Articles 9 and 10: Problems Solved and Problems Created. Barkley Clark, 38 U.Colo.L.Rev. 99 (1965–66).

PART 1
1966 CODE

§ 4–10–101. Effective date

(1) This title shall take effect at 12:01 a.m. on July 1, 1966. The provisions of this title apply to transactions entered into and events occurring after such date.

(2) Transactions validly entered into prior to the effective date of this title and the rights, duties, and interests flowing from them remain valid thereafter and may be terminated, completed, consummated, or enforced as required or permitted by any statute or other law amended or repealed by the enactment of this title as though such repeal or amendment had not occurred.

(Laws 1965, S.B.104, § 1.)

Prior Compilations: C.R.S.1963, § 155–10–101.

Official Comment

This effective date is suggested so that there may be ample time for all those who will be affected by the provisions of the Code to become familiar with them.
Variations from Official Text
The official text of § 10–101 of the Uniform Commercial Code provides:

"This Act shall become effective at midnight on December 31st following its enactment. It applies to transactions entered into and events occurring after that date."

*Reprinted from *West's Colorado Revised Statutes Annotated,* © 1989, with permission of West Publishing Company.

In analyzing this statute, first determine the relationship among its parts. What is the relationship between subsections (1), (2), and (3) and, within subsection (3), the relationship between paragraphs (a), (b), and (c)?

The first line of paragraph 1 answers the first of these two questions: The phrase "Except as otherwise provided in this section" indicates that the first subsection sets out the general rule and that subsections 2 and 3 set out the exceptions. To answer the second question, look at the words used to connect paragraphs (3)(a), (3)(b), and (3)(c). Because the three paragraphs are connected by the word "or," we know that they set out alternatives. Even if the formal requirements set out in subsection (1) are not met, the contract may still be enforceable if the requirements set out in paragraph (3)(a), (3)(b), or (3)(c) are met.

Now analyze the first subsection. What is the general rule? A careful reading reveals that subsection (1) sets out a rule rather than a standard. When you break apart the first sentence, you see that [a contract] [for the sale of goods] [for more than $500] is not enforceable unless certain requirements are met. The requirements are (1) that there be some writing sufficient to indicate that the parties entered into a contract for the sale of the goods and (2) that this writing be signed by the party against whom enforcement is sought.

Questions

1. If there is no "writing," is a contract for the sale of goods for $450.00 enforceable?

2. Can a seller enforce a contract for the sale of goods for $1,000 if the writing is signed by the seller but not by the buyer?

3. Is a contract for the sale of standard machine parts enforceable if the seller orally agreed to buy 15,000 parts but the writing says that the buyer agrees to buy 10,000 parts?

Step 3: Apply the Statute to the Facts of Your Case

The next step is to break the statute into its component parts. For most statutes, this step entails identifying the requirements, or elements. To obtain the benefit of the statute, what must be proved? To avoid the penalties, what must happen?

Once you have broken the statute apart, test each part against the facts of your case, determining which requirements are clearly met, which are clearly not met, and which will be disputed. For many attorneys, a chart like the one in Exhibit 4.2 simplifies the process.

EXHIBIT 4.2	Applying the Statute to the Facts in Your Case

Statutory Language	*Facts in Your Case*
Unless otherwise provided in this section	
a contract for the sale of goods	contract was for the sale of three rugs
for the price of $500 or more	total price for the three rugs was $16,875.00
is not enforceable unless there is a writing	
signed by the party against whom enforcement is sought	although the seller sent the buyers a written proposal, the buyers did not sign anything

Step 4: Determine How Ambiguous Language Has Been (Or Can Be) Interpreted

When the statutory language is ambiguous, look beyond the particular statutory section for help in interpreting it. In some instances, the ambiguous language will have been defined in a definitions section at the beginning of the act. In other instances, the legislature's intent can be determined from the purpose section at the beginning of the act, the official comments accompanying either the act or the particular section, or from a legislative history. In still other instances, the answer can be found in court opinions in which the court defines the ambiguous language.

Sometimes this search will result in a definitive answer. Given the statutory or court definition, the application of the language to the facts of your case is clear. For example, given the definition of "goods" set out in section 2-105, rugs are goods. They are "things," and they are moveable at the time of identification to the contract for sale. At other times, the answer is less clear. Is a contract for the sale and installation of wall-to-wall carpeting a contract for the sale of goods? To find the answer to this question, you would have to look to the case law.

Question

Is any of the language used in section 2-201(3)(a) ambiguous?

§4.3   ANALYZING CASES

Cases must be read as carefully as statutes. You must ask the relevant questions and analyze the language. What issue was before the court? What rule or test did the court apply? Given that rule or test, what facts were important? What was the court's holding and its rationale for that holding? Is any of the language in the opinion dicta, that is, observations or statements by the court that are not necessary to its holding? In addition, you must read between the lines. What doesn't the court say? What assumptions or inferences has the court made or drawn?

§4.3.1   Format of a Court Opinion

Like a statute, a court opinion has three parts: (1) the caption, which identifies the parties, the court issuing the decision, and the date of the decision; (2) prefatory information written by either the court reporter or the company publishing the opinion; and (3) the text of the court's opinion. The following opinion is typical.

COLORADO CARPET INSTALLATION, INC., d/b/a Sierra Range Carpets, Inc., a Colorado corporation, Petitioner,

v.

Fred PALERMO and Zuma Palermo, Respondents.

No. 82SC168.

Supreme Court of Colorado.

Sept. 12, 1983.*

The Court of Appeals, 647 P.2d 686, held that an oral contract involving purchase and installation of carpeting and other flooring materials was contract for sale of goods and that the contract was unenforceable by reason of the "writing" requirement of the Uniform Commercial Code. Certiorari was granted to review the decision of the Court of Appeals. The Supreme Court, Quinn, J., held that: (1) where agreement for installation of carpet

Caption

The caption identifies the parties, the docket number, the court issuing the opinion, and the date on which the opinion was issued. If there is a parallel cite, that cite may also be included.

Syllabus (Synopsis)

The syllabus is not part of the court's opinion; it is prepared by either the "reporter" or an attorney working for the company that publishes the reporter in which the opinion appears. In the summary, the reporter or attorney summarizes the case's history and the court's decision.

Because the syllabus is not part of the court's opinion, it cannot be cited as authority.

*Reprinted from *West's Colorado Revised Statutes Annotated,* © 1989, with permission of West Publishing Company.

contemplated that title to carpeting and other materials would pass to buyers, the agreement constituted "contract for sale," and, sale of goods being primary purpose of the contract, contract was within statute of frauds provisions of the Uniform Commercial Code, and (2) evidence did not permit finding that carpet which was to be installed in buyer's home was "specially manufactured" within "specially manufactured goods" exception to such statute of frauds.

Judgment of Court of Appeals affirmed. . . .

4. Frauds, Statute of ☞82

To satisfy "specially manufactured goods" exception to statute of frauds, goods must be specially made for buyer, goods must be unsuitable for sale to others in ordinary course of seller's business, seller must have substantially begun to manufacture goods or must have made commitment for their procurement, and manufacture or commitment must have been commenced under circumstances reasonably indicating that goods are for buyer and prior to seller's receipt of notification of repudiation. C.R.S. 4-2-201(1), (3)(a).

5. Frauds, Statute of ☞82

Term "specially manufactured" as used in "specially manufactured goods" exception to statute of frauds in Uniform Commercial Code refers to character of goods as specially made for particular buyer, and not to whether they were "specially made" in usual course of seller's business. C.R.S. 4-2-201(1), (3)(a).

> See publication Words and Phrases for other judicial constructions and definitions.

6. Frauds, Statute of ☞82

Evidence did not permit finding that carpet which was to be installed in buyer's home was "specially manufactured" within "specially manufactured goods" exception to statute of frauds in Uniform Commercial Code. C.R.S. 4-2-201(1), (3)(a).

Louis A. Weltzer, Denver, for petitioner.

Joseph P. Constantine, Denver, for respondents.

Headnotes

Like the syllabus, the headnotes are not part of the court's opinion; they are written by an attorney who works for the publisher. The attorney reads the opinion and, for each rule set out by the court, prepares a one-sentence "note."

For each headnote number there is a corresponding number in the text where the court discusses the rule summarized in the headnote. See, for example, pages 78-79.

Because headnotes are not part of the court's opinion, they cannot be cited as authority.

Attorneys' Names

The names of the attorneys representing the parties

QUINN, Justice.

We granted certiorari to review the decision of the court of appeals in *Colorado Carpet Installation, Inc. v. Palermo*, 647 P.2d 686 (Colo.App.1982). The court of appeals, in reversing the trial court, held that an oral agreement involving the purchase and installation of carpeting and other flooring materials was a contract for the sale of goods within the meaning of section 4–2–201(1), C.R.S.1973, of the Uniform Commercial Code, rather than a service contract, and that the contract was unenforceable because the goods did not qualify under section 4–2–201(3)(a), C.R.S.1973, for the "specially manufactured goods" exception to the "writing" requirement of section 4–2–201(1), C.R.S.1973. We affirm the judgment of the court of appeals.

I.

In July 1980 Colorado Carpet Installation, Inc., doing business as Sierra Range Carpets, Inc. (Colorado Carpet), commenced an action in the District Court of Adams County against Fred and Zuma Palermo for breach of contract. The claim was based on an alleged oral agreement in which the Palermos agreed to pay $4,775.75 to Colorado Carpet for the purchase and installation of carpeting, other flooring materials, and bathroom tile for the Palermo home in Thornton, Colorado. The Palermos in their answer denied the existence of a contract and affirmatively asserted that the statute of frauds, section 4–2–201(1), C.R.S.1973, rendered any such agreement unenforceable.

The controversy was tried to the court and arose as follows. Colorado Carpet is a Colorado corporation engaged in the business of selling and installing carpeting, tile and other flooring materials. In April 1980,

Justice's Name
The name of the justice writing the majority opinion

Text of the Opinion
Although the content and organization will vary, the following information is usually included in the text of the opinion:

a. a summary of the facts;
b. a statement of issues before the court;
c. a summary of the applicable law;
d. an application of the law to the facts of the case; and
e. the court's holding.

1386 Colo.   **668 PACIFIC REPORTER, 2d SERIES**

Jack Duran, the president of Colorado Carpet, began negotiations with the Palermos for the sale and installation of carpeting, carpet padding, tile and vinyl floor covering in the downstairs and upstairs areas of their home. Colorado Carpet did not maintain an actual retail store or warehouse for these materials, but arranged to purchase them from other distributors. In the course of his negotiations with the Palermos, Duran delivered carpet samples to the Palermo home, measured the home, and assisted Mrs. Palermo in locating at local retail outlets the type and brand of flooring materials that she wanted. Further negotiations ensued, including a written proposal from Duran.

This written proposal, which referred to Colorado Carpet as "the seller" and to the Palermos as "the customer," stated that Colorado Carpet offered for the Palermos' acceptance the following items: a total of 195 square yards of Seduction and Amaretto carpeting, along with padding, at $15.95 per square yard, for a total price of $3110.45; 48 square yards of kitchen carpeting at $8.50 per square yard, for a total price of $399.50;[1] 55 square yards of deck carpeting at $7.50 per square yard, for a total price of $412.50; approximately 220 square feet of ceramic tile at $3.50 per square foot, for a total price of $770; and 9 square yards of vinyl floor covering at $9.50 per square yard, for a total price of $85.50. The proposal expressly included all labor. According to Duran, the source of Colorado Carpet's profit from such a transaction would be the markup on the sale of the materials and not their installation, the latter being provided at cost. He estimated the labor cost at $2.00 per square yard for installing the upstairs, downstairs and kitchen carpeting, and $1.50 per square foot for installing the tile.

Although the Palermos never made a written acceptance of Colorado Carpet's proposal, Duran testified that Mrs. Palermo orally accepted the proposal on or about April 25, 1980, shortly after he submitted it to her. Mrs. Palermo, in contrast, denied accepting the written proposal. It was her testimony that neither she nor her husband ever agreed to purchase any carpeting from Colorado Carpet and that she had contacted Duran only about a tiling job for the upstairs and downstairs bathrooms.

On April 30 and May 1, 1980, Colorado Carpet placed orders with Georgia and California manufacturers for the Seduction (downstairs) and the Amaretto (upstairs) carpeting. These orders called for both carpets to be cut into segments measuring 12 feet by 73 feet in order to permit effective installation in the upstairs and downstairs sections of the Palermo home.[2] The orders were filled in due course, and the carpets were eventually delivered to a Denver warehouse. Colorado Carpet deferred ordering the carpet padding and kitchen carpet at this time because these were stock items and could be purchased immediately before the installation was to commence.

Colorado Carpet purchased and delivered the ceramic tile to the Palermo home for eventual installation in the upstairs and downstairs bathrooms. Mrs. Palermo, however, had a disagreement with Colorado Carpet's tile man over some repair work in connection with the tile installation and arranged with some other contractor to supply and install other tile. Duran, on behalf of Colorado Carpet, attempted unsuccessfully to renegotiate with the Palermos but to no avail. Colorado Carpet removed its tile from the home, returned half of it to the supplier for a refund and sold the other half. It also shipped the Seduction carpeting back to the California manufacturer in

1. At $8.50 per square yard, the price of 48 square yards of kitchen carpeting should have been $408.

2. Colorado Carpet paid a more expensive "cut price" rather than the usual "roll price" for the orders. Mr. Duran testified that an order based

on the "roll price" would be cut from that size of available roll that most nearly approximates the dimensions requested in the cut. The "special cut" price, in contrast, is based upon an order cut to the dimensions requested.

COLORADO CARPET INSTALLATION, INC. v. PALERMO Colo. **1387**
Cite as 668 P.2d 1384 (Colo. 1983)

exchange for some credit and was able to sell the Amaretto carpeting to a local purchaser.

The trial court found that Colorado Carpet's proposal for the sale and installation of the carpeting and other materials had been orally accepted by the Palermos, thereby resulting in a contract, and determined that the contract was enforceable for two reasons: first, the agreement constituted a service contract for the performance of labor, rather than a contract for the sale of goods, and thus was not subject to the "writing" requirement of the statute of frauds section of the Uniform Commercial Code, section 4–2–201(1), C.R.S.1973; and second, even if the entire agreement was construed as a contract for the sale of goods, that part of the agreement relating to the purchase and installation of carpeting fell within the "specially manufactured goods" exception to the statute of frauds, section 4–2–201(3)(a), C.R.S.1973, and thus was enforceable on that basis.[3] The court awarded damages to Colorado Carpet in the amount of $1,356.50, based upon lost profits, labor, and storage and shipping costs in connection with all the carpeting and padding ordered under the contract, not just the upstairs and downstairs carpeting. The court of appeals reversed the judgment, reasoning that although the agreement was a contract for the sale of goods, it did not satisfy the "specially manufactured goods" exception to the statute of frauds. We granted certiorari to consider whether the

oral agreement in question constituted a contract for the sale of goods within the meaning of section 4–2–201(1) of the Uniform Commercial Code, and, if so, whether it qualified for the "specially manufactured goods" exception of section 4–2–201(3)(a).

II.

We first address the court of appeals' determination that the contract was one for the sale of goods, rather than for the performance of labor or services. We conclude that the agreement in question involved a contract for the sale of goods as contemplated by section 4–2–201(1), C.R.S.1973.

[1] This section prohibits the enforcement of contracts "for the sale of goods for the price of $500 or more ... unless there is some writing sufficient to indicate that a contract for sale has been made between the parties and signed by the party against whom enforcement is sought ...." By its terms, the statute applies only to contracts for the sale of goods, and not to contracts for labor or services. *E.g., Robertson v. Ceola,* 225 Ark. 703, 501 S.W.2d 764 (1973); *George F. Mueller & Sons, Inc. v. Northern Illinois Gas Co.,* 12 Ill.App.3d 362, 299 N.E.2d 601 (1973); 3 R. Duesenberg & L. King, *Bender's Uniform Commercial Code Service* § 2.02[4] at 2–24 (1982); *cf. Samuelson v. Chutich,* 187 Colo. 155, 529 P.2d 631 (1974) (statutory warranties imposed by Uniform Sales Act not applicable to *service*

---

3. The trial court also concluded that the entire oral agreement was excepted from the statute of frauds by reason of the doctrine of part performance. Section 4–2–201(3)(c), C.R.S. 1973, states that a contract not satisfying the "writing" requirement of section 4–2–201(1), C.R.S.1973, is nevertheless enforceable "[w]ith respect to goods for which payment has been made and accepted or which have been received and accepted (section 4–2–606)." Official Comment 2 to section 4–2–201 states that "'[p]artial performance' as a substitute for the required memorandum can validate the contract only for the goods which have been accepted or for which payment has been made and accepted." The only material actually received and accepted was the tile, but Colorado Carpet, as the trial court found, was able to

return or resell the tile and suffered no damages on this item. The court of appeals resolved the part performance issue as follows:

"Here, the tile was the only item which was delivered to and initially accepted by the defendants. However, plaintiff removed the tile, and payment for the tile forms no part of plaintiff's present claim. As the carpeting was neither received nor accepted by the defendant, the part performance exception cannot apply to validate that portion of the contract." 647 P.2d at 688.

Colorado Carpet has not requested certiorari review on the part performance issue, and we do not address it in this opinion.

contracts). The Uniform Commercial Code defines "goods" to mean "all things (including specially manufactured goods) which are movable at the time of identification to the contract for sale other than the money in which the price is to be paid, investment securities ... and things in action." Section 4-2-105(1), C.R.S.1973. A "sale," by statutory definition, "consists in the passing of title from the seller to the buyer for a price," and a "contract for sale" includes a present sale of goods as well as a contract to sell goods at a future time. *Id.* 4-2-106(1).

[2, 3] In this case the subject of the contract involved "goods" because the carpeting and other materials were movable at the time that Colorado Carpet procured them for installation pursuant to the agreement. Since the agreement contemplated that title to the carpeting and other materials would pass to the Palermos, it constituted a "contract for sale." The scope of the contract, however, included not only the sale of goods but also the performance of labor or service. Thus, we must determine whether such a mixed contract qualified as a contract for the sale of goods or, instead, constituted a contract for labor or service outside the scope of section 4-2-201(1), C.R.S.1973.

The performance of some labor or service frequently plays a role in sales transactions. "Goods," however, are not the less "goods" merely because labor or service may be essential to their ultimate use by the purchaser. The mere furnishing of some labor or service, in our view, should not determine the ultimate character of a contract for purposes of section 4-2-201(1) of the Uniform Commercial Code. Rather, the controlling criterion should be the primary purpose of the contract—that is, whether the circumstances underlying the formation of the agreement and the performance reasonably expected of the parties demonstrates the primary purpose of the contract as the sale of goods or, in contrast, the sale of labor or service. We agree in this re-

spect with the following statement in *Bonebrake v. Cox,* 499 F.2d 951, 960 (8th Cir. 1974):

"The test for inclusion or exclusion is not whether [goods and services] are mixed, but, granting that they are mixed, whether their predominant factor, their thrust, their purpose, reasonably stated, is the rendition of service, with goods incidentally involved (*e.g.,* contract with artist for painting) or is a transaction of sale, with labor incidentally involved (*e.g.,* insulation of a water heater in a bathroom)."

Accord, e.g., Care Display, Inc. v. Didde-Glaser, Inc., 225 Kan. 232, 589 P.2d 599 (1979); *Burton v. Artery Co., Inc.,* 279 Md. 94, 367 A.2d 935 (1977); *Meyers v. Henderson Construction Co.,* 147 N.J.Super. 77, 370 A.2d 547 (1977). *See generally* Annot., *Applicability of U.C.C. Article 2 to Mixed Contracts for Sale of Goods and Services,* 5 A.L.R. 4th 501 (1981).

This "primary purpose" test, we believe, is designed to promote one of the expressed statutory policies of the Uniform Commercial Code—"[t]o simplify, clarify, and modernize the law governing commercial transactions." Section 4-1-102(2)(a), C.R.S.1973. Useful factors to consider in determining whether "goods" or "service" predominates include the following: the contractual language used by the parties, *see, e.g., Triangle Underwriters, Inc. v. Honeywell, Inc.,* 604 F.2d 737 (2d Cir.1979); *Bonebrake v. Cox, supra; Fifteenth Street Investment Co. v. People,* 102 Colo. 571, 81 P.2d 764 (1938); whether the agreement involves one overall price that includes both goods and labor or, instead, calls for separate and discrete billings for goods on the one hand and labor on the other, *see, e.g., Triangle Underwriters, Inc. v. Honeywell, Inc., supra; Aluminum Company of America v. Electro Flo Corp.,* 451 F.2d 1115 (10th Cir.1971); the ratio that the cost of goods bears to the overall contract price, *see, e.g., Lincoln Pulp & Paper Co., Inc. v. Dravo Corp.,* 436 F.Supp. 262 (D.Me.1977); *Van Sistine v.*

COLORADO CARPET INSTALLATION, INC. v. PALERMO Colo. **1389**
Cite as 668 P.2d 1384 (Colo. 1983)

Tollard, 95 Wis.2d 678, 291 N.W.2d 636 (Wis.Ct.App.1980); and the nature and reasonableness of the purchaser's contractual expectations of acquiring a property interest in goods (goods being defined as things that are movable at the time of identification to the contract, section 4–2–105(1), C.R. S.1973), *see generally* Marshall, *The Applicability of the Uniform Commercial Code to Construction Contracts,* 28 Emory L.J. 335, 365–76 (1979).

Considering the contract under these guidelines, we are satisfied that, as a matter of law, its primary purpose was the sale of goods and not the sale of labor or service.[4] The language in Colorado Carpet's proposal referred to the parties as "seller" and "customer." In addition, the agreement called for an overall contract price that included both the cost of goods and labor, and, as the trial evidence established, the charge for labor was slight in relation to the total contractual price.[5] Finally, the carpeting and other materials were movable when Colorado Carpet procured them for the purpose of selling them to the Palermos. The fact that these materials might later be installed in the Palermo home and assume the character of fixtures does not undermine the primary purpose of the contract as one for a sale of goods. *See Saliba v. Reed Electric Co.,* 90 Colo. 287, 8 P.2d 1095 (1932). We therefore agree with the court of appeals that the agreement between Colorado Carpet and the Palermos constituted a contract for the sale of goods, with labor or service only incidentally involved, and thus within the statute of frauds provisions of the Uniform Commercial Code.

III.

We turn now to the question whether the contract qualified for the "specially manufactured goods" exception to the statute of frauds. Section 4–2–201(3)(a), C.R.S.1973, states that a contract for the sale of goods which does not meet the "writing" requirements of section 4–2–201(1), C.R.S.1973, is nonetheless enforceable under the following circumstances:

"If the goods are to be specially manufactured for the buyer and are not suitable for sale to others in the ordinary course of the seller's business and the seller, before notice of repudiation is received and under circumstances which reasonably indicate that the goods are for the buyer, has made either a substantial beginning of their manufacture or commitments for their procurement ...."

[4] The plain terms of section 4–2–201(3)(a), C.R.S.1973, make clear that four distinct criteria are necessary to satisfy the "specially manufactured goods" exception to the statute of frauds: (1) the goods must be specially made for the buyer; (2) the goods must be unsuitable for sale to others in the ordinary course of the seller's business; (3) the seller must have substantially begun to have manufactured the goods or to have made a commitment for their procurement; and (4) the manufacture or commitment must have been commenced under circumstances reasonably indicating that the goods are for the buyer and prior to the seller's receipt of notification of contractual repudiation. In this case there is no dispute that the third and fourth statutory criteria have been established. There is evidence

---

4. While some cases have concluded that certain installation agreements involving flooring materials are service contracts, we find them distinguishable from the instant case. *See, e.g., Ranger Construction Co. v. Dixie Floor Co., Inc.,* 433 F.Supp. 442 (D.S.C.1977) (emphasizing that the agreement was a "construction contract" and not a contract for the sale of goods, one party being referred to as a "subcontractor" rather than a "materialman"); *Dionne v. Columbus Mills, Inc.,* 311 So.2d 681 (Fla.Dist.Ct.App.1975) (installer provided all

materials except the carpet itself which was furnished by the hiring party).

5. At the rate of $2.00 per square yard as the labor charge for installation of the upstairs, downstairs and kitchen carpets, and $1.50 per square foot for installation of the tile, the contract price of $4,777.75 represents a total labor charge of $926 ($596 for 298 square yards of carpeting and $330 for 220 square feet of tile). The record contains no evidence of a labor charge for installation of the vinyl floor covering.

demonstrating that Colorado Carpet, before receipt of the Palermos' repudiation of the agreement and under circumstances reasonably indicating that the upstairs and downstairs carpeting was for them, placed special orders with carpet manufacturers for the procurement of these two pieces of carpeting. There being no controversy about these matters, we confine our consideration to the statutory provisions requiring the goods to be "specially manufactured for the buyer" and "not suitable for sale to others in the ordinary course of the seller's business."

A.

The "specially manufactured goods" exception is premised on notions of both evidentiary reliability and fairness. Certain marketing practices provide sufficiently reliable evidence on the matter of a contractual relationship as to dispense with the written requirements of the statute of frauds. It is a reasonable assumption, for example, that a seller will not make or procure goods not suitable for sale to others in the normal course of the seller's business unless a purchaser has contracted with the seller to purchase these goods. *See Impossible Electronics Techniques, Inc. v. Wackenhut Protective Systems, Inc.,* 669 F.2d 1026 (5th Cir.1982); 3 R. Duesenberg & L. King, *supra,* § 2.02[4] at 2–30. Denying enforcement of the contract under such circumstances can result in unfairness to the seller by encumbering him with unsalable goods. *Impossible Electronics Techniques, Inc. v. Wackenhut Protective Systems, Inc.,* 669 F.2d at 1037. There is no unfairness in nonenforcement, however, when the goods are of a class customarily sold by the seller and are readily marketable to others in the ordinary course of the seller's business.

[5] The term "specially manufactured" refers to the character of the goods as specially made *for a particular buyer,* and not to whether they were "specially made" in the usual course of the seller's business.

Id. Thus, although not articulated in the Uniform Commercial Code, "the unsalable quality of the goods presumably must be found in their characteristics of special manufacture and not in such tests as lost markets, passed seasons, or the objective inability of the particular seller to dispose of the goods for reasons unrelated to their nature as prescribed by the buyer." 2 R. Duesenberg & L. King, *supra,* § 2.02[4] at 2–32. It has been held that "[i]f with slight alterations the goods could be sold, then they are not specially manufactured; if, however, essential changes are necessary to render the goods marketable by the seller to others, then the exception does apply." *Impossible Electronic Techniques, Inc. v. Wackenhut Protective Systems, Inc.,* 669 F.2d at 1037. It is in the light of these standards that the evidentiary state of the record must be considered.

B.

[6] There is no evidence from which one may reasonably conclude that the upstairs and downstairs carpets were "specially made" within the intendment of section 4–2–201(3)(a), C.R.S.1973. These styles of carpets had been observed by Mrs. Palermo in retail carpeting outlets in the Denver area, and both carpets were ordered by Colorado Carpet as stock items from carpet manufacturers in California and Georgia. No special dying, weaving or other treatment was required to fill the orders. The carpeting was not cut to any unusual shape nor even to the precise dimensions of the rooms where they were to be installed, but rather was cut in a rectangular shape with footage adequate for the entire project. *In* short, there is no showing of any unusual or special features of the carpeting that might attest to its character as specially made for a particular buyer. *See, e.g., Maderas Tropicales v. Southern Crate & Veneer Co.,* 588 F.2d 971 (5th Cir.1979); *Saliba v. Reed Electric Co., supra.*

The record is similarly deficient in establishing that the upstairs and downstairs car-

COLORADO CARPET INSTALLATION, INC. v. PALERMO Colo. **1391**
Cite as **668 P.2d 1384 (Colo. 1983)**

peting satisfied the other statutory requirement of section 4–2–201(3)(a), C.R.S.1973: "not suitable for sale to others in the ordinary course of the seller's business." The business of Colorado Carpet was to purchase carpeting from wholesalers or manufacturers and then to resell the carpeting to retail purchasers at a price inclusive of a labor charge for installation. As a dealer in carpeting and other flooring materials, Colorado Carpet continually dealt with goods of this nature and reasonably could be expected to find a buyer for them. There certainly was nothing in the character of the upstairs and downstairs carpeting that required basic or essential changes to be made in order to render them marketable to other purchasers. The dimensions of both pieces of carpeting were such that each could be easily recut, if necessary, to accommodate retail purchasers who might be looking for these particular brands in different dimensions. Indeed, the record shows that Colorado Carpet received credit from the manufacturer upon its return of the upstairs carpet and had little difficulty in selling the downstairs carpet to a local purchaser. This state of the record is manifestly insufficient to support the trial court's determination that the upstairs and downstairs carpeting qualified for the "specially manufactured goods" exception to the statute of frauds.

We also conclude that there was no evidence to support the trial court's inclusion

of the carpet padding and the kitchen carpet in the "specially manufactured goods" category. The record shows that these materials were stock items, and, far from being cut or processed to conform to the needs of the customer, they were never ordered or obtained by Colorado Carpet in connection with the Palermo agreement.[6]

It was the burden of Colorado Carpet to present sufficient evidence permitting the fact finder to reasonably conclude by a preponderance of the evidence that the goods included in its sales agreement with the Palermos satisfied the statutory criteria for the "specially manufactured goods" exception to the statute of frauds. It failed to carry its burden of proof on this issue, and, as the court of appeals correctly ruled, the trial court erred in enforcing the contract.

The judgment of the court of appeals is affirmed.

---

6. Mr. Duran testified that he usually ordered kitchen carpets C.O.D. and the cutting would take place when the supplier was actually paid. Since the kitchen carpets had been neither ordered nor paid for, they obviously had not been cut for installation in the Palermo home.

When, as in *Colorado Carpet,* the judges hearing the case concur in both the result and the rationale for that result, there is only one opinion. When they do not agree, there will be multiple opinions: In addition to the majority opinion, there may be concurring opinions, which are written or signed by judges who agree with the result but not the rationale, and dissenting opinions, which are written or signed by judges who disagree both with the result and the rationale.

Note

When a majority of the judges hearing a case cannot agree on a single opinion, there will be a plurality opinion and not a majority opinion.

_____

§4.3.2   Briefing Cases

Briefing is a process that attorneys use to analyze a case. By preparing a brief, they force themselves to read the case carefully.

As a general rule, you will need to read a case more than once. When reading a case for a law school class, use the first reading to determine what the case is about and why it was included in your casebook. What point does the case raise or illustrate? Similarly, when reading a case for a research project, use the first reading to determine whether the case is potentially useful. Does it discuss the same issue that you have been asked to research? If it does, does it set out or interpret the rule? Can you use the case to make an argument based on precedent? How might the other side use the case?

Then read the case again, this time looking at (a) the name of the court and date the opinion was issued; (b) the case's procedural posture; (c) the issue or issues that were before the court; (d) the rule or test that the court applied in resolving each; (e) the facts that the court found legally significant; (f) the court's holding; (g) the court's reasoning; and (h) the disposition of the case.

a.   The name of the court and the date the opinion was issued.   Although you should always note the name of the court issuing the opinion and the date of issuance, this information will be used differently depending on whether you are briefing the case for a law school class or for a research project.

If you are briefing the case for class, the name of the court and date of the opinion may help explain why the result in the case that you are reading is different from the result in the preceding case or the case that follows: It is not unusual for different jurisdictions to have different rules (either statutory or common law), and in later cases courts can overrule their earlier decisions.

In contrast, if you are briefing the case for a research project, the court and date of the opinion will be used to determine whether the case is mandatory authority (authority that the court must follow) or only persuasive authority (authority that the court will consider but that is not binding on the court). (See section 2.3 for a complete discussion of mandatory and persuasive authority.)

b. The case's procedural posture.   Note also the case's procedural posture. Is the decision a decision of a trial or an appellate court? If it is a decision of an appellate court, is the appellate court reviewing a procedural ruling before there has been a final judgment, or is the court reviewing the final judgment itself?

c. The issue(s) before the court.   The issue can almost always be stated in more than one way. It can focus on the procedural aspects (did the trial court err in granting the motion for summary judgment?) or on the substantive issue (what test did the court apply in determining whether the goods were specially manufactured?). In addition, it can be stated either narrowly or broadly.

If you are stating the issue for class, consider both the issue as stated by the court and the reason that the case was included in the casebook. If the case is in your civil procedure casebook, you will want to frame the issue so that it highlights the procedural issue; if it is in your contracts book, frame the issue so that it highlights the substantive rules.

In stating the issue for a research brief, consider two things. First, make sure that you understand the case's procedural posture. Did the court decide that goods were specially manufactured or only that the trial court erred in granting summary judgment? Second, remember that the issue determines the holding. How can you state the issue so that the court's holding supports your client's position? How will the other side characterize the issue and the holding?

d. The rule or test that the court applied.   Once you have identified the issue before the court, the next step is to determine what law the court applied in resolving that issue. In some cases, the law is not in dispute. Both sides agree that the case is governed by a particular statute or well-established common law rule. In other cases, the parties disagree over what the law is. If there is no law, they may each advocate a different approach; if there is law, they may disagree over how that law should be interpreted or applied.

In the former instance, you need note only the rule or test that the court applied; in the latter, note which rule each side advocated and which rule the court ultimately applied.

e. The facts that the court found legally significant.   The next step is to identify the legally significant facts. Which facts did the court rely on in deciding the case?

To determine which facts the court relied on, look at both the facts that the court recited in its fact summary at the beginning of the case and at the facts that it refers to in its holding and reasoning. Also look at the facts set out in any concurring or dissenting opinions. Sometimes it is the absence of a fact that is legally significant.

f. The court's holding.   The holding is the answer to the question before the court. If the question was whether the court erred in granting summary judgment, the holding is that the court did (or did not) err in granting the motion. Similarly, if the issue is whether there was sufficient evidence to support a finding that the rugs were specially manufactured when they were stock items and not subjected to any special dyeing or weaving, the holding is that there was (or was not) sufficient evidence.

g. The court's reasoning.   In addition to setting out the court's holding, also set out its reasoning. Why did the court decide the issue as it did? Did it rely on an established rule or test? If not, why did it adopt the rule or test that it did? Also look at how broadly or narrowly the court stated its holding and the policies that it considered.

h. The disposition of the case.   The final section is the disposition of the case. What was the court's decision and how did that decision affect the parties?

Although the format will vary from person to person and even from class to class, the following brief is representative.

EXAMPLE

Colorado Carpet Installation, Inc.
v. Palermo

Colorado Supreme Court
1983
668 P.2d 1384 (Colo. 1983)

Procedural Posture

Colorado Carpet brought suit against Palermo, asking the trial court to enforce an oral contract for the sale and installation of carpeting and other materials. The trial court found the contract enforceable for two reasons: (1) it was a contract for services and not goods and (2) even if the contract was a contract for goods, it was enforceable under the exception for specially manufactured goods. Damages in the amount of $1,356.50 were awarded to plaintiff.

On appeal, the Colorado Court of Appeals reversed, holding that the contract was a contract for the sale of goods and not services and that the goods did not qualify under the exception for specially manufactured goods. The Colorado Supreme granted certiorari to review the Court of Appeals' decision.

Issues

1. Is a contract for the sale and installation of carpeting and other materials a contract for services or for goods?

2. Does a contract for the sale of carpeting that is a stock item available at other retail outlets and that has not been cut to a specific size or subjected to any special dyeing, weaving, or other treatment qualify for the exception for specially manufactured goods set out in 2-201(3)(a)?

Rule or Test

Issue 1

The court does not set out a specific rule or test. Instead, it considered the following factors:

a. the contract's primary purpose,
b. the cost of the goods versus the cost of the services,
c. the fact that the carpeting and other materials were moveable when Colorado Carpet procured them, and
d. the labels used to describe the parties (see footnote 4 in opinion).

Issue 2

Element 1 (specially manufactured for the buyer).   The term "specially manufactured" refers to the character of the goods as specially made for a particular buyer and not to whether they were "specially made" in the usual course of the seller's business. (Cites *Impossible Electronics Techniques, Inc. v. Wackenhut Protective Systems, Inc.,* 669 F.2d 1026 (5th Cir. 1982) and 3 R. Duesenberg & L. King, *Bender's Uniform Commercial Code Service § 2.02*[4].

Element 2 (not suitable for resale in the ordinary course of the seller's business).   The unsalable quality must be found in the goods' characteristics of special manufacture and not in such tests as lost markets, passed seasons, or the objective inability of the particular seller to dispose of the goods for reasons unrelated to their nature as prescribed by the buyer. Cites to *Bender.* If with slight alterations the goods can be sold, the goods are not specially manufactured. Cites *Impossible Electronics.*

Legally Significant Facts

Issue 1

1. primary purpose of contract was sale of goods and not services (this is stated as a fact)

2. cost of services slight in comparison to cost of goods
3. carpet and other materials moveable at the time they were procured
4. parties referred to as "seller" and "customer"

Issue 2

1. Mrs. Palermo had observed the same style of carpets at other retail carpeting outlets in the Denver area
2. Colorado Carpet ordered carpets as stock items from manufacturers in California and Georgia
3. no special dyeing, weaving, or other treatment required to fill orders
4. carpeting not cut to any unusual shapes or even to the dimensions of the rooms
5. Colorado Carpet's ordinary course of business was to purchase carpeting from wholesalers and resell it to retail customers
6. Colorado Carpet continually dealt with goods of same nature and could reasonably be expected to find a buyer for the carpet
7. essential changes not needed to make carpets marketable
8. Colorado Carpet received credit when it returned some of carpeting to manufacturer and sold rest of carpeting to retail customer

Holding

Issue 1

The contract was a contract for the sale of goods and not services.

Issue 2

Colorado Carpet did not meet its burden of proving by a preponderance of the evidence that the goods satisfied the criteria for exception to the Statute of Frauds.

Disposition

Decision of the Colorado Court of Appeals affirmed.

A copy of a brief prepared for a research project is set out in section 5.6.1.

The Legal Writing Process

Chapter 5

The Objective Memorandum

§5.1 INTRODUCTION

Writing an objective memorandum is a multi-step process involving research, analysis, writing, and rewriting. In this chapter, we walk through that process, explaining, in the context of a single example, each of the steps.

You can use this chapter in one of several ways: You can use it to obtain an overview of the process, reading the entire chapter before you begin working on your own memorandum problem; you can use it as you would a cookbook, reading a section and then applying what you have learned before moving on to the next section; or you can use it as a reference, referring to it on an "as needed" basis.

No matter which way you use the material, keep in mind that writing an office memorandum is not a linear process: You will seldom be able to march through the process step-by-step without backtracking. Rather, the process is recursive. After analyzing the statutes, you may find it necessary to do more research, and after writing the first draft of the discussion section, you may find it necessary to rewrite the statement of facts, adding or deleting facts. Exhibit 5.1 illustrates the process.

Also keep in mind that not everything that you need is contained in this chapter. As you do the research, you will want to refer to Chapters 9 through 16, and as you write, you will want to refer to Chapters 18 through 27. Cross-references have been included to help you move from chapter to chapter and section to section.

§5.2 THE OBJECTIVE MEMORANDUM: ITS PURPOSE, AUDIENCE, AND FORMAT

Objective memoranda, also called office memos, are usually written by legal interns (law students working for a law firm or agency) or

EXHIBIT 5.1   The Steps in Writing an Objective Memorandum

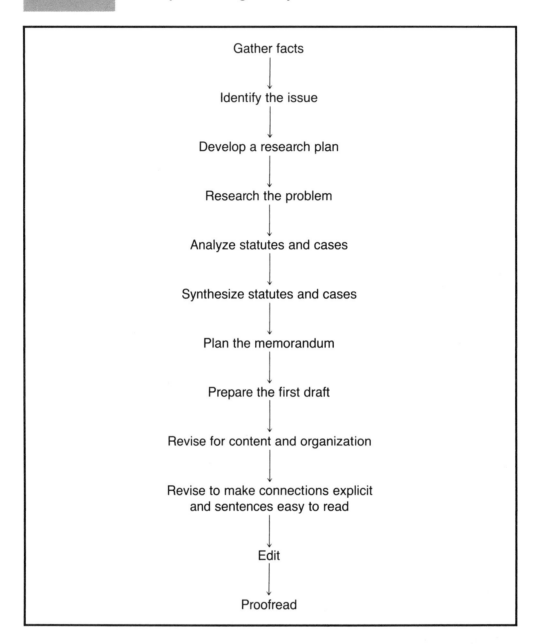

Gather facts

↓

Identify the issue

↓

Develop a research plan

↓

Research the problem

↓

Analyze statutes and cases

↓

Synthesize statutes and cases

↓

Plan the memorandum

↓

Prepare the first draft

↓

Revise for content and organization

↓

Revise to make connections explicit
and sentences easy to read

↓

Edit

↓

Proofread

by new associates. In them, the intern or associate sets out the applicable rules of law, describes how those rules have been applied in other similar cases, and applies those rules to the facts of the client's case, setting out each side's arguments and then evaluating those arguments.

When the memo is completed, the attorney who assigned the memo reads through it and then uses the information contained in it to advise the client or to draft another document, such as a letter to the client, a letter to an opposing party, or a brief to a trial or appellate court. Thus, objective memoranda are in-house documents. They are directed to the attorney handling the case and not the client, opposing party, or court.

Although the format of a memo will vary from law firm to law firm, most attorneys want the following sections in an objective memorandum: a heading, a statement of facts, a formal statement of the issue, a brief answer, a discussion section, and a formal conclusion.

| **Section Summary** | *The Office Memorandum* |

Audience

Primary Audience: an attorney within a law firm
Secondary Audience: may be sent to the client

Purpose

To provide the attorney with the information that he or she needs to evaluate the case, advise the client, or prepare another document, such as a letter to the client, a letter to opposing counsel, or a brief to the trial or appellate court.

Conventions

Although the format varies from firm to firm, most attorneys want the following sections:

1. heading
2. statement of facts
3. question(s) presented
4. brief answer(s)
5. discussion
6. conclusion.

A.   PREWRITING

Just as the artist begins "painting" long before paint is put to canvas, the writer begins "writing" long before the first word is put on paper. The artistic process begins with an image, an idea, or an insight that is shaped and then reworked many times before the project is finished. The writing process begins with a question that is focused and refocused through research and analysis.

In both instances, the process takes place in context. The artist's work is influenced by training, by the expectations of the artistic community, and by the reactions of viewers to past works. Similarly, your work will be shaped by your knowledge of the law, the conventions governing both the format and content of a legal memorandum, and by your understanding of your audience and how your audience will use the memo.

Thus, like the artist, you begin work with a vision, albeit a preliminary one. Although you do not yet know what the final product will look like, you have an idea of where you want to go. You know the attorney's question, the types of information the attorney needs, and how the memo will be used. This information is your touchstone, your point of reference, and as such can guide most if not all of the decisions you make throughout the writing process.

§5.3   THE ASSIGNMENT

The process begins with the assignment. A senior attorney asks an intern or associate to research an issue and prepare a memorandum.

In the sample problem that follows, the assignment is given to the intern in writing. After interviewing the client, the attorney, Connie Krontz, prepared the following memo.

EXAMPLE

To: Summer Intern

From: Connie Krontz

Date: September 21, 1993

Re: Beaver Custom Carpets, File No. 93-478

I just finished interviewing Jim Beaver, the owner of Beaver Custom Carpets. Mr. Beaver wants our help in collecting money owed him by the McKibbins.

The McKibbins first contacted Beaver Custom Carpets (BCC) in June of this year. The McKibbins had purchased the Reutlinger Mansion, which is located at 43 Oak Street in Denver, in early January and were turning the mansion into a bed and breakfast. Because they wanted their bed and breakfast to be "something special," the McKibbins were trying to replicate the mansion's original furnishings.

As originally furnished, the mansion had large area rugs in the parlor, library, and dining room. Around the perimeter of each rug was a twelve-inch maroon strip; in the center was beige carpet with the Reutlinger family flower woven into the carpet at one-foot intervals. The original rugs had been custom-made, and similar rugs were not available from carpet outlets.

The McKibbins showed a BCC sales representative a picture in which the original rugs were visible and asked whether BCC could produce such rugs. The sales representative called BCC's manufacturer and was told that the manufacturer could produce such rugs: Although the looms would have to be specially set, standard dyes could be used.

The sales representative relayed this information to the McKibbins and then went to the mansion and measured the rooms. Two days later, on June 19, the sales representative sent the McKibbins a "proposal" setting out the specifications for the three rugs and the price: $16,875.00.

On June 29, Mrs. McKibbin called the sales representative and told him that she and her husband wanted to purchase the rugs. BCC did not send her a contract or obtain a down payment. The sales representative simply called the manufacturer and placed the order.

On August 4, Mrs. McKibbin called the sales representative and told him that she and her husband were cancelling their order. Mr. McKibbin had fallen from the roof of the mansion and was in the hospital.

The sales representative immediately called the manufacturer. Unfortunately, the manufacturer had already produced the rugs, and BCC was, therefore, forced to take delivery of the three rugs at a cost of $13,500.

On August 15, BCC sent the McKibbins a bill for the proposal price. Last week, BCC received a letter from the McKibbins' attorney, stating that because there was no written contract, the contract was unenforceable under the UCC Statute of Frauds.

On September 1, BCC sold the rugs to a carpet wholesaler for an even $10,000.00. (BCC had sold carpet to this wholesaler on only one prior occasion. On that occasion, the same sales representative made an error in writing down the number of the dye; as a consequence, the carpet did not meet the customer's specifications.)

BCC is a specialty carpet firm located in Denver, Colorado. It has been in business for about one year and caters primarily to businesses, helping those businesses design and obtain carpet in non-standard colors or with unique patterns. For example, it has helped design carpet for a hotel that wanted its corporate emblem woven into the carpet and for a department store that wanted strips of standard carpet sewn into a bold contemporary design.

Although BCC carries no stock, it has carpet samples, photographs, and catalogs in its showroom. BCC also employs its own designer, who is available to work with customers.

BCC is in financial trouble and needs to recover at least the difference between what it paid the manufacturer and what it received when it sold the rugs to the wholesaler.

It seems to me that the contract should be enforceable under the UCC Statute of Frauds exception for specially manufactured goods. Please see if I am right.

§5.4   PREPARING A RESEARCH PLAN

The first step is the preparation of a research plan. Before going into the library, you need to (1) prepare a preliminary issue statement, (2) identify both the jurisdiction and type of law, (3) decide which sources you are going to use, and (4) prepare a list of search terms.

§5.4.1   Preparing a Preliminary Issue Statement

Good research begins with a good preliminary issue statement. Although you will not be able to draft the final version of the question presented until after you have completed your research, by drafting a preliminary one now, you force yourself to focus. What is it that you have been asked to determine?

Often the issue can be stated in a number of different ways. It can be stated broadly or narrowly, or it can find its focus somewhere in between.

EXAMPLE 1

How can BCC recoup its losses?

EXAMPLE 2

Were the rugs "specially manufactured" within the meaning of the Statute of Frauds?

EXAMPLE 3

Is the contract enforceable under the exception for specially manufactured goods?

Example 1 is very broad: If you used this version as your preliminary issue statement, you would need to research a number of different
legal theories. In contrast, Example 2 is very narrow: If the issue were
framed this way, you would need to research only one of the exception's
four elements, that the goods be specially manufactured for the buyer.
The third example finds the middle ground. In doing the research, you
need not consider all of the ways in which BCC might recoup its losses;
you need determine only whether the contract is enforceable under the
exception for specially manufactured goods.

Because the way in which the issue is framed determines how
broad or narrow the research will be, you must know what the attorney
does and does not want researched. If the issue is framed too broadly,
you may spend too much time — not to mention too much of the
client's money — on the project; if the issue is framed too narrowly, you
may not answer the attorney's question. Consequently, read the instructions carefully and, when necessary, ask the questions needed to clarify
those instructions.

§5.4.2   Determining What Law Governs

The next step is to determine which jurisdiction's law governs. Is
the question governed by federal or state law? If state law governs,
which state's law will be applied?

In the statute of frauds problem, the answer is Colorado state law.
Contracts between private parties (in contrast to contracts with the
state or federal government) are governed by state law. And when both
the parties are from the same state, the law of that state almost always
governs.

Having determined which jurisdiction's law governs, you must
then determine whether the problem is governed by that jurisdiction's
enacted law (the constitution, statutes, regulations) or by its common
law (rules or doctrines created by the courts).

Although in the statute of frauds problem the answer is easy (the
Statute of Frauds is a statute), in many problems it is more difficult. You
may not know whether the question is governed by enacted or common
law. In these cases, play it safe. Look first for enacted law. If you don't
find any, look for common law.

§5.4.3   Deciding What Sources to Use

You also need to determine which sources you are going to use and the order in which you are going to use them.

a. Background Reading

If you know little or nothing about the area of law, you should begin your research with background reading.

In doing this reading, you are looking for several things. First, you want information. You want to learn the vocabulary, and you want an overview of the area of law. Second, you want the questions. What are the issues, and what are the steps in the decisionmaking process? Third, you want citations to authority. Is there a citation to the governing statute or case?

Depending on the problem, you will be able to find the answers to these questions in a legal encyclopedia, a hornbook, a practice book, or American Law Reports (A.L.R.). These sources are discussed in more detail in the next section, section 5.5, and in Chapter 13.

Note

If you are familiar with the area of law, you can skip this step and begin your research with the search for the applicable law.

b. Locating the Applicable Statute or Common Law Rule

The next step is to locate the governing law. Where will you find the applicable statute or common law rule?

If the problem is governed by federal statute, you will begin your research in the United States Code, a multivolume set that contains federal statutes. In contrast, if the problem is governed by state common law, you will begin your search in the state's case digest (a subject index to the state's court opinions), LEXIS, or Westlaw.

For the purposes of this discussion, let's assume that you find mandatory authority: a constitutional provision, statute, or common law rule that is "on point." Having found such authority, you must do two things: (1) shepardize to determine if the statute or case is still "good law," and (2) analyze that law. When does the law apply and who must prove what? You must also determine whether both sides are likely to agree on how that law will be applied to the facts of the case. If both sides will agree, no further research is needed. The issue can simply be raised and dismissed. If, however, such agreement is unlikely, you need to con-

tinue, this time looking for analogous cases. How has the law been applied in cases that are factually similar to the client's?

c. Locating Analogous Cases

The method of finding analogous cases is determined by the type
of law. When the "law" is a constitutional provision or a statute, you can
find analogous cases by looking at the notes of decision that follow the
constitutional provision or statute in an annotated code; in contrast,
when the "law" is a common law rule, you will use a case digest, LEXIS,
or Westlaw.

After selecting the analogous cases that you want to use in your
memo, you must shepardize those cases to see (a) whether the cases
are still good law and (b) whether there are more recent cases. If they
are good law, you can stop; if they are not, you must continue your
search.

You will also need to do more research if you were unable to find
any analogous cases in your jurisdiction or if the cases that you found
are of little use. In such instances, look for persuasive authority: cases
from other jurisdictions applying a similar rule of law or law review
articles or other commentary discussing and analyzing the issue.

d. Locating Arguments

Although there is no "Book of Arguments," as you do your research
you need to think about the arguments that each side can make. How
can each side argue the plain language of the statute or rule? How can
each side use the analogous cases? What types of policy arguments can
be made?

§5.4.4 Developing a List of Search Terms

The last step is preparing a list of search terms, that is, words and
phrases that can be used to locate the applicable sections in the codes
or digests.

The two major legal publishing companies, West Publishing Company and Lawyers Co-operative Publishing Company (Bancroft-Whit-
ney), suggest techniques for developing such lists. West recommends
listing words describing (1) the parties involved, (2) the places where
the facts arose and the objects and things involved, (3) the acts of omissions that gave rise to the legal action or issue, (4) the defense to the
action or issue, and (5) the relief sought. Lawyers Co-op recommends
looking up descriptive words that suggest the Thing, the Act, the Person,
or the Place involved (TAPP).

The end product of this thinking process is a research plan that
looks something like this.

EXAMPLE

Research Plan
for the Statute of Frauds Problem

Legal Question: Is the contract between BCC and the Mc-Kibbins enforceable under the Statute of Frauds exception for specially manufactured goods?

Jurisdiction: Colorado

Type of Law: Enacted law

Search Terms: Uniform Commercial Code, Statute of Frauds, Specially Manufactured Goods

Step 1:   Read about the UCC Statute of Frauds in a legal encyclopedia, hornbook, practice book, or A.L.R.

Step 2:   Using the index to the state code, locate the section of the UCC that sets out the Statute of Frauds.

Step 3:   Update the statute to be sure that the statute is the most recent version.

Step 4:   Read and analyze the statute. What are the elements? Is the application of law to fact clear? If the application is clear, no further research is needed on that element. If application is not clear, look for analogous cases.

Step 5:   Read through the notes of decision following the applicable statutes, identifying analogous cases.

Step 6:   Locate analogous cases in either state or regional reporters. Read the relevant portion of each case.

Step 7:   Shepardize the cases to determine (1) whether the case is still good law and (2) whether there are any additional cases.

Step 8:   Look up and, if appropriate, shepardize any additional cases.

Step 9:   Stop research unless no analogous cases have been located or cases that have been located are not useful. In such instances, look for persuasive authority, that is, cases from other jurisdictions, law review articles, or treatises. Locate additional cases by using A.L.R., Uniform Laws, law reviews, LEXIS, or Westlaw.

Step 10:   Shepardize the cases to make sure they are still good law.

Note

At first, your research plan should be in writing. Although you will always need to plan, as you become more proficient, you may find that a written plan is not necessary.

Section Summary

Before going into the library, prepare a research plan containing the following information:

1. a preliminary issue statement;
2. the jurisdiction and type of law;
3. a list of sources and the order in which you will consult them; and
4. search terms.

§5.5   RESEARCHING THE PROBLEM

Research plan in hand, it is now time to go into the library.

§5.5.1   Background Reading

When you are researching a problem in an area of law with which you are unfamiliar, begin by doing some background reading to familiarize yourself with the concepts, terminology, and common questions.

This background reading can be done in a number of different sources. Depending on the topic, the best source may be a legal encyclopedia, a hornbook, a practice book, or American Law Reports (A.L.R.). See Chapter 13.

§5.5.2   Locating the UCC Statute of Frauds

In Colorado, the Statute of Frauds can be found in one of three sets: Session Laws of Colorado, Colorado Revised Statutes, or West's Colorado Revised Statutes Annotated.

The Session Laws of Colorado contains the Colorado statutes in chronological order. There are volumes for each legislative session, and within each volume, the statutes are arranged in date order. For example, an act signed into law on January 24, 1985, precedes an act signed into law on January 25, 1985, and an act signed into law on February 19, 1992, precedes one signed into law on February 20, 1992.

Because the session laws use a chronological rather than a topical organizational scheme, they are not usually the best source. Unless you are doing a legislative history or looking for a statute that is no longer in effect, the better source is a code.

In a code, the statutes that are currently in effect are grouped by topic. For example, all the statutes relating to criminal law are placed under one title, those relating to corporations under another, and those relating to the dissolution of marriage and child custody under still another.

Like many states, Colorado has two codes: its official code, Colorado Revised Statutes, and an unofficial code, West's Colorado Revised Statutes Annotated. The first is published by the State of Colorado and the second by a commercial publishing company, West.

Both sets have the following: the text of the United States Constitution, the text of the Colorado state constitution, the text of the Colorado statutes currently in effect, historical notes for each statute, and a subject index. In addition, West's Colorado Revised Statutes Annotated contains additional finding tools: cross-references to other West materials; notes of decision, which are one-sentence descriptions of cases that have interpreted or applied the statutes; and case name tables. (See section 10.1.2.)

Question

When might you choose an official code over an unofficial one? An annotated code over one that is not annotated?

These codes can be accessed in one of two ways. If you already know the number of the applicable statute, go directly to the volume that contains that title, chapter, and section number. If you don't know the section number, begin your search in the subject index, using your search terms to find a reference to the applicable statute.

For the purposes of this chapter, let's assume that you do not know the section number; you did not find the number during your background reading. Consequently, you begin with the subject index, looking up the most specific of the search terms: "specially manufactured goods."

**SPECIALIZED TELECOMMUNICA-
TIONS EQUIPMENT**
Defined,
    Disabled telephone users fund,
        40–17–102
    Telecommunications, **40–17–102**

SPECIALLY MANUFACTURED GOODS
Sales Act, exception, **4–2–201**

SPECIALTY FERTILIZER
Defined, fertilizers, **35–12–103**

SPECIALTY PET
Defined, commercial feed, **35–60–102**

In this instance, the search is successful. The phrase "specially manufactured goods" is listed.

Note

If the phrase "specially manufactured goods" had not been listed, you would have needed to look up other, broader search terms. For example, if there had been no entry under "Specially Manufactured Goods," the next place to look would have been "Statute of Frauds," and if there had been no entry under "Statute of Frauds," the next place would have been "Uniform Commercial Code."

The next step is to locate the statute itself. This is done using the citation that follows the subject entry: 4-2-201. Although different states use differing numbering systems, in Colorado, the first number is the reference to the title and the second is the reference to the specific section within that title. Thus, we want to find the volume containing Title 4, section 2-201, of the Colorado Revised Statutes. (See Exhibit 5.2.)

The next step is to determine whether the section that we have located is, in fact, the applicable section. In this instance, 4-2-201 is the applicable section. Paragraph (1) lists the formal requirements for a contract for goods priced at $500 or more, and paragraph (3)(a) sets out the exception for specially manufactured goods.

§5.5.3   Updating the Statute

Before going further, we must make sure that we have the current version of the statute.

There are two steps in this process. The first is to look up the statutory number in the supplement, or pocket part, which is located inside the back cover. If the section was amended or repealed after the bound volume was published but before the pocket part was issued, you will find the amended version of the statute or a note indicating the date the statute was repealed. If the statute has not been amended or repealed, there will be nothing or only additional notes of decision. (See Exhibit 5.3.)

In this case, there are only notes of decision. We can, therefore, infer that the statute was not amended or repealed before the date covered by the pocket part.

The second step is to shepardize the statute to determine whether it has been amended or repealed since the pocket part was issued. (See Chapter 14.)

We begin by locating the appropriate volume or volumes of *Shepard's*. In this instance, we are looking for the volumes containing the Colorado Code Annotated covering the time period since the pocket part was issued. Using the information printed on the front cover of each volume of *Shepard's*, we determine that we need only the most recent supplement. (Text resumes on page 107. — ED.)

EXHIBIT 5.2   Colorado Revised Statutes § 4-2-201*

§ 4–2–107

UNIFORM COMMERCIAL CODE

goods in that Article differs from the definition of goods in this Article.

However, both Articles treat as goods growing crops and also timber to be cut under a contract of severance.

Official Reasons for Changes made by 1977 Amendment

Several timber-growing states have changed the 1962 Code to make timber to be cut under a contract of severance goods, regardless of the question who is to sever them. The section is revised to adopt this change. Financing of the transaction is facilitated if the timber is treated as goods instead of real estate. A similar change is made in the definition of "goods" in Section 9–105. To protect persons dealing with timberlands, filing on timber to be cut is required in Part 4 of Article 9 to be made in

real estate records in a manner comparable to fixture filing.

Cross References:

Point 1: Section 2–201.

Point 2: Section 2–105.

Point 3: Articles 9 and 9–105.

Definitional Cross References:

"Buyer". Section 2–103.

"Contract". Section 1–201.

"Contract for sale". Section 2–106.

"Goods". Section 2–105.

"Party". Section 1–201.

"Present sale". Section 2–106.

"Rights". Section 1–201.

"Seller". Section 2–103.

Historical and Statutory Notes

The 1977 amendment, which conformed this section to the 1972 changes made in the official text of § 2–107 of the Uniform Commercial Code, in subsec. (1), substituted "minerals or the like (including oil and gas)" for "timber, minerals or the like", and in subsec. (2), inserted "or of timber to be cut". See Official Comment, ante.

Library References

Sales ⟜10, 11.
WESTLAW Topic No. 343.
C.J.S. Sales § 13 et seq.

Colorado Methods of Practice, 3d Ed., Vol. 2 (1983), Krendl, § 2707.

Notes of Decisions

Natural gas 1
Refineries 2

---

1. Natural gas

Extrinsic evidence was admissible in action for breach of contract for sale of natural gas to determine intent of parties despite lack of facial ambiguity in the contract language where there was no finding that parties intended contract to be completely integrated. Amoco Production Co. v. Western Slope Gas Co., D.C. (Colo.) 1985, 754 F.2d 303.

2. Refineries

The sale of an oil refinery did not involve the sale of "goods" and thus was not covered by Article II of the Uniform Commercial Code. McClanahan v. American Gilsonite Co., D.C. Colo.1980, 494 F.Supp. 1334.

PART 2

FORM, FORMATION, AND READJUSTMENT OF CONTRACT

Law Review Commentaries

U.N. Convention on the Sale of Goods and the Battle of the Forms. Paul C. Blodgett, 18 Colo.Law. 421 (March 1989).

§ 4–2–201. Formal requirements—statute of frauds

(1) Except as otherwise provided in this section, a contract for the sale of goods for the price of five hundred dollars or more is not enforceable by way of action or defense unless there is some writing sufficient to indicate that a contract for sale has been made between the parties and signed by the party against whom enforcement is sought or by his authorized agent or broker. A writing is not insufficient because it omits or incorrectly states a term agreed

EXHIBIT 5.2   *(continued)*

SALES   **§ 4-2-201**

upon, but the contract is not enforceable under this paragraph beyond the quantity of goods shown in such writing.

(2) Between merchants, if within a reasonable time a writing in confirmation of the contract and sufficient against the sender is received and the party receiving it has reason to know its contents, it satisfies the requirements of subsection (1) of this section against such party unless written notice of objection to its contents is given within ten days after it is received.

(3) A contract which does not satisfy the requirements of subsection (1) of this section but which is valid in other respects is enforceable:

(a) If the goods are to be specially manufactured for the buyer and are not suitable for sale to others in the ordinary course of the seller's business and the seller, before notice of repudiation is received and under circumstances which reasonably indicate that the goods are for the buyer, has made either a substantial beginning of their manufacture or commitments for their procurement; or

(b) If the party against whom enforcement is sought admits in his pleading, testimony, or otherwise in court that a contract for sale was made, but the contract is not enforceable under this provision beyond the quantity of goods admitted; or

(c) With respect to goods for which payment has been made and accepted or which have been received and accepted (section 4-2-606).

(Laws 1965, S.B.104, § 1.)
Prior Compilations: C.R.S.1963, § 155-2-201.

Official Comment

Prior Uniform Statutory Provision: Section 4, Uniform Sales Act (which was based on Section 17 of the Statute of 29 Charles II).
Changes: Completely rephrased; restricted to sale of goods. See also Sections 1-206, 8-319 and 9-203.
Purposes of Changes: The changed phraseology of this section is intended to make it clear that:

1. The required writing need not contain all the material terms of the contract and such material terms as are stated need not be precisely stated. All that is required is that the writing afford a basis for believing that the offered oral evidence rests on a real transaction. It may be written in lead pencil on a scratch pad. It need not indicate which party is the buyer and which the seller. The only term which must appear is the quantity term which need not be accurately stated but recovery is limited to the amount stated. The price, time and place of payment or delivery, the general quality of the goods, or any particular warranties may all be omitted.

Special emphasis must be placed on the permissibility of omitting the price term in view of the insistence of some courts on the express inclusion of this term even where the parties have contracted on the basis of a published price list. In many valid contracts for sale the parties do not mention the price in express terms, the buyer being bound to pay and the seller to accept a reasonable price which the trier of the fact may well be trusted to determine. Again, frequently the price is not mentioned since the parties have based their agreement on a price list or catalogue known to both of them and this list serves as an efficient safeguard against perjury. Finally, "market" prices and valuations that are current in the vicinity constitute a similar check. Thus if the price is not stated in the memorandum it can normally be supplied without danger of fraud. Of course if the "price" consists of goods rather than money the quantity of goods must be stated.

Only three definite and invariable requirements as to the memorandum are made by this subsection. First, it must evidence a contract for the sale of goods; second, it must be "signed", a word which includes any authentication which identifies the party to be charged; and third, it must specify a quantity.

2. "Partial performance" as a substitute for the required memorandum can validate the contract only for the goods which have been accepted or for which payment has been made and accepted.

EXHIBIT 5.2   *(continued)*

§ 4–2–201

Receipt and acceptance either of goods or of the price constitutes an unambiguous overt admission by both parties that a contract actually exists. If the court can make a just apportionment, therefore, the agreed price of any goods actually delivered can be recovered without a writing or, if the price has been paid, the seller can be forced to deliver an apportionable part of the goods. The overt actions of the parties make admissible evidence of the other terms of the contract necessary to a just apportionment. This is true even though the actions of the parties are not in themselves inconsistent with a different transaction such as a consignment for resale or a mere loan of money.

Part performance by the buyer requires the delivery of something by him that is accepted by the seller as such performance. Thus, part payment may be made by money or check, accepted by the seller. If the agreed price consists of goods or services, then they must also have been delivered and accepted.

3. Between merchants, failure to answer a written confirmation of a contract within ten days of receipt is tantamount to a writing under subsection (2) and is sufficient against both parties under subsection (1). The only effect, however, is to take away from the party who fails to answer the defense of the Statute of Frauds; the burden of persuading the trier of fact that a contract was in fact made orally prior to the written confirmation is unaffected. Compare the effect of a failure to reply under Section 2–207.

4. Failure to satisfy the requirements of this section does not render the contract void for all purposes, but merely prevents it from being judicially enforced in favor of a party to the contract. For example, a buyer who takes possession of goods as provided in an oral contract which the seller has not meanwhile repudiated, is not a trespasser. Nor would the Statute of Frauds provisions of this section be a defense to a third person who wrongfully induces a party to refuse to perform an oral contract, even though the injured party cannot maintain an action for damages against the party so refusing to perform.

5. The requirement of "signing" is discussed in the comment to Section 1–201.

6. It is not necessary that the writing be delivered to anybody. It need not be signed or authenticated by both parties but it is, of course, not sufficient against one who has not signed it. Prior to a dispute no one can determine which party's signing of the memorandum may be necessary but from the time of contracting each party should be aware that to him it is signing by the other which is important.

7. If the making of a contract is admitted in court, either in a written pleading, by stipulation or by oral statement before the court, no additional writing is necessary for protection against fraud. Under this section it is no longer possible to admit the contract in court and still treat the Statute as a defense. However, the contract is not thus conclusively established. The admission so made by a party is itself evidential against him of the truth of the facts so admitted and of nothing more; as against the other party, it is not evidential at all.

Cross References:

See Sections 1–201, 2–202, 2–207, 2–209 and 2–304.

Definitional Cross References:

"Action". Section 1–201.

"Between merchants". Section 2–104.

"Buyer". Section 2–103.

"Contract". Section 1–201.

"Contract for sale". Section 2–106.

"Goods". Section 2–105.

"Notice". Section 1–201.

"Party". Section 1–201.

"Reasonable time". Section 1–204.

"Sale". Section 2–106.

"Seller". Section 2–103.

Law Review Commentaries

Breach of Contract: Statute of Frauds and Damages. 55 Den.L.J. 415 (1978).

Uniform Commercial Code and Sales Warranties in Colorado. Morris B. Hecox, Jr., 38 U.Colo.L.Rev. 7 (1965–66).

Library References

Frauds, Statute of ⬤81 et seq.
WESTLAW Topic No. 185.
C.J.S. Frauds, Statute of § 138 et seq.

Colorado Methods of Practice, 3d Ed., Vol. 2 (1983), Krendl, §§ 2634, 2655.

WESTLAW Electronic Research

See WESTLAW Electronic Research Guide following the Preface.

Notes of Decisions

Burden of proof 8

Confirmation 3

EXHIBIT 5.2   *(continued)*

SALES

§ 4-2-201
Note 5

1. Scope

Where agreement for installation of carpet contemplated that title to carpeting and other materials would pass to buyers, the agreement constituted "contract for sale," and, sale of goods being primary purpose of the contract, contract was "contract for the sale of goods" within statute of frauds provisions of the Uniform Commercial Code. Colorado Carpet Installation, Inc. v. Palermo, 1983, 668 P.2d 1384.

Contract furnishing installed carpeting, primary purpose of which was sale of goods rather than rendering of services in installation of carpeting, came within statute of frauds and without a writing signed by party to be charged, was unenforceable. Colorado Carpet Installation, Inc. v. Palermo, App.1982, 647 P.2d 686, affirmed 668 P.2d 1384.

2. Sufficiency of writing, generally

Note and chattel mortgage describing property and parties but failing to mention purchase price was insufficient to take out of statute of frauds contract sought to be enforced by action. Howse v. Crumb, 1960, 352 P.2d 285, 143 Colo. 90.

3. Confirmation

Substantial evidence supported trial court's finding that wheat buyer's delay in delivery of confirmation of sale was the result of erroneous addressing on the part of the buyer, and that its confirmation was not received by defendant seller within a "reasonable time" under statute of frauds provision of the Uniform Commercial Code; furthermore, there was substantial evidence to support the finding that the seller's objections to the buyer's confirmation because of a cancellation clause therein was within the ten-day period provided in the aforesaid provision. Cargill, Inc. v. Stafford, C.A. (Colo.) 1977, 553 F.2d 1222.

In respect to July 23 wheat purchase, defendant seller, the owner and operator of a grain elevator, never admitted the existence of a valid contract, where the seller, upon being called by the buyer's agent on July 23, said that he might make the sale, that he would check over the written confirmation, and that "if it looks all right, I will sign it and send it back," but where the seller did not sign the confirmation or return it to the buyer. Cargill, Inc. v. Stafford, C.A. (Colo.) 1977, 553 F.2d 1222.

To constitute sufficient writing to take oral contract outside statute of frauds, writing must be in confirmation of contract. Nations Enterprises, Inc. v. Process Equipment Co., 1978, 579 P.2d 655, 40 Colo.App. 390.

Purchase order was not sufficient confirmatory memorandum to satisfy statute of frauds requirement of writing in absence of showing that parties had entered into oral contract. Nations Enterprises, Inc. v. Process Equipment Co., 1978, 579 P.2d 655, 40 Colo.App. 390.

4. Specially manufactured goods

To satisfy "specially manufactured goods" exception to statute of frauds, goods must be specially made for buyer, goods must be unsuitable for sale to others in ordinary course of seller's business, seller must have substantially begun to manufacture goods or must have made commitment for their procurement, and manufacture or commitment must have been commenced under circumstances reasonably indicating that goods are for buyer and prior to seller's receipt of notification of repudiation. Colorado Carpet Installation, Inc. v. Palermo, 1983, 668 P.2d 1384.

Term "specially manufactured" as used in "specially manufactured goods" exception to statute of frauds in Uniform Commercial Code refers to character of goods as specially made for particular buyer, and not to whether they were "specially made" in usual course of seller's business. Colorado Carpet Installation, Inc. v. Palermo, 1983, 668 P.2d 1384.

Contract under which plaintiff sold defendants carpeting, which was not specially cut to fit defendants' room, was a stock item carried by number of carpeting distributors, and was suitable for sale to others in ordinary course of business, did not fall within specially manufactured goods exception to statute of frauds and, due to lack of a signed writing, was unenforceable. Colorado Carpet Installation, Inc. v. Palermo, App.1982, 647 P.2d 686, affirmed 668 P.2d 1384.

5. Payment

Where concrete had been delivered in accordance with terms of the contract and payment had been received and accepted, formal requirements of the statute of frauds did not apply to the case and neither the contract nor an asserted modification was required to be in writing. U. S. for Use of Mobile Premix Concrete, Inc. v. Santa Fe Engineers, Inc., D.C. Colo.1981, 515 F.Supp. 512.

Oral sales agreement with respect to automobile was a sale contract covered by the Uniform Commercial Code, so that contract became enforceable by virtue of payment of $200 coupled with buyer's taking possession of the automobile, despite contention that agreement was unenforceable under statute of frauds because it was not in writing. Morrison v. Droll, 1978, 588 P.2d 383, 41 Colo.App. 354.

Promissory note, merely indicating balance which would be owing if and when buyer made down payment agreed upon, was given

EXHIBIT 5.2   *(continued)*

§ 4–2–201
Note 5

UNIFORM COMMERCIAL CODE

to evidence an obligation and did not constitute such part "payment" as would take oral purchase contract out of statute of frauds. Howse v. Crumb, 1960, 352 P.2d 285, 143 Colo. 90.

6. Receipt of goods

Evidence supported determination that first dress shop intended to retain ownership of merchandise supplied to second dress shop and that sale of merchandise by second dress shop, in light of first dress shop's actions, did not constitute acceptance of the merchandise; therefore, statute of frauds provisions in the Uniform Commercial Code precluded recovery by first dress shop, which unilaterally determined nature, quantity, and resale prices of merchandise supplied, for purchase price of merchandise supplied to second dress shop under alleged oral agreement. Lockhart v. Elm, App.1987, 736 P.2d 429.

While part performance can be sufficient to remove the bar of the statute of frauds, it will remove only that portion of the contract which relates to goods which have actually been received and accepted. Colorado Carpet Installation, Inc. v. Palermo, App.1982, 647 P.2d 686, affirmed 668 P.2d 1384.

Receipts and acceptance of tile did not operate to make part performance exception to statute of frauds applicable to sales contract, which was unenforceable due to lack of a signed writing; plaintiff's offer to furnish and install carpeting was orally accepted by defendants, but only tile was received and accepted, though later removed, and claim for breach of contract related only to carpeting. Colorado

Carpet Installation, Inc. v. Palermo, App.1982, 647 P.2d 686, affirmed 668 P.2d 1384.

Manufacturer of pumps which were shipped to buyer and accepted by it was entitled to recover purchase price of pumps although contract for their sale was not in writing. Nations Enterprises, Inc. v. Process Equipment Co., 1978, 579 P.2d 655, 40 Colo.App. 390.

To satisfy statute of frauds exception, acceptance must be voluntary and unconditional; but such acceptance may be inferred from buyer's conduct in taking physical possession of goods or some part of them. Howse v. Crumb, 1960, 352 P.2d 285, 143 Colo. 90.

Evidence, that defendant had picked up one of trucks at the ranch and had driven it back when it ran out of gasoline, was at least prima facie evidence requiring finding as to whether there had been such receipt and acceptance of part of goods as would take oral contract to buy trucks and trailers out of statute of frauds. Howse v. Crumb, 1960, 352 P.2d 285, 143 Colo. 90.

7. Unjust enrichment

Unjust enrichment cannot be used to gain benefits from executory oral contracts barred enforcement by a statute of frauds. Cargill, Inc. v. Stafford, C.A. (Colo.) 1977, 553 F.2d 1222.

8. Burden of proof

Party attempting to prove purchase order was confirmatory memorandum satisfying statute of frauds requirement of writing had burden to prove that oral contract had been entered into before purchase order was drawn. Nations Enterprises, Inc. v. Process Equipment Co., 1978, 579 P.2d 655, 40 Colo.App. 390.

§ 4–2–202. Final written expression—parol or extrinsic evidence

Terms with respect to which the confirmatory memoranda of the parties agree or which are otherwise set forth in a writing intended by the parties as a final expression of their agreement with respect to such terms as are included therein, may not be contradicted by evidence of any prior agreement or of a contemporaneous oral agreement but may be explained or supplemented:

(a) By course of dealing or usage of trade (section 4–1–205) or by course of performance (section 4–2–208); and

(b) By evidence of consistent additional terms unless the court finds the writing to have been intended also as a complete and exclusive statement of the terms of the agreement.

(Laws 1965, S.B.104, § 1.)
Prior Compilations: C.R.S.1963, § 155–2–202.

Official Comment

Prior Uniform Statutory Provision: None.

Purposes:

1. This section definitely rejects:

EXHIBIT 5.3   **Pocket Part for § 4-2-201***

§ 4–2–201. **Formal requirements—statute of frauds**

Law Review Commentaries

Judicial admissions exception to the statute of frauds: An Update. Peter J. Shedd, 12 Whittier L.Rev. 131 (1991).

U.N. Convention on the sale of goods and the "Battle of the Forms". Paul C. Blodgett, 18 Colo.Law. 421 (1989).

Library References

Colorado Methods of Practice, Rev.3d Ed., Vol. 2A (1991), Krendl, § 2655.

*Reprinted from *West's Colorado Revised Statutes Annotated: 1991 Cumulative Pocket Part,* © 1991, with permission of West Publishing Company.

Note

Shepard's volumes are not cumulative. Each volume covers a different time period.

Having located the appropriate volume, we turn to the page covering Title 4, section 2-201. (See Exhibit 5.4.) Although to the uninitiated these entries may appear meaningless, for the person trained to use *Shepard's,* they contain a wealth of information: The entries give both the current "status" of the statute and a list of cases in which the court has cited the statute.

At this point, we are interested only in the status entries. These entries, if there are any, always precede the references to cases and have a single-letter code in the left-hand margin. Exhibit 5.5, taken from the front of *Shepard's,* explains the codes.

If section 2-201 had been recently repealed, amended, or declared unconstitutional, there would be a status entry immediately under the heading for section 2-201. This entry would be preceded by a code describing the action that had been taken, and to the right of this code would be a reference to the session of the Colorado State Legislature in which that action had been taken and to the chapter number where the new language, if any, appears.

In our example, there are no status entries. The statute has not been amended or appealed since the pocket part was issued. (Text resumes on page 111. — ED.)

Question

Which version of the statute would you look for — the statute that was in effect at the time the cause of action arose or the statute that is currently in effect?

EXHIBIT 5.4 **Excerpt from *Shepard's* Volume***

COLORADO REVISED STATUTES (AS AMENDED BY REPLACEMENT VOLUMES TO 1984) AND SUPPLEMENT, 1984

4-2-706

4-2-101 to	553F2d1222	**4-2-209**	555P2d195	40CoA372	**4-2-402**	**4-2-603**	98Æ1211n
4-2-725	515FS515	40CoA114	651P2d415	530P2d991	Subd. 3	35CoA202	¶ a
587FS49	46CUR338	575P2d858	524FS1156	575P2d863	¶ a	530P2d991	35CoA200
4-2-101	Subd. 1	515FS515	595FS1314	5CoL1775	42CoA411	653P2d753	530P2d992
39CoA12	668P2d1385	52DJ448	¶ b	Subd. 3	599P2d943	Subd. 1	693P2d394
563P2d369	Subd. 2	46CUR341	737F2d873	190Col65	46CUR333	47CUR580	¶ b
4-2-102	40CoA394	Subd. 1	595FS1314	544P2d989	46CUR333	Subd. 2	40CoA529
Rs	579P2d656	52DJ478	Subd. 2	¶ a	**4-2-403**	47CUR580	41CoA576
[1977HB1400	553F2d1222	46CUR341	684P2d208	41CoA575	38CoA73	**4-2-604**	578P2d670
39CoA11	Subd. 3	47CUR566	**4-2-314**	589P2d74	552P2d314	35CoA202	589P2d74
563P2d369	¶ a	Subd. 2	190Col66	¶ b	687P2d964	530P2d991	Subd. 2
648P2d163	647P2d687	46CUR342	38CoA445	41CoA575	11CoL1165	47CUR580	35CoA200
675P2d334	668P2d1385	Subd. 3	40CoA18	589P2d74	46CUR335	**4-2-605**	530P2d992
687P2d536	¶ b	40CoA114	40CoA113	¶ c	Subd. 1	47CUR579	693P2d394
687P2d966	553F2d1222	575P2d861	536P2d864	41CoA575	42CoA411	**4-2-606**	47CUR586
754F2d307	¶ c	46CUR342	544P2d990	589P2d74	599P2d943	41CoA575	65Æ366n
494FS1349	40CoA395	Subd. 4	561P2d357	**4-2-317**	46CUR333	589P2d74	Subd. 3
46CUR335	41CoA357	40CoA114	570P2d1311	39CoA12	Subd. 1.5	Subd. 3	35CoA202
4Æ935n	540P2d356	575P2d861	575P2d858	563P2d369	Ad	668P2d976	530P2d990
4-2-103	579P2d656	46CUR342	624P2d1315	4CoL45	[1975HB1365	643F2d1391	8CoL1414
46CUR361	588P2d383	Subd. 5	648P2d683	**4-2-318**	648P2d164	Subd. 1	13CoL1155
Subd. 1	668P2d1387	40CoA114	687P2d536	190Col67	87YLJ965	643F2d1391	47CUR580
¶ a	515FS515	575P2d861	690P2d1282	38CoA445	Subd. 2	¶ b	54CUR517
40CoA113	97Æ948n	**4-2-210**	524FS1157	40CoA18	640P2d268	653P2d753	Subd. 1
575P2d858	**4-2-202**	Subd. 1	4CoL45	40CoA113	648P2d163	**4-2-607**	47CUR591
¶ b	40CoA114	46CUR344	9CoL458	40CoA134	687P2d965	536P2d867	54CUR535
687P2d967	40CoA372	Subd. 5	46CUR360	544P2d990	46CUR333	643F2d1391	Subd. 4
553F2d1227	40CoA410	47CUR590	Subd. 1	561P2d357	87Æ28n	47CUR585	47CUR593
46CUR360	575P2d861	**4-2-302**	91Æ883n	570P2d1310	93Æ376n	Subd. 1	**4-2-610**
¶ d	575P2d863	192Col124	91Æ884n	574P2d103	687P2d966	653P2d753	653P2d757
40CoA113	579P2d88	43CoA463	Subd. 2	575P2d858	46CUR338	Subd. 2	10CoL970
575P2d858	737F2d871	556P2d474	¶ c	640P2d221	Subd. 4	35CoA200	47CUR580
684P2d206	754F2d307	608P2d827	196Col175	684P2d208	46CUR333	530P2d992	Subd. a
4-2-104	581FS595	659P2d671	38CoA129	580FS525	**4-2-504**	542F2d829	553F2d1226
Subd. 1	55DJ62	8CoL2373	552P2d1026	595FS1312	47CUR589	Subd. 3	**4-2-611**
687P2d966	46CUR340	**4-2-305**	583P2d277	596FS1475	**4-2-507**	536P2d864	47CUR579
553F2d1222	Subd. a	Subd. 1	684P2d208	4CoL45	38CoA71	47CUR586	**4-2-612**
592F2d1144	698P2d779	574F2d583	47CUR219	100Æ757n	552P2d314	Subd. 2	47CUR589
46CUR338	**4-2-204**	¶ c	¶ e	100Æ774n	Subd. 2	39CoA546	Subd. 2
4-2-105	40CoA395	91Æ1258n	**4-2-326**	**4-2-508**	38CoA73	40CoA134	47CUR580
39CoA109	528P2d417	**4-2-306**	684P2d208	10CoL968	552P2d314	570P2d1305	Subd. 3
564P2d965	579P2d656	Subd. 2	¶ f	Subd. 1	31BRW680	574P2d103	47CUR580
494FS1349	553F2d1223	653P2d756	665P2d127	¶ a	**4-2-508**	618P2d661	47CUR580
4Æ935n	47CUR580	**4-2-312 to**	684P2d208	11CoL2949	47CUR580	633P2d518	**4-2-614**
Subd. 1	**4-2-206**	**4-2-317**	**4-2-315**	¶ b	54CUR547	648P2d683	47CUR580
39CoA12	40CoA393	5CoL1767	196Col175	11CoL2948	Subd. 1	678P2d561	**4-2-702**
563P2d369	579P2d656	**4-2-312**	35CoA199	Subd. 3	47CUR588	684P2d201	38CoA71
648P2d163	653P2d754	55CUR97	40CoA113	46CUR354	Subd. 2	643F2d1391	552P2d315
668P2d1388	**4-2-207**	Subd. 3	530P2d990	100Æ1072n	47CUR586	595FS1313	8CoL1417
675P2d334	653P2d754	599FS375	536P2d864	Subd. 5	**4-2-511**	47CUR585	47CUR575
687P2d536	553F2d1223	**4-2-313**	575P2d858	Ad	Subd. 3	¶ b	Subd. 1
4-2-106	Subd. 1	198Col394	583P2d277	[1982HB1181	38CoA73	599FS375	54CUR517
Subd. 1	553F2d1223	35CoA201	665P2d127	38CoA73	39CoA62	Subd. 5	Subd. 3
668P2d1388	592F2d1148	35CoA405	684P2d208	38CoA222	552P2d314	¶ a	A
Subd. 3	Subd. 2	37CoA558	687P2d516	38CoA222	564P2d959	38CoA162	[1977HB1400
599FS373	553F2d1225	38CoA160	687P2d536	552P2d314	Subd. 4	555P2d195	744F2d690
4-2-107	592F2d1144	40CoA113	524FS1157	556P2d93	Ad	**4-2-608**	**4-2-703**
494FS1349	¶ b	41CoA575	595FS1312	687P2d966	[1975HB1365	35CoA38	47CUR590
Subd. 1	660P2d911	530P2d993	4CoL45	Subd. 1	87YLJ965	35CoA105	Subd. f
A	**4-2-208**	536P2d842	46CUR361	39CoA48	**4-2-513**	35CoA200	653P2d757
[1977HB1400	661P2d691	553P2d836	47CUR581	560P2d856	41CoA576	40CoA529	**4-2-704**
754F2d307	698P2d779	555P2d190	**4-2-316**	Subd. 2	589P2d74	528P2d942	Subd. 2
Subd. 2	581FS596	575P2d858	40CoA113	38CoA222	**4-2-601**	530P2d990	47CUR559
A	46CUR340	589P2d75	40CoA372	556P2d93	643F2d1391	536P2d864	**4-2-705**
[1977HB1400	47CUR589	604P2d676	575P2d858	640P2d268	47CUR589	578P2d669	11CoL1165
47CUR580	Subd. 1	640P2d221	575P2d863	648P2d163	Subd. a	678P2d561	693P2d395
4-2-201	581FS595	687P2d536	737F2d873	Subd. 5	**4-2-602**	693P2d393	47CUR581
et seq.	46CUR340	737F2d873	524FS1157	Ad	47CUR585	542F2d829	Subd. 1
494FS1349	Subd. 2	524FS1156	580FS524	[1975HB1365	Subd. 1	643F2d1391	676P2d1268
4-2-201	698P2d779	595FS1312	4CoL46	648P2d164	653P2d753	47CUR586	47CUR580
40CoA114	46CUR341	4CoL45	11CoL2120	87YLJ965	668P2d976	47CUR586	Subd. 3
40CoA394	Subd. 3	5CoL1775	55CUR97		47CUR585	65Æ399n	47CUR581
575P2d861	598FS1568	Subd. 1	Subd. 1		Subd. 2	98Æ1198n	
579P2d656	46CUR339	684P2d207	737F2d873		¶ a	Subd. 1	
647P2d687		¶ a	Subd. 2		35CoA202	35CoA200	
668P2d1387		38CoA162	35CoA199		530P2d990	530P2d990	Continued

293

EXHIBIT 5.5   **Explanation of Codes in *Shepard's****

ILLUSTRATIVE STATUTE

Colorado Revised Statutes (as amended by Replacement Volumes to 1984) and Supplement, 1984

38-26-105

A1975SB163
A1979HB
[1146   1
A1979SB306
A1981HB
[1502

199Col38
39CoA565
40CoA363
41CoA167
44CoA468
574P2d507   2
578P2d664
580P2d1278
604P2d684
615P2d69
651P2d427
685P2d785

592F2d1146   3
33BRW540

4CoL2327
8CoL582   4
11CoL2313

Subd. 1   7
33BRW540

Citations to section 38-26-105 of the Colorado Revised Statutes (as amended by Replacement Volumes to 1984) and Supplement, 1984 are shown in the left margin of this page in the same form in which they appear in the division for that code in this volume.

Citations to each cited statutory provision are grouped as follows:

1. amendments, repeals, etc. by the Colorado General Assembly;
2. citations by the Colorado courts analyzed as to constitutionality or validity;
3. citations by the federal courts analyzed as to constitutionality or validity;
4. citations in articles in legal periodicals;
5. citations in annotations of Lawyers' Edition, United States Supreme Court Reports and the American Law Reports
6. citations in selected legal texts; and
7. citations to specific subdivisions.

For the purpose of illustration only, this grouping has been indicated by bracketing the citations accordingly. It will be noted that as yet there are no citations in groups five and six.

In indicating the legislative and judicial operation of a cited statute, the letter-form abbreviations shown on page xiii are used.

In using the statute divisions of Shepard's Colorado Citations, Statute Edition, it is important to remember that the language of any section of a particular Colorado code or session law may appear in the same or substantially the same form in corresponding sections of one or more other Colorado codes or laws to which citations are shown separately in Shepard's Colorado Citations, Statute Edition and that to obtain all relevant citations one should run down not only the particular section in which one is interested but any such corresponding sections of other codes or laws as well.

An examination of the citations in group one indicates the section was amended "A" by the Colorado General Assembly in acts appearing in Senate Bill "SB" 163 of the 1975 Colorado Laws. It was also amended in House Bill "HB" 1146 and Senate Bill 306 of the 1979 Colorado Laws, and again amended in House Bill 1502 of the 1981 Colorado Laws.

The section is then shown as having been cited by the Colorado Supreme Court in a case reported in 199 Colorado Reports "Col" at page 38. This is followed by other citations in the Colorado Court of Appeals Reports "CoA." The same citing cases are also shown as reported in Pacific Reporter, Second Series "P2d." The section has also been cited by the lower federal courts in cases reported in 592 Federal Reporter, Second Series "F2d" 1146 and 33 Bankruptcy Reporter (West) "BRW" 540.

The absence of letter-form abbreviations indicating judicial operation of statute shows that an analysis of the citing references has disclosed no holding as to the constitutionality or validity of the cited section in any of the citing cases shown.

Citations in articles in legal periodicals are illustrated by the references shown in 4 Colorado Lawyer "CoL" 2327, 8 CoL 582 and 11 CoL 2313.

A citation to a specific subdivision of section 38-26-105 is illustrated by the reference to subdivision "Subd." 1 which appears in 33 BRW 540.

EXHIBIT 5.5   *(continued)*

ABBREVIATIONS-ANALYSIS
STATUTES

Form of Statute

Amend.	Amendment		p	Page
Appx.	Appendix		¶	Paragraph
Art.	Article		P. L.	Public Law
Ch.	Chapter		RCP	Rules of Civil Procedure
Cl.	Clause		§	Section
Div.	Division		S. B.	Senate Bill
Ex	Extra Session		S. C. R.	Senate Concurrent
H. B.	House Bill			Resolution
H. C. R.	House Concurrent		Sent.	Sentence
	Resolution		S. J. M.	Senate Joint Memorial
H. J. M.	House Joint Memorial		S. J. R.	Senate Joint Resolution
H. J. R.	House Joint Resolution		S. R.	Senate Resolution
H. M.	House Memorial		St.	Statute or Statutes at Large
H. R.	House Resolution		Subd.	Subdivision
No.	Number		Sub ¶	Subparagraph
			Subsec.	Subsection

Operation of Statute

Legislative

A	(amended)	Statute amended.
Ad	(added)	New section added.
E	(extended)	Provisions of an existing statute extended in their application to a later statute, or allowance of additional time for performance of duties required by a statute within a limited time.
L	(limited)	Provisions of an existing statute declared not to be extended in their application to a later statute.
R	(repealed)	Abrogation of an existing statute.
Re-en	(re-enacted)	Statute re-enacted.
Rn	(renumbered)	Renumbering of existing sections.
Rp	(repealed in part)	Abrogation of part of an existing statute.
Rs	(repealed and superseded)	Abrogation of an existing statute and substitution of new legislation therefor.
Rv	(revised)	Statute revised.
S	(superseded)	Substitution of new legislation for an existing statute not expressly abrogated.
Sd	(suspended)	Statute suspended.
Sdp	(suspended in part)	Statute suspended in part.
Sg	(supplementing)	New matter added to an existing statute.
Sp	(superseded in part)	Substitution of new legislation for part of an existing statute not expressly abrogated.
Va	(validated)	

Judicial

C	Constitutional.		V	Void or invalid.
U	Unconstitutional.		Va	Valid.
Up	Unconstitutional in part.		Vp	Void or invalid in part.

§5.5.4   Analyzing the Statute

The next step is to analyze the statute, breaking it apart and iden-tifying each of its requirements, or elements. We begin with paragraph (1), which sets out the formal requirements. After a close reading of the section, we come up with the following list.

EXAMPLE

FORMAL REQUIREMENTS

a. unless otherwise provided in this section (2-201)
b. a contract for the sale of goods
c. for the price of $500 or more
d. is not enforceable unless there is a writing signed by the party against whom enforcement is sought

---

In the BCC case, the formal requirements are not met. Even though there was a contract for the sale of goods priced at $500 or more, there is no writing signed by the McKibbins, the party against whom enforce-ment is sought. The contract is not, therefore, enforceable unless one of the exceptions applies.

We turn, therefore, to paragraph (3)(a), the paragraph that con-tains the exception for specially manufactured goods. Once again, we read the paragraph carefully, identifying the parts.

EXAMPLE

EXCEPTION FOR SPECIALLY MANUFACTURED GOODS

A contract which does not satisfy the requirements of para-graph 1 but which is valid in other respects is enforceable if

a. the goods are to be specially manufactured for the buy-er,
b. the goods are not suitable for sale to others in the ordi-nary course of the seller's business, and
c. the seller has made either a substantial beginning of their manufacture or commitments for their procurement
   1. before notice of repudiation and
   2. under circumstances that reasonably indicate that the goods are for the buyer.

Note

As in many cases, in this case there is more than one way of listing the elements. For example, item (c) could be divided into either two or three elements. In this case, we listed it as one because, given the facts of the case, the element does not appear to be in dispute. If it were, we probably would have divided it into at least two parts. The goal is to identify those elements that are, and are not, in dispute and to divide them into manageable, and logical, research units.

Also note that because an "and" and not an "or" joins the elements, the exception applies only if all of the requirements are met.

We must now test each of these elements against the facts of the case, determining which elements are in dispute and which are not.

In the BCC case, the first two elements are in dispute. BCC will claim that the rugs were specially manufactured for the McKibbins and that it could not resell them in the ordinary course of its business; the McKibbins will argue that regular manufacturing procedures were used and that BCC did sell the rugs to a party with whom it had done business on a previous occasion. Only the third element will not be in dispute: The rugs had been manufactured at the time the McKibbins repudiated, and the pattern woven into the rugs is evidence that the rugs were manufactured for the McKibbins.

For more on analyzing statutes, see section 4.2.

§5.5.5   Researching the Disputed Elements

The next step is to research each of the disputed elements, looking first for statutory definitions and official comments, and then looking for cases that have interpreted or applied the statute.

a.   Locating Definitions and Comments

In researching the first disputed element, whether the goods were specially manufactured for the buyer, look first for a definition. Has the Colorado State Legislature defined the phrase "goods specially manufactured for the buyer"? To find out whether it has, we look first at the list of cross-references set out after the text of the statute. (See page 104.)

In this instance, the phrase is not statutorily defined. We must, therefore, look further — this time to the official comments that follow section 2-201. (Look again at pages 103-104.) Is the phrase "specially manufactured" discussed? Once again we come up empty-handed. There is nothing in the comments that tells us how the phrase should be interpreted.

b. Identifying Potentially Applicable Cases

Not finding a statutory definition, we look next to the cases. Are there any Colorado cases that have interpreted or applied section 4-2-201(3)(a)?

Although cases can be found using a number of different sources (for example, case digests and LEXIS and Westlaw), the most efficient and least expensive source is the notes of decision that follow the text of the statute in an annotated code. (Look again at pages 104-106.)

These notes, or annotations, are not part of the court's decision; they are written by attorneys who work for the company that published the set of books in which the annotations appear. Thus, the annotations in Colorado Revised Statutes Annotated were not written by the judges or their staffs but by attorneys employed by West Publishing Company.

When West Publishing Company receives a decision from the Colorado courts, the case is assigned to an attorney who prepares a one-sentence summary for each "point of law" set out in the case. If the case contains just one point of law, the attorney prepares only one note of decision; if the case contains twenty points of law, he or she prepares twenty notes.

These notes are then classified by topic. For example, if in the case the court mentions section 4-2-201, then the note of decision that discusses that particular point of law will be placed after the text of section 4-2-201. Similarly, if in the case the court mentions section 4-2-105, the note of decision that discusses that point will be placed after the text of section 4-2-105. As a result, the same case may be found after more than one statutory section or, if in discussing a particular statutory section the court makes more than one point, there may be more than one reference to a case in any given set of notes of decision.

If there are only a few notes of decision for a particular statutory section, those notes will be arranged only by court and date. Decisions from higher courts will be listed before decisions from lower courts and, within each of these classifications, more recent decisions will be listed before older decisions. If, however, there are a number of notes of decision, the notes will be arranged by topic. A list of topics with their corresponding section numbers will precede the notes themselves. Then, within each topic, the decisions of higher courts will be listed before decisions of lower courts, and more recent cases will be listed before older cases. (For more information on annotated codes, see section 10.1.2.)

Now look again at page 105, at the top of column one. The topic heading "specially manufactured goods" is directly on point. Consequently, we look first at the notes of decision listed under "4. Specially Manufactured Goods" in both the bound volume and the pocket part.

The first thing we note is that although there are three notes of decision in the bound volume, all three cite to the same case, *Colorado*

Carpet Installation, Inc. v. Palermo. While the first two notes of decision cite to a 1983 decision, the third note cites both to a 1982 appellate decision and the 1983 decision. From these cites, we deduce that there are two different decisions: a 1982 Colorado Court of Appeals decision and a 1983 Colorado Supreme Court decision.

Question

Are these cases mandatory or persuasive authority? (For a discussion of mandatory and persuasive authority, see section 2.3.)

We also note that there are no cases listed in the pocket part. Although there are entries, the citations are to law review articles and a practice book and not to court decisions. (See Exhibit 5.3 on page 107.)

4-2-201
40CoA114
40CoA394
575P2d861
579P2d656
647P2d687
668P2d1387
553F2d1222
515FS515
46CUR338
Subd. 1
668P2d1385
Subd. 2
40CoA394
579P2d656
553F2d1222
Subd. 3
¶ a
647P2d687
668P2d1385
¶ b
553F2d1222
¶ c
40CoA395
41CoA357
540P2d356
579P2d656
588P2d383
668P2d1387
515FS515
97A3948n

There is, however, one more place that we can look for Colorado cases. By shepardizing section 4-2-201, we can determine whether there have been any cases since the pocket part was issued. Thus, we look once again at *Shepard's*.

The entries under "Subd. 3, ¶a" refer the reader to the Colorado cases that have cited 4-2-201(3)(a). Section 2-201(3)(a) is cited on page 687 of volume 647 of the *Pacific Reporter, Second Series* (the Colorado Court of Appeals decision in *Colorado Carpet*) and on page 1385 of volume 668 of the *Pacific Reporter, Second Series* (the Colorado Supreme Court's decision in *Colorado Carpet*).

At this point, we can draw only one conclusion. There are only two Colorado decisions discussing the exception for specially manufactured goods: the Colorado Court of Appeals and the Colorado Supreme Court's decisions in *Colorado Carpet*.

c. Locating the Potentially Applicable Cases

Cases are published in sets of books called reporters. Like session laws (see page 99), reporters are organized chronologically: Instead of being arranged under topics, decisions are presented in date order.

In some states, decisions are published in only one reporter. For example, since 1980, the decisions of the Colorado Court of Appeals and Colorado Supreme Court have been published in only the *Pacific Reporter, Second Series,* a West publication containing cases from thirteen western states. In other states, decisions are published in more than one reporter. For example, the decisions of the Oregon Supreme Court are published in both *Oregon Reports* (the official reporter for Oregon's Supreme Court decisions) and in the *Pacific Reporter*. (See Chapter 12.)

Note

Prior to 1980, Colorado decisions were published in both an official reporter, *Colorado Reports* or *Colorado Court of Appeals Reports,* and the Pacific Reporter. To determine the name or names of the reporters publishing a particular court's decisions, see Table T.1 in *The Bluebook: A Uniform System of Citation* (15th ed.).

Cases are located using the citation. For example, to find the decisions cited in *Colorado Carpet,* we would use the citations found at the end of the notes of decision. The 1982 Court of Appeals decision is published in volume 647 beginning at page 686, and the 1983 Supreme Court decision in volume 668 beginning at page 1384.

Note

The Colorado Supreme Court's decision is set out in Chapter 4 at pages 72-80.

d. Analyzing the Cases

The final step is to read and, if appropriate, analyze each analogous case.

As a general rule, begin by reading the syllabus and headnotes that precede the text of the decision. Although they are not part of the court's decision and cannot, therefore, be cited as authority, they can help you determine whether the case might be useful.

If after reading the syllabus and headnotes you determine that the case is not useful, discard it, noting in your research notes that you looked at the case but did not find it useful. If, however, the case appears to be useful, the next step is to read the opinion itself. When the opinion is short (three to five pages), you will usually want to read the entire opinion. If it is longer, begin by reading the portions (1) stating the issue or issues, (2) summarizing the facts, and (3) discussing the relevant points of law. (Use the headnote numbers to find relevant discussions of the law. See Chapter 4, page 73.)

In doing this reading, you should look for a number of different things. First, make sure that the opinion is "on point." Is it discussing the statute that you are researching or, in a common law case, the cause of action in which you are interested? Second, make sure that you understand the question before the court. Was the court determining whether a particular good was specially manufactured or only whether the trial court erred in granting the defendant's motion for summary judgment?

Also determine how you might be able to use the case. Is this a case that you can cite as authority for the general rule? Does the opinion set out the rule or test that should be used in determining whether a particular element is or is not met? Are the facts close enough to the facts in your case that you (or the other side) can use the case to argue by analogy, comparing or contrasting the facts in the analogous case with the facts in your case? Are the arguments that the parties made arguments that either you or the other side might also make?

Finally, look at the statutes, cases, and secondary authorities that the court cites. If any of them look promising, copy the citations and look them up later.

If, after reading for these things, you still think that the case might be useful, either take notes on the decision or photocopy the relevant sections. (See section 5.5.8, below.)

Note

Never photocopy a case that you haven't read. Although the copy-now-and-read-later approach may seem efficient, it almost never is. You need to find out what you have before you know where to go next.

§5.5.6   Locating Persuasive Authority

Because we found only one Colorado case on point, *Colorado Carpet,* we decide to look for persuasive authority, specifically, cases from other jurisdictions. Because the UCC is a uniform act, the law in most other states is the same as it is in Colorado.

Cases from other jurisdictions can be found using a number of sources. We found some when we did the background reading: Legal encyclopedias, treatises, hornbooks, A.L.R., and practice books all contain case citations. Cases can also be found using a regional digest, the Decennial Digest, law reviews, and LEXIS or Westlaw. (See Chapters 12 and 15.) In addition, when the case involves the application of a uniform law, cases from other jurisdictions can be found using a set called *Uniform Laws Annotated.* (See section 13.3.3.)

Question

How do you decide which source to use?

In the BCC problem, we decide to locate cases using the *Uniform Laws Annotated.* Of the sources available, it is the most specific and the most comprehensive.

The *Uniform Laws Annotated* is organized much as a state code is organized. As in the *Colorado Code Annotated,* there is a volume containing the subject index and volumes containing the text of the uniform acts.

When we look up section 2-201 of the Uniform Commercial Code, we find the text of section 2-201, the official comments, cross-references, a list of law review articles, and notes of decision. Excerpts from the notes of decision section are set out in Exhibit 5.6.

Note

Always remember to check the supplement or pocket part.

We find a wealth of cases. In just the bound portion of the volume, there are references to more than fifteen different cases.

EXHIBIT 5.6   **Excerpt from Notes of Decision for UCC § 2-201***

§ 2–201
Note 20

UNIFORM COMMERCIAL CODE

General contractor, though it could not be described as a steel merchant because it was not in business of buying and selling steel, was nonetheless a "merchant" within exception to statute of frauds pertaining to a merchant who fails to give written notice of its objection to a writing in confirmation of an oral contract where general manager for contractor conceded in cross-examination that general contractor was familiar with steel business and with work of steel subcontractors. Pecker Iron Works, Inc. v. Sturdy Concrete Co. Inc., 1978, 410 N.Y.S.2d 251, 96 Misc.2d 998.

Purchaser of goods was bound to proceed to arbitration, in relation to dispute over whether goods were defective, where paragraph of contract sent by seller to purchaser following oral orders stated that any controversy arising in relation to the contract could be settled only by arbitration, and where purchaser did not object to contents of the contract within ten days of its receipt. Trafalgar Square, Limited v. Reeves Bros., Inc., 1970, 315 N.Y.S.2d 239, 35 A.D.2d 194.

Where letter sent from materials supplier to highway construction contractor regarding supplier's need and intention to increase amount charged by supplier pursuant to contract for furnishing of materials for use in highway construction project met requirements of Uniform Commercial Code regarding unsigned written modification of contract, supplier's claim for modified price as to materials delivered after date of letter was not barred by statute of frauds in absence of written objection from contractor. A. & G Const. Co., Inc. v. Reid Bros. Logging Co., Inc., Alaska 1976, 547 P.2d 1207.

Where written confirmation by plaintiff highway contractor was received by defendant supplier on July 15, 1968, relating to telephone call in which supplier orally quoted a price to plaintiff for certain sealcoat chips, letter of supplier mailed on July 25, 1968, rejecting the confirmation, was timely under section of statute of frauds stating that a written confirmation of the contract satisfies the requirements of the statute unless written notice of objection to its contents is given within 10 days after it is received. Tiffany Inc. v. W.M.K. Transit Mix, Inc., 1972, 493 P.2d 1220, 16 Ariz.App. 415.

Material issue of fact precluding summary judgment existed as to whether invoice price for merchandise was binding on buyer who failed to object within 90 days of accepting delivery of goods. Hinson–Barr, Inc. v. Pinckard, 1987, 356 S.E.2d 115, 292 S.C. 267.

If merchant sending confirmatory memorandum has met statute of frauds requirements by sending memorandum stating quantity term and sufficiently indicating that contract for sale has been made, and if merchant receiving writing does not give timely notice of objection, then confirmatory writing need not be signed by receiving merchant to satisfy statute of frauds. Howard Const. Co. v. Jeff-Cole Quarries, Inc., Mo.App.1983, 669 S.W.2d 221.

That cotton farmer was astute in selling his own product was not sufficient to make him a "dealer" in goods within statute of frauds provision defining "merchant" as person who deals in goods of the kind; thus his oral contract to sell cotton was unenforceable although he did not within ten days give written notice of objection to buyer's written confirmation of the oral contract. Loeb & Co., Inc. v. Schreiner, 1975, 321 So.2d 199, 294 Ala. 722.

21. Specially manufactured goods

Spare parts accepted by middleman for benefit of retailer's ongoing retailing of private label electronic products and in context of middleman's compliance with retailer's request that middleman not do business with retailer's competitors might be considered "unique" goods and subject to statute of frauds under New York law, even if buy-back arrangement by which retailer repurchased parts from middleman were construed as one for purchase of goods rather than one for purchase of services. Esquire Radio & Electronics, Inc. v. Montgomery Ward & Co., Inc., C.A.2 (N.Y.) 1986, 804 F.2d 787.

Term "specially manufactured," as used in exception to writing requirement of Florida statute of frauds for sales of goods refers to the nature of the particular goods in question and not to whether the goods were made in an unusual, as opposed to the regular, business operation or manufacturing process of the seller. Impossible Electronics Techniques, Inc. v. Wackenhut Protective Systems, Inc., C.A.Fla. 1982, 669 F.2d 1026.

Those pump parts which were not shipped by manufacturer to buyer fell into the category of goods "specifically manufactured for the buyer and not suitable for sale to others in the ordinary course of business" within meaning of statute of frauds provision of the Uniform Commercial Code. Rust Engineering Co. v. Lawrence Pumps, Inc., D.C.Mass.1975, 401 F.Supp. 328.

Under Indiana law, where object of contract is manufacture of something to be made especially for buyer, on his special order, and object is not suitable for sale to others in ordinary course of business, contract is not a sale within meaning of Uniform Sales Act. Aghnides v. Marmon Group, Inc., D.C.W.Va.1972, 344 F.Supp. 829.

EXHIBIT 5.6 *(continued)*

SALES

§ 2–201

Uniqueness of cargo of cork waste and its intended use for grinding, compressing and peeling into sheets by consignee's buyer made latter's contract with consignee-seller a contract for "special manufacture" within this section and relevant state statute then in effect, and because reprocessing of undamaged as well as water damaged bales was all but required, consignee-seller could maintain suit and recover certain items of damages without being able to prove exact number of bales damaged by stevedore's negligence. Consolidated Cork Corp. v. Jugoslavenska Linijska Plovidba, D.C.N.Y.1970, 318 F.Supp. 1209.

Contract for purchase of lighting fixtures was not within either the Connecticut or New York statute of frauds since the goods were to be fabricated especially for the buyer and could not be sold to others in the ordinary course of business. Franklin Research & Development Corp. v. Swift Elec. Supply Co., D.C. N.Y.1964, 236 F.Supp. 992, affirmed 340 F.2d 439.

Sale of steel reinforcing rods for retaining wall at site of residence that defendant was contemplating building for himself fell within either or both of two exceptions to writing requirement, in that goods were either specially manufactured and not suitable for sale to others or were received and accepted. Frank Adams & Co., Inc. v. Baker, 1981, 439 N.E.2d 953, 1 Ohio App.3d 137, 1 O.B.R. 444.

Oral contract for purchase of special printed merchandise which identified seller and which was sent and accepted by seller was enforceable over objection that it violated statute of frauds. Burger Man, Inc. v. Jordan Paper Products, Inc., App. 1 Dist. 1976, 352 N.E.2d 821, 170 Ind.App. 295.

Blacktop packed down and laid in place was goods manufactured specially for buyer, and where, also, landowner accepted blacktopping work, contract price was recoverable though it was more than $500 and there was no contract signed by party against whom enforcement was sought or by his authorized agent or broker, as required by statute in case of contract for sale with price of more than $500. Rose Acre Farms, Inc. v. L.P. Cavett Co. of Ind., 1972, 279 N.E.2d 280, 151 Ind.App. 268.

Since machine was to be specially manufactured for buyer and was not suitable for sale in ordinary course of seller's business, modifications of contract for manufacture of machine did not have to be in writing to satisfy statute of frauds. S. C. Gray, Inc. v. Ford Motor Co., 1979, 286 N.W.2d 34, 92 Mich.App. 789.

Statute of frauds was not defense to suit to recover on contract for sale of printing services where printed materials delivered under such contract were specially manufactured and not suitable for sale to others and where buyer gave no notice of repudiation before there had been substantial beginning in the printing. Associated Lithographers v. Stay Wood Products, Inc., Minn.1979, 279 N.W.2d 787.

To satisfy "specially manufactured goods" exception to statue of frauds, goods must be specially made for buyer, goods must be unsuitable for sale to others in ordinary course of seller's business, seller must have substantially begun to manufacture goods or must have made commitment for their procurement, and manufacture or commitment must have been commenced under circumstances reasonably indicating that goods are for buyer and prior to seller's receipt of notification of repudiation. Colorado Carpet Installation, Inc. v. Palermo, Colo.1983, 668 P.2d 1384.

Unsigned invoice sent to buyer was not writing in confirmation of contract. Camera Haus, Inc. v. Olympus Corp., 1985, 333 S.E.2d 22, 175 Ga.App. 166.

Oral contract for sale of wrapping material from manufacturer to operator of bakery was not barred by statute of frauds and was enforceable against operator, where wrapping material was manufactured to size required by operator's containers, was imprinted with operator's name and unique "artwork," and was completely produced by seller. Flowers Baking Co. of Lynchburg, Inc. v. R–P Packaging, Inc., 1985, 329 S.E.2d 462, 229 Va. 370.

Evidence showed that merchandise allegedly ordered by buyer was suitable for sale to others, so that company with whom order was allegedly placed could not recover on alleged oral purchase contract under exception to statute of frauds, where president of company testified that merchandise was not "specially manufactured" for alleged buyer, and where some of the merchandise, though slow moving, had already been sold to other parties. Mel-Tex Valve, Inc. v. Rio Supply Co., Inc., Tex. App. 1 Dist.1986, 710 S.W.2d 184.

Contract for export-shipping crates for vehicles manufactured by defendant, which did not sign plaintiff's written bid, was governed by that subsection of statute rendering enforceable unwritten contracts for goods specially manufactured for buyer and not suitable for sale to others in the ordinary course of seller's business, where containers were manufactured according to detailed specifications required by defendant and plaintiff made a substantial beginning before any notice of repudiation. LTV Aerospace Corp. v. Bateman, Tex.Civ.App. 1973, 492 S.W.2d 703.

If our case were a big one and the client had unlimited resources, we might take the time to locate and read each of the cases listed in the notes. This is not, however, a reasonable course of action in the BCC case. We need to be more selective. Instead of locating all of the cases, we need to select those that are "best."

In selecting the best cases, we are looking for several things. First, we are looking for cases that set out the "law," that is, cases that set out a definition of "specially manufactured" or the test that the courts use in determining whether a particular good is "specially manufactured for the buyer." Second, we are looking for cases in which the court has applied the "law" to facts that are similar to the facts in the client's case. Are there any cases in which the courts have decided whether a particular rug or set of rugs was "specially manufactured"? If not, are there any cases in which a symbol, logo, or company name was placed on stationery, cartons, or T-shirts? Finally, we are looking for cases in which the court summarizes each side's arguments.

There are several other factors that should be considered in selecting cases. When there are numerous cases on point, select decisions from higher courts over those from lower courts, more recent decisions over older decisions, and more factually analogous cases over cases that are less factually analogous.

In addition, in selecting analogous cases, try to select at least one case in which the court held that the definition or test was met and one in which the court held that it was not. You can place the client's case in the middle, comparing the facts in the client's case to those in the case in which the court found that the test was met and those in the case in which the court held that the test was not met.

X	X	X
Case A (test not met)	Client's case	Case B (test met)

Criteria for Selecting Cases

1. Know what information you need, and select cases that appear to contain that information.
2. Select decisions from higher courts over decisions from lower courts.
3. Select recent decisions over older decisions.
4. Select cases that are more factually analogous over cases that are less factually analogous.
5. Select cases in which the court has found that the disputed element was met and cases in which it has found it was not met.

In the BCC case, we select the following cases for the memorandum.

1. *Impossible Electronics Techniques, Inc. v. Wackenhut Protective Systems,* 669 F.2d 1026 (5th Cir. 1982). Defines the phrase "specially manufactured."

   2. *Flowers Baking Co. of Lynchburg, Inc. v. R-P Packaging, Inc.,*
      229 Va. 30, 329 S.E.2d 42 (1985). This case appears to be fac-
      tually analogous. Like the rugs, the goods were manufactured
      to the buyer's specifications and imprinted with the buyer's
      "artwork." The exception applied.
   3. *LTV Aerospace Corp. v. Bateman,* 492 S.W.2d 703 (Tex. Civ.
      App. 1973). This case appears to be factually analogous. Like
      the rugs, the containers were manufactured according to the
      defendant's detailed instructions.

The next step is to locate and read the cases themselves.

Note

As in most sources, in the *Uniform Laws Annotated,* the citations
are not in *Bluebook* form. For the correct way of citing cases, see Chapter 17 and *The Bluebook: A Uniform System of Citation* (15th ed.).

As we just saw in the analysis of *Colorado Carpet,* reading the cases
is a three-step process: (1) begin by reading the headnotes, using them
to locate the relevant portions of the opinion; (2) read the relevant portions of the opinion to determine if the case might be useful; and (3) if
a case appears useful, brief it, noting not only the tests that the court
applied but also the facts that the court considered significant and the
cases that the court cited as authority.

The last step is to shepardize the cases that you plan to use in your
memo, determining whether they are still good law and whether there
are more recent cases that might be useful.

§5.5.7   Shepardizing the Cases

Just as you must shepardize a statute to determine if it is "good
law," you must also shepardize each case that you plan to use, determining (1) the current status of the case (whether the decision has been
reversed or overruled) and (2) whether there are other, more recent
cases that are on point. (For more on shepardizing, see Chapter 14.)

Exhibit 5.7, taken from the front of a *Shepard's* case citator, shows
the order in which the entries appear and explains the abbreviations
that are used.

Using the information in Exhibit 5.7, we shepardize *Colorado Carpet,* one of the cases that we plan to use in the memorandum. We begin
by noting the relevant information from *Colorado Carpet.* What is the
cite, and what are the numbers of the applicable headnotes? (Look again
at page 73.)

Using the citation, we then locate the applicable volumes of
Shepard's, in this instance the *Shepard's* for the *Pacific Reporter, Second
Series* that includes references to volume 668.

EXHIBIT 5.7   Guide to Using a *Shepard's* Case Citator*

ILLUSTRATIVE CASE

**Pacific
Reporter,
Second
Series**

Vol. 553

-423-
(87Wsh2d298)
D430US952
D5ILℰ801
D97SC1594
s510P2d233   1
cc553P2d442
cc554F2d369

559P2d⁴²602
564P2d838
566P2d²¹1264
578P2d⁴¹878
583P2d²¹625
589P2d¹⁹262
d589P2d²¹287
j589P2d288
f599P2d1274
605P2d²⁶1277
627P2d²⁶577
628P2d¹513
628P2d²¹817
638P2d1216
639P2d²¹773
639P2d²789
639P2d²⁶840
639P2d²¹841   2
j639P2d843
e649P2d832
652P2d²⁶967
655P2d³⁷1181
655P2d³⁸1181
658P2d¹1261
668P2d²⁹576
675P2d²¹202
675P2d²²202
j675P2d207
676P2d⁶499
j676P2d973
680P2d²¹420
683P2d³⁸209
704P2d³⁷692
719P2d²⁶535

Idaho
615P2d⁶123   4
Nev
582P2d²⁵792

La
354So2d775   5
Md
501A2d73

58.42 1024s
89.43 467n
89.43 487n
9.41 1152n   7
9.41 1165n
23.41 298n
35.41 29n
35.41 44n

Citations to the case of *State of Washington v. Ralph Williams' North West Chrysler Plymouth, Inc.* as reported in Volume 553 Pacific Reporter, Second Series at page 423 are shown in the left margin of this page in the same form in which they appear in the Pacific Reporter, Second Series division of this edition.

Cross references to a cited case as also reported in a series of state reports and the American Law Reports are shown enclosed in parentheses immediately following the page number of that case when first available and are not repeated in subsequent volumes. Thus the reference "(87 Wsh2d 298)" immediately following the –423– page number of the *Ralph Williams'* case indicates that that case is also reported in Volume 87 Washington Reports, Second Series at page 298 and the absence of an American Law Reports reference enclosed in parentheses indicates that the *Ralph Williams'* case is not also reported in the American Law Reports.

Citations to each cited case are grouped as follows:

1. citations by state and federal courts analyzed as to the history of the cited case;
2. other citations by courts of the state in which the cited case was decided analyzed as to the treatment accorded the cited case;
3. other citations by federal courts analyzed as to the treatment accorded the cited case;
4. citations, arranged alphabetically by states, by courts of states covered by the Pacific Reporter other than the state in which the cited case was decided analyzed as to the treatment accorded the cited case;
5. citations, arranged alphabetically by states, by courts of states covered by any units of the National Reporter System other than Pacific Reporter;
6. citations in articles in the American Bar Association Journal;
7. citations in annotations of Lawyers' Edition, United States Supreme Court Reports and the American Law Reports; and
8. citations in selected legal texts.

For the purpose of illustration only, this grouping has been indicated by bracketing the citations accordingly. It will be noted that as yet there are no citations in groups three and six.

In indicating the history and treatment of a cited case, the letter-form abbreviations shown on page xvi are used.

An examination of the citations relating to the history of the cited case indicates that an appeal was dismissed "D" by the United States Supreme Court in a case reported in 430 United States Supreme Court Reports "US" 952 as well as in 51 Lawyers' Edition, United States Supreme Court Reports, Second Series "Lℰ" 801 and in 97 Supreme Court Reports "SC" 1594. Another phase of the same case "s" is shown in a case reported in 510 Pacific Reporter, Second Series "P2d" 233. Connected cases "cc" are reported in 553 P2d 442 and 554 Federal Reporter, Second Series "F2d" 369.

An examination of the treatment accorded the cited case in subsequent Washington cases reported in the Pacific Reporter, Second Series indicates that it has been distinguished "d" in a case reported in 589 P2d 287, followed "f" in a case reported in 599 P2d 1274 and explained "e" in a case reported in 649 P2d 832. The *Ralph Williams'* case was also cited in

EXHIBIT 5.7 *(continued)*

ABBREVIATIONS—ANALYSIS

History of Case

a   (affirmed)   Same case affirmed on appeal.
cc (connected   Different case from case cited but arising out of same subject
        case)   matter or intimately connected therewith.
D   (dismissed)   Appeal from same case dismissed.
De (denied)   Review or rehearing denied.
Gr (granted)   Review or rehearing granted.
m   (modified)   Same case modified on appeal.
Np (not published)   Reporter of Decisions directed not to publish this opinion.
Op (original   Citation of original opinion.
        opinion)
r   (reversed)   Same case reversed on appeal.
Re (republished)   Reporter of Decisions directed to publish opinion previously
                              ordered not published.
s   (same case)   Same case as case cited.
S   (superseded)   Substitution for former opinion.
v   (vacated)   Same case vacated.
US cert den   Certiorari denied by U. S. Supreme Court.
US cert dis   Certiorari dismissed by U. S. Supreme Court.
US reh den   Rehearing denied by U. S. Supreme Court.
US reh dis   Rehearing dismissed by U. S. Supreme Court.

Treatment of Case

c   (criticised)   Soundness of decision or reasoning in cited case criticised for
                              reasons given.
d   (distinguished) Case at bar different either in law or fact from case cited for
                              reasons given.
e   (explained)   Statement of import of decision in cited case. Not merely a
                              restatement of the facts.
f   (followed)   Cited as controlling.
h   (harmonized)   Apparent inconsistency explained and shown not to exist.
j   (dissenting   Citation in dissenting opinion.
        opinion)
L   (limited)   Refusal to extend decision of cited case beyond precise issues
                              involved.
o   (overruled)   Ruling in cited case expressly overruled.
p   (parallel)   Citing case substantially alike or on all fours with cited case in
                              its law or facts.
q   (questioned)   Soundness of decision or reasoning in cited case questioned.

ABBREVIATIONS—COURTS

Cir. DC–U.S. Court of Appeals, District of Columbia Circuit
Cir (number)–U.S. Court of Appeals Circuit (number)
Cir. Fed.–U.S. Court of Appeals, Federal Circuit
CCPA–Court of Customs and Patent Appeals
CIT–United States Court of International Trade
ClCt–Claims Court (U.S.)
CtCl–Court of Claims (U.S.)
CuCt–Customs Court
ECA–Temporary Emergency Court of Appeals
ML–Judicial Panel on Multidistrict Litigation
RRR–Special Court Regional Rail Reorganization Act of 1973

Note

If a decision is printed in more than one reporter, you can shepardize the case using either citation. You will, however, find different information depending on which citation you use. Because the different sets have different coverage, entries that appear under one cite may not appear under the other. To determine the coverage of a particular set, check the table in the front of the volume.

If an opinion is printed in more than one reporter, you must also make sure that you use headnote numbers that correspond to the citation that you are using. What may be headnote 3 in the official reporter may be headnote 5 in the unofficial reporter.

Looking in the oldest volume first, we locate the page that includes volume 668, page 1384. (See Exhibit 5.8.)

Having found the right set of entries, we look first at the case history. Were there any lower court decisions? Has the decision been appealed to a higher court? If there was an appeal, did the higher court agree to hear the case? If it did, what was the outcome of that appeal?

If there are "history" entries, these entries will appear before the references to other cases that have cited the case being shepardized. For example, in Exhibit 5.8, the first entry is a "history of the case" entry. The "s" tells us that the citation is to the same case, and the "647P2d686" that the same case can be found in volume 647 of the *Pacific Reporter, Second Series,* beginning on page 686. When we look up this citation, we find the first page of the Colorado Court of Appeals' decision in *Colorado Carpet Installation, Inc. v. Palermo.* After the Colorado Court of Appeals decided the case, its decision was appealed to the Colorado Supreme Court.

At this point, we also need to note what we don't see. In the history of the case section, there are no entries preceded by the letter "r." The absence of such an entry tells us that the Colorado Supreme Court's decision was not reversed by a higher court.

Although we now know that the case was not reversed, we do not know whether, in a different case decided at a later date, a court overruled the Colorado Supreme Court's decision in *Colorado Carpet.* To determine whether this has happened, we scan the abbreviations preceding the "nonhistory" entries, looking for an "o" or even a "q." If we find an "o," it means that in the case cited after the "o," the court overruled, either in part or in whole, the Colorado Supreme Court's decision in *Colorado Carpet.* If we find a "q," it means that the rule set out in *Colorado Carpet* was questioned. In Exhibit 5.8 there are no "o"s or "q"s; thus, the court's decision in *Colorado Carpet* is still good law.

Question

Why do we distinguish cases that have been reversed from cases that have been overruled? What difference does it make to the parties? What difference does it make to you as a researcher?

EXHIBIT 5.8 ***Shepard's* Citator for the *Pacific Reporter, Second Series****

Vol. 668 PACIFIC REPORTER, 2d SERIES

Volume number

Vt
477A2d633

– 1126 –
Case 2
s464US1073
s79LE222
s104SC986
cc693P2d4
669P2d299
674P2d[6]1141
674P2d[7]1141
675P2d[19]447
676P2d[17]860
690P2d[17]471
690P2d[26]473
692P2d[5]562
693P2d[26]628
695P2d[27]548
695P2d[9]552
695P2d[22]552
695P2d[27]555
698P2d[5]25
698P2d[5]33
699P2d662
701P2d[24]422
701P2d[18]425
e701P2d[27]428
702P2d1036
706P2d[5]164
713P2d1045
714P2d
[[26]1042
714P2d
[[26]1042
718P2d[16]362
719P2d[19]842
720P2d337
720P2d741
723P2d[26]287
724P2d[27]787
NM
712P2d[12]794
SD
391NW679
74ALR3d1138s

– 1139 –
2ALR4th27s

– 1144 –
702P2d[2]375

– 1147 –
cc679P2d278
668P2d[3]1152

– 1150 –
e672P2d[1]306
26ALR3d951s

– 1152 –
Cir. 10
791F2d[4]1581

– 1157 –
US cert den
in104SC977
in464US1070
684P2d560
43ALR3d385s

– 1164 –
674P2d[1]1150
683P2d[1]988

– 1165 –
702P2d[4]1058
721P2d[1]421

– 1172 –
26ALR3d951s

– 1175 –
700P2d[3]671

– 1186 –
(295Or467)
s648P2d388
670P2d[3]141
693P2d1316
703P2d[3]250
705P2d[2]1146
714P2d266
j719P2d860
Calif
208CaR402

– 1197 –
(295Or524)
s659P2d1010
684P2d[1]17
j684P2d18
698P2d959
708P2d619

– 1201 –
(295Or580
s642P2d692
671P2d[1]118
672P2d[3]377
681P2d[1]1156

– 1206 –
(295Or553)
m677P2d671
s656P2d955
669P2d1146
Ariz
722P2d[1]981

– 1210 –
(295Or574)

– 1214 –
(295Or561)

– 1217 –
(295Or604)
f678P2d[4]1221
690P2d[4]502
f690P2d[7]504
691P2d[4]99
96ALR2d823s

– 1224 –
(295Or594)
e682P2d256
682P2d[1]261

– 1225 –
(295Or598)
f669P2d330
f671P2d[4]703
e701P2d434
701P2d[3]436
701P2d[4]437
717P2d[2]622

– 1228 –
(295Or588)
s652P2d1
701P2d782
907
1032

1 –
(64OrA420)

– 1232 –
(64OrA439)
cc655P2d
[1103
711P2d199

– 1233 –
(64OrA443)
s672P2d1193
cc663P2d
[1291

– 1236 –
(64OrA448)
s672P2d1193

– 1242 –
(64OrA478)

– 1245 –
(64OrA493)
s675P2d491
cc675P2d508
712P2d[2]152

– 1249 –
(64OrA487)
679P2d[3]350
679P2d[6]350
682P2d[6]829
709P2d[1]765

– 1254 –
Cir. 10
758F2d[4]1384

– 1258 –
f674P2d[4]133
e675P2d1205
681P2d[4]1266
700P2d[4]1111
701P2d[1]1101
709P2d319
718P2d[3]392

– 1266 –
(100Wsh2d
232)
j694P2d32

– 1278 –
(100Wsh2d
263)
692P2d197
693P2d[4]134
711P2d1055
c711P2d1056
716P2d[2]946

– 1285 –
(35WAp592)
675P2d[1]1254

– 1286 –
(35WAp678)

– 1292 –
(35WAp557)

– 1294 –
(35WAp598)
702P2d[1]1220
702P2d[2]1220

– 1301 –
(35WAp626)
s627P2d136

– 1304 –
(35WAp610)
700P2d[7]346
708P2d[19]664
Cir. 9
761F2d1323
DC
511A2d396
23ALR3d932s

– 1311 –
(35WAp673)

– 1315 –
(35WAp643)

– 1319 –
(35WAp650)
r683P2d189

Page number

324 –
2d 10
'2d[1]917
e692P2d932
f694P2d[2]121
f694P2d[1]122
e694P2d[1]124
f695P2d[2]1028
695P2d[2]1030
715P2d[2]238
j715P2d243
715P2d[2]249

– 1333 –
692P2d[13]235
692P2d[15]236
695P2d[2]628
719P2d617
Nev
714P2d[9]572

– 1343 –
680P2d[8]488
d693P2d[10]853
f699P2d337

– 1351 –
j679P2d484
78ALR3d846s

– 1362 –
s720P2d999
690P2d[8]1255
690P2d[7]1256
d697P2d[3]27
708P2d1368
f708P2d
[[14]1370
713P2d[7]1332
713P2d
[[11]1333

718P2d[9]1056
719P2d[4]715
j722P2d400
725P2d[4]1176

– 1371 –
f686P2d
[[22]1366
689P2d[18]694
692P2d
[[16]1051
697P2d[19]741
698P2d
[[10]1339
699P2d[1]1339
701P2d[22]274
701P2d
[[22]1267
703P2d650
703P2d[4]671
703P2d[5]671
703P2d[6]671
704P2d[4]332
706P2d[4]408
706P2d[4]769
f713P2d[6]870
713P2d[4]1335
716P2d[6]1116
716P2d[4]1118
721P2d[4]1203
722P2d448
725P2d[5]783
j725P2d785
Ore
696P2d
[[10]1123
80ALR2d1428s

– 1384 –
s647P2d686
675P2d[2]334
687P2d[2]536
690P2d[1]1282
718P2d[2]264

Vol. 669

– 1 –
(34C3d644)
(194CaR765)
s185CaR184
674P2d[2]1317
f678P2d892
e684P2d[3]830
693P2d248
693P2d[3]249
e702P2d[1]617
198CaR701
199CaR[2]59
f199CaR[1]533
200CaR[2]200
f201CaR317
e205CaR[3]269
209CaR669
209CaR[3]670
e216CaR[1]459
216CaR875
229CaR[1]109

– 9 –
(34C3d554)
(194CaR773)
f721P2d592
200CaR[4]633
206CaR[2]749

206CaR[1]750
206CaR[4]751
209CaR123
210CaR811
e213CaR714
215CaR[6]705
d215CaR[4]905
218CaR502
j218CaR520
218CaR[1]900
f221CaR343
221CaR[4]346
222CaR366
223CaR884
228CaR[2]344
f228CaR506
229CaR[1]629

– 17 –
(34C3d658)
(194CaR781)
683P2d[1]1157
686P2d614
686P2d[1]614
j686P2d629
694P2d753
j696P2d122
718P2d[4]74
36CaR[1]904
197CaR[4]700
d200CaR[4]514
206CaR[1]94
j206CaR109
210CaR[1]240
210CaR640
j211CaR730
f217CaR792
221CaR[3]619
226CaR[4]87
229CaR703
j229CaR714
Colo
700P2d516
Idaho
d725P2d[1]528
j725P2d533
Mich
353NW460

– 41 –
(34C3d695)
(194CaR805)
681P2d[5]903
709P2d[2]474
196CaR[4]658
196CaR[5]658
197CaR[4]35
197CaR[5]35
202CaR[4]904
203CaR[5]636
j206CaR9
d208CaR[6]28
209CaR196
210CaR[6]824
214CaR[5]731
216CaR[4]588
220CaR[2]670
229CaR[5]769
Alk
721P2d[6]1129
Ala
457So2d399
Mich
390NW223

Vt
499A2d427
80ALR2d320s
6COA695§13

– 51 –
(137Az73)
s669P2d90
717P2d[3]445
720P2d[5]89
722P2d[5]362
724P2d[3]1247

– 58 –
(137Az80)
s691P2d689
cc672P2d
[1311
669P2d[1]74
676P2d[16]627
676P2d
[[16]1117
678P2d
[[16]1378
679P2d[15]495
f682P2d[3]420
682P2d[15]421
689P2d[16]577
d691P2d[3]300
700P2d[6]869
700P2d[12]869
702P2d[6]687
702P2d[7]687
704P2d[7]275
711P2d[7]584
713P2d[6]286
f714P2d[6]397
717P2d[8]886

– 68 –
(137Az90)
US cert den
in104SC985
in464US1073
678P2d[5]447
d691P2d[3]300
697P2d[1]333
703P2d[11]477
706P2d[8]391
Fla
449So2d886
NC
333SE234
54ALR3d612s
18ALR4th743s

– 78 –
(137Az100)
e674P2d[1]848
674P2d[2]849
f678P2d[2]942
f691P2d1085
691P2d[1]1086
691P2d[2]1086
f691P2d1103
f697P2d[2]1078
j697P2d1084

– 83 –
(137Az105)
671P2d905
672P2d967
673P2d[8]11
691P2d[8]693
692P2d[4]1006

– 89 –
(137Az111)
s669P2d94

– 90 –
(137Az112)
v669P2d51

– 94 –
(137Az116)
D669P2d89

– 99 –
(137Az121)

– 102 –
(137Az124)

– 108 –
(137Az130)
77ALR3d1290s

– 111 –
(137Az133)
674P2d[2]331
674P2d[1]333

– 113 –
(137Az135)

– 115 –
(137Az137)
Wyo
j678P2d879
Ind
496NE1351

– 121 –
(137Az143)

– 126 –
671P2d[6]952
676P2d[2]704
676P2d[3]704
678P2d[3]1005
f678P2d[5]1019
681P2d[7]935
f681P2d[8]936
f683P2d[5]767
f683P2d[7]767
f683P2d[5]1194
697P2d395
697P2d[7]741
f703P2d[5]1285
714P2d[4]492
Kan
724P2d702
Wyo
f678P2d[7]869
706P2d[7]261

– 130 –
713P2d[3]379

– 135 –
m710P2d488
680P2d[3]1301
59ALR3d152s

– 141 –
682P2d[1]499
682P2d[1]1240

796

*Reproduced from Shepard's *Pacific Reporter Citations,* 4th ed. 1987, by permission of Shepard's/McGraw-Hill, Inc. Further reproduction is strictly prohibited.

Shepard's can also be used to find additional cases. Having found one case that discusses a particular rule, we can use *Shepard's* to locate other cases discussing that same rule. For example, if in a case decided after *Colorado Carpet* a court cites *Colorado Carpet,* a reference to that later case will appear in the *Shepard's* entries for *Colorado Carpet.*

Note

The preceding sentence is somewhat of an overstatement. See the Note on page 107 regarding the coverage of different sets of *Shepard's.*

Thus, we look once again at the entries under " — 1384 — ":

```
– 1384 –
s647P2d686
675P2d²334
687P2d²536
690P2d¹1282
718P2d²264
```

*Reproduced from Shepard's *Pacific Reporter Citations,* 4th ed. 1987, by permission of Shepard's/McGraw-Hill, Inc. Further reproduction is strictly prohibited.

The second entry is "675P2d²334." In this citation, the "675" is the volume number; the "P2d" is the abbreviation for the reporter; the superscript "2" is a reference to the headnote for which the case was cited; and the "334" is the page number on which the *Colorado Carpet* citation appears.

Because we are interested only in the exception for specially manufactured goods, we do not need to look up all of the entries in *Shepard's.* We can be selective, looking only at those entries that discuss the headnotes relating to specially manufactured goods and that were decided after the notes of decision were published.

Because we are interested only in cases that discuss the points of law set out in headnotes 4, 5, and 6 in *Colorado Carpet,* we scan the *Shepard's* entries, looking for citations with one of these three numbers printed as a superscript following the abbreviation for the reporter. If we find one, we will check the volume number to see if the case was decided before or after the notes of decision were published.

In Exhibit 5.8, there are no entries corresponding to headnotes 4, 5, or 6. The only entries are for headnotes 1 and 2. Because we are not interested in cases that cite *Colorado Carpet* for the rules set out in either of these headnotes, we do not look up any of these cases. Instead, we move to the supplements, once again looking up volume 668, page 1384.

Reminder

Shepard's volumes are not cumulative. You must, therefore, check each volume and supplement that contains your citation.

───────────

Note

As you now know, shepardizing can be tedious. Fortunately, the process is being made easier. You can now shepardize both statutes and cases using LEXIS or Westlaw. Although this computer-assisted shepardizing is expensive, it requires less time and may reduce the potential for error. Remember too that the paper (book) versions of *Shepard's* are not completely up-to-date. To locate the most recent cases, you will need to use LEXIS or Westlaw.

───────────

§5.5.8   Keeping Track of What You Have Found

In doing legal research, you must have a system. You must know where you have already looked and what it is that you found, and you must keep track of which statutes and cases you have shepardized and which you haven't.

In addition, you must think as you research. Although it may seem easier to photocopy everything and then read it, it isn't. Read as you go, analyzing each piece and trying to put the pieces together. You won't know what else you need until you know what you already have.

One way of keeping yourself organized is to develop a structured note-taking system. For example, many researchers find it helpful to create a sheet like the one in Exhibit 5.9 for each element.

Most researchers also make it a practice to write down the full citation for each case (there is nothing worse than having to run back to the library to locate the parallel cite or to get the year the decision was issued) and to make a list of the statutes and cases that they have shepardized.

§5.6   UNDERSTANDING WHAT YOU HAVE FOUND

At this point, you may feel overwhelmed. You have spent hours in the library, and your desk is stacked with notes and photocopies. The

---

EXHIBIT 5.9	**Format for Research Notes**

Research Notes

Element 1
Goods specially manufactured for the buyer

Definition, Rule or Test:

Analogous Cases:

Arguments that we can make:

Arguments that the other side can make:

---

question is, now what? Is it time to start drafting the memo? The answer is, not yet. Before you begin drafting, you must analyze and synthesize the statutes and cases that you have found.

§5.6.1   Analyzing the Pieces

Simply put, analysis is examining something closely, identifying each part or component and determining how the parts are related.

In law, there are two types of analysis: statutory analysis and case analysis. We did statutory analysis when we took apart paragraph three of section 2-201, identifying each of the elements and determining whether all or only some of them had to be met. (See pages 111 and 112.) We must now analyze each of the cases.

In analyzing, or briefing, a case, the first step is to identify the issue. What was the court asked to decide? The next step is to identify the rule or test. What rule or test did the court apply and, if the court could select from several rules or tests, why did it select the one it did? The last step is to look at the court's conclusion. What did the court decide and how did it reach that conclusion?

In the following example, the writer has analyzed *Colorado Carpet.*

Note

Compare this brief, which is done for the purpose of writing the memo, with the more general case brief presented on pages 83-85.

EXAMPLE

BRIEF FOR *COLORADO CARPET INSTALLATION, INC. V. PALERMO*

Issue No. 1:

Whether Colorado Carpet met its burden of proving the first element, that the goods were specially manufactured for the buyer.

Rule:

The term "specially manufactured" refers to the character of the goods as made for a particular buyer and not to whether they were specially made in the usual course of the seller's business. (p. 1390)

Holding:

The seller did not meet its burden of proving the first element, that the goods be specially manufactured for the buyer.

Reasoning:

There was no evidence from which one could reasonably conclude that the carpets were specially manufactured.

- The same carpets were available from other retail outlets.
- Both carpets were ordered as stock items.
- No special dyeing, weaving, or other treatment was required to fill orders.
- The carpets were not cut to unusual shapes or sizes.

Because the carpets had no special features, they did not provide evidence that they were made for a particular buyer.

Issue No. 2:

Whether Colorado Carpet met its burden of proving the second element, that the goods were not suitable for resale in the ordinary course of its business.

Rules:

The unsalable quality of the goods presumably must be found in their characteristic of special manufacture and not in such tests as lost markets, passed seasons, or the objective inability of the particular seller to dispose of the goods for reasons unrelated to their nature.

If with slight alterations the goods can be sold, then they are not specially manufactured. If essential changes are needed to make the goods marketable, this element is met. (Court cites *Impossible Electronics Techniques, Inc. v. Wackenhut Protective Systems, Inc.*)

Holding:

The seller did not meet its burden of proving the second element, that the goods were not suitable for resale in the ordinary course of its business.

Reasoning:

The evidence did not support a finding that the goods were not suitable for resale in the ordinary course of the seller's business.

- Colorado Carpet's ordinary course of business was the buying of carpet from wholesalers and the reselling of that carpet to retail customers.
- As a retailer of carpet, Colorado Carpet dealt with this type of carpet regularly and could reasonably be expected to find a buyer for it.
- Essential changes were not necessary to make the carpet marketable to other buyers.
- The record shows that Colorado Carpet was able to return some of the carpet to the manufacturer for a credit and that it had no difficulty selling the rest of the carpet to another retail customer.

Notes:

The court began its discussion by setting out underlying policies.

- Certain marketing practices provide sufficiently reliable evidence of a contract.
- In such situations, denying enforcement of the contract would be unfair.

Question

Why did the writer divide the brief into two parts, analyzing the first and second elements in separate sections?

§5.6.2   Putting the Pieces Together

The second step is synthesis. Having analyzed each piece, you must put those pieces together. When read as a whole, what do the statutes and cases "say"?

In some instances, you will find that the same rule has been applied in each case. The rule, which has first set out in Case A, is repeated in Cases B and C.

Case A (Establishes the Rule):

The term refers to the nature of the goods and not to whether the goods were made in an unusual, as opposed to the regular, operation or manufacturing process of the seller.

Case B:

Although the term is not statutorily defined, other courts have held that it refers to the nature of the goods and not to whether the goods were made in an unusual, as opposed to the regular, operation or manufacturing process of the seller. (Court cites Case A as authority.)

Case C:

The courts have repeatedly held that the phrase "specially manufactured" refers to the nature of the goods and not to whether the goods were made in an unusual, as opposed to the regular, operation or manufacturing process of the seller. (Court cites Case A and Case B as authority.)

In this situation, the synthesis — if it can be called that — is easy. All three cases set out the same rule.

Not all synthesis is this easy. Sometimes, each court sets out a slightly different rule. Assume for a moment that the same court has decided each of the following cases.

Case D:

The seller, a printer, asked the court to find that an oral contract for 500,000 fliers was enforceable under the UCC exception for specially manufactured goods. The court found that the first element, that the goods be specially manufactured for the buyer, was met even though the seller used its usual printing processes in producing the fliers. In reaching its conclusion, the court stated, "In this case the nature of the goods themselves is evidence that a contract was formed. It is unlikely that the seller would have produced fliers printed with a specific buyer's name, address, and logo if it had not had a contract for such an order."

Case E:

The seller, a manufacturer of custom T-shirts, asked the court to find that an oral contract for 500 T-shirts with a happy face printed on the front of them was enforceable under the UCC exception for specially manufactured goods. The court held that the contract was not enforceable: "In this case, the goods do not specifically identify the buyer. Because the shirts could be used by any number of other potential purchasers, the first element, that the goods be specially manufactured for the buyer, is not met."

Case F:

The seller, a manufacturer of packaging materials, asked the court to find that an oral contract for wrapping material was enforceable under the UCC exception for specially manufactured goods. The court found that the first element, that the goods be specially manufactured for the buyer, was met. "Because the wrapping material was cut to the size specified by the buyer and has the buyer's logo printed on it, it is not likely that it could be used by other buyers. Consequently, we find that the goods were in fact specially manufactured for the buyer."

Unlike Cases A, B, and C, in these cases the court does not repeat the same rule in each case. Even so, the court may be applying a single principle. To find out if it is, analyze the cases, identifying the significant facts in each.

Case D	*Case E*	*Case F*
Fliers printed with the buyer's name, address, and logo	T-shirts with a happy face printed on the front	Wrapping material cut to size specified by buyer and printed with buyer's logo

The next step is to identify the court's conclusion and reasoning.

Case D	*Case E*	*Case F*
First element met.	First element not met.	First element met.
Nature of goods provides evidence of contract. Not likely that seller would have produced fliers had there been no contract.	Shirts could be used by a number of other purchasers.	Wrapping material could not be used by other buyers.

Finally, you must synthesize. When the cases are read together, what principles can be inferred? Is there a principle or rule that explains all three of the court's decisions?

In the above cases, there are a couple of possibilities. The narrowest is that the first element is met when the goods are printed with the buyer's logo and not met when such a logo is not present. The cases support such a rule: In the cases in which the goods were printed with the buyer's logo, the court held that the first element was met, and in the case in which the goods were not printed with the buyer's logo, the court held that the element was not met.

It is, however, possible to conclude that the court applied a broader, less fact-specific rule. The determining factor may not have been whether the goods had the buyer's logo printed on them but whether they specifically identified the buyer. If through a logo, name, or other characteristic the goods specifically identify the buyer, then they are specially manufactured. Conversely, if they do not specifically identify the buyer, the first element is not met.

A third possibility is that the court looked to whether the goods could be used by another buyer. If they could be used by another buyer, then the element is not met. If, however, they cannot (because they have another's logo or name printed on them), then the element is met.

Let's look at another example.

Case A:

Williams sued James Salons, alleging that James Salons acted outrageously when it refused to serve Williams, an African-American. The court dismissed the claim, holding that because Williams had not been publicly humiliated, the salon's conduct was not so outrageous in character and so extreme in degree as to go beyond all possible bounds of decency.

Case B:

Contreras sued his employer, Crown Zellerbach, alleging that Crown Zellerbach acted outrageously when, during work hours and in front of customers, it permitted its employees to direct racial slurs at Contreras, a Mexican-American. In finding that Crown Zellerbach's conduct was outrageous, the court considered (1) that, as an employer, Crown Zellerbach was in a position of authority and (2) that, because he was a Mexican-American, Contreras was particularly susceptible.

Case C:

Yi sued his neighbor, Brown, alleging that Brown acted outrageously when he sent Yi, an Asian-American, a letter containing racial slurs. The court dismissed the claim, holding that because copies of the letter were not distributed to others, the conduct was not extreme and outrageous.

Case D:

Gomez, a Mexican-American, sued the university that he attended, alleging that the University acted outrageously when it did not stop Gomez's teammates from calling him a "fucking spic" during games. In finding that the University's conduct was outrageous, the court considered the public nature of the insults and the University's relationship with Gomez. Because of its position, a university has a duty to protect its students from racial slurs.

Once again, we begin by identifying the key facts and the court's conclusions and reasoning.

Facts:

Case A	*Case B*	*Case C*	*Case D*
Service refused to African-American	Racial slurs directed at Mexican-American	Letter containing racial slurs sent to Asian-American	Racial slurs directed at Mexican-American
Conduct "private"	Conduct "public"	Conduct "private"	Conduct "public"

Holding:

Not outra-geous be-cause not publicly humiliated	Outrageous be-cause em-ployer in position of authority and plaintiff par-ticularly sus-ceptible	Not outrageous because let-ter not dis-tributed to others	Outrageous be-cause of the University's relationship and public nature of slurs

In this example, the cases in which the courts found the conduct to be outrageous have three facts in common: In each there was a racial slur, made in public, directed at a Mexican-American. The cases in which the court found that the conduct was not outrageous also have a fact in common. In each, the conduct was private: Neither Brown nor Yi was publicly humiliated.

There are also some common threads in the reasons that the court set out to support its holdings. In Cases A and C, the court explained its decisions by saying, in effect, that the conduct was not outrageous be-cause it was not public; in contrast, in Case D, the court based its deci-sion that the conduct was outrageous, at least in part, on the fact that the slurs were public. Similarly, in Cases B and D the court expressly considered the defendant's relationship with the plaintiff. The conduct was found to be outrageous when the defendant was in a position of power over the plaintiff.

When these common threads are collected, several "principles" ap-pear. The court finds conduct to be outrageous when it occurs in public and when the defendant is in a position of power over the plaintiff. Thus, in Case A, the significant facts are not that the plaintiff was denied ser-vice or that she was an African-American but that the conduct was pri-vate, rather than public, and that the defendant was not (at least arguably) in a position of power. Similarly, in Case C, the significant facts are that the letter was not made public and that it was sent by a neighbor and not an employer or other person in a position of power over the plaintiff.

Question

Do you agree with this reading of the cases? Can the cases be read in another way? What do you do if there is more than one way of putting the pieces together?

In writing your memo, it is the principles, not the individual rules, that you want to set out.

The following examples illustrate the difference between a discus-sion in which there is no synthesis or minimal synthesis and one in which the synthesis is good. (Complete citations have not been included.)

In Example 1, there is no synthesis. The writer simply summarizes the case (the "book report" format).

EXAMPLE 1 **NO SYNTHESIS**

In Case A, the court held that because the plaintiff, an African-American, had not been publicly humiliated, the defendant's conduct was not so extreme and outrageous as to go beyond all bounds of decency.

In Case B, a case in which an employer did not prevent its employees from directing racial slurs against a Mexican-American employee during work hours and in front of customers, the court held that the conduct was outrageous. In reaching its decision, the court considered two factors: that the defendant was in a position of authority over the plaintiff and that because the plaintiff was a Mexican-American, he was particularly susceptible.

In Case C, a case in which a letter containing racial slurs was sent to an Asian-American, the court held that the conduct was not outrageous because the letter had not been sent to others.

In Case D, the court held that because of its relationship to the plaintiff, a student, the defendant, a university, acted outrageously when it did not stop teammates from directing racial slurs toward the plaintiff during games.

In Example 2, there is minimal synthesis. Although the writer has included topic sentences and organized cases around the holdings, the emphasis is still on the cases themselves and not on the principles that can be drawn from those cases.

EXAMPLE 2 **MINIMAL SYNTHESIS**

In determining whether conduct is outrageous, the courts have applied several different tests.

In Case A, the court held that because the plaintiff, an African-American, had not been publicly humiliated, the defendant's conduct was not so extreme and outrageous as to go beyond all bounds of decency. Similarly, in Case C, a case in which a letter containing racial slurs was sent to an Asian-American, the court held that the conduct was not outrageous because the letter had not been sent to others.

In contrast, in Case B, a case in which an employer did not prevent its employees from directing racial slurs against a Mexican-American employee during work hours and in front of customers, the court held that the conduct was outrageous. In reaching its decision, the court considered two factors: that the defendant was in a position of authority over the plaintiff and that because he was a Mexican-American, the defendant was particularly susceptible. The court reached a similar result in Case D when it held that because of its relationship to the plaintiff, a student, a university acted outrageously when it did not stop teammates from directing racial slurs toward the plaintiff during games.

Example 3 is much better. The writer has organized the discussion around the principles that can be drawn from the cases, only using the cases to illustrate the application of those principles.

EXAMPLE 3   GOOD SYNTHESIS

In determining whether racial discrimination or slurs are outrageous, the courts consider two factors: (1) whether the plaintiff was publicly humiliated and (2) whether the defendant was in a position of power over the plaintiff. See Case A; Case B; Case C; Case D.

In the cases in which the plaintiff was publicly humiliated and the defendant was in a position of power over the defendant, the courts have found the conduct to be outrageous. For example, in Case B, a case in which an employer did not prevent its employees from directing racial slurs against a Mexican-American employee during work hours and in front of customers, the court held that the conduct was outrageous because the employer was in a position of power over the plaintiff. Similarly, in Case D, the court found that a university acted outrageously when it did not stop teammates from directing racial slurs toward the plaintiff, a student, during games.

When the plaintiff was not publicly humiliated, the courts have reached the opposite conclusion. In Case A, a case in which the defendant refused to serve the plaintiff, the court held that the conduct was not outrageous because the plaintiff was not publicly humiliated. The court reached the same conclusion in Case D, holding that because a letter containing racial slurs had not been made public, the defendant's conduct was not extreme and outrageous. Although in these two cases the court did not expressly consider the defendant's relationship to the plaintiff, the facts indicate that the defendant was not in a position of authority over the plaintiff. In Case A, the defendant was a beauty salon and the plaintiff was a potential customer; in Case C, the plaintiff and defendant were neighbors.

Synthesis becomes even more difficult when the cases come from different jurisdictions. In addition to looking for common factors, you must consider the court that decided the case.

Case X:

Kwak sued a gymnastics club, alleging that the club acted outrageously when it allowed one of its coaches to direct racial slurs at Kwak, a Korean-American. In affirming the trial court's order dismissing the case, the court held that racial slurs are not, by themselves, sufficient to support a cause of action.

Case Y:

Johnson, an African-American, sued Easy-Mart Stores, Inc., alleging that it acted outrageously when it permitted one of its security guards to direct racial slurs at Johnson, whom they had detained without cause. In reversing the trial court's order dismissing the case, the court held that Johnson's complaint stated facts sufficient to support a cause of action for the tort of outrage.

Case Z:

Aziz, an Iraqi, sued Martin, alleging that Martin acted outrageously when he directed racial slurs at Aziz in the hallway outside their university classroom. In reversing the trial court's order dismissing the claim, the court held that racial slurs are no longer tolerated and that they can, by themselves, provide the basis for a cause of action.

In this situation, the cases cannot be reconciled. Although Cases X and Y may be reconciled, Cases X and Z cannot. If all three cases were decided by State A's Supreme Court, State A's lower courts would be bound by the most recent of the decisions. For example, if Case Z were the most recent, the lower courts would be bound by that decision; if, however, Case X were the most recent, the lower courts would be bound by it.

The result is different if cases are from different jurisdictions. If Cases X and Y were decided by State A's courts and Case Z by State B's Supreme Court, there would be no need to reconcile the cases. State A's courts would simply follow the rule set out in Cases X and Y, State B's courts the rule set out in Case Z.

Question

Assume that State C has never decided a tort of outrage case based on racial slurs. When a case does arise, how can the attorneys use the cases from States A and B? _____

For a complete discussion of mandatory and persuasive authority, see section 2.3.

§5.6.3   Preparing a Decision Chart

The final step is the preparation of a decision chart. In deciding the case, what are the questions and in what order will they be asked?

The scope of your decision chart is determined by the issue that you were asked to discuss. (See page 94.) If you had been asked to determine whether the BCC contract was barred by the UCC Statute of Frauds, you would have had to determine (1) whether the UCC applied; (2) if it did, whether the formal requirements of the Statute of Frauds had been met; and (3) if they had not, whether any of the exceptions would apply.

Exhibit 5.10 illustrates the decisionmaking process.

> ### Section
> ### Summary

Before writing:

1. Analyze each piece, "tearing apart" each statute and briefing each case.
2. Synthesize. Put the pieces together, determining what the cases "say" when read together. Have each of the courts applied the same rules and tests? If they haven't, what common principles can be derived?
3. Prepare a decision chart that identifies each question and the order in which those questions would be asked.

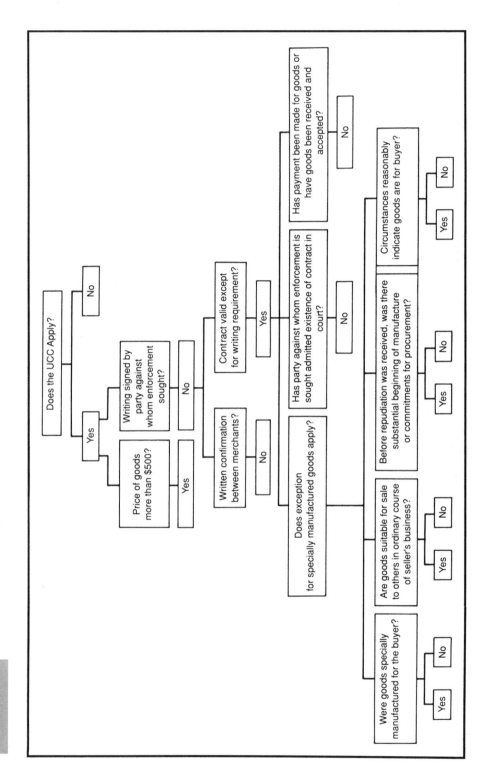

EXHIBIT 5.10 The Decisionmaking Process

B.　DRAFTING

　　With the prewriting stage behind you, it is now time to put pen to paper or fingers to keyboard.

　　As you begin writing, there are several things that you should keep in mind. First, remember your audience. In writing an objective memorandum, you are not writing for the client, the other side, or even a judge. You are writing to an attorney in your firm.

　　Second, remember how the attorney will use the memo. Your purpose is not persuasion. It is to give the attorney the information that he or she needs to objectively evaluate the case and advise the client. Consequently, in writing the memo, you must present the law objectively. This is not the time or place to omit or even de-emphasize unfavorable precedent or facts. If the attorney is to accurately evaluate the case, you must present both the favorable and unfavorable information.

　　Third, remember that unlike briefs, there are no court rules specifying the format of an objective memorandum. There are only conventions. Although these conventions are useful for both the writer and the reader, once you understand them, you should feel free to break them when appropriate. When the convention does not serve its purpose, don't use it.

　　Finally, and perhaps most important, remember that writing a memo is a recursive process. Writing is not just a process of putting completely formed ideas on paper. It is a process of discovery. As a result, as you write you will begin thinking about the problem in new ways, which may necessitate doing more research or rethinking your analysis or synthesis of the law.

　　Similarly, because the process is recursive, there is no right order in which to write the sections. While some writers draft the sections in the order in which they appear in the memo, others begin with the brief answer, the discussion section, or even the conclusion. Because each section is connected to the others, wherever you start, you will have to go back to that section at the end, revising it in light of what you wrote in the other sections.

§5.7　Drafting the Heading

　　The heading is the easiest section to write. It consists of only four entries: the name of the person to whom the memo is addressed, the name of the person who wrote the memo, the date, and an entry identifying the client and the issue or issues discussed in the memo. Although the first three entries are self-explanatory, the fourth needs some explanation.

　　In some firms, the memo is filed only in the client's file. If you work for one of these firms, the "Re:" entry should be quite specific: It should identify both the client and the issues discussed in the memo.

EXAMPLE 1

To: Connie Krontz
From: Thomas McMurty
Date: September 28, 1993
Re: Beaver Custom Carpets, File No. 93-478
           Whether oral contract for three rugs is enforceable under
           UCC Statute of Frauds exception for specially manufac-
           tured goods when the rugs have the Reutlinger family
           flower woven into them at one-foot intervals.

In other firms, the memo is filed not only in the client's file but also in a "memo bank," that is, a computer or paper file in which all memos are filed by topic. In these offices, the "Re:" section serves two purposes. Within the client's file, it distinguishes the memo from any other memos that may have been or will be written, and in the memo bank, it provides either the database for a word search or topic categories under which the memo will be filed. To serve this last purpose, the heading needs to be less specific; instead of including specific facts, it should refer to more general categories.

EXAMPLE 2

To: Connie Krontz
From: Thomas McMurty
Date: September 28, 1993
Re: Beaver Custom Carpets, File No. 93-478
           Contract Law; UCC Statute of Frauds;
           Exception for Specially Manufactured Goods.

---

§5.8 DRAFTING THE STATEMENT OF FACTS

The first question is, why is there a statement of facts? Why include a fact statement when the attorney already knows what the facts are?

There are several answers. The easiest is tradition, or convention. Because most memos have a fact statement, you should include one in your memo. The attorneys expect to see a statement of facts and, unless they have told you not to include one, will note its absence. There are, however, better answers. As in many situations, there are reasons for the convention.

The first has its source in the structure of our legal system. In the United States, courts do not decide legal questions in the abstract. Decisions are always made in the context of a specific dispute. Consequently, to predict what a court might do, the attorneys need to know both the law and the facts that, given that law, the court would find significant. The statement of facts gives the attorneys this last piece of information. In writing the statement of facts, you do not simply parrot back the facts that were given to you. Instead, you sort through them, including in the memo only those that are legally significant.

The second is more practical. In larger firms, more than one attorney may work on a case. As a result, the attorney who ultimately reads and uses your memo may not be the attorney who assigned it. In such situations, that attorney relies on your statement of facts when evaluating the case and talking to the client. In addition, memories fade. Given the fast pace of law practice, neither you nor the attorney may be able to recall the facts even a few weeks after the memo is written.

§5.8.1   Deciding What Facts to Include

A typical statement of facts includes three types of facts: facts that are legally significant, facts that are emotionally significant, and background facts that, although not legally or emotionally significant, are necessary to "tell the story."

a.   *Legally Significant Facts*

A legally significant fact is a fact that a court would consider significant either in deciding that a statute or rule was applicable or in applying that statute or rule. For example, in the BCC case, a court would find it legally significant that the rugs were made to the buyer's specifications and that the same type of rug was not available at other outlets. The court would not, however, find it legally significant that the rugs were maroon and beige rather than, say, light and dark blue.

Either of two techniques can be used to determine whether a fact is legally significant. The first technique, which is used before the discussion section has been written, is to prepare a two-column chart. In the first column, list the legal requirements, and in the second, the facts that the court would consider in deciding whether the requirement was met.

EXAMPLE

Law	*Facts*
"Specially manufactured" refers to the nature of the goods and not to whether they were made in the usual course of the seller's business.	The rugs were unique; made to buyer's specifications; and apparently not available from other outlets.
Goods are not specially manufactured if, with slight alterations, they can be sold.	Because the rugs had already been completed, they could not be altered.

The second technique is used after the discussion section has been completed. To ensure that you have included all of the legally significant facts, go through your discussion section, listing each fact that you used in applying law to fact; then check this list against your statement of facts. If you used a fact in applying law to fact, that fact is legally significant and should be included in the statement of facts. (Remember, writing a memo is a recursive process. Even though you may write the statement of facts first, you will need to revise it after you have completed the discussion section.)

EXAMPLE

FACTS USED IN DISCUSSION SECTION

1. BCC had to make special arrangements with the manufacturer
2. the manufacturer had to specially set its looms
3. identical rugs could not be found at other carpet outlets
4. the rugs were made to fit specific rooms and special weaving was required
5. the rugs had the Reutlinger family flower woven into them
6. if the contract is not enforced, BCC, a small business, will suffer a loss
7. BCC is in the business of producing custom goods

b. *Emotionally Significant Facts*

An emotionally significant fact is one that, while not legally significant, may affect the way the judge or jury decides the case.

In the statute of frauds case, several facts could be considered emotionally significant. For example, although it is not legally significant that Mr. McKibbin was injured, if the case were to go to trial, jurors might view him more sympathetically than they would a person who had not been injured. Similarly, jurors might empathize with BCC if they learn that the firm is in financial trouble. Because either of these facts might affect the outcome of the case, the attorney needs to consider them in evaluating the case.

c. *Background Facts*

In addition to including the legally and emotionally significant facts, you also need to include those facts that are needed to tell the story and that provide the context for the legally and emotionally significant facts. Thus, although it is not legally significant that the McKibbins planned to turn the mansion into a bed and breakfast, this fact helps explain why the rugs were ordered.

§5.8.2 Organizing the Facts

In writing a statement of facts, most writers use one of three organizational schemes. They arrange the facts chronologically, they arrange them topically, or they combine the two schemes, organizing the facts by topic and then presenting the facts chronologically within each topic.

The facts themselves usually dictate which organizational scheme will work best. If the case involves a series of events related by date, then the facts should be presented chronologically. If, however, there are a number of facts that are not related by date (for example, the description of several different pieces of property) or a number of unrelated events that occurred during the same time period (for example, four unrelated crimes committed by the defendant over the same two-day period), the facts should be organized by topic.

EXAMPLE 1   **FACTS PRESENTED CHRONOLOGICALLY**

STATEMENT OF FACTS

Our client, Beaver Custom Carpets (BCC), wants to know whether it can enforce an oral contract for three rugs that were manufactured to the buyers' specifications.

The buyers, Mr. and Mrs. McKibbin, first contacted BCC in June of this year, asking whether BCC could replicate the original rugs in the Reutlinger Mansion, which Mr. and Mrs. McKibbin were refurbishing and turning into a bed and breakfast. Around the perimeter of each rug was a twelve-inch maroon strip; in the center was beige carpet with the Reutlinger family flower woven into the carpet at one-foot intervals.

After examining a picture of the rugs, BCC called its manufacturer. The manufacturer told BCC's sales representative that it could produce the rugs. Although the looms would have to be specially set, standard dyes could be used. On June 19, the sales representative sent the McKibbins a proposal setting out the specifications and the price, $16,875.

On June 29, Mrs. McKibbin called the sales representative and told him that she and her husband wanted to purchase the rugs. The next day, the salesperson ordered the rugs from the manufacturer. A written contract was not sent to the McKibbins.

On August 4, Mrs. McKibbin called BCC and told the sales representative that because her husband had fallen from the roof of the mansion, they were canceling their order. Although BCC called its manufacturer the same day, the rugs had already been completed, and BCC was forced to accept delivery of the rugs at a cost of $13,500.

On August 15, BCC sent the McKibbins a bill for the proposal price of the rugs. Last week, BCC received a letter from the McKibbins' attorney stating that because the contract was not in writing, it was not enforceable under the UCC Statute of Frauds.

BCC sold the rugs to a wholesaler on September 1 for $10,000. BCC has done business with this wholesaler on one prior occasion. Similar rugs are not available from other carpet stores.

BCC is a specialty carpet firm that specializes in custom work. It has been in business for only one year and is in financial trouble.

In the BCC case, common sense dictated that the facts be presented chronologically. Most of the facts could be tied to a particular date, and the story makes the most sense when the facts are related in date order. The facts that could not be tied to particular date (for example, the description of the rugs) were placed in the paragraphs where they could be most easily integrated into the story.

EXAMPLE 2　FACTS ARRANGED TOPICALLY

STATEMENT OF FACTS

We represent Judith Davis, the petitioner in a divorce action. Although Ms. Davis and her husband, Frank Davis, agree that the marriage is irretrievably broken, they disagree on who should get custody of their children and on the distribution of their property.

The couple have two children: Jason, age 11, and Elizabeth, age 5. When the children were very young, Ms. Davis stayed home with them. Three years ago, though, she decided to fulfill a lifelong goal to become a doctor. Despite the fact that her husband disagreed with this plan, she applied to and was accepted into medical school. She is now in the second year of an eight-year program. The program is a demanding one, and Ms. Davis currently spends approximately twelve hours a day at school, either in class or studying. She admits that she finds this schedule exhausting and that when she is home she has very little energy. She says, though, that what energy she has goes into caring for the children. She still fixes their dinner, helps with homework, and puts them to bed.

Mr. Davis is a partner in a local law firm. Although he too has a demanding schedule, he has always played an active role in raising the children. He has spent whatever free time he has with them, and he has accompanied them to the doctor's and dentist's offices and has been active in their school activities. Although Ms. Davis says that Mr. Davis is a good father, she believes that on occasion he drinks too much.

Both parents agree that the parent who gets custody of the two children should get possession of the family home. They disagree, though, on how the other assets should be divided. Mr. Davis wants to split the remaining property in half. Ms. Davis wants fifty percent plus the cost of her medical school education. She states that because the cost of her husband's law school education was paid from community funds, the cost of her medical school education should also be paid from community funds.

In this example, the facts could not be presented chronologically. Only a few of them could be tied to a particular date, and the dates that were available were not particularly important. Consequently, the author organized the facts by topic, selecting the topics on the basis of the issues discussed in the memo — the custody of the children and the distribution of property. The facts relating to custody were placed in one block of paragraphs and the facts relating to the distribution of the property in another.

EXAMPLE 3   **FACTS PRESENTED BOTH CHRONOLOGICALLY AND TOPICALLY**

STATEMENT OF FACTS

Our clients, Elizabeth and Jeff Bovee, want to bring a medical malpractice claim against Dr. Stephen O'Toole. They allege that Dr. O'Toole negligently performed a vasectomy, which resulted in an unexpected pregnancy.

Elizabeth and Jeff Bovee are established professionals who live in Gainesville, Florida. Jeff works as an urban planner for the City of Gainesville and, until last September, Elizabeth worked as a veterinarian at a local clinic. In September, Elizabeth quit her job as a veterinarian and began working as a Professor of Veterinary Science at the University of Florida. With her new job, Elizabeth's salary increased from $35,000 a year to $48,000 a year.

Between 1983 and 1991, Elizabeth gave birth to three congenitally deformed children, each of whom died in infancy. In 1991, Dr. O'Toole told the Bovees that there was a seventy-five percent probability that any child that they conceived would suffer from the same deformity. Relying on this information, Jeff and Elizabeth decided that Jeff should have a vasectomy. On August 15, 1991, Dr. O'Toole performed a vasectomy on Jeff Bovee. Three months later, Dr. O'Toole performed a sperm count on Jeff and informed him that the operation had rendered him sterile.

However, in January 1992, Elizabeth discovered that she was pregnant. For religious reasons, the couple decided not to abort the fetus; they also chose not to have amniocentesis performed. After a difficult pregnancy, Elizabeth gave birth to a healthy boy on August 2, 1992.

The Bovees have consulted us to evaluate the possibility of recovering damages from Dr. O'Toole for the injuries they suffered as a result of the unwanted pregnancy and birth. While Jeff and Elizabeth love their son, they claim that his conception and birth have caused them severe emotional, physical, and financial harm. They wish to recover the substantial medical expenses related to the pregnancy and birth, and they seek to recover for lost time and wages. Elizabeth also contends that the leave that she had to take in conjunction with the pregnancy has put her new job in jeopardy. In addition, the Bovees claim to have suffered considerable trauma from the conception and birth of a child whom they expected to be deformed.

In this example, it was not possible to present the facts strictly chronologically or topically. Although some facts were tied to dates, many were not. The solution was to arrange the facts by topic, for example, background information, information about the Bovees, a description of Elizabeth's prior pregnancies, and a description of the alleged malpractice, and then, within each of these topics, to present the facts chronologically.

Whichever organizational scheme you use, you will usually want to begin the statement of facts with a sentence or paragraph that introduces the case or sets the stage for the rest of the facts. In the following examples, the introductory paragraphs introduce the "cast of characters" and establish a context for the facts that follow.

EXAMPLE 1

Our client, Beaver Custom Carpets (BCC), wants to know whether it can enforce an oral contract for three rugs that were manufactured to the buyers' specifications.

EXAMPLE 2

We represent Judith Davis, the petitioner in a divorce action. Although Ms. Davis and her husband, Frank Davis, agree that the marriage is irretrievably broken, they disagree on who should get custody of their children and on the distribution of their property.

EXAMPLE 3

Our clients, Elizabeth and Jeff Bovee, wish to bring a medical malpractice claim against Dr. Stephen O'Toole. They allege that Dr. O'Toole negligently performed a vasectomy on Jeff Bovee, resulting in an unexpected pregnancy.

---

§5.8.3　Presenting the Facts

Once you have decided which facts to include and the order in which you will present those facts, it is time to begin writing.

a.   Present Facts Accurately and Objectively

The first rule is that the facts must be presented accurately and objectively. This means that you must include all of the legally significant facts, even if some of them do not favor your client or are offensive. It also means that you should use neutral language. Although in a brief you will want to present the facts in the light most favorable to your client, in a memo you need to present the facts unembellished.

In the following example, the facts have been presented neither accurately nor objectively.

EXAMPLE 1

> Three weeks ago, Mrs. McKibbin called, alleging that her husband had fallen from the roof of the mansion. Using this fall as an excuse, she told BCC that she and her husband were canceling their rug order.
>
> The salesperson immediately called the manufacturer. Unfortunately, her call came too late. The manufacturer had already completed the rugs. Although BCC tried to sell the rugs to other retail customers, it was not able to do so. Consequently, it was forced to sell the rugs at a substantial loss to a wholesaler with whom it had done business on only one prior occasion.

The writer has done several things wrong. First, he or she has added facts. There was nothing in the memo from the senior partner that said that BCC had tried to sell the rugs to other retail customers. Second, the writer slanted the facts: BCC is presented in a favorable light and the McKibbins in an unfavorable one. Mrs. McKibbin "alleges" that her husband has been injured and then uses this injury "as an excuse." "Unfortunately," the rugs had already been completed, and BCC was forced to sell to a wholesaler with whom it had done business on "only" one prior occasion at a "substantial loss."

The following example is much better: The facts are presented accurately, and the language is neutral.

EXAMPLE 2

> Three weeks ago, Mrs. McKibbin called BCC, telling BCC that because her husband had fallen from the roof of the mansion, they were canceling the order.

Although the sales representative immediately called the manufacturer, the rugs had already been completed, and BCC was forced to take delivery of them at a cost of $13,500. BCC subsequently sold the rugs for $10,000 to a wholesaler with whom it had done business on one prior occasion.

b. Do Not Include Legal Conclusions in the Statement of Facts

The second rule is that you cannot state as a fact something that is, in the context of the case, a legal conclusion. For example, in the BCC case, you cannot say in your statement of facts that the rugs were specially manufactured. Although in some problems it might be a fact that something was, or was not, specially manufactured, in this problem "specially manufactured" is an element under the statute and whether this element is met is a legal conclusion. Instead of saying that the rugs were specially manufactured, set out the facts that the court would consider in determining whether this element is met.

Question

In the statute of frauds problem, which of the following are facts and which are legal conclusions?

    a. BCC is a specialty carpet company that caters to customers who want to purchase custom-made carpets in nonstandard colors or patterns.

    b. BCC was not able to sell the rugs in the ordinary course of its business.

    c. The manufacturer had completed the rugs before Mrs. McKibbin called to cancel the order.

c. Make the Statement of Facts as Interesting as Possible

Like other human beings, attorneys enjoy a story. Consequently, in writing the statement of facts, do not simply list the facts. Although you must present the facts accurately and objectively, your statement does not need to be dull. BCC has a story, and it is your job to tell it.

Checklist for Critiquing the Statement of Facts

I. Organization

- The writer has included an introductory sentence or paragraph that identifies the parties and the nature of the dispute.
- The writer has used one of the conventional organizational schemes: chronological, topical, or a combination of chronological and topical.

II. Content

- All of the legally significant facts have been included.
- When appropriate, emotionally significant facts have been included.
- Enough background facts have been included so that a person not familiar with the case can understand what happened.
- The facts are presented accurately.
- The facts are presented objectively.
- The writer has not included legal conclusions in the statement of facts.

III. Writing

- The attorney can understand the facts of the case after reading the statement of facts once.
- The paragraph divisions are logical, and the paragraphs are neither too long nor too short.
- Transitions and dovetailing have been used to make clear the connections between ideas.
- In most sentences, the writer has used the actor as the subject of the sentence, and the subject and verb are close together.
- The writer has varied the length of the sentences and the sentence patterns so that each sentence flows smoothly from the prior sentence.
- The writing is concise and precise.
- The statement of facts is grammatically correct.
- The statement of facts is correctly punctuated.
- The statement of facts has been proofread.

§5.9 DRAFTING THE QUESTION PRESENTED

The question presented establishes the memo's focus. It identifies the applicable statute or common law rule, it defines the precise legal question, and it summarizes the facts that will be significant in deciding the legal question.

Note

The phrases "question presented" and "issue statement" are often used interchangeably.

_____

§5.9.1   Determining the Number of Issues and the Order in Which They Should Be Presented

By convention, you should have the same number of questions presented as parts to the discussion section. Accordingly, if in the discussion section you discuss three unrelated issues — whether service of process was adequate, whether the statute of limitations has run, and whether the defendant was negligent — you should have three separate questions presented, one corresponding to each of the three issues. If, however, you discuss only one issue, whether the contract is enforceable under UCC Statute of Frauds exception for specially manufactured goods, you will have only one formal issue statement. You will not prepare a question presented for each of the sub-issues.

Convention also dictates that in a multi-issue memo you list the questions presented in the same order in which you discuss those issues in the discussion section. The first question presented will correspond to the first section of the discussion section, the second will correspond to the second section, and so on.

§5.9.2   Writing the Question Presented

Although different readers prefer different formats, the easiest type of question presented to write is one using the "under-does-when" format.

"Under-does-when" Format

The "under-does-when" format forces you to include all the essential information in the question presented: After the "under," insert a reference to the applicable law; after the "does," "is," or "can," insert the legal question, and after the "when," insert the most important of the legally significant facts.

Under	(insert reference to applicable law) _____
does/is/can	(insert legal question) _____
when	(insert most important legally significant facts)? _____

a. Applicable Law

The first question is, what law applies? Consequently, a well-written question presented begins with a reference to the applicable law. In the under-does-when format, this reference follows "under."

In deciding how specific the reference should be, you need to find the middle ground. If the reference is too specific, the reader will not understand it. For example, few attorneys would know, without looking up the section number in the code, that section 4-2-201(3)(a) is the section setting out the exception to the Statute of Frauds. A reference that is too general is equally useless. Hundreds of thousands of cases are filed each year in which the problem is governed by Colorado law.

EXAMPLE   REFERENCES THAT ARE TOO SPECIFIC

"Under 2-201, . . ."

"Under Colo. Rev. Stat. § 4-2-201, . . ."

EXAMPLE   REFERENCES THAT ARE TOO GENERAL

"Under Colorado law, . . ."

"Under Colorado statutory law, . . ."

"Under the Uniform Commercial Code, . . ."

EXAMPLE   THE MIDDLE GROUND

"Under Article 2 of the UCC, . . ."

"Under the UCC Statute of Frauds, . . ."

"Under the Colorado UCC Statute of Frauds, . . ."

"Under the UCC Statute of Frauds exception for specially manufactured goods, . . ."

b. The Legal Question

The next component is the legal question. What is the court being asked to decide?

In framing the question, do not state it too narrowly or too broadly. If stated too narrowly, the question will not cover all of the issues and sub-issues in the discussion section; if stated too broadly, the statement will be meaningless.

EXAMPLE   QUESTIONS THAT ARE TOO NARROW

"are the rugs specially manufactured . . ."

"are the rugs suitable for sale in the ordinary course of the seller's business . . ."

"did the seller, under circumstances that reasonably indicate that the goods are for the buyer, make a substantial beginning of their manufacture or commitments for their procurement before notice of the buyer's repudiation . . ."

EXAMPLE   QUESTIONS THAT ARE TOO BROAD

"can BCC sue . . ."

"will BCC win . . ."

"can BCC recover the purchase price . . ."

EXAMPLE   QUESTIONS THAT ARE PROPERLY FRAMED

"is a contract enforceable under the exception for specially manufactured goods . . ."

"will the court find that the contract is enforceable under the UCC Statute of Frauds exception for specially manufactured goods . . ."

"is an oral contract for three rugs manufactured to the buyer's specifications enforceable under the UCC Statute of Frauds exception for specially manufactured goods . . ."

Note

In the last example, the writer included legally significant facts as part of the legal question. ⸻⸻⸻

c. Legally Significant Facts

The question presented is not yet complete. In our judicial system, legal questions are never decided in the abstract. They are decided in terms of specific facts. Thus, in writing the question presented, you cannot just ask the legal question. You must ask it in terms of the facts of the particular case.

The problem lies in deciding which facts should be included in the question presented. If there are only two or three facts that are legally significant, the answer is easy. Include all the legally significant facts. What do you do, though, if there are five to ten facts that are, at least arguably, legally significant? And even worse, what do you do if there are fifteen legally significant facts? You cannot include them all in your question presented — if you did, you would have a question presented that was as long as your statement of facts.

Occasionally, you will be able to include all of the legally significant facts by either summarizing the facts or by categorizing them and listing only the categories. There will, however, be times when neither of these techniques works. In these situations, you will simply have to leave some facts out. Not all legally significant facts are equally significant.

EXAMPLE 1

Under Florida tort law, do the parents of a healthy child have a cause of action for wrongful pregnancy when (1) during the years 1983 through 1991, the couple had three congenitally deformed children who died as infants; (2) after the birth of the third child, the doctor told the couple that there was a 75 percent chance that any other children that the couple had would suffer from the same deformity; (3) relying on this information, the couple decided that the husband should have a vasectomy to prevent future pregnancies; (4) after performing the vasectomy and subsequent sperm count, the doctor told the couple that the husband was sterile; (5) one year after the operation, the wife became pregnant by the husband; and (6) after a difficult pregnancy, the wife gave birth to a healthy boy?

Most attorneys would not read the above question presented. Although the writer has included only legally significant facts, the statement is simply too long and, though enumerated, too difficult to wade through. The following question presented is much better.

EXAMPLE 2

Under Florida tort law, do parents have a cause of action for wrongful pregnancy when, after a doctor performs a vasectomy on the husband, the wife becomes pregnant by the husband and gives birth to a healthy child?

Although not all the legally significant facts are included, the most important ones are.

There are several other situations that may cause problems. First, you may encounter a situation in which it is not clear which rule of law the court will apply: If the court adopts one rule, one set of facts will be significant, and if it adopts the other rule, another set of facts will be significant. In such a situation, include only those facts that the court would consider significant in determining which rule to apply.

Second, you may encounter a situation in which the facts are in dispute: The plaintiff alleges that things happened this way, and the defendant alleges that they happened that way. In such a case, summarize each side's allegations. If you cannot, simply state the facts that are not disputed and indicate which facts, or categories of facts, are in dispute.

You may also be tempted to state as a fact something that is a legal conclusion. For example, the first time you write a question presented you may write something like the following.

EXAMPLE   INCORRECT

Under the UCC Statute of Frauds, is an oral contract enforceable when the goods were specially manufactured for the buyer and not suitable for resale in the ordinary course of the seller's business?

Common sense tells you that the answer to this question must always be yes. If the elements are met, the exception applies. If your issue statement is to be meaningful, you must set out the facts that the court will consider in determining whether the elements are met and not the elements themselves.

Note

One of the "facts" that you will usually include in your question presented is the identity of the client. There are two schools of thought about how this fact should be handled. One says that the issue statement should be case-specific and that the client should be referred to by name. The other says that the question presented should be generic. Proponents of this school say that the client should not be referred to by name; instead you should determine what role the client plays and then use that label. The following examples illustrate the two methods.

EXAMPLE 1

Under the UCC Statute of Frauds exception for specially manufactured goods, is the oral contract between **BCC** and the **McKibbins** for the sale of rugs enforceable when (1) the rugs were manufactured to the **McKibbins'** specifications, (2) the same rugs are not available at other outlets, (3) the **McKibbins** told **BCC** that they did not want the rugs after the rugs had been completed, and (4) **BCC** sold the rugs to a wholesaler with whom it had done business on one prior occasion?

EXAMPLE 2

Under the UCC Statute of Frauds exception for specially manufactured goods, is an oral contract for the sale of rugs enforceable when (1) the rugs were manufactured to the **buyers'** specifications, (2) the same rugs are not available at other outlets, (3) the **buyers** told the **seller** that they did not want the rugs after the rugs had been completed, and (4) the **seller** sold the rugs to a wholesaler with whom it had done business on one prior occasion?

The "Whether" Format

Although the "under-does-when" format is the easiest format to use, some readers prefer the more traditional "whether" format.

If you use this format, begin the question presented with the word "whether"; the "whether" is then followed by a statement of the legal question and the legally significant facts.

EXAMPLE

Whether a contract for the sale of three rugs is enforceable under the Statute of Frauds exception for specially manufactured goods when (1) the rugs were manufactured to the buyers' specifications, (2) the same rugs were not available at other outlets, (3) the buyers told the seller that they did not want the rugs after the rugs had been completed, and (4) the seller sold the rugs to a wholesaler with whom it had done business on one prior occasion.

As you read through this question presented, you probably noticed two things: first, that the legal question and the reference to the rule of law are combined, and second, that because the statement begins with the word "whether," the question presented is an incomplete sentence.

Note

At first, you may be bothered by the fact that your question presented is an incomplete sentence. If you are, keep in mind (1) that, by convention, this format is not only acceptable but preferred by many attorneys and (2) that if you read in the words "the issue is . . ." before "whether," the sentence is complete.

The Multisentence Format

In both of the formats described above, the question presented is a single sentence. Although this format often works well, some writers are now rebelling against it because they find that single-sentence questions presented are too long and too difficult to read and write. To make their questions presented easier to read, these writers use the multisentence format.

When using this format, begin with one or more factual statements, and then ask the legal question.

EXAMPLE

The buyers entered into an oral contract with the seller for three rugs, each with the buyers' emblem woven into the rugs at one-foot intervals. Although standard dyes could be used, the manufacturer had to specially set its looms to produce the rugs. After the rugs were completed, the buyers repudiated. The seller has since sold the rugs at a loss to a wholesaler with whom it had done business on one prior occasion. Under these circumstances, is the contract enforceable under the Statute of Frauds exception for specially manufactured goods?

---

§5.9.3 Revising and Editing the Question Presented

Whether your question presented is a single sentence or several sentences, you will probably spend more time writing it than you will any other sentence in your memo. You will spend considerable time making sure that the question is properly focused, that you have included all the essential information, and that your writing is both concise and precise.

To ensure that your question presented is good, you should write several drafts. In writing the first draft, make sure that you have included all the essential information (namely, a reference to the applicable law, the legal question, and the legally significant facts). Then go back and revise and edit what you have written, making sure that your statement is easy to read and understand.

In particular, look at your subject and verb. Have you used the actor as the subject of the sentence? Have you used an action verb? In addition, look at the placement of your subject and verb. Are they close together? If not, rewrite your sentence so that the subject and verb are no more than seven words apart. (See sections 5.23.1(a) and 22.4.)

EXAMPLE 1

Under federal counterfeiting law, **is it** a violation of the law to hang a black-and-white photocopy of a $1,000 bill on the wall?

In this example, the writer has not used the actor as the subject of the sentence: "it" is the subject and "is" is the verb. Both are weak.

EXAMPLE 2

Under federal counterfeiting statutes, **did John Gundy,** the person who allowed the black-and-white photocopy of a $1,000 bill to hang on the wall of his office, **violate** the law?

Although the writer has used the actor, John Gundy, as the subject of the sentence, the subject (Gundy) and verb (violate) are far apart.

EXAMPLE 3

Under federal law, **is** a **person** guilty of counterfeiting if he allows a black-and-white photocopy of a $1,000 bill to hang on the wall of his office?

Although in this example the writer has used a form of the verb "to be," he or she has chosen a strong subject, and the subject and verb are close together.

Question

Which example uses the under-does-when format?

Also look at the facts you included in the question presented. In listing facts, have you used parallel constructions and when appropriate have you repeated structural clues? (See section 25.7.)

EXAMPLE

    Whether a contract for the sale of three rugs is enforceable under the Statute of Frauds exception for specially manufactured goods when (1) the buyers told the seller that they did not want the rugs after the rugs had been completed, (2) the seller sold the rugs to a wholesaler with whom it had done business on one prior occasion, (3) the rugs were manufactured to the buyers' specifications, and (4) were not available at other outlets.

    In this example, the writer has not used parallel constructions in setting out the facts. Although the first three items are parallel, the fourth is not.

1. the buyers told the sellers . . .
2. the sellers sold the rugs . . .
3. the rugs were manufactured to the buyers' specifications . . .
4. were not available at other outlets.

Although the writer has included both a subject and a verb in the first three, in the fourth there is only a verb. It could be revised as follows.

4. the rugs were not available at the outlets.

Checklist for Critiquing the Question Presented

I. Format

- The writer has used one of the conventional formats: under-does-when, whether, or multisentence.

II. Content

- The reference to the rule is neither too broad nor too narrow.
- The legal question is stated neither too broadly nor too narrowly.
- The most significant facts have been included.
- Legal conclusions have not been stated as fact.
- The references to the rule of law and the facts are accurate.
- The question is presented objectively: It does not favor one side.

III. Writing

- The reader can understand the question presented after just one reading.
- When appropriate, the writer has used all three slots in the sentence: the opening, the middle, and the end.
- The writer has used a concrete subject and action verb, and the subject and verb are close together.
- In presenting the facts, the writer has used parallel constructions.
- The question presented is grammatically correct.
- The question presented is correctly punctuated.
- The question presented has been proofread.

§5.10   DRAFTING THE BRIEF ANSWER

§5.10.1   Purpose of the Brief Answer

The brief answer serves a purpose similar to that served by the formal conclusion: It tells the attorney how you think each issue will be decided and why you think it will be decided that way. It is not, however, as detailed as the conclusion.

§5.10.2   Format of the Brief Answer

A brief answer should be included for each issue stated in the question presented section of the memo. If there is one issue statement, there should be one brief answer; if there are two issues, there should be two brief answers.

§5.10.3   Content of the Brief Answer

By convention, most writers begin each of their brief answers with a one- or two-word answer to the question. The words that are typically used are "yes," "no," "probably," "probably not," and "maybe." After this one- or two-word answer, the writer then explains the answer in one, or sometimes two, sentences.

EXAMPLE

QUESTION PRESENTED

Under the UCC Statute of Frauds exception for specially manufactured goods, is an oral contract for the sale of rugs enforceable when (1) the rugs were manufactured to the buyers' specifications, (2) the same rugs are not available at other outlets, (3) the buyers told the seller that they did not want the rugs after the rugs had been completed, and (4) the seller sold the rugs to a wholesaler with whom it had done business on one prior occasion?

BRIEF ANSWER

Probably. Although the formal requirements of the Statute of Frauds are not met, the contract is probably enforceable under the exception for specially manufactured goods: To produce the rugs, the manufacturer had to specially set its looms, and the rugs were sold not to a retail customer but to a wholesaler at a loss.

Checklist for Critiquing the Brief Answer

I. Format

- A separate brief answer has been included for each question presented.

II. Content

- The writer has used the conventional format: a one- or two-word answer followed by a short explanation.
- The writer has predicted, but not guaranteed, how the issue will be decided.
- The writer has briefly explained his or her prediction. For example, which elements will be easy to prove and which will be more difficult?

III. Writing

- The reader can understand the brief answer after just one reading.
- The writer has used a concrete subject and action verb, and the subject and verb are close together.
- When appropriate, the writer has used parallel constructions.
- The brief answer is grammatically correct.
- The brief answer is correctly punctuated.
- The brief answer has been proofread.

§5.11　THE DISCUSSION SECTION: AN INTRODUCTION

In reading the discussion section, attorneys have certain expectations. They expect to see certain types of information, and they expect to see that information presented in a particular order.

These expectations are not born of whim. Instead, they are based on conventional formats, which are themselves based on the way attorneys approach legal questions. In analyzing a legal problem, the lawyer begins with the law. What is the applicable statute or common law rule? The lawyer then applies that law to the facts of the client's case. Are both sides likely to agree on the conclusion, or will the application of the law be in dispute?

If the application is in dispute, the attorney looks to see how the law has been applied in similar cases. Because our system is a system based on precedent, the courts usually decide like, or analogous, cases in a like manner.

The attorney then considers the arguments that each side is likely to make. What types of factual arguments or arguments based on the analogous cases are each side likely to make? Given the purpose and policies underlying the statute or rule, what type of policy arguments might each side make?

Finally, the attorney makes a prediction. Given the law, cases, and arguments, how will a court decide the case?

The discussion section reflects this process. It contains the same components — rules, analogous cases, arguments, and mini-conclusion — in the same order. At its simplest, and at its best, it analyzes the problem for the attorney, walking the attorney step-by-step through the law, cases, and arguments to the probable outcome. See Exhibits 5.11 and 5.12.

The example on the next page illustrates how the writer uses the discussion section to analyze the legal question.

EXHIBIT 5.11　　How an Attorney Approaches a Legal Problem

1. Identifies applicable law
2. Determines whether the application of law to facts is likely to be in dispute
3. If the application is in dispute, looks at analogous cases to determine how like cases have been decided
4. Determines what arguments that each side is likely to make
5. Predicts the outcome: Given the law, analogous cases, and arguments, how is the court likely to decide the case?

EXHIBIT 5.12   **The Components of the Discussion Section**

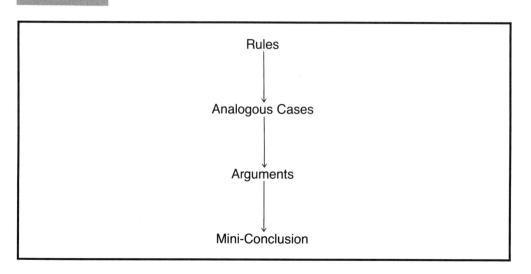

DISCUSSION

General rule
section

Even if the formal requirements of the UCC Statute of Frauds are not met, a contract is enforceable if the goods were specially manufactured. The applicable portion of the statute is as follows:

> (3) A contract which does not satisfy the requirements of subsection (1) but which is valid in other respects is enforceable
>
> (a) if the goods are to be specially manufactured for the buyer and are not suitable for sale to others in the ordinary course of the seller's business and the seller, before notice of repudiation is received and under circumstances which reasonably indicate that the goods are for the buyer, has made either a substantial beginning of their manufacture or commitments for their procurement; . . .

Colo. Rev. Stat. § 4-2-201(3)(a).

Specially manufactured goods are exempt from the writing requirement because the very nature of the goods serves as a reliable indication that a contract was indeed formed. When the goods conform to the special needs of a particular buyer and are not, therefore, suitable for sale to others, not only is the likelihood of a perjured claim diminished, but denying enforcement of such a contract would impose a substantial hardship on the aggrieved party. *Impossible Electronics Techniques, Inc. v. Wackenhut Protective Systems, Inc.,* 669 F.2d 1026, 1037 (5th Cir. 1982).

Consequently, if we can establish (1) that BCC specially manufactured the rugs for the McKibbins, (2) that BCC was not able to resell the rugs in the ordinary course of its business, (3) that the rugs had been completed before BCC received the McKibbins' notice of repudiation, and (4) that the evidence reasonably indicates that the rugs were for the McKibbins, then the contract will be enforceable.

Policies underlying general rule

1. Specially Manufactured for the Buyer

The first requirement is that the goods be specially manufactured for the buyer. Although the term "specially manufactured" is not defined in the statute, the Colorado Supreme Court has held that the term refers to the nature of the goods and not to whether the goods were made in the usual course of the seller's business. *Colorado Carpet Installation, Inc. v. Palermo,* 668 P.2d 1384, 1390 (Colo. 1983). *Accord, Impossible Electronics Techniques, Inc. v. Wackenhut Protective Systems, Inc.,* 669 F.2d 1026, 1037 (5th Cir. 1982).

Rule section for the first element

In the only Colorado case discussing the exception for specially manufactured goods, the Colorado Supreme Court held that carpeting that was available from other carpet outlets and that had not been cut to unusual shapes or subjected to special dyeing, weaving, or other procedures was

Analogous case section for the first element

not specially manufactured. *Colorado Carpet v. Palermo,* 668 P.2d 1384 (Colo. 1983). In contrast, in a Virginia case, the Virginia Supreme Court held that wrapping material imprinted with the buyer's name and unique artwork and cut to the buyer's specifications was "specially manufactured because the wrapping material was personalized and of little value to a third party." *Flowers Baking Co. of Lynchburg, Inc. v. R-P Packaging, Inc.,* 329 S.E.2d 462, 464 (Va. 1985).

Plaintiff's arguments for the first element

In the present case, we will argue that the rugs were specially manufactured for the buyer. Relying on the plain language of the statute, we will argue that the rugs were in fact specially manufactured: BCC had to make special arrangements with the manufacturer and, to produce the rugs, the manufacturer had to specially set its looms.

We will also contrast the facts in our case to the facts in *Colorado Carpet.* Unlike *Colorado Carpet,* in our case, identical rugs are not available from other carpet outlets. The rugs in question are one of a kind: They were made to fit specific rooms, and special weaving was required. Our case is more like *Flowers.* Like the wrapping material, the rugs were personalized. The Reutlinger family flower is as distinctive as any company name or logo and, as a consequence, rugs with such a flower woven into them are of little value to a third party.

Finally, we can argue policy. In this instance, the rugs themselves are evidence that a contract was formed. BCC probably would not have produced rugs matching the original rugs in the Reutlinger Mansion had there not been a contract. In addition, if the court does not enforce the contract, BCC, a small business, will suffer a substantial loss.

Defendant's arguments for the first element

The McKibbins will try to distinguish the facts in our case from the facts in *Flowers.* Unlike *Flowers,* in our case it is only the Reutlinger family flower and not the Reutlinger name that is woven into the rugs. Furthermore, the flower is not particularly unusual; consequently, the wholesaler was able to sell the rugs to a third party with little or no difficulty.

The McKibbins' best argument is, however, a policy argument. They can argue that under the UCC, oral contracts should be the exception rather than the rule. Thus, a seller whose only business is custom or specially manufactured goods should not be exempt from the Statute of Frauds because its goods are specially manufactured. For, if all of such a seller's goods are custom, a written contract will never be necessary, and written contracts will become the exception and not the rule. In addition, the McKibbins can argue that a seller who deals in only custom goods is just as likely to fabricate a contract for custom goods as is a seller who deals in ready-made merchandise.

We can respond to such an argument by citing *Wackenhut,* a case in which the seller sold custom closed-circuit television cameras. In holding that the cameras were specially manufactured, the court said that the fact that the seller is in the business of manufacturing custom-designed and made goods does not necessarily preclude a finding that the goods are specially manufactured. *Id.* at 1037.

> Plaintiff's counter-argument

The court will probably find that the rugs were specially manufactured for the McKibbins. The rugs were not available from other outlets and, to produce the rugs, the manufacturer had to specially set its looms. Although BCC is in the business of producing custom carpets, it is not likely that it would have produced rugs with the Reutlinger family flower woven into them unless it had been requested to do so.

> Mini-conclusion for the first element

---

§5.12   THE DISCUSSION SECTION: THE PLANNING STAGE

The first step in writing the discussion section is planning. You must select the organizational plan that best fits your problem, and then, using that plan as a guide, prepare an outline.

§5.12.1   Selecting an Organizational Plan

Most problems involve one of three types of analysis: (a) an analysis of a series of requirements or elements, (b) a balancing of competing interests, or (c) when the case raises an issue not previously decided in that jurisdiction, a discussion and evaluation of the rules from other jurisdictions.

Plan A: Elements Analysis

The most commonly used plan is the one for an elements analysis. It is used when a statute or common law rule requires that the court determine whether a series of elements or requirements has been satisfied. For example, an elements analysis is used in applying a criminal statute, in determining whether a person has committed an intentional tort or was negligent, and in applying most court rules.

When this plan is used, the discussion begins with a statement of the general rule and a list of the elements. The writer then discusses each element, setting out the applicable rules, the analogous cases, each side's arguments, and a mini-conclusion for each element. The following outline illustrates the organizational structure.

PLAN A

I. **Statement of general rule and list of elements**
     A.   First element
         1.   Rule
         2.   Analogous cases (if appropriate)
         3.   Arguments
         4.   Mini-conclusion
     B.   Second element
         1.   Rule
         2.   Analogous cases (if appropriate)
         3.   Arguments
         4.   Mini-conclusion
     C.   Third element
         1.   Rule
         2.   Analogous cases (if appropriate)
         3.   Arguments
         4.   Mini-conclusion

Plan B: Balancing of Competing Interests

Another common plan is the plan that is used to balance competing interests, such as the rights of competing landowners in nuisance cases or, in litigation, the parties' interests in admitting or excluding evidence.

PLAN B

(Version 1)

A. statement of general rules including a description of the interests that are balanced
B. description of analogous cases
C. the plaintiff's or moving party's arguments
D. the defendant's or responding party's arguments
E. an evaluation and balancing of each side's arguments

In balancing competing interests, the courts often consider a list of factors. For example, in deciding which parent should be granted child custody, the courts are usually required to consider the child's wishes, the wishes of the parents, and each parent's relationship with the child. In these cases, the discussion section is structured very much like the discussion section for an elements analysis.

PLAN B

(Version 2)

I. **Statement of general rule including (1) interests that are balanced and (2) factors that are considered in balancing these interests**
     A. First factor
          1. Description of factor or rule or test
          2. Analogous case(s) (if appropriate)
          3. Arguments
          4. Mini-conclusion
     B. Second factor
          1. Description of factor or rule or test
          2. Analogous case(s) (if appropriate)
          3. Arguments
          4. Mini-conclusion
     C. Third factor
          1. Description of factor or rule or test
          2. Analogous case(s) (if appropriate)
          3. Arguments
          4. Mini-conclusion
     D. Fourth factor
          1. Description of factor or rule or test
          2. Analogous case(s) (if appropriate)
          3. Arguments
          4. Mini-conclusion
II. **Evaluation of factors and balancing of interests**

Plan C: Issue of First Impression

The most complex of the plans is Plan C, the plan that is used when the problem raises an issue of first impression and other jurisdictions have adopted different rules. Before you can apply law to fact, you must determine what the law is.

When working on a problem of this type, begin by describing the status of the law in your jurisdiction. The attorney needs to know that the issue is one of first impression. Then outline the rules that other jurisdictions have adopted, briefly describing each rule and the reasons that have been given by the courts in adopting it. End with an evaluation of each rule and a prediction: Which rule is your jurisdiction likely to adopt and why?

Having determined what the law is, or is likely to be, you must then apply that law to the facts of your client's case. In doing so, you can take one of two approaches. You can either present and apply only the rule that you think the court will adopt, or you can apply each rule. Whichever approach you take, organize your application-of-law-to-fact section by incorporating Plan A or Plan B into Plan C.

PLAN C

  I. **Status of law in governing jurisdiction**
  II. **Rules adopted in other jurisdictions**
      A. List of rules
      B. Statement regarding which rule the majority of courts have adopted
      C. Reasons courts have given for adopting a particular rule
  III. **Critical evaluation of each rule and prediction about which rule the court would adopt**
  IV. **Application of rule most likely to be adopted by court**
      [Plan A or Plan B, depending on whether rule requires elements analysis or the balancing of competing interests.]
  V. **Application of other rules (optional)** [Plan A or Plan B, depending on whether the approach requires elements analysis or the balancing of competing interests.]

In the statute of frauds problem, the plan that works best is Plan A. In determining whether the exception for specially manufactured goods applies, the court will consider the elements set out in section 2-201(3)(a).

ORGANIZATIONAL PLAN FOR THE STATUTE OF FRAUDS PROBLEM

  I. **Exception for specially manufactured goods**
      A. General rule
      B. First element (in dispute)
          1. Rules
          2. Analogous cases
          3. Arguments
          4. Mini-conclusion
      C. Second element (in dispute)
          1. Rules
          2. Analogous cases
          3. Arguments
          4. Mini-conclusion

    D.   Third element (not in dispute)
       1. Rule
       2. Application

§5.12.2　Preparing an Outline

The next step is to prepare a detailed outline. In the statute of frauds problem, the first part of the completed outline looks like this.

EXAMPLE

DETAILED OUTLINE

  I. Exception for specially manufactured goods
    A. General rule
      1. Set out applicable portion of 2-201(3)(a)
      2. Set out policies underlying exception
      3. List elements (this list will provide a roadmap for the rest of discussion)
    B. First element
      1. Applicable rules
        a. Sentence identifying element to be discussed (could use subheading)
        b. Statement that phrase "specially manufactured" is not statutorily defined
        c. Rule from *Colorado Carpet*
      2. Analogous cases
        a. Description of *Colorado Carpet,* the only Colorado case discussing the exception for specially manufactured goods. (Court held that goods were not specially manufactured)
        b. Description of case in which court held that goods were specially manufactured for buyer (*Flowers*)
      3. Application of law to fact
        a. BCC's arguments
          i. Plain language argument
          ii. Arguments based on *Colorado Carpet* and *Flowers*
          iii. Policy arguments
        b. The McKibbins' arguments
          i. Arguments based on *Colorado Carpet* and *Flowers*
          ii. Policy arguments

     4.   Mini-conclusion
         The court will probably rule that rugs were specially manufactured because they were personalized and because the goods themselves are evidence that a contract was formed.

   C.   Second element . . . .

Note

Although not all good writers write from an outline, they all plan. Through experience they have learned that not planning is costly. When they don't plan, it takes them longer to complete the project and the product is less sophisticated.

Section Summary

Planning the discussion section is a two-step process. First, select one of the following three organizational plans, and then modify that plan to fit your problem:

Plan A   Use this plan when the problem requires an analysis of elements or requirements.

Plan B   Use this plan when the problem requires the balancing of competing interests.

Plan C   Use this plan when the issue is one of first impression and other jurisdictions have adopted different rules.

These plans can be combined in a number of different ways.
     Second, prepare a detailed outline.

§5.13   THE DISCUSSION SECTION: PRESENTING THE RULES

§5.13.1   Placement of the Rule Paragraph

Each section and subsection begins with a statement of the applicable rule. The general rule is set out at the beginning of the section and the more specific rules at the beginning of each subsection.

PLAN A

I. **Issue No. 1**
    A. General rule
    B. First element (not in dispute)
        1. **Specific rule**
        2. Application of specific rule to facts of case
    C. Second element (in dispute)
        1. **Specific rule**
        2. Description of analogous cases
        3. Application of law to fact (each side's arguments)
        4. Mini-conclusion
    D. Third element (in dispute)
        1. **Specific rule**
        2. Description of analogous cases
        3. Application of law to fact (each side's arguments)
        4. Mini-conclusion

EXAMPLE

DISCUSSION

Even if the formal requirements of the UCC Statutes of Frauds are not met, a contract is enforceable if the goods were specially manufactured. The applicable portion of the statute is as follows:

    (3) A contract which does not satisfy the requirements of subsection (1) but which is valid in other respects is enforceable

    (a) if the goods are to be specially manufactured for the buyer and are not suitable for sale to others in the ordinary course of the seller's business and the seller, before notice of repudiation is received and under circumstances which reasonably indicate that the goods are for the buyer, has made either a substantial beginning of their manufacture or commitments for their procurement; . . .

Colo. Rev. Stat. § 4-2-201(3)(a).

    Specially manufactured goods are exempt from the writing requirement because the very nature of the goods serves as a re-

General rule

Policies underlying general rule

liable indication that a contract was indeed formed. When the goods conform to the special needs of a particular buyer and are not, therefore, suitable for sale to others, not only is the likelihood of a perjured claim diminished, but denying enforcement of such a contract would impose a substantial hardship on the aggrieved party. *Impossible Electronics Techniques, Inc. v. Wackenhut Protective Systems, Inc.,* 669 F.2d 1026, 1037 (5th Cir. 1982).

Consequently, if we can establish (1) that BCC specially manufactured the rugs for the McKibbins, (2) that BCC was not able to resell the rugs in the ordinary course of its business, (3) that the rugs had been completed before BCC received the Mc-Kibbins' notice of repudiation, and (4) that the evidence reasonably indicates that the rugs were for the McKibbins, then the contract will be enforceable.

1. Specially Manufactured for the Buyer

Rule section for the first element

The first requirement is that the goods be specially manufactured for the buyer. Although the term "specially manufactured" is not defined in the statute, the Colorado Supreme Court has held that the term refers to the nature of the goods and not to whether the goods were made in the usual course of the seller's business. *Colorado Carpet Installation, Inc. v. Palermo,* 668 P.2d 1384, 1390 (Colo. 1983). *Accord, Impossible Electronics Techniques, Inc. v. Wackenhut Protective Systems, Inc.,* 669 F.2d 1026, 1037 (5th Cir. 1982).

Do not set out all of the rules (the general rule and all of the specific rules) at the beginning of the discussion. If you do, you will overwhelm even the brightest of attorneys. Instead, give the attorney the rules on an "as needed" basis.

EXAMPLE　　INCORRECT

I.　First issue
 A.　Rules
  1.　General rule
  2.　Specific rules for the first element
  3.　Specific rules for the second element
  4.　Specific rules for the third element
 B.　Analogous cases
  1.　Analogous case descriptions for the first element
  2.　Analogous case descriptions for the second element
  3.　Analogous case descriptions for the third element
 C.　Application of law to facts
  1.　Application of law to fact for the first element
  2.　Application of law to fact for the second element
  3.　Application of law to fact for the third element
 D.　Mini-conclusions
  1.　Mini-conclusion for the first element
  2.　Mini-conclusion for the second element
  3.　Mini-conclusion for the third element

---

§5.13.2　Types of Rule Paragraphs

The rule can take one of several forms: It can be a statute, a statute plus cases, or a common law doctrine.

a.　Single Statutory Section

When the rule is a single statute, introduce the statute and then quote the relevant portions.

In the following example, the writer has not introduced the statute.

EXAMPLE 1　　WEAK

Discussion

 (3) A contract which does not satisfy the requirements of subsection (1) but which is valid in other respects is enforceable
  (a) if the goods are to be specially manufactured for the buyer and are not suitable for sale to others in the ordinary

course of the seller's business and the seller, before notice of repudiation is received and under circumstances which reasonably indicate that the goods are for the buyer, has made either a substantial beginning of their manufacture or commitments for their procurement; . . .

Colo. Rev. Stat. § 4-2-201(3)(a).

The following example is much better. In addition to setting out the text of the statute, the writer has introduced the statute, explaining how section 2-201(3)(a) fits with the section just discussed, 2-201(1), and foreshadowing what is to follow.

EXAMPLE 2 **BETTER**

Even if the formal requirements are not met, the contract is enforceable if the goods were specially manufactured.

(3) A contract which does not satisfy the requirements of subsection (1) but which is valid in other respects is enforceable
(a) if the goods are to be specially manufactured for the buyer and are not suitable for sale to others in the ordinary course of the seller's business and the seller, before notice of repudiation is received and under circumstances which reasonably indicate that the goods are for the buyer, has made either a substantial beginning of their manufacture or commitments for their procurement; . . .

Colo. Rev. Stat. § 4-2-201(3)(a).

Even though Example 2 is better, it is not as good as it might be. When the statute is long and the text difficult to read, you can help the attorney by paraphrasing the statute, stating the rule in terms of the facts of your case.

EXAMPLE 3 **BEST**

Even if the formal requirements are not met, the contract is enforceable if the goods were specially manufactured.

(3) A contract which does not satisfy the requirements of subsection (1) but which is valid in other respects is enforceable

(a) if the goods are to be specially manufactured for the buyer and are not suitable for sale to others in the ordinary course of the seller's business and the seller, before notice of repudiation is received and under circumstances which reasonably indicate that the goods are for the buyer, has made either a substantial beginning of their manufacture or commitments for their procurement; . . .

Colo. Rev. Stat. § 4-2-201(3)(a).

Thus, if we can establish (1) that BCC specially manufactured the rugs for the McKibbins, (2) that BCC was not able to resell the rugs in the ordinary course of its business, and (3) that the rugs had been completed before BCC received the McKibbins' notice of repudiation, the contract will be enforceable.

---

b. Multiple Statutory Sections

The format is similar when there is more than one applicable statutory section. Introduce the statutes and then quote the relevant portions, starting with the more general sections and ending with the more specific.

EXAMPLE 1   WEAK

9A.40.010 reads as follows:

(1) "Restrain" means to restrict a person's movements without consent and without legal authority in a manner which interferes substantially with his liberty.
(2) "Abduct" means to restrain a person by either (a) secreting or holding him in a place where he is not likely to be found, or (b) using or threatening to use deadly force.

Section 9A.40.030 states that

(1) A person is guilty of kidnapping in the second degree if he intentionally abducts another person under circumstances not amounting to kidnapping in the first degree.

In this example, the writer made two mistakes. The more general statutory section is not presented first (the sections are presented in number order), and the introductions are weak. The following example is much better.

EXAMPLE 2   **BETTER**

A person is guilty of kidnapping in the second degree if "he intentionally abducts another person under circumstances not amounting to kidnapping in the first degree." 9A.40.030(1).

The term "abducts" is defined in section 9A.40.010(2):

> (2) "Abduct" means to restrain a person by either (a) secreting or holding him in a place where he is not likely to be found, or (b) using or threatening to use deadly force.

"Restrain" is defined in 9A.40.010(1).

> (1) "Restrain" means to restrict a person's movements without consent and without legal authority in a manner which interferes substantially with his liberty.

Note

Most attorneys want to see the text of the statute. Consequently, if the statute is short, you should quote it in full. If the statute is longer, you have some options. You can set out only the applicable portions; you can set out the full text but italicize those portions that are applicable; or you can paraphrase the statute and attach a photocopy of the text of the statute to the memo.

---

c. Statutes Plus Cases

In some problems you will have to present not only the statute but also rules from cases that have interpreted or applied the statute. In these situations, quote the statute and then set out the rules from the cases.

EXAMPLE

Section 402 sets out the standard that the trial court must use in awarding child custody.

SECTION 402: BEST INTEREST OF CHILD

The court shall determine custody in accordance with the best interest of the child after considering all relevant factors including:
> (1) the wishes of the child's parent or parents as to his custody;

(2) the wishes of the child as to his custodian;

(3) the interaction and interrelationship of the child with his parent or parents, his siblings, and any other person who may significantly affect the child's best interest;

(4) the child's adjustment to his home, school, and community; and

(5) the mental and physical health of all individuals involved.

The court shall not consider conduct of a proposed custodian that does not affect his relationship to the child.

Because this statute supersedes the common law, there is no longer a presumption that the custody of young children should be awarded to the mother. *In re Marriage of Huen,* 24 Official Reporter 9, 678 Regional Reporter 68 (1986). The Supreme Court has, however, held that if the child is too young to express his or her preference, the best interests of the child mandate that the trial court award custody of the child to the primary custodian absent a finding that the custodian is unfit to have custody. *Id.*

d. Common Law Rules

Common law rules are handled in one of two ways. If the rule is well established, most writers just set out the rule, either stating it in general terms or personalizing it by using the names of the parties.

EXAMPLE 1   GENERIC

To establish title through adverse possession, the party claiming title must establish that its possession was (1) exclusive, (2) actual and uninterrupted, (3) open and notorious, and (4) hostile and under claim of right for the statutory period. *Williams v. Howell,* 108 N.M. 225, 770 P.2d 870 (1989).

EXAMPLE 2   PERSONALIZED

To establish title through adverse possession, the Kearneys must establish that their possession was (1) exclusive, (2) actual and uninterrupted, (3) open and notorious, and (4) hostile and under claim of right for the statutory period. *See Williams v. Howell,* 108 N.M. 225, 770 P.2d 870 (1989).

When the rule is not so well established, you must synthesize the cases, identifying the common principles. (See section 5.6.)

EXAMPLE 1   WEAK, NO SYNTHESIS

In Case A, the court held that because the plaintiff, an African-American, had not been publicly humiliated, the defendant's conduct was not so extreme and outrageous as to go beyond all bounds of decency.

In Case B, a case in which an employer did not prevent its employees from directing racial slurs against a Mexican-American employee during work hours and in front of customers, the court held that the conduct was outrageous. In reaching its decision, the court considered two factors: that the defendant was in a position of authority over the plaintiff and that because the plaintiff was a Mexican-American, he was particularly susceptible.

In Case C, a case in which a letter containing racial slurs was sent to an Asian-American, the court held that the conduct was not outrageous because the letter had not been sent to others.

In Case D, the court held that because of its relationship to the plaintiff, a student, the defendant, a university, acted outrageously when it did not stop teammates from directing racial slurs toward the plaintiff during games.

EXAMPLE 2   BETTER, RULES SYNTHESIZED

In determining whether racial discrimination or slurs are outrageous, the courts consider two factors: (1) whether the plaintiff was publicly humiliated and (2) the defendant's relationship to the plaintiff. *See* Case A; Case B; Case C; Case D.

When it is appropriate to trace the history of the rule, the following approach should be taken.

EXAMPLE

In the older cases, the courts refused to find exclusive possession if both the adverse possessor and the title owner used the land. "[S]hared occupancy of the disputed property by the adverse possessor and the title owner precludes a finding of exclusive possession." *Scott v. Slater,* 42 Wash. 2d 366, 369, 255 P.2d 377, 378 (1953), *overruled on other grounds, Chaplin v. Sanders,* 100 Wash. 2d 853, 676 P.2d 431 (1984). However, more recently, the Washington courts have held that the claimant's possession need not be absolutely exclusive. The possession need only be of a type that would be expected of an owner under the circumstances. *See ITT Rayonier, Inc. v. Bell,* 51 Wash. App. 124, 752 P.2d 398, *cert. denied,* 111 Wash. 2d 1001 (1988); *Crites v. Koch,* 49 Wash. App. 171, 741 P.2d 1005 (1987).

---

e.   Rules Plus Policy

In some instances, it is not enough to just set out the rule. The application of the rule is uncertain, and in arguing to the court, the parties will make arguments based on either the intent of the legislature or the policies underlying the common law rule. In such a situation, the policies may be presented either before or after the rule.

EXAMPLE 1   POLICY USED TO INTRODUCE RULE

A writing is not, however, always required. An exception is made when, because they were specially manufactured, the goods themselves serve as a reliable indication that a contract was indeed formed. In such situations, not only is the likelihood of a perjured claim minimal, but denying enforcement would impose a substantial hardship on the aggrieved party. *Impossible Electronics Techniques, Inc. v. Wackenhut Protective Systems, Inc.,* 669 F.2d 1026, 1037 (5th Cir. 1982).

The exception for specially manufactured goods is set out in section 2-201(3)(a):

> (3) A contract which does not satisfy the requirements of subsection (1) but which is valid in other respects is enforceable
> (a) if the goods are to be specially manufactured for the buyer and are not suitable for sale to others in the ordinary course of the seller's business and the seller, before notice of repudiation is received and under circumstances which reasonably indicate that the goods are for the buyer, has made either

a substantial beginning of their manufacture or commitments for their procurement; . . .

EXAMPLE 2   **POLICIES EXPLAINED AFTER RULE**

Even if the formal requirements are not met, the contract is enforceable if the goods were specially manufactured.

(3) A contract which does not satisfy the requirements of subsection (1) but which is valid in other respects is enforceable
(a) if the goods are to be specially manufactured for the buyer and are not suitable for sale to others in the ordinary course of the seller's business and the seller, before notice of repudiation is received and under circumstances which reasonably indicate that the goods are for the buyer, has made either a substantial beginning of their manufacture or commitments for their procurement; . . .

Colo. Rev. Stat. § 4-2-201(3)(a).
Specially manufactured goods are exempt from the writing requirement because the very nature of the goods serves as a reliable indication that a contract was indeed formed. When the goods conform to the special needs of a particular buyer and are not, therefore, suitable for sale to others, not only is the likelihood of a perjured claim diminished, but denying enforcement of such a contract would impose a substantial hardship on the aggrieved party. *Impossible Electronics Techniques, Inc. v. Wackenhut Protective Systems, Inc.*, 669 F.2d 1026, 1037 (5th Cir. 1982).

---

§5.13.3   Citation to Authority

Every rule must be supported by a citation to authority. If the source of the rule is a statute, cite the statute; if the source is a case, cite the case.

Although the citation can go either before or after the rule, it is usually best to put it after. In the rule section, you want the focus on the rule and not on the authority for that rule.

EXAMPLE 1   **FOCUS ON THE CITATION AND NOT THE RULE**

In *Impossible Electronics Techniques, Inc. v. Wackenhut Protective Systems, Inc.*, 669 F.2d 1026, 1037 (5th Cir. 1982), the court stated that specially manufactured goods are exempt from the writing requirement because the very nature of the goods serves as a reliable indication that a contract was indeed formed. When the goods conform to the special needs of a particular buyer and are not, therefore, suitable for sale to others, not only is the likelihood of a perjured claim diminished, but denying enforcement of such a contract would impose a substantial hardship on the aggrieved party.

EXAMPLE 2   **FOCUS ON THE RULE AND NOT THE CITATION**

Specially manufactured goods are exempt from the writing requirement because the very nature of the goods serves as a reliable indication that a contract was indeed formed. When the goods conform to the special needs of a particular buyer and are not, therefore, suitable for sale to others, not only is the likelihood of a perjured claim diminished, but denying enforcement of such a contract would impose a substantial hardship on the aggrieved party. *Impossible Electronics Techniques, Inc. v. Wackenhut Protective Systems, Inc.*, 669 F.2d 1026, 1037 (5th Cir. 1982).

Section Summary

1. Begin each section and subsection with a statement of the applicable rules.
2. In presenting a series of rules, set out the general rules and then the more specific rules and exceptions.
3. When the "rule" is a statute, introduce the statute and then quote the relevant portions.
4. If the statute is long or difficult to understand, quote the relevant portions and then, using your own language, list the elements.
5. If a common law rule is well established, simply set out the rule.
6. If the common law rule is not well established, synthesize the cases and present the common principles.
7. Include a citation to authority for each rule stated.

§5.14   THE DISCUSSION SECTION: DESCRIBING THE ANALOGOUS CASES

Cases can be used in two ways. They can be used as the authority for a rule, and they can be used to show how a rule has been applied.

EXAMPLE

Cases used as authority for rule

The first requirement is that the goods be specially manufactured for the buyer. Although the term "specially manufactured" is not defined in the statute, the Colorado Supreme Court has stated that it refers to the nature of the goods and not to whether the goods were made in the usual course of the seller's business. *Colorado Carpet Installation, Inc. v. Palermo,* 668 P.2d 1384, 1390 (Colo. 1983). *Accord, Impossible Electronics Techniques, Inc. v. Wackenhut Protective Systems, Inc.,* 669 F.2d 1026, 1037 (5th Cir. 1982).

Case used to show how rule was applied

In the only Colorado case discussing the exception for specially manufactured goods, the Colorado Supreme Court held that carpeting that was available from other carpet outlets and that had not been cut to unusual shapes or subjected to special dyeing, weaving, or other procedures was not specially manufactured. *Colorado Carpet v. Palermo,* 668 P.2d 1384 (Colo. 1983).

Case used to show how rule was applied

In contrast, in a Virginia case, the Virginia Supreme Court held that wrapping material imprinted with the buyer's name and unique artwork and cut to the buyer's specifications was "specially manufactured because the wrapping material was personalized and of little value to a third party." *Flowers Baking Co. of Lynchburg, Inc. v. R-P Packaging, Inc.,* 329 S.E.2d 462, 464 (Va. 1985).

When the application of the rule to the facts is clear, descriptions of analogous cases are not needed. The attorney does not need analogous cases to determine that the requirement is met.

Analogous cases can, however, be helpful when the application of the rule to the facts is not so clear. By comparing (or contrasting) the facts in the analogous case to the facts in the client's case, the attorney can better predict how a court might decide the issue. If the legally significant facts are similar, the second court is likely to reach the same result as the court did in the analogous case; if the legally significant facts are different, the outcome is less certain.

§5.14.1 Placement of Case Descriptions

Descriptions of analogous cases can go in one of two places. If the case will be used by both sides, it usually works best to describe the case in a separate "analogous case section" immediately following the rule.

PLAN A

I. **Issue No. 1**
    A. General rule
    B. First element (not in dispute)
        1. Specific rule
        2. Application of specific rule to the facts of the case
    C. Second element (in dispute)
        1. Specific rule
        2. Description of analogous cases
        3. Application of law to fact (each side's arguments)
        4. Mini-conclusion
    D. Third element (in dispute)
        1. Specific rule
        2. Description of analogous cases
        3. Application of law to fact (each side's arguments)
        4. Mini-conclusion

Note that because the first element is not in dispute, an analogous case section is not needed.

If the case will be used by only one side, the case description can be placed in a separate analogous case section or integrated into the application-of-law-to-fact section as part of the argument.

§5.14.2 Types of Case Descriptions

Case descriptions vary in length, content, and form. At their shortest, they are no more than a word or phrase and describe only a significant fact; at their longest, they run a page or more and include not only the facts but also the court's holding and reasoning. The key is to give the attorneys what they need, no more and no less.

In the following examples, Example 1 is the best choice if, in applying law to fact, the writer refers only to the facts of the case, comparing the facts in his or her case to the facts in the analogous case. In contrast, Example 2 or Example 3 is best if, in addition to comparing the facts, the writer uses the courts' reasoning.

EXAMPLE 1

In applying this rule, the courts have found that carpeting that has not been specially cut or dyed or woven to meet the buyer's specifications is not specially manufactured, *Colorado Carpet v. Palermo,* 668 P.2d 1384 (Colo. 1983), but that wrapping paper that has been specially cut and imprinted with the buyer's logo is, *Flowers Baking Co. of Lynchburg, Inc. v. R-P Packaging, Inc.,* 329 S.E.2d 462 (Va. 1985).

EXAMPLE 2

In the only Colorado case discussing the exception for specially manufactured goods, the Colorado Supreme Court held that carpeting that was available from other carpet outlets and that had not been cut to unusual shapes or subjected to special dyeing, weaving, or other procedures was not specially manufactured. *Colorado Carpet v. Palermo,* 668 P.2d 1384 (Colo. 1983). In contrast, in a Virginia case, the Virginia Supreme Court held that wrapping material imprinted with the buyer's name and unique artwork and cut to the buyer's specifications was "specially manufactured because the wrapping material was personalized and of little value to a third party." *Flowers Baking Co. of Lynchburg, Inc. v. R-P Packaging, Inc.,* 329 S.E.2d 462, 464 (Va. 1985).

EXAMPLE 3

This rule was applied in *Colorado Carpet,* a case in which the seller, Colorado Carpet, asserted that the contract for the sale and installation of flooring material was enforceable because the carpet was specially manufactured. In affirming the Court of Appeals, the Colorado Supreme Court held that the carpet was not specially manufactured. The same carpet was available from other retail outlets, and although the carpet had been cut, it had not been cut to the buyer's specifications. In addition, the carpet had not been subjected to any special dyeing or weaving.

In contrast, in *Flowers Baking Co. of Lynchburg, Inc. v. R-P Packaging, Inc.,* 329 S.E.2d 462 (Va. 1985), the court held that R-P Packaging's claim against Flowers was not barred by the UCC Statute of Frauds. Even though the contract was not in writing, the court found that the contract was enforceable because the goods were "specially manufactured": the wrapping paper had been cut to the size specified by Flowers and had been imprinted with Flowers's name and unique artwork. Because it had been personalized, the court concluded that paper would be of little value to a third party and that, under such circumstances, it would be unfair to deny enforcement of the contract.

Note

One way of checking your case descriptions is to compare the information set out in your case description with the information used in the application-of-law-to-fact section. If you have set out information that you have not used, you have one of two problems: Either you have included irrelevant information in your case description or your application-of-law-to-fact section is incomplete.

---

§5.14.3　Introducing Analogous Cases

When an attorney reads a description of an analogous case, he or she should know, from the very first line, why that case has been included in the memo. The relationship between the rule and the case should be clear and, if more than one case is described, the relationship between the cases should be explained.

Consider the following examples. In the first, the writer lays out the rule in one paragraph and then abruptly shifts to the analogous case, *Colorado Carpet.*

EXAMPLE 1　**ABRUPT SHIFT TO CASE**

The first requirement is that the goods be specially manufactured for the buyer. Although the term "specially manufactured" is not defined in the statute, the Colorado Supreme Court has stated that it refers to the nature of the particular goods in question and not to whether the goods were made in an unusual, as opposed to the regular, business operation or manufacturing process of the seller. *Id.* at 1390.

In *Colorado Carpet,* the Colorado Supreme Court affirmed the Court of Appeals, holding that the evidence was not sufficient to support a finding that the carpet was "specially manufactured" within the "specially manufactured exception" to the Statute of Frauds. The same carpet was available from other retail outlets, and although the carpet had been cut, it had not been cut to the buyer's specifications. In addition, the carpet had not been subjected to any special dyeing or weaving.

In this example, the writer has not made explicit the connection between the rule and the description of the analogous case. Instead of explaining up front that the case is being used to illustrate how the rule has been applied, the writer begins by reciting the case's procedural history.

In the following examples, the writers introduce the cases, making explicit the connection between the rule and the case.

EXAMPLE 2   SEPARATE ANALOGOUS CASE SECTION

The first requirement is that the goods be specially manufactured for the buyer. In *Colorado Carpet,* the court stated that the term "specially manufactured" refers to the nature of the particular goods in question and not to whether the goods were made in an unusual, as opposed to the regular, business operation or manufacturing process of the seller. *Id.* at 1390.

In the only Colorado case discussing the exception for specially manufactured goods, the Colorado Supreme Court held that carpeting that was available from other carpet outlets and that had not been cut to unusual shapes or subjected to special dyeing, weaving, or other procedures was not specially manufactured. *Colorado Carpet v. Palermo,* 668 P.2d 1384 (Colo. 1983).

In contrast, in a Virginia case, *Flowers Baking Co. of Lynchburg, Inc. v. R-P Packaging, Inc.,* 329 S.E.2d 462, 464 (Va. 1985), the Virginia Supreme Court held that wrapping material imprinted with the buyer's name and unique artwork and cut to the buyer's specifications was "specially manufactured because the wrapping material was personalized and of little value to a third party."

EXAMPLE 3   CASE INTEGRATED INTO APPLICATION-OF-LAW-TO-FACT SECTION

The University will argue that Gomez's emotional distress is not severe. In doing so, it will rely on *Spurrell,* a case in which the court held that one sleepless night, tears, loss of appetite, and anxiety were not enough to establish severe emotional distress, and *Lawson,* a case in which loss of appetite, sleeplessness, and increased headaches were considered not above "that level which is a fact of life." *Id.* at 263.

Section Summary

1. Cases can be used in two ways: as authority for a rule and as examples to show how a rule has been applied.
2. If the application of the rule is clear, case descriptions are not needed; if the application is unclear, case descriptions can help the attorney to predict how the court is likely to rule.
3. The case description should include only the information the attorney needs. (You can check case descriptions by comparing information included in the description against information used in applying law to fact. If the information was not used, it can probably be deleted from the case description.)

4. Each case should be introduced. From the first line, the attorney should know why the case was included at that point in the memo.

§5.15   THE DISCUSSION SECTION: APPLYING LAW TO FACT

The attorney now knows the rules and how those rules have been applied in similar cases. What the attorney doesn't know is how the rule will be applied in the client's case.

§5.15.1   Element Not in Dispute

In some cases, the application of one or more elements is not in dispute. Both sides agree that the element is, or is not, met. For example, in the statute of frauds case, both sides will agree that the third element, that the rugs were completed before the McKibbins canceled the order, has been met.

In such a situation, the application is simple: Set out the applicable portion of the rule, a "connector," and the legally significant facts.

Legal Analysis = Rule "applied to" Legally Significant Facts

EXAMPLE 1

Incomplete (no reference to rule)

In this case, the first element is not in dispute. The rugs were completed before the McKibbins canceled their order.

Complete (reference to both the rule and the legally significant facts)

In this case, the first element is not in dispute. Because the McKibbins canceled their order after the rugs had been completed, BCC will be able to prove that it had made a substantial beginning of their manufacture before notice of repudiation was received.

EXAMPLE 2

Incomplete (no reference to rule)

Several elements are not in dispute. The government will be able to show that the photocopy was hanging on the wall in

Gundy's office, and Gundy has admitted that he did not have possession under the "authority of the Secretary of the Treasury or other authorized official."

Complete (includes references to both the rule and the legally significant facts)

Several elements are not in dispute. The government will be able to prove the first element, possession or custody, by showing that the photocopy was hanging on the wall in Gundy's office. It will also be able to prove the second element, lack of authority. Gundy has admitted that he did not ask for permission to hang the copy on his wall.

---

§5.15.2   Element in Dispute

When the element is in dispute, the analysis must be much more sophisticated. As the writer, you must anticipate and explain the arguments that each side is likely to make.

These arguments can be presented using either the "script" or "integrated" format.

a. The Script Format

Many attorneys use the script format. Because the arguments are set out as they would be presented to a court, the format itself helps the attorney evaluate the case.

When you use the script format, you do what the name implies: You prepare a "script," presenting the arguments as they would be presented to a court. The moving party's arguments are presented first, the responding party's answer is presented next, and, if appropriate, the discussion ends with the moving party's rebuttal. The court's ruling, or at least the writer's prediction about how the court will rule, is set out in the mini-conclusion. (See section 5.16.)

Script Format

A. Rules

B. Descriptions of analogous cases

C. Application of law to fact

    1. Moving party's argument
    2. Responding party's argument or answer
    3. Moving party's rebuttal (if needed)

D. Mini-conclusion

| EXAMPLE | APPLICATION-OF-LAW-TO-FACT SECTION — SCRIPT FORMAT |

In the present case, we will argue that the rugs were specially manufactured for the buyer. Relying on the plain language of the statute, we will argue that the rugs were in fact specially manufactured: BCC had to make special arrangements with the manufacturer and, to produce the rugs, the manufacturer had to specially set its looms.

> Moving party's first argument

We will also distinguish the facts in our case from the facts in *Colorado Carpet.* Unlike the carpet in *Colorado Carpet,* in our case, identical rugs are not available from other carpet outlets. The rugs in question are one-of-a-kind: They were made to fit specific rooms, and special weaving was required. Our case is more like *Flowers.* Like the wrapping material, the rugs were personalized. The Reutlinger family flower is as distinctive as any company name or logo and, as a consequence, rugs with such a flower woven into them are of little value to a third party.

> Moving party's second argument

Finally, we can argue policy. In this instance, the rugs themselves are evidence that a contract was formed. BCC probably would not have produced rugs matching the original rugs in the Reutlinger Mansion had there not been a contract. In addition, if the court does not enforce the contract, BCC, a small business, will suffer a substantial loss.

> Moving party's third argument

The McKibbins will try to distinguish the facts in our case from the facts in *Flowers.* Unlike *Flowers,* in our case it is only the Reutlinger family flower and not the Reutlinger name that is woven into the rugs. Furthermore, the flower is not particularly unusual; the wholesaler was able to sell the rugs to a third party with little or no difficulty.

> Responding party's first argument

The McKibbins' best argument is, however, a policy argument. They can argue that under the UCC, oral contracts should be the exception rather than the rule. Thus, a seller whose only business is custom or specially manufactured goods

> Responding party's second argument

should not be exempt from the Statute of Frauds because its goods are specially manufactured. For, if all of such a seller's goods are custom, a written contract will never be necessary and written contracts will become the exception and not the rule. In addition, the McKibbins can argue that a seller who deals in only custom goods is just as likely to fabricate a contract for custom goods as is a seller who deals in ready-made merchandise.

Moving party's rebuttal

We can respond to such an argument by citing *Wackenhut,* a case in which the seller sold custom closed-circuit television cameras. In holding that the cameras were specially manufactured, the court said the fact that the seller is in the business of manufacturing custom-designed and made goods does not necessarily preclude a finding that the goods are specially manufactured. *Id.* at 1037.

Mini-conclusion

The court will probably find that the rugs were specially manufactured for the McKibbins. The rugs were not available from other outlets and, to produce the rugs, the manufacturer had to specially set its looms. Although BCC is in the business of producing custom carpets, it probably would not have produced rugs with the Reutlinger family flower woven into them unless it had been requested to do so.

If you use this format, make sure that you avoid the "ping pong" effect. Do not bounce back and forth between the moving and responding parties' arguments. At best, most attorneys find the following organizational scheme merely annoying.

C. Application of law to fact
1. Moving party's plain language argument
2. Responding party's plain language argument
3. Moving party's arguments based on analogous cases
4. Responding party's arguments based on analogous cases
5. Moving party's policy arguments
6. Responding party's policy arguments

The arguments would not be presented in this order to a court, and they should not be presented in this order to the attorney.

b.   *The Integrated Format*

The second format is the "integrated" format. Instead of presenting the moving party's arguments in one paragraph or paragraph block, the responding party's in a second, and the rebuttal in a third, the arguments are presented without reference to the parties. The writer begins with the conclusion and then explains how he or she reached that conclusion, integrating the presentation of each side's arguments with the evaluation of those arguments.

**EXAMPLE   APPLICATION-OF-LAW-TO-FACT SECTION —
INTEGRATED FORMAT**

The court will probably find that the first requirement, that the goods be specially manufactured for the buyer, is met.

Mini-conclusion

The court will base its conclusion on several factors. First, like the wrapping material in *Flowers,* the rugs were personalized. In *Flowers,* the wrapping paper was imprinted with the buyer's name and unique artwork; in this case, the rugs had the Reutlinger family flower woven into them. Although it was the Reutlinger family flower and not the Reutlinger name that was woven into the rugs, a court is not likely to find this difference determinative. The rule requires only that the goods be personalized, not that they have the buyer's name on them.

First reason

Second, the rugs were, in fact, specially manufactured. Although standard dyes were used, the manufacturer did specially set its looms. In addition, instead of being manufactured to standard dimensions, the rugs were made to fit the rooms in the Reutlinger Mansion.

Second reason

Finally, in this case, the goods themselves are evidence that a contract was formed. Even though BCC produces only custom carpets, it probably would not have manufactured the rugs without a contract to do so. Further, as the court noted in *Wackenhut,* the fact that the seller is in the business of manufacturing custom-designed and made goods does not necessarily preclude a finding that the goods are specially manufactured. *Id.* at 1037.

Third reason

---

§5.15.3   Structuring the Arguments

As the preceding examples demonstrate, there is more than one type of argument. Attorneys make arguments based on the plain language of the statute or rule, analogous cases, and policy.

a.   *Plain Language Arguments*

The easiest argument is a plain language, or factual, argument. You take the plain language of the statute or rule and apply it to the facts of the case.

In the following example, the writer gives the phrase "specially manufactured" its plain meaning. The rugs were specially manufactured because the buyer had to make "special" arrangements with the "manufacturer," and the "manufacturer" had to "specially" set its looms.

EXAMPLE

In the present case, we will argue that the rugs were **specially manufactured** for the buyer. Relying on the plain language of the statute, we will argue that the rugs were in fact **specially manufactured:** BCC had to make **special** arrangements with the **manufacturer,** and to produce the rugs, the **manufacturer** had to **specially** set its looms.

Similarly, in the next example, the writer gives the phrase "any person" its plain meaning.

EXAMPLE

We will ask the court to give the phrase "any person" its plain meaning. "Any person" means any person.

Note that in each of these examples, the writers used the key phrase both in setting out the rule and in applying the facts. In making an argument, use the language of the law whenever you can reasonably do so. (See section 5.17.4.)

b. *Arguments Based on Analogous Cases*

If plain language arguments are the easiest to structure, arguments based on analogous cases are the most difficult. It is not enough just to repeat the facts of the cases. You must explain why the factual similarities (or differences) are significant.

EXAMPLE 1   SCRIPT FORMAT

Ineffective Use of Analogous Cases

In *Colorado Carpet,* identical carpets were available from other carpet outlets. In our case, the rugs were one-of-a-kind. In *Flowers,* the material had the buyer's name and unique artwork printed on it. In our case, the Reutlinger family flower was woven into the rugs.

More Effective Use of Analogous Cases

We will distinguish *Colorado Carpet.* Unlike *Colorado Carpet,* in our case, identical rugs are not available from other carpet outlets. The rugs in question are one-of-a-kind: They were made to fit specific rooms, and special weaving was required. Our case is more like *Flowers.* Like the wrapping material, the rugs were personalized. The Reutlinger family flower is as distinctive as any company name or logo and, as a consequence, rugs with such a flower woven into them are of little value to a third party.

EXAMPLE 2   INTEGRATED FORMAT

The court will base its conclusion on several factors. First, like the wrapping material in *Flowers,* the rugs were personalized. In *Flowers,* the rugs were imprinted with the buyer's name and unique artwork; in this case, the rugs had the Reutlinger family flower woven into them. Although it was the Reutlinger family flower and not the Reutlinger name that was woven into the rugs, a court is not likely to find this difference determinative. The rule requires only that the goods be personalized, not that they have the buyer's name on them.

Second, the rugs were, in fact, specially manufactured. Although standard dyes were used, the manufacturer in our case, unlike the manufacturer in *Colorado Carpet,* did specially set its looms. In addition, instead of being manufactured to standard dimensions, the rugs were made to fit the rooms in the Reutlinger Mansion.

Also make sure that the facts that you are comparing are legally significant. In the above examples, the writer has not compared the quantities ordered; in the client's case, the amount ordered is not significant. Instead, the writer has compared the facts that are legally significant. Because it was important to the Colorado court that the same carpet was available from other outlets, the writer has compared this fact with the facts in the client's case. Similarly, because in *Flowers* it was important that the goods had been personalized, in comparing the cases, the writer focuses on this aspect.

Finally, note how the writer tied the facts to the law. Because the rugs had the flower woven into them, they were of "little value to a third party," and because the flower was not particularly unusual, "the wholesaler was able to sell the rugs to a third party with little or no difficulty."

Thus, in structuring an argument based on analogous cases, you want to do three things: (1) tell the attorney whether the analogous case is like or unlike the client's case, (2) compare only those facts that are legally significant, and (3) tie the facts back to the law.

c. Arguments Based on Policy

The third type of argument is an argument based on public policy. In enacting the statute, what was the legislature's intent? What interests was the common law rule designed to promote?

In making a policy argument, identify the policy and then show how, given the facts of the case, that policy would be promoted. The following examples show how this can be done. The writer identifies the policy (to reduce the number of fraudulent claims by making oral contracts for goods valued at more than $500 unenforceable unless the goods themselves provide sufficient evidence of a contract) and then shows how enforcement of the contract would be consistent with that policy.

EXAMPLE 1

Finally, we can argue policy. In this instance, the rugs themselves are evidence that a contract was formed. It is not likely that BCC would have produced rugs matching the original rugs in the Reutlinger Mansion had there not been a contract.

EXAMPLE 2

The McKibbins' best argument is, however, a policy argument. They can argue that under the UCC, oral contracts should be the exception rather than the rule. Thus, a seller whose only business is custom or specially manufactured goods should not be exempt from the Statute of Frauds because its goods are specially manufactured. For, if all of such a seller's goods are custom, a written contract will never be necessary and written contracts will become the exception and not the rule. In addition, the McKibbins can argue that a seller who deals in only custom goods is just as likely to fabricate a contract for custom goods as is a seller who deals in ready-made merchandise.

Section Summary

1. Always apply the rules to the facts of the client's case.
2. If the application of the rule to the facts is not in dispute, simply set out the rule, a "connector," and the legally significant facts.
3. If the application of the rule to the facts is in dispute, identify and present the arguments that each side is likely to make.
4. There are three categories of arguments: (1) plain language, or factual, arguments, (2) arguments based on analogous cases, and (3) policy arguments.
5. In presenting the arguments, use either the script or the integrated format.

§5.16   THE DISCUSSION SECTION: DRAFTING THE MINI-CONCLUSION

Each time you apply law to fact, you need to state your conclusion. Given the arguments, how is the court likely to rule on that element?

§5.16.1   Placement of Mini-conclusions

When you use the script format, the mini-conclusions follow the application-of-law-to-fact section.

PLAN A

I. **Issue No. 1**
    A. General rule
    B. First element (not in dispute)
        1. Specific rule
        2. Application of specific rule to the facts of the case
    C. Second element (in dispute)
        1. Specific rule
        2. Description of analogous cases
        3. Application of law to fact (each side's arguments)
        4. Mini-conclusion
    D. Third element (in dispute)
        1. Specific rule
        2. Description of analogous cases
        3. Application of law to fact (each side's arguments)
        4. Mini-conclusion

Note

Because the first element is not in dispute, the mini-conclusion is incorporated into the application-of-law-to-fact section. (See section 5.15.1.)

---

§5.16.2 Structure of Mini-conclusions

The structure of the mini-conclusion depends on whether the element is in dispute.

a. Element Not in Dispute

If the element is not in dispute, the application-of-law-to-fact section and the mini-conclusion can be combined. In the following examples, the mini-conclusion has been highlighted.

EXAMPLE 1

In this case, the first element is not in dispute. Because the McKibbins canceled their order after the rugs had been completed, BCC will be able to prove that it had made a substantial beginning of their manufacture before notice of repudiation was received.

EXAMPLE 2

Several elements are not in dispute. The government will be able to prove the first element, possession or custody, by showing that the photocopy was hanging on the wall in Gundy's office. **It will also be able to prove the second element.** Gundy has admitted that he did not have possession under the "authority of the Secretary of the Treasury or other authorized official."

---

b. Element in Dispute

When the element is in dispute, you must do more than tell the attorneys that it is in dispute. You must evaluate each side's arguments and predict how the court is likely to rule.

EXAMPLE 1

This element is in dispute.

Although this sentence can be used to introduce an element that is in dispute, it is not a mini-conclusion. When the element is in dispute, the attorneys want to know how the court will rule and why.

EXAMPLE 2

Because both sides have strong arguments, it is impossible to predict how the court will rule.

If an element is in dispute, you cannot guarantee how a court will rule. You can, however, make some predictions. Does the moving party have the stronger arguments, or is the court more likely to be persuaded by the arguments of the responding party?

EXAMPLE 3

Although this element is in dispute, the court will probably find that the rugs were specially manufactured for the buyer.

In this example the writer has made a prediction. He or she has not, however, given the attorney the basis for this prediction. In addition to making a prediction, you need to explain why you think the court will rule as you have predicted.

EXAMPLE 4

The court will probably find that the rugs were specially manufactured for the McKibbins. The rugs were not available from other outlets and, to produce the rugs, the manufacturer had to specially set its looms. In addition, although BCC is in the business of producing custom carpets, it is not likely that it would have produced rugs with the Reutlinger family flower woven into them unless it had been requested to do so.

When the script format is used, this is what a mini-conclusion should look like. The writer makes a prediction and then explains why the court is likely to rule that way.

In contrast, when you use the integrated format, the mini-conclusion precedes the application of law to fact. The following example contains not only a mini-conclusion for the element ("The court will probably find that the first requirement, that the goods be specially manufactured for the buyer, is met"), but also a mini-conclusion for each argument.

EXAMPLE   **INTEGRATED FORMAT**

Mini-conclusion for the first element	The court will probably find that the first requirement, that the goods be specially manufactured for the buyer, is met.
Mini-conclusion for the first argument	The court will base its conclusion on several factors. First, like the wrapping material in *Flowers,* the rugs were personalized. In *Flowers,* the wrapping material was imprinted with the buyer's name and unique artwork; in this case, the rugs had the Reutlinger family flower woven into them. Al-

though it was the Reutlinger family flower and not the Reutlinger name that was woven into the rugs, a court is not likely to find this difference determinative. The rule requires only that the goods be personalized, not that they have the buyer's name on them.

Second, the rugs were, in fact, specially manufactured. The manufacturer did specially set its looms. In addition, instead of being manufactured to standard dimensions, the rugs were made to fit the rooms in the Reutlinger Mansion.

Mini-conclusion for the second argument

Finally, in this case, the goods themselves are evidence that a contract was formed. Even though BCC produces only custom carpets, it is unlikely that it would have manufactured the rugs without a contract to do so. Further, as the court noted in *Wackenhut,* the fact that the seller is in the business of manufacturing custom-designed and made goods does not necessarily preclude a finding that the goods are specially manufactured. *Id.* at 1037.

Mini-conclusion for the third argument

Whichever format you use, keep in mind that these mini-conclusions are in addition to the formal conclusion that follows the discussion section. (See section 5.19.) In your formal conclusion, collect and summarize your mini-conclusions.

Section Summary

1. Each time you apply law to fact, state your conclusion.
2. If the element is not in dispute, the application-of-law-to-fact section and the mini-conclusion can be combined.
3. If the element is in dispute, evaluate each side's arguments and predict how the court will rule.

§5.17   THE DISCUSSION SECTION: AVOIDING THE COMMON PROBLEMS

Although the path to writing a good discussion section is filled with pitfalls, if you know about them, you can avoid them.

§5.17.1   Speak for Yourself

The temptation to string together a series of quotations is always there. Instead of putting the rules into your words, it seems easier to pluck a series of quotations from the cases.

Quoting almost always creates more problems than it solves. Writers who overrely on quotes usually do so because they do not understand the law. They have not figured out the individual rules, and they have not figured out how the rules fit together. (See section 5.6.) Although the quotations get them through the rule section, these writers are lost when it comes time to apply law to fact.

Overquoting also causes writing problems. In quoting, you almost inevitably run into problems with verb tenses and pronouns. In setting out the rules, one judge uses the past tense and another the present tense, and instead of using the proper noun, a judge will use a pronoun that does not have, at least in the quoted language, a referent. In addition, the writing usually becomes a mish-mash of writing styles. Judge A has one writing style, Judge B another, and Judge C still another. Because the judges were writing to a different audience and for a different purpose, it is unlikely that what worked for them will work for you.

Because of these problems, use quotations sparingly. Quote statutes but little else.

Note

When you do quote a case, include a pinpoint, or jump cite, for all quoted language.

---

§5.17.2   Lay It Out

Most attorneys are bright. Given piece A, piece B, and enough time, they can figure out how the two go together. A discussion section is not, however, a puzzle. Attorneys don't want you to hand them the pieces in a box; they want you to put the puzzle together. It is you, and not they, who should be doing the work.

Study the following examples.

| EXAMPLE 1 | INFORMATION JUST HANDED TO THE ATTORNEY |

In our case, it is only the Reutlinger family flower and not the Reutlinger name that is woven into the carpet. The McKibbins might try to distinguish the facts in our case from the facts in *Flow-*

ers. The flowers are not particularly unusual; the wholesaler was able to sell the rugs to a third party with little or no difficulty. The McKibbins might argue that a seller who deals only in custom-made goods is as likely to fabricate a contract for custom-made goods as a seller of ready-made goods is to fabricate a contract for its regular merchandise. A seller whose only business is custom or specially manufactured goods should not be exempt from the Statute of Frauds just because its goods are specially manufactured. Written contracts will become the exception and not the rule. If all of such a seller's goods are custom-made, a written contract will never be necessary. The McKibbins can argue that under the UCC, oral contracts should be the exception rather than the rule.

As written, this part of the discussion section makes no sense, even to the brightest attorney. Although all of the pieces are there, they are not presented in a logical order.

EXAMPLE 2　　**INFORMATION ORDERED BUT NOT CONNECTED**

The McKibbins might try to distinguish the facts in our case from the facts in *Flowers.* In our case, it is only the Reutlinger family flower and not the Reutlinger name that is woven into the carpet. The flower is not particularly unusual; the wholesaler was able to sell the rugs to a third party with little or no difficulty.

The McKibbins can argue that under the UCC, oral contracts should be the exception rather than the rule. A seller whose only business is custom or specially manufactured goods should not be exempt from the Statute of Frauds simply because its goods are specially manufactured. If all of such a seller's goods are custom-made, a written contract will never be necessary. Written contracts will become the exception and not the rule. The McKibbins might argue that a seller who deals only in custom-made goods is as likely to fabricate a contract for custom-made goods as a seller of ready-made goods is to fabricate a contract for its regular merchandise.

In this example the writer has sorted and ordered the pieces. The sentences are now in order, and they have been placed into two different paragraphs. Although the resulting text is more understandable, the attorney still has to work to figure out how the pieces go together.

EXAMPLE 3   **INFORMATION ORDERED AND
EXPLICITLY CONNECTED**

**The McKibbins might try to distinguish the facts in our
case from the facts in *Flowers*. Unlike *Flowers*,** in our case, it
is only the Reutlinger family flower and not the Reutlinger name
that is woven into the carpet. **In addition,** the flower is not particularly unusual; the wholesaler was able to sell the rugs to a third
party with little or no difficulty.

**The McKibbins' best argument is, however, a policy ar-
gument.** The McKibbins can argue that under the UCC, oral contracts should be the exception rather than the rule. **Thus,** a seller
whose only business is custom or specially manufactured goods
should not be exempt from the Statute of Frauds simply because
its goods are specially manufactured. **For,** if all of such a seller's
goods are custom-made, a written contract will never be necessary: written contracts will become the exception and not the rule.
In addition, the McKibbins might argue that a seller who deals
only in custom-made goods is as likely to fabricate a contract for
custom-made goods as a seller of ready-made goods is to fabricate a contract for its regular merchandise.

This example is much better than the previous two. By adding topic sentences and transitions (the language that has been highlighted),
the writer has made the connections between ideas explicit. (For more
on topic sentences and transitions see sections 5.22.2 and 5.22.3 and
Chapters 19 and 21.)

§5.17.3   Show How You Reached
Your Conclusions

After you have spent days researching and thinking about a problem, the answer often seems obvious. The client has a cause of action
or it does not, the element is met or it is not. Because the answer is so
clear, when it comes time to write the discussion section, the natural
tendency is to jump from the rule directly to the conclusion. If the answer is clear to you, it seems that it will also be clear to the attorney.

You cannot do this. Although the attorneys want a conclusion,
what they are most interested in is how you reached that conclusion.
They want you to think through the problem for them, rehearsing and
evaluating each side's arguments.

The following examples illustrate the difference between analysis
that is conclusory and analysis that gives the attorneys what they
need.

EXAMPLE 1

BCC will argue that the goods were specially manufactured. In contrast, the McKibbins will argue that the goods were not specially manufactured. The court will probably agree with BCC and find that the goods were specially manufactured.

In this example, the analysis is conclusory. Instead of setting out each side's arguments, the writer simply states their positions. Without knowing what the arguments are, the attorneys have no basis for evaluating the conclusion.

EXAMPLE 2

In arguing that the rugs were specially manufactured, BCC will rely on *Flowers,* arguing that its case is like *Flowers.* BCC will also distinguish *Colorado Carpet.*

In contrast, the McKibbins will argue that the goods were not specially manufactured. In doing so, they will argue that their case is more like *Colorado Carpet* than *Flowers.*

This example is only marginally better. It is not enough to tell the attorney which cases each side will use. You must use them.

EXAMPLE 3

BCC will rely on *Flowers.* In *Flowers,* the wrapping paper was imprinted with the buyer's name and artwork and was cut to the buyer's specifications. In our case, the rugs had the Reutlinger family flower woven into them and were manufactured to fit the rooms in the Reutlinger Mansion.

The McKibbins will, however, try to distinguish this case from the *Flowers* case. They will point out that in *Flowers* the wrapping material was imprinted with the buyer's name while in this case the rugs had only the Reutlinger family flower woven into them. Instead, the McKibbins will rely on *Colorado Carpet:* In both that case and our case standard dyes were used.

BCC will respond, arguing that while standard dyes were used in both cases, unlike the manufacturer in *Colorado Carpet,* in this case the manufacturer had to specially set its looms.

This example is better than the first two. In addition to identifying the cases, the writer has used them, comparing the facts in the analogous cases with the facts in the client's case. The writer has not, however, explained why the factual similarities and differences are significant. Why is it significant that in *Flowers* the wrapping material was imprinted with the buyer's name and art work while in the client's case it was only the family flower that was woven into the rugs? Similarly, why is it significant that in *Colorado Carpet* standard dyes and manufacturing processes were used while in the client's case the manufacturer had to specially set the looms?

EXAMPLE 4

BCC will argue that the rugs were specially manufactured because they were personalized and because they were of little value to a third party. Like the wrapping material in *Flowers,* the rugs were personalized: The Reutlinger family flower was woven into the carpet at one-foot intervals. In addition, the rugs were of little value to a third party. BCC did not resell them to a retail customer; it resold them to a wholesaler.

The McKibbins will distinguish the facts in this case from the facts in *Flowers.* In *Flowers,* the wrapping material was imprinted with the buyer's name and artwork; as a consequence, the material could not be resold to a third party. In contrast, here the rugs had only the Reutlinger flower and not the Reutlinger name woven into them. Because this flower was not particularly distinctive, BCC was able to resell the rugs.

Example 4 illustrates good application of law to fact. The writer sets out the test from *Flowers* — whether the goods were personalized and therefore of little value to a third party — and then applies each part of that test to the facts of the case, discussing both whether the rugs were personalized and whether they were of value to a third party. In doing so, the writer refers to specific facts and explains why the factual similarities and differences are significant.

§5.17.4   Use the Language of the Law

In some types of writing, elegant variation is desirable. You want to vary the words you use, at different times calling the lake a shimmering pond, a foreboding sea, and an environmental waste. The same is not true in law. In law, a lake is a lake. If you use a different word, the attorney (and in interpreting a contract, the court) will assume that you meant something different.

This means that as a writer, you need to find the right word and then use that word throughout the discussion. For example, in the discussion of the first element (whether the goods were specially manufactured for the buyer), the phrase "specially manufactured" should appear in the rule section, in the description of analogous cases, in the application-of-law-to-fact section, and in the mini-conclusion.

EXAMPLE

The first requirement is that the goods be **specially manufactured** for the buyer. Although the term **"specially manufactured"** is not defined in the statute, the courts have held that it refers to the nature of the goods and not to whether the goods were made in the usual course of the seller's business. *See Impossible Electronics Techniques, Inc. v. Wackenhut Protective Systems, Inc.,* 669 F.2d 1026, 1037 (5th Cir. 1982); *Colorado Carpet Installation, Inc. v. Palermo,* 668 P.2d 1384, 1390 (Colo. 1983). If, with slight alterations, the goods can be sold, they are not **specially manufactured.** *Id.*

Applying this standard, the Virginia Supreme Court held that wrapping material imprinted with the buyer's name and unique artwork and cut to the buyer's specifications was **"specially manufactured** because the wrapping material was personalized and of little value to a third party." *Flowers Baking Co. of Lynchburg, Inc. v. R-P Packaging, Inc.,* 329 S.E.2d 462, 466 (Va. 1985). However, in a case involving carpeting, the Colorado Supreme Court held that because the carpeting was available from other carpet outlets and had not been cut to unusual shapes or subjected to special dyeing, weaving, or other procedures, it could be resold and was not, therefore, **specially manufactured.** *Colorado Carpet v. Palermo,* 668 P.2d 1384 (Colo. 1983).

In the present case, we will argue that the rugs were **specially manufactured for the buyer.** Relying on the plain language of the statute, we will argue that the rugs were in fact **specially manufactured:** BCC had to make special arrangements with the manufacturer and, to produce the rugs, the manufacturer had to specially set its looms.

The McKibbins' best argument is, however, a policy argument. They can argue that under the UCC, oral contracts should be the exception rather than the rule. Thus, a seller whose only business is custom or specially manufactured goods should not be exempt from the Statute of Frauds just because its goods are **specially manufactured.** For, if all of such a seller's goods are custom, a written contract will never be necessary and written contracts will become the exception and not the rule. In addition, the McKibbins can argue that a seller who deals in only custom goods is just as likely to fabricate a contract for custom goods as is a seller who deals in ready-made merchandise.

We can respond to such an argument by citing *Wackenhut,* a case in which the seller sold custom closed-circuit television cameras. In holding that the cameras were **specially manufactured,** the court said the fact that the seller is in the business of manufacturing custom-designed and made goods does not necessarily preclude a finding that the goods are **specially manufactured.** *Id.* at 1037.

The court will probably find that the rugs were **specially manufactured** for the McKibbins. The rugs were not available from other outlets and, to produce the rugs, the manufacturer had to specially set its looms. Although BCC is in the business of producing custom carpets, it probably would not have produced rugs with the Reutlinger family flower woven into them unless it had been requested to do so.

You should also use other terms consistently. If something is an element refer to it as an element and not as a requirement or a factor. (See section 23.1.4.)

§5.17.5   See More Than the Obvious

Finally, look beyond the obvious. The difference between an acceptable memo and one that wins praise is often the depth of the analysis. The second author sees, and then presents, arguments that the first author does not.

Compare, for example, the following discussions, taken from a memo analyzing Oregon's recreational use statute.

EXAMPLE 1

The second element is met. The statute only requires that the landowner permit "any person" to use the land, and OWW's members are people.

EXAMPLE 2

We may also have difficulty proving the second element, that the use was by "any person." We will ask the court to give the phrase its plain meaning. "Any person" means any person, and OWW's members are persons. OWW will counter, arguing that the language should be read in light of the legislature's intent, which was to protect landowners who allowed the public to use their land for recreational purposes. Although Murphy allowed OWW members to use the path, he did not open it to the general public. As a consequence, he is not entitled to the benefit of the statute.

In the first example, the writer saw only the obvious: a plain language argument; in the second, the writer went beyond the plain language and made an argument based on the legislature's intent.

Section Summary

In writing the discussion section,

1. paraphrase rules instead of pulling quotations and stringing them together;
2. present the information in a logical order and make the connections between ideas explicit;
3. set out the reasoning and not just the conclusion;
4. use the language of the law and use it consistently; and
5. see more than the obvious.

§5.18 WRITING THE DISCUSSION SECTION: THE FIRST DRAFT

At last it is time to write. Working from the outline, the writer prepares the first draft of the discussion section.

In writing this draft, the goal is not perfection. It makes no sense to work and rework a sentence that may, later in the process, be edited out. Instead, the goal is to get the draft written. Once that is done, you can go back through the draft, revising and editing it.

EXAMPLE

FIRST DRAFT OF THE DISCUSSION

Exception for Specially Manufactured Goods

The exception for specially manufactured goods applies if the goods were specially manufactured and are not suitable for resale in the ordinary course of the seller's business. The applicable portion of the statute is as follows:

> (3) A contract which does not satisfy the requirements of subsection (1) but which is valid in other respects is enforceable
>
> > (a) if the goods are to be specially manufactured for the buyer and are not suitable for sale to others in the ordinary course of the seller's business and the seller, before notice of repudiation is received and under circumstances which reasonably indicate that the goods are for the buyer, has made either a substantial beginning of their manufacture or commitments for their procurement; . . .

Colo. Rev. Stat. § 4-2-201(3)(a).

Thus, if we can establish (1) that BCC specially manufactured the rugs for the McKibbins, (2) that BCC was not able to resell the rugs in the ordinary course of its business, and (3) that the rugs had been completed before BCC received the McKibbins' notice of repudiation, the contract will be enforceable.

1. Were the Rugs Specially Manufactured For the Buyer?

The first requirement is that the goods be specially manufactured for the buyer. Although the term "specially manufactured" is not defined in the statute, the Colorado courts have held that it refers to the nature of the goods and not to whether the goods were made in the usual course of the seller's business. *Colorado Carpet Installation, Inc. v. Palermo,* 668 P.2d 1384, 1390 (Colo. 1983).

In *Impossible Electronics Techniques, Inc. v. Wackenhut Protective Systems,* 669 F.2d 1026 (5th Cir. 1982), a case in which plaintiff IET brought suit for breach of an oral contract for the purchase of closed-circuit cameras by defendant Wackenhut, the court explained why specially manufactured goods are exempt from the Statute of Frauds. The court said:

> The Statute exempts contracts involving "specially manufactured" goods from the writing requirement because in these cases the very nature of the goods serves as a reliable indication that a contract was indeed formed. Where the seller has commenced or completed the manufacture of goods that conform to the special needs of a particular buyer, and thereby are not suitable for sale to others, not only is the likelihood of a perjured claim of a contract diminished, but denying enforcement to such a contract would impose substantial hardship on the aggrieved party.

Id. at 1036-37 (applying Florida law). The court further stated:

> That the seller may be in the business of manufacturing custom designed and made goods does not necessarily preclude his goods from being deemed specially manufactured.

Id. at 1037.

In our case, it is not a defense that BCC is in the business of producing custom carpets.

This rule was applied in *Flowers Baking Co. of Lynchburg, Inc. v. R-P Packaging, Inc.,* 329 S.E.2d 462 (Va. 1985). In the *Flowers* case, it was held that R-P Packaging, a manufacturer of customized wrapping paper, had a valid cause of action against Flowers. Flowers had asserted that the Statute of Frauds barred R-P's claim for payment. However, it was found that wrapping material manufactured by R-P was to the size required by Flowers and was imprinted with Flowers' name and unique artwork. *Id.* at 466. The court further concluded that the paper was personalized for Flowers and of little value to a third party. In *Colorado Carpet,* it was determined that the specially manufactured standard set out in *Wackenhut* was not met: It was asserted that *Colorado Carpet* had a strictly oral contract with defendant Palermo for the sale and installation of flooring materials but that the contract was enforceable because the goods were specially manufactured. However, the court found that the specially manufactured exception did not apply because the same carpet style was available from other carpet outlets in the Denver area and the carpets had not been cut to unusual shapes or subjected to special dyeing, weaving, or other procedures. *Id.* at 1391.

In the present case, it can be argued that the rugs were specially manufactured. Similar to the situation in *Flowers,* where R-P provided paper to Flowers printed with Flowers' name and unique art work, in our case, the rugs that were procured by BCC had the Reutlinger family flower woven into them.

It is likely that BCC will prevail. It is clear that BCC did have the carpet manufactured exclusively for the McKibbins. In BCC's order to the manufacturer, both the dimensions and the flower pattern of the rugs met the specifications provided by defendant. The fact that BCC had to check with the manufacturer to confirm that the rugs could be made is a further indication that these rugs were not available "off-the-shelf" from local carpet sellers, contrary to the situation in *Colorado Carpet.*

Even though the McKibbins will argue that this case is different from the *Flowers* case, we should win. Unlike *Flowers,* in this case the Reutlinger name was not woven into the rugs. The carpet may, therefore, not be so unique or specific in design that it could qualify as specially manufactured under the *Wackenhut* rule.

---

§5.19   DRAFTING THE CONCLUSION

In a one-issue memo, the conclusion is used to summarize your analysis of that one issue. For example, in the statute of frauds case, the

conclusion is used to tell the attorney that although the formal requirements of the Statute of Frauds are not met, the contract is probably
enforceable under the exception for specially manufactured goods.

EXAMPLE

CONCLUSION

Although the formal requirements of the UCC Statute of
Frauds are not met, the contract between BCC and the McKibbins
is probably enforceable under the exception for specially manufactured goods.

We should be able to prove the first element, that the rugs
were specially manufactured for the McKibbins. The rugs were
made to the McKibbins' specifications: The manufacturer specially set its looms to weave the Reutlinger family flower into the rugs.

We should also be able to prove the second element, that
the goods are not suitable for sale in the ordinary course of BCC's
business. BCC's ordinary course of business is selling carpets to
retail customers, not wholesalers.

The third element, that there had been a substantial beginning prior to repudiation, and the fourth element, that the evidence
reasonably indicates that the goods were for the McKibbins, are
also not in dispute. The rugs had been completed at the time Mrs.
McKibbins canceled the order, and the family flower is evidence
that the goods were for the McKibbins.

While some attorneys will want you to stop there, others will want
you to go one step further, telling (advising) the attorney what you think
should be done next. What should the attorney tell the client? What
action should the attorney take next? Is this the type of case that the
firm should, or wants to, handle? When you are asked to include this
type of information in your conclusion, add a paragraph like the following.

EXAMPLE

Because it is likely that a court would enforce the contract,
we should advise BCC to pursue this action. We can either contact the McKibbins' attorney and attempt to settle the matter or
file a complaint.

In a multi-issue memo, the conclusion takes a slightly different form. You will devote one paragraph or paragraph block to each issue, summarizing in each paragraph or block your analysis of one of the issues. You will then, in a final paragraph, summarize your analysis. Given your conclusion on each of the issues, how is the case likely to be resolved?

Checklist for Critiquing the Conclusion

I. Organization

- The conclusion is organized logically.

II. Content

- In a one-issue memorandum, the conclusion is used to predict how the issue will be decided and to summarize the reasons supporting that prediction.
- In a multi-issue memorandum, the conclusion is used to predict the decision on each issue and the overall result in the case.
- When appropriate, the writer includes not only the conclusion but also strategic advice.

C. REVISING

§5.20 REVISING: CHECKING CONTENT AND LARGE-SCALE ORGANIZATION

§5.20.1 Checking Content

In revising a draft, the first thing that should be checked is its content. If there are problems with content, nothing else matters.

a. *Have You Given the Attorneys the Information That They Need?*

In checking content, the first question to ask yourself is whether you have given the attorneys the information that they requested. Did you research the assigned issue or issues? Did you locate all of the applicable statutes and cases? Did you identify and present the arguments that each side is likely to make? Did you evaluate those arguments and predict how the court is likely to rule?

In the statute of frauds problem, the writer has given the attorney the information that she requested. See page 94. The research is complete: The writer found not only the applicable statute but also the key cases.

The discussion also begins at the right place. Like most attorneys, Ms. Krontz is familiar with the UCC: She knows that it applies to the sale of goods. Consequently, it was not necessary to make this point in the discussion section. Nor was it necessary to discuss whether rugs are goods. All of the law indicates that they are. The discussion also stops where it should. Ms. Krontz did not ask for a discussion of damages. The assignment was to determine whether the exception applied.

Last but not least, the writer included all of the pieces. He included both the general and specific rules and, when appropriate, descriptions of analogous cases. In addition, he applied those rules and cases to the facts of the client's case, anticipating the arguments that each side was likely to make and then evaluating those arguments and predicting how the court was likely to rule.

Thus, when the writer asks himself whether he has given the attorney the information she needs, the answer is yes. He knew the law, and in presenting that law, he used good judgment.

b. *Is the Information Presented Accurately?*

In law, small errors can have serious consequences. An overlooked "o" in *Shepard's,* an omitted "not," or an "or" when it should have been "and" can make the difference between winning and losing, competent lawyering and malpractice.

As a consequence, in writing the memo, you must exercise great care. Because the attorneys are relying on you, your research must be thorough and your presentation accurate. Every statute and case must be shepardized, each quotation copied accurately, and each paraphrase a fair statement of the law. You must also use cases carefully. The facts must be presented accurately, and the holding correctly identified. Unless the attorneys read the statutes and cases that you cite, they may not see an error until it is too late.

In the following example, the writer has made a number of mistakes. If you were the attorney, would you see them?

EXAMPLE

The exception for specially manufactured goods applies if the goods were specially manufactured and are not suitable for resale.

Although the term "specially manufactured" is not defined in the UCC, it has been defined by the courts. The courts have held that a good is specially manufactured if it is personalized and of little value to a third party. *Flowers Baking Co. of Lynchburg, Inc. v. R-P Packaging, Inc.*, 329 S.E.2d 462 (Va. 1958).

The first paragraph contains two errors: (1) the writer implies that there are only two requirements when in fact there are three or four, and (2) the requirements are not presented accurately. It is not enough that the goods were specially manufactured. They must have been specially manufactured for the buyer. Similarly, it is not enough that the goods are not suitable for resale; they cannot be suitable for resale in the ordinary course of the seller's business.

The second paragraph also contains two errors. First, the writer implies that all courts have defined "specially manufactured" in the same way. This is not true. Second, the writer has made an error in citing *Flowers.* The case was decided in 1985, not 1958.

Question

Why is each of the above errors significant? Which is the most serious?

---

§5.20.2   Checking Large-scale Organization

The next step is to check the discussion section's large-scale organization. Has the information been presented in a logical order? Does the information appear in the order that the attorney expects to see it?

The easiest way to check large-scale organization is to prepare an after-the-fact outline. This is done by identifying the subject matter of each paragraph and then listing those labels in outline form.

The following example shows how this is done.

EXAMPLE

FIRST DRAFT OF DISCUSSION SECTION

Exception for Specially Manufactured Goods

The exception for specially manufactured goods applies if the goods were specially manufactured and are not suitable for

General rule
introduction

resale in the ordinary course of the seller's business.

Text of statute

     (3) A contract which does not satisfy the requirements of subsection (1) but which is valid in other respects is enforceable

     (a) if the goods are to be specially manufactured for the buyer and are not suitable for sale to others in the ordinary course of the seller's business and the seller, before notice of repudiation is received and under circumstances which reasonably indicate that the goods are for the buyer, has made either a substantial beginning of their manufacture or commitments for their procurement; . . .

Colo. Rev. Stat. § 4-2-201.

List of elements

     Thus, if we can establish (1) that BCC specially manufactured the rugs for the McKibbins, (2) that BCC was not able to resell the rugs in the ordinary course of its business, and (3) that the rugs had been completed before BCC received the McKibbins' notice of repudiation, the contract will be enforceable.

First element

1. Were the Rugs Specially Manufactured For the Buyer?

     The first requirement is that the goods be specially manufactured for the buyer. Although the term "specially manufactured" is not defined in the statute, the courts have held that it refers to the nature of the goods and not to whether the goods were made in the usual course of the seller's business. *See Impossible Electronics Techniques, Inc. v. Wackenhut Protective Systems, Inc.,* 669 F.2d 1026, 1037 (5th Cir. 1982); *Colorado Carpet Installation, Inc. v. Palermo,* 668 P.2d 1384, 1390 (Colo. 1983). If, with slight alterations, the goods can be sold, they are not specially manufactured. *Id.*

Tests that courts use in determining whether goods are specially manufactured

Facts of *IET*

     In *Wackenhut,* a case in which plaintiff IET brought suit for breach of an oral contract for the purchase of closed-circuit cameras by defendant Wackenhut, the court explained why specially manufactured goods are exempt from the Statute of Frauds. The court said:

> The Statute exempts contracts involving "specially manufactured" goods from the writing requirement because in these cases the very nature of the goods serves as a reliable indication that a contract was indeed formed. Where the seller has commenced or completed the manufacture of goods that conform to the special needs of a particular buyer, and thereby are not suitable for sale to others, not only is the likelihood of a perjured claim of a contract diminished, but denying enforcement to such a contract would impose substantial hardship on the aggrieved party.

Reasons why specially manufactured goods are exempt from Statute of Frauds

Id. at 1036-1037 (applying Florida law).

That the seller may be in the business of manufacturing custom designed and made goods does not necessarily preclude his goods from being deemed specially manufactured. *Id.* at 1037.

Rule: exception can apply even if seller's business is selling custom goods

In our case, it is not a defense that BCC is in the business of producing custom carpets.

Application of rule to our facts

This rule was applied in *Flowers Baking Co. of Lynchburg, Inc. v. R-P Packaging, Inc.,* 329 S.E.2d 462 (Va. 1985). In the *Flowers* case, it was held that R-P Packaging, a manufacturer of customized wrapping paper, had a valid cause of action against Flowers. Flowers had asserted that the Statute of Frauds barred R-P's claim for payment. However, it was found that wrapping material manufactured by R-P was to the size required by Flowers and was imprinted with Flowers' name and unique artwork. *Id.* at 466. The court further concluded that the paper was personalized for Flowers and of little value to a third party.

Description of *Flowers*

In *Colorado Carpet,* it was determined that the specially manufactured standard set out in *Wackenhut* was not met: it was asserted that *Colorado Carpet* had a strictly oral contract with defendant Palermo for the sale and installation of flooring materials but that the contract was enforceable because the goods were specially manufactured.

Description of *Colorado Carpet*

Argument based on *Flowers*

However, the court found that the specially manufactured exception did not apply because the same carpet style was available from other carpet outlets in the Denver area and the carpets had not been cut to unusual shapes or subjected to special dyeing, weaving, or other procedures. *Id.* at 1391.

In the present case, it can be argued that the rugs were specially manufactured. Similar to the situation in *Flowers,* where R-P provided paper to Flowers printed with Flowers' name and unique artwork, in our case, the rugs that were procured by BCC had the Reutlinger family flower woven into them.

Original Outline

I. **Exception for specially manufactured goods**
  A. General rule
    1. Set out applicable portion of 2-201(3)(a)
    2. Set out policies underlying the exception
    3. List elements (this will provide a roadmap for the rest of the discussion)
  B. First element
    1. Applicable rules
      a. Sentence identifying the element to be discussed (could use subheading)
      b. Rules as set out in *Colorado Carpet* and *Wackenhut*
    2. Analogous cases
      a. Paragraph describing case in which court held that goods were specially manufactured for buyer (*Flowers*)
      b. Paragraph describing case in which court held that goods were not specially manufactured (*Colorado Carpet*)
    3. Application of law to fact
      a. BCC's arguments
        i. Plain language argument
        ii. Arguments based on *Flowers* and *Colorado Carpet*
        iii. Policy arguments
      b. The McKibbins' arguments
        i. Arguments based on *Flowers* and *Colorado Carpet*
        ii. Policy arguments
    4. Mini-conclusion
    Court will probably rule that rugs were specially

manufactured — they were personalized and the goods themselves are evidence that contract was formed.

 C. Second Element . . .

After-the-Fact Outline

 I. General rule
  A. Introduction
  B. Text of statute
  C. List of elements
 II. First element (specially manufactured)
  A. Tests that courts use in determining whether goods are specially manufactured
  B. Facts of *IET*
  C. Reasons why specially manufactured goods are exempt from Statute of Frauds
  D. Rule: exception can apply even if seller's business is selling custom goods
  E. Application of rule to facts
  F. Description of *Flowers*
  G. Description of *Colorado Carpet*
  H. Argument based on *Flowers*

When the after-the-fact outline is compared with the original outline, several differences are apparent. First, in writing the draft, the writer has set out the policies under the first element and not under the general rule. Second, the writer has inserted both the description of a case (facts of *IET*) and the application of a rule in the rule section.

In this instance, the organization set out in the original outline is better than that used in the draft. It is, therefore, necessary to revise the draft, reordering some of the sections.

Checklist for Critiquing the Discussion Section: Content and Large-scale Organization

 I. Content

  General Rule Section
  ● The writer has included a sentence or paragraph establishing a context and introducing the statute or common law rule.
  ● The writer has set out the general rule, quoting the applicable statutory sections and quoting or paraphrasing the common law rule.

- When the elements of the statute (or common law rule) are not easily identified, the writer goes beyond simply quoting the statute (or common law rule) and adds a paraphrase that lists the elements.
- When appropriate, the writer has explained the policies underlying the rule.
- When appropriate, the writer has told the attorney who has the burden of proof and what the burden is.
- The writer has not included rules or information that the attorney does not need.
- The rules are stated accurately and objectively.
- For each rule stated, the writer has included a citation to authority.

Discussion of Each Element
- For each element, the writer has set out the applicable definitions, rules, and tests.
- When an element is in dispute, the writer has included descriptions of analogous cases, setting these descriptions out before the arguments (script format) or integrating the descriptions into the discussion (integrated format).
- In describing analogous cases, the writer has given the attorney the information that he or she needs: no more and no less.
- The descriptions of the analogous cases are accurate.
- The writer has applied the law to the facts of the client's case, either by setting out each side's arguments and counter arguments (script format) or by setting out the support for the conclusion (integrated format).
- The analysis is not conclusory: The writer has explained why the plain language supports the conclusion, why the factual similarities between the analogous cases and the client's case are significant, why it would be consistent with the policies underlying the statute or rule to decide the case in a particular way.
- The analysis is sophisticated: The writer has addressed more than the obvious arguments.
- The writer has included mini-conclusions in which he or she predicts how the question will be decided and gives reasons to support those predictions.
- In setting out the rules, analogous cases, arguments, and mini-conclusions, the writer has used the language of the law.

II. Large-scale Organization
- The writer has used an organizational scheme that is logical: Threshold questions are discussed first and when issues build on each other, they are discussed in the appropriate order.
- The writer has presented the information in the order in which the attorney expects to see it. For example, the gen-

eral rule is stated first, and specific rules are set out before the arguments based on those rules.

§5.21   REVISING: THE SECOND DRAFT

Having identified the problems with content and large-scale organization, the writer prepares the second draft.

EXAMPLE

SECOND DRAFT OF THE DISCUSSION

Even if the formal requirements of the UCC Statute of Frauds are not met, a contract is enforceable if the goods were specially manufactured.

> (3) A contract which does not satisfy the requirements of subsection (1) but which is valid in other respects is enforceable
> (a) if the goods are to be specially manufactured for the buyer and are not suitable for sale to others in the ordinary course of the seller's business and the seller, before notice of repudiation is received and under circumstances which reasonably indicate that the goods are for the buyer, has made either a substantial beginning of their manufacture or commitments for their procurement; . . .

Colo. Rev. Stat. § 4-2-201(3)(a).

Specially manufactured goods are exempt from the writing requirement because the very nature of the goods serves as a reliable indication that a contract was indeed formed. When the goods conform to the special needs of a particular buyer and are not, therefore, suitable for sale to others, not only is the likelihood of a perjured claim diminished, but denying enforcement of such a contract would impose a substantial hardship on the aggrieved party. *Impossible Electronics Techniques, Inc. v. Wackenhut Protective Systems, Inc.,* 669 F.2d 1026, 1037 (5th Cir. 1982).

If we can establish (1) that BCC specially manufactured the rugs for the McKibbins, (2) that BCC was not able to resell the rugs in the ordinary course of its business, and (3) that the rugs had been completed before BCC received the McKibbins' notice of repudiation, the contract will be enforceable.

1. Were the Rugs Specially Manufactured For the Buyer?

Although the term "specially manufactured" is not defined in the statute, the Colorado Supreme Court has held that it refers to the nature of the goods and not to whether the goods were made in the usual course of the seller's business. *Colorado Carpet Installation, Inc. v. Palermo,* 668 P.2d 1384, 1390 (Colo. 1983). *Accord, Impossible Electronics Techniques, Inc. v. Wackenhut Protective Systems, Inc.,* 669 F.2d 1026, 1037 (5th Cir. 1982). In a case involving carpeting, it was held that carpeting that was available from other carpet outlets and had not been cut to unusual shapes or subjected to special dyeing, weaving, or other procedures was not specially manufactured. *Colorado Carpet v. Palermo,* 668 P.2d 1384 (Colo. 1983).

Wrapping material imprinted with the buyer's name and unique artwork and cut to the buyer's specifications was held to be "specially manufactured" because the wrapping material was personalized and of little value to a third party. *Flowers Baking Co. of Lynchburg, Inc. v. R-P Packaging, Inc.,* 329 S.E.2d 462 (Va. 1985).

BCC had to make special arrangements with the manufacturer and, to produce the rugs, the manufacturer had to specially set its looms. Thus, in this case, the goods were specially manufactured.

Unlike the carpet in *Colorado Carpet,* in our case identical rugs could not be found at other carpet outlets. The rugs in question were one-of-a-kind. They were made to fit specific rooms, and special weaving was required. Our case is more like the *Flowers* case. Like the wrapping material in *Flowers,* the carpet was personalized: The Reutlinger family flower is as distinctive as any company name or logo and, as a result, carpet with the flower woven into it is of little value to a third party.

The rugs themselves provide the necessary evidence of a contract. It is not likely that BCC would have produced carpet matching the original carpet in the Reutlinger Mansion had it not been requested to do so. In addition, if the court does not enforce the contract, BCC, a small business, will suffer a loss.

Unlike *Flowers,* in our case, it is only the Reutlinger family flower and not the Reutlinger name that is woven into the carpet. Further, the flower is not particularly unusual; the wholesaler was able to sell the rugs to a third party with little or no difficulty.

Under the UCC, oral contracts should be the exception rather than the rule. Thus, a seller whose only business is custom or specially manufactured goods should not be exempt from the Statute of Frauds simply because its goods are specially manufactured. For, if all of such a seller's goods are custom-made, a written contract will never be necessary: Written contracts will become the exception and not the rule. In addition, the McKibbins might argue that a seller who deals only in custom goods is as likely to fabricate a contract for custom goods as a seller of ready-made goods is to fabricate a contract for its regular merchandise.

In *Wackenhut,* the court held that goods produced by a firm specializing in the manufacture of closed-circuit television cameras were specially manufactured for the buyer. "That the seller may be in the business of manufacturing custom-designed and made goods does not necessarily preclude his goods from being deemed specially manufactured." *Id.* at 1037.

It is likely that a court will find that the rugs were specially manufactured for the McKibbins. The rugs were not available on the general market: To produce the rugs, the manufacturer had to specially set its looms. Although BCC is in the business of producing custom carpets, it would not have produced a carpet with the Reutlinger family flower woven into it unless it had been requested to do so.

§5.22   REVISING: MAKING THE CONNECTIONS EXPLICIT

Having revised for content and organization, the next step is to look at the draft through the reader's eyes. Will the organizational scheme be apparent to the reader? Can the reader determine how paragraphs, sentences, and even the parts of sentences are related? If the connections are not explicit, more roadmaps, signposts, and transitions are needed.

§5.22.1   Roadmaps

A roadmap is just what the term implies: a "map" providing the reader with an overview of the document.

To be effective, a roadmap should be short and substantive in nature. Although the following roadmap meets the first criterion, it fails the second.

EXAMPLE 1

This memo is divided into two parts. In the first part, I discuss whether the formal requirements set out in 2-201(1) are met; in the second part, I discuss the exception for specially manufactured goods.

The following roadmap satisfies both criteria.

EXAMPLE 2

In deciding whether the contract is enforceable, the court will first determine whether the formal requirements of the Statute of

Frauds are met. If they are, the contract is enforceable; if they are not, the contract is not enforceable unless one of the exceptions, for example, the exception for specially manufactured goods, applies.

In addition to being short, the second example is substantive in nature. The writer does not just describe how the section is organized; she describes the decisionmaking process. Also note that in the second example, the writer does not use the personal pronoun "I." By convention, personal pronouns are not usually used in the discussion section of memoranda and briefs. (See section 19.2.1.)

§5.22.2   Topic Sentences and Other Signposts

Topic sentences and signposts serve the same function that directional signs serve on a freeway. They tell the attorneys where they are and what to expect. (See Chapter 19 and section 20.5.)

As you discovered when you read the second draft (see section 5.21), these directional signs are particularly important in legal writing. Without them, the connections between paragraphs and between sentences are not clear.

In Example 1 the writer has not included topic sentences or signposts.

EXAMPLE 1

EXCERPT FROM THE SECOND DRAFT OF THE DISCUSSION

Although the term "specially manufactured" is not defined in the statute, the Colorado Supreme Court has held that it refers to the nature of the goods and not to whether the goods were made in the usual course of the seller's business. *Colorado Carpet Installation, Inc. v. Palermo*, 668 P.2d 1384, 1390 (Colo. 1983). Accord, *Impossible Electronics Techniques, Inc. v. Wackenhut Protective Systems, Inc.*, 669 F.2d 1026, 1037 (5th Cir. 1982).

In a case involving carpeting, it was held that carpeting that was available from other carpet outlets and had not been cut to unusual shapes or subjected to special dyeing, weaving, or other procedures, was not specially manufactured. *Colorado Carpet v. Palermo*, 668 P.2d 1384 (Colo. 1983). Wrapping material imprinted with the buyer's name and unique artwork and cut to the buyer's specifications was held to be "specially manufactured" because the wrapping material was personalized and of little value to a third party. *Flowers Baking Co. of Lynchburg, Inc. v. R-P Packaging, Inc.,* 329 S.E.2d 462 (Va. 1985).

BCC had to make special arrangements with the manufacturer and, to produce the rugs, the manufacturer had to specially set its looms. Thus, in this case, the goods were specially manufactured.

Unlike the carpet in *Colorado Carpet,* in our case identical rugs could not be found at other carpet outlets. The rugs in question were one-of-a-kind. They were made to fit specific rooms, and special weaving was required. Our case is more like the *Flowers* case. Like the wrapping material in *Flowers,* the carpet was personalized: the Reutlinger family flower is as distinctive as any company name or logo and, as a result, carpet with the flower woven into it is of little value to a third party.

In Example 2 the writer has included topic sentences and signposts. The new language is in boldface type. Language that can be deleted is in brackets.

EXAMPLE 2

EXCERPT FROM THE SECOND DRAFT OF THE DISCUSSION

The first requirement is that the goods be specially manufactured for the buyer. Although the term "specially manufactured" is not defined in the statute, the Colorado Supreme Court has held that it refers to the nature of the goods and not to whether the goods were made in the usual course of the seller's business. *Colorado Carpet Installation, Inc. v. Palermo,* 668 P.2d 1384, 1390 (Colo. 1983). *Accord, Impossible Electronics Techniques, Inc. v. Wackenhut Protective Systems, Inc.,* 669 F.2d 1026, 1037 (5th Cir. 1982).

In the only Colorado case discussing the exception for specially manufactured goods, the Colorado Supreme Court held that carpeting that was available from other carpet outlets and that had not been cut to unusual shapes or subjected to special dyeing, weaving, or other procedures was not specially manufactured. *Colorado Carpet v. Palermo,* 668 P.2d 1384 (Colo. 1983). **In contrast, in a Virginia case,** the Virginia Supreme Court held that wrapping material imprinted with the buyer's name and unique artwork and cut to the buyer's specifications was "specially manufactured because the wrapping material was personalized and of little value to a third party." *Flowers Baking Co.*

of Lynchburg, Inc. v. R-P Packaging, Inc., 329 S.E.2d 462, 464 (Va. 1985).

In the present case, we will argue that the rugs were specially manufactured for the buyer. Relying on the plain language of the statute, we will argue that the rugs were in fact specially manufactured: BCC had to make special arrangements with the manufacturer and, to produce the rugs, the manufacturer had to specially set its looms. [Thus, in this case, the goods were specially manufactured.]

We will also contrast the facts in our case to the facts in *Colorado Carpet.* Unlike the carpet in *Colorado Carpet,* in our case, identical rugs could not be found at other carpet outlets. The rugs in question were one-of-a-kind. They were made to fit specific rooms, and special weaving was required. Our case is more like the *Flowers* case. Like the wrapping material in *Flowers,* the carpet was personalized: The Reutlinger family flower is as distinctive as any company name or logo and, as a result, carpet with the flower woven into it is of little value to a third party.

---

§5.22.3   Transitions

You can also use transitions to explain the relationship between ideas. (See Chapter 21.)

In Example 1, the writer has not included sufficient transitions. As a result, the attorney must do extra work. She must mentally make the connections that the writer has left out.

EXAMPLE 1

The McKibbins may try to distinguish the facts in our case from the facts in *Flowers.* In our case, it is only the Reutlinger family flower and not the Reutlinger name that is woven into the carpet. The flower is not particularly unusual; the wholesaler was able to sell the rugs to a third party with little or no difficulty.

The McKibbins can argue that under the UCC, oral contracts should be the exception rather than the rule. A seller whose only business is custom or specially manufactured goods should not be exempt from the Statute of Frauds simply because its goods are specially manufactured. If all of such a seller's goods are custom-made, a written contract will never be necessary. Written contracts will become the exception and not the rule. The McKibbins may argue that a seller who deals only in custom-made goods is as likely to fabricate a contract for custom-made goods as a seller of ready-made goods is to fabricate a contract for its regular merchandise.

In Example 2, the writer has made the connections between ideas explicit. By adding transitions (in boldface type), the analysis is more sophisticated and the attorney's job easier.

EXAMPLE 2

The McKibbins may try to distinguish the facts in our case from the facts in *Flowers*. **Unlike *Flowers,*** in our case, it is only the Reutlinger family flower and not the Reutlinger name that is woven into the carpet. **In addition,** the flower is not particularly unusual; the wholesaler was able to sell the rugs to a third party with little or no difficulty.

The McKibbins can **also** argue that under the UCC, oral contracts should be the exception rather than the rule. **Consequently,** a seller whose only business is custom or specially manufactured goods should not be exempt from the Statute of Frauds because its goods are specially manufactured. **For,** if all of such a seller's goods are custom-made, a written contract will never be necessary: written contracts will become the exception and not the rule. **In addition,** the McKibbins may argue that a seller who deals only in custom-made goods is as likely to fabricate a contract for custom-made goods as a seller of ready-made goods is to fabricate a contract for its regular merchandise.

Note

Punctuation can be used as a transition. Note how in the previous example, the colon is used to explain how the two parts of the sentence are related. (See section 26.3.)

---

§5.22.4　Dovetailing

Transitions are not the only device that can be used to make the connections between ideas clearer. As is explained in section 21.3, dovetailing can also be used.

EXAMPLE 1

Without Dovetailing

The McKibbins had purchased the Reutlinger Mansion with the intention of restoring it. The McKibbins wanted to replicate the original rugs, which were beige with a twelve-inch maroon strip around the perimeter and the family emblem woven in at one-foot intervals.

With Dovetailing

The McKibbins had purchased the Reutlinger Mansion with the intention of **restoring** it. **As part of this restoration,** the Mc-Kibbins wanted to replicate the original rugs, which were beige with a twelve-inch maroon strip around the perimeter and the family emblem woven in at one-foot intervals.

Frequently, the second half of a dovetail, the reference to what was previously stated, also serves as a signpost. In the following example, the phrase "In the only Colorado case discussing the exception for specially manufactured goods" is both a dovetail referring the reader to the information contained in the prior paragraph and a signpost, telling the attorney what to expect in the paragraph that it introduces.

EXAMPLE 2

   The first requirement is that the goods be specially manufactured for the buyer. Although the term "specially manufactured" is not defined in the statute, the Colorado Supreme Court has held that it refers to the nature of the goods and not to whether the goods were made in the usual course of the seller's business. *Colorado Carpet Installation, Inc. v. Palermo,* 668 P.2d 1384, 1390 (Colo. 1983). *Accord, Impossible Electronics Techniques, Inc. v. Wackenhut Protective Systems, Inc.,* 669 F.2d 1026, 1037 (5th Cir. 1982).
   In the only Colorado case discussing the exception for specially manufactured goods, the Colorado Supreme Court held that carpeting that was available from other carpet outlets and that had not been cut to unusual shapes or subjected to special dyeing, weaving, or other procedures was not specially manufactured. *Colorado Carpet v. Palermo,* 668 P.2d 1384 (Colo. 1983).

Checklist for Revising the Discussion Section

Small-Scale Organization

- When appropriate, the writer has included a roadmap.
- Roadmaps are short and describe the decisionmaking process.
- Signposts and topic sentences have been used to tell the attorney where he or she is in the discussion and what to expect next.
- Transitions and dovetailing have been used to make clear the connections between sentences and paragraphs.

D.　EDITING

The work is now almost done. When you step back from the memo and look at it through the attorney's eyes, you are pleased with its content, organization, and presentation.

The last steps in the process are editing and proofreading your work. Like the painter preparing to have his work judged by a critic, you go back through your memo once again, correcting errors in grammar, punctuation, and usage and checking your citations. You also read your memo for style. Does each sentence flow smoothly from the prior sentence? Do the words create vivid images? Does the writing engage the reader? In sum, is the memo the work of an artisan or an artist?

§5.23　Editing and Proofreading

Although some writers mistakenly believe that revising, editing, and proofreading are all the same skill, they are not. Revising is literally "re-seeing" your creation. It is stepping back and examining the "vision" that you have.

Editing, on the other hand, is more a shaping of the vision, making the vision clearer, more concise, more precise, more accessible to a reader.

Proofreading is different yet again. It is the search for error. When you proofread, you are not asking yourself "Is there a better way of saying this?" Instead, you are looking to see if what you intended to have on the page is, in fact, there.

Although the lines between revising and editing and between editing and proofreading are blurry at times, the distinctions among these three skills are important to keep in mind, if for no other reason than to remind you that there are three distinct ways of making changes to a draft and that the best written documents undergo all three types of change.

§5.23.1   Editing

Editing, like revising, requires that you look at your work through fresh eyes. At this stage, however, the focus is not on the larger issues of content and organization but on sentence construction, precision and conciseness, grammar, and punctuation. The goal is to produce a professional product that is easily read and understood.

a. *Make the Sentences Readable*

Most writers can substantially improve their sentences by following four simple rules:

1. Use the actor as the subject of most sentences.
2. Keep the subject and verb close together.
3. Put old information at the beginning of the sentence and new information at the end.
4. Vary sentence length and pattern.

Rule 1   **Use the Actor as the Subject of Most Sentences**

By using the actor as the subject of most of your sentences, you can avoid many of the constructions that make legal writing hard to understand: overuse of the passive voice and expletive constructions, most nominalizations, and many misplaced modifiers.

1. Passive Constructions

In a passive construction, the actor appears in the object, rather than the subject, slot of the sentence or is not named at all. For example, in the following sentence, although the jury is the actor, the word "jury" is used as the object rather than the subject.

EXAMPLE   **PASSIVE VOICE**

A verdict was reached by the jury. *OR*

A verdict was reached.

To use the active voice, simply identify the actor (in this case, the jury) and use it as the subject of the sentence.

EXAMPLE   **ACTIVE VOICE**

The jury reached a verdict.

Now read each of the following sentences, marking the subject and verb and deciding whether the writer used the actor as the subject of the sentence. If the writer did not use the actor, decide whether the sentence should be rewritten.

EXAMPLE

(1) These rules were applied in *Flowers Baking Co. of Lynchburg, Inc. v. R-P Packaging, Inc.,* 329 S.E.2d 462 (Va. 1985). (2) In *Flowers,* it was held that R-P Packaging, a manufacturer of customized wrapping paper, had a valid cause of action against Flowers. (3) Flowers had asserted that the Statute of Frauds had barred R-P's claim for payment. (4) However, it was found that wrapping material manufactured by R-P was to the size required by Flowers and was imprinted with Flowers' name and unique artwork. *Id.* at 466. (5) The court further concluded that the paper was personalized for Flowers and that it had little value to a third party.

Sentence 1:

These rules were applied in *Flowers Baking Co. of Lynchburg, Inc. v. R-P Packaging, Inc.,* 329 S.E.2d 462 (Va. 1985).

In this sentence, the writer used the passive voice: The actor (the court) is not used as the subject of the sentence.

In this instance, the writer's decision to use the passive voice was a good one. By placing the phrase "These rules" at the beginning of the sentence, the writer was able to use dovetailing to make the connection between the information in this paragraph and the prior paragraph explicit.

Sentence 2:

In *Flowers,* it was held that R-P Packaging, a manufacturer of customized wrapping paper, had a valid cause of action against Flowers.

Sentence (2) is another sentence in which the writer did not use the actor (the court) as the subject of the sentence. In this instance, however, the decision to use the passive voice was not a good one: Use of the passive voice does not improve the transition between sentences or emphasize what was done.

EXAMPLE

Passive

it was held [by the court] that R-P

Active

the court held that R-P

Sentence 3:

Flowers had asserted that the Statute of Frauds had barred R-P's claim for payment.

In this sentence, the writer uses the active voice: The actor, Flowers, is used as the subject of the sentence. Here, the use of the active voice is effective. Not only does it result in a strong subject-verb unit (Flowers had asserted), but it also allows the writer to use dovetailing ("... against **Flowers. Flowers** had asserted ...") to make the connection between the two sentences clear.

Sentence 4:

However, it was found that wrapping material manufactured by R-P was to the size required by Flowers and was imprinted with Flowers' name and unique artwork.

Like sentences (1) and (2), this sentence is written in the passive voice. The actor (the court) is not used as the subject of the sentence.

In this instance, the passive voice is inappropriate for several reasons: The passive voice was not used to make the connections between the sentences explicit or to emphasize what was done. In addition, the passive voice was not needed to break the pattern established in the earlier sentences. (If "the court" had been used as the actor in each of preceding sentences, the writer might have elected to use the passive voice to relieve the monotony.)

Instead, the active voice would work better for both the writer and the reader. The writer wants to emphasize what the court did and, after reading the third sentence ("Flowers asserted ....) the reader is looking for the court's response.

Sentence 5:

The court further concluded that the paper was personalized for Flowers and of little value to a third party.

In this sentence the writer has used the actor as the subject. By doing so, the writer makes the connection between this sentence and the other sentence clear (by using a parallel construction, the writer makes it clear that this sentence develops the topic introduced in the prior sentence) and places the emphasis on what the court did.

For more on active and passive voice, see section 22.1.

2.　Nominalizations

You are guilty of using nominalizations if you turn a word that is usually used as a verb into a noun. For example, in the following sentence, the words "application" and "conclusion" are nominalizations.

EXAMPLE

Application of the same principles here dictates the **conclusion** that the rugs were not suitable for resale in the ordinary course of the seller's business.

To make this sentence better, identify the actor (the court, you, ????) and then, in the verb, specifically state what action that actor has taken or will take (see section 22.1).

EXAMPLE

If it **applies** the same principles to this case, the court will **conclude** that the rugs were not suitable for resale in the ordinary course of BCC's business.

3.　Expletive Constructions

In an expletive construction, the phrase "it is" or "there are" is used as the subject and verb for the sentence. Although it is sometimes necessary to use such a construction (note the use of expletive constructions in this paragraph), such a construction gives the reader almost no information. It is, therefore, much better to use a concrete subject and verb — that is, a subject and verb that describe something the reader can "see" in his or her mind (see sections 22.2 and 23.2.4).

EXAMPLE

Expletive

It is BCC's argument that . . .

Corrected

BCC will argue that . . .

---

4. Dangling Modifiers

A dangling modifier is a modifier that does not reasonably modify anything in the sentence. For example, in the following sentence, the phrase "Applying this definition" does not reasonably modify anything in the sentence. It is not "it was held" that is doing the applying.

EXAMPLE 1

Applying this definition, it was held that the wrapping material was not specially manufactured for the buyer.

The dangling modifier can be eliminated if the actor is used as the subject of the sentence.

EXAMPLE 2

Applying this definition, the court held that the wrapping material was specially manufactured for the buyer.

Now the phrase "Applying this definition" modifies something in the sentence: the court.

Rule 2	**Keep the Subject and Verb Close Together**

Researchers have established that readers cannot understand a sentence until they have located both the subject and the verb. In addition, readers have difficulty remembering the subject if it is separated from the verb by more than seven words. If there are more than seven words between the subject and the verb, the reader must go back and relocate the subject after finding the verb.

The lesson to be learned from this research is that, as a writer, you should try to keep your subject and verb close together.

EXAMPLE 1

The **court** in *Colorado Carpet Installation, Inc. v. Palermo*, 668 P.2d 1384 (Colo. 1983), a case involving the sale of carpet, **held** that the goods were not specially manufactured because no special dyeing or weaving was required and because the carpet was not cut to specified shapes.

Even without the full citation, this sentence is difficult to read.

EXAMPLE 2

The **court** in *Colorado Carpet,* a case involving the sale of carpet, **held** that the goods were not specially manufactured because no special dyeing or weaving was required and because the carpet was not cut to specified shapes.

The sentence reads more smoothly if the subject (court) is placed next to the verb (held).

EXAMPLE 3

In a case involving the sale of carpet, the **court held** that the goods were not specially manufactured because no special dyeing or weaving was required and because the carpet was not cut to specified shapes. *Colorado Carpet Installation, Inc. v. Palermo,* 668 P.2d 1384 (Colo. 1983).

For more information on the distance between subjects and verbs, see section 22.4.

Rule 3	**Put Old Information at the Beginning of the Sentence and New Information at the End**

Sentences, and the paragraphs that they create, make more sense when the old information is placed at the beginning of sentences and the new information is placed at the end. When this pattern is used, the development progresses naturally, from left to right, without unnecessary backtracking.

EXAMPLE 1

The McKibbins had purchased the Reutlinger Mansion with the intention of **restoring** it. **As part of this restoration,** the McKibbins wanted to replicate the original rugs, which were beige with a twelve-inch maroon strip around the perimeter and the family emblem woven in at one-foot intervals.

Old information	*New information*
The McKibbins had purchased the Reutlinger Mansion	with the intention of restoring it.
As part of this restoration,	the McKibbins wanted to replicate . . .

EXAMPLE 2

Unlike *Flowers,* in our case, it is only the Reutlinger family flower and not the Reutlinger name that is woven into the carpet. Furthermore, the flower is not particularly unusual; the wholesaler was able to sell the rugs to a third party with little or no difficulty.

Old information	*New information*
Unlike *Flowers,*	in our case, it is only the Reutlinger family flower and not the Reutlinger name that is woven into the carpet.
Furthermore, the flower	is not particularly unusual; the wholesaler was able to sell . . .

Note how this rule is consistent with dovetailing. (See sections 5.22 and 21.3.)

Rule 4	**Vary Both the Length of Your Sentences and the Sentence Patterns**

Even if writing is technically correct, it is not considered good if it isn't pleasing to the ear.

EXAMPLE 1

We represent Beaver Custom Carpets (BCC). BCC is a specialty carpet firm that helps businesses obtain specialty carpets. BCC has been in business for one year.

The McKibbins purchased the Reutlinger Mansion earlier this year. They wanted to restore the mansion to its original condition.

The McKibbins contacted BCC in June of this year. They asked BCC if it could obtain rugs matching the rugs that were originally in the mansion. BCC contacted its manufacturer. The manufacturer told BCC that it could produce the rugs. Although standard dyes could be used, special weaving would be required.

In the above example, the writing is not pleasing because the sentences are similar in length and because, except for the last sentence, each sentence follows the same pattern (subject-verb-object). Although short, uncomplicated sentences are usually better than long, complicated ones, the use of too many short sentences results in writing that sounds sophomoric. As the following example illustrates, the passage is much better when the writer varies sentence length and pattern.

EXAMPLE 2

We represent Beaver Custom Carpets (BCC), a specialty carpet firm that helps businesses obtain specialty carpets. BCC has been in business for one year.

Earlier this year, the McKibbins purchased the Reutlinger Mansion. They wanted to restore the mansion to its original condition and then use it as a bed and breakfast.

> In June of this year, the McKibbins contacted BCC, asking BCC whether it could obtain rugs matching the rugs that were originally in the mansion. After contacting its manufacturer, BCC told the McKibbins that it could obtain the rugs. Although standard dyes could be used, special weaving would be required.

For more on sentence construction see Chapters 21 and 22.

b. Write Concisely and Precisely

The editing stage is also the red pen stage. Working from hard copy, go back through the draft, making sure that you have used language consistently and precisely and crossing out unnecessary words and phrases. (For a more complete discussion see sections 23.1 and 23.2.)

1. Conciseness

Although writing sentences with strong subject-verb units eliminates much unnecessary language, you also need to take your red pen to such throat-clearing expressions as "it is expected that . . ." and "it is generally recognized that . . ." and to redundancies like "combined together" and "depreciate in value." (See sections 23.2.5 and 23.2.7.) In the following example, language that should be deleted has been crossed out.

EXAMPLE

> ~~It is also important to note that~~ unlike the carpet in the *Colorado Carpet* case, in our client's case identical-looking rugs were not available at other carpet ~~outlet~~ stores. The rugs in question were one-of-a-kind. They were made to fit specific rooms, and they were specially woven. Our case is more like the *Flowers* case. Like the wrapping material in *Flowers,* the rugs were personalized: The Reutlinger family flower is as unique ~~and distinctive~~ as any company name or logo and, as a result, rugs with the flower woven into them are of little or no value to a third party.

In addition, more often than not you can reduce a sentence to a clause, a clause to a phrase, and a phrase to a word. (See section 23.2.9.)

Reducing a Sentence to a Clause

`EXAMPLE`

Original

This rule was applied in the *Flowers* case. In the *Flowers* case, the court held that R-P Packaging had a valid cause of action against Flowers. Flowers had asserted that the Statute of Frauds barred R-P's claim for payment. However, it was found that wrapping material manufactured by R-P was to the size required by Flowers and was imprinted with Flowers' name and unique artwork. The court further concluded that the paper was personalized for Flowers and of little value to a third party.

Rewrite

Applying this rule, the *Flowers* court denied Flowers' motion to dismiss, ruling that R-P's claim was not barred by the Statute of Frauds. Because the wrapping material had been personalized with Flowers' name and unique artwork, it was of little value to a third party.

Reducing a Clause to a Phrase

`EXAMPLE`

Original

R-P Packaging, which is a company that produces wrapping materials, sought to enforce an oral contract for wrapping material that had Flowers' name and unique artwork printed on it.

Rewrite

R-P Packaging, a company that produces wrapping materials, sought to enforce an oral contract for wrapping material imprinted with Flowers' name and unique artwork.

Reducing a Phrase to a Word

EXAMPLE

Original

It is not likely that BCC would have produced rugs duplicating those in the Reutlinger Mansion when the mansion was originally built in the absence of the McKibbins' calling and placing an order for such rugs.

Rewrite 1

It is unlikely that BCC would have produced these unique rugs unless it had been requested to do so.

Rewrite 2

BCC probably would not have produced these unique rugs unless it had been requested to do so.

---

2. Preciseness

Equally important is preciseness. You must select the correct term and then use that term consistently. For example, do not use the term "holding" to refer to something that is not in fact the court's holding and, once you have labeled something as an "element," do not later refer to it as a "requirement" or "factor." (See section 23.1.4.)

EXAMPLE

In denying the motion to dismiss, the trial court held that the first requirement, that the goods be specially manufactured for the buyer, was not met because the element requires a judgment that the goods were personalized.

In this example, in misusing the words "held" and "judgment," the writer demonstrates his or her lack of understanding of the judicial process. In deciding a motion, a court "rules," not "holds," and a judgment is entered not on a single element, but at the close of the case. In addition, the writer switches from "requirement" to "element," leaving the reader wondering whether the terms refer to the same or to different things.

You must also look carefully at your subject-verb-object units to make sure that the subject goes with the verb and the verb with the object.

EXAMPLE 1

Although the court might argue that the exception does not apply because BCC is in the business of manufacturing custom goods, such an argument would be inconsistent with the language of the statute and the decisions of other courts.

EXAMPLE 2

In the absence of a written contract, the goal behind the exception has been established when the goods themselves provide evidence that a contract was indeed formed.

In the first example, the writer has the court arguing: "the court might argue." Although courts "state," "find," "rule," and "hold," they rarely "argue." Only the parties argue. In the second example, the writer states that "the goal" "has been established" when in fact he or she wants to say the "exception applies" or "enforcement of the contract is consistent with the legislature's intent in enacting the exception." (See section 23.1.6.)

c. Correct Errors in Grammar and Punctuation

For a moment, imagine that you have received the following letter from a local law firm.

Dear Student:

Thank you for submitting an application for a position as a law clerk with are firm. Your grades in law school are very good, however, at this time we do not have any positions available. Its possible, however, that we may have a opening next summer and we therefore urge you to reapply with us then.

Sincerely,

Senior Partner

No matter how bad the market is, most students would not want to be associated with a firm that sends out a five-line letter containing three major errors and several more minor ones. Unfortunately, the reverse is also true. No matter how short-handed they are, most law firms do not want a law clerk who has not mastered at least the basic rules of grammar and punctuation. Most firms cannot afford a clerk who makes careless errors or one who lacks basic writing skills.

Consequently, at the editing stage you need to go back through your draft, correcting errors. Look first for the errors that potentially affect meaning (misplaced modifiers, incorrect use of "which" and "that") and for errors that the well-educated reader is likely to notice (incomplete sentences, comma splices, incorrect use of the possessive, lack of parallelism). Then look for the errors that you know, from past experience, you are likely to make.

§5.23.2 Proofreading

Most writers learn the importance of proofreading the hard way. A letter, brief, or contract goes out with the client's name misspelled, with an "or" where there should have been an "and," or without an essential "not." At a minimum, these errors cause embarrassment; at worst, they result in a lawsuit.[1]

To avoid such errors, treat proofreading as a separate step in the revising process. After you have finished revising and editing, go back through your draft, looking not at content, organization, or sentence style, but for errors. Have you written what you intended to write?

Proofreading is most effective when it is done on hard copy several days (or when that is not feasible, several hours) after you have finished editing. Force yourself to read slowly, focusing not on the sentence, but on the individual words in the sentence. Is a word missing? Is a word repeated? Are letters transposed?

Note

You can force yourself to read slowly by covering up all but the line you are reading, by reading from right to left, or by reading from the bottom of the page to the top.

Also force yourself to begin with the sections that caused you the most difficulty or that you wrote last. Because you were concentrating on content or were tired, these sections probably contain the most errors.

Finally, when you get into practice, make it a habit to have a second person proofread your work. Not only will such a person see errors that

---

[1] See, for example, *Emter v. Columbia Health Services,* 63 Wash. App. 378, 819 P.2d 390 (1991).

you did not, he or she is also less likely than you to "read in" missing words. Although you are responsible for every word that goes out under your name, a trusted proofreader is worth his or her weight in chocolate bars.

§5.23.3   A Note About Citations

As a legal writer, you have an extra burden. In addition to editing and proofreading the text, you must also edit and proofread your citations to legal authorities.

At the editing stage, focus on selection and placement of citations. Is the authority that you cited the best authority? Did you avoid string cites (the citing of multiple cases for the same point)? Have you included a citation to authority for every rule stated? Did you include the appropriate signal? Have you over- or under-emphasized the citation? (You emphasize a citation by placing it in the text of a sentence; you de-emphasize it by placing it in a separate citation sentence.)

In contrast, at the proofreading stage focus on the citation itself. Are the volume and page numbers correct? Are the pinpoint cites accurate? Have you included the year of the decision and any subsequent history? Is the spacing correct?

For a complete discussion of citations, see Chapter 17.

Checklist for Editing the Discussion Section

I.   Editing

- The attorney can understand the sentences after reading them only once.
- In most sentences, the writer has used the actor as the subject of the sentence.
- In most sentences the subject and verb are close together.
- The writer has used the passive voice when he or she wants to emphasize what was done rather than who did it or when the passive voice facilitates dovetailing.
- In most sentences, the old information is at the beginning of the sentence and the new information is at the end.
- The writer has varied both sentence length and sentence structure so that each sentence flows smoothly from the prior sentence.
- The writing is concise: When appropriate, sentences have been reduced to clauses, clauses to phases, and phrases to words.
- The writer has used language precisely: The writer has selected the correct term and used that term consistently.
- The memorandum is grammatically correct.
- The memorandum is correctly punctuated.

II. Proofreading

- The memorandum has been proofread.

§5.24   THE FINAL DRAFT

The final draft of the memo looks like this.

EXAMPLE

To: Connie Krontz

From: Thomas McMurty

Date: September 28, 1993

Re: Beaver Custom Carpets, File No. 93-478

Whether oral contract for three rugs is enforceable under UCC Statute of Frauds exception for specially manufactured goods when the rugs have the Reutlinger family flower woven into them at one-foot intervals.

Statement of Facts

Our client, Beaver Custom Carpets (BCC), wants to know whether it can enforce an oral contract for three rugs that were manufactured to the buyers' specifications.

The buyers, Mr. and Mrs. McKibbin, first contacted BCC in June of this year, asking whether BCC could replicate the original rugs in the Reutlinger Mansion, which Mr. and Mrs. McKibbin were refurbishing and turning into a bed and breakfast. Around the perimeter of each rug was a twelve-inch maroon strip; in the center was beige carpet with the Reutlinger family flower woven into the carpet at one-foot intervals.

After examining a picture of the rugs, BCC called its manufacturer. The manufacturer told BCC's sales representative that it could produce the rugs. Although the looms would have to be specially set, standard dyes could be used. On June 19, the sales representative sent the McKibbins a proposal setting out the specifications and the price, $16,875.

On June 29, Mrs. McKibbin called the sales representative and told him that she and her husband wanted to purchase the rugs. The next day, the salesperson ordered the rugs from the manufacturer. A written contract was not sent to the McKibbins.

On August 4, Mrs. McKibbin called BCC and told the sales representative that because her husband had fallen from the roof of the mansion, they were canceling their order. BCC called its manufacturer the same day. Unfortunately, the rugs had already been completed, and BCC was forced to accept delivery of the rugs at a cost of $13,500.

On August 15, BCC sent the McKibbins a bill for the proposal price of the rugs. Last week, BCC received a letter from the McKibbins' attorney stating that because the contract was not in writing, it was not enforceable under the UCC Statute of Frauds.

BCC sold the rugs to a wholesaler on September 1 for $10,000. BCC has done business with this wholesaler on only one prior occasion. Similar rugs are not available from other carpet stores.

BCC is a specialty carpet firm that specializes in custom work. It has been in business for only one year and is in financial trouble.

Question Presented

Under the UCC Statute of Frauds exception for specially manufactured goods, is an oral contract for the sale of rugs enforceable when (1) the rugs were manufactured to the buyers' specifications, (2) the same rugs are not available at other outlets, (3) the buyers told the seller that they did not want the rugs after the rugs had been completed, and (4) the seller sold the rugs to a wholesaler with whom it had done business on one prior occasion?

Brief Answer

Probably. Although the formal requirements of the Statute of Frauds are not met, the contract is probably enforceable under the exception for specially manufactured goods: To produce the rugs, the manufacturer had to specially set its looms, and the rugs were sold not to a retail customer but to a wholesaler at a loss.

Discussion

Even if the formal requirements of the UCC Statute of Frauds are not met, a contract is enforceable if the goods were specially manufactured. The applicable portion of the statute reads as follows.

> (3) A contract which does not satisfy the requirements of subsection (1) but which is valid in other respects is enforceable
>> (a) if the goods are to be specially manufactured for the buyer and are not suitable for sale to others in the ordinary course of the seller's business and the seller, before notice of

repudiation is received and under circumstances which reasonably indicate that the goods are for the buyer, has made either a substantial beginning of their manufacture or commitments for their procurement; . . .

Colo. Rev. Stat. § 4-2-201(3)(a).

Specially manufactured goods are exempt from the writing requirement because the very nature of the goods serves as a reliable indication that a contract was indeed formed. When the goods conform to the special needs of a particular buyer and are not, therefore, suitable for sale to others, not only is the likelihood of a perjured claim diminished, but denying enforcement of such a contract would impose a substantial hardship on the aggrieved party. *Impossible Electronics Techniques, Inc. v. Wackenhut Protective Systems, Inc.,* 669 F.2d 1026, 1037 (5th Cir. 1982).

Consequently, if we can establish (1) that BCC specially manufactured the rugs for the McKibbins, (2) that BCC was not able to resell the rugs in the ordinary course of its business, (3) that the rugs had been completed before BCC received the McKibbins' notice of repudiation, and (4) that the evidence reasonably indicates that the rugs were for the McKibbins, the contract will be enforceable.

1. Specially Manufactured for the Buyer

The first requirement is that the goods be specially manufactured for the buyer. Although the term "specially manufactured" is not defined in the statute, the Colorado Supreme Court has held that it refers to the nature of the goods and not to whether the goods were made in the usual course of the seller's business. *Colorado Carpet Installation, Inc. v. Palermo,* 668 P.2d 1384, 1390 (Colo. 1983). *Accord, Impossible Electronics Techniques, Inc. v. Wackenhut Protective Systems, Inc.,* 669 F.2d 1026, 1037 (5th Cir. 1982).

In the only Colorado case discussing the exception for specially manufactured goods, the Colorado Supreme Court held that carpeting that was available from other carpet outlets and that had not been cut to unusual shapes or subjected to special dyeing, weaving, or other procedures was not specially manufactured. *Colorado Carpet v. Palermo,* 668 P.2d 1384 (Colo. 1983). In contrast, in a Virginia case, the Virginia Supreme Court held that wrapping material imprinted with the buyer's name and unique artwork and cut to the buyer's specifications was "specially manufactured because the wrapping material was personalized and of little value to a third party." *Flowers Baking Co. of Lynchburg, Inc. v. R-P Packaging, Inc.,* 329 S.E.2d 462, 464 (Va. 1985).

In the present case, we will argue that the rugs were specially manufactured for the buyer. Relying on the plain language of the statute, we will argue that the rugs were in fact specially manufactured: BCC had to make special arrangements with the manufacturer and, to produce the rugs, the manufacturer had to specially set its looms.

We will also contrast the facts in our case to the facts in *Colorado Carpet.* Unlike *Colorado Carpet,* in our case, identical rugs are not available from other carpet outlets. The rugs in question are one-of-a-kind: They were made to fit specific rooms, and special weaving was required. Our case is more like *Flowers.* Like the wrapping material, the rugs were personalized. The Reutlinger family flower is as distinctive as any company name or logo and, as a consequence, rugs with such a flower woven into them are of little value to a third party.

Finally, we can argue policy. In this instance, the rugs themselves are evidence that a contract was formed. BCC probably would not have produced rugs matching the original rugs in the Reutlinger Mansion had there not been a contract. In addition, if the court does not enforce the contract, BCC, a small business, will suffer a substantial loss.

The McKibbins will try to distinguish the facts in our case from the facts in *Flowers.* Unlike *Flowers,* in our case it is only the Reutlinger family flower and not the Reutlinger name that is woven into the rugs. Furthermore, the flower is not particularly unusual; the wholesaler was able to sell the rugs to a third party with little or no difficulty.

The McKibbins' best argument is, however, a policy argument. They can argue that under the UCC, oral contracts should be the exception rather than the rule. Thus, a seller whose only business is custom or specially manufactured goods should not be exempt from the Statute of Frauds simply because its goods are specially manufactured. For, if all of such a seller's goods are custom, a written contract will never be necessary and written contracts will become the exception and not the rule. In addition, the McKibbins can argue that a seller who deals in only custom goods is just as likely to fabricate a contract for custom goods as is a seller who deals in ready-made merchandise.

We can respond to such an argument by citing *Wackenhut,* a case in which the seller sold custom closed-circuit television cameras. In holding that the cameras were specially manufactured, the court said the fact that the seller is in the business of manufacturing custom-designed and made goods does not necessarily preclude a finding that the goods are specially manufactured. *Id.* at 1037.

The court will probably find that the rugs were specially manufactured for the McKibbins. The rugs were not available from other outlets and, to produce the rugs, the manufacturer had to specially set its looms. Although BCC is in the business of producing custom carpets, it is not likely that it would have produced rugs with the Reutlinger family flower woven into them unless it had been requested to do so.

2. Not Suitable for Sale to Others in the Ordinary Course of the Seller's Business

Conclusion

Although the formal requirements of the UCC Statute of Frauds are not met, the contract between BCC and the McKibbins is probably enforceable under the exception for specially manufactured goods.

We should be able to prove the first element, that the rugs were specially manufactured for the McKibbins. The rugs were made to the McKibbins' specifications: The manufacturer specially set its looms to weave the Reutlinger family flower into the rugs.

We should also be able to prove the second element, that the goods are not suitable for sale in the ordinary course of BCC's business. BCC's ordinary course of business is selling carpets to retail customers, not wholesalers.

The third element, that there had been a substantial beginning prior to repudiation, and the fourth element, that the evidence reasonably indicates that the goods were for the McKibbins, are also not in dispute. The rugs had been completed at the time Mrs. McKibbins canceled the order, and the family flower is evidence that the goods were for the McKibbins.

Because it is likely that a court would enforce the contract, we should advise BCC to pursue this action. We can either contact the McKibbins' attorney and attempt to settle the matter or file a complaint.

Chapter 6

The Opinion Letter

What happens to an objective memorandum once it is completed? In some instances, the attorney uses it to prepare for a meeting with the client. The attorney reads the memo and then conveys the information to the client orally. More frequently, however, the attorney uses the memorandum to write an opinion letter to the client.

This was the situation in the BCC case. After studying the memorandum, the attorney wrote a letter to Mr. Beaver, the owner of Beaver Custom Carpets.

Question

Why are more and more attorneys putting their advice in writing?

In writing this letter, the attorney took the information contained in the memorandum and repackaged it so that it better met the needs of its new audience: the client. A memorandum is written to a particular audience (the attorney) for a particular purpose (to help the attorney evaluate the case and advise the client); an opinion letter is written to a different audience for a different purpose.

§6.1 AUDIENCE

Although the primary audience for an opinion letter is the client, there may be a secondary audience. The letter may be read not only by the client but also by an interested third party or, in some cases, by the other side. Consequently, in writing the letter, you must write for both the client and for anyone else who may read the letter.

§6.2 PURPOSE

For a moment, assume that the audience is the client and no one else. In writing to that client, what is your purpose? Is it to inform? To persuade? To justify the bill? To keep the client? Should you be giving the client only your conclusions, or should you be giving the client the information that he or she needs to reach his or her own conclusions?

Your role is determined, at least in part, by your state's Rules of Professional Conduct. The following rules are representative.

Rule 1.4 Communication . . .

(b) A lawyer shall explain a matter to the extent reasonably necessary to make informed decisions regarding the representation.

Rule 1.13 Client Under a Disability

(a) When a client's ability to make adequately considered decisions in connection with the representation is impaired, whether because of minority, mental disability or for some other reason, the lawyer shall, as far as reasonably possible, maintain a normal client-lawyer relationship with the client.

Rule 2.1 Advisor

In representing a client, a lawyer shall exercise independent professional judgment and render candid advice. In rendering advice, a lawyer may refer not only to law but to other considerations such as moral, economic, social, and political factors that may be relevant to the client's situation.

Question

How would you write the following letters?

1. A letter to a banker who wants to discharge an employee with AIDS. On the basis of your research, you have determined that a discharge based on the fact that the employee has AIDS would violate state law. There may, however, be ways of getting around state law.

2. A letter to a person with Alzheimer's disease who wants to know the tax consequences of giving real estate valued at $400,000 to his son.

3. A letter to a college-educated woman who is divorcing her spouse about her rights to marital property. The woman, who was

abused, has told you that she wants you to make the decisions for her. What would you tell the client if you believe the husband's offer is fair? unfair?

———————

§6.3   CONVENTIONS

Just as convention dictated the content and form of the objective memorandum, convention also dictates the content and form of the opinion letter. Most opinion letters have (1) an introductory paragraph identifying the issue and, most often, the attorney's opinion; (2) a summary of the facts on which the opinion is based; (3) an explanation of the law; (4) the attorney's advice; and (5) a closing sentence or paragraph. Note the similarities between the objective memorandum and the opinion letter.

Objective Memorandum	*Opinion Letter*
heading	name
	address
	file reference
	salutation
question presented	introductory paragraph
brief answer	opinion
statement of facts	summary of facts on which opinion is based
discussion section	explanation
conclusion	advice
	closing

§6.3.1   The Introductory Paragraph

In writing the introductory paragraph, you have two goals: to establish the appropriate relationship with the reader and to define the issue or goal. In addition, you will often include substantive information. When the news is favorable, you will almost always want to set out your opinion in the introductory paragraph.

Because the introductory paragraph is so important, avoid "canned" openings. Do not begin all of your letters with "This letter is in response to your inquiry of . . ." or "As you requested . . . ." Instead of beginning with platitudes, begin by identifying the topic or issue. Compare the following examples.

EXAMPLE 1

This letter is in response to your inquiry of September 10, 1993. I have now completed my research and have formed an opinion. The issue in your case is whether you can enforce your "contract" with the McKibbins. It is my opinion that you can.

EXAMPLE 2

Since our visit two days ago, I have researched the Uniform Commercial Code's Statute of Frauds. Based on this research, I believe that your oral contract with the McKibbins is enforceable under the exception for specially manufactured goods.

EXAMPLE 3

I have researched your potential claim against the McKibbins, and I think that you will be pleased with the results.

The first two sentences of Example 1 could be used to open almost any letter. The sentences could have been typed into the computer, the attorney filling in the blanks with the appropriate information each time that he or she writes a letter. Because these types of sentences subtly suggest to the reader that he or she is just one more client to whom the attorney is cranking out a response, most successful attorneys avoid them. Instead, like the authors of the Examples 2 and 3, they personalize their openings.

§6.3.2 Statement of the Issue

Although you need to identify the issue, you do not want to include a formal issue statement. The under-does-when format used in office memos is inappropriate in an opinion letter.

In deciding how to present the issue, keep in mind your purpose, both in including a statement of the issue and in writing the letter itself. You are including an issue statement because you want the client to know that you were listening and because you want to protect yourself. Thus, you include a statement of the issue for both rhetorical and practical reasons. You use it to establish the relationship with the client and to limit your liability.

Look again at the examples above. In each, how did the writer present the issue?

In Example 1, the attorney was explicit in setting out the issue. He states: "The issue in your case is whether you can enforce your 'contract' with the McKibbins." The issue statement is not as readily identified in Examples 2 and 3. Instead of setting out the issue, the writers simply identify the topic that they researched.

Question

Which approach is better? Why? When?

§6.3.3   Opinion

The client is paying you for your opinion. It is, therefore, essential that you include your opinion, or conclusion, in the letter.

When the news is good, you will usually put your opinion in the introductory paragraph; having had his or her question answered, the client can then concentrate on the explanation. You may, however, want to use a different strategy when the news is bad. Instead of putting your opinion "up front," you may choose to put it at the end, hoping that having read the explanation, the client will better understand the conclusion.

Whatever your opinion, present it as your opinion. Because you are in the business of making predictions and not guarantees, never tell the client that he will or will not win. Instead, present your opinion in terms of probabilities: "The court will probably find that the goods were specially manufactured." "It is not likely that you would win on appeal."

§6.3.4   Summary of the Facts

There are two reasons for including a summary of the facts. As with the statement of the issue, the first is rhetorical: You want the client to know that you heard his or her story. The second is practical. You want to protect yourself. Your client needs to know that your opinion is based on a particular set of facts and that if the facts turn out to be different, your opinion might also be different.

Just as you do not include all of the facts in the statement of facts written for an objective memorandum, you do not include all of the facts in an opinion letter. Include only those that are legally significant or that are important to the client. Because the letter itself should be short, keep your summary of facts as short as possible.

§6.3.5 Explanation

Under the rules of professional responsibility, you must give the client the information that he or she needs to make an informed decision. It is essential, therefore, that you give not only your opinion but also the basis for your opinion. The explanation section is not, however, just a repeat of the discussion section from your memorandum. It is usually much shorter and much more client-specific.

When the explanation requires a discussion of more than one or two issues, you will usually want to include a roadmap. (See section 5.22.1.) Before beginning your explanation, outline the steps in the analysis.

EXAMPLE 1

As a general rule, only written contracts are enforceable. Because your contract was not in writing, it will be enforceable only if the court finds that the exception for specially manufactured goods applies. For this exception to apply, we must prove that the rugs were "specially manufactured," that they were not suitable for sale in the ordinary course of your business, and that you had . . .

EXAMPLE 2

If you decide to go to trial, the court must decide two questions. The first is whether your actions constitute an assault. If the court finds that they do, it must then determine whether Mr. Hoage was damaged. For you to be held liable, both questions must be answered affirmatively.

Having outlined the steps, you can then discuss each step in more detail.

The amount of detail will depend on the question, the subject matter, and the client. Although there are exceptions, as a general rule, do not set out the text of the statute or include specific references to cases. Instead, just tell the client what the statutes and cases say, without citation to authority.

After explaining the law, do some basic application of law to fact. If a particular point is not in dispute, explain why it isn't; if it is in dispute, summarize each side's arguments. The difference between the analysis in an objective memorandum and in an opinion letter is a difference in degree, not kind. In each instance, give the reader what he or she needs — nothing more and nothing less.

§6.3.6   Advice

When there is more than one possible course of action, include an advice section in which you describe and evaluate each option. For example, if there are several ways in which your client could change its business operations to avoid liability, describe and evaluate each of those options. Similarly, if your client could choose negotiation over arbitration or arbitration over litigation, describe and evaluate each option. Having described the options, you can then advise the client as to which option you think would be in his or her best interest.

§6.3.7   Concluding Paragraph

Just as you should avoid canned openings, also avoid canned closings. Instead of using stock sentences, use the concluding paragraph to affirm the relationship that you have established with the client and to confirm what, if anything, is to happen next. What is the next step and who is to take it?

§6.3.8   Warnings

Some firms will want you to include explicit warnings: They will want you to tell the client that your opinion is based on the facts currently available and that your opinion might be different if the facts turn out to be different, or that your opinion is based on current law. Other firms believe that these warnings, when set out explicitly, set the wrong tone. Because practice varies, determine which approach your firm takes before writing the letter.

Note

In writing your letter you can use the modified semi-block format, the full block (the date, the paragraphs, and the signature block are not indented), or the modified block (paragraphs are not indented but the date and signature block are). For examples of each format, see *Webster's Legal Secretaries Handbook* 298-305 (1981).

§6.4   WRITING STYLE

It is not enough that the law be stated correctly and that your advice be sound. The client must be able to understand what you have written.

As with other types of writing, a well-written letter is one that is well organized. As a general rule, you will want to present the information in the order listed above: an introductory paragraph in which you identify the issue and give your opinion followed by a summary of the facts, the explanation of the law, your advice, and a concluding sentence or paragraph. You will also want to structure each paragraph carefully, identifying the topic in the first sentence and making sure that each sentence builds on the prior one. Transitions are also important. Use them to keep your reader on track and to make the connections between ideas explicit.

Also take care in constructing your sentences. You can make the law more understandable by using concrete subjects and verbs and relatively short sentences. When longer sentences are needed, manage those sentences by using punctuation to divide the sentence into shorter units of meaning.

Finally, remember that you will be judged by the letter you write. Although clients may not know whether you have the law right, they will know whether you have spelled their name correctly. In addition, most will note other mistakes in grammar, punctuation, or spelling. If you want to be known as a competent lawyer, make sure that your letters provide the proof.

§6.5 TONE

In addition to selling competence, you are selling an image. As you read each of the following letters, picture the attorney who wrote it.

EXAMPLE   **LETTER A**

Dear Mr. and Mrs. McDonald:

This letter is to acknowledge receipt of your letter of February 17, 1993, concerning your prospects as potential adoptive parents. The information that you provided about yourself will need to be verified through appropriate documentation. Furthermore, I am sure that you are cognizant of the fact that there are considerably more prospective adoptive placements than there are available adoptees to fill those placement slots.

Nonetheless, I will be authorizing my legal assistant to keep your correspondence on file. One can never know when an opportunity may present itself and, in fact, a child becomes unexpectedly available for placement. If such a opportunity should arise, please know that I would be in immediate contact with you.

Very sincerely yours,

Kenneth Q. Washburn, III
Attorney at Law

EXAMPLE   **LETTER B**

Dear Bill and Mary,

    Just wanted you to know that I got your letter asking about adopting a baby. I can already tell that you two would make great parents. But, as you probably know, there are far more "would be" parents out there than there are babies.

    But I don't want you to lose hope. You might be surprised. Your future little one may be available sooner than you think. It has happened before! And you can be sure that I'll call you the minute I hear of something. Until then, I'll have Marge set up a file for you.

                              All the best,

                              Ken Washburn

EXAMPLE   **LETTER C**

Dear Mr. and Mrs. McDonald:

    Your letter about the possibility of adopting a baby arrived in my office yesterday. The information in your letter indicates that you would be ideal adoptive parents. However, I am sure that you realize that there are more couples who wish to adopt than there are adoptable babies. For this reason, you may have to wait for some time for your future son or daughter.

    Even so, occasionally an infant becomes available for adoption on short notice. For this reason, I will ask my legal assistant to open a file for you so that we can react quickly if necessary. Because we do not know exactly when an infant will become available, I recommend that we begin putting together the appropriate documentation as soon as possible. In the meantime, please know that I will call you immediately if I learn of an available infant who would be a good match for you.

                        Sincerely,

                        Kenneth Washburn

Questions

    1. How does your image of Mr. Washburn change from letter to letter? In each letter, which words or phrases are key in creating an

image of Mr. Washburn? How might you explain the difference in content among the three letters?

2. How do you think Mr. and Mrs. McDonald will respond to each of the letters? If you were Mr. or Mrs. McDonald, in what types of cases would you want the Mr. Washburn of letter A to represent you? of letter B? of letter C?

3. Why might an attorney elect to adopt the writing style of letter A? letter B? Is letter C the "perfect" letter?

Checklist for Critiquing the Opinion Letter

I.   Organization

- The information has been presented in a logical order: The letter begins with an introductory sentence or paragraph that is followed, in most instances, by the attorney's opinion, a summary of the facts, an explanation, the attorney's advice, and a concluding paragraph.

II.   Content

- The introductory sentence identifies the topic and establishes the appropriate relationship with the client.
- The attorney's opinion is sound and is stated in terms of probabilities.
- The summary of the facts is accurate and includes both the legally significant facts and the facts that are important to the client.
- The explanation gives the client the information that he or she needs to make an informed decision.
- The options are described and evaluated.
- The concluding paragraph states who will do what next and sets an appropriate tone.

III.   Writing

- The client can understand the letter after reading it once.
- When appropriate, the attorney has included roadmaps.
- The paragraph divisions are logical, and the paragraphs are neither too short nor too long.
- Signposts and topic sentences have been used to tell the client where he or she is in the explanation and what to expect next.
- Transitions and dovetailing have been used to make clear the connections between sentences.
- In most sentences, the writer has used the actor as the subject of the sentence.
- In most sentences, the subject and verb are close together.
- The writer has used the passive voice when he or she

wants to emphasize what was done rather than who did it or when the passive voice facilitates dovetailing.

- In most sentences, the old information is at the beginning of the sentence and the new information is at the end.
- The writer has varied both sentence length and sentence structure so that each sentence flows smoothly from the prior sentence.
- The writing is concise: When appropriate, sentences have been reduced to clauses, clauses to phrases, and phrases to words.
- The writer has used language precisely: The writer has selected the correct term and used that term consistently.

Chapter 7

Trial and Appellate Briefs

§7.1 AN INTRODUCTION TO ADVOCACY

Advocacy is not something unique to the law. As small children, we acted as advocates when we tried to persuade our parents to buy us a particular toy or to stay up past our bedtime; as teenagers, we perfected the art as we tried to persuade our parents to buy us the latest fashions, to stay out past our curfews, or to let us use the family car.

As the following example illustrates, we knew the standard "moves" long before we came to law school.

Jon, a 17-year-old junior, wants to use his father's sports car for the junior prom. Because he knows that persuading his father will be difficult, Jon plans his strategy carefully. During the week before he makes his request, Jon is on his best behavior. He is easy to get along with, does his homework without being nagged, and even volunteers to mow the lawn.

When he finally approaches his father, he begins by setting the stage. He subtly reminds his father of how mature and reliable he has become and then begins talking about Sarah, his date for the prom, and about the importance of the event. Isn't Sarah beautiful and intelligent? Isn't your junior prom something you remember for the rest of your life?

He then poses the question. He isn't asking for himself; he is asking for Sarah. Wouldn't it be so much nicer for Sarah if he could take her to the prom in his father's sports car rather than the family's other car, which shows the effect of years of hauling kids from one event to another?

When his father doesn't immediately agree, Jon launches into his first argument. Although Jon's father has said that neither Jon nor his older brothers can drive the sports car, Jon knows that there have been exceptions. Both of Jon's older brothers were allowed to drive the car to their proms. Thus, Jon's version of the rule is not that he and his brothers cannot drive the car but that they can drive the car only on prom nights.

Jon supports his argument by reminding his father that both of his older brothers used the sports car for their proms. Although his father acknowledges that this is true, he distinguishes the cases. Both of Jon's brothers had excellent driving records, while Jon has had two speeding tickets. Thus, Jon's father's version is not that the children can drive the sports car only on prom nights but that a child can drive the car on prom night provided that he has a good driving record.

Instead of accepting defeat and walking away, Jon tries a couple of other approaches. He begins by conceding that in the past he did not have a good driving record. Recently, however, his driving record has been very good. In the last nine months, he has not had any tickets. Thus, his argument is that, in fact, he falls within the rule set out by his father. Because he currently has a good driving record, he should be allowed to use the sports car on prom night.

Jon also tries a couple of policy arguments. If his parents want to promote safe driving, he should be rewarded for his recent behavior. In addition, his parents can promote participation in social activities that they approve of by allowing him to use the car.

He also refers his father to the decision of the family's neighbors, the Morgans. Although the Morgans' son David has a worse driving record than Jon, the Morgans have told David that he can use their Lincoln Continental for the prom.

Persuading a trial or appellate court is not that much different from persuading a parent. In both instances, the appeals that work best are those that have been carefully planned.

§7.1.1   Presenting the Facts in a Favorable Light

The good advocate begins with a statement of the facts, doing what he or she did intuitively as a child: presenting the facts in the light most favorable to his or her side. Is Jon the immature and reckless driver he was nine months ago, or has he matured? Is the defendant a sexual psychopath who attacks young women in broad daylight or a devoted new husband working his way through college? Depending on which characterization the court believes, the plaintiff wins or loses.

§7.1.2   Asking the Right Question in the Right Way

The advocate then moves to the question itself. As most advocates have learned, getting the right answer is often a function of asking the right question. Jon knew this when he asked his father for the car. Does his father really want Sarah to go to the prom in a junker? The same is true in other cases. If you were the judge, how would you rule after reading the first of the following two issue statements? After reading the second?

EXAMPLE 1

Do electric light equipment and chandeliers become fixtures when they are attached in the usual manner to the walls and ceiling of a dwelling?

EXAMPLE 2

Should a chandelier and sidelights that have belonged to a family for thirty years and that have been moved by the family from house to house four times become fixtures in the last house when the family had no intention that they should remain with the house?

In some cases, the fact and issue statements are enough to persuade the court. In these instances, the arguments simply provide the support for the already reached conclusion. In other cases, like Jon's above, the arguments must also persuade.

§7.1.3 Selecting the Right Arguments

Courts can be persuaded by a variety of arguments: plain language or factual arguments, arguments based on analogous cases, or policy arguments. The trick is in knowing which argument or arguments to make and when to make them.

The answer can usually be found by putting yourself in the position of the decision-maker. How does the parent see his or her role? What is it that he or she values? Similarly, how does a trial or appellate judge see his or her role and what does he or she value?

Although the answers will vary from decision-maker to decision-maker, most urban trial judges see themselves as being on the front line, a small platoon holding off chaos. Their job is to apply existing law, deciding cases quickly and making decisions that will not result in unfavorable headlines or reversals on appeal. Thus, the arguments that work best are those based on established law. A trial court is much more likely to find that a case fits within an existing rule than it is to create a new one.

In contrast, supreme court justices are more likely to see themselves as protectors, either of the language of the constitution, the rights of states or individuals, or of a particular set of values. As a general rule, they are more interested in the law that a case creates than the case itself. As a consequence, a supreme court justice may be more easily persuaded by policy arguments than by factual arguments or arguments based on analogous cases.

It is not, however, enough to know in general what the typical trial or appellate judge values. The good advocate also knows the values motivating the particular decision-maker before whom he or she will be arguing. What is Jon's father more interested in promoting, Jon's social life or safe driving? Does the judge before whom you will be arguing a criminal case believe that the United States Supreme Court has gone too far in protecting the rights of criminal defendants? How will your judge, herself a working mother, respond to an argument that it would be in the child's best interest to grant custody to a nonworking mother? Not only must the arguments that the advocate makes be sound, they must be consistent with the decision-maker's own values.

§7.1.4 The Power of Reputation and Conviction

Two other characteristics distinguish the good advocate. First, since before Aristotle, advocates have known the importance of their own reputation. By being on good behavior for the week before making his request, Jon demonstrated that he knew the importance of his own reputation both to the merits of his argument and to his ability to present that argument successfully. So it is with attorneys. Although judges do not decide cases based on who the attorney is, they take more seriously arguments presented by attorneys with good reputations and view more skeptically those by attorneys whose professional reputations are tarnished. Thus, the good advocate is always prepared, does not step over the line between advocacy and misleading the court, and concedes those points that he or she cannot or need not win.

Second, the good advocate understands the power of his or her own conviction. The reason teenagers are so often successful in persuading their parents is that they believe completely (if sometimes unreasonably) in the point they are arguing. For attorneys, it is often more difficult to develop the same level of conviction. After all, attorneys don't always get to pick their cases. Even so, a judge is unlikely to accept an argument if the attorney, its advocate, doesn't believe in it. Thus, the good advocate always finds something in the case on which to hang his or her conviction: If the advocate doesn't believe in the individual case, he or she may find conviction in the principle behind it or in the system itself.

Thus, the good advocate is a person who knows not only the law and the standard moves but also people and what persuades them. He or she looks at the case not just through his or her own eyes but also through the eyes of the parties and the court.

Question

The following statement was set out in your information packet at the beginning of the semester.

> If a paper is turned in after the time it is due, a late penalty of one full letter grade will be imposed for every twenty-four-hour period that the assignment is late. For example, if a paper receiving a grade of B is turned in two hours after it is due, the grade on the paper will be reduced from a B to a C.
>
> Extensions will be granted only when requested in advance and when illness or an emergency has substantially interfered with the student's ability to complete the assignment on time.

In explaining this policy, the professor stated that the policy existed for two reasons: She wanted to simulate the constraints that the students would encounter in practice (in practice, sanctions may be imposed if deadlines are not met), and she wanted to be fair to students who met the deadlines.

You know of two instances in which students turned in their briefs late. In the first, the student was involved in a serious automobile accident while driving to school to turn in her brief. The accident occurred at 9:00 a.m.; the brief was due at 1:00 p.m.; the brief was turned in at 3:00 p.m. In this instance, the professor waived the late penalty.

In the second case, the student underestimated the amount of time that it would take to have the brief copied. As a result, the brief was turned in ten minutes late. In this instance, the professor did not waive the late penalty.

You completed writing the brief at 10:00 p.m. on the day before it was due. Unfortunately, when you began to print it out, your hard disk crashed, and you lost your entire twenty-five-page brief. Although you worked all night trying to recreate the brief, your brief was one hour late. Because you thought that you might make the deadline, you did not call the professor to request an extension.

How would you argue your case?

§7.2   TYPES OF BRIEFS

The brief is one of the attorney's most powerful tools. In an age of crowded dockets and noisy courtrooms, the attorney's voice is most clearly heard in the quiet of the judge's chambers. A good brief can persuade the court to dismiss the case or grant a motion for summary judgment, keep key evidence from the ears of the jury, or reverse a lower court's ruling. If the brief does not persuade, it is unlikely that the oral argument will.

Unfortunately, goods briefs are hard to write. Writing one requires knowledge, skill, and insight. You must understand both your audience and your purpose in writing to that audience; you must know the facts of your case as well as the law; and you must be a skilled writer.

In this section, we describe two types of briefs: briefs in support of or in opposition to a motion and appellate briefs.

§7.2.1   Briefs in Support of or in Opposition to a Motion

Much of litigation is motions practice. As a litigator, you will file motions for temporary relief, to compel discovery, to suppress evidence, for summary judgment, and to set aside a verdict. Although not all of these motions will be supported by briefs, many will.

a.   Audience

In writing a brief in support of or in opposition to a pretrial or trial motion, you are writing to the trial judge. Although your brief may be read by your client, opposing counsel, and perhaps an appellate court, the trial judge is your primary audience.

Sometimes you will know to which trial judge you are writing: either the case will have been assigned to a specific judge or a specific judge will have requested the brief. At other times, you will not know which judge will read your brief: The case will not be assigned until the day the motion is heard.

When you find yourself in the first situation, write for the specific judge. Learn that judge and then craft a brief that he or she will find persuasive. In the latter case, write a brief that will play well before any of the judges who may end up reading it. Although a particular approach might work well with one judge, do not risk it if it might offend others.

Whichever situation you find yourself in, keep the judge's schedule in mind. It is not uncommon for a judge hearing civil motions to hear 20 motions in a single day. If in each of these cases each party filed a 20-page brief, the judge would have 800 pages to read. Given this work-load, it is not surprising that for most judges the best brief is the short brief. Make your point and then stop.

Also keep in mind the constraints placed on trial judges. Because trial judges must apply mandatory authority, they want to know what the law is — not what you think it should be. Thus, whenever possible, make the easy argument. Set out and apply existing law.

EXHIBIT 7.1   **Format of a Brief in Support of or Opposition to a Pretrial Motion**

IN THE SUPERIOR COURT FOR KING COUNTY, STATE OF WASHINGTON

STATE OF WASHINGTON,	)	
	)	
Plaintiff,	)	NO. 93-3456
	)	
v.	)	BRIEF IN
	)	SUPPORT OF MOTION
DEAN EUGENE PATTERSON,	)	TO SUPPRESS
	)	
	)	
Defendant.	)	
	)	

This memorandum is submitted in support of Defendant's motion to suppress the show-up, line-up, and in-court identifications of Beatrice Martinez and Chester Clipse.

<u>Statement of the Case</u>

[See section 7.5.]

<u>Question Presented</u>

[See section 7.6.]

<u>Argument</u>

[See sections 7.7, 7.8, and 7.9.]

<u>Prayer for Relief</u>

[See section 7.10.]

Attorney's Signature

---

b. Purpose

In writing to a trial judge, you have two goals: to educate and to persuade. You are the teacher, teaching the judge both the applicable law and the facts of the case. But your position is not neutral. As you teach, you must persuade. You want the judge to take an action on your client's behalf.

c. Conventions

The format of the brief will vary from jurisdiction to jurisdiction and sometimes within a jurisdiction from judge to judge. Consequently, you must check the local rules. Is there a local rule specifying the format of the brief? If not, have individual judges established their own guidelines?

In the county in which the *Patterson* case was tried, there are no local rules governing the format of a brief. There are, however, conventions. Exhibit 7.1 shows the sections that are included.

§7.2.2 Appellate Briefs

Although you will probably write fewer appellate briefs than briefs in support of motions, when you write an appellate brief the stakes are high: You will be trying to regain what has been lost or to keep what has already been won.

a. Audience

The audience for a brief in support of a motion differs significantly from the audience for an appellate brief. In writing a brief in support of a motion, you are writing to a single judge; to win, you need persuade only that one judge. In contrast, in writing an appellate brief you are writing to a panel of three or more judges. You cannot, therefore, tailor your brief to one particular judge. If you are to be successful, you must persuade a majority of the judges hearing the case.

In addition, you have another audience. In most appellate courts, the first reader of the brief is the judge's law clerk. Each appeal is assigned to a particular judge; that judge then assigns the case to one of his or her law clerks. After reading the briefs and independently researching the issues, the clerk prepares a memo to the judge (often called a bench memo) that summarizes the law and each side's arguments and, in some courts, recommends how the appeal should be decided. Because law clerks can shape how the judges view the appeal, they are some of your most significant readers.

You also need to keep in mind that like the trial judges, appellate judges have substantial workloads. Most intermediate appellate judges hear between 100 and 150 cases a year, writing opinions in approximately one third of those cases. If each party submits a 50-page brief, each judge would read between 10,000 and 15,000 pages in the course of a year. Length is, therefore, once again an issue. One of the most common complaints from judges is that briefs are too long. Appellate judges want briefs that are brief.

Also like the trial judges, appellate judges must work within certain constraints, the most significant of which is the standard of review. Although in some cases the court's review is *de novo,* in most cases the review is more limited: Instead of making its own determination, the appellate court looks to see if the trial judge abused his or her discretion or if there is substantial evidence to support the jury's verdict. (See section 7.11.)

In addition, in some cases the appellate court is itself bound by mandatory authority. State intermediate courts of appeal are bound by the decisions of the state's supreme court, and both the state courts and the United States Court of Appeals are bound by decisions of the United States Supreme Court.

b. Purpose

Once again, your purpose is twofold: to educate and to persuade. In addition to explaining the facts and the law, you must explain what happened at the trial court level, persuading the appellate court that the decision of the trial court was correct and should be affirmed; that the trial court's decision was wrong and that the case should, therefore, be remanded back to the trial court; or that the trial court's decision should be reversed.

c. Conventions

The format of appellate briefs is governed by rule. These rules are usually quite specific and govern everything from the types of briefs that may be filed to the sections that must be included, the type of paper, and citation form. These rules are discussed in more detail in section 7.12, Preparing the Appellate Brief.

§7.3 State v. Patterson

In this section, we set out the facts of the case that is used as the example for this chapter.

§7.3.1 The Assault

The first time the station wagon drove by, 17-year-old Beatrice Martinez barely noticed it. She had gotten a late start and was hurrying to get to work by 5:00 p.m. She became more alert a few minutes later. As she turned the corner from Howell onto Belmont, Martinez saw the older model red station wagon once again. This time, the car was moving slowly, and the driver was staring at her.

When his car was just a few feet from her, the driver pulled in front of Martinez, blocking the sidewalk. As Martinez watched, he got out of his car, walked one or two steps toward her, and then, reaching into his pocket, pulled out a gun and pointed it at her. Martinez screamed, took a step back, and ran.

At about the same time, Chester Clipse turned the corner onto Belmont. He had just gotten off work and was walking from the bus stop to his apartment, which was in the middle of the block. When he was thirty to forty feet away, Clipse saw a red station wagon pull into his parking stall. His curiosity aroused, Clipse watched as the driver got out of the car and walked toward a young woman on the sidewalk. A moment later, his curiosity turned to horror. As he watched, Clipse saw the man pull a gun and point it at the woman. Without thinking, Clipse yelled "hey" and simultaneously pushed a nearby teenager, Richard Martin, out of harm's way. Startled by the scream, the gunman pushed the gun back into his pocket, ran back to his car, and drove away.

Although both Clipse and Martin tried to get the car's license number, they were unable to do so. They were, however, able to flag down a passing parking enforcement officer who, after being given a description of the car, went looking for it. Several minutes later, the officer found a car similar to the one Clipse and Martin had described. The car was parked on Howell Street, and a man was taking a brown paper bag from the passenger side of the car. As the parking officer drove by, the man nodded and smiled.

While the parking enforcement officer was looking for the car, Clipse took Martinez up the stairs to his landlady's apartment. Clipse called the police and then went back downstairs.

§7.3.2 The Show-up

The police arrived about ten minutes later. After talking to Clipse, Martin, and the parking enforcement officer, the police had the station wagon impounded. They then followed Clipse upstairs, where they interviewed both Clipse and Martinez.

Clipse and Martinez gave the police similar descriptions. Martinez told the police that her assailant was a medium-built white male with blondish-brown wavy hair, a dark jacket, and glasses; Clipse described the gunman as being a white male about 5'9" tall and weighing between 180 and 185 pounds with brown curly hair, a dark green jacket, and glasses. Martinez estimated that her assailant was in his early forties; Clipse guessed that he was in his late thirties.

After talking to Martinez and Clipse, the officers asked Martinez whether she wanted a ride home. Too shaken to go to work, Martinez accepted the offer.

While Clipse watched from his landlady's apartment balcony, Martinez accompanied the officers down the stairs and into the police car. As Officer Hume pulled out, Officer Moffat noticed a pedestrian wearing a green denim jacket. Turning to Martinez, Moffat asked, "Does that look like the guy?" Although unable to see the man's face, Martinez told the officer that from behind, it did. A moment later, the police car pulled next to the man, and Officer Moffat asked, "Is he the one?" Shaken, Martinez answered yes.

Upon hearing her response, the police officers stopped the car and got out. As they did so, they heard Clipse yelling. He was standing on the balcony of his landlady's apartment pointing at the same pedestrian. The officers motioned Clipse back inside and then, while Martinez watched from inside the police car, questioned and took the pedestrian into custody.

§7.3.3   The Arrest

After sending Martinez back to the landlady's apartment, the officers placed the pedestrian, Dean Patterson, in the police car and took him to the county jail, where he was fingerprinted and booked.

Martinez and Clipse arrived at the station a short time later. The statements that they gave to the police are set out on pages 274 and 275.

The police interviewed Patterson the next day. In the presence of his attorney, Patterson gave the statement set out on page 276.

§7.3.4   The Arraignment

On August 15, the State filed an information charging Patterson with assault with a deadly weapon.

At his arraignment, Patterson pleaded not guilty. Unable to post bail, Patterson was held in jail.

§7.3.5   The Line-up

A line-up was conducted on August 17. The officer in charge of the line-up, Detective Gerdes, selected the participants from the inmate population at the county jail. Although all four of the men who were selected were of medium build, three were taller than Patterson and one was shorter. In addition, although all four men had brown hair, Patterson's hair was noticeably shorter. All four were in their early twenties.

Despite protests from Terry Kellogg, the representative from the public defender's office who had been assigned to observe the line-up, the line-up proceeded with Patterson in position number five. In that position, Patterson was the first to enter and, because of a change in procedure, the last to leave.

Although neither Richard Martin nor the parking enforcement officer was able to identify Patterson, Beatrice Martinez and Chester Clipse made positive identifications. See Exhibits 7.2 and 7.3.

§7.3.6   Planning the Defense

The Public Defender's office filed its Notice of Appearance and Request for Discovery on August 27. Soon thereafter, Patterson's attorney, Sarah Fisher, began developing her strategy.

Her first step was to talk to her client. Fisher began the interview by explaining her role and the charge that had been filed. She then told Patterson about his options: they could proceed to trial; she could try to arrange a plea bargain; or, if she could not arrange a plea bargain,

Form 9.28   **SEATTLE POLICE DEPARTMENT**   Case Number

CSS 21.122   93-49721

DATE 08-13-93   **TIME** 6:05 P.M.   **PLACE** Police Headquarters

STATEMENT OF: Beatrice Marie Martinez

     My name is Beatrice Marie Martinez, and I live at 801 East Harrison #202, and my phone number is 329-9679. I am 17 years old. Today, at 4:30 p.m. I left my apartment, beginning my walk to work; Angelo's Restaurant at 5th & Pike. I walked southbound on Harvard to Denny Way, then westbound on Denny Way to Boylston. I again walked southbound on Boylston, until I came to East Howell Street. As I was walking westbound on East Howell Street, a red, old station wagon was going eastbound, and it attracted my attention because it slowed down and the driver was looking at me. I didn't think much of it, and turned the corner, now walking southbound in the 1700 block of Belmont. As I turned the corner, I again saw the old red station wagon, coming northbound on Belmont. As I came to an apartment, the station wagon pulled in front of me, blocking the side-walk, and the driver kept looking at me. The driver jumped out of the car, and shouted "Hey." I looked at him, and he had what looked to me to be a .38, pointed at my stomach. I stepped back, and heard someone else yell "Hey," and I ran across the street and hid behind a wall. I also pushed buttons, trying to get someone to let me inside the apartment house. The man who appeared to be in his early 40s, white, 165-170 lbs., 5'7-8 blondish brown hair, wearing dark jacket, and glasses, jumped back into the station wagon, and took off down the street. A man ran up, and took me to his apartment to call police. The police came, and took a report and were taking me home, when I saw the man, walking in front of us. Police arrested him, and I again went back to the apartment, at the request of the police. I was brought downtown by the man who had the apartment, to give this statement. This is a true and correct statement, to the best of my knowledge.

STATEMENT
TAKEN BY: *Det. Al Gerdes*   **SIGNED:** *Beatrice Martinez*

WITNESS: **WITNESS:**

Form 9.28   **SEATTLE POLICE DEPARTMENT**   Case Number

CSS 21.122   93-49721

DATE 08-13-93   **TIME** 6:47 P.M.   **PLACE** Police Headquarters

STATEMENT OF: Chester Joseph Clipse

    My name is Chester Joseph Clipse, I'm a 19 year old white male. I live at 600 E. Olive St., Apt. 110. Today at about 4:50 p.m., I was walking home, and as I approached my apartment building, at Corner of E. Olive St. and Belmont, I saw a man in a red dodge wagon driving up the street slowly. He pulled into my parking stall, so I approached, to see what he was doing. He approached a girl, who was on the sidewalk, and she screamed. At this time, I saw the man had a gun, and I yelled "Hey." He turned, and ran to his car, putting the gun under his coat. The girl ran across the street, and the guy backed out, and took off down the street, northbound. At that moment, a meter maid came down street, and I flagged him down, telling him what happened. The meter maid took off after the man, and I took the girl to my apartment house to get her off the street. I went with officers and positively identified the car, which was parked in the 600 Block of E. Howell. The driver was a white man about late 30's or early 40's. He was about 5'9 or 5'10, and about 180-185 lbs. He had brown wavy hair, and was wearing a green outfit. After the officers had left, I saw him walking up the street, and I saw officers confront him. The officers sent me back inside with the girl.

    This is a true and correct statement to the best of my knowledge.

STATEMENT
TAKEN BY: Det. Al Gerdes   **SIGNED:** Chester Clipse

WITNESS: **WITNESS:**

Form 9.28   **SEATTLE POLICE DEPARTMENT**   Case Number

CSS 21.122   93-49721

DATE 08-14-93   **TIME** 3:22 P.M.   **PLACE** Police Headquarters

STATEMENT OF: Dean Patterson

On August 13, I worked my usual 11-7 shift as a security guard. When I got home, I went to bed and slept until about 1:00 p.m. At 1:30, my wife, a nurse at a nearby hospital, received a call asking her to come to work at 3:00 p.m. She told them that she could come in and, at about 2:45, I drove her to work. When I got back, I couldn't find a parking spot in front of our building and was forced to park almost a block away. Between 3:00 and 4:30 I did two loads of laundry, watched an old movie on T.V., and talked on the phone with both a friend, Karen Callendar, and my wife. I made my last trip to the laundry room at about 4:30 p.m.. On my way back, I decided to check my car to see how much gas I had. After I checked the gas, I moved the car to a parking spot right in front of our building. At about 5:30, I left the apartment and began walking toward the hospital, where I planned to join my wife at 6:00 for her dinner break. When I was about two blocks from our apartment, I was stopped and arrested. The gun that was found in my apartment is the gun that I was issued by the security company that I work for.

**STATEMENT
TAKEN BY:** Det. Al Gerdes   **SIGNED:** Dean Patterson

WITNESS: **WITNESS:**

**IN THE SUPERIOR COURT OF THE STATE OF WASHINGTON
FOR KING COUNTY**

STATE OF WASHINGTON,	)	
	)	
Plaintiff,	)	NO. 93-49721
	)	
vs.	)	INFORMATION
	)	
DEAN EUGENE PATTERSON,	)	
	)	
Defendant.	)	
	)	

I, Norm Mason, Prosecuting Attorney for King County, in the name and by the authority of the State of Washington, by this Information do accuse Dean Eugene Patterson of the crime of assault in the second degree, committed as follows:

That the defendant Dean Eugene Patterson, in King County, Washington, on or about August 13, 1993, did knowingly assault Beatrice Martinez, a human being, with a weapon and other instrument or thing likely to produce bodily harm, to-wit: a revolver;

Contrary to RCW 9A.36.021 (1)(C), and against peace and dignity of the State of Washington.

Norm Mason

NORM MASON
Prosecuting Attorney

Michael T. Frankel

Witnesses for state:

By Michael T. Frankel
MICHAEL T. FRANKEL
Chester Joseph Clipse
Assistant Chief Criminal Deputy
Beatrice Marie Martinez
Prosecuting Attorney
Richard Edward Martin
Terry William Hindman
William P. Moffat
Al Gerdes
Roy Moran

Information

EXHIBIT 7.2 **Line-up Identification of Beatrice Martinez**

Line-Up Document

SHOW-UP IDENTIFICATION
Seattle Police Department
Criminal Investigation Division

Form 9.3
CSS 21.53
Rev. 9-72

Case Number: _93-49721_

Date: _8-17-93_
Time: _1400_

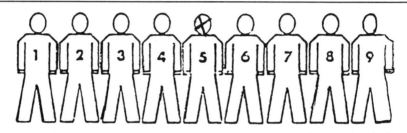

I have just witnessed a show-up consisting of _5_ person(s).

I identify the above number(s) _5_

the person(s) who _assaulted me_

(robbed me, assaulted me, etc.)

on _August 13_   _4:40_   at _1700 Belmont_
   (date)   (time)   (address)

The person(s) I have indicated above have been identified
to me as: _____
          Dean Patterson

Witness
   or
(Victim) _Beatrice Martinez_ _801 E. Harrison # 202_
        (Signature)   (address)
                                      _329-9679_
                                      (phone)

Statement taken by: _Det. Al Gerdes_ Witness: _____

Show-up prepared by: _"   "_   Location: _____

Photographs taken by: _Det. R. Reed_
                      (name)   (division)

Attorney present: _Jerry Kellogg_
                  (name)

Waiver signed: Yes _____   No _X_

EXHIBIT 7.3   **Line-up Identification of Chester Clipse**

Line-Up Document

Form 9.3
CSS 21.53
Rev. 9-72

SHOW-UP IDENTIFICATION
Seattle Police Department
Criminal Investigation Division

Case Number: _93-49721_   Date: _8-17-93_
        Time: _1400_

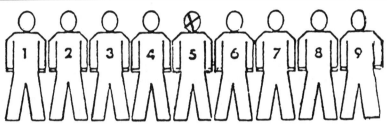

I have just witnessed a show-up consisting of _five_ person(s).

I identify the above number(s) _5_

the person(s) who _I saw attempt to assault a girl_
               (robbed me, assaulted me, etc.)

on _8/13/93_   _16:45_   at _600 East Olive Street_
  (date)   (time)   (address)

The person(s) I have indicated above have been identified
to me as: _____
     Dean Patterson

(Witness)
or
Victim: _Chester Clipse_, _600 East Olive Street_
    (Signature)   (address)   (phone)

Statement taken by: _Det. Al Gerdes_ Witness: _____

Show-up prepared by: _″   ″_   Location: _____

Photographs taken by: _Det. R. Reed_
         (name)   (division)

Attorney present: _Terry Kellogg_
       (name)

Waiver signed: Yes _____   No _X_

Patterson could plead guilty. Patterson told Fisher that he was not interested in a plea bargain. He was innocent, and he wanted to be vindicated.

Patterson also told Fisher a little bit about himself. He told her that he was a junior at the University and that he had only been married since May. He also told her that a year earlier he had been charged with rape. The charges had been dropped, however, when he passed a polygraph test and the complaining witness did not.

After listening, Fisher told Patterson that at this point they had only two options: She could try to get the State to voluntarily dismiss the charges, or she could try to get the identification evidence suppressed, thus forcing the State to dismiss the charges. Because a voluntary dismissal seemed unlikely, Patterson asked Fisher to pursue the second option.

Knowing what her client wanted, Fisher began to determine whether she had grounds for bringing a Motion to Suppress. She began with the law. Like most courts, the Washington courts apply the test set out in *Manson v. Braithwaithe*, 432 U.S. 98 (1972). Under the first part of this test, the defendant has the burden of showing that the identification procedure was unnecessarily suggestive. If the defendant meets this burden, the State then has the burden of showing that, under the totality of the circumstances, the reliability of the identification outweighs the suggestiveness of the police procedure.

Fisher then reviewed the file. Was there evidence indicating that the police procedures were suggestive? And if there was, under the totality of the circumstances, were the identifications reliable? On the basis of her review, Fisher determined that she had an argument. Show-ups are inherently suggestive, and there were problems with the line-up. In addition, the witnesses' opportunity to view was limited, and their descriptions were inaccurate. She just might be able to persuade the court to suppress both the line-up and show-up identifications.

Question

Why wouldn't it be enough to get the line-up identifications suppressed? Just Martinez's identifications suppressed? Just Clipse's identifications suppressed?

Having determined that she had grounds for filing a Motion to Suppress, Fisher's next step was to file the motion. She did this as part of her omnibus application. (See item 10 of the application).

IN THE SUPERIOR COURT OF WASHINGTON FOR
KING COUNTY

STATE OF WASHINGTON,   )
)
        Plaintiff,   )   NO. 93226

```
                    )
                    )
                    )        OMNIBUS APPLICATION OF
         v.         )        DEFENDANT
                    )
DEAN PATTERSON,     )
                    )
                    )
                    )
    Defendant       )
_____ )
```

COMES NOW the defendant by and through his attorney and makes the following motions, requests and representatives.

A.   The defendant may call as witnesses:

Name   Address   Phone
Gail Patterson, Seattle   363-2594
Karen Callender, Seattle, 584-1360

B.   The following exhibits, obtained or prepared as indicated, may be offered at trial by the defendant:

Exhibit   Source

None

C.   The results of the following scientific tests, experiments or comparisons may be offered by the defendant:

None

D.   The general nature of the defenses that may be raised at trial are the following:

   A.   Alibi defense _____
   B.   Incompetency to stand trial _____
   C.   Mental responsibility in any respect _____
   D.   Entrapment
   E.   Other:

COMES NOW the defendant pursuant to CrR 4.5 and makes the applications or motions checked off below:

_____   1.   To dismiss for failure of the indictment (or information) to state an offense.
_____   2.   To sever defendant's case and for separate trial.
_____   3.   To sever counts and for a separate trial.

_____ 4. To make more definite and certain by providing a Bill of Particulars.

__✓__ 5. For discovery of all oral, written or recorded statements made by defendant and all witnesses to investigating officers or to third parties and in the possession of the plaintiff.

__✓__ 6. For discovery of the names and addresses of all plaintiff's witnesses questioned in this matter.

__✓__ 7. To inspect all physical or documentary evidence in plaintiff's possession relating to this case.

_____ 8. To suppress physical evidence in plaintiff's possession because of (1) illegal search, (2) illegal arrest.

_____ 9. For a hearing under Rule 3.5.

__✓__ 10. To suppress evidence of the identification of the defendant.

_____ 11. To take the deposition of witnesses.

_____ 12. To secure the appearance of material witnesses at trial or hearing.

_____ 13. To inquire into the conditions of pretrial release.

That the Court Requires the Prosecutor:

__✓__ 14. To state —
   (a) If there was an informer involved;
   (b) Whether he will be called as a witness at the trial; and,
   (c) The name and address of the informer or claim the privilege.

__✓__ 15. To disclose all evidence within his knowledge or in plaintiff's possession, favorable to defendant or which tends to negate defendant's guilt as to the offense charged.

__✓__ 16. To disclose whether it will rely on prior acts or convictions of a similar nature for proof of knowledge or intent.

__✓__ 17. To advise whether any expert witness will be called, and if so, supply
   (a) Name of witness, qualifications and subject of testimony;
   (b) Report.

__✓__ 18. To supply any reports or tests of physical or mental examinations in the control of the prosecution.

__✓__ 19. To supply any reports of scientific tests, experiments, or comparisons and other reports to experts in the control of the prosecution pertaining to this case.

_____✓___ 20.   To permit inspection and copying of any books, papers, documents, photographs or tangible objects which the prosecution —
(a)   Obtained from defendant or belonging to the defendant, or
(b)   Which will be used at the hearing or trial.

_____✓___ 21.   To supply any information known concerning a prior conviction of persons whom the prosecution intends to call as witnesses at the hearing or trial.

_____✓___ 22.   To inform the defendant of any information he has indicating entrapment of the defendant.

_____✓___ 23.   To provide prior records on witnesses that may be called by the state at trial.

_____ 24.   To compel the prosecutor to hold a line-up.

_____ 25.   To allow the defendant to pose for a photograph in jail.

_____ 26.   To permit the defendant to compel examination, tests or comparisons of evidence in the prosecutor's control by experts of the defendant's selection.

Explain:

_____✓___ 27.   To indicate the relationship, if any, of the State's witnesses to the prosecuting authority.

_____ 28.   To indicate any electronic surveillance including but not limited to wiretapping of the defendant's premises or conversations to which defendant was a party and any record thereof.

_____✓___ 29.   To disclose any information which the prosecutor has indicating entrapment of the defendant.

_____✓___ 30.   To compel the prosecutor to attempt to cause such material or information in the knowledge, possession or control of other persons which would be discoverable if in the knowledge, possession or control of the prosecutor and relevant to the issue of innocence or guilt.

E.   A jury (   ) will not be waived
       (✓) may be waived
       (   ) jury of ____ will be waived.

F.   It is estimated the trial will last __2__ days.

DATED: This __11th__ day of __October, 1993__

Sara Fisher.

Attorney for Defendant

The evidentiary hearing on the Motion to Suppress was held on October 10. The State presented four witnesses: Beatrice Martinez, Chester Clipse, Detective Gerdes, and Terry Kellogg. Although the presiding judge, the Honorable Frank D. Schmit, could have ruled on the motion at the close of the hearing, he elected not to do so. Instead, he asked the parties to brief the issue and to appear two weeks later for oral argument.

In the following sections, sections 7.4 through 7.9, we walk you through the process that the attorneys went through in planning and writing the briefs.

§7.4   Planning the Brief

Good briefs don't just happen. They are planned. The planning begins with the theory of the case. Before beginning to write, the attorney selects both a legal theory and an approach that is emotionally appealing. This theory of the case then becomes the focus of the brief, every word, sentence, paragraph, and section supporting and fostering the development of that theory.

In the *Patterson* case, Patterson's options are limited. If he is to win the Motion to Suppress, he must establish both that the police procedures were impermissibly suggestive and that, under the totality of the circumstances, all of the identifications were unreliable. In addition, he must get the judge to view him sympathetically. He must persuade the judge that, like Martinez, he is a victim. His only crime was to be at the wrong place at the wrong time.

The State has more options. In arguing the law, it can argue either that the police procedures were not impermissibly suggestive or, even if they were, that under the totality of the circumstances the identifications are nonetheless reliable. In deciding which approach to take, the prosecutor selects the one he thinks will be both legally and emotionally appealing.

Thus, before they begin to write, both sides must decide what message they want to communicate and what image they want to create. With this message and image in mind, they can then draft the brief.

§7.5   Drafting the Statement of the Case

Never underestimate the importance of the facts. At both the trial court and the appellate court levels, it is the facts and not the law that usually determine the outcome.

§7.5.1   Creating a Context

The statement of the case does more than give the judge the facts of the case. It provides the context. Consider the following sentence:

EXAMPLE

He pulled out his gun and, at point-blank range, shot the woman in the head.

After reading this sentence, what is your reaction? Who is the "bad guy"? Who is the victim? For most, it is the gunman who is the bad guy. Having shot a woman at point-blank range, he is a cold-blooded killer who should be found guilty of murder.

Now read the following sentence.

EXAMPLE

Pushing his young son out of harm's way, he pulled out his gun and, at point-blank range, shot the woman in the head.

Although he has shot a woman, our gunman is no longer a cold-blooded killer; he is a father shooting to save his son. The context has changed, and our father is no longer the bad guy; he and his son are the victims.

Consider one final sentence.

EXAMPLE

Having stalked his victim for days, the gunman pushed his young son behind him, pulled out his gun and, at point-blank range, shot the woman in the head.

Do we still have a father shooting to save his son? The answer is no. Now we have a gunman who is worse than the cold-blooded killer in the first example: We have a man who shoots a woman in front of his own son. Another context, a different verdict.

In the *Patterson* case, context is equally important. Is Patterson a clean-cut newlywed who is working nights to put himself through college, or is he a misfit who attacks young women in broad daylight? Are Martinez and Clipse reliable witnesses, or are they two impressionable teenagers who have allowed themselves to be influenced by the police? Each attorney must get his or her client's story before the court.

§7.5.2 Selecting the Facts

Like the statement of facts in an objective memo, the statement of the case in a persuasive document such as a brief contains three types of facts: legally significant facts, emotionally significant facts, and background facts.

a. Legally Significant Facts

Most court rules require that the statement of the case be "fair." For example, Washington Rule on Appeal 10.4 requires a "fair statement of the facts"; California Rule on Appeal 13, an "accurate" "summary of material facts"; and Federal Circuit Rule 28, a "fair summary of facts relevant to issues presented for review." Thus, in writing the statement of the case, you must include all of the legally significant facts, both favorable and unfavorable.

b. Emotionally Significant Facts

You do not, however, need to include all of the emotionally significant facts. Although as a defensive move you may sometimes include an emotionally significant fact that is unfavorable, recharacterizing it or minimizing its significance, most of the time you will not. You will only include those emotionally significant facts that favor your client.

The harder question is how to handle emotionally significant facts that are unfavorable to the other side. Should you sling mud, or should you take a higher road, omitting any reference to those facts? The answer is that it depends: It depends on the fact, on the case, and on the attorney. If the case is strong and the fact's connection to the case is tenuous, most attorneys would not include the fact. If, however, the case is weak and the fact's connection is closer, many attorneys would include it, some using it as a sword, others much more subtly.

c. Background Facts

Background facts play a different role in persuasive writing than they do in objective writing. In an objective statement of facts, the writer includes only those facts that are needed for the story to make sense. In a persuasive statement of facts, you want to do more. You want to use background facts to create a favorable context.

§7.5.3 Selecting an Organizational Scheme

The next step is to select an organizational scheme. Should the facts be presented chronologically, topically, or in an organizational scheme that combines the two?

Unlike the objective statement of facts, in which the only selection criterion is logic, in writing a persuasive statement of the case there are two criteria: You want to select a scheme that (1) is logical and (2) allows you to present the facts in an order most favorable to the client.

In the *Patterson* case, the scheme that works best is chronological. Because there was only one event, the assault, and because the timing is significant, logic dictates that the facts be presented chronologically. A chronological scheme also allows both defense counsel and the State to present the facts in a favorable context. By starting the story early in the day, defense counsel can begin her statement of facts with facts that favor Patterson; similarly, by starting the story with the assault, the State starts with the facts that support its view of the case. See section 7.5.5(b) on use of positions of emphasis.

EXAMPLE

THE INTRODUCTORY PARAGRAPHS OF THE DEFENDANT'S STATEMENT OF THE CASE

On Monday morning, August 13, 1993, twenty-two-year-old Dean Patterson returned home from working the graveyard shift as a security guard at Seattle University, where he is also a student. He went to bed and slept until about one o'clock that afternoon. At about 2:30, his wife received a phone call asking her to come to work at the local hospital where she is employed as a nurse. She got ready, and Mr. Patterson dropped her off at the hospital at about 3:10.

At about 3:30, Mr. Patterson called his wife to find out how long she would have to work; they had plans to go to a movie with a friend that evening, and he wanted to find out if he would have to change them. At about 3:40, Patterson called the friend, telling the friend that his wife would have to work that evening. After talking for about ten minutes, Mr. Patterson and his friend decided that they would go to the movie by themselves.

At about 3:50, Mr. Patterson took a load of wash to the apartment complex laundry room. When he returned to the apartment, he watched part of an old movie. At about 4:20, Mr. Patterson went again to the laundry room, putting the laundry in the dryer. On his way back, he went outside to check his car for gas. In doing so, he noticed a parking spot much closer to his apartment and, after checking his gas, moved his car to that spot. After parking his car, he got out of the car and, because his driver's side door does not lock from the outside, walked to the passenger side to lock the doors. As he did so, he nodded to a parking enforcement officer who passed by.

By this time, it was 4:30, and Mr. Patterson decided to phone his wife again. They arranged to meet at 5:15 for her dinner break. Patterson cleaned up and left his apartment a little after five to walk to the hospital to meet his wife. He never made it.

EXAMPLE

THE FIRST PARAGRAPH OF THE STATE'S STATEMENT OF THE CASE

On Monday, August 13, 1993, seventeen-year-old Beatrice Martinez was assaulted with a deadly weapon. At a show-up thirty to forty minutes after the attack, Ms. Martinez positively identified the defendant, Dean E. Patterson, as her assailant. Four days after the assault, Ms. Martinez again positively identified Patterson as her assailant at a line-up conducted by the police.

---

§7.5.4   Writing a Persuasive Statement of the Case

Although the statement of the case must be fair, it need not be objective. As an advocate, you are not only permitted, but expected, to present the facts in the light most favorable to your client.

Compare, for example, the following excerpts from the Defendant's and the State's briefs. In both, the attorneys have included the legally significant facts, presenting those facts accurately and without argument. Each has, however, a goal in mind. While defense counsel wants to create the impression that Martinez had only a limited opportunity to view her assailant, the prosecutor wants to create the opposite impression. He wants the judge to believe that Martinez had a good opportunity to view him.

EXAMPLE

EXCERPT FROM THE DEFENDANT'S STATEMENT OF THE CASE

Ms. Martinez stated that she was walking down Belmont when a car that she had previously seen pulled in front of her and a man jumped out. Taking one or two steps toward her, the man suddenly pulled a gun out of his pocket. As soon as she spotted the gun, Martinez screamed, looked away, and then, crying hysterically, ran across the street. The entire encounter was over in one or two seconds.

EXAMPLE

EXCERPT FROM THE STATE'S STATEMENT OF THE CASE

Ms. Martinez was assaulted at approximately 4:30 p.m. on August 13, 1993.

As she walked north on Belmont, Ms. Martinez observed an older model red station wagon with a chrome luggage rack as it passed slowly by her. Moments later, the same car came down the street again. This time, the driver pulled his car in front of Ms. Martinez, stopping his car so that it blocked Ms. Martinez's path. As Ms. Martinez watched, the driver got out of his car and walked toward her. The man then took a gun from his coat pocket and pointed it at Ms. Martinez. Ms. Martinez stared at the gun, looked back up at her assailant, and then ran across the street to safety.

In crafting the above paragraphs, the attorneys used a number of persuasive techniques.

a.　*The Visual Image*

The visual image is often more powerful than the words themselves. Thus, the advocate must be concerned not only with the words but with how those words appear on the page.

In the example set out above, defense counsel wanted to emphasize that Martinez had only a short period of time to view her assailant. She chose, therefore, to keep the paragraph describing the assault short. In contrast, the prosecutor used a long paragraph to create the impression that a substantial period of time elapsed. Similarly, while defense counsel elected to use short phrases and sentences to speed up the sequence of events, the prosecutor elected to use longer ones to slow it down.

b.　*Airtime*

Just as listeners remember best the songs that get the most airtime, readers remember best the facts that get the most words. Consequently, favorable facts should be given considerable "airtime"; unfavorable ones should get little or no "play."

Look again at the example set out above. Note that while defense counsel dismisses Martinez's initial observations in just two words ("previously seen"), the prosecutor uses a full sentence ("As she walked north on Belmont, Ms. Martinez observed an older model red station wagon with a chrome luggage rack as it passed slowly by her").

c. Detail

Readers tend to remember events described in detail better than those that are described without it. The more detail, the more vivid the picture, and the more vivid the picture, the more memorable the picture. Consequently, you want to use detail, or the absence of detail, to your best advantage. Favorable facts should be described in detail; unfavorable ones, in only general terms.

The above examples illustrate the technique. Defense counsel says only that the man jumped out of a car that Martinez had previously seen. Because the fact is not favorable, the car is not described. In contrast, the prosecutor describes the car in detail: Martinez didn't just see a car, she "observed an older model red station wagon with a chrome luggage rack." The inference is that if Martinez is able to provide this much detail about the car, her opportunity to observe was good.

d. Word Choice

Words are powerful. Not only do they convey information, they also create images. Consider, for example, the words listed below. Although they all convey essentially the same information, their connotations are very different.

EXAMPLE 1

Says	Makes a statement
Alleges	Makes a controversial charge or statement without presentation of proof
Asserts	States or expresses positively
Affirms	States or expresses positively but with less force than *asserts*
Declares	Carries the approximate force of *asserts* but suggests a more formal statement
Claims	Maintains a position in the face of an argument
Maintains	Declares to be true
Avers	Declares in a positive or dogmatic manner
Argues	Implies intent to persuade an adversary through debate

---

EXAMPLE 2

Dean Patterson
Mr. Patterson
Dean
the young man
the defendant
the suspect
the accused
the man charged with the assault
the man charged with the assault of the seventeen-year-old
     girl

In the excerpts from the briefs, reproduced below, each side chose its words carefully. Note the words that are in boldface type.

EXAMPLE

EXCERPT FROM THE DEFENDANT'S STATEMENT OF THE CASE

Ms. Martinez **said** that she was walking down Belmont when a car that she had previously seen pulled in front of her, and **a man jumped out.** Taking one or two steps toward her, the man **suddenly pulled** a gun out of his pocket. As soon as she **spotted** the gun, Martinez screamed, looked away, and then, **crying hysterically,** ran across the street. The entire **encounter** was over in one or two seconds.

In writing her statement of facts, defense counsel selected words that convey the impression that events happened very quickly:

EXAMPLE

the man **jumped** out of the car

the man **suddenly pulled** a gun out of his pocket

As soon as she **spotted** the gun

The entire **encounter** was over in one or two seconds.

Question

Why did defense counsel use the word "stated" rather than "testified" and the phrase "crying hysterically" rather than just "crying" or just "hysterical"?

> **EXAMPLE**
>
> ### EXCERPT FROM THE STATE'S STATEMENT OF THE CASE
>
> Ms. Martinez was assaulted at approximately 4:30 p.m. on August 13, 1993.
>
> As she walked north on Belmont, Ms. Martinez **observed** an older model red station wagon with a chrome luggage rack as it passed slowly by her. Moments later, the same car came down the street again. This time, the driver pulled his car in front of Ms. Martinez, **stopping** his car so that it blocked Ms. Martinez's path. As Ms. Martinez **watched,** the driver **got out** of his car and **walked toward** her. The man then **took** a gun from his coat pocket and **pointed** it at Ms. Martinez. Ms. Martinez **stared** at the gun, **looked back up** at her assailant, and then ran across the street to safety.

In writing his statement of facts, the prosecutor took a different approach. He selected the following words because they create the impression that Ms. Martinez was somewhat calmer than the defense makes her out to be and that the opportunity to view was good.

> **EXAMPLE**
>
> Ms. Martinez **observed** an older model red station wagon
>
> As Ms. Martinez **watched,** the driver **got out** of his car and **walked toward** her.
>
> The man then **took** a gun from his coat pocket and **pointed** it at Ms. Martinez.
>
> Ms. Martinez **stared** at the gun, **looked back up** at her assailant

Questions

1. Why didn't the prosecutor introduce the paragraph with the phrase "Ms. Martinez stated . . . ."

2. If you were defense counsel, how would you have referred to Martinez and the assailant? Would you have used the same terms if you were the prosecutor?

———————

§7.5.5   Other Persuasive Techniques

a.   Point of View

Perhaps one of the most powerful persuasive devices is point of view. To create a favorable context, tell the story as the client would tell it.

When you want to emphasize what your client did, make your client the actor. Look again at the introductory paragraphs, noting the subject of each main clause.

———————

EXAMPLE 1

THE INTRODUCTORY PARAGRAPHS OF THE
DEFENDANT'S STATEMENT OF THE CASE

On Monday morning, August 13, 1993, twenty-two-year-old **Dean Patterson** returned home from working the graveyard shift as a security guard at Seattle University, where he is also a student. **He** went to bed and slept until about one o'clock that afternoon. At about 2:30, **his wife** received a phone call asking her to come to work at the local hospital, where she is employed as a nurse. **She** got ready, and **Mr. Patterson** dropped her off at the hospital at about 3:10.

At about 3:30, **Mr. Patterson** called his wife to find out how long she would have to work; **they** had plans to go to a movie with a friend that evening, and **he** wanted to find out if he would have to change them. At about 3:40, **Patterson** called the friend, telling the friend that his wife would have to work that evening. After talking for about ten minutes, **Mr. Patterson and his friend** decided that they would go to the movie by themselves.

———————

THE FIRST PARAGRAPH OF THE STATE'S STATEMENT OF THE CASE

On Monday, August 13, 1993, seventeen-year-old **Beatrice Martinez** was assaulted with a deadly weapon. At a show-up thirty to forty minutes after the attack, **Ms. Martinez** positively identified the defendant, Dean E. Patterson, as her assailant. Four days after the assault, **Ms. Martinez** again positively identified Patterson as her assailant at a line-up conducted by the police.

In these examples, the subjects of the main clauses are as follows:

Example 1	*Example 2*
Dean Patterson	Beatrice Martinez
he	Ms. Martinez
his wife	Ms. Martinez
she	
Mr. Patterson	
Mr. Patterson	
they	
he	
Patterson	
Mr. Patterson and his friend	

By using your client as the actor, you make it his or her story.

b. Positions of Emphasis

Readers tend to remember best the information that is presented at the beginning and at the end. Thus, in writing the statement of the case, try to place favorable facts at the beginning and the end of the fact statement, at the beginning and the end of paragraphs, and at the beginning and the end of sentences. Conversely, place less favorable facts in the middle of a sentence, paragraph, or fact statement.

Note

The position of emphasis within a sentence is determined in large part by the sentence's placement within the paragraph and section. If the sentence is the first sentence in a paragraph or section, the position of emphasis is at the beginning of the sentence. In contrast, if the sentence is the last sentence in a paragraph, the position of emphasis is the end of the sentence.

EXAMPLE 1

EXCERPT FROM THE STATE'S STATEMENT OF THE CASE

Ms. Martinez told the police that her assailant was a white male about 5′7″ tall, that her assailant had wavy blondish-brown hair, that her assailant appeared to be in his early forties, and that, at the time of the assault, her assailant was wearing a dark jacket and wire-rim glasses.

EXAMPLE 2

EXCERPT FROM THE DEFENDANT'S STATEMENT OF THE CASE

Because she was upset, Ms. Martinez was able to give the police only a general description of her assailant. She described him as being a short, white male with blondish-brown hair who was wearing glasses and a dark jacket. In addition, she told police that her assailant was in his early forties. Mr. Patterson is twenty-two years old.

In Example 1, the State wanted to de-emphasize the discrepancy between Martinez's statement regarding her assailant's age and Patterson's actual age. To do this, the prosecutor placed the fact in the middle of a sentence in the middle of a paragraph. In contrast, defense counsel wanted to emphasize the discrepancy. She did so by using the positions of emphasis: she placed the key facts at the end of sentences and the key sentence at the end of the paragraph.

c. Sentence Construction

In writing an objective memorandum, your primary concern is that your sentences be well written. As an advocate, you still want your sentences to be well written. However, you also want them to persuade. As a consequence, as you write each sentence, think about whether the sentence should be long or short, whether it should be written in the active or passive voice, and what information should be placed in the main, or independent, clause.

1. Sentence Length

Readers remember short sentences better than they do long ones. Therefore, if you want to emphasize a fact, place that fact in a short sentence. (See section 22.5.3.) Similarly, if you want to deflect attention from a particular fact, place the fact in a long sentence. Look again at the following examples.

EXAMPLE 1

EXCERPT FROM THE STATE'S STATEMENT OF THE CASE

Ms. Martinez told the police that her assailant was a white male about 5'7" tall, that her assailant had wavy blondish-brown hair, that her assailant appeared to be in his early forties, and that, at the time of the assault, her assailant was wearing a dark jacket and wire-rim glasses.

EXAMPLE 2

EXCERPT FROM THE DEFENDANT'S STATEMENT OF THE CASE

Because she was upset, Ms. Martinez was able to give the police only a general description of her assailant. She described him as being a short white male with blondish-brown hair who was wearing glasses and a dark jacket. In addition, she told police that her assailant was in his early forties. Mr. Patterson is twenty-two years old.

While the prosecutor uses one long sentence, defense counsel uses several short ones. The difference is striking. After reading the State's version, most readers remember only that Martinez described her assailant; they cannot recount the details of that description. Their reaction to the second example is very different. After reading it, readers recall the discrepancy in ages.

Note

In the examples set out above, the writers combined the two persuasive techniques just discussed: positions of emphasis and sentence length. You can do the same thing. To emphasize a fact, place it in a short sentence at the beginning or end of a section or paragraph block. Similarly, to de-emphasize a fact, bury it in the middle of a long sentence in the middle of a paragraph in the middle of a section.

2.   Active Voice and Passive Voice

You should also use the active voice and passive voice to your advantage, using the active voice when you want to emphasize what the actor did and the passive voice when you want to draw the reader's attention away from his or her actions. Consider the following examples.

EXAMPLE 1

Patterson assaulted Martinez.

EXAMPLE 2

Martinez was assaulted by Patterson.

EXAMPLE 3

Martinez was assaulted.

The prosecutor would want to use Example 1. By using Patterson as the actor, he emphasizes what Patterson did. In contrast, defense counsel would want to use Example 3. Example 1 is written in the active voice. The actor, Patterson, is used as the subject of the sentence. In contrast, Examples 2 and 3 use the passive voice. In Example 2, the actor is used as the object, and in Example 3, the actor is omitted.

Although in an objective memo Example 1 might be the best choice, in persuasive writing the answer is not that easy. While the State would want to use the active voice, thereby emphasizing that it was Patterson who assaulted Martinez, defense counsel would want to use the passive. (See section 22.1 for more on active voice and passive voice.)

A Final Note

As you write the statement of the case, remember that the facts must be presented without argument. You do not persuade by arguing. In fact, arguing facts has the opposite effect. When you argue the facts, you lose your credibility and, with it, your ability to persuade.

---

§7.5.6   Writing the Statement of the Case for an Appellate Brief

In writing the statement of the case for an appellate brief, you must comply with court rules. In most jurisdictions, this means that in addition to presenting a fair statement of the case you must also include (1) references to the record and (2) a procedural history.

a.   References to the Record

Most court rules require that each statement of fact be supported by a reference to the record. For example, Washington Rule on Appeal 10.4(a)(4) states: "Reference to the record must be included for each factual statement." References may be either to the Clerk's Papers (the documents filed with the clerk of the court, for example, the complaint or information, motions, written orders, findings of fact and conclusions of law, judgment and sentence); to the Verbatim Report of Proceedings (the trial transcript); or to an exhibit that was properly admitted. In some jurisdictions, failure to include references to the record may result in the striking (return) of the brief.

Note

The abbreviations that should be used are usually set out in the court rules. For example, in Washington, clerk's papers are designated using "CP," the verbatim report of proceedings is "RP," and exhibits are "Ex." See RAP 10.4(f).

---

b.   *Procedural History*

Court rules also often require a procedural history. In addition to describing the underlying event (for example, the assault), the writer must summarize the history of the case. What have been the relevant procedural actions to date?

The following example is from the State's appellate brief.

EXAMPLE   **EXCERPT FROM THE STATE'S APPELLATE BRIEF**

STATEMENT OF THE CASE

Procedural History

On August 13, 1993, the Defendant, Dean Eugene Patterson, was charged under Wash. Rev. Code § 9A.36.020(1) with the second-degree assault of Beatrice Martinez. CP 1. On October 11, 1993, Defendant filed a motion asking the court to suppress the identifications made at the time of the arrest and at a line-up four days later. CP 9. After an evidentiary hearing, Judge Schmit denied the motion. RP 43.

The case went to trial on October 21, 1993. RP 45. On October 25, 1993, a jury entered a guilty verdict. The Notice of Appeal was filed on November 15, 1993. CP 41.

Statement of Facts . . .

Note that in this example, the State does not set out all of the procedural facts. It sets out only those that are relevant to the appeal: the trial court's ruling on the motion, the jury's verdict, and the date the appeal was filed.

Also note that the procedural facts are set out in a separate section at the beginning of the statement of the case. In some jurisdictions, this is required by rule. In others, the advocate has more latitude. The procedural facts can be placed in a separate section at the beginning or at the end or integrated into the statement of facts.

Question

Why might a judge want the procedural facts set out in a separate section at the beginning of the statement of the case?

Checklist for Critiquing the Statement
of the Case

I. Organization

- The facts have been presented in a logical order (chronologically, topically).
- When possible, the facts have been presented in an order that favors the client.

II. Content

- The writer has included both the relevant procedural facts (procedural history) and the facts on which the case is based (statement of facts).
- All of the legally significant facts have been included.
- The emotionally significant facts that favor the client have been included.
- An appropriate number of background facts have been included.

III. Persuasiveness

- The writer has presented the facts so that they support the writer's theory of the case.
- The writer has begun the statement of facts by creating an appropriate context.
- The writer has presented the facts from the point of view that favors the client. (In telling the client's story, the writer has often used the client as the subject of the sentence.)
- Paragraph and sentence length have been adjusted to create the appropriate visual images.
- Favorable facts have been given more airtime than facts that do not support the client's position.
- Favorable facts have been described in detail; unfavorable facts have been described more generally.
- Words have been selected not only for their denotation but also for their connotation.
- The positions of emphasis have been used effectively. When possible, favorable facts have been placed at the beginning and end of the statement of the case, at the beginning and end of a paragraph, and at the beginning and end of a sentence.
- Short sentences and short paragraphs have been used to emphasize favorable facts; unfavorable facts have been placed in longer sentences in longer paragraphs.
- Favorable information has been emphasized by placing it in the main, or independent, clause; unfavorable facts have been placed in dependent clauses.
- The active and passive voices have been used effectively.

§7.6　Drafting the Question Presented

§7.6.1　Selecting the Lens

The question presented is the lens through which the court views the case. Select the correct lens, and chances are that the court will see the case as you do and rule in the client's favor.

Look, for example, at the questions presented from *Hishon v. King & Spaulding,* a 1982 case in which the United States Supreme Court was asked to decide whether law firms were subject to federal civil rights laws prohibiting discrimination in employment on the basis of sex, race, religion, or national origin.

Petitioner's Issue Statement

Whether King and Spaulding and other large institutional law firms that are organized as partnerships are, for that reason alone, exempt from Title VII of the Civil Rights Act of 1964, and are free (a) to discriminate in the promotion of associate lawyers to partnership on the basis of sex, race or religion; and (b) to discharge those associates whom they do not admit to partnership based on reasons of sex, race or religion under an established "up-or-out" policy.

Respondent's Issue Statements

Whether law partners organized for advocacy are entitled to constitutionally protected freedom of association.

Whether Congress intended through Title VII of the Civil Rights Act of 1964 to give the Equal Employment Opportunity Commission, a politically appointed advocacy agency engaged in litigation, jurisdiction over invitations to join law firm partnerships.

In *Hishon,* each side viewed the case through a different lens. For Petitioner, the issue was whether law firms are free to discriminate on the basis of sex, race, religion, or national origin. In contrast, Respondent saw two issues: (1) whether the partners in a law firm are entitled to their constitutionally protected right of freedom of association and (2) whether members of a politically appointed advocacy agency have the right to determine who is invited to join a law firm. The result was determined by the lens that the court selected.

The difficulty, of course, is in selecting the lens. How do you select just the right one? Unfortunately, there is no easy answer. Because selecting the lens is, at least in part, a creative act, there is no foolproof formula.

There are, however, some strategies you can try. Begin by looking at the case through the client's eyes. How does the client see the case? In the *Patterson* case, Patterson sees himself as an innocent victim — a man at the wrong place at the wrong time. In contrast, the State sees this case as another attempt to restrain the activities of the police: How can the police do their job if they can't stop and question a suspect?

Also study the analogous cases carefully. In the cases in which the courts suppressed identification evidence, how did the courts "present" the issue? Did they focus on the rights of the defendant? the police's abuse of its power? the discrepancies in the testimony? the unreliability of the witnesses? Make a similar study of the cases in which the court suppressed the identifications. In those cases, what lens did the court use?

Finally, brainstorm. From what other angles can you view the case? What other labels can you attach? In the *Hishon* case, the defendant had to break out of the structure established by the plaintiff. It simply could not argue that a law firm had a right to discriminate. To win, it had to recharacterize the case. This was not a case about discrimination; it was a case about freedom of association and the power of administrative agencies.

§7.6.2   Writing the First Draft: Selecting a Format

Most courts allow the advocate considerable latitude in selecting a format for the question. Although there should be a direct correlation between the issue statements and argumentative headings (if there is one question presented, there should be one main heading; if there are two questions presented, there should be two main headings), the advocate can state the question using the under-does-when format, the whether format, or several sentences. (See section 5.9.2.)

EXAMPLE   **"UNDER-DOES-WHEN" FORMAT**

Under Washington law, did the trial court act properly when it denied Defendant's Motion to Suppress when the police merely asked the victim whether a pedestrian looked like her assailant and when the victim observed her assailant on two occasions for several seconds in broad daylight from a distance of two or three feet?

In this example, the reference to the rule of law was omitted because it adds so little.

EXAMPLE   **"WHETHER" FORMAT**

Whether the trial court acted properly when it denied defendant's Motion to Suppress when the police merely asked the victim whether a pedestrian looked like her assailant and when the victim observed her assailant on two occasions for several seconds in broad daylight from a distance of two or three feet.

EXAMPLE　　**MULTISENTENCE FORMAT**

At approximately 4:30 p.m. on August 13, the victim noticed a man in an old red station wagon staring at her as he drove by. A few minutes later, the victim saw the station wagon drive by again. This time, however, the man pulled the car in front of the victim, blocking her path. The man then got out of the car and approached the victim. When he was two or three feet from her, he pulled a gun. The victim stared at the man for a moment and then ran. A short time later, the police asked the victim whether a pedestrian looked like her assailant. After looking closely at the pedestrian, the victim identified him as her assailant. Under these circumstances, did the trial court act properly when it denied Defendant's Motion to Suppress?

Note

Although you may use any format, once you select one, use it for each of your questions. Do not write one issue using the under-does-when format and another using the whether format. Also remember that you are not bound by your opponent's choices. You do not need to use the format that he or she used, and you do not need to have the same number of issues. Do not let your opponent dictate your strategy.

---

§7.6.3　Writing the Second Draft: Making the Question Presented Subtly Persuasive

The question presented should be subtly persuasive. After reading it, the judge should be inclined to rule in favor of the party who prepared the statement.

Two techniques can be used to make the question persuasive: (1) state the question so that it suggests the answer that supports your client's position and (2) present the facts that support that answer in the light most favorable to your client.

a. State the Question So That It Suggests a Favorable Answer

The question presented should be framed so that the question itself suggests the conclusion the advocate wants the court to reach. For example, Patterson's attorney would frame the legal question in terms of whether the court should grant the Motion to Suppress. In contrast, the prosecutor would frame the question in terms of whether the court should deny the motion.

EXAMPLE 1   **(FROM DEFENDANT'S BRIEF IN SUPPORT OF THE MOTION TO SUPPRESS)**

Whether the identification evidence should be suppressed when . . .

EXAMPLE 2   **(FROM THE STATE'S BRIEF IN OPPOSITION TO THE MOTION TO SUPPRESS)**

Should identification evidence be admitted when . . .

EXAMPLE 3   **(FROM APPELLANT'S BRIEF)**

Did the trial court err when . . .

EXAMPLE 4   **(FROM RESPONDENT'S BRIEF)**

Did the trial court act properly when . . .

---

b. Present the Facts in the Light Most Favorable to the Client

In addition to stating the question so that it suggests a favorable answer, the advocate needs to present the facts in the light most favorable to the client.

For example, to get Martinez's show-up identification suppressed, the defendant must persuade the court that the police procedures were unnecessarily suggestive and that Martinez's identification was unreliable. Accordingly, in writing the questions presented, defense counsel includes the facts that establish that the procedure was suggestive (instead of allowing Martinez to identify Patterson independently, the police pointed out Patterson and repeatedly asked the shaken Martinez whether he looked like her assailant). Similarly, defense counsel emphasizes the facts that establish that Martinez had a limited opportunity to view her assailant and that her description was inaccurate. Defense counsel also omits the unfavorable facts that at the time of the assault it was light and that Martinez was only a few feet from her assailant.

EXAMPLE 1   (FROM DEFENDANT'S BRIEF IN SUPPORT OF THE MOTION TO SUPPRESS)

Under the Fourteenth Amendment to the Constitution, should the court grant Defendant's motion to suppress Martinez's show-up identification when (1) the police pointed out Patterson to Martinez, repeatedly asking the shaken Martinez whether Patterson looked like her assailant and (2) during the second or two that Martinez viewed her assailant, her attention was focused on the gun and not on his face?

In contrast, the prosecutor downplays the police officer's questions, emphasizing instead that Martinez had a good opportunity to view her assailant.

EXAMPLE 2   (FROM THE STATE'S BRIEF IN OPPOSITION TO THE MOTION TO SUPPRESS)

Under Washington law, did the trial court act properly when it denied Defendant's Motion to Suppress when the police merely asked the victim whether a pedestrian looked like her assailant and when the victim observed her assailant on two occasions for several seconds in broad daylight from a distance of two or three feet?

Question

Is it ethical to omit a legally significant fact? If it is, is it strategically wise?

Thus, writing a persuasive issue statement is a three-step process: you must (1) select the appropriate lens, (2) select a format, and (3) craft your statement so that it is subtly persuasive. (See sections 7.6.4 and 7.6.5.)

Checklist for Critiquing the Question Presented

I.   Format

- The writer has used one of the conventional formats: under-does-when, whether, or multisentence.
- The same format has been used for each question presented.

II.   Content

- The question presented states the legal question and includes references to the legally significant facts. In addition, when appropriate, it also includes a reference to the rule of law.
- The legal questions have been framed so that they support the writer's theory of the case: Both the lens and the focus are effective.

III.   Persuasiveness

- The legal question has been framed so that it suggests an answer favorable to the client.
- The question presented includes references to the facts that support the client's position; unfavorable facts are de-emphasized or omitted.
- Favorable facts have been placed in the positions of emphasis.
- Favorable facts have been described vividly and in detail.
- Words have been selected both for their denotation and their connotation.

IV.   Writing

- The judge can understand the question presented after reading it through once.
- Punctuation has been used to divide the question presented into manageable units of meaning.
- When appropriate, parallel constructions have been used.
- In both the main and subordinate clauses, the subject and verb are close together.
- The question presented is grammatically correct and correctly punctuated.

§7.7 ORDERING THE ISSUES AND ARGUMENTS

§7.7.1 Presenting the Issues and Arguments in a Logical Order

In many cases, logic dictates the order of both the issues and, under each issue, the arguments. Threshold questions (for example, issues relating to subject matter jurisdiction, service of process, and the statute of limitations) must be discussed before questions relating to the merits of the case. Similarly, the parts of a test must be discussed in order and, when one argument builds on another, the foundation arguments must be put first.

Although in the *Patterson* case there is only one issue before the trial court — whether the identifications should be suppressed — there are a number of subissues. The court must decide not only whether it should suppress Martinez's and Clipse's show-up and line-up identifications but also whether it should prevent Martinez and Clipse from making in-court identifications.

Logic dictates, at least in part, the order in which these six subissues should be discussed. Because an impermissibly suggestive show-up would taint the line-up and in-court identifications, the show-up should be discussed before the line-up, and both the show-up and line-up should be discussed before the in-court identifications.

Logic also dictates the order of the arguments. To suppress an identification, the court must find (1) that the police procedures were impermissibly suggestive and (2) that under the totality of the circumstances the resulting identifications are unreliable. Because a finding of suggestiveness is a prerequisite to the court's consideration of reliability, Patterson's attorney must discuss suggestiveness first. She cannot start with reliability and then work her way back.

Question

In deciding whether an identification is nonetheless reliable, the courts consider five factors: (1) the witness's opportunity to view; (2) the witness's degree of attention; (3) the accuracy of the witness's description; (4) the witness's level of certainty; and (5) the length of time between the crime and the confrontation. Does logic dictate that these factors be discussed in the order set out above?

---

§7.7.2 Deciding Which Issues and Arguments Should Be Presented First

Because you want the court's first impression of your case to be a good one, when logic does not dictate the order, put your strongest arguments first.

What this means in practice is that the moving party's first argument will often be the responding party's last and vice versa. For example, while Patterson's attorney might want to start with Martinez's show-up, the prosecutor would want to start with Clipse's.

Note

Some attorneys believe that you should take advantage of the positions of emphasis, starting and ending with the strong issues and within each issue the strong arguments. Others believe that this strategy is dangerous. If the judges do not finish the brief, they may never see the final strong issue or argument.

Question

Think again about the five factors that the courts consider in determining whether an identification is reliable. If you were Patterson's attorney, which factor would you discuss first? What would you do if you were the prosecutor? Do both sides have to discuss each of the factors? Can some factors be grouped together?

---

§7.7.3 Putting the Pieces Together

Even with these guidelines, there may be several ways in which the pieces can be put together. For example, in the *Patterson* case, the sub-issues can be organized around the event (that is, the show-up, line-up, and in-court identification) or around the witnesses (that is, Martinez and Clipse).

EXAMPLE   **PLAN A:**
SUBISSUES ORGANIZED AROUND EVENTS

I. **Test the court applies in determining whether the identifications should be suppressed**
   A. Show-up
      1. Martinez
      2. Clipse
   B. Line-up
      1. Martinez
      2. Clipse
   C. In-court identification
      1. Martinez
      2. Clipse

EXAMPLE	**PLAN B:**

SUBISSUES ORGANIZED AROUND WITNESSES

I. **Test the court applies in determining whether the identifications should be suppressed**
   A. Martinez
       1. Show-up
       2. Line-up
       3. In-court identification
   B. Clipse
       1. Show-up
       2. Line-up
       3. In-court identification

In such a situation, select the organizational scheme that best allows you to implement your overall strategy (see section 7.4) and that is the most concise. Although repetition can be an effective tool of persuasion, repeating rules and tests is not.

§7.8   DRAFTING THE ARGUMENTATIVE HEADINGS

§7.8.1   Using Argumentative Headings to Define the Structure of the Arguments

Just as posts and beams define the form of a building, argumentative headings define the form of the argument. When properly drafted, they identify the main points and tell the judge the order in which those points are discussed.

EXAMPLE	**ARGUMENTATIVE HEADINGS WITHOUT INTERVENING TEXT**

I. **THE TRIAL COURT SHOULD EXCLUDE MARTINEZ'S SHOW-UP IDENTIFICATION BECAUSE THE SHOW-UP WAS IMPERMISSIBLY SUGGESTIVE AND BECAUSE, UNDER THE TOTALITY OF THE CIRCUMSTANCES, MARTINEZ'S IDENTIFICATION IS NOT RELIABLE.**
   A. The police procedure was unnecessarily suggestive because, in the absence of exigent circumstances, the police drew Martinez's attention to Patterson,

> the sole person on the street, repeatedly asking Martinez whether Patterson looked like her assailant.
>
> B.   Martinez's identification is not reliable because she viewed her assailant for only one or two seconds and because Patterson does not resemble the person Martinez described shortly after the crime.

In addition to defining the structure, argumentative headings serve as locators. By using the headings, the judge can find the section of the argument that he or she is interested in reading.

Note

Argumentative headings also help the writer. As a practicing lawyer, you will seldom have large blocks of time available for writing. Instead, you will squeeze in an hour here or two hours there. If you prepare your argumentative headings first, you can use this time effectively, writing the argument one section at a time.

§7.8.2   Using Argumentative Headings to Persuade

In addition to providing structure, argumentative headings persuade. They allow the attorney to state his or her position and, at least in summary form, the reasons that support it.

a.   The Heading Should Be in the Form of a Positive Assertion

If a heading is to be persuasive, it needs to be in the form of a positive assertion. If you want the court to suppress the identification evidence, make that statement in the affirmative: "The court should suppress the identification evidence . . . ." In contrast, if you want the court to admit the evidence, state that conclusion affirmatively.

EXAMPLE   **INCORRECT**

Not a Positive Assertion:

The court should not suppress the identification evidence . . .

The court should not grant defendant's motion to suppress . . .

EXAMPLE   **CORRECT**

Positive Assertion:

The court should admit the identification evidence . . .

The court should deny defendant's motion to suppress . . .

The heading should also state the reasons that support that conclusion. The most common format is as follows:

> Legal conclusion   because   reasons.

EXAMPLE 1

THE SHOW-UP IDENTIFICA- TION SHOULD BE SUP- PRESSED	BECAUSE	THE POLICE PROCEDURE WAS UNNEC- ESSARILY SUGGESTIVE AND THE WIT- NESSES' IDENTIFICA- TIONS ARE UNRELIABLE.

EXAMPLE 2

Martinez's identifi- cation was not reliable	because	she viewed her assailant for only one or two seconds and because Patter- son does not look like the man she de- scribed.

In both examples, the format is correct: There is a conclusion followed by a "because" clause. Let's look, though, at the substance of each heading.

Although the first example has a "because" clause, that clause does not contain reasons. The issue in *Patterson* is not whether an identification should be suppressed if it was the result of unnecessarily suggestive police procedures and the identifications are unreliable. That is the law. The issue is whether, given the facts, the police procedure was unnecesarily suggestive and, if it was, whether the identifications were unreliable.

Because Example 1 only restates the law, it has little or no persuasive value if left standing by itself. It works well, however, when followed by subheadings. In such a situation, the main heading acts as a roadmap, outlining the argument, and the subheadings set out the more specific conclusions and reasons.

b. Make the Heading as Specific as Possible

As a general rule, headings should be case-specific. They should explain why, given the facts of this particular case, the court should reach the conclusion that has been set out.

To make a heading specific, use the parties' names and describe the facts in detail. Compare the following examples.

Too General

The witness's identification is reliable because she had a good opportunity to view her assailant.

More Specific

Martinez's identification is reliable because she was able to view her assailant, face-to-face, for several seconds.

---

c. *Present the Facts in the Light Most Favorable to the Client*

The facts should also be presented in the light most favorable to the client. Select your words carefully and use the positions of emphasis to your best advantage. See section 7.6.5.

EXAMPLE   **DEFENSE COUNSEL'S HEADINGS**

Version 1:

Martinez's show-up identification is unreliable because Martinez was able to view her assailant for only one or two seconds.

Version 2:

Martinez's show-up identification is unreliable because after being startled by a gunman, Martinez only glanced at the gunman before screaming and running to safety.

EXAMPLE   **THE PROSECUTOR'S HEADINGS**

Version 1:

Martinez's identification is reliable because she was able to view her assailant, face-to-face, for several seconds in broad daylight.

Version 2:

Because Martinez was able to view her assailant, face-to-face for several seconds in broad daylight, her identification is reliable.

Question

Which of the examples is most effective? When might you want to put the "because" clause first?

_____

d. Make Your Heading Readable

A heading that is not read is not persuasive. To ensure that the heading is read, keep it short, no more than two or three lines.

EXAMPLE **TOO LONG**

The police procedures were unnecessarily suggestive because the witness viewed only one person, the police asked the witness whether that person looked like her assailant, and because the person was simply walking down the street and not trying to escape and the witness was not likely to die or disappear, there was no reason to conduct a one-person show-up.

Also use a sentence construction that makes the reader's job easier. Use parallel constructions (see section 25.7) and, when appropriate, repeat the words that highlight the parallel structure (for example, "that" or "because"). When appropriate, also use commas, semicolons, and colons to divide the sentence into more manageable units of meaning.

§7.8.3 Following the Conventions: Number, Placement, and Typeface

By convention, there should be one, and only one, main heading for each question presented. The issue is set out in the question presented and the answer in the main heading. Although subheadings and sub-subheadings are optional, if there is one, there should be at least two. There may or may not be text between the main heading and the first subheading or between the subheading and the first sub-subheading.

Convention also governs the typefaces used. Although practice varies from jurisdiction to jurisdiction, in most persuasive memoranda and briefs, main headings are in all caps, subheadings are in regular type and underlined, and sub-subheadings are in regular type but not underlined.

Argument

I. FIRST MAIN HEADING [corresponds to first question presented]

[If appropriate, text of argument]

    A. First subheading

        [If appropriate, text of argument]

        1. First sub-subheading

            [Text of argument]

        2. Second sub-subheading

            [Text of argument]

    B. Second subheading

        [Text of argument]

    C. Third subheading

        [Text of argument]

II. SECOND MAIN HEADING [corresponds to second question presented]

[If appropriate, text of argument]

    A. First subheading

        [Text of argument]

    B. Second subheading

        [If appropriate, text of argument]

        1. First sub-subheading

            [Text of argument]

        2. Second sub-subheading

            [Text of argument]

Checklist for Critiquing
Argumentative Headings

I. Format and Content

- When read together, the headings provide the judge with an outline and overview of the argument.
- Each heading and subheading is in the form of a positive assertion: It includes an assertion, a connector, and the support for the assertion.
- The headings are neither too narrow nor too broad.
- The writer has used the typefaces that are required by court rule or by local convention.

II. Persuasiveness

- The headings support and emphasize the writer's theory of the case.

- As a general rule, the headings are case-specific.
- The facts that support the client's position are included; unfavorable facts are de-emphasized or omitted if not legally significant.
- Favorable facts have been placed in the positions of emphasis.
- Favorable facts have been described vividly and in detail.
- Words have been selected both for their denotation and their connotation.

III. Writing

- The judge can understand the heading after reading it through once. (Headings are not more than two or three lines long.)
- Punctuation has been used to divide the heading into manageable units of meaning.
- When appropriate, parallel constructions have been used.
- In both the main and subordinate clauses, the subject and verb are close together.
- The headings are grammatically correct and correctly punctuated.

§7.9   DRAFTING THE ARGUMENTS

We have all had arguments. As children, we fought with our parents over cleaning our rooms and about how late we could stay out; as adults we have fought with roommates and spouses over household tasks, budgets, and world events. We know how to express anger and frustration.

Unfortunately, most of us have had far less experience making arguments. In everyday life we do not set out conclusions and then systematically walk our listeners through the "proof." We make our point and then move on. Even less frequently do we pay attention to the language that we use in setting out either the conclusion or the proof. Instead of picking our words, we let the words pick themselves.

Picking words and walking another through a proof, however, are exactly the skills that are needed to make an argument. Good advocates do both. They have the mental discipline of a mathematician. They think linearly, identifying each of the steps in the analysis and setting them out in order. They also have the insight of an advertising executive. They know their market, and they know both the image they want and how to use language to create it. In short, they have mastered both the science and the art of advocacy.

§7.9.1   The Science: The Content and Structure of an Argument

a.   *Supporting Your Conclusions*

An argument has two parts: a conclusion and the support for that conclusion.

As the following examples illustrate, a conclusion can take one of two forms. It can be procedural, suggesting an action, or it can be substantive, stating a legal conclusion (the legal requirements are or are not met).

EXAMPLE

Procedural:

The court should suppress Martinez's show-up identification.

The court should deny Defendant's Motion to Suppress.

Substantive:

The police procedures were impermissibly suggestive.

Martinez's identification is unreliable.

Although the conclusion is an integral part of the argument, it is not, by itself, an argument. How many judges would be persuaded by the following exchange?

Defense Counsel: Your honor, the court should suppress Martinez's show-up identification.

Prosecutor: Your honor, we respectfully disagree. The court should deny the motion.

Defense Counsel: No, your honor, the court should grant the motion.

Prosecutor: No. The court should deny the motion.

An exchange in which defense counsel claims that the police procedures were impermissibly suggestive and the prosecutor claims that they were not is no more persuasive. Standing alone, conclusions do not persuade. They must be supported.

In law, that support can take several forms: You can support a conclusion by setting out and applying a statute or common law rule, by comparing the facts in your case to the facts in analogous cases, or by explaining how the conclusion is consistent with public policy. Compare the following examples.

EXAMPLE 1

Conclusion

The police procedures were impermissibly suggestive.

Support

Rules: One-person show-ups are inherently suggestive. *State v. Hanson,* 46 Wash. App. 656, 731 P.2d 1140 (1987). When the police present the witness with a single suspect, the witness will probably infer that the police believe that the person being presented committed the crime. *Id.*

Application: In this case, the police presented only a single suspect: Mr. Patterson. Therefore, Martinez probably inferred that the officers believed that it was Mr. Patterson who committed the crime.

EXAMPLE 2

Conclusion

The police procedures were impermissibly suggestive.

Support

Analogous case: In *State v. Booth,* 36 Wash. App. 66, 671 P.2d 1218 (1983), the police brought the witness to the scene of the arrest and showed him a single suspect, who was sitting with his back to the witness in the back seat of the police car. The court held that the police procedures were impermissibly suggestive.

Application: As in *Booth,* in this case the police showed the witness a single suspect and asked her to identify him before she had had an opportunity to see his face. The only difference between the two cases is the identity of the person in the police car. While in *Booth* it was the suspect, in this case it was Martinez.

EXAMPLE 3

Conclusion

The police procedures were impermissibly suggestive.

Support

Policy: To protect the rights of defendants, the courts should not admit those identifications that are unreliable.

Application: Because the identifications are unreliable, Patterson will be denied his right to a fair trial if they are admitted.

Note that in each of these examples, the support had two components: a "citation to authority" and an application of that "authority" to the facts of the case. Also note that there is often more than one way of supporting a conclusion. In such instances, you are faced with a decision. Should you set out all of the arguments or only some of them? (Identifying the arguments is part of the science, deciding which to present is the art.)

b. Structuring the Argument

In making an argument, most advocates use one of two forms of reasoning: deductive or inductive.

The first type, deductive reasoning, is the most common. You set out the conclusion and then the support for it. There are, however, times when inductive reasoning works best. For example, it makes no sense to begin with the conclusion if you know that the conclusion will, on its face, be rejected. (In 1950, you would not have wanted to begin by stating that separate but equal schools are unconstitutional.) In such instances, it makes more sense to start with support, if you can, leading the judge one small step at a time to the final conclusion.

EXAMPLE   **DEDUCTIVE REASONING**

Conclusion:	The identification was not reliable.
Support:	The identification was not reliable because Martinez was able to view her assailant for only one or two seconds.
	The identification was not reliable because Martinez's attention was focused on the assailant's gun and not on his face.
	The identification was not reliable because Martinez's description of her assailant was inaccurate.
	The identification was not reliable because at the show-up Martinez was, at least at first, uncertain whether Patterson was her assailant.

EXAMPLE   **INDUCTIVE REASONING**

Support:	Martinez was able to view her assailant for only one or two seconds.
	Martinez's attention was focused on the assailant's gun and not on his face.
	Martinez's description of her assailant was inaccurate.
	At the show-up Martinez was, at least at first, uncertain whether Patterson was her assailant.
Conclusion:	Because Martinez had only a limited opportunity to view her assailant, because her attention was diverted, because her description was inaccurate, and because she was not certain that Patterson was her assailant, Martinez's identification is not reliable.

When deductive reasoning is used, the argument section is organized in much the same way as the discussion section of an objective memo: Model A is used when the problem requires an analysis of elements and Model B is used for a problem that requires the balancing of competing interests. (See section 5.11.3.)

As Exhibit 7.4 illustrates, the main structural difference between the discussion section of an objective memo and an argument is the addition of a new piece, the assertion.

§7.9.2 The Art: Presenting the Argument

Although the structure of an argument is similar to the structure of a discussion section, the presentation is very different. While in an objective memo the rules, cases, and arguments are presented objectively, in a brief they are not. Without misrepresenting either, the advocate packages both the law and the facts so that they favor the client.

a. Stating the Rule

The rules should be presented in the light most favorable to the client. Favorable rules should be stated broadly, making it easier for the court to find that the case falls within the scope of the rule, and unfavorable rules should be stated narrowly, making it less likely that the rule applies. Study the following examples, identifying the differences.

EXAMPLE 1

OBJECTIVE STATEMENT OF RULE

In deciding whether identification testimony is admissible, the court applies a two-part test. Under the first part of the test, the defendant must prove that the procedure was impermissibly suggestive. If the court finds that the procedure was impermissibly suggestive, the State then has the burden of showing that, under the totality of the circumstances, the reliability of the identification outweighs the suggestive police procedure. *Manson v. Braithwaithe,* 432 U.S. 98 (1972).

EXHIBIT 7.4	Comparison of the Analysis in an Objective Memo and a Persuasive Brief

MODEL A
Problem Requiring Analysis of Elements or Factors

Objective Memo	*Persuasive Brief*
	Assertion
General rule	General rule
First element	*First element*
(Suggestiveness)	(Suggestiveness)
	Assertion
Rule	Rule
Analogous case(s)	Analogous case(s)
Defendant's argument	Your argument (including response to other side's argument)
State's argument	
Mini-conclusion	Mini-conclusion
Second element	*Second element*
(Reliability)	(Reliability)
	Assertion
General rule	General rule
First factor	*First factor*
(Opportunity to view)	(Opportunity to view)
	Assertion
Rule	Rule
Defendant's argument	Your argument (including response to other side's argument)
State's arguments	
Mini-conclusion	Mini-conclusion
Second factor	*Second factor*
(Attention)	(Attention)
	Assertion

EXHIBIT 7.4   *(continued)*

Objective Memo	Persuasive Brief
Rule	Rule
Defendant's argument	Your argument (including response to other side's argument)
State's arguments	
Mini-conclusion	Mini-conclusion
Third factor	*Third factor*
(Accuracy of description)	(Accuracy of description)
	Assertion
Rule	Rule
Defendant's argument	Your argument (including response to other side's argument)
State's arguments	
Mini-conclusion	Mini-conclusion

EXAMPLE 2

RULE STATED IN THE LIGHT MOST FAVORABLE TO THE DEFENDANT

The United States Supreme Court has developed a two-part test to ensure a criminal defendant the procedural due process guaranteed to every individual by the Fourteen Amendment. *Manson v. Braithwaithe,* 432 U.S. 98 (1972).

Under the first part of the test, the defendant need show only that the identification that he seeks to suppress was obtained through the use of unnecessarily suggestive police procedures. *Id.* Once this has been established, the onus shifts to the State to prove that, under the totality of the circumstances, the witness's identifications are so reliable that they should be admitted even though they were obtained through impermissibly suggestive means. *Id.*

EXAMPLE 3

RULE STATED IN THE LIGHT MOST FAVORABLE TO THE STATE

Identification evidence should not be kept from jury consideration unless the procedures used in obtaining the identification were so suggestive and unreliable that a substantial likelihood of irreparable misidentification exists. *See Simon v. United States,* 390 U.S. 377 (1968).

In deciding whether identification evidence is admissible, the courts employ a two-part test. Under the first part of the test, the defendant has the burden of proving that the identification evidence that he seeks to suppress was obtained through impermissibly suggestive procedures. *Manson v. Braithwaithe,* 432 U.S. 98 (1972). Only if the defendant satisfies this substantial burden is the second part of the test applied.

Even if the court determines that the police procedures were impermissibly suggestive, the evidence is admissible if, under the totality of the circumstances, the identifications are reliable. Due process does not compel the exclusion of an identification if it is reliable. *Id.*

Let's begin by comparing the opening sentences of all three examples. In Example 1, the writer simply states that the court applies a two-part test. There is no attempt to create a favorable context.

EXAMPLE 1   **OBJECTIVE**

In deciding whether identification testimony is admissible, the court applies a two-part test.

In contrast, in Examples 2 and 3, the writers package the statements, using policy to create a context that favors their respective clients. The key language is highlighted.

EXAMPLE 2   DEFENDANT

The United States Supreme Court has developed a two-part test to ensure a criminal defendant the **procedural due process guaranteed to every individual by the Fourteenth Amendment.**

EXAMPLE 3   THE STATE

Identification **evidence should not be kept from jury consideration** unless the procedures used in obtaining the identification were so suggestive and unreliable that a substantial likelihood of irreparable misidentification exists.

In addition to creating a favorable context, the two advocates have focused on different parts of the rule, highlighting what is favorable to their client and minimizing what isn't. Compare the highlighted passages.

EXAMPLE 1   OBJECTIVE

Under the first part of the test, **the defendant must prove** that the procedure was unnecessarily suggestive.

EXAMPLE 2   DEFENDANT

Under the first part of the test, **the defendant need show only** that the identification that he seeks to suppress was obtained through the use of unnecessarily suggestive police procedures.

EXAMPLE 3   THE STATE

Under the first part of the test, **the defendant has the burden of proving** that the identification evidence that he seeks to suppress was obtained through impermissibly suggestive procedures.

Similarly, both sides try to lead the court to the desired conclusion. Defense counsel presumes that the defendant will meet its burden; the State presents the second part of the test as an alternative. Even if it loses on the first part of the test, it wins on the second. Once again, the key language is highlighted.

EXAMPLE 1   DEFENDANT

Once this has been established, the onus shifts to the State to prove that, under the totality of the circumstances, the witness's identifications are so reliable that they should be admitted even though they were obtained through impermissibly suggestive means.

EXAMPLE 2   THE STATE

Only if the defendant satisfies this substantial burden is the second part of the test applied.
Even if the court determines that the police procedures were unnecessarily suggestive, the evidence is admissible if, under the totality of the circumstances, the identifications are reliable.

Question

How far can you go in characterizing the law? Is either of the following statements permissible?

1. Under the first part of the test, the State must prove that the police procedures were not unnecessarily suggestive.

2. Under the first part of the test, the court must determine whether the police procedures were unnecessarily suggestive.

If you were defense counsel, what factors would you consider in deciding how to state the law? _____

Finally, look at the words that each side has used.

Defendant	The State
ensure	so suggestive
guaranteed	burden
onus shifts	substantial burden
so reliable	compel

Instead of using the language they had seen in the cases or the first thing that came to mind, each side selected its words carefully and with the goal of subtly influencing the decisionmaking process.

Question

Note that in setting out the first part of the test defense counsel uses the phrase "unnecessarily suggestive" while the State uses the phrase "impermissibly suggestive." What might account for the difference in language? If the courts have used the phrase "impermissibly suggestive," is defense counsel misrepresenting the law if she uses the phrase "unnecessarily suggestive"? _____

b.　Using Cases

When you use an analogous case to support your argument, present the case in the light most favorable to the client.

In *Patterson,* both sides used analogous cases. Defense counsel used cases to support defendant's assertion that the identification was unreliable; the prosecutor used them to support its claim that identification was reliable.

One of the cases both sides used was *State v. Booth,* 36 Wash. App. 66, 671 P.2d 1218 (1983), a case in which the court held that the identification was reliable. The relevant portion of the court's opinion is set out below.

EXCERPT FROM *STATE V. BOOTH*

The facts provide several indicia of reliability. Ms. Thomas was driving slowly, it was a clear day and she observed Booth for approximately 45 seconds. Her attention was greater than average because he had money in his hands and was running. In addition, her attention was particularly drawn to the car with Missouri plates because she had lived in Missouri. Finally, the identification took place 30 to 40 minutes later and was unequivocal. On the basis of these facts we find that reliability outweighed the harm of suggestiveness and the identification was properly admitted.

Because the *Booth* court found that the identification was reliable, the State wants to emphasize the similarities between the two cases.

EXAMPLE

EXCERPT FROM THE STATE'S BRIEF

The courts do not require that the witness have viewed the defendant for an extended period of time. For example, in *State v. Booth,* the court found the witness's identification reliable when she viewed the defendant for less than a minute. Because her attention was drawn to the fleeing man and because she viewed him in broad daylight, the court found that the identification was reliable despite an impermissibly suggestive show-up.

In contrast, defense counsel distinguishes the case.

EXAMPLE

EXCERPT FROM THE DEFENDANT'S BRIEF

An identification will not be found to be reliable unless the witness had an adequate opportunity to view the defendant. This was the situation in *State v. Booth.* In that case, a bystander was able to view the defendant for almost a minute. Because she was able to view the defendant for an extended period of time under good conditions, the court found that her identification was reliable.

---

c. Presenting the Arguments

In an objective memo, you set out each side's arguments: As Exhibit 7.4 indicates, you set out the moving party's arguments, the responding party's arguments, and then the court's ruling. This is not the case in persuasive writing. In a brief, make only your client's case; do not do the other side's work.

This does not mean that you ignore the other side's arguments. In addition to making your own affirmative case, you will usually want to respond to the arguments that the other side has made. The key is in how you do this.

1.   Present Your Own Arguments First

You will almost always set out your own arguments first. By doing so, you remain on the offensive, rather than the defensive, and you take advantage of the positions of emphasis.

EXAMPLE   **INEFFECTIVE**

EXCERPT FROM THE STATE'S BRIEF

The defendant argues that the police procedures were impermissibly suggestive because the police showed Martinez a single suspect, Patterson, and because they asked Martinez whether Patterson "was the one."

It is our contention that the police procedures were not impermissibly suggestive. One-person show-ups are not *per se* impermissibly suggestive; if the show-up occurs shortly after the commission of a crime during a search for the suspect, it is permissible. *See State v. Booth,* 36 Wash. App. 66, 671 P.2d 1218 (1983); *United States v. Hines,* 455 F.2d 1317 (1971), *cert. denied,* 406 U.S. 975 (1972).

EXAMPLE   **MORE EFFECTIVE**

EXCERPT FROM THE STATE'S BRIEF

One-person show-ups are not *per se* impermissibly suggestive; a show-up is permissible if it occurs shortly after the commission of a crime during a search for the suspect. *See State v. Booth,* 36 Wash. App. 66, 671 P.2d 1218 (1983); *United States v. Hines,* 455 F.2d 1317 (1971), *cert. denied,* 406 U.S. 975 (1972).

In this case, the show-up occurred within forty-five minutes of the assault. It also occurred before the police had completed their investigation: The police saw Patterson as they were leaving the crime scene to take Martinez home.

In such circumstances, the police would have been negligent if they had not looked for a person who matched the description given by Martinez and, having seen someone who did, if they had not asked Martinez whether he looked like her assailant. If they were not permitted to conduct one-person show-ups, the police would be unable to do their job. The officer's question, "Does that look like him?" was not enough to turn a permissible show-up into one that was impermissibly suggestive.

2.   Spend Most of Your Time Making Your Own Case

Spend more time making your own affirmative case than respond-ing to points raised by your opponent. Your goal is to counter your opponent's argument without giving it undue attention. In the following examples, note the difference in airtime the State gives to the age dis-crepancy in the ineffective and effective excerpts.

EXAMPLE   **INEFFECTIVE**

EXCERPT FROM THE STATE'S BRIEF

On the whole, Ms. Martinez's description was accurate. When she was interviewed, Ms. Martinez told the police that her assailant was a white male, that he was approximately 5'7" weigh-ing between 165 and 170 pounds, that he had blondish-brown hair and was wearing a dark jacket, and that he appeared to be in his early 40's. **In fact, Patterson is 22.**

This discrepancy in age is insignificant. It is often diffi-cult to guess a person's age. Some people appear older than they are, while others appear younger. Thus, the court should give little weight to the fact that Ms. Martinez misjudged the defendant's age. On the basis of the other information that Ms. Martinez gave the police, the police were able to identify Patter-son as the assailant.

EXAMPLE   **MORE EFFECTIVE**

EXCERPT FROM THE STATE'S BRIEF

Ms. Martinez was able to give the police a detailed descrip-tion of her assailant. When interviewed, she told the police that her assailant was a white male with blondish-brown hair; that he was approximately 5'7" tall and weighed between 165 and 170 pounds; **that he appeared to be in his early 40's;** and that he was wearing a dark green jacket.

This description is accurate **in all but one respect. Al-though Ms. Martinez misjudged Patterson's age,** she accu-rately described his hair, his height and weight, and his clothing.

---

3. Use Language That Undermines Your Opponent's Arguments and Strengthens Your Own

When you do explicitly discuss a point made by your opponent, use words like "alleges" or "contends": "Although the defendant alleges . . ." or "The plaintiff contends . . . ." By doing so, you remind the court that your opponent is simply making an argument — which the court can either accept or reject.

Conversely, do not use such words when you make your own argument. You are stating the "truth," not an allegation or a contention.

EXAMPLE

Ineffective:

It is our contention that the police procedures were impermissibly suggestive.

More Effective:

The police procedures were impermissibly suggestive.

Similarly, do not use phrases like "we believe" or "I feel." When you are in the courtroom, your beliefs and feelings are immaterial.

4. Use the Persuasive Devices That Were Discussed in Section 7.6, Drafting the Statement of the Case

Finally, when appropriate, use the same persuasive devices that you used in writing the statement of the case. (See sections 7.6.4 and 7.6.5.) Use the positions of emphasis to your best advantage; place favorable information in short sentences and paragraphs and bury unfavorable information in long sentences and long paragraphs; place favorable information in the main clause and unfavorable information in subordinate clauses; and select your words carefully, selecting those that convey not only the right denotation but also the right connotation.

Also remember that persuasive arguments are not written, they are crafted. On the first drafts, concentrate on content and organization; on subsequent drafts work on persuasiveness.

§7.10 DRAFTING THE PRAYER FOR RELIEF OR CONCLUSION

§7.10.1 The Prayer for Relief or Conclusion

The final section of the brief is the prayer for relief or conclusion. The form of this section varies depending on the jurisdiction. In some jurisdictions, this section is very short: The attorney simply sets out the desired relief.

EXAMPLE

PRAYER FOR RELIEF

For the reasons set out above, Defendant respectfully requests that the Court suppress Beatrice Martinez's and Chester Clipse's show-up and line-up identifications.

In other jurisdictions, in addition to setting out the desired relief, the attorney summarizes the arguments.

EXAMPLE

CONCLUSION

The court should suppress Beatrice Martinez's show-up identification because the police officer's questions were impermissibly suggestive and because, given Ms. Martinez's limited opportunity to view her assailant and the inaccuracies in her description, her identification is unreliable.

The court should also suppress Chester Clipse's show-up identification. Like Ms. Martinez's identification, Mr. Clipse's identification was influenced by the police officers' actions. In addition, Mr. Clipse's identification is unreliable: Like Ms. Martinez, he had only a limited opportunity to view the assailant, and his description is inaccurate.

Finally, the court should suppress both Ms. Martinez's and Mr. Clipse's line-up identifications. The court can do so on either of two grounds: It can find that the line-up was tainted by the impermissibly suggestive show-up, or it can find that the line-up was itself impermissibly suggestive.

Whichever format you use, it is permissible to ask for alternative relief. If the court will not suppress all of the identifications, you can ask that it suppress at least some of them; if, on appeal, the court does not reverse, you can ask that it remand the case for a new trial.

§7.10.2   Signing the Brief

Although the prayer for relief or conclusion is the final section, it is not the end of the brief. The brief still must be signed. The following format is appropriate.

Submitted this _____ day of _____, 199 __.

_____

Attorney for Defendant

§7.11   DETERMINING THE ISSUES ON APPEAL

In the *Patterson* case, Judge Schmit denied Defendant's Motion to Suppress, and the case went to trial. After deliberating for less than three hours, the jury found Patterson guilty as charged. Two weeks later, Judge Schmit sentenced Patterson to a twenty-four-month term of imprisonment.

Soon thereafter, Ms. Fisher met with Patterson to talk about an appeal. She described the appeals process and told Patterson that he could now appeal Judge Schmit's denial of the Motion to Suppress. She also told Patterson that she might be able to identify other errors after she had looked at the trial record.

Patterson decided that he wanted to appeal, and on October 21, Fisher filed a Notice of Appeal with the trial court.

Fisher's next step was to request copies of the verbatim report of proceedings (the trial transcript) and the clerk's papers (the documents that had been filed with the trial court).

§7.11.1   Reviewing the Record for Error

Fisher received her copy of the record on November 16. Several days later, she began reviewing it.

Like most attorneys, Fisher reviews the record for error using a four-step process. She begins by reviewing her trial notes, writing down the errors that she identified during the trial. She then begins a systematic review of the record, highlighting in some way

a.   each motion that she made that was denied,
b.   each motion that the State made that was granted,

c. each objection that she made that was denied,

d. each objection that the State made that was granted,

e. each request for a jury instruction that she made that was denied, and

f. each request for a jury instruction that the State made that was granted.

EXCERPT FROM VERBATIM REPORT OF PROCEEDINGS

Q: And you stated that when the police stopped you, you never asked them what was going on?

A: After I was put in the back seat of the patrol car and they had began asking me what had happened, I asked them what was the charge, what was I being arrested for.

Q: But you just stood there and let them stop you and frisk you and plunge you in the patrol car and never asked what was going on?

A: I did later. I just explained that.

Q: But when they read you your rights you didn't say anything did you?

Ms. Fisher: Objection.

The Court: Overruled.

Q: You didn't tell them the story you've told the jury today did you?

Ms. Fisher: Objection, he is allowed to remain silent.

The Court: Overruled, answer the question.

A: Not at that moment, no. I did later.

Q: You indicated that you told the officers where the gun was?

A: Yes, I did.

Q: And you have seen the gun we have marked as an exhibit in this action?

A: From a distance, yes.

As her third step, Fisher looks for the other, less obvious types of errors.

- Were Patterson's constitutional rights violated? (Was the defendant read his Miranda rights? Was he represented by counsel at all significant stages in the process? Was he tried within the appropriate time period? Was he given the right to confront the witnesses against him? Is his sentence cruel and unusual?)
- Is the statute under which Patterson was charged constitutional?
- Was there misconduct on the part of the judge, opposing counsel, or the jury?

Finally, she examines her own actions. Did she miss a defense or fail to object to a motion or a piece of evidence? If she did, Patterson might be able to argue that he was denied effective assistance of counsel.

Having identified the potential errors, Fisher can analyze them and decide which of them she should raise on appeal.

§7.11.2   Selecting the Issues on Appeal

As an appellate judge, whom would you find more credible: the attorney who lists twenty-three issues or the one who lists three?

Most appellate judges take the attorney who lists two, three, or four issues more seriously than the attorney who lists a dozen or more. Instead of describing the attorney who lists numerous issues as "thorough" or "conscientious," judges use terms such as "inexperienced," "unfocused," and "frivolous." When so many issues are listed, the appellate court is likely to think that the problem is not the trial court but the attorney bringing the appeal.

But how do you decide which issues and arguments to include?

a.   Was There an Error?

The first question that should be asked is whether there was in fact an error. Can you make a credible argument that the trial judge's ruling was erroneous? If you cannot, do not raise the issue.

Note

Although you want to be selective, do not be too quick to dismiss an issue. If you are not familiar with the governing law, don't guess about what the law might be. Look it up. Also keep in mind that the law is not static. What might have been permissible yesterday may be impermissible tomorrow.

_____

b.   If There Was an Error, Was the Error Preserved?

It is not enough that there was an error. Unless the error involves an issue of constitutional magnitude, that error must have been preserved. Defense counsel must have objected, or in some other manner brought the alleged error to the attention of the trial court.

In *Patterson*, defense counsel did object to the prosecutor's questions.

EXCERPT FROM THE VERBATIM REPORT OF PROCEEDINGS

Q: But you just stood there and let them stop and frisk you and plunge you in the patrol car and never asked what was going on?

A: I did later. I just explained that.

Q: But when they read you your rights you didn't say anything did you?

Ms. Fisher: Objection.
The Court: Overruled.

> *Q:*   You didn't tell them the story you've told the jury today did you?
>
> *Ms. Fisher:*   Objection, he is allowed to remain silent.
> *The Court:*   Overruled, answer the question.

The question is whether the objections were enough. Did defense counsel correctly identify the error? Should she have also requested a mistrial? The answer is in the rules and cases. In arguing an appeal, you must research both the substance and the procedure.

c. If the Error Was Preserved, Was the Error Harmless?

The next question is whether the error was harmless. As the courts have often said, "A defendant is entitled to a fair trial, not a perfect one."

> The reversal of a conviction entails substantial social costs: it forces jurors, witnesses, courts, the prosecution, and the defendants to expend further time, energy, and other resources to repeat a trial that has already once taken place.... These societal costs of reversal and retrial are an acceptable and often necessary consequence when an error ... has deprived the defendant of a fair determination of the issue of guilt or innocence. But the balance of interest tips decidedly the other way when the error has had no effect on the outcome of the trial.

William Rehnquist, *Harmless Error, Prosecutorial Misconduct, and Due Process: There's More to Due Process Than the Bottom Line,* 88 Colum. L. Rev. (1988).

In determining whether an error is harmless, most courts apply either the contribution test or the overwhelming untainted evidence test. Under the contribution test, the appellate court looks at the tainted evidence to determine whether that evidence could have contributed to the factfinder's determination of guilt. If it could have, reversal is required. *See Price v. Georgia,* 398 U.S. 323, 331 (1970). The courts that apply the overwhelming untainted evidence test take a different approach: Instead of looking at the tainted evidence, they look at that which is untainted. If the untainted evidence is sufficient to support a finding of guilt, reversal is not required. *See Brown v. United States,* 411 U.S. 223, 231 (1973).

Thus, as an advocate, you need to weed out those errors that were harmless. Although the court may have acted improperly when it allowed a particular piece of testimony, you don't have a case if that same testimony was properly elicited from several other witnesses.

d. What Is the Standard of Review?

The last thing that you need to consider is the standard of review. In deciding whether there was an error, what standard will the appellate court apply? Will it review the issue *de novo,* making its own independent determination, or will it defer to the trial court, affirming the trial court unless the trial court's finding was clearly erroneous or the trial court judge abused his or her discretion?

As a general rule, an appellate court will review questions of law *de novo.* As a consequence, when the issue is whether the jury was properly instructed, the appellate court will make its own independent determination. The standard is much higher when the question is one of fact. In most circumstances, an appellate court will not disturb factual findings unless such findings are "clearly erroneous" or "contrary to law." Similarly, the appellate courts give great deference to the trial court judge's evidentiary rulings, not reversing unless the judge abused, or manifestly abused, his or her discretion.

Because the rules set out above are general, you must research the standard of review. Sometimes this research will be easy. In one of its opinions, the court will state the standard that is to be applied. At other times, the research is much more difficult. Although the court decides the issue, it does not explicitly state what standard it is applying. In such cases, read between the lines. Although the court does not state that it is reviewing the issue *de novo,* is that in fact what the court has done?

Because very few issues are pure questions of law or pure questions of fact, you may be able to argue the standard of review. As the appellant, you can argue that the appellate court should review the question *de novo;* as the respondent you can argue that the appellate court should affirm unless the trial court's ruling was clearly erroneous or the trial court abused its discretion.

Having done this analysis, Patterson's attorney is ready to select the issues on appeal. She decides that the only two that are viable are the trial court's denial of the Motion to Suppress and the prosecutor's references to Patterson's post-arrest silence. In each instance, she has strong arguments that there was an error and that the error was prejudicial. In addition, because both issues raise questions of constitutional magnitude, she can argue that the standard of review is *de novo,* a standard that favors her client.

§7.11.3   Preparing an Abstract of the Record

Before beginning the brief, Patterson's attorney does one last thing: She prepares an abstract of the record, noting each piece of relevant testimony.

EXAMPLE

Excerpt from Abstract of Record

Martinez (direct)

> RP 57   First noticed old red station wagon while walking down Howell. Noticed that driver was staring at her.
>
> RP 57   Saw car again after turning onto Belmont. Car was moving slowly.
>
> RP 57   Car pulled in front of her and man jumped out. He hollered, "Hey." Victim saw gun.

Although preparing such an abstract is time-consuming, it forces Fisher to go through the record carefully, identifying each piece of relevant testimony. It also makes brief writing and preparation for oral argument easier. Instead of having to search through the entire record for the testimony she needs, she can refer to her abstract.

As the preceding materials illustrate, attorneys do not just sit down and write an appellate brief. Just as they developed a pretrial strategy and a plan for the brief in support of or opposition to the Motion to Suppress, they plan the appeal, deciding what issues they can raise and how they can best be argued.

§7.12   PREPARING THE APPELLATE BRIEF

In almost every jurisdiction, the form of the appellate brief is governed by court rule. The rules describe the types of briefs that may be filed, the sections that should be included and the order of those sections, and the length and typeface. The following rules, Rules 10.1, 10.3, and 10.4 of the Washington Rules on Appeal, are representative.

RULE 10.1: BRIEFS WHICH MAY BE FILED

(a) **Scope of Title.** The rules in this title apply only to the briefs referred to in this rule, unless a particular rule indicates a different application is intended.

(b) **Briefs Which May Be Filed in Any Review.** The following briefs may be filed in any review: (1) a brief of appellant or petitioner, (2) a brief of respondent, and (3) a reply brief of appellant or petitioner.

(c) **Reply Brief of Respondent.** If the respondent is also seeking review, the respondent may file a brief in reply to the response the appellant or petitioner has made to the issues presented by respondent's review.

(d) **Pro Se Supplemental Brief in Criminal Case.** A defendant in a review of a criminal case may file a brief supplementing the brief filed by the defendant's counsel, but only if the defendant files a notice of intention to file a pro se supplemental brief. The notice of intent should be filed within 30 days after the defendant has received the brief prepared by defendant's counsel, a notice from the clerk of the appellate court advising the defendant of the substance of this section, Rule 10.2(e), and 10.3(d), and a form of notice of intention to file a pro se supplemental brief. The clerk will advise all parties if the defendant files the notice of intention.

(e) **Amicus Curiae Brief.** An amicus curiae brief may be filed only if permission is obtained as provided in Rule 10.6. If an amicus curiae brief is filed, a brief in answer to the brief of amicus curiae may be filed by a party.

RULE 10.3: CONTENT OF BRIEF

(a) **Brief of Appellant or Petitioner.** The brief of the appellant or petitioner should contain under appropriate headings and in the order here indicated:

(1) *Title Page.* A title page, which is the cover.

(2) *Tables.* A table of contents, with page references, and a table of cases (alphabetically arranged), statutes and other authorities cited, with references to the pages of the brief where cited.

(3) *Assignment of Error.* A separate concise statement of each error a party contends was made by the trial court, together with the issues pertaining to the assignments of error.

(4) *Statement of the Case.* A fair statement of the facts and procedure relevant to the issues presented for review, without argument. Reference to the record must be included for each factual statement.

(5) *Argument.* The argument in support of the issues presented for review, together with citations to legal authority and references to relevant parts of the record. The argument may be preceded by a summary.

(6) *Conclusion.* A short conclusion stating the precise relief sought.

(7) *Appendix.* An appendix to the brief if deemed appropriate by the party submitting the brief.

(b) **Brief of Respondent.** The brief of respondent should conform to section (a) and answer the brief of appellant or petitioner. A statement of the issues and a statement of the case need not be made if respondent is satisfied with the statement in the brief of appellant or petitioner. If a respondent is also seeking review, the brief of respondent must state the assignments of error and the issues pertaining to those assignments of error presented for review by respondent and include argument of those issues.

(c) **Reply Brief.** A reply brief should be limited to a response to the issues in the brief to which the reply brief is directed.

RULE 10.4: PREPARATION AND FILING OF BRIEF BY PARTY

(a) **Typing and Filing Brief.** One legible, clean, and reproducible copy of the brief must be filed with the appellate court. The brief should be typed in black on 20-pound substance 8½ by 11-inch white paper. Type must be pica type or its equivalent, with no more than 10 characters an inch. Lines should not generally exceed 5 inches in length. Margins 2 inches on the left side and 1½ inches on the right side and on the top and bottom of each page are preferred. Lines should be double spaced. Quotations may be single spaced and footnotes should be single spaced.

(b) **Length of Brief.** A brief of appellant, petitioner, or respondent, and a pro se brief in a criminal case should not exceed 50 pages. A reply brief should not exceed 25 pages. An amicus curiae brief, or answer thereto, should not exceed 20 pages. For the purpose of determining compliance with this rule appendices, the title sheet, table of contents, and table of authorities are not included. For compelling reasons the court may grant a motion to file an over-length brief.

(c) **Text of Statute, Rule, Jury Instruction, or the Like.** If a party presents an issue which requires study of a statute, rule, regulation, jury instruction, finding of fact, exhibit, or the like, the party should type the material portions of the text out verbatim or include them by facsimile copy in the text or in an appendix to a brief.

(d) **Motion in Brief.** A party may include in a brief only a motion which, if granted, would preclude hearing the case on the merits.

(e) **Reference to Party.** References to parties by such designations as "appellant" and "respondent" should be kept to a minimum. It promotes clarity to use the designations used in the lower court, the actual names of the parties, or descriptive terms such as "the employee," "the injured person," and "the taxpayer."

(f) **Reference to Record.** A reference to the record should designate the page and part of the record. Exhibits should be referred to by number. The clerk's papers should be abbreviated as "CP"; exhibits should be abbreviated as "Ex"; and the report of proceedings should be abbreviated as "RP." Suitable abbreviations for other recurrent references may be used.

(g) **Citations.** Citations must be in conformity with the form used in current volumes of the Washington Reports. Decisions of the Supreme Court and of the Court of Appeals must be cited to the official report thereof and should include the national reporter citation and the year of the decision. The citation of other state court decisions should include both the state and national reporter citations. The citation of a United States Supreme Court decision should include the United States Reports, the United States Supreme Court Reports Lawyers' Edition.

§7.12.1 The Cover

The cover must comply with the requirements set out in the court rules. In Washington, this means that the appellant's brief has a gray cover and the respondent's brief a green one. It also means that only certain information is included and that that information is presented in a specific way. The following example shows the correct format.

No. I-93423

COURT OF APPEALS, DIVISION I,
OF THE STATE OF WASHINGTON

State of Washington, Respondent,
v.
Dean E. Patterson, Appellant.

BRIEF OF APPELLANT

Sarah Fisher
Attorney for
Appellant

Office of Public Defender
623 Second Ave.
Seattle, WA 98104

See Washington Rules on Appeal, Form 5.

§7.12.2   Table of Contents

The first page of your brief should be the table of contents. Page 342 shows the table of contents from the Respondent's brief. *See* Washington Rules on Appeal, Form 6.

§7.12.3   Table of Authorities

Like most jurisdictions, Washington requires a table of authorities listing the cases, constitutional provisions, statutes, rules, and other authorities cited in the brief.

Page 343 shows an example from an Appellant's brief. *See* Washington Rules on Appeal, Form 6.

Table of Contents

TABLE OF AUTHORITIES

Table of Cases

§7.12.4   Assignments of Error

In some states, the court rules require the appellant to set out assignments of error.

RAP 10.3(A)(3)

The brief of the appellant or petitioner should contain . . .
    (3) *Assignments of Error.* A separate concise statement of each error a party contends was made by the trial court.

RAP 10.3(G)

Special Provision for Assignments of Error. A separate assignment of error for each instruction which a party contends was improperly given or refused must be included with reference to each instruction or proposed instruction by number. A separate assignment of error for each finding of fact a party contends was improperly made or refused must be included with reference to the finding or proposed finding by number. The appellate court will only review a claimed error which is included in an assignment of error or clearly disclosed in the associated issue pertaining thereto.

The Washington courts have held that such assignments of error are jurisdictional. If error is not assigned, the court need not consider the issue, even if the issue is argued in the brief.
    The format of such assignment of errors is simple. Each begins with the assertion "The trial court erred when . . . ."

EXAMPLE

The trial court erred when it denied Defendant's Motion to Suppress.

The trial court erred when it overruled defense counsel's timely objections to the prosecutor's references to Defendant's post-arrest silence.

There need not be the same number of assignments of error as there are issues. (One assignment of error could raise a number of issues, or a number of assignments of error could give rise to a single issue.) Unless the Respondent is counter-appealing, the Respondent should not include assignments of error in its brief.

§7.12.5   Issues or Questions Presented

In writing the issue, follow the guidelines set out in section 7.6. If your jurisdiction requires assignment of errors, include a reference to the relevant assignment(s) of error in a parenthetical after the issue statement.

EXAMPLE

Whether the trial court's failure to prevent the prosecutor's repeated references to Mr. Patterson's post-arrest silence violated Mr. Patterson's constitutional rights and deprived him of a fair trial. (Assignment of Error No. 2)

---

§7.12.6   Statement of the Case

In an appellate brief, the statement of the case has two parts: a procedural history and a statement of facts.

RAP 10.3.(A)(4)

Statement of the Case. A fair statement of the facts and procedure relevant to the issues presented for review, without argument. Reference to the record must be included for each factual statement.

In writing the procedural history and statement of facts, follow the advice set out in section 7.5.

§7.12.7   Summary of the Argument

The summary of the argument is just what the title implies: It is a summary of the advocate's argument. Although some courts do not require one (the Washington rules state that the "argument *may* be preceded by a summary"), a summary can be a useful tool. For those judges who read the entire brief, it provides an overview of the arguments and authorities that support those arguments; for those judges who do not read everything, it provides the arguments in a nutshell.

You may want to write your summary of the argument twice. By writing a draft before you write the argument section, you will force yourself to focus. If you understand what it is that you want to argue, you should be able to set out the argument in a paragraph or two. If you can't, more thinking and outlining are needed.

Preparing a draft after you have written the argument section is equally useful. When strung together, the opening sentences of your paragraphs or paragraph blocks should provide the reader with a summary of the argument. If they don't, it is the argument section itself, and not the summary, that needs work.

The most common problem that writers have with the summary of the argument is length. They write too much. The summary of the argument should be no more than one or two pages long with one or two paragraphs for each argument. Citations to authority should also be kept to a minimum. Although you may want to refer to key cases and statutes, the focus should be on the arguments and not the cites.

§7.12.8 The Argument

The argument section has two parts: the argumentative, or point, headings and the arguments themselves. The material on how to write effective argumentative headings is set out in section 7.8. The drafting of the arguments is discussed in section 7.9.

§7.12.9 The Conclusion or Prayer for Relief

The last section of the brief is the conclusion or the prayer for relief. In most jurisdictions, this section is short. Unlike the conclusion in an objective memo, you do not include a summary of the arguments; you did that in the summary of the argument. Instead, you set out the precise relief requested. Are you asking the court to reverse? to remand? to affirm? If you wish, you may make alternative requests, requesting that the appellate court reverse the trial court or, in the alternative, that the case be remanded for a new trial. See section 7.10.

§7.12.10 Signature

The brief must be signed by the attorney who is presenting it. Thus, the following information should be set out after the conclusion.

Date

Respectfully submitted,

[signature]

Name of Attorney
Attorney for [Appellant or Respondent]

§7.12.11　Appendix

If appropriate, you may include an appendix containing the material that the court needs during its review but that might not be readily available to the individual judges. Thus, if the case requires the study of a particular statute, jury instruction, finding of fact, or exhibit, a copy of the relevant material should be placed into the appendix. Each item should be separately labeled (Appendix A, Appendix B), and the items should be listed in the table of contents under the heading "Appendix."

§7.13　Reaching for Excellence

Like pornography, we know it when we see it. We know a superb brief when we read it, an excellent oral argument when we hear it. We have, however, a much harder time defining it. What is it that distinguishes competent advocacy from that which is excellent? And more important, how does one move from being a competent advocate to an excellent one?

§7.13.1　Defining the Differences: The Characteristics of Excellent Advocacy

Excellent advocacy has three characteristics: (1) it is focused; (2) it is insightful; and (3) it is engaging. Instead of just laying out the facts and the law, the advocate weaves them together into a single story that can't be put down.

a.　*Excellent Advocacy Is Focused*

Over and over again, judges tell attorneys the same thing. Don't raise every issue. Don't make every argument. Be selective. Know what you want to say and say it — no more.

The first two parts of this advice create a dilemma for attorneys. If they don't raise an issue or make an argument, they may leave the door open to a claim that they did not effectively represent the client. If they do raise all the issues and make all of the arguments, they probably will not be persuasive. The weak issues will draw the court's attention away from the strong, and the weak arguments will dilute those with merit.

Excellent advocates find one of two solutions: Either they trust their own judgment and raise only the best issues, or they find an umbrella under which numerous issues or arguments can be gathered into one coherent whole. Either way, the argument is kept focused. The advocate tells one story, not five or six.

The last part of this advice, know what you want to say and say it — no more, creates its own set of problems. It presumes expertise not often possessed by the beginning advocate as well as the time needed to revise and rehearse, something often in short supply or difficult for the client to finance. The weak or mediocre advocate's solution is the long, unfocused brief. It is easier, and much faster to write. The writer simply includes everything, hoping that somewhere in the heap the court will find a gem it likes. Doing the sorting oneself is much harder: Not only must the advocate know much more, but he or she must take the time to find the diamond or to polish a stone until it shines like one.

b.　Excellent Advocacy Is Insightful

Insight. Excellent advocates have lots of it. Not only do they know the law, the facts, and their audience, but they see things that others don't. They are able to see beyond the obvious, beyond the conventional arguments.

The source of this insight is difficult to pinpoint. Those who have it have mastered the conventions. They don't just apply them mechanically; they understand the rationale underlying them. (See page 349, below.) But there is more. Most of the people who fall within this group share several other characteristics: they are bright; they read widely, not just in law but in numerous other fields; and they have common sense. In addition, they are often the people for whom law was, at least initially, the most difficult. The holistic style of thinking that may have initially caused them problems in law school now works to their advantage.

c.　Excellent Advocacy Is Engaging

By definition, a brief or argument that is focused and insightful is engaging. We are drawn naturally to the advocate and his or her argument.

Often, however, there is even more. The best advocates are almost always great storytellers. Although their style is not that of a mystery writer, their writing is lively, their words and phrases carefully chosen to create the desired mood, image, and nuance. In addition, the best advocates believe, or at least appear to believe, in their argument, their case, their client. And because they believe, their readers are engaged — they read or listen, looking for the source of the advocate's enthusiasm and conviction.

§7.13.2　Breaking Through: Moving from Competence to Excellence

An even more difficult question than what is excellent advocacy is the question of how one moves from being a mechanic to an inventor, from an artisan to an artist, from writing a "B" brief to one that deserves an "A+."

EXHIBIT 7.5   The Stages of Advocacy — I

**Stage 2
(Competence)**

Knows the standard moves and the rationale underlying them

Is able to adapt rules and conventions to new situations

**Stage 1
(The Beginning)**

Knows the standard moves but does not understand the rationale underlying them

Applies rules and conventions mechanically

Foundation

Knows the structure of the United States system of government and legal system

---

Many argue that the move from competent to excellent cannot be taught. Although you can teach people to paint, you cannot teach them to be Michelangelo.

Others disagree. Although Michelangelo was born with talent, he was not born a great artist. Like so many others of his day, he learned his craft as an apprentice, studying under both Domenico Ghirlandaio and Bertoldo, a pupil of Donatello. In addition, he worked in an environment that both nurtured his talent and pushed him to excellence. Supported by the Medici and driven by his competition with Leonardo da Vinci, Michelangelo developed his craft and took art where it had not been before.

a. Developing Competence

In moving toward excellence, most advocates go through two stages. During the first stage, the advocate is like the novice cook, only able to follow the recipe set out in the cookbook. This changes, however, as the advocate moves to the second stage. As the advocate learns why certain ingredients are added in certain amounts at certain times, he or she is able to adapt the "recipe" to meet new situations, new demands. See Exhibit 7.5.

At the first stage, the beginning advocate might write a heading like the following.

EXAMPLE

The Identifications Should Be Suppressed Because They Are Suggestive.

Although the advocate used the conventional format, he or she did so mechanically. The heading does not reflect an understanding of the rationale for including a heading or even of the law itself.

This changes as advocates move to the next stage. As they begin to understand that argumentative headings are more than just a requirement under the rules, the headings change. The advocate uses the headings both to structure the argument and to persuade the court. Similarly, instead of parroting the law, the advocate begins to understand the rule (it is the police procedures that are suggestive, not the identification) and the reasons for it (evidence is suppressed to deter inappropriate police conduct). The revised heading reflects the change.

EXAMPLE

The evidence should be suppressed because the police acted inappropriately when, through their conduct and words, they suggested to Martinez that Patterson was the person who had assaulted her.

This heading is the work of a competent advocate. It follows the conventions (assertion, connector, support), but it does not do so mechanically. The advocate understands both the function argumentative headings serve and the law itself.

b. Breaking Through

For some advocates, competence is not enough. They want to break through the steel barrier that separates competence from excellence. See Exhibit 7.6.

1. Breakthrough Thinking

The people who cross the barrier separating competence from excellence are those who are capable of breakthrough thinking. They are

EXHIBIT 7.6   **The Stages of Advocacy — II**

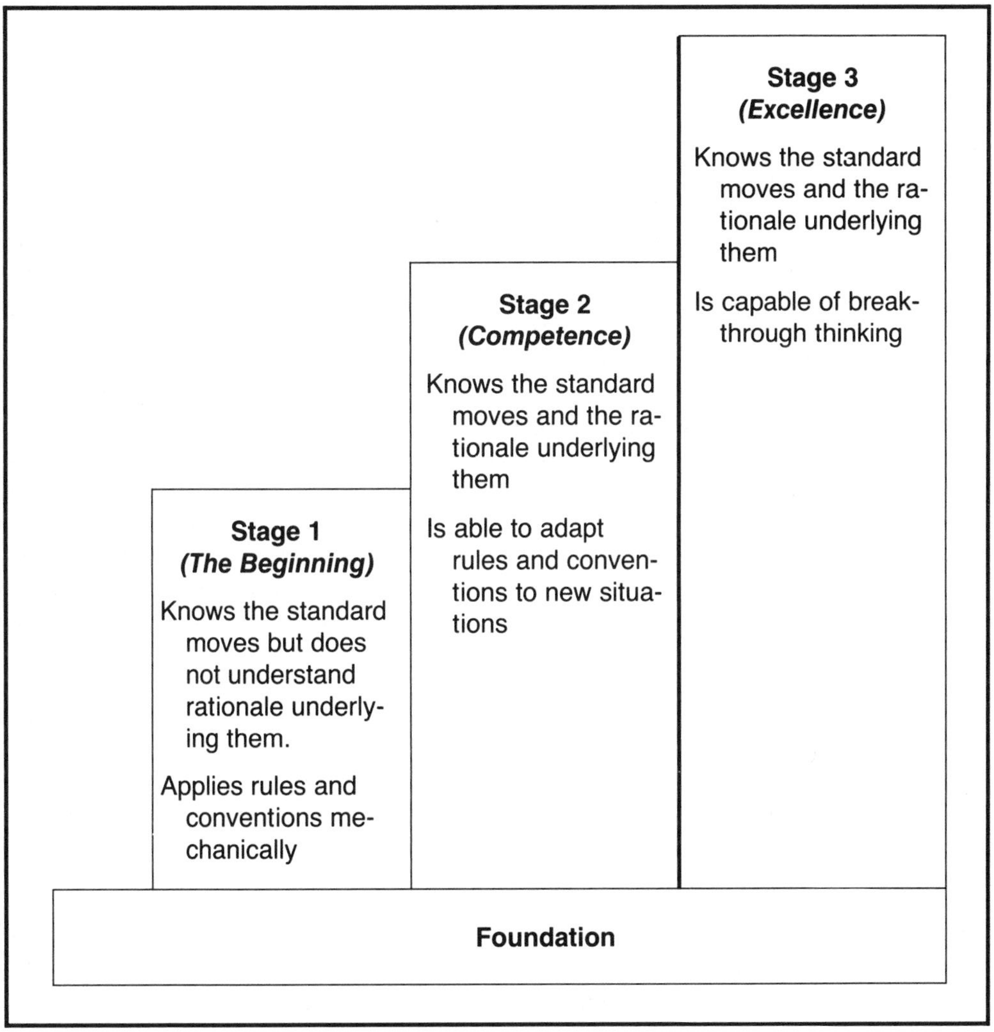

**Stage 3
(Excellence)**

Knows the standard moves and the rationale underlying them

Is capable of breakthrough thinking

**Stage 2
(Competence)**

Knows the standard moves and the rationale underlying them

Is able to adapt rules and conventions to new situations

**Stage 1
(The Beginning)**

Knows the standard moves but does not understand rationale underlying them.

Applies rules and conventions mechanically

Foundation

the children who, when challenged to think of ten ways of using a pencil other than as a writing implement, can come up with twenty-five; the military officer who, when told that he will be shot at dawn, responds by thinking about how he can use the guns to facilitate his own escape; the defense attorney who sees the Rodney King videotape not as a problem but as an opportunity. In sum, they are the people who see past the obvious, past the conventional barriers. They can adopt a totally new perspective and turn seeming liabilities into assets.

Breakthrough thinking occurs differently for different people. Sometimes, it is a matter of being willing to take risks, as Michelangelo did when he did autopsies on human cadavers in order to study anatomy. Although this breakthrough allowed him to take his art to a new level, it came at the risk of excommunication and ostracization.

At other times, breakthrough thinking requires seeing what others do not see. When Alexander Fleming saw mold growing in a laboratory dish containing bacteria, he did not see the obvious, a ruined experiment; instead, he noticed that all the bacteria around the mold had been killed, a breakthrough that led to penicillin.

At still other times, breakthrough thinking occurs when a person uses a metaphor or analogy to see the problem in a new light or when, like a computer, a person arranges and rearranges information until a solution appears. It occurs when a person brings two previously distinct bodies of information together for the first time, or when a person is the first to name a previously amorphous concept, such as police brutality or battered woman's syndrome, so that once named, the concept can be explored and understood at a new level.

However it occurs, breakthrough thinking goes beyond the established standard moves, creating new ones. Once those children who are trying to come up with twenty-five ways of using a pencil "break through" the idea that the pencil must remain whole, they see several new categories of use. A pencil broken in half can be used as popsicle sticks or even corn-on-the-cob holders. And once this new move is established — breaking the item into smaller pieces — it is only a small step to thinking of grinding up that once-whole pencil and using it as sawdust.

The most common type of breakthrough, however, is to turn an apparent liability into an asset. When the people at the 3-M corporation tried to make a super glue that would bond with anything, they accidentally invented one of the weakest adhesives known. Instead of discarding the adhesive as a failure, the chemists explored possible uses for a weak glue — a classic example of breakthrough thinking — and put the weak adhesive on the backs of what later became Post-it Notes.

Similarly, once the defense lawyers in the Rodney King case broke through the idea that the videotape was a liability, they saw how they could use it to their advantage. Step one was to play and replay the videotape to desensitize the jury to its violence, and thus to neutralize its effect as evidence for the prosecution. But the attorneys for the police officers went even further. They replayed the tape over and over *very slowly,* using it to enhance their theory of the case, which was that Rodney King was in control of the situation.

2. The Right Case

Although competence can win routine cases, the tough ones not only require, but inspire, excellence. Faced with a flawed piece of marble that had stymied several other sculptors before him, Michelangelo rose to the challenge and created the *David.* Faced with a birth defect (a missing right hand) that would have prevented most people from even considering a career as an athlete, Jim Abbot became not just a professional baseball player but an outstanding pitcher. Faced with what everyone considered a losing case, the counsel for the police officers rose to the occasion and won the Rodney King case.

3.   The Right Environment

It is not a coincidence that some of the world's greatest artists — Donatello, Raphael, da Vinci, and Michelangelo — were working at approximately the same time in roughly the same place. The move from competence to excellence seldom occurs in a vacuum.

Instead, it most often occurs in an environment that is supportive as well as competitive. Up against a deadline, the engineer solves a problem while talking with colleagues at lunch; matched against the best prosecutor in the county, defense counsel tries out numerous ideas on the "best and brightest" in the office before coming up with the winning theory of the case.

4.   The Right Person

It is also not a coincidence that people who are capable of breakthrough thinking share certain personal characteristics. They are the people who are willing to look for multiple solutions to a problem and who have the discipline to do so. They work independently, but when they hit a dead end, seek out others, both sharing their own ideas and listening to the ideas of others.

They are also committed, energetic, and hardworking. They may work on a problem for days at a time, taking only short breaks and shrugging off initial failures. Excellence seldom comes easily. As Thomas Edison noted, "genius is 1 percent inspiration and 99 percent perspiration."

Finally, most breakthrough thinkers are experts in their field, knowing not only the subject matter but also the "culture." Michelangelo knew not only the techniques of his art, but also the values of the community that would receive and judge it. Similarly, the excellent advocate knows not only what types of arguments can be made, but also how a particular argument may be received by the legal community as a whole and, in many instances, by its specific audience.

Thus, breakthrough thinking builds on more than just the first two stages. Although it cannot occur without them, more is required. Breakthrough thinking occurs when the right people in the right environments tackle the right problems.

§7.13.3   Facilitating the Breakthrough

So how does one move from writing the competent brief to writing one that is excellent?

Although the answer is far from clear, there are some things that we do know. Those making the move create opportunities for success. Some seek out the master teacher, the right mentor; others look for colleagues who will support, challenge, and inspire them. Some chose a job not just for what it will pay, but also for what it will demand from them and how it will make them grow.

Still others make it a point to look for the tough cases, the ones that demand excellence, rather than backing away from them. They develop their ability to brainstorm and make a regular practice of looking at problems from new perspectives. They cultivate the ability to stick with a tough problem, thinking and rethinking it, sounding out others, gleaning information from multiple sources.

And, to a one, they strive for more than they can achieve, knowing that even if they fall short of the "Michelangelo standard" they have set for themselves, they will have accomplished more by aiming high.

> Ah, but a man's reach should exceed his grasp,
> Or what's a heaven for?
>
> — Robert Browning, *Andrea del Sarto*

§7.13.4 The All-Important Lingering Question

In the hands of an advocate, excellence is a powerful tool and perhaps a powerful weapon. Used appropriately, it can be a force for finding truth and justice and improving the human condition; used inappropriately, it can harm and destroy. The genius that led to the Sistine Chapel has much in common with the genius that led to nuclear weapons.

The question then for all breakthrough thinkers, particularly those in law, is one of the ethics of excellence.

Consider, for example, the Rodney King case. There is no doubt that in that case defense counsel broke through the barrier between competence and excellence. They took a case that no one imagined they could win and won.

But did their excellence foster or hinder justice? We will let history answer that question, but the larger question — how one should use the power of excellence — is one that every excellent attorney must face.

Chapter 8

Oral Advocacy

Oral argument. For some, it is the part of practice that they most enjoy; for others, it is the part they most dread.

Whichever group you fall into, oral argument is probably not what you expect. It is not a speech, a debate, or a performance. Instead, when done right, it is a dialogue between the attorneys, who explain the issues, law, and facts, and the judges, who ask questions, not because they want to badger the attorney or because they want to see how much he or she knows, but because they want to make the right decision.

§8.1 AUDIENCE

In making an oral argument, who is your audience?

At the trial court level, the audience is the trial judge who is hearing the motion; at the appellate level, it is the panel of judges hearing the appeal. In both instances, the audience is extremely sophisticated. Although an eloquent oral argument is more persuasive than one that isn't, form seldom wins out over substance. If you don't have anything to say, it doesn't matter how well you say it.

At oral argument, the court can be either "hot" or "cold." The court is hot when the judges come to the oral argument prepared. The judges have studied the briefs and, at least in some appellate courts, have met in a pre-oral argument conference to discuss the case. In contrast, a cold court is not as prepared. The judge or judges are not familiar with the case and if they have read the briefs, have done so only quickly.

As a general rule, hot courts are more active than cold ones. Because they have studied the briefs, they often have their own agenda. They want to know more about point A, or they are concerned about how the rule being advocated might be applied in other cases. As a consequence, they often take more control over the argument, directing counsel to discuss certain issues and asking a number of questions. A cold court is usually comparatively passive. Because the judges are not as familiar with the case, most of their questions are informational. They want counsel to clarify the issue, supply a fact, or explain in more detail how the law should be applied.

§8.2 PURPOSE

In making your oral argument, you have two goals: to educate and to persuade. You want to explain the law and the facts in such a way that the court rules in your client's favor.

§8.3 PREPARING FOR ORAL ARGUMENT

The key to a good oral argument is preparation. You must know what you must argue to win; you must know your case; and you must have practiced both the text of your argument and your responses to the questions the court can reasonably be expected to ask.

§8.3.1 Deciding What to Argue

In making your argument, you will have only a limited amount of time. Depending on the case and the court, you will be granted ten, fifteen, or thirty minutes to make your points, answer the judge or judges' questions and, if you are the appellant, to make your rebuttal. Because time is so limited, you will not be able to make every argument that you made in your brief. You must be selective.

In selecting the issues and arguments that you will make, choose those that are essential to your case. Don't spend your time on the easy argument if, to get the relief you want, you must win on the hard one. Make the arguments that you must make to win.

Also anticipate the arguments that the other side is likely to make. Although you don't want to make the other side's arguments, try to integrate your responses into your argument. Similarly, anticipate the court's concerns and decide how they can best be handled.

§8.3.2 Preparing an Outline

Do not write out your argument. If you do, you will either read it, or perhaps worse yet, memorize and recite it. Neither is appropriate. A dialogue does not have a predetermined text. Instead, prepare either a list of the points that you want to cover or an outline.

Because it is difficult to predict how much of the time will be spent answering the court's questions, most advocates prepare two lists or outlines: a short version, in which they list only those points that they must make, and a long version, in which they list the points that they would like to make if they have time. If the court is hot and asks a number of questions, they argue from the short list or outline; if the court is cold, they use the long one.

§8.3.3   Practicing the Argument

The next step is to practice, both by yourself and with colleagues. Working alone, practice your opening, your closing, your statements of the law, and the arguments themselves. Think carefully about the language that you will use and about how you will move from one issue to the next and, within an issue, from argument to argument. Also list every question that a judge could be reasonably expected to ask, and decide (1) how you will respond and (2) how you can move from the answer to another point in your argument. (See page 364.)

Then, with colleagues, practice delivering the argument. Ask your colleagues to play the role of the judge(s), sometimes asking almost no questions and at other times asking many. As you deliver the argument, concentrate on "reading" the court, adjusting your argument to meet its concerns; on responding to questions; and on the transitions between issues and arguments. Before a major argument, you will want to go through your argument five to ten times, practicing in front as many different people as you can.

§8.3.4   Reviewing the Facts and Law

You will also want to review the facts of the case, the law, and both your brief and your opponent's brief. When you walk into the courtroom, you should know everything that there is to know about your case.

Note

In practice, months or years may pass between the writing of the brief and the oral argument. When this is the case, it is essential that you update your research, when appropriate filing a supplemental brief with the court.

——————————

§8.3.5   Organizing Your Materials

Part of the preparation is getting your materials organized. You do not want to be flipping through your notes or searching the record during oral argument.

a. Notes or Outline

To avoid the "flipping pages syndrome," limit yourself to two pages of notes: a one-page short list or outline and a one-page long list or outline. These pages can then be laid side-by-side in front of you on the podium. (So that they don't blow off, many advocates staple the pages to the inside of a manila folder.) Colored markers can be used to highlight the key portions of the argument.

b. The Briefs

You will want to take a copy of your brief and your opponent's brief with you to the podium, placing them on the inside shelf. Make sure that you know both what is in the briefs and where that information is located.

c. The Record

In arguing an appeal, you will usually want to have the relevant portions of the record in the courtroom, either on the podium shelf or on counsel table. You should also be fully familiar with the record, as with the briefs, knowing both what is in the record and where particular information can be found. To assist them in quickly locating information, many attorneys tab the record or prepare a quick index.

d. The Law

Although you do not need to have copies of all of the statutes and cases with you, you should be familiar with both the statutes and cases that you cited in your brief and those on which your opponent's case is based. If you do bring cases with you, have them indexed and highlighted for quick reference.

§8.4   COURTROOM PROCEDURES AND ETIQUETTE

Like much of law, oral argument has its own set of conventions and procedures.

§8.4.1   Seating

In most jurisdictions, the moving party sits on the left (when facing the court) and the responding party sits on the right.

§8.4.2   Before the Case Is Called

If court is not in session, sit at counsel table, reviewing your notes or quietly conversing with co-counsel. If court is in session, sit in the audience until the prior case is completed. When your case is called, rise and move to counsel table.

§8.4.3   Courtroom Etiquette

Stand each time you are instructed to do so by the bailiff. For example, stand when the bailiff calls court into session and announces the judge or judges, and stand when court is recessed or adjourned. In the first instance, remain standing until the judges are seated, and in the latter instance, remain standing until the judges have left the courtroom.

Also stand each time you address the court, whether it be to tell the court that you are ready to proceed, to make your argument, or to respond to a question.

In addressing the court, you will want to use the phrases "Your Honor," "Your Honors," "this Court," "the Court," or, occasionally, the judge's name: "Judge Brown" or "Justice Smith." Never use a judge or justice's first name.

Finally, never speak directly to opposing counsel. While court is in session, all your comments must be addressed to the court. Also remember that you are always "on." While opposing counsel is arguing, sit attentively at counsel table, listening and, if appropriate, taking notes.

§8.4.4   Appropriate Dress

As a sign of respect, both for the court and the client, most attorneys dress for oral argument. Men wear conservative suits and ties, and women wear conservative dresses or suits. The key is to look professional but not severe. During oral argument, the judge's attention should be focused on your argument and not your attire.

§8.5   MAKING THE ARGUMENT

Like the brief, the oral argument has a prescribed format.

§8.5.1   Introductions

Begin your oral argument by introducing yourself and your client. At the trial court level, the language is relatively informal. Most attorneys say "Good morning, Your Honor," and then introduce himself or herself and the client. At the appellate level, the language is more formal.

EXHIBIT 8.1   **Outline of Oral Argument**

Outline of Oral Argument

A. *Moving party* (party bringing the motion or, on appeal, the appellant)
    1. Introductions
    2. Opening
    3. Statement of the issue(s)
    4. Brief summary of the significant facts
    5. Argument
    6. Conclusion and request for relief
B. *Responding party* (party opposing the motion or, on appeal, in the respondent or appellee)
    1. Introductions
    2. Opening
    3. Statement of position
    4. Brief summary of significant facts (when appropriate)
    5. Argument
    6. Conclusion and request for relief
C. *Moving party's rebuttal*
D. *Sur-rebuttal* (when allowed)

By convention, most attorneys begin by saying, "May it please the Court, my name is _____, and I represent the [appellant] [respondent], _____."

In many courts, the introduction is also used to reserve rebuttal time. The attorney for the moving party reserves rebuttal either before introducing himself or herself or immediately afterwards. "Your Honor, at this time, I would like to reserve _____ minutes for rebuttal."

§8.5.2   Opening

The first minute of your argument should be memorable. The opening sentences should catch the judge's attention, making the case's importance clear, establishing the theme, and creating the appropriate context for the argument that follows.

§8.5.3   Statement of the Issues

a.   *The Moving Party*

If you are the moving party, you need to set out the issues. Sometimes this is best done as part of the opening. From the issue statement alone, the case's importance is clear: "In this case, the appellant asks the Court to overrule *Roe v. Wade.*" At other times, such a strategy is not effective. For example, few trial judges would find the following opening memorable: "In this case, the defendant asks the court to suppress identification testimony." In such cases, the opening and the statement of the issues should not be combined.

Note

As a general rule, the statement of the issues should precede the summary of the facts. Before hearing the facts, the court needs a context. There are times, however, when it is more effective to set out the issues after the summary of the facts.

Wherever they are presented, the issue statements must be tailored to oral argument. What is effective in writing may not be effective when spoken. For example, although the under-does-when format works well in a brief, it does not work well orally. In oral argument, the issue needs to be presented more simply. "In this case, the court is asked to decide whether . . ." or "This case presents two issues: first, whether . . . and second, whether . . . ."

Even though they are streamlined, the issues should be presented in the light most favorable to the client. The questions should be framed as they were in the brief, and the significant and emotionally favorable facts should be included. (Review section 7.6.)

b.　The Responding Party

As a general rule, the responding party does not restate the issue or issues. Instead, it states its position, either as part of its opening or as a lead-in to its arguments: "Martinez's show-up identification need not be suppressed: The police procedures were not impermissibly suggestive and, under the totality of the circumstances, the identification is reliable."

§8.5.4　Summary of Facts

a.　The Moving Party

When arguing to a cold court, you will want to include a summary of the facts, in one to three minutes telling the court what the case is about. You may also want to include a summary of the facts when arguing to a hot court. If the facts are particularly important, you will want to summarize them, refreshing the court's memory and presenting the facts in the light most favorable to the client. There will, however, be times when a separate summary of the facts is not the best use of limited time. In these cases, instead of presenting the facts in a separate summary at the beginning, integrate them into the argument.

b. The Responding Party

As the responding party, you do not want to use your time repeating what opposing counsel just said. Consequently, for you a summary of the facts is optional, even if the court is cold. If opposing counsel set out the facts accurately, the summary can be omitted. Just integrate the significant facts into the argument. You will, however, want to include a summary if opposing counsel misstated key facts or omitted facts that are important to your argument or if you need to present the facts from your client's point of view.

c. References to the Record

In presenting the facts, you will not, as a matter of course, include references to the record. You must, however, be able to provide such references if asked to do so by the court or if you are correcting a misstatement made by opposing counsel.

§8.5.5 The Argument

Unless the issues and arguments build on each other, start with your strongest issue and in discussing that issue, your strongest argument. This allows you to take advantage of the positions of emphasis and ensures that you will have the opportunity to make your best, or most crucial, arguments. In addition, it usually results in better continuity. Because the moving party's strongest issue is usually the responding party's weakest, the moving party's final issue will be the responding party's first, providing the responding party with an easy opening for its argument.

Moving Party   *Responding Party*

Issue 1 ⟶ Issue 2   Issue 2 ⟶ Issue 1

In presenting the arguments, do what you did in your brief, but in abbreviated form. When the law is not in dispute, begin by presenting the rule of law, presenting that law in the light most favorable to your client (see section 7.9.2, page 321). Then argue that law, explaining why the court should reach the result that you advocate (see section 7.9.2, page 328). When it is the law itself that is in dispute, argue your interpretation.

In both instances, you must support your position, presenting arguments based on the plain language of the statute or rule, legislative intent, policy, the facts of the case, or analogous cases. When appropriate, cite to the relevant portions of a statute or to a common law rule and, in using analogous cases, be specific, explaining the rule that the court applied, the significant facts, and the court's reasoning. Although you should have the full case citations available, you do not need to include them in your argument.

Although you want to cite to the relevant authorities, you do not, as a general rule, want to quote them or your brief. Reading more than a line is seldom effective. If it is important that the court have specific language before it, refer the judge or judges to the appropriate page in the brief or, better yet, prepare a visual aid.

There are several other things that you need to keep in mind in making your argument. First, it is usually more difficult to follow an oral argument than a written one. As a result, it is important to include sufficient roadmaps, signposts, and transitions. Make both the structure of your argument and the connections between ideas explicit.

Second, you need to manage your time. Do not spend so much time on one issue or argument that you do not have time for the other issue or issues or other arguments. Because it is difficult to predict how many questions the court will ask, practice a short and a long version of each argument.

§8.5.6 Answering Questions

You should welcome the court's questions. They tell you how the court is thinking about your case, what the judges understand, and what they still question. If you're not getting questions, it is usually a bad sign. The judges have either already made up their minds or are not listening.

Questions from the bench fall into several categories. Some are mere requests for information. The judge wants to clarify a fact or your position on an issue or wants to know more about the rule or how you think it should be applied.

Other questions are designed to elicit a particular response from you: Judge A agrees with your position and wants you to pursue a particular line of argument for the benefit of Judge B, who is not yet persuaded. Still other questions are designed to test the merits of your argument. These questions can have as their focus your case or, at the appellate level, future cases. If the court applies rule A, what does that mean for cases X, Y, and Z?

Whatever the type of question, when the judge begins to speak, you must stop. Although judges can interrupt you, you should not interrupt them. As the judge speaks, listen, not only to the question that is being asked but also for clues about how the judge is perceiving the case.

The hardest part comes next. Before answering the judge, think through your answer. Although the second or two of silence may make you uncomfortable, the penalty for answering too quickly can be severe. Although few cases are won at oral argument, some are lost, usually because in answering a question the attorney conceded or asserted too much. The second or two of silence is by far better than an unfavorable ruling.

When you know what you want to say, answer. In most instances, you will want to begin by giving the judge a one-, two-, or three-word answer. "Yes." "No." "Yes, but . . . ." "No, but . . . ." "In some cases, ..." Then explain or support your answer, integrating the points that you want to make into your answer when possible. Instead of thinking of questions as interruptions, think of them as another vehicle for making your argument.

There are a number of things that you should not do in responding to question. First, do not tell the judge that you will answer the question later. It is you and not the judge who must be flexible.

Second, do not argue with the judge. Answer all questions calmly and thoughtfully. Do not raise your voice, and even if you are frustrated, don't let it show. If one line of argument isn't working and the point is essential to your case, try another, and if that line doesn't work, try still another. When the point is not important or you have given all the answers that you have, answer, and then without pausing move as smoothly as you can into the next part of your argument.

Third, after answering the question, don't stop and wait for the judge's approval or permission to continue. Answer the question, and then, unless asked another question, move to the next part of your argument.

Finally, don't answer by asking the judge a question. In oral argument, it is inappropriate to question a judge.

§8.5.7 Closing

The closing is as important as the opening. Because it is a position of emphasis, you want to end on a favorable point.

One way of doing this is to end with a summary of your arguments, reminding the court of your strongest points and requesting the appropriate relief. Although this is often effective, it can also be ineffective. Many judges stop listening when they hear the phrase "In conclusion" or "In summary." Consequently, when using a summary, avoid stock openers. Catch the court's attention by repeating a key phrase, weaving the pieces together, or returning to the points made in your opening.

Another way is to end on a strong point. If you are running out of time, it may be better to stop at the end of an argument or after answering a question than to rush through a prepared closing. Like a good comedian, a good advocate knows when to sit down.

§8.5.8 Rebuttal

Perhaps the hardest part of the oral argument is rebuttal. In one or two minutes you must identify the crucial issues and make your strongest argument or response.

As a general rule, do not try to make more than one or two points during rebuttal. The points should be selected because of their importance to your case: Do not merely repeat what you said in the main portion or your argument or respond to trivial points made by opposing counsel. Instead, make your rebuttal a true rebuttal, responding to significant points made by opposing counsel or questions or concerns raised by the court during opposing counsel's argument.

Because time is so limited, most advocates begin their rebuttal by telling the court how many points they plan to make: "I would like to make two points." This introduction tells the court what to expect. The advocate then makes his or her first point and supports it and, unless interrupted by a question, moves to the second point. Most advocates close by quickly repeating their request for relief.

§8.6　DELIVERING THE ARGUMENT

Every advocate has his or her own style. While some are soft-spoken, others are dynamic; while some are plain-speaking, others strive for eloquence. As an advocate, you will need to develop your own style, building on your strengths and minimizing your weaknesses.

Whatever your style, there are certain "rules" that you should follow.

§8.6.1　Do Not Read Your Argument

The first, and perhaps most important, rule is not to read your argument. Similarly, do not try to deliver a memorized speech. Know what you want to say and then talk to the court. You are a teacher, sharing information and answering the court's questions.

§8.6.2　Maintain Eye Contact

If you don't read, you will be able to maintain eye contact with the court. This is important for several reasons. First, it helps you keep the court's attention. It is very difficult not to listen to a person who is looking you in the eye. Second, it helps you "read" the court. By studying the judges, you can often determine (1) whether they already agree with you on a point and you can move to the next part of your argument; (2) whether they are confused; or (3) whether you have not yet persuaded them. Finally, eye contact is important because of what it says about you and your argument. An advocate who looks the judges in the eye is perceived as being more confident and more competent than one who doesn't.

Note

When you are arguing to an appellate court, maintain eye contact with all of the judges. Even when answering a specific judge's question, maintain eye contact with all of the judges.

---

§8.6.3   Do Not Slouch, Rock, or Put Your Hands in Your Pockets

In delivering an oral argument to the court, stand erect, but not stiffly, behind the podium. Do not rock from foot to foot, and do not put your hands in your pockets.

Although it may be appropriate to move around the courtroom when arguing to a jury, you should not do so when arguing to the court.

§8.6.4   Limit Your Gestures and Avoid Distracting Mannerisms

Gestures are appropriate in an oral argument. They should, however, be natural and relatively constrained. If you talk with your hands, mentally put yourself inside a small telephone booth.

You also want to avoid distracting mannerisms. Do not play with a pen, the edge of your notes, or the keys in your pocket. In addition, do not repeatedly push hair out of your eyes or glasses back up on your nose.

§8.6.5   Speak So That You Can Be Easily Understood

In delivering your oral argument, speak loudly and clearly enough that you can be easily heard by the judges.

Also try to modulate your voice, varying both the pace and how loudly you speak. If you want to emphasize a point, speak more slowly and either more softly or more loudly.

§8.7   Making Your Argument Persuasive

In delivering your oral argument, you will want to use many of the same techniques that you used in writing your brief. In stating the issue, frame the question so that it suggests the answer favorable to your client and, in presenting the facts, emphasize the favorable facts by placing them in positions of emphasis and by using detail and sentence structure to your advantage. Review sections 7.5 and 7.6. Also present the law in the light most favorable to your client. State favorable rules broadly, use cases to your advantage, and emphasize the policies that support your client's position. (See section 7.9.)

You should also pick your words carefully. Select words both for their denotation and their connotation and avoid words and phrases that undermine the persuasiveness of your argument. If you are the plaintiff, don't say, "It is the plaintiff's position that the line-up was suggestive." Say "The line-up was suggestive." Similarly, don't say, "We feel that the prosecutor acted improperly when she referred to the defendant's post-arrest silence." Say instead, "The prosecutor acted improperly when she referred to the defendant's post-arrest silence."

§8.8   HANDLING THE PROBLEMS

Because an oral argument isn't scripted, you need to prepare for the unexpected, deciding in advance how you will handle the problems that might arise.

§8.8.1   Counsel Has Misstated Facts or Law

If opposing counsel misstates an important fact or the governing law, you will usually want to bring the error to the attention of the court. This should, however, be done carefully.

First, make sure that you are right. If there is time, double-check the record, the statute, or the case. Second, make sure that you are correcting a misstatement of fact or law and not opposing party's interpretation of a fact, statute, or case. Third, correct the mistake and not opposing counsel. Instead of criticizing or attacking opposing counsel, simply provide the court with the correct information and, if possible, the citation to the record or the language of the statute or case.

EXAMPLE

"Ms. Martinez did not see the assailant three times. She testified that she saw him twice: once when he drove by slowly and then when he pulled in front of her."

Finally, correct only those errors that are significant.

§8.8.2   You Make a Mistake

If you make a significant mistake, correct it as soon as you can.

§8.8.3 Not Enough Time

Despite the best of planning, you will sometimes run out of time. You may have gotten more questions than you expected, leaving you little or no remaining time for your last issue or your final points. When this happens, you have two options. You can either quickly summarize the points that you would have made, or you can tell the court that, because you are out of time, you will rely on your brief for the issues and arguments that you didn't cover.

What you don't want to do is exceed the time that you have allotted. Unless the court gives you permission to continue, you must stop when your time is up.

§8.8.4 Too Much Time

This is not a problem. You do not need to use all of your allotted time. When you have said what you need to say, thank the court and sit down.

§8.8.5 You Don't Know the Answer to a Question

Occasionally you will be asked a question that you can't answer. If it is a question about the facts of your case or about the law, don't try to bluff. Instead, do one of the following: (1) if you can do so in a few seconds, look up the answer; (2) tell the judge that at this point you can't answer the question but that you will be glad to provide the information after oral argument, or (3) give the best answer that you can.

EXAMPLE

"So that I may answer correctly, let me quickly check the record."

"I'm not sure what the actual words were. I will check and provide you with that information after oral argument."

"As I recall, the police officer testified that he asked the question twice."

If the question raises an issue you hadn't considered, the options are slightly different. You can either trust yourself and, on the spot, give your best answer or tell the court that you need to give the question some thought.

§8.8.6 You Didn't Understand the Question

If you don't understand a question, tell the judge and either ask him or her to repeat the question or repeat the question in your own words, asking the judge whether you understood correctly. "I'm sorry, I'm not sure that I understand your question. Could you please rephrase it?" "If I am correct, you are asking whether . . . ."

§8.8.7 You Become Flustered or Draw a Blank

It happens, at some time or another, to almost everyone. You become flustered or draw a blank. When this happens, "buy" a few seconds by either taking a drink of water or taking a deep breath and looking down at your notes. If you still can't continue with the point that you were making, move to another one.

§8.8.8 You're Asked to Concede a Point

Concessions can work both to your advantage and to your disadvantage. You will win points by conceding points that you can't win or that are not important to your argument. You can, however, lose your case if you concede too much. You must, therefore, know your case, conceding when appropriate and otherwise politely, but firmly, standing your ground.

§8.9 A FINAL NOTE

No matter how much they dread it, most individuals end up enjoying oral argument for what it is, a stimulating dialogue among intelligent people.

Checklist for Critiquing the Oral Argument

I. Preparation

- The advocate knows the law and the facts of the case.
- The advocate has anticipated and prepared rebuttals for the arguments that the other side is likely to make.
- The advocate has anticipated and prepared responses to the questions that the court is likely to ask.
- The advocate has determined what arguments he or she needs to make to win.

- The advocate has prepared two outlines: a long outline, which can be used if the court asks only a few questions, and a short outline, which can be used in case the court asks more questions.

II. Content and Organization

A. *Introduction*
- The advocate identifies himself or herself and his or her client.
- When appropriate, the advocate requests rebuttal time.

B. *Opening and Statement of Issues or Position*
- The advocate begins the argument with a sentence or phrase that catches the attention of the court and establishes the client's theory of the case.
- The advocate then presents the question or states his or her position.
- The question or statement of position is framed so that it supports the advocate's theory of the case and suggests an answer favorable to the client.
- The question or statement of position is presented using language that is easily understood.

C. *Summary of Facts*
- When appropriate, the advocate includes a short summary of the facts in which he or she explains the case and establishes an appropriate context. When a separate summary of the facts is not appropriate, the advocate weaves the facts into the argument.
- The facts are presented accurately but in the light most favorable to the client. The positions of emphasis and detail are used effectively, and words have been selected for both their denotation and connotation.

D. *Argument*
- The advocate discusses the issues and makes the arguments needed to win.
- The argument is structured in such a way that it is easy to follow: (1) issues and arguments are discussed in a logical order and (2) sufficient roadmaps, signposts, and transitions are used.
- The arguments are supported. The advocate uses the law, analogous cases, policy, and the facts to support each of his or her assertions.
- The law, analogous cases, policies, and facts are presented accurately.
- The law, analogous cases, policies, and facts are presented in the light most favorable to the client.

  E. *Questions from the Bench*
- When a judge asks a question, the advocate immediately stops talking and listens to the question.
- The advocate thinks before answering.
- As a general rule, the advocate begins his or her answer with a short response (Yes, No, In this case) and then supports that answer.
- After answering the question, the advocate moves back into his or her argument without pausing or waiting for the judge to give permission to continue.
- The advocate sees questions not as an interruption but as another opportunity to get his or her argument before the court.
- As he or she listens to the questions, the advocate adjusts the argument to match the concerns and interests of the court.

  F. *Closing*
- The advocate ends the argument by summarizing the main points or on a strong point.
- When appropriate, the advocate includes a request for relief.

  G. *Rebuttal*
- The advocate uses rebuttal to respond to the one or two most important points raised by opposing counsel or the court.

III. Delivery

- The advocate treats the argument as a dialogue; he or she does not read or recite the argument.
- The advocate maintains eye contact with all of the judges.
- The advocate has good posture, uses gestures effectively, and speaks so that he or she can be easily understood.
- The advocate is composed and treats the court and opposing counsel with respect.
- The advocate does not use phrases like "I think," "We maintain," or "It is our position that."

Part III

A Guide to Legal Research

Most legal researchers remember their first trip to the law library. Problem in hand, they stood among the stacks, staring at row after row of books. What filled those thousands of volumes? Where to begin?

Although you may learn to do research through trial and error, that method is time-consuming and unreliable. You will become a better researcher faster if you go into the library knowing what types of material are there and the weight that should be given to each.

This part of the book gives you much of that information. The first four chapters in Part III describe the various types of primary authority. Chapter 9 discusses constitutions and charters, and Chapters 10 through 12 discuss primary authorities from the three branches of government. The final four chapters discuss the most frequently used secondary sources, *Shepard's* citators, computer-assisted research, and research strategies.

Although these chapters can be used alone, they work best when read in conjunction with sections 5.4 and 5.5, which show how these tools are used to research a legal problem.

Chapter 9

Constitutions
and Charters

§9.1 THE UNITED STATES CONSTITUTION

We begin with most primary of the primary sources: the United States Constitution.

The United States Constitution is the supreme law of the land. The principles that it announces bind the federal government as well as the states, local governments, and private individuals. The Constitution, however, does more than establish the basic principles of law; it establishes the framework within which our governments and our systems of law operate. By dividing the power of the government between a federal government and states and among the legislative, executive, and judicial branches, the Constitution created our multilayered legal system. It is because of our Constitution that we have both federal and state statutes, federal and state regulations, and federal and state court decisions.

The text of the United States Constitution can be found in numerous places. Copies can be found in both general and legal encyclopedias, at the front of most state codes, in separately published pamphlets and, at least at one time, on the tray liners at McDonald's.

Commentary, although plentiful, is not as generally available. The most readily available sources are the annotated United States codes. In addition to setting out the text of the Constitution, both the United States Code Annotated (U.S.C.A.) and United States Code Service (U.S.C.S.) (see pages 376-377) go through the Constitution clause by clause, for each clause listing cases that have interpreted or applied that particular clause. See Exhibit 9.1.

A more comprehensive source, at least for commentary, is *The Constitution of the United States of America: Analysis and Interpretation,* which is published by the Government Printing Office. This multivolume set goes through the Constitution clause by clause, providing the researcher not only with the text of the Constitution and citations to significant cases but also with commentary. See Exhibit 9.2.

REPRESENTATIVES—QUALIFICATIONS   Art I, § 2, cl 2, n 2

seq.) was not illegal on ground that minors were unable to vote for Congress, which passed Act. George v United States (1952, CA9 Cal) 196 F2d 445, cert den 344 US 843, 97 L Ed 656, 73 S Ct 58 (disagreed with United States v Seeger (CA2 NY) 326 F2d 846, affd 380 US 163, 13 L Ed 2d 733, 85 S Ct 850 (ovrld Welsh v United States, 398 US 333, 26 L Ed 2d 308, 90 S Ct 1792) as stated in United States ex rel. Foster v Schlesinger (CA2 NY) 520 F2d 751).

Where candidate for office of Representative in United States Congress was registered as affiliated with the Republican Party, but not as Democrat, and received nomination of both parties, his certification as candidate of Democratic Party did not deprive any voters of right to vote for candidates for that office at general election, and it did not deprive them of any other rights; thus, political party can lawfully nominate, as its candidate for Representative in Congress, person not registered as affiliated with that party, but registered as affiliated with another political party, as such nominations are not contrary to federal Constitution or of any law of United States. Shaffer v Jordan (1954, CA9 Cal) 213 F2d 393.

> Text of the Constitution

Sec. 2, Cl. 2. Qualifications of Representatives.

No person shall be a Representative who shall not have attained to the Age of twenty five Years, and been seven Years a Citizen of the United States, and who shall not, when elected, be an Inhabitant of that State in which he shall be chosen.

CROSS REFERENCES

Power of each House to judge qualifications of its own members, USCS Constitution, Art. I, § 5, cl. 1.

RESEARCH GUIDE

> Annotations

Federal Procedure L Ed:
Government Officers and Employee, Fed Proc, L Ed, § 40:579.

INTERPRETIVE NOTES AND DECISIONS

1. Generally
2. Validity of qualifications or requirements established by state law
3. —Residency
4. —Candidate's moral qualifications
5. —Prohibiting office holder from running for Congress

> Annotations

1. Generally

Word "State" is used in Art. 1, § 2, cl. 2, of Constitution in its geographical sense. Texas v White (1869) 74 US 700, 19 L Ed 227, cause dismd 77 US 68, 19 L Ed 839 and (ovrld on other grounds Morgan v United States, 113 US 476, 28 L Ed 1044, 5 S Ct 588).

Representative, duly elected and meeting all constitutional requirements for service as such, could not legally be excluded by House of Representatives, and because he had properly alleged claim for back wages, fact that new Congress had convened in which he had been seated did not render his case moot. Powell v McCormack (1969) 395 US 486, 23 L Ed 2d 491, 89 S Ct 1944.

Portions of plea agreement entered by member of Congress who pled guilty to several federal crimes, pertaining to resignation from Congress and withdrawal as candidate for re-election are void since they represent unconstitutional interference by executive with legislative branch of government and with rights of defendant's constituents. United States v Richmond (1982, ED NY) 550 F Supp 605.

Since Congressman must be resident of state from which he is chosen, it is presumed that Congressman from Arkansas is resident thereof when elected and as such is subject to state income taxes. Cravens v Cook (1947) 212 Ark 71, 204 SW2d 909.

2. Validity of qualifications or requirements established by state law

As applied to persons seeking ballot positions as independent candidates for United States Congress, state election statute requiring that independent candidate, to obtain ballot status, must file nomination papers signed by specified percentage of vote cast in preceding general elec-

EXHIBIT 9.2	**Sample Page from *The Constitution of the United States of America: Analysis and Interpretation* (U.S. Government Printing Office)**

ART. I—LEGISLATIVE DEPARTMENT   107

Sec. 2—House of Representatives   Cl. 2—Qualifications

Notwithstanding the vesting of discretion to prescribe voting qualifications in the States, conceptually the right to vote for United States Representatives is derived from the Federal Constitution [13] and Congress has had the power under Article I, § 4, to legislate to protect that right against both official [14] and private denial.[15]

Text of Constitution —

Clause 2. No person shall be a Representative who shall not have attained to the Age of twenty-five Years, and been seven Years a Citizen of the United States, and who shall not, when elected, be an inhabitant of the State in which he shall be chosen.

QUALIFICATIONS OF MEMBERS OF CONGRESS

When the Qualifications Must Be Possessed

Commentary —

A question much disputed but now seemingly settled is whether a condition of eligibility must exist at the time of the election or whether it is sufficient that eligibility exist when the Member-elect presents himself to take the oath of office. While the language of the clause expressly makes residency in the State a condition at the time of election, it now appears established in congressional practice that the age and citizenship qualifications need only be met when the Member-elect is to be sworn.[1] Thus, persons elected to either the House of Representatives or the Senate before attaining the required age or term of citizenship have been admitted as soon as they became qualified.[2]

Exclusivity of Constitutional Qualifications

Congressional Additions.—Writing in *The Federalist* with reference to the election of Members of Congress, Hamilton firmly stated that "[t]he qualifications of the persons who may . . . be

---

[13] "The right to vote for members of the Congress of the United States is not derived merely from the constitution and laws of the state in which they are chosen, but has its foundation in the Constitution of the United States." *Ex parte Yarbrough*, 110 U.S. 651, 663 (1884). *See also Wiley* v. *Sinkler*, 179 U.S. 58, 62 (1900); *Swafford* v. *Templeton*, 185 U.S. 487, 492 (1902); *United States* v. *Classic*, 313 U.S. 299, 315, 321 (1941).

[14] *United States* v. *Mosley*, 238 U.S. 383 (1915).

[15] *United States* v. *Classic*, 313 U.S. 299, 315 (1941).

[1] *See* S. Rept. No. 904, 74th Congress, 1st sess. (1935), reprinted in 79 *Cong. Rec.* 9651–9653 (1935).

[2] 1 A. Hinds' *Precedents of the House of Representatives* (Washington: 1907), § 418; 79 *Cong. Rec.* 9841–9842 (1935); cf. Hinds' *Precedents, supra,* § 429.

Section Summary	***The United States Constitution***

Type: Primary authority

Sources: Unannotated copies can be found in general and legal encyclopedias, in most state codes, and in separately publisheᵈ pamphlets.

Annotated copies can be found in the United States Code Annotated (U.S.C.A.) and the United States Code Service (U.S.C.S.).

Commentary can be found in *The Constitution of the United States of America: Analysis and Interpretation.*

§9.2   STATE CONSTITUTIONS

Like the United States Constitution, state constitutions are primary authority. Within the state, they are the supreme law of the land, binding both the government and the people of the state and creating the state's system of government.

Note

Although state constitutions cannot limit the rights granted by the United States Constitution, they can grant additional rights. For example, in some states, the state's Due Process Clause grants criminal defendants more rights than they have under the Due Process Clause of the United States Constitution.

The easiest place to find a copy of a particular state's constitution is in the state code for that state. If the code is unannotated, you will find only the text of the constitution; if the code is annotated, you will find both the text and annotations to cases that have interpreted it.

When you want to compare the text of the constitutions of the various states, the best source is *Constitutions of the United States, National and State,* which is published by Oceana. Although unannotated, this book collects in one place the constitutions of all fifty states.

Section Summary	*State Constitutions*

Type: Primary authority

Sources: The easiest place to find a copy of a particular state's constitution is in that state's code.

           If you want to compare the text of several states' constitutions, the best source is *Constitutions of the United States, National and State.*

§9.3   CHARTERS

Although not usually thought of as constitutions, charters serve the same function, granting and limiting power, but at the county or municipal level. Copies of city and county charters are not usually widely distributed; they are usually published as part of the county or city code.

Section Summary	*Charters*

Type: Primary authority

Source: Published in the county or city code, which can usually be obtained at the local law library or the offices of the city or county executive.

Chapter 10

The Legislative Branch

The first of the three branches of government is the legislative branch.

If constitutional, the statutes enacted by the legislative branch are primary authority, binding both the judicial and executive branches. The judiciary interprets the statutes enacted by the legislature, and the executive branch enforces them. (See Exhibit 10.1.)

§10.1   LOCATING STATUTES

Most statutes can be found in more than one source: in the session laws, in an unannotated code, and in an annotated code.

§10.1.1   Session Laws

Session laws are the statutes published in chronological order. At the end of a legislative session, the statutes enacted during that session are collected and arranged, not by topic, but by date.

The following example is taken from the *Statutes at Large,* the session laws of the United States Congress. Note that the statutes are indexed by their Public Law Number, a number that is assigned at the time the law is enacted. The first of the two numbers identifies the Congress, the second the particular statute. Thus, in the following example, the statute was the 352d statute enacted during the 88th Congress.

Public Law   88-352

Congress   Statute Number

Similar numbering systems are used for state statutes.

EXHIBIT 10.1   **The Branches of Government**

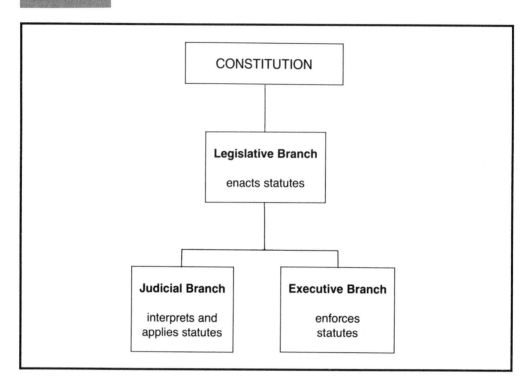

Although session laws are the "first" place that a statute appears, they are not usually the source of first choice. Because the statutes are arranged by date and not by topic, you will usually need to check several volumes to find the current version of the statute. The original version of the statute will be found in one volume and amendments in later ones. Consequently, session laws should be used only when (1) you are preparing a legislative history, (2) you are looking for a copy of a statute that is no longer in effect, or (3) you are looking for a copy of statute that has just been enacted.

Note

The text of newly enacted federal statutes can be found in the slip laws for the *Statutes at Large,* the advance sheets for U.S.C.A. and U.S.C.S., and the advance sheets for *United States Code Congressional and Administrative News* (USCCAN).

§10.1.2   Codes

When you want the text of a current statute, the best source is a code.

Unlike session laws, codes are organized by topic and not by date. All statutes on the same topic that are currently in effect are placed together, with amending language inserted where appropriate and repealed language deleted.

The numbering system used in codes reflects the difference in organization. Instead of using numbers that indicate the order in which the statutes were enacted, codes use a numbering system based on subject matter.

The United States Code, for example, uses a two-part numbering system. The first number identifies the title or topic, and the second identifies the particular section. For example, in the citation 42 U.S.C. § 2000e, the first number, 42, identifies the title. Title 42 of the United States Code deals with Public Health and Welfare. Section 2000e is the Definitions section for Title VII of the Civil Rights Act.

Some states have numbering systems similar to the United States Code. Others include chapters or articles to further break down their titles. For example, in Washington, Title 46 concerns motor vehicles; Chapter 61 concerns the rules of the road; section 130 concerns passing zones. Thus, the citation to the Revised Code of Washington for no passing zones is Wash. Rev. Code § 46.61.130 (title, chapter, section).

Finally, some states do not use titles at all. Instead, they break down the state code into smaller codes denominated by name. California, for example, calls its traffic rules and regulations its Vehicle Code. The citation to California's code concerning passing, then, is Cal. Veh. Code § 21.750.

a.   *Unofficial versus Official Codes*

In those jurisdictions with more than one version of the code, one will be designated as the official code and the other or others as the unofficial code. For example, in the federal system, Congress has designated the *United States Code,* which is published by the Government Printing Office, as the official code and *United States Code Annotated* (U.S.C.A.) and *United States Code Service* (U.S.C.S.) as unofficial. Although you can do your research in any of these three codes (the text of the statutes should be identical), the citation should be to the official code. (See section 17.3.)

b.   *Unannotated versus Annotated Codes*

When you are interested in only the text of an act, the best source is an unannotated code. Because there are no annotations, the relationship among individual sections is more easily seen. See Exhibit 10.2.

EXHIBIT 10.2 Sample Page from an Unannotated Code (*Revised Code of Washington*)

Sales 62A.2–202

to contract; "termination"; "cancellation". (1) In this Article unless the context otherwise requires "contract" and "agreement" are limited to those relating to the present or future sale of goods. "Contract for sale" includes both a present sale of goods and a contract to sell goods at a future time. A "sale" consists in the passing of title from the seller to the buyer for a price (RCW 62A.2–401). A "present sale" means a sale which is accomplished by the making of the contract.

(2) Goods or conduct including any part of a performance are "conforming" or conform to the contract when they are in accordance with the obligations under the contract.

(3) "Termination" occurs when either party pursuant to a power created by agreement or law puts an end to the contract otherwise than for its breach. On "termination" all obligations which are still executory on both sides are discharged but any right based on prior breach or performance survives.

(4) "Cancellation" occurs when either party puts an end to the contract for breach by the other and its effect is the same as that of "termination" except that the cancelling party also retains any remedy for breach of the whole contract or any unperformed balance. [1965 ex.s. c 157 § 2–106. Subd. (1) cf. former RCW 63.04-.020; 1925 ex.s. c 142 § 1; RRS § 5836–1. Subd. (2) cf. former RCW sections: (i) RCW 63.04.120; 1925 ex.s. c 142 § 11; RRS § 5836–11. (ii) RCW 63.04.450; 1925 ex.s. c 142 § 44; RRS § 5836–44. (iii) RCW 63.04.700; 1925 ex.s. c 142 § 69; RRS § 5836–69.]

62A.2–107 Goods to be severed from realty: Recording. (1) A contract for the sale of minerals or the like including oil and gas or a structure or its materials to be removed from realty is a contract for the sale of goods within this Article if they are to be severed by the seller but until severance a purported present sale thereof which is not effective as a transfer of an interest in land is effective only as a contract to sell.

(2) A contract for the sale apart from the land of growing crops or other things attached to realty and capable of severance without material harm thereto but not described in subsection (1) or of timber to be cut is a contract for the sale of goods within this Article whether the subject matter is to be severed by the buyer or by the seller even though it forms part of the realty at the time of contracting, and the parties can by identification effect a present sale before severance.

(3) The provisions of this section are subject to any third party rights provided by the law relating to realty records, and the contract for sale may be executed and recorded as a document transferring an interest in land and shall then constitute notice to third parties of the buyer's rights under the contract for sale. [1981 c 41 § 3; 1965 ex.s. c 157 § 2–107. Cf. former RCW sections: (i) RCW 63.04.755(1); 1925 ex.s. c 142 § 76; RRS § 5836–76; formerly RCW 63.04.010. (ii) RCW 65.08-.040; Code 1881 § 2327; 1863 p 413 § 4; 1854 p 404 § 4; RRS § 5827.]

Effective date——1981 c 41: See RCW 62A.11–101.

(1989 Ed.)

PART 2
FORM, FORMATION AND READJUSTMENT OF CONTRACT

62A.2–201 Formal requirements; statute of frauds. (1) Except as otherwise provided in this section a contract for the sale of goods for the price of five hundred dollars or more is not enforceable by way of action or defense unless there is some writing sufficient to indicate that a contract for sale has been made between the parties and signed by the party against whom enforcement is sought or by his authorized agent or broker. A writing is not insufficient because it omits or incorrectly states a term agreed upon but the contract is not enforceable under this paragraph beyond the quantity of goods shown in such writing.

(2) Between merchants if within a reasonable time a writing in confirmation of the contract and sufficient against the sender is received and the party receiving it has reason to know its contents, it satisfies the requirements of subsection (1) against such party unless written notice of objection to its contents is given within ten days after it is received.

(3) A contract which does not satisfy the requirements of subsection (1) but which is valid in other respects is enforceable

(a) if the goods are to be specially manufactured for the buyer and are not suitable for sale to others in the ordinary course of the seller's business and the seller, before notice of repudiation is received and under circumstances which reasonably indicate that the goods are for the buyer, has made either a substantial beginning of their manufacture or commitments for their procurement; or

(b) if the party against whom enforcement is sought admits in his pleading, testimony or otherwise in court that a contract for sale was made, but the contract is not enforceable under this provision beyond the quantity of goods admitted; or

(c) with respect to goods for which payment has been made and accepted or which have been received and accepted (RCW 62A.2–606). [1965 ex.s. c 157 § 2–201. Cf. former RCW 63.04.050; 1925 ex.s. c 142 § 4; RRS § 5836–4; prior: Code 1881 § 2326.]

Statute of frauds: RCW 19.36.010.

62A.2–202 Final written expression: Parol or extrinsic evidence. Terms with respect to which the confirmatory memoranda of the parties agree or which are otherwise set forth in a writing intended by the parties as a final expression of their agreement with respect to such terms as are included therein may not be contradicted by evidence of any prior agreement or of a contemporaneous oral agreement but may be explained or supplemented

(a) by course of dealing or usage of trade (RCW 62A.1–205) or by course of performance (RCW 62A.2–208); and

(b) by evidence of consistent additional terms unless the court finds the writing to have been intended also as

[Title 62A RCW—p 9]

The format used in the Revised Code of Washington is similar to that used in other unannotated codes. The section number and title are set out first; the text of the statute second; and the history of the statute (the information in brackets) last. (See section 4.1.)

Note

The bracketed material following 62A.2-201 tells you that section 62A.2-201 was enacted during the 1965 extraordinary session; that its session law number was chapter 157, section 2-201; and that 62A.2-201 replaced former Revised Code of Washington section 63.04.050, which had been enacted during the 1925 extraordinary session as chapter 142, section 4.

When you need not only the text of the statute but also citations to cases interpreting and applying it, the best source is an annotated code. Like an unannotated code, an annotated code sets out the text of the statute. In addition, most annotated codes provide you with cross-references to other potentially applicable statutory sections; a list of law review articles citing the section; references to other materials produced by the same publisher that may provide useful information; and, in the Notes of Decision section, one-paragraph annotations for cases that have interpreted or applied the statute. See Exhibit 10.3.

c. Updating Unannotated and Annotated Codes

Codes are updated in one of two ways: through the use of pocket parts and supplements or, if the code is published in a loose-leaf binder, by replacing pages. To find the most recent version of a statute, check the pocket parts and supplements through the date the legislative body last met.

d. Research Strategies

A particular statutory section can be located in a number of different ways, through the use of (1) the subject index, (2) the popular name table, or (3) codification tables. If you already know the statute's title and section number, look up that title and section number in the main volumes.

1. Subject Index

The most common way of locating a particular statutory section is through the subject index, which, depending on the code, either precedes or follows the main volumes. Subject indices are arranged alpha-

EXHIBIT 10.3 Pages from an Annotated Code*

62A.2-107 UNIFORM COMMERCIAL CODE

32 Wn LR 30 (Washington timber deed and contracts).
34 Wn LR 78 (Sales and Uniform Commercial Code).

Annotations:

25 ALR 1133, 1157, 57 ALR 535, 537, 57 ALR 1308, 1312, 148 ALR 375, 13 ALR2d 1312 (conflict of laws as to effect of failure to comply with local statute as to filing and recording).

65 ALR 714, 717 (sufficiency of description of property in recorded conditional sales contract to give notice to third person).

95 ALR 1197 (when transfer of account or other chose in action is deemed a sale rather than a pledge as security for a loan, and vice versa).

136 ALR 821 (constructive notice from filing and recording where chattel left in possession of dealer).

4 ALR2d 213 (what amounts to acknowledgment by third person that he holds goods on buyer's behalf within provision respecting delivery when goods are in possession of third person).

10 ALR2d 764 (statute respecting registration in case of nonresidents).

58 ALR2d 1351, 1388 (effect of failure to record automobile liens).

72 ALR2d 727 (size and kind of trees contemplated by contracts or deeds in relation to standing timber).

87 ALR2d 732 (validity, construction, and effect of contract between grower of vegetable or fruit crops, and purchasing processor, packer, or canner).

Key Number Digests:
Sales ⟜10, 11.

NOTES OF DECISIONS

DECISIONS IN OTHER JURISDICTIONS

Contract for sale of logs to be severed and removed from realty by seller is considered contract for sale of goods. Coos Lbr. Co. v Builders Lbr. & Supply Corp. (1963) 104 NH 404, 188 A2d 330.

Wall to wall carpeting constitutes fixture. Vincent (Dean), Inc. v Redisco, Inc (1962) 232 Ore 170, 373 P2d 995.

122

PART 2
FORM, FORMATION AND READJUSTMENT OF CONTRACT

62A.2-201 Formal requirements; statute of frauds

(1) Except as otherwise provided in this section a contract for the sale of goods for the price of $500 or more is not enforceable by way of action or defense unless there is some writing sufficient to indicate that a contract for sale has been made between

Text

SALES 62A.2-201

the parties and signed by the party against whom enforcement is sought or by his authorized agent or broker. A writing is not insufficient because it omits or incorrectly states a term agreed upon but the contract is not enforceable under this paragraph beyond the quantity of goods shown in such writing.

(2) Between merchants if within a reasonable time a writing in confirmation of the contract and sufficient against the sender is received and the party receiving it has reason to know its contents, it satisfies the requirements of subsection (1) against such party unless written notice of objection to its contents is given within ten days after it is received.

(3) A contract which does not satisfy the requirements of subsection (1) but which is valid in other respects is enforceable

(a) if the goods are to be specially manufactured for the buyer and are not suitable for sale to others in the ordinary course of the seller's business and the seller, before notice of repudiation is received and under circumstances which reasonably indicate that the goods are for the buyer, has made either a substantial beginning of their manufacture or commitments for their procurement; or

(b) if the party against whom enforcement is sought admits in his pleading, testimony or otherwise in court that a contract for sale was made, but the contract is not enforceable under this provision beyond the quantity of goods admitted; or

(c) with respect to goods for which payment has been made and accepted or which have been received and accepted (RCW 62A.2-606).

LEGISLATIVE HISTORY

Enacted Laws 1st Ex Sess 1965 ch 157 § 2-201, effective midnight June 30, 1967. Similar to:
(a) Laws Ex Sess 1925 ch 142 § 4 p 356.
(b) Code 1881 § 2326.
(c) Uniform Sales Act § 4.
See RRS § 5836-4 and former RCW 63.04.050.

WASHINGTON COMMENTS

(1) This subsection changes Washington law in three important respects.

First, this statute of frauds section is limited to contracts for the sale of goods. USA 4(1) (RCW

123

Legislative History

62A.2-201 UNIFORM COMMERCIAL CODE

to him it is signing by the other which is important.

7. If the making of a contract is admitted in court, either in a written pleading, by stipulation or by oral statement before the court, no additional writing is necessary for protection against fraud. Under this section it is no longer possible to admit the contract in court and still treat the Statute as a defense. However, the contract is not thus conclusively established. The admission so made by a party is itself evidential against him of the truth of the facts so admitted and of nothing more; as against the other party, it is not evidential at all.

Cross References:

See Sections 1—201, 2—202, 2—207, 2—209 and 2—304.

Definitional Cross References:

"Action". Section 1—201.
"Between merchants". Section 2—104.
"Buyer". Section 2—103.
"Contract". Section 1—201.
"Contract for sale". Section 2—106.
"Goods". Section 2—105.
"Notice". Section 1—201.
"Party". Section 1—201.
"Reasonable time". Section 1—204.
"Sale". Section 2—106.
"Seller". Section 2—103.

CROSS REFERENCES

General definitions: RCWA 62A.1-201.
Modification, rescission and waiver: RCWA 62A.2-209.
Parol or extrinsic evidence: RCWA 62A.2-202.
Price payable in an interest in realty: RCWA 62A.2-304.
Sale or return contracts: RCWA 62A.2-326.
Secured transactions: RCWA 62A.9-101 et seq.
Security interests, formal requirements: RCWA 62A.9-203, 62A.9-302.
Statute of frauds: RCWA 19.36.010(1).
Terms in acceptance additional to or different from those agreed upon: RCWA 62A.2-207.

COLLATERAL REFERENCES

Am Jur 2d Commercial Code § 11, Crops §§ 47 et seq.; Am Jur Mines and Minerals § 29, Sales §§ 12, 20, 33, 343, 450, 861, 901, 904, 907, 908, Statute of Frauds §§ 236 et seq.
CJS Frauds, Statutes of §§ 138 et seq.

Forms:

2 Am Jur Legal Forms, Nos. 2:28-2:34 (memorandum of sale by auction).
11 Am Jur Legal Forms, Nos. 11:1171 et seq. (sales contracts).
13A Am Jur Legal Forms, Nos. 2:42 et seq. (instruments and provisions meeting requirements of, and pertaining to, statute of frauds).
6 Am Jur Pl & Pr Forms, No. 6:653 (form of defendant's allegation that contract illegal because in violation of statute of frauds).

128

SALES 62A.2-201

17 Am Jur Pl & Pr Forms, Nos. 17:1321 et seq. (forms relating to sales), Nos. 17:1344 et seq. (complaints for refusal to accept and pay for goods).
19 Am Jur Pl & Pr Forms, Nos. 19:1 et seq. (forms relating to statute of frauds), Nos. 19:4-19:26 (complaint, answer, etc., in suits for sale of goods under statute of frauds).
Modern Legal Forms, § 8198 (acceptance).

Law Review Articles:

20 Ala Law 355 (application of this section).
17 Alb LR 16 (new statute of frauds under the Uniform Commercial Code).
2 Bost Col Ind & Com LR 59 (freedom of contract under the Uniform Commercial Code).
4 Bost Col Ind & Com LR 381 (anatomy of §§ 2-201, 2-202 of Uniform Commercial Code).
30 Brooklyn LR 177 (impact of the Code on the law of contracts).
2 Cal LR 159 (memorandum signed by one party and statute of frauds).
4 Cal LR 260 (relinquishment of property rights as part performance).
6 Cal LR 37 (adoption of the Uniform Sales Act with respect to auctions and the statute of frauds).
9 Cal LR 27, 31 (need for revision of the statute of frauds in relation to sales of personalty and advantages of the Uniform Sales Act).
43 Cal LR 295 (statute of frauds and conflict of laws).
37 Cal St BJ 141 (Commercial Code's Statute of Frauds).
58 Dick LR 373 (comparison of the statute of frauds sections of the Uniform Sales Act and Uniform Commercial Code in Pennsylvania).
62 Dick LR 170 (inadvertent acceptance of buyer's terms).
36 Fla BJ 1020 (effect of the Uniform Commercial Code on Florida's existing law of sales).
63 Harv LR 573 (statute of frauds under the proposed Commercial Code).
5 Hast LJ 258 (part performance of oral land contracts as sufficient to take transaction out of the statute of frauds and justify specific performance).
16 Hast LJ 569 (Statute of Frauds in Uniform Commercial Code).
52 Ill BJ 660 (battle of the forms under the Code).
15 Maine LR 21 (formation of sales contracts).
40 Mich S BJ 12 (formation of contract).
35 NY U LR 1477 (commercial law).
39 ND LR 7 (impact of the Uniform Commercial Code on the law of contracts).
15 Ohio S LJ 12 (law of sales in the Uniform Commercial Code).
15 Ohio S LJ 19 (this section criticized).
33 Ore LR 113 (suggested changes in Uniform Commercial Code: sales).
4 Pers Fin LQ Rep 1, 4 (Williston on Commercial Code).
10 Pract Law 73 (major changes under the Code in sales contracts).
17 Rutgers LR 14, 18 (merits of this section).
10 St Louis ULJ 30, 45 (contract formation under the Code).

T. 62 to 62A (1-101 to 2-725) Wash Code—9 129

References

Law Review Articles

*Reprinted from *Revised Code of Washington Annotated*, © 1966, and 1992 *Cumulative Annual Pocket Part*, © 1992, with permission of West Publishing Company.

387

EXHIBIT 10.3 *(continued)*

62A.2–201 UNIFORM COMMERCIAL CODE

5 So Cal LR 233 (validity of oral agreement authorizing broker to sell stock).

9 So Cal LR 172 (portrait commissions).

27 So Cal LR 128, 131 (express contracts and the statute of frauds).

27 So Cal LR 471 (estoppel to assert statute of frauds).

3 Stan LR 281 (part performance, estoppel, and the statute of frauds).

4 Stan LR 142 (intent, acceptance, and statute of frauds).

4 Stan LR 416 (mistake in statute of frauds memorandum).

5 Stan LR 811 (sale as transaction whereby one party acquires property in thing sold and other parts with it for valuable consideration).

36 Temp LQ 75 (changes effected in statute of frauds by enactment of the Uniform Commercial Code in Pennsylvania).

18 U Pitt LR 293 (sales contracts).

22 U Pitt LR 201 (contracts, sales, and insurance).

3 Vill LR 1 (contract formalities and the Uniform Commercial Code).

2 Wn LR 69 (Washington Uniform Sales Act).

34 Wn LR 124 (English statute of frauds in Washington).

34 Wn LR 345 (contracts in Washington).

1952 Wis LR 209 (sales: "from status to contract").

15 Wyo LJ 1 (sales, bulk sales and documents of title under the Uniform Commercial Code).

59 Yale LJ 829 (new formal requirements: statute of frauds).

Annotations:
1. In General.
2. Particular Transactions.
3. Writing or Memorandum.
4. — Signature.
5. Acceptance—Payment or Performance.
6. Procedure.

1. IN GENERAL.

13 ALR 271 (alternative oral agreement, one of the alternatives being within statute of frauds).

17 ALR 10, 29 ALR 1095, 80 ALR 539, 118 ALR 1511 (right to modify by subsequent parol agreement a contract required to be in writing).

17 ALR 1299, 1333, 79 ALR 1346, 1351, 8 ALR2d 787 (moral obligation connected with contract within statute of frauds as consideration for executory promise).

71 ALR 479 (failure to comply with statute of frauds as part of contract within statute as affecting enforceability of another part not covered by statute).

105 ALR 652, 161 ALR 820 (statute of frauds and conflict of laws).

148 ALR 1325 (retrospective applicability of statute of frauds).

169 ALR 187 (vendor's willingness and ability to perform contract which does not satisfy statute of frauds as precluding purchaser's recovery back of payments made thereon).

25 ALR2d 672 (construction and effect of exception making statute of frauds provision inapplicable where goods are manufactured by seller for buyer).

130

62A.2–201 UNIFORM COMMERCIAL CODE

85 ALR 1184 (necessity that each of several papers constituting contract be signed by party to be charged).

112 ALR 937 (place of signature on memorandum to satisfy statute of frauds).

114 ALR 1005 (who must sign and form of signature, in case of partnership, in order to comply with statute of frauds).

159 ALR 253 (initials as sufficient signature under statute of frauds).

171 ALR 334 (printed, stamped or typewritten name as satisfying requirement of statute of frauds as regards signature).

5. ACCEPTANCE—PAYMENT OR PERFORMANCE

4 ALR 902 (when goods remaining in custody of seller or a third person deemed to have been received by buyer).

23 ALR 473 (discharge of existing debt as part-payment).

36 ALR 649, 111 ALR 1312 (acceptance which will satisfy statute of frauds where purchaser of goods is in possession at time of sale).

38 ALR 693 (part performance of contract embracing more than one subject matter).

59 ALR 1305 (doctrine of part performance as sustaining action of law).

113 ALR 810 (acceptance as affected by cancellation of contract before goods were shipped).

131 ALR 1252, 170 ALR 245 (money or other property in possession of seller, before contract was made, as satisfying condition of part payment which will take oral contract for sale of goods out of statute of frauds).

166 ALR 443 (irreparable injury as necessary condition of part performance which will take oral contract out of statute of frauds).

6 ALR2d 1053, 1108, 1156, 1176 (oral contract of sale not to be performed within a year as taken out of statute of frauds by performance).

8 ALR2d 251 (check as payment of consideration).

30 ALR2d 972 (oral acceptance of written offer by party sought to be charged as satisfying statute of frauds).

81 ALR2d 1355 (buyer's note as payment within statute of frauds).

6. PROCEDURE

22 ALR 723 (admission by pleading or parol contract as preventing pleader from taking advantage of statute of frauds).

49 ALR 1121 (contract which violates statute of frauds as evidence of value in action not based on contract).

158 ALR 89 (manner of pleading statute of frauds as defense).

15 ALR2d 1330 (failure to object parol evidence, or voluntary introduction thereof, as waiver of defense statute of frauds).

81 ALR2d 991 (parol evidence to connect signed and unsigned documents relied upon as memorandum to satisfy statute of frauds).

Key Number Digests:
Frauds, Statute of ⊐81 et seq.

132

A.L.R. Annotations

Key Number Reference

NOTES OF DECISIONS

A. **DECISIONS UNDER FOR-MER WASHINGTON STAT-UTES** (See Former RCWA 63.04.050).

B. **DECISIONS IN OTHER JU-RISDICTIONS.**

A. **DECISIONS UNDER FOR-MER WASHINGTON STAT-UTES** (See Former RCWA 63.04.050).

1. In General.
2. Acceptance and Receipt of Goods.
3. Part Payment—"Something in Earnest."
4. Memorandum.
5. Goods Manufactured Especially for Buyer.
6. Particular Transactions.
7. Modification of Contract.
8. Procedure.

1. IN GENERAL.

Where goods sold for more than $50 are at distance from place of contract, or are of such nature that they cannot be immediately delivered, and seller authorizes buyer to take possession, and he does take possession with all reasonable dispatch after making contract, sale is not void by reason of statute, because at time of making contract there was no earnest payment and no acceptance and receipt of part of goods. Hosner v McDonnell (1921) 114 Wn 489, 195 P 231.

Fact that one of parties contemplated more formal contract does not affect contract of sale that satisfies statute of frauds. Wash-

133

ington Dehydrated Food Co. v Triton Co. (1929) 151 Wn 613, 276 P 562.

Statute of frauds has no applicability to contract of sale where buyer has received goods and made payment therefor, and only issue between buyer and seller is whether amount paid was contract price. Dodd v Polack (1964) 63 Wn 2d 828, 389 P2d 289.

It was immaterial, in determining seller's obligation to buyer, that promise to place machine in workable condition was parol agreement inconsistent with terms of purchase order, where buyer's right to purchase machine was established by prior lease-option agreement which contained warranties that machine would be capable of doing work for which it was designed, since, by signing purchase order, buyer merely exercised option provision of lease agreement, and parol agreement of seller was simply promise to perform obligations that were already owed. Case (J. I.) Credit Corp. v Stark (1964) 64 Wn 2d 470, 392 P2d 215.

2. ACCEPTANCE AND RECEIPT OF GOODS

To satisfy this statute where contract is unwritten, there must be not only delivery by seller, but actual acceptance by buyer with intent to take possession as owner. Adams County Mercantile Co. v Walla Walla Livestock Co. (1911) 64 Wn 285, 116 P 669.

Though delivery is direct by party from whom seller purchases, such delivery to ultimate buyer takes oral contract out of statute of frauds. First Nat. Bank v Geske

UNIFORM COMMERCIAL CODE 62A.2-201

(3) The provisions of this section are subject to any third party rights provided by the law relating to realty records, and the contract for sale may be executed and recorded as a document transferring an interest in land and shall then constitute notice to third parties of the buyer's rights under the contract for sale.

Amended by Laws 1981, ch. 41, § 3, eff. June 30, 1982 (midnight).

Historical and Statutory Notes

Effective date—Laws 1981, ch. 41: See § 62A.11-101.

Notes of Decisions

The granting of a right to cut standing timber for a limited period with uncut timber reverting to the "grantor" does not convert the timber into personal property but rather passes an interest in real property, viz., the right to take the profits of the land by entering onto it and cutting and removing the timber. Trees remain part of the real property until severed and any transfer of the land passes title to the standing timber, subject to the exercise of any remaining

cutting right. Layman v. Ledgett (1978) 89 Wash.2d 906, 577 P.2d 970.

Prior to the enactment of provisions of this section, which governs the determination of the property character of goods which are to be severed from realty, perennial uncultivated vegetation, such as peat, not yet severed from the soil, was considered a part of the real property and not personal property. Clarke v. Alstores Realty Corp. (1974) 11 Wash.App. 942, 527 P.2d 698.

PART 2—FORM, FORMATION AND READJUSTMENT OF CONTRACT

62A.2-201. Formal requirements; statute of frauds

Law Review Commentaries

California's version of part payment rule under the code. 23 Hast.L.J. 633.

Judicial admissions exception to the statute of frauds: An Update. Peter J. Shedd, 12 Whittier L.Rev. 131 (1991).

Partial payment exception to U.C.C. sale-of-goods statute of frauds. 13 UCC L.J. 135 (1980).

Promissory estoppel, Article 2 of the U.C.C., and the Restatement (Third) of Contracts. Michael Gibson, 73 Iowa L.Rev. 674 (1988).

Promissory estoppel in Washington. 55 Wash.L.Rev. 795 (1980).

Promissory estoppel versus the statute of frauds. 17 Gonzaga L.Rev. 937 (1982).

Proposal to repeal § 2-201. Roger S. Cunningham, 85 Com.L.J. 361 (1980).

"Special order provisions" of Uniform Commercial Code, affecting operation of statute of frauds. 2 Gonzaga L.Rev. 127.

Notes of Decisions

A.1. DECISIONS UNDER PRESENT STATUTE

Promissory estoppel cannot be used to overcome the statute of frauds contained in this § 62A.2-201 in a case which involves the sale of goods, since to adopt Restatement (Second) of Contracts provision authorizing enforcement of a promise which induced action or forbearance by a promisee notwithstanding the statute of frauds would allow parties to circumvent this section. Lige Dickson

Co. v. Union Oil Co. of California (1981) 96 Wash.2d 291, 635 P.2d 103.

Under this section, a writing is enforceable as a contract of sale only if it evidences a sale of goods, it is signed, and it specifies quantity. Quantity need not be precisely stated, however, and parol evidence is admissible to show the parties' intention as to the exact quantity. Hankins v. American Pacific Sales Corp. (1972) 7 Wash.App. 316, 499 P.2d 214.

23

Pocket Part

Court Decisions

389

betically by topic and for each topic include references to the appropriate title and section number.

The subject index may itself be periodically updated through the use of pocket parts or supplements.

2. Popular Name Table

When an act has a popular name (Social Security Act, Civil Rights Act, Superfund Act), the easiest way of finding the act is to use the Popular Name Table, which is found in the index volumes of most codes. This table lists acts by their popular name, for each act listing the title(s) and section number(s) where the act, or parts of it, can be found. See Exhibit 10.4.

Note

Popular names are not usually listed in the subject index. For example, although "Superfund" is listed in the Popular Name Table, it is not listed in the subject index.

---

3. Codification Tables

If you know the public law number, the title and section numbers can be located using the codification tables accompanying the code.

For example, if you knew the public law number for the Civil Rights Act of 1964 was Pub. L. 88-352, you could look in the codification tables and find that it is codified, among other places, at 42 U.S.C. § 2000e (in the note to the section). See Exhibit 10.4.

Statutes can also be located using LEXIS and Westlaw. Although using these services is more expensive than looking up the statute in printed form, LEXIS and Westlaw are useful when you want to find the text of a statute from another jurisdiction and you do not have access to that jurisdiction's printed code or when you want to find all the places in the code in which a particular word or phrase appears. In addition, because LEXIS and Westlaw are updated frequently, they can be used to find the most recent version of a statute.

Section Summary   *Statutes*

Type: Primary authority

Sources: *Session Laws:* Statutes presented in the order in which they were enacted. Used when you need to find the text of a statute that is not currently in effect or when compiling a legislative history.

POPULAR NAME TABLE   866

Civil Obedience Act of 1968
  Pub. L. 90–284, title X, Apr. 11, 1968, 82 Stat. 90 (Title 18, §§ 231–233)

Civil Relief Act (Soldiers and Sailors)
  See Soldiers' and Sailors' Civil Relief Acts of 1918 and 1940

Civil Rights Acts
  See Title 42, §§ 1971 et seq., 1981 et seq.
  Apr. 9, 1866, ch. 31, 14 Stat. 27
  May 31, 1870, ch. 114, 16 Stat. 140
  Feb. 28, 1871, ch. 99, 16 Stat. 433
  Apr. 20, 1871, ch. 22, 17 Stat. 13
  Mar. 1, 1875, ch. 114, §§ 3–5, 18 Stat. 336, 337

Civil Rights Act of 1957
  Pub. L. 85–315, Sept. 9, 1957, 71 Stat. 634 (See Title 5, § 5315(19); Title 28, §§ 1343, 1861;
        Title 42, §§ 1971, 1975, 1975a, 1975b, 1975c, 1975d, 1975e, 1995)
  Pub. L. 86–383, title IV, § 401, Sept. 28, 1959, 73 Stat. 724 (Title 42, § 1975c)
  Pub. L. 86–449, May 6, 1960, title IV, title VI, 74 Stat. 89 (Title 42, §§ 1971, 1975d)
  Pub. L. 87–264, title IV, Sept. 21, 1961, 75 Stat. 559 (Title 42, § 1975c)
  Pub. L. 88–152, § 2, Oct. 17, 1963, 77 Stat. 271 (Title 42, § 1975c)
  Pub. L. 88–352, title V, July 2, 1964, 78 Stat. 249 (Title 42, §§ 1975a–1975d)
  Pub. L. 90–198, § | Amendments | Stat. 582 (Title 42, §§ 1975c, 1975e)
  Pub. L. 91–521 | | 84 Stat. 1356, 1357 (Title 42, §§ 1975a, 1975b, 1975d,
        1975e)
  Pub. L. 92–64, Aug. 4, 1971, 85 Stat. 166 (Title 42, § 1975e)
  Pub. L. 92–496, Oct. 14, 1972, 86 Stat. 913 (Title 42, §§ 1975a–1975e)
  Pub. L. 94–292, § 2, May 27, 1976, 90 Stat. 524 (Title 42, § 1975e)
  Pub. L. 95–132, § 2, Oct. 13, 1977, 91 Stat. 1157 (Title 42, § 1975e)
  Pub. L. 95–444, §§ 2–7, Oct. 10, 1978, 92 Stat. 1067, 1068 (Title 42, §§ 1975b, 1975c, 1975d,
        1975e)
  Pub. L. 96–81, §§ 2, | Name of act | Stat. 642 (Title 42, §§ 1975c, 1975e)
  Pub. L. 96–447, § 2, | | tat. 1894

Civil Rights Act of 1960
  Pub. L. 86–449, May 6, 1960, 74 Stat. 86 (Title 18,   Public law number,   §§ 241, 640;
        Title 42, §§ 1971, 1974–1974e, 1975d)   Statutes at Large
                                                           citation, and location
                                                           in U.S.C.

Civil Rights Act of 1964
  Pub. L. 88–352, July 2, 1964, 78 Stat. 241 (Title 28, § 1447; Title 42, §§ 1971, 1975a–1975d,
        2000a–2000h–6)
  Pub. L. 92–261, §§ 2–8, 10, 11, 13, Mar. 24, 1972, 86 Stat. 103–113 (Title 42, §§ 2000e,
        2000e–1 to 2000e–6, 2000e–8, 2000e–9, 2000e–13 to 2000e–17)
  Pub. L. 92–318, title IX, § 906(a), June 23, 1972, 86 Stat. 375 (Title 42, §§ 2000c, 2000c–6,
        2000c–9, 2000h–2)
  Pub. L. 93–608, § 3(1), Jan. 2, 1975, 88 Stat. 1972 (Title 42, § 2000e–4)
  Pub. L. 94–273, § 3(24), Apr. 21, 1976, 90 Stat. 377 (Title 42, § 2000e–14)
  Pub. L. 95–251, § 2(a)(11), Mar. 27, 1978, 92 Stat. 183 (Title 42, § 2000e–4)
  Pub. L. 95–555, § 1, Oct. 31, 1978, 92 Stat. 2076 (Title 42, § 2000e)
  Pub. L. 95–598, title III, § 330, Nov. 6, 1978, 92 Stat. 2679 (Title 42, § 2000e)
  Pub. L. 95–624, § 5, Nov. 9, 1978, 92 Stat. 3462 (Title 42, § 2000g)
  Pub. L. 96–191, § 8(g), Feb. 15, 1980, 94 Stat. 34 (Title 42, § 2000e–16)
  Pub. L. 100–259, § 6, Mar. 22, 1988, 102 Stat. 31 (Title 42, § 2000d–4a)
  Pub. L. 102–166, Title I, § 104, 105(a), 106 to 108, 109(a), (b)(1), 110(a), 111, 112, 113(b), 114,
        Nov. 21, 1991, 105 Stat. 1074 to 1079 (Title 42, §§ 2000e, 2000e–1, 2000e–2, 2000e–4,
        2000e–5, 2000e–16)

Civil Rights Act of 1968
  Pub. L. 90–284, Apr. 11, 1968, 82 Stat. 73–92 (Title 18, §§ 231–233, 241, 242, 245, 1153, 2101,
        2102; Title 25, §§ 1301–1303, 1311, 1312, 1321–1326, 1331, 1341; Title 28, § 1360 note;
        Title 42, §§ 1973j, 3533, 3535, 3601–3619, 3631)
  Pub. L. 93–265, Apr. 12, 1974, 88 Stat. 84 (Title 25, § 1341)
  Pub. L. 93–383, title VIII, § 808(b), Aug. 22, 1974, 88 Stat. 729 (Title 42, §§ 3604–3606, 3631)
  Pub. L. 100–430, §§ 4, 5, 6(a), (b)(1), (2), (c) to (e), 7 to 10, 15, Sept. 13, 1988, 102 Stat. 1619 to
        1636 (Title 42, §§ 3601 note, 3602, 3604, 3605, 3607, 3608, 3610 to 3614a, 3615 to 3619,
        3631)

Unannotated Codes: Statutes currently in effect organized by subject matter (codified). Use when only the text of the statute is needed.

Annotated Codes: Same as unannotated codes but also include cross-references to other sources and notes of decision for cases citing the statute.

§10.2 Compiling a Legislative History

Legislative histories. The thought of doing one makes the blood pressure of even the most experienced researchers rise. For most interns, being sent to do a legislative history is the most severe of punishments.

Although compiling a legislative history can be time-consuming and frustrating, such histories are often essential. The court needs to know what the legislature intended when it enacted the statute.

§10.2.1 The Legislative Process

a. Introduction of a Bill

The first step in the legislative process is the drafting of a bill. This may be done by a private individual; a special interest group; a legislator; or at the request of a legislator, a legislative staff member, or the code reviser's office.

The second step is the introduction of the bill. Although the drafting of a bill can be done by anyone, bills can only be introduced by a member of the legislative body. At the time the bill is introduced, it is given a number. At the federal level, bills introduced into the House are designated with "H.R." and bills introduced into the Senate are designated "S.": H.R. 21, S. 129. Note that although the number identifies the chamber into which the bill was introduced, it does not identify the Congress.

The third step is the assignment to committee. After a bill has been introduced, it is assigned to the appropriate standing or ad hoc committee.

b. Consideration by a Committee

Much of the work on a bill is done at the committee level. Members of the committee's staff may research the bill; the committee may hold hearings; and in some cases, the committee may issue a report in which it (a) discusses the need or lack of need for such legislation, (b) explains the bill and its individual provisions, and (c) recommends passage or nonpassage. Two things can happen as a result of the committee's work. The committee can allow the bill to "die," or the committee can refer it back to the originating house.

c. *Floor Debates*

When a bill is referred back to the originating house, the presiding officer reads the bill into the record and opens the floor for debate. At the federal level, these debates are published in the *Congressional Record,* which appears in two forms. The daily version is published at the end of each day that Congress is in session, and the multivolume edition is published at the end of the session. The pagination in the two versions is different, and there is no cross-referencing system.

Note

The material that appears in the *Congressional Record* may not accurately reflect what was said on the floor. Members of Congress are permitted to edit their remarks and to add additional information or statements. Consequently, the *Congressional Record* is often not given great weight in determining what Congress actually intended in enacting a particular statute.

---

d. *Consideration by the Other House*

If a bill passes one house, it is then referred to the next, where it is "read" for the first time and then referred to committee. The second committee has the same options as the first: the bill may be researched by the committee's staff, hearings may be held, and a report may be issued.

At this point, one of four things can happen: (1) the bill can die in the second committee, (2) the bill can be forwarded to the floor of the second house where, after debate, it fails to pass, (3) the bill passes the second house and is forwarded to the President (or the governor, at the state level) for signature, or (4) the bill is passed in a different form.

In the latter case, the bill is returned to the originating house for consideration. If the originating house passes it in its amended form, the bill is forwarded for signature; if it is not passed, it is sent to a conference committee made up of members from both houses.

e. *Approval or Veto by the President or the Governor*

After a bill has been passed by both houses, it is sent to the executive branch: at the federal level to the President (or, at the state level, to the governor). The President may (1) sign the bill, in which case the bill becomes law; (2) veto the bill, in which case the bill dies unless the Congress overrides the veto by a two-thirds majority vote; or (3) take no action. If the President takes no action within ten days, the bill becomes law without the President's signature.

Note

There is one exception to the ten-day rule. If Congress adjourns within the ten-day period, the bill dies. This is known as the pocket veto.

The documents produced at any one of these stages can be used in compiling a legislative history. The sponsor's intent can be drawn from the initial language of the bill, the committee's intent from its report, and the house's intent from its debate (see the Note on page 393) or from the amendments it rejected or accepted.

§10.2.2   Compiled Legislative Histories

Whenever possible, use a compiled legislative history. Don't do work that others have done for you.

The best source of compiled legislative histories is *Sources of Compiled Legislative Histories* by Nancy Johnson. This looseleaf publication includes, in chart form, a list of all public laws in which a legislative history has been compiled, telling the researcher where the history was published.

Another source is CCH's *Public Laws—Legislative Histories on Microfiche.* This source, which covers laws beginning with the 96th Congress, provides the researcher with the text of the House or Senate bill as introduced; the reported House or Senate bill; committee reports and conference reports, if any; and relevant legislative debate as reported in the *Congressional Record.*

§10.2.3   Sources for Federal Legislative Histories

At the federal level, the most comprehensive source is the Congressional Information Service (CIS). The bound volumes contain references to congressional documents; the documents themselves are available on microfiche. Unfortunately, CIS includes only documents published since 1970.

Another source is *United States Code Congressional and Administrative News* (USCCAN). Begun in 1941, it provides a history of bills, providing references to committee reports and to the dates a particular bill was considered in Congress. In addition, it selectively publishes some committee reports.

For additional sources, consult your law librarian.

§10.2.4   Sources for State Legislative Histories

Compiling a legislative history for a state statute is even more difficult than compiling one for a federal statute. Many states have few or no published legislative histories, and what is available is often stored in the state archives, accessible only to the state archivists.

Consequently, if you need to do a legislative history for a state statute, start with your law librarian. He or she can tell you what sources are available and how they can be accessed.

Chapter 11

The Executive Branch

The second branch of the government is the executive branch. Article II of the United States Constitution grants the President all executive powers including the power to execute, or enforce, all laws.

Although the Constitution grants the President only the power to execute laws, in practice the President also creates law. The President issues executive orders and proclamations. In addition, administrative agencies, which act under the power granted to them by the executive and legislative branches, routinely promulgate regulations, which are similar in form and content to statutes.

§11.1 PRESIDENTIAL DOCUMENTS

Presidents issue a variety of documents. Some, like speeches and formal statements, are not law. At best, they are persuasive authority, indicating general policy or the executive branch's opinion about how a particular statute should be interpreted. Others, like executive orders and proclamations, have the effect of law and, as such, are primary authority.

The best source of presidential documents is the *Weekly Compilation of Presidential Documents,* published by the United States Government Printing Office. It is published weekly and includes the text of all presidential documents issued during the prior week.

Executive orders and proclamations are also published in the *Federal Register* and, subsequently, under Title 3 in the *Code of Federal Regulations.* Title 3 is not, however, cumulative. Unlike other titles, which include the text of all regulations currently in effect, Title 3 contains only the executive orders and proclamations issued during the previous year.

A particular presidential document can be located using one of several sources: (1) the *CIS Index to Presidential Executive Orders and Proclamations;* (2) *Codification of Presidential Proclamations*

397

and Executive Orders, which is published by the Office of the Federal Register; or (3) a carefully worded search on either LEXIS or Westlaw.

Section Summary	*Executive Orders and Proclamations*

Type: Primary authority

Source: The most comprehensive source for presidential documents is the *Weekly Compilation of Presidential Documents* published by the Office of the Federal Register.

   Executive orders and proclamations are also published in the *Federal Register* and Title 3 of the *Code of Federal Regulations.*

§11.2   FEDERAL REGULATIONS

When acting pursuant to the power granted them by the legislative or executive branch, administrative agencies have the power to promulgate regulations that, when specified procedures have been followed, have the effect of law and are, therefore, primary authority.

For most agencies, the procedures for promulgating regulations are set out in the Administrative Procedure Act. This Act, which is codified at 5 U.S.C. § 551 *et seq.,* requires (1) that notice of a proposed rule be published in the *Federal Register,* (2) that there be time for comment and hearings, and (3) that the enacted version of the regulation be published initially in the *Federal Register* and permanently in the *Code of Federal Regulations.*

§11.2.1   The *Federal Register*

The *Federal Register,* which is published every working day, contains both notices of proposed rules and the text of those that have been enacted. As in the *Statutes at Large,* the material is organized chronologically. See Exhibit 11.1.

Copies of the *Federal Register* are available at Government Depository Libraries, at many law libraries, and online on LEXIS and Westlaw. Although the Government Printing Office publishes an index to the *Federal Register,* many researchers prefer the more detailed *CIS Federal Register Index,* which is published by Congressional Information Service.

EXHIBIT 11.1   Sample Page from the *Federal Register*

8428   Federal Register / Vol. 53, No. 50 / Tuesday, March 15, 1988 / Rules and Regulations

comparison to the amounts permitted by an applicable standard, the amounts found in a market-basket survey, or the amounts in a similar product or class of products as found in recent applicable reference sources. FSIS believes that this requirement provides sufficient information for consumers to make informed choices.

2. Requirements for Other Sausages

Comment: Several commenters stated that the new requirement may be unfair in comparison to other sausage-type products such as salami that will continue to have to comply with the 10 percent maximum on added moisture.

Response: The petition from AMI related specifically to frankfurters and similar cooked sausages which have both fat and water restrictions. FSIS recognizes that other cooked sausage products could also be formulated with more water. However, other cooked sausage standards do not include an analogous fat content limit. In this rulemaking, FSIS has focused its attention on cooked sausages of those types which have both fat and water limitations. Petitions to change the regulations for other sausage-type products would be evaluated by FSIS on their own merits.

3. Non-meat Proteins

Comment: A number of commenters stated that the proposal failed to address the issue of non-meat proteins. Use of certain non-meat proteins can increase the amount of added water since their protein content is not deducted from the total protein prior to calculations for added water. However, other commenters saw no need to address non-meat proteins in this rulemaking since the concern is not limited to one category of products.

Response: FSIS recognizes the importance of non-meat proteins as functional ingredients. However, as several commenters pointed out, the focus of this proposal was to permit the replacement of fat with added water. Also, concerns about non-meat proteins are not limited to a single category of products and should be more comprehensively addressed. FSIS has concluded delay impl address th

Text of Regulation

FSIS is ad issue for all cooked sausage products subject to added moisture controls in a rulemaking proceeding initiated on August 18, 1987 (52 FR 30925).

4. Product Name Qualifiers

Comment: Several commenters objected to the requirement that if

binders and extenders such as vegetable protein products are used, the name of each must prominently appear on the label contiguous to the product name, but there is no such requirement when ingredients such as poultry products and Mechanically Separated (Species) are used. One of these commenters also believed that FSIS should eliminate the current use limitations on vegetable protein products and credit in the calculations for added moisture the protein from ingredients such as soy protein isolate, which the commenter considered to be equivalent to meat from a protein quality standpoint.

Response: FSIS recognizes the apparent inconsistency of restrictions imposed on the use of vegetable protein products due to labeling requirements and product standards. However, these issues are not limited to a single category of product. Allowing credit for vegetable proteins, believed by some commenters to be equivalent in quality to meat protein, would allow for the replacement of livestock and poultry product ingredients with other sources of protein, such as hydrated vegetable protein products. Such a change would have broad policy implications, well beyond the scope of this rulemaking. For these reasons, FSIS believes it to be inappropriate to incorporate or consider these changes in this final rule. However, due to the merit of these comments, FSIS intends to pursue a rulemaking proceeding regarding the current use limitations on vegetable protein products and the requirements for product name qualifiers when these products are used.

Final Rule

For reasons set out in the preamble, Title 9, Part 319 of the Code of Federal Regulations is amended as set forth below.

List of Subjects in 9 CFR Part 319

Meat and meat food products, Standards of identity, Food labeling.

PART 319—DEFINITIONS AND STANDARDS OF IDENTITY OR COMPOSITION

1. The authority citation for Part 319 continues to read as follows:

Authority: 34 Stat. 1260, 81 Stat. 584, as amended (21 U.S.C. 601 *et seq.*); 72 Stat. 862, 92 Stat. 1069, as amended (7 U.S.C. 1901 *et seq.*), 76 Stat. 663 (7 U.S.C. 450 *et scq.*)

§ 319.180   [Amended]

2. In § 319.180, paragraphs (a) and (b) are amended by removing that portion of the fourth sentence in paragraph (a) and that portion of the fifth sentence in paragraph (b) reading: "but the sausage

shall contain no more than 10 percent of added water" and substituting therefor the following: "but the sausage shall contain no more than 40 percent of a combination of fat and added water".

§ 319.181   [Amended]

3. Section 319.181 is amended by removing that portion of the last sentence reading: "These products shall contain no more than 10 percent of added water and/or ice, 30 percent fat" and substituting therefor the following: "These products shall contain no more than 40 percent of a combination of fat and added water, and no more than 30 percent fat".

Done at Washington, DC, on March 10, 1988.

Lester M. Crawford,

Administrator, Food Safety and Inspection Service.

[FR Doc. 88–5656 Filed 3–14–88; 8:45 am]

BILLING CODE 3410-DM-M

COMMODITY FUTURES TRADING COMMISSION

17 CFR Parts 3 and 145

Registration Requirements for Futures Commission Merchants, Introducing Brokers, Commodity Pool Operators, Commodity Trading Advisors, Leverage Transaction Merchants and their Associated Persons; Commission Records and Information

AGENCY: Commodity Futures Trading Commission.

ACTION: Final rules.

SUMMARY: The Commodity Futures Trading Commission ("Commission") has adopted amendments to its rules governing the registration under the Commodity Exchange Act, 7 U.S.C. 1 *et seq.* ("Act"), of futures commission merchants, introducing brokers, commodity trading advisors, commodity ated the

Source of Delegation   ("NFA")

transaction merchants and their associated persons by the Commission. This action is being taken in order to authorize the implementation of certain registration rules which have been submitted by NFA for Commission approval and thereby eliminate any inconsistency between the Commission's rules and those of NFA. The amendments specifically are intended to streamline the registration process by narrowing the circumstances requiring a new registration, eliminating

§11.2.2   The *Code of Federal Regulations*

Permanent regulations are published in the *Code of Federal Regulations* (C.F.R.), which is published by the United States Government Printing Office. Like the *United States Code,* it is organized by topic, each regulation being codified under one of fifty titles.

	Statutes	*Regulations*
Organized Chronologically	*Statutes at Large*	*Federal Register*
Organized Topically	*United States Code*	*Code of Federal Regulations*

There is not an annotated version of the *Code of Federal Regulations.* To find a case interpreting or applying a particular regulation, use either *Shepard's Citator to the Code of Federal Regulations* or LEXIS or Westlaw.

a.   *Search Tools*

Regulations can be found using either of two methods. When the question is whether there is a regulation implementing a particular federal statute, the best source is the *Index and Finding Aids to the Code of Federal Regulations* volume of the *United States Code Service* (U.S.C.S.). See Exhibit 11.2. By using the tables in this volume, you can move from the *United States Code* section to the C.F.R. section or from the C.F.R. section to the *United States Code* section.

Regulations can also be found using the C.F.R. subject index, which is published annually by the United States Government Printing Office, or one of the more detailed indices published by Congressional Information Service.

b.   *Updating the C.F.R.*

Because regulations are promulgated almost daily, updating the C.F.R. is a complicated and sometimes tiresome process.

Instead of publishing a new set once a year, the Government Printing Office updates the C.F.R. in stages, revising one-quarter of the volumes every three months. Thus, although each volume is revised once a year, at any given time some volumes will be three months old, others six months old, and still others nine or twelve months old. Because of this, the updating process begins with the date on the front of the C.F.R. volume. Once you know that date, you know how much updating is necessary.

EXHIBIT 11.2   **Sample Pages from U.S.C.S.** *Index and Finding Aids to the Code of Federal Regulations* **Volume**

TABLE I—AUTHORITIES

CFR	USCS	CFR
	21 USCS—Continued	
.....21 Parts 1, 2, 225, 226, 250, 299, 514, 520, 522, 524, 539, 540, 544, 546, 556, 558, 801, 809		872, 874, 876, 878, 880, 882, 884, 886, 888, 890, 892, 895, 1003, 1010, 1020, 1030, 1040, 1050, 1240, 1250
...... 21 Part 814		40 Parts 23, 160, 177-180
...... 21 Parts 50, 320, 361, 510, 813	372............................ 21 Part 814	
.. 21 Parts 20, 860	372a........................... 21 Part 197	
. 21 Parts 809, 861	373—375 .... 21 Part 814	
......21 Part 807, 868, 870, 872, 874, 882, 884, 886, 888, 890, 892	373—374 .... 21 Part 179	
	374—375 .... 21 Part 200	
	374........................... 21 Parts 2, 20, 110, 113, 114, 129, 197, 201, 205, 207, 211, 225, 226, 310, 507, 600, 601, 606, 607, 700, 701, 710, 720, 801, 803, 809, 812, 813, 820, 860, 861	
....21 Parts 1010,), 1030, 1040, 1050	375...................... 21 Parts 250, 310	
. 21 Parts 60, 200, 864, 866, 868, 870, 978, 880, 882, 884, 886, 888, 890, 892	376........................... 21 Parts 50, 56, 58, 60, 70, 73, 74, 80-82, 103, 105, 131, 133, 135-137, 139, 145, 146, 161, 163, 164, 166, 168, 169-171, 175, 312, 314, 320, 361, 430, 431, 500, 510, 511, 514, 571, 812-814, 1003, 1010	
...... 21 Part 895		
...... 21 Parts 50, 171, 180, 320, 361, 12, 813, 820, 1003,		
Parts 170, 571, 895	376 note .... 21 Part 81	
Parts 20, 801, 860	377............................ 21 Part 2	
	379............................ 21 Part 814	
	381............................ 19 Part 12	

Authorizing statute in U.S.C. → ... ← C.F.R. section

TABLE II—AUTHORITIES

CFR	USCS	CFR
9 Part 310 .... 33 § 1254		9 Part 391 ....
9 Part 310 .... 21 §§ 601—695		9 Part 391 ....
9 Part 310 .... 7 § 450 et seq.		10 Parts 0-2 ....
9 Part 310 .... 7 § 1901 et seq.		10 Part 0.............
9 Parts 311-316............. 21 § 601 et seq.		10 Parts 0-2 ....
9 Part 311 .... 33 §§ 466—466k		10 Parts 0-2 ....
9 Parts 311-316............. 21 § 71 et seq.		10 Part 0.............
9 Part 313 .... 7 §§ 1901—1906		10 Parts 0-2 ....
9 Parts 314-317.......... 33 §§ 466—466k		10 Part 1.............
9 Part 316 .... 21 § 621		10 Part 1.............
9 Part 317 .... 21 §§ 601—695		10 Part 1.............
9 Part 317 .... 33 § 1171		10 Part 1.............
9 Part 317 .... 21 § 607		
9 Part 317 .... 21 § 457		10 Part 1.............
9 Part 318 .... 21 §§ 451—470		10 Part 1.............
9 Part 318 .... 21 §§ 601—695		10 Part 2.............
9 Part 318 .... 7 §§ 1901—1906		10 Part 2.............
9 Part 318 .... 7 § 450		10 Part 2.............
9 Part 319 .... 7 § 450 et seq.		10 Part 2.............
9 Part 319 .... 21 § 621		10 Part 2.............
9 Parts 319-322............. 21 § 601 et seq.		10 Part 2.............
9 Part 319 .... 7 § 1901 et seq.		10 Part 2.............
9 Parts 319-321.......... 33 §§ 466—466k		10 Part 2.............
9 Part 319 .... 33 § 1254		10 Part 2.............
9 Part 320 .... 33 § 1254		10 Part 2.............
9 Part 320 .... 44 § 3506		10 Part 2.............
9 Part 320 .... 21 § 621		10 Part 2.............

C.F.R. section → ... ← Authorizing statute in U.S.C.

EXHIBIT 11.3 **Sample Page from C.F.R. *List of Sections* *Affected* Volume**

DECEMBER 1991   **67**

CHANGES JANUARY 2, 1991 THROUGH DECEMBER 31, 1991

Page

317.19 Regulations at 55 FR 49834 and 50081 effective date delayed to 1-2

317.20 Regulations a ⌐C.F.R. citation 49833, 49834 and being updated fective date delaye 92...22638

(a) and (c) regulations at 55 FR 49833, 49834, 50081 and 56 FR 22638 effective date delayed to 3-2-92.................. 67485

317.21 Regulations at 55 FR 49834 and 50081 effective date delayed to 1-2-92............. 22638

Regulations at 55 FR 49833, 49834, 50081 and 56 FR 22638 effective date delayed to 3-2-92.................................67485

317.22 Regulations at 55 FR 49834 and 50081 effective date delayed to 1-2-92............. 22638

317.23 Regulations at 55 FR 49833 and 50081 effective date delayed to 1-2-92............. 22638

317.24 Regulations at 55 FR 49833 and 50081 effective date delayed to 1-2-92............. 22638

318 Authority citation revised; sectional authority citations removed.......................................3195

319 Authority citation revised; sectional authority citations removed.......................................3195

319.180 (e) revised..........................41448
319.181 Amended........................... 41448
319.281 (b)(9) revised................... 41448

320 Authority citation revised; sectional authority citations removed.......................................3195

321 Authority citation revised; sectional authority citations removed.......................................3195

322 Authority citation revised; sectional authority citations removed.......................................3195

325 Authority citation revised; sectional authority citations removed.......................................3195

325.1 (b)(2) revised; eff. 1-15-92..65180

327 Authority citation revised; sectional authority citations removed.......................................3195

Page

327.3 (d) removed..........................38335

327.7 **Heading revised; (a), (b), (c), and (h) removed; (d), (e),** as (⌐Page in the 1-15 Federal Register on which to locate change .65180

327.22   .65180

329 Authority citation revised; sectional authority citations removed......................................3195

331 Authority citation revised; sectional authority citations removed......................................3195

331.2 Table amended.....................8909
331.6 Table amended.....................8908

335 Authority citation revised; sectional authority citations removed......................................3195

350 Authority citation revised; sectional authority citations removed......................................3195

381 Authority citation revised; sectional authority citations removed......................................3195

381.118 Regulation at 55 FR 26422 effective date delayed to 9-3-91.....................................1359

381.121a Regulations at 55 FR 49835 and 50081 effective date delayed to 1-2-92............. 22638

381.121b Regulations at 55 FR 49835 and 50081 effective date delayed to 1-2-92............. 22638

381.121c Regulations at 55 FR 49836 and 50081 effective date delayed to 1-2-92............. 22638

(a) and (c) regulations at 55 FR 49833, 49834, 50081 and 56 FR 22638 effective date delayed to 3-2-92.................. 67485

381.121d Regulations at 55 FR 49836 and 50081 effective date delayed to 1-2-92............. 22638

Regulations at 55 FR 49833, 49834, 50081 and 56 FR 22638 effective date delayed to 3-2-92.................................67485

381.121e Regulations at 55 FR 49836 and 50081 effective date delayed to 1-2-92............. 22638

NOTE: **Boldface entries indicate December changes.**

To determine whether new regulations have been proposed or promulgated since the date the C.F.R. volume was revised, use the *List of Sections Affected* volumes, which are published monthly and which are usually shelved at the end of the C.F.R. See Exhibit 11.3. If a new regulation has been proposed or promulgated, there will be a page reference to the *Federal Register.*

Note

Depending on when the C.F.R. volume was revised, it may be necessary to consult more than one *List of Sections Affected* volume. It will also be necessary to consult the "C.F.R. Parts Affected During the Month" table that is published at the back of each *Federal Register* issue. You will need to look at the most recent issue of the *Federal Register* to update through the current month. It may also be necessary to use the last issue of the preceding month to update for that month.

———————

The C.F.R. can also be updated using LEXIS and Westlaw. Once a regulation is on the screen, you can update it using a single update command.

Section Summary	*Federal Regulations*

Type: Primary authority

Source: Proposed rules and enacted rules are published in chronological order in the *Federal Register.*

        Permanent enacted rules are also published in the *Code of Federal Regulations,* which is organized by topic.

Finding Tools: A particular regulation can be found using the *Index and Finding Tools* volume of the U.S.C.S., the C.F.R. subject index, or LEXIS or Westlaw.

        To find a case interpreting or applying a particular regulation, use *Shepard's Citator for the Code of Federal Regulations* or LEXIS or Westlaw.

§11.3   STATE REGULATIONS

Like their federal counterparts, many state agencies promulgate regulations. As in the federal system, these regulations are usually published first in the state register and then in the state administrative code. The name of each state's register and administrative code is set out in the Tables section of the *Bluebook.*

Section Summary	*State Regulations*

Type: Primary authority

Source: State register and state administrative code

§11.4   ADMINISTRATIVE DECISIONS

In addition to their legislative role, many state and federal administrative agencies serve a judicial function, deciding disputes that arise under the statutes that they are responsible for implementing or the regulations that they have themselves promulgated.

Although copies of these decisions are on file in the agency, the agency is usually not the best source for these decisions. For the federal agencies, better sources are decisions disseminated by the Government Printing Office, looseleaf services published by commercial publishing companies (see section 13.2), and LEXIS and Westlaw.

Note

A list of federal administrative agencies and where their decisions are available can be found in the appendix of West's hornbook, *How to Find the Law.*

Section Summary	*Decisions of Federal Administrative Agencies*

Type: Primary authority

Source: The best sources of administrative decisions are the decisions published by the Government Printing Office, commercially produced looseleaf services, and LEXIS and Westlaw. Copies of decisions can also be obtained from the agency itself or in government depository libraries.

Chapter 12

The Judicial Branch

The third branch of the government is the judicial branch. Article III of the United States Constitution created the Supreme Court and gave Congress the power to create such inferior courts as it might "from time to time ordain and establish," giving those courts the power to hear all cases arising under the Constitution and the laws of the United States and between citizens of different states. Similarly, through its constitution each state created its own judiciary, giving its supreme and inferior courts the power to hear cases arising under the state constitution, state statutes, and state common law.

Like constitutions, statutes, and administrative regulations, cases are primary authority. Each time a court decides a case, it creates law.

§12.1 Court Decisions

Just as statutes and regulations are published at different times in different forms, so are cases. Cases are initially published as slip opinions. Reported cases are then collected and published in advance sheets and then in bound reporters.

§12.1.1 Slip Opinions

A "slip opinion" is the opinion in the form in which it is released by the court. Each opinion is issued individually and, as a general rule, the opinions are typed rather than printed. Because the opinions have not yet been "processed," there is no syllabus, no headnotes, and no citation.

Although the slip opinions of the United States Supreme Court are widely distributed, the slip opinions of the other federal and most state court are not. As a general rule, slip opinions are sent only to the parties, to the reporter, to other courts and, when special arrangements have been made, to local or law school libraries.

§12.1.2   Advance Sheets

Bimonthly or monthly, the slip opinions for reported cases are collected and published in softbound pamphlets known as "advance sheets." These advance sheets are part of a particular reporter: Opinions from the federal district courts are published in the advance sheets for the Federal Supplement, opinions from the Virginia Supreme Court in the Southeastern Reporter.

Unlike slip opinions, the opinions that appear in the advance sheets have been processed. A citation has been assigned, and a syllabus and headnotes have often been added.

Most advance sheets are widely distributed. In law firms, advance sheets are circulated among the attorneys, each attorney reading those cases that relate to his or her area of practice; in law libraries, they are filed at the end of the bound reporters.

§12.1.3   Bound Reporters

When a sufficient number of decisions have been issued, the advance sheets are replaced by a bound volume, which then becomes a permanent part of that reporter.

Although the bulk of each volume is taken up by opinions, other information is included. In a typical reporter, you will find the following information:

1. a list of the courts whose opinions appear in that reporter;
2. a list of the judges or justices sitting at the time the opinions were issued;
3. a table listing, in alphabetical order, the cases appearing in that volume;
4. in many state reporters, the names of the attorneys just admitted to the bar;
5. amendments to existing court rules or new or proposed court rules; and
6. a subject index for the cases in that volume.

§12.1.4   The National Reporter System

In most law libraries, reporters fill row after row in stack after stack. There are reporters for federal cases, reporters for state cases, regional reporters, and specialized reporters. A particular opinion may appear in only one of these reporters or in several different ones.

Although some reporters are published by the courts themselves, most are published by West Publishing Company. Its network of reporters, which is known as the National Reporter System, includes the following:

Regional Reporters:

Atlantic Reporter (begun in 1886)
    Connecticut
    Delaware
    District of Columbia
    Maine
    Maryland
    New Hampshire
    New Jersey
    Pennsylvania
    Rhode Island
    Vermont

California Reporter (begun in 1960)

New York Supplement (begun in 1888)

North Eastern Reporter (begun in 1885)
    Illinois
    Indiana
    Massachusetts
    New York (only Court of Appeals after 1888)
    Ohio

North Western Reporter (begun in 1885)
    Iowa
    Michigan
    Minnesota
    Nebraska
    North Dakota
    South Dakota
    Wisconsin

Pacific Reporter (begun in 1884)
    Alaska
    Arizona
    California (after 1960, Supreme Court only)
    Colorado
    Hawaii
    Idaho
    Kansas
    Montana
    Nevada
    New Mexico
    Oklahoma
    Oregon
    Utah
    Washington
    Wyoming

South Eastern Reporter (begun in 1887)
Georgia
North Carolina
South Carolina
Virginia
West Virginia

South Western Reporter (begun in 1887)
Arkansas
Kentucky
Missouri
Tennessee
Texas

Southern Reporter (begun in 1887)
Alabama
Florida
Louisiana
Mississippi

Federal Reporters:

Supreme Court Reporter (S. Ct.): decisions of the United States
Supreme Court
Federal Reporter and *Federal Reporter, Second Series* (F. and F.2d):
decisions of the United States Court of Appeals
Federal Supplement (F. Supp.): decisions of the United States District
trict Court
Bankruptcy Reporter (begun in 1980): decisions of the United
States Bankruptcy Courts and other decisions involving bankruptcy issues
ruptcy issues
Claims Court Reporter (begun in 1982): decisions of the Claims
Court (formerly Court of Claims)
Federal Rules Decisions (begun in 1940): decisions from the
United States district courts on issues related to the federal
rules of criminal and civil procedure

Each of these reporters uses the West Key Number System, a system that allows West to categorize each rule of law set out in a case.
The system works as follows. When West receives a case, the case is assigned to an editor. The editor identifies each rule of law set out by the court and then categorizes each rule, assigning both a topic and, within that topic, a key number. This information is then used in two ways: (1) the rules, with their topic and key numbers, become the headnotes that appear at the beginning of each West opinion and (2) the headnotes are collected and printed in digests, the subject indices for cases. See pages 414-415. Exhibit 12.1 illustrates West Key Numbers as they appear at the beginning of a case; Exhibit 12.2 illustrates West Key Numbers as they appear in a digest.

By using the West Key Number System, a researcher can quickly locate that portion of the opinion in which the court sets out a particular rule and, having identified the relevant topic and key number, can use a digest to locate other cases in which the court has applied or discussed the same rule of law. Given the usefulness of West's Key Number System, it is not surprising that many researchers still follow Horace Greeley's advice and "go West."

Note

A list of the topics that West uses appears at the front of most West digest volumes.

---

§12.1.5   Other Reporters

West's major commercial competitor is Lawyers Co-operative, which publishes two annotated reporters, the *Supreme Court Reporter, Lawyer's Edition* and *American Law Reports.* The *Supreme Court Reporter, Lawyer's Edition* (L. Ed. or L. Ed. 2d) contains the text of all United States Supreme Court decisions plus, at the end of the volume, annotations discussing issues raised in selected opinions appearing in that volume. *American Law Reports* (A.L.R., A.L.R.2d, A.L.R.3d, A.L.R.4th, A.L.R.5th, and A.L.R. Fed.) selects noteworthy decisions from both the federal and state courts. For each of these decisions, it publishes a summary of the attorneys' arguments, the text of the court's opinion, and an annotation collecting and summarizing other cases discussing the same issue. (For more on A.L.R., see pages 426-430.)

Section Summary	*Reporters*

Type: Primary authority

Sources: *United States Supreme Court: United States Reports* (U.S.), *Supreme Court Reporter* (S. Ct.), *Supreme Court Reporter, Lawyer's Edition* (L. Ed. or L. Ed. 2d), or LEXIS or Westlaw

United States Court of Appeals: Federal Reporter (F. or F.2d) or LEXIS or Westlaw

United States District Court: Federal Supplement (F. Supp.) or LEXIS or Westlaw

EXHIBIT 12.1   Key Numbers in a Case*

COLORADO CARPET INSTALLATION, INC. v. PALERMO   Colo.   **1385**
Cite as 668 P.2d 1384 (Colo. 1983)

nates in contract include contractual language used by parties, whether agreement involves one overall price that includes both goods and labor or calls for separate and discrete bills for goods on one hand and labor on the other, ratio that cost of goods bears to overall contract price and nature and reasonableness of buyer's contractual expectations of acquiring property interest in goods. C.R.S. 4–2–102(2)(a), 4–2–101 et seq., 4–2–105(1), 4–2–106(1), 4–2–201(1).

4. Frauds, Statute of ⟨key⟩82

To satisfy "specially manufactured goods" exception to statute of frauds, goods must be specially made for buyer, goods must be unsuitable for sale to others in ordinary course of seller's business, seller must have substantially begun to manufacture goods or must have made commitment for their procurement, and manufacture or commitment must have been commenced under circumstances reasonably indicating that goods are for buyer and prior to seller's receipt of notification of repudiation. C.R.S. 4–2–201(1), (3)(a).

5. Frauds, Statute of ⟨key⟩82

Term "specially manufactured" as used in "specially manufactured goods" exception to statute of frauds in Uniform Commercial Code refers to character of goods as specially made for particular buyer, and not to whether they were "specially made" in usual course of seller's business. C.R.S. 4–2–201(1), (3)(a).

> See publication Words and Phrases for other judicial constructions and definitions.

6. Frauds, Statute of ⟨key⟩82

Evidence did not permit finding that carpet which was to be installed in buyer's home was "specially manufactured" within "specially manufactured goods" exception to statute of frauds in Uniform Commercial Code. C.R.S. 4–2–201(1), (3)(a).

———————

Louis A. Weltzer, Denver, for petitioner.

Joseph P. Constantine, Denver, for respondents.

EN BANC.

QUINN, Justice.

We granted certiorari to review the decision of the court of appeals in *Colorado Carpet Installation, Inc. v. Palermo*, 647 P.2d 686 (Colo.App.1982). The court of appeals, in reversing the trial court, held that an oral agreement involving the purchase and installation of carpeting and other flooring materials was a contract for the sale of goods within the meaning of section 4–2–201(1), C.R.S.1973, of the Uniform Commercial Code, rather than a service contract, and that the contract was unenforceable because the goods did not qualify under section 4–2–201(3)(a), C.R.S.1973, for the "specially manufactured goods" exception to the "writing" requirement of section 4–2–201(1), C.R.S.1973. We affirm the judgment of the court of appeals.

I.

In July 1980 Colorado Carpet Installation, Inc., doing business as Sierra Range Carpets, Inc. (Colorado Carpet), commenced an action in the District Court of Adams County against Fred and Zuma Palermo for breach of contract. The claim was based on an alleged oral agreement in which the Palermos agreed to pay $4,775.75 to Colorado Carpet for the purchase and installation of carpeting, other flooring materials, and bathroom tile for the Palermo home in Thornton, Colorado. The Palermos in their answer denied the existence of a contract and affirmatively asserted that the statute of frauds, section 4–2–201(1), C.R.S.1973, rendered any such agreement unenforceable.

The controversy was tried to the court and arose as follows. Colorado Carpet is a Colorado corporation engaged in the business of selling and installing carpeting, tile and other flooring materials. In April 1980,

EXHIBIT 12.2   **Key Numbers in a Digest***

30 P.D.(585 P.2d)—487   **FRAUDS, STATUTE OF**   ⬚84

For references to other topics, see Descriptive-Word Index

any extrinsic evidence for proof of essential terms of a contract to make a will unless a writing is produced and signed by decedent which evidences the essential terms of the contract. NMSA 1978, §§ 45–2–701, 45–2–701, subd. A(1–3).

> Matter of Estate of Vincioni, 698 P.2d 446, 102 N.M. 576, certiorari denied 698 P.2d 886, 102 N.M. 613.

Wyo. 1989. Disclaimer signed by surviving husband regarding property in wife's estate consisting of $200,000 cash and certain real property did not establish enforceable contract between husband and wife to make will leaving property to specific residuary beneficiaries for statute of frauds purposes; disclaimer was not consistent with what reciprocal wills of spouses provided, under which all of wife's property was to go to husband, and disclaimer by husband was gratuitous act which did not support or corroborate notion of contract between spouses. W.S.1977, § 1–23–105.

> Sievers v. Barton, 775 P.2d 489.

⬚76. —— **Partnership contracts and lands.**

Ariz.App. 1980. Alleged oral contract requiring transfer of land from one joint venturer to another was within statute of frauds. A.R.S. § 44–101.

> Johnson v. Gilbert, 621 P.2d 916, 127 Ariz. 410.

⬚77–80. *For other cases see earlier editions of this digest, the Decennial Digests, and WESTLAW.*

VII. SALES OF PERSONAL PROPERTY.

(A) CONTRACTS WITHIN STATUTE.

⬚81. **Statutory provisions.**

Library references

> C.J.S. Frauds, Statute of § 138 et seq.

⬚82. **Nature of property.**

Library references

> C.J.S. Frauds, Statute of § 142.

Colo. 1983. To satisfy "specially manufactured goods" exception to statute of frauds, goods must be specially made for buyer, goods must be unsuitable for sale to others in ordinary course of seller's business, seller must have substantially begun to manufacture goods or must have made commitment for their procurement, and manufacture or commitment must have been commenced under circumstances reasonably indicating that goods are for buyer and prior to seller's receipt of notification of repudiation. C.R.S. 4–2–201(1), (3)(a).

> Colorado Carpet Installation, Inc. v. Palermo, 668 P.2d 1384.

Term "specially manufactured" as used in "specially manufactured goods" exception to statute of frauds in Uniform Commercial Code refers to character of goods as specially made for particular buyer, and not to whether they were "specially made" in usual course of seller's business. C.R.S. 4–2–201(1), (3)(a).

> Colorado Carpet Installation, Inc. v. Palermo, 668 P.2d 1384.

Evidence did not permit finding that carpet which was to be installed in buyer's home was "specially manufactured" within "specially manufactured goods" exception to statute of frauds in Uniform Commercial Code. C.R.S. 4–2–201(1), (3)(a).

> Colorado Carpet Installation, Inc. v. Palermo, 668 P.2d 1384.

Colo.App. 1982. The specially manufactured goods exception to the statute of frauds applies only when goods are not a stock item and they are unsuitable for sale to others in the ordinary course of business. C.R.S.1973, 4–2–201, 4–2–201(3)(a).

> Colorado Carpet Installation, Inc. v. Palermo, 647 P.2d 686, affirmed 668 P.2d 1384.

Contract under which plaintiff sold defendants carpeting, which was not specially cut to fit defendants' room, was a stock item carried by number of carpeting distributors, and was suitable for sale to others in ordinary course of business, did not fall within specially manufactured goods exception to statute of frauds and, due to lack of a signed writing, was unenforceable. C.R.S.1973, 4–2–201, 4–2–201(3)(a).

> Colorado Carpet Installation, Inc. v. Palermo, 647 P.2d 686, affirmed 668 P.2d 1384.

⬚83. **Existence and condition of goods.**

Library references

> C.J.S. Frauds, Statute of § 142.

Colo.App. 1988. While subsequent conduct can modify a written warranty, such modification must still meet requirements of statute of frauds. C.R.S. 4–2–201, 4–2–209, 4–2–313.

> Cooley v. Big Horn Harvestore Systems, Inc., 767 P.2d 740, certiorari granted.

⬚84. **Nature of contract.**

Library references

> C.J.S. Frauds, Statute of §§ 139, 141.

Colo. 1983. Uniform Commercial Code section prohibiting enforcement of oral contracts for sale of goods for price of $500 or more applies by its terms only to contracts for sale of goods, and not to contracts for labor or

State Court Decisions: Regional reporter and, in some states, official state reporter; also LEXIS or Westlaw

Recent decisions can be found in the advance sheets, in the form of a slip opinion, or on LEXIS or Westlaw.

§12.2   COURT RULES

The judicial branch does, however, do more than just decide cases. It also promulgates the procedural rules that govern the cases that come before it. The United States Supreme Court promulgates the rules that govern federal cases, and the state supreme courts promulgate the rules that govern cases in their state systems.

Note

Lower courts and, even within a court, particular judges, may promulgate their own local rules.

Court rules can be found in a number of different places. The Federal Rules of Civil Procedure are published as an appendix to Title 28 in both the *United States Code* and the *United States Code Annotated* and as separate volumes in the *United States Code Service.* The rules also appear in commercial publications, including supplements to Civil Procedure case books and *Federal Civil Judicial Procedure and Rules* by West.

Another good source is treatises. *Federal Practice and Procedure* (also known as Wright and Miller) and *Moore's Federal Practice* are multivolume sets containing not only the text of the rules but also commentary and references to cases that have interpreted or applied the rules. Cases can also be found in West's *Federal Rules Decisions* (locate cases using the *Federal Practice Digest*) and in Callaghan's *Federal Rules Service.*

State rules are usually published at the beginning of the state's code and in separate publications, published either by the court or by a commercial publisher. Local rules are available either from the court or the judge or, for the larger courts, from the local entity or a commercial publisher.

Section Summary	*Court Rules*

Type: Primary authority

Sources: The Federal Rules of Civil Procedure can be found in the appendix to Title 28 in the *United States Code* (U.S.C.) and the

FOOD———□ Topic

SUBJECTS INCLUDED

Regulation of manufacture, sale or use of articles of food and drink and of substitutes and imitations thereof

Rights of property and traffic in unwholesome or adulterated articles used as food, etc.

Liabilities for injuries from the sale, use, etc., thereof

Violations of laws relating to such articles, and prosecution and punishment thereof as public offenses

SUBJECTS EXCLUDED AND COVERED BY OTHER TOPICS

Adulteration as a public offense, see ADULTERATION

Inspection for prevention of fraud or commercial purposes, see INSPECTION

Interstate commerce, regulations regarding commodities as articles of, see COMMERCE

Intoxicants, see INTOXICATING LIQUORS

Medicines, see DRUGS AND NARCOTICS   □ Cross-references

Poisons, see POISONS

Unfair trade practices under statutes, see TRADE REGULATION

Warranties on sale, see SALES

For detailed references to other topics, see Descriptive-Word Index

Analysis

⚎½. What is food.
  1. Power to make regulations.
  1.5. —— State power in general.
  1.6. —— Municipal power in general.
  1.7. —— Administrative power in general.
  1.8. —— Milk products and substitutes.
    (1). In general.
    (2). State power.
    (3). Municipal power.   □ Topic analysis
    (4). Administrative power.   (subject outline)
  1.9. —— Milk marketing and price.
    (1). In general.
    (2). State power.
    (3). Administrative power.
  1.10. —— Meat and poultry.
  2. Statutory and municipal regulations in general.
  3. License and inspection.
  4. Quantity and price.

51 West's Fed.Pr.Dig.3d—23

*Reprinted from West's *Federal Practice Digest 3d*, © 1985 (West's National Reporter System), with permission of West Publishing Company.

EXHIBIT 12.4   **Entries in Main Volumes of West's *Federal Practice Digest 3d***

51 F P D 3d—691

FOOD ☞1

For references to other topics, see Descriptive-Word Index

Research Notes

Food; Food, Drug and Cosmetic Act, see West's Federal Forms.

Practice under Food, Drug and Cosmetic Law, see West's Federal Practice

> Key number

☞½. **What is food.**

Library references

C.J.S. Food § 1.

C.A.N.Y. 1984. "Starchblockers" are "drug," not "food," for purposes of Federal Food, Drug, and Cosmetic Act. Federal Food, Drug, and Cosmetic Act, § 201(g)(1)(C), 21 U.S.C.A. § 321(g)(1)(C).

American Health Products Co. v. Hayes, 744 F.2d 912.

D.C.Ill. 1982. If a product is intended by user and manufacturer or distributor to be used as a drug, it would be regulated as such; conversely, if it is intended that the product be used as a food, it will be so considered. Federal Food, Drug, and Cosmetic Act, § 201(f, g), 21 U.S.C.A. § 321(f, g).

Nutrilab, Inc. v. Schweiker, 547 F.Supp. 880, affirmed 713 F.2d 335.

The Food and Drug Administration, in determining whether a product is a food or a drug, may consider manufacturers' subjective intent as well as actual therapeutic intent based upon objective evidence in this determination. Federal Food, Drug, and Cosmetic Act, § 201(f, g), 21 U.S.C.A. § 321(f, g).

Nutrilab, Inc. v. Schweiker, 547 F.Supp. 880, affirmed 713 F.2d 335.

D.C.Tex. 1976. Frog legs are a "food" within meaning of Federal Food, Drug and Cosmetic Act provision which defines "food" for purposes of the Act as including "articles used for food or drink for man or other animals." Federal Food, Drug, and Cosmetic Act, § 201(f)(1), 21 U.S.C.A. § 321(f)(1).

U. S. v. 76,552 Pounds of Frog Legs, 423 F.Supp. 329.

☞1. **Power to make regulations.**

> Citation

Library references

C.J.S. Food § 4(1) et seq.

U.S.Minn. 1981. Equal protection clause did not deny the state of Minnesota authority to ban one type of milk container, i. e., plastic nonreturnable containers, conceded to cause environmental problems merely because another type, i. e., paperboard containers already established in the market was permitted to continue in use; whether in fact the act would promote more environmentally desirable milk packaging was not the question as equal protection clause was satisfied by Supreme Court's conclusion that the state legislature could rationally have decided that its ban on the plastic

nonreturnable jugs might foster greater use of environmentally desirable alternatives. M.S.A. §§ 116F.01, 116F.22; U.S.C.A.Const. Amend. 14.

Minnesota v. Clover Leaf Creamery Co., 101 S.Ct. 715, 449 U.S. 456, 66 L.Ed.2d 659, rehearing denied 101 S.Ct. 1735, 450 U.S. 1027, 68 L.Ed.2d 222, on remand 304 N.W.2d 915.

> Cross-references (to *Corpus Juris Secundum*)

nonreturnable conomic dislo- ent toward the superior containers, a stated purpose for Minnesota legislature's ban on plastic nonreturnable milk containers, was a valid justification for the ban and would further state statutory purposes, including promoting resource conservation, as plastic nonreturnables had only recently been introduced on a wide scale in the state and while legislature was considering the act many state dairies were preparing to invest large amounts of capital in plastic container production. M.S.A. §§ 116F.01, 116F.21, 116F.22; U.S.C.A.Const. Amend. 14.

Minnesota v. Clover Leaf Creamery Co., 101 S.Ct. 715, 449 U.S. 456, 66 L.Ed.2d 659, rehearing denied 101 S.Ct. 1735, 450 U.S. 1027, 68 L.Ed.2d 222, on remand 304 N.W.2d 915.

> Squib (abstract)

ffect, Minnesota legislature aperboard containers, at least temporarily, did not make legislature's ban on use of plastic nonreturnable, nonrefillable milk containers arbitrary or irrational; state legislature could reasonably conclude that nonreturnable, nonrefillable containers imposed environmental hazards and by banning the most recent entry while permitting paperboard containers the state could prevent the industry from becoming reliant on the new container while avoiding severe economic dissolution as few dairies were presently able to package their products in refillable bottles or plastic pouches. M.S.A. § 116F.22; U.S.C.A. Const. Amend. 14.

Minnesota v. Clover Leaf Creamery Co., 101 S.Ct. 715, 449 U.S. 456, 66 L.Ed.2d 659, rehearing denied 101 S.Ct. 1735, 450 U.S. 1027, 68 L.Ed.2d 222, on remand 304 N.W.2d 915.

Minnesota statute banning retail sale of milk in plastic nonreturnable, nonrefillable containers, but permitting such sales in other nonreturnable, nonrefillable containers such as paperboard cartons, bore a rational relation to stated objectives of promoting resource conservation, easing solid waste disposal problems and conserving energy and, hence, passed muster under the equal protection rationality test.

United States Code Annotated (U.S.C.A.) and as separate volumes in *United States Code Service* (U.S.C.S.).

The Federal Rules can also be found in commercial publications like *West's Federal Civil Judicial Procedure and Rules,* which contain just the text of the rule, or in treatises like West's *Federal Practice and Procedure* and *Moore's Federal Practice,* which have not only the text of the rules but also commentary and citations to cases.

State rules can be found in most state codes or in separately bound pamphlets or books.

Local rules can be obtained from the clerk of the court.

§12.3   DIGESTS

Cases can be found in a variety of ways: (1) by using the annotations that follow the text of the statute or court rule in an annotated code; (2) by looking up the citations found in a legal encyclopedia, hornbook, treatise, or other secondary source; (3) by using LEXIS or Westlaw; or (4) by using a digest.

Digests are the subject indices for case reporters. Abstracts of cases are arranged by topic and, within each topic, by subtopic. See Exhibits 12.3 and 12.4.

Just as there are numerous reporters, there are also numerous digests. The most comprehensive (and the most time-consuming to use) is the *Dicennial Digest,* which lists cases from both the federal courts and all of the state courts. Smaller in scope but easier to use are the federal digests, the regional digests, and the state digests.

Federal Digests:

> *Federal Digest.* Through 1940.
> *Modern Federal Practice Digest.* 1940-1960.
> *Federal Practice Digest 2d.* 1961-November 1975.
> *Federal Practice Digest 3d.* 1975- (no specific cutoff date).
> *Federal Practice Digest 4th.* Supplements *Federal Practice Digest 3d.*

Regional Digests: The digests that are available vary from region to region.

State Digests: Some states have their own digest; others do not.

Specialized Digests (representative examples):

> *Bankruptcy Digest*
> *Education Law Digest*
> *United States Claims Court Digest*

Most digests have the same format. They are almost always multi-volume sets containing descriptive word index volumes, volumes containing the case abstracts, and volumes containing other finding tools (for example, tables of cases, plaintiff-defendant tables, and a words and phrases volume). With the exception of the Dicennial and General Digests, all digests are kept current through the use of pocket parts, which are usually published yearly, and supplemental pamphlets, which may be published monthly or quarterly.

The best way to use a digest depends on what you already know and what it is that you are looking for.

1. Location of a specific case.   If you know the name of a case but not the citation, the best source is the Table of Cases or the Defendant-Plaintiff table. By looking up either the case name or the plaintiff's or defendant's name, you can find the case citation.

2. Other cases discussing the same point of law.   If you have found one case that is on point, you can find others discussing the same point by looking up the topic and key number in the main volumes of the digests. For example, if you want to find other cases discussing the point of law set out in headnote 4 in *Colorado Carpet,* you would locate the digest volume containing the topic "Frauds, Statute of." You would then locate that topic and, within that topic, key number 82. See pages 410 and 411.

3. Cases discussing a particular point of law.   If you have not yet found a case discussing a particular point of law, you can use a digest to find the first case. The best way of doing this is through the digest's descriptive word index. Look up your search terms in the index, for each term noting the topic and key number references. Then look up the topic and key numbers that appear to be most on point in the main volumes of the digest.

4. Cases defining a particular word or phrase.   If you are looking for a definition, the best source is the words and phrases volume. If the word or phrase has been defined, the word or phrase and the citation to the case or cases in which it has been defined will be listed.

Section Summary	*Digests*

Type: Finding tool

Sources: Digests are subject indices for cases. Federal cases can be found using one of the federal digests (for example, recent cases can be found using *Federal Practice Digest 3d* or *4th*);

state cases can be located using the state's own digest or the appropriate regional digest.

Most digests contain a number of finding tools; for example, most digests have a table of cases, defendant-plaintiff tables, and a words and phrases volume.

Chapter 13

Secondary Sources

Unlike primary sources, secondary sources do not contain the law itself. Instead, they summarize, explain, or comment on the law.

As a researcher, you will use secondary sources in a variety of ways. When you are unfamiliar with a particular area of law, you can use secondary sources to obtain an overview of the area of law. See section 5.6.1. Secondary sources can, however, be used in other ways: They can be used to locate the key cases in your, or other, jurisdictions and, at times, as authority. When there is no mandatory authority, or the mandatory authority does not support the position you are advocating, secondary sources can be cited as persuasive authority.

Although any given source can be used for more than one purpose, some are better for one purpose than they are for another. For example, although a legal encyclopedia may be a good source for background reading, you would not want to cite it as persuasive authority.

To help you determine which sources are best for particular purposes, this chapter groups and discusses secondary sources according to their primary purpose: Secondary sources that can be used for background reading are discussed first, secondary sources that are effective finding tools are discussed second, and secondary sources that can be used as persuasive authority are discussed third.

§13.1 SOURCES FOR BACKGROUND READING

Probably the best sources for background reading are legal encyclopedias, hornbooks, and practice books. There are, however, a variety of other sources that can be used. Depending on the problem, useful background information can be found in a legal dictionary, in *American Law Reports* (A.L.R.), or in a law review or book.

67 Am Jur 2d   SALES   § 194

on the other hand, often construed as rendering the contract enforceable in its entirety.[29] A downpayment on an automobile takes the transaction outside the statute of frauds.[30] And a check for $2,325 bearing the legend "deposit on aux. sloop, D'Arc Wind, full amount $4,650" would constitute partial performance sufficient to uphold the entire contract calling for the sale of this boat, as against a statute of frauds objection.[31] It has, however, been held that a partial payment and acceptance upon an oral contract for the sale of indivisible goods does not take the contract out of the operation of the statute of frauds.[32]

A mere tender of payment by the buyer is not sufficient to constitute "payment" within the meaning of Uniform Commercial Code § 2-201(3)(c),[33] but the delivery of a check by the buyer to the seller constitutes a "payment",[34] and the fact that the buyer stops payment on a check for the purchase price, or part of the purchase price, of an oral contract for the sale of goods has no effect on the application of the proposition that the delivery of a check by the buyer to the seller constitutes a "payment" within the meaning of Uniform Commercial Code § 2-201(3)(c).[35]

It has been held that the endorsement by the seller of a check given by the buyer under an oral contract for the sale of goods is necessary in order for the retention of the check by the seller to constitute an acceptance of payment within the meaning of the statute herein discussed,[36] but other cases have held to the contrary.[37]

§ 194. Specially manufactured goods.

A contract which does not satisfy the requirements of the Uniform Commercial Code statute of frauds,[38] but which is valid in other respects, is enforceable if the goods are to be specially manufactured for the buyer and are not

---

000, under which buyer gave seller check for $1,000 as earnest money, was unenforceable under UCC § 2-201(1), except to extent that buyer's check for $1,000 earnest money could constitute partial payment for cattle within meaning of UCC § 2-201(3)(c). Anthony v Tidwell **(Tenn)** 560 SW2d 908, 23 UCCRS 561.

29. Paloukos v Intermountain Chevrolet Co., 99 **Idaho** 740, 588 P2d 939, 25 UCCRS 655; Sedmak v Charlie's Chevrolet, Inc. **(Mo** App) 622 SW2d 694, 31 UCCRS 851, 26 ALR4th 284; Gulden v Sloan **(ND)** 311 NW2d 568.

30. Lockwood v Smigel (2d Dist) 18 **Cal** App 3d 800, 96 Cal Rptr 289, 9 UCCRS 452 (stating that the statutory policy which under the old law permitted the enforcement of oral contracts upon proof of part payment was equally sound under the Uniform Commercial Code, as applied to the sale of an indivisible unit); Morrison v Droll, 41 **Colo** App 354, 588 P2d 383; Thomaier v Hoffman Chevrolet, Inc. (2d Dept) 64 App Div 2d 492, 410 NYS2d 645, 25 UCCRS 44; Starr v Freeport Dodge, Inc., 54 Misc 2d 271, 282 NYS2d 58, 4 UCCRS 644.

31. Cohn v Fisher, 118 **NJ** Super 286, 287 A2d 222, 10 UCCRS 372.

32. Part payment of $100 on two vats orally sold for a total of $1,600 does not take the transaction out of the statute of frauds. Williamson v Martz, 11 **Pa** D & C2d 33.

33. Presti v Wilson (ED NY) 348 **F** Supp 543, 11 UCCRS 716.

34. Kaufman v Solomon (CA3 Pa) 524 F2d 501, 17 UCCRS 1159 (applying Pennsylvania statute); Mann v Commissioner (CA8) 483 F2d 673, 73-2 USTC ¶ 9618, 13 UCCRS 630 (applying Iowa statute); Shipman v Craig Ayers Chevrolet, Inc. **(Okla** App) 541 P2d 876, 17 UCCRS 1169.

35. Presti v Wilson (ED NY) 348 **F** Supp 543, 11 UCCRS 716 (applying New York statute); Cohn v Fisher, 118 **NJ** Super 286, 287 A2d 222, 10 UCCRS 372.

36. Presti v Wilson (ED NY) 348 **F** Supp 543, 11 UCCRS 716 (applying New York statute).

37. Kaufman v Solomon (CA3 Pa) 524 F2d 501, 17 UCCRS 1159 (applying Pennsylvania statute).

Annotation: 97 ALR3d 908, 933 § 14[c].

38. Uniform Commercial Code § 2-201(1).

§ 141   *FRAUDS, STATUTE OF*   37 C.J.S

This conflict has been largely settled by the fairly widespread adoption of the Uniform Sales Act, under the provisions of which the contract must be in writing although the goods may be intended to be delivered at some future time or may not at the time of the contract or sale be actually made, procured, or provided, or fit or ready for delivery, or some act may be requisite for the making or completing thereof, or rendering the same fit for delivery; but if the goods are to be manufactured by the seller especially for the buyer and are not suitable for sale to others in the ordinary course of the seller's business a parol agreement may be enforced.[34] Under the act, for a parol contract for the sale of future goods to be enforceable, it must be shown both that the goods are to be manufactured by the seller especially for the buyer and that they are not suitable for sale to others in the ordinary course of the seller's business.[35] Moreover, if the goods are not to be manufactured by the seller, but are to be procured by him from another, the agreement must be in writing to be enforceable.[36]

In jurisdictions where the Uniform Sales Act has not been adopted and in other jurisdictions prior to its adoption, the authorities have largely followed one of three rules, known respectively as the English, the New York, and the Massachusetts rules.[37]

The Massachusetts rule, which the Uniform Sales Act adopted,[38] is that a contract for the sale of articles then existing, or such as the seller in the ordinary course of his business manufactures or procures for the general market, whether on hand at the time or not, is a contract for the sale of goods, to which the statute of frauds applies, but that, on the other hand, if the goods are to be manufactured especially for the buyer, and on his special order, and are not suitable for the general market, the case is not within the statute.[39]

---

34. Md.—Poole Engineering & Machine Co. v. Swindell, 157 A. 763, 161 Md. 571.
Mich.—Shirek v. Roesink, 235 N.W. 818, 254 Mich. 105.
N.J.—Bauer v. Victory Catering Co., 128 A. 262, 101 N.J.Law 364.
N.Y.—Berman Stores Co. v. Hirsh, 148 N.E. 212, 240 N.Y. 209, reversing 203 N.Y.S. 815, 208 App.Div. 622.
27 C.J. p 236 note 22 [b] (3), (4).

Enforceable by either party
N.Y.—Indiana Limestone Co. of New York v. Harry Bernstein Cut Stone Co., 32 N.Y.S.2d 956, 263 App.Div. 312.

35. N.Y.—Berman Stores Co. v. Hirsh, 148 N.E. 212, 240 N.Y. 209.

Goods held specially manufactured and not suitable for sale to others
(1) Cider tank.—M. K. Smith Corporation v. Ellis, 153 N.E. 548, 257 Mass. 269.

(2) Contract to cut, shape, sew, and make carpet for designated rooms.—Brooks v. Stone, 152 N.E. 59, 256 Mass. 167.

(3) Diamond bracelet.—Gura v. Herman, 238 N.Y.S. 230, 227 App.Div. 452, affirmed 171 N.E. 808, 253 N.Y. 618.

(4) Furniture ordered in particular styles.—Morris Furniture Co. v. Braverman, 230 N.W. 356, 210 Iowa 946.

(5) Limestone to be quarried and cut to special sizes.—Indiana Limestone Co. of New York v. Harry Bernstein Cut Stone Co., 32 N.Y.S.2d 956. 263 App.Div. 312.

(6) Motor truck parts.—Carrollton Acceptance Co. v. Ruggles Motor Truck Co., 234 N.W. 134, 253 Mich. 1.

(7) Novelty clothing.—Shirek v. Roesink, 235 N.W. 818, 254 Mich. 105.

(8) Shoes stamped with buyer's name.—Roth Shoe Co. v. Zager & Blessing, 193 N.W. 546, 195 Iowa 1238.

Goods held saleable in usual course of business
N.J.—Bauer v. Victory Catering Co., 128 A. 262, 101 N.J.Law 364.

Goods of less value to others
Although statute requiring written contracts of sale of goods provides that it shall not apply to goods "specially manufactured" by the seller for the buyer, and not suitable for sale to others in the ordinary course of the seller's business, it applies to a sale of machinery of a standard type manufactured by the seller of less value to others than the buyer, and the contract must be in writing.—Saco-Lowell Shops v. Clinton Mills Co., C.C.A.Mass., 277 F. 349.

Minor changes required to make goods saleable to others
(1) Goods may be suitable for sale to others although minor changes at small expense may be necessary to suit the customer.—Clinton Mills Co. v. Saco-Lowell Shops, C.C.A.Mass., 3 F.2d 410.

(2) Where goods were of type manufactured in ordinary course and had market value, fact that suits were specially manufactured for buyer and that sellers agreed to place buyer's labels and lot numbers on goods was insufficient to take contract out of statute.—Berman Stores Co. v. Hirsh, 148 N.E. 212, 240 N.Y. 209, reversing 203 N.Y.S. 815, 208 App.Div. 622.

(3) A transaction whereby plaintiff received an order for ladies' coats, which plaintiff made up for the trade in general, using certain style numbers, which a number of salesmen were exhibiting by samples throughout the country, was an agreement of sale, and within the statute of frauds, although defendant ordered a button to be put on the label of one of the styles chosen, and the sizes ordered were all large sizes.—Brody & Funt Co. v. Schondorf, 187 N.Y.S. 672, affirmed 193 N.Y.S. 927, 201 App.Div. 880.

36. Mass.—Pope v. Brooks, 144 N.E. 214, 249 Mass. 381—Atlas Shoe Co. v. Rosenthal, 136 N.E. 107, 242 Mass. 15.
N.Y.—Brook Iron Works v. Cohen, 246 N.Y.S. 329, 138 Misc. 416.

37. Okl.—Kansas Flour Mills Corporation v. Dreyfus Bros., 40 P.2d 20, 170 Okl. 325—Linstroth Wagon Co. v. Rives, 226 P. 1057, 100 Okl. 18.
27 C.J. p 234 note 5.

38. Md.—Poole Engineering & Machine Co. v. Swindell, 157 A. 763, 161 Md. 571.
Mass.—Atlas Shoe Co. v. Rosenthal, 136 N.E. 107, 242 Mass. 15.

39. Cal.—Flynn v. Dougherty, 2 P. 1080, 91 Cal. 669, 14 L.R.A. 230— Golden Eagle Milling Co. v. Old Homestead Bakery, 211 P. 56, 59 Cal.App. 541.
Ga.—Lingo v. Phœnix Hermetic Co., 121 S.E. 253, 31 Ga.App. 547— Schreiber v. Wolf, 113 S.E. 53, 28 Ga.App. 817.
Okl.—Kansas Flour Mills Corporation v. Dreyfus Bros., 40 P.2d 20, 170 Okl. 325—Linstroth Wagon Co. v. Rives, 226 P. 1057, 100 Okl. 18.
27 C.J. p 235 notes 16, 18.

Manufacture by third person
Where there is an understanding

628

§13.1.1   Legal Encyclopedias

Like other encyclopedias, legal encyclopedias are sources of information. They provide the researcher with a summary of the law on a wide range of topics. There are two major legal encyclopedias: *Corpus Juris Secundum* (C.J.S.), which is published by West, and *American Jurisprudence* (now Am. Jur. 2d), which is published by Lawyers Co-operative. See Exhibits 13.1 and 13.2.

The two sets are very similar. Both have subject indices, both are organized topically by subject, both have textual material supported by footnotes, and both are kept current through annual pocket parts. The major difference is in the cross-references. While C.J.S. provides cross-references to other West publications (West digests, West practice books), Am. Jur. 2d provides cross-references to other Lawyers Co-operative publications (*American Law Reports, Am. Jur. Proof of Facts,* and *Am. Jur. Legal Forms*).

Note

The topic and section numbers in C.J.S. are not part of West's Key Number System. The key numbers are set out in the "Library References" section that follows some sections.

———————

As Exhibits 13.1 and 13.2 illustrate, legal encyclopedias do not provide the researcher with a state-by-state or circuit-by-circuit summary of the law. Instead, they set out general rules. Because of this general approach, you should not use an encyclopedia as the source, or authority, for a particular rule of law. Although the rules set out in the encyclopedia may be the rules followed in most jurisdictions, they may not be the law in yours. Use a legal encyclopedia only as a source of information and not as a source of law.

§13.1.2   Hornbooks

Like legal encyclopedias, hornbooks are a source of information. In one volume, they provide the researcher with an overview of a particular area of law.

Because the primary market for hornbooks is law students, there are hornbooks for most of the subjects taught in law school, for example, basic property, tort, and contract law and the uniform commercial and tax codes.

Most of these books are written by well-known experts in the area and most use the same format: textual material at the top of the page and footnotes citing to representative cases at the bottom. See Exhibit 13.3. Information can be found using either the table of contents at the beginning of the volume or the subject index at the back.

EXHIBIT 13.3 Sample Page from *Uniform Commercial Code* (White & Summers), a Hornbook*

the writing be "sufficient to indicate" a contract. Admittedly this latter language is not identical with the former, but it is submitted that our earlier analysis of the meaning of the "sufficient to indicate" language [9] applies to the "in confirmation" language of 2–201(2). An early case under 2–201(2) sets a rational standard. In Harry Rubin & Sons, Inc. v. Consolidated Pipe Co. of America,[10] the buyer sent a letter to the seller that referred to the buyer's earlier oral "order" as a closed deal rather than merely as a pending offer. The court rejected seller's argument that because the buyer used the word "order" in his letter rather than "agreement" or "contract," the letter was not a writing "in confirmation of a contract sufficient to satisfy 2–201(2)." [11] The court perceived that the true test was whether "the writing offered a basis for believing that the offered oral evidence rested on a real transaction" and observed that the buyer "must still sustain the burden of persuading the trier of fact that the contracts were in fact made prior to the written confirmation." [12]

Section 2–201(3) provides:

A contract which does not satisfy the requirement of subsection (1) but which is valid in other respects is enforceable

(a) if the goods are to be specially manufactured for the buyer and are not suitable for sale to others in the ordinary course of the seller's business and the seller, before notice of repudiation is received and under circumstances which reasonably indicate that the goods are for the buyer, has made either a substantial beginning of their manufacture or commitments for their procurement; or

(b) if the party against whom enforcement is sought admits in his pleading, testimony or otherwise in court that a contract for sale was made, but the contract is not enforceable under this provision beyond the quantity of goods admitted; or

(c) with respect to goods for which payment has been made and accepted or which have been received and accepted (Sec. 2–606).

price and goods description constituted "writing in confirmation").

9. See text accompanying notes 18–22 supra section 2–4.

10. 396 Pa. 506, 153 A.2d 472, 1 UCC 40 (1959). But see, Trilco Terminal v. Prebilt Corp., 167 N.J.Super. 449, 400 A.2d 1237, 26 UCC 616 (1979), aff'd, 174 N.J.Super. 24, 415 A.2d 356 (1980) ("a more stringent writing requirement under subsection (2) can be justified by the statutory language and the fact that its effect is to bind a merchant to a writing he did not sign," but "whether more is required of a writing under subsection (2) than subsection (1) is not yet clear").

11. Id. at 511, 153 A.2d at 475, 1 UCC at 43.

12. Id. at 512, 153 A.2d at 476, 1 UCC at 44. See also, Perdue Farms, Inc. v. Motts, Inc. of Mississippi, 459 F.Supp. 7, 25 UCC 9 (N.D.Miss.1978), aff'd, 459 F.Supp. 7, 25 UCC 33 (N.D.Miss.1978); Spinnerin Yarn Co., Inc. v. Apparel Retail Corp., 614 F.Supp. 1174, 42 UCC 65 (S.D.N.Y.1985); Triangle Marketing, Inc. v. Action Industries, Inc., 630 F.Supp. 1578, 1 UCC2d 36 (N.D.Ill.1986) ("absent prior agreement purchase orders are not in confirmation of anything and Triangle cannot claim the benefit of 2–201(2)'s exception to the statute of frauds").

*Reprinted from James J. White and Robert S. Summers, *Uniform Commercial Code*, 3d ed. (Hornbook Series Student Ed.), © 1988, with permission of West Publishing Company.

Although hornbooks are not usually cited as authority, they are a better source than a legal encyclopedia. An up-to-date hornbook can be cited as authority when describing the history of particular rule or doctrine, for the policies underlying a common law rule, or for the general rule in other jurisdictions.

§13.1.3   Practice Books

Practice books are books that are written for practitioners. Although they take many different forms, the types that are most useful for background reading are deskbooks and practice manuals.

Unlike legal encyclopedias and hornbooks, most practice books are jurisdiction-specific. They are usually written by local practitioners and explain what the law is in that practitioner's state. For example, many state bar associations publish deskbooks summarizing their state's criminal, property, commercial, and family law. In addition, in many states, West publishes a set of practice books that summarize both the state's substantive law and its criminal and civil procedural rules. See Exhibit 13.4.

As a general rule, practice books should not be cited as authority. Use them to obtain an overview of the law and to locate sources of primary authority.

Section Summary	*Background Reading*

Type: Finding tool and persuasive authority

Sources: *Legal Encyclopedias:* The two major legal encyclopedias are C.J.S. and Am. Jur. 2d. Both provide the researcher with a summary of the law on a wide range of topics. Neither is jurisdiction-specific.

Hornbooks: Hornbooks are written primarily for law students and are available for most subjects taught in law school. Like legal encyclopedias, they provide the researcher with a summary of the law. Also like encyclopedias, they are not jurisdiction-specific.

Practice Books: Practice books are written for practitioners, providing the practitioner with an overview of the law on a particular topic. Unlike encyclopedias and hornbooks, most practice books are jurisdiction-specific.

or act inconsistent with the claim afterwards asserted; (2) action by the other party on the faith of such admission, statement, or act; and (3) injury to such other party resulting from permitting the first party to contradict or repudiate such admission, statement, or act.[22]

§ 23.7   Statute of Frauds

Even though the Code has made it easier for the courts to find a binding contract for the purchase or sale of goods, Article 2 still requires in certain situations that there be a writing between the parties in order to satisfy the Code's version of the statute of frauds. Generally, in contracts involving the sale of goods where the price is $500 or more, the Code requires a writing sufficient to show a contract for sale signed by the party against whom enforcement is sought. The writing must contain a statement of the quantity of goods.[1] The Supreme Court of Washington has held that if a contract for the purchase or sale of goods is subject to the requirements of the Code's statute of frauds, no substitute for compliance with the statute of frauds, such as promissory estoppel, can be used to render the contract enforceable if the statute of frauds is not otherwise complied with.[2]

Despite these general rules, the Code has a number of exceptions and limitations on the statute of frauds itself. First, if the writing omits or incorrectly states a term agreed upon by the parties to the contract, the writing is not void under the statute of frauds; the only limitation is that the writing is not enforceable beyond the quantity of goods shown on its face.[3]

Second, there is a somewhat different rule for merchants. Between merchants, (1) if a writing and confirmation of the contract is sent within a reasonable time, (2) the writing is sufficient against the sender, (3) the writing is received, and (4) the party receiving it has reason to know its contents, then a writing will be considered by the courts to satisfy the statute of frauds under the Code, unless the party receiving the writing gives written notice of objection to its contents within 10 days after receipt.[4]

Third, when the seller is specially manufacturing goods for the buyer, and these goods are not suitable for sale to others in the ordinary course of the seller's business, then the seller may enforce the contract against the buyer if the seller has made a substantial beginning of manufacture or commitments for production of specially manu-

---

22. Wilson v. Westinghouse Elec. Corp., 85 Wn.2d 78, 530 P.2d 298 (1975); Farm Crop Energy, Inc. v. Old Nat. Bank of Wash., 38 Wn. App. 50, 685 P.2d 1097 (1984), *new trial granted* 109 Wn.2d 923, 750 P.2d 231 (1988).

§ 23.7

1. RCWA 62A.2-201(1).

2. Lige Dickson Co. v. Union Oil Co. of Cal., 96 Wn.2d 291, 635 P.2d 103 (1981). The court, however, did not consider whether fraud, deceit, or equitable estoppel might be available to overcome the statute of frauds.

3. RCWA 62A.2-201(1).

4. RCWA 62A.2-201(2).

*Reprinted from Barbara Barker and Irene Scharf, 1 *Washington Practice — Methods of Practice*, 3d ed., © 1989, with permission of West Publishing Company.

§13.2   SOURCES THAT CAN BE USED AS FINDING TOOLS

Legal encyclopedias, hornbooks, and practice books can, however, be used for more than background reading. They are also finding tools. Legal encyclopedias and hornbooks cite to landmark or representative cases from a variety of jurisdictions, practice books to the key cases within the jurisdiction.

In addition, there are several other secondary sources that can be used as finding tools.

§13.2.1   *American Law Reports*

American Law Reports (A.L.R.) was first published in 1919 to compete against West's National Reporter System. Instead of publishing every state and federal appellate opinion, A.L.R. is selective, publishing only "significant" cases.

Today, most researchers do not use A.L.R. as a source for the text of an opinion. Instead, they use it for the annotations that follow the opinions. These annotations, which are researched and written by attorneys employed by Lawyers Co-operative, explain and discuss the issue raised in the selected case and provide summaries and lists of cases from other jurisdictions dealing with the same issue. See Exhibit 13.5.

Like other reporters, A.L.R. is organized chronologically. The oldest cases and annotations are printed in A.L.R. and the most recent in A.L.R.5th or A.L.R. Fed.

A.L.R.	1919-1948
A.L.R.2d	1948-1965
A.L.R.3d	1965-1980
A.L.R.4th	1980-1991
A.L.R.5th	1992-current
A.L.R. Fed.	1969-current

Annotations can be located in a number of different ways. The easiest is through the subject indices that accompany the various sets. Recent annotations can be found using the Index to Annotations, which includes references to annotations published in A.L.R.2d, A.L.R.3d, A.L.R.4th, A.L.R.5th, and A.L.R. Fed. Older annotations can be found using the Quick Index for the individual set.

Annotations can also be found using one of the tables contained in the index volume. Annotations discussing a particular section of the United States Code or the Code of Federal Regulations or a particular court rule, uniform act, or restatement section can be located using the Table of Laws, Rules, and Regulations; in the older sets, annotations discussing a particular case can be found using the Table of Cases.

EXHIBIT 13.5	Sample Pages from *American Law Reports* (Lawyers Co-operative) (continues on next page)*

ANNOTATION

SALES: "SPECIALLY MANUFACTURED GOODS" STATUTE OF FRAUDS EXCEPTION IN UCC § 2-201(3)(a)

by

Thomas R. Malia, J.D.

TOTAL CLIENT-SERVICE LIBRARY® REFERENCES

67 Am Jur 2d, Sales § 194; 72 Am Jur 2d, Statute of Frauds § 142

Annotations: See the related matters listed in the annotation, infra.

23 Am Jur Pl & Pr Forms (Rev), Statute of Frauds, Forms 1, 4

4 Am Jur Proof of Facts 2d 641, Detrimental Reliance on Promise; 5 Am Jur Proof of Facts 2d 727, Promise Made With Intent Not to Perform; 6 Am Jur Proof of Facts 2d 215, Breach in Regard to Accepted Goods

3 Am Jur Trials 637, Selecting the Remedy; 3 Am Jur Trials 681, Tactics and Strategy of Pleading

US L Ed Digest, Contracts §§ 39, 40; Statute of Frauds § 16

ALR Digests, Contracts § 100

L Ed Index to Annos, Contracts; Sales; Uniform Commercial Code

ALR Quick Index, Contracts; Statute of Frauds; Merchandise or Goods; Sales; Uniform Commercial Code

Federal Quick Index, Agreements; Contracts; Sales; Statute of Frauds; Uniform Commercial Code

Auto-Cite®: Any case citation herein can be checked for form, parallel references, later history, and annotation references through the Auto-Cite computer research system.

Finally, annotations can be found using LEXIS. Because the full text of each annotation is online, use standard search procedures to find annotations. (See Chapter 15.)

Through the years, different methods have been used to keep the annotations up to date. In some instances, older annotations have been superseded by newer annotations in later volumes. (To determine whether an annotation has been superseded, use the Annotation History Table, which is located in the Index to Annotations.) In other instances, the annotations have been supplemented.

EXHIBIT 13.5   *(continued)*

EXHIBIT 13.5   *(continued)*

45 ALR4th   UCC—Statute of Frauds   § 1[a]
45 ALR4th 1126

TABLE OF JURISDICTIONS REPRESENTED

Consult POCKET PART in this volume for later cases

US: §§ 3, 4, 7[a, b], 8, 9, 12, 14, 15
Cal: §§ 3, 6, 11
Colo: §§ 3, 5, 7[a, b], 8, 11
Fla: §§ 3, 7[a, b], 9
Ga: §§ 8, 15
Ind: §§ 2[b], 10, 14
Md: § 2[b]
Mass: § 12

Mich: § 13
Minn: § 14
NY: § 10
Ohio: §§ 10, 14
Pa: §§ 4, 12
Tex: § 15
Wash: § 14

I. Preliminary matters

§ 1. Introduction

[a] Scope

This annotation[1] collects and an-alyzes the state and federal cases in which the courts have construed or applied the "specially manufac-tured goods" statute of frauds ex-ception contained in § 2-201(3)(a) of the Uniform Commercial Code[2]

1. The present annotation super-sedes § 59[b] of the annotation at 17 ALR3d 1010.

2. UCC § 2-201 provides in full:
Formal Requirements; Statute of Frauds

"(1) Except as otherwise provided in this section a contract for the sale of goods for the price of $500 or more is not enforceable by way of action or defense unless there is some writing sufficient to indicate that a contract for sale has been made between the par-ties and signed by the party against whom enforcement is sought or by his authorized agent or broker. A writing is not insufficient because it omits or incorrectly states a term agreed upon but the contract is not enforceable under this paragraph beyond the quan-tity of goods shown in such writing.

"(2) Between merchants if within a reasonable time a writing in confirma-tion of the contract and sufficient against the sender is received and the party receiving it has reason to know its contents, it satisfies the require-ments of subsection (1) against such party unless written notice of objection to its contents is given within ten days after it is received.

"(3) A contract which does not sat-isfy the requirements of subsection (1) but which is valid in other respects is enforceable

(a) if the goods are to be specially manufactured for the buyer and are not suitable for sale to others in the ordinary course of the seller's business and the seller, before notice of repudi-ation is received and under circum-stances which reasonably indicate that the goods are for the buyer, has made either a substantial beginning of their manufacture or commitments for their procurement; or

(b) if the party against whom en-forcement is sought admits in his pleading, testimony or otherwise in court that a contract for sale was made, but the contract is not enforceable

A.L.R.	Supplemented through use of *A.L.R. Blue Book of Supplemental Decisions.* (Note: These supplements are not cumulative.)
A.L.R.2d	Supplemented using A.L.R.2d Later Case Service. A.L.R.2d Later Case Service is kept current through the use of cumulative pocket parts.
A.L.R.3d, A.L.R.4th, A.L.R.5th, A.L.R. Fed., L. Ed., and L. Ed. 2d	Updated through the use of pocket parts at the back of each volume. Lawyers Co-operative also maintains a toll-free number (listed on the front of the pocket part) for cases decided since the pocket part was published.
Quick Index for A.L.R.3d, A.L.R.4th, A.L.R.5th, and A.L.R. Fed.	The index is kept current through the use of pocket parts at the end of each index volume.

Although A.L.R.'s primary use is as a finding tool, the annotations are sometimes cited as persuasive authority. For example, an author may cite an annotation as authority for what the majority and minority rules are or to support a statement about current trends. You should not, however, cite A.L.R. as the source of a rule. Instead, cite the primary authority, that is, the statutes, regulations, and cases discussed in the annotation.

Note

Although the A.L.R. annotations are usually well researched and well written, do not cite a source discussed in the annotation without reading the source itself. Never cite a statute, regulation, or case that you have not read in its primary form.

---

§13.2.2   Looseleaf Services

Looseleaf services can be used both as a finding tool and as a source of primary authority. They provide a researcher with up-to-date information on a particular area of law.

There are almost as many looseleaf services as there are areas of law. There are looseleaf services for most areas of administrative law (see, for example, BNA's *Environment Reporter*) and for many specialized areas of practice (see CCH's *Standard Federal Tax Reporter* and Lawyers Co-operative's *Social Security Law and Practice*). See Exhibit 13.6. In addition, some looseleaf services have as their primary purpose providing up-to-date information about court decisions (see, for example, *United States Law Week*). To determine whether there is a looseleaf

18,007

INCOME ● GROSS INCOME

[¶ 5502] GROSS INCOME DEFINED

Sec. 61 [1986 Code]. (a) GENERAL DEFINITION.—Except as otherwise provided in this subtitle, gross income means all income from whatever source derived, including (but not limited to) the following items:

(1) Compensation for services, including fees, commissions, fringe benefits, and similar items;

(2) Gross income derived from business;

(3) Gains derived from dealings in property;

(4) Interest;

(5) Rents;

(6) Royalties;

(7) Dividends;

(8) Alimony and separate maintenance payments;

(9) Annuities;

(10) Income from life insurance and endowment contracts;

(11) Pensions;

(12) Income from discharge of indebtedness;

(13) Distributive share of partnership gross income;

(14) Income in respect of a decedent; and

(15) Income from an interest in an estate or trust.

(b) CROSS REFERENCES.—

For items specifically included in gross income, see part II (sec. 71 and following). For items specifically excluded from gross income, see part III (sec. 101 and following).

.01 Amended by P.L. 98-369.

.10 Committee Reports on P.L. 98-369 are at 1984-3 CB 420.

.20 Committee Reports on 1954 Code Sec. 61 as originally enacted were reproduced at 571 CCH ¶ 601.20.

● *Regulations*

[¶ 5503] § 1.61-1. **Gross income.**—(a) *General definition.* Gross income means all income from whatever source derived, unless excluded by law. Gross income includes income realized in any form, whether in money, property, or services. Income may be realized, therefore, in the form of services, meals, accommodations, stock, or other property, as well as in cash. Section 61 lists the more common items of gross income for purposes of illustration. For purposes of further illustration, § 1.61-14 mentions several miscellaneous items of gross income not listed specifically in section 61. Gross income, however, is not limited to the items so enumerated.

(b) *Cross references.* Cross references to other provisions of the Code are to be found throughout the regulations under section 61. The purpose of these cross references is to direct attention to the more common items which are included in or excluded from gross income entirely, or treated in some special manner. To the extent that another section of the Code or of the regulations thereunder, provides specific treatment for any item of income, such other provision shall apply notwithstanding section 61 and the regulations thereunder. The cross references do not cover all possible items.

(1) For examples of items specifically included in gross income, see part II (section 71 and following), subchapter B, chapter 1 of the Code.

(2) For examples of items specifically excluded from gross income, see part III (section 101 and following), subchapter B, chapter 1 of the Code.

431

service covering the topic that you are researching, check *Legal Loose-leafs in Print* or your library's card catalog, or ask a person who practices in that area.

Although each service is unique, they share some common characteristics. First, most are difficult to use, at least initially. Many have multiple parts and the index or indices may be difficult to use. Consequently, before attempting to use a particular service, either read the "How to Use This Service" section that is at the beginning of most services or ask an experienced researcher or librarian to walk you through the service, explaining how the material is organized and indexed.

Second, most looseleaf services are published in notebook form, the subscriber being sent additional or replacement pages regularly. Although this format causes some of the indexing problems noted above, it allows the publisher to keep the set up to date.

Finally, most looseleaf services contain several types of information; any given service may have within it the text of court and administrative decisions, current and proposed statutes, regulations and rules, information about court judgments or the settlement of particular cases, and commentary.

Section Summary	*Finding Tools*

Type: Finding tools and, in some instances, persuasive authority

Sources: *American Law Reports (A.L.R.): American Law Reports* is an annotated reporter. The annotations explain and discuss the issue raised in the selected case and provide summaries and lists of cases from other jurisdictions dealing with the same issue.

         Looseleaf Services: Looseleaf services are commercial publications that index and collect primary and secondary authority for a specialized area of practice and that provide researchers with up-to-date information.

§13.3   Sources That Can Be Cited as Persuasive Authority

Some of the most frequently cited secondary sources are treatises and other books, law reviews, and the comments accompanying uniform acts and the restatements.

§13.3.1   Treatises and Other Books

Most treatises are multivolume works on a single topic. Written by recognized experts in the area, treatises provide the researcher with an in-depth explanation of even narrow issues, citations to supporting cases and statutes, and, at least in some treatises, the author's comments or other commentary. Books are what the name implies. They are single volumes written by scholars, practitioners, or nonlawyers.

Treatises and books can be located through the library's card catalog using the author, title, or subject index. (To determine which sources are considered best, ask the law librarian or consult with someone who is familiar with the area of law.) To find the relevant sections within a treatise or book, use the index.

Although treatises and books are not primary authority, they can be used as persuasive authority. The weight that will be given to a particular treatise or book depends on its author. The more respected the author, the more persuasive the source.

§13.3.2   Law Reviews and Other Legal Periodicals

Like treatises and books, law reviews are a source of in-depth information, citations to supporting authority, and commentary. The difference is in their scope. While treatises and books cover broad topics (the Federal Rules of Evidence), law reviews focus on much narrower issues (the application of a particular rule in a particular circumstance).

Most law reviews are published by law schools. Some of these journals are general in nature, publishing articles on a wide range of topics. Others deal with a specific subject area, for example, international or environmental law.

In most law reviews, there are four types of "articles": (1) lead articles, which are written by professors, judges, or practitioners; (2) comments, which are written by students and which focus on a particular legal topic; (3) notes, which are written by students about a particular case or statute; and (4) book reviews, which are usually written by professors, judges, or practitioners. The students who are on law reviews decide which articles are published.

Like treatises, law review articles have two parts: text and footnotes. In the text, the author usually defines the issue or problem, summarizes and comments on the existing law, and proposes a solution to the issue or problem. The footnotes provide supporting documentation and, for the researcher, additional research sources.

Law review articles can be located using a number of different indices.

> *Index to Legal Periodicals (I.L.P.).* Prior to 1980, the *Index to Legal Periodicals* was the only index. In book form, it provides access to most law review articles through author, title, subject, case name, and statute indices. The *Index to Legal Periodicals* is now available on CD-ROM disks.
>
> *Current Law Index (C.L.I.).* In 1980, Information Access Company began publishing the *Current Law Index.* Like the *Index to Legal Periodicals,* this index is available in both book and CD-

ROM form. Unlike the *Index to Legal Periodicals,* which uses its own index system, the *Current Law Index* uses the Library of Congress subject headings. As a consequence, its headings are usually more specific, making it easier to locate relevant articles. (Note: C.L.I. indexes only articles published after 1980.)

LEXIS and Westlaw. LEXIS and Westlaw now have the full text of a number of law reviews online. This allows a researcher to locate information contained in the text or footnotes that might not be identifiable through the other indices.

Current Index to Legal Periodicals (C.I.L.P.). This index, which is published by the University of Washington Law Library, is a weekly publication listing just-published law review articles. C.I.L.P. is available both in paper and via computer-assisted research.

Index to Foreign Legal Periodicals. This index can be used to locate articles relating to foreign, comparative, or international law published in the major legal periodicals of foreign countries. Some of the articles have English translations; many do not.

Index to Periodical Articles Related to Law. This publication lists articles relating to law or having an impact on the law that are published in nonlaw publications.

In addition to law reviews, there are a number of other legal periodicals published by national, state, and local bar associations, special interest groups, and commercial publishers. These publications usually contain information of a more practical nature and may include articles on law office management, courtroom tips, or the handling of particular types of cases. Two of the most popular legal periodicals are the *American Bar Association Journal,* which is published by the American Bar Association, and *Trial,* which is published by the Association of Trial Lawyers of America.

§13.3.3 Uniform Laws and Model Acts

Another frequently cited secondary source is the official comments accompanying uniform laws. If a state has enacted the uniform law, these comments can be used as evidence of "legislative intent."

Uniform laws are drafted by the Commission on Uniform Laws, which was established in 1912 to "promote uniformity in the law among the several states on subjects where uniformity is desirable and practicable."

Once a year, commissioners from each of the fifty states and the District of Columbia meet to consider drafts of proposed uniform laws. If the commissioners approve a draft, they then take the draft to their own state legislatures, urging their legislatures to enact it. As of this date, the commissioners have approved more than 200 uniform laws.

Note

A proposed uniform law does not become law until it has been enacted by the legislature.
_____

If your state has adopted a uniform act, the commissioners' comments can usually be found in your state's annotated code following the text of the statute. (See page 385.) They can also be found in *Uniform Laws Annotated* (U.L.A.), a multivolume set that contains the text of the uniform laws, the commissioners' official comments, a list of the states that have enacted the uniform law in whole or in part, and annotations, or notes of decisions, for cases and law review articles interpreting or applying the uniform law. The set also contains, in pamphlet form, a Directory of Uniform Acts and a Table of Adopting Jurisdictions.

Model acts are similar to uniform laws: They propose legislation. Some model acts are put forward by the Commission on Uniform Laws, others by sections of the American Bar Association or by special interest groups.

Most model acts adopted by the Uniform Commission on State Laws are published in *Uniform Laws Annotated;* other model acts are separately published. To find a copy, use your library's card catalog.

§13.3.4   Restatements

While uniform laws are prospective, restatements are retrospective. Drafted by the American Law Institute, a consortium of legal scholars, the restatements describe existing common law on a wide range of topics.

Because the drafters of the restatements are so well respected, the restatements and the reporter's notes and illustrations that accompany them are given more weight than a typical treatise. A restatement is usually the most persuasive of persuasive authority.

Each of the restatements is published separately. The main volumes of the restatements contain the restatement sections themselves and the reporter's comments. Annotated volumes contain citations to cases, cross-references to West's Key Number System and *American Law Reports* (A.L.R.), and an index. To find a particular restatement, use your library's card catalog.

Note

Restatement sections can be shepardized using *Shepard's Restatement of the Law Citations.*
_____

Section Summary	*Secondary Sources That Can Be Cited as Persuasive Authority*

Type: Persuasive authority

Sources: *Treatises:* Treatises are in-depth summaries or commentary on specific areas of law written by recognized experts.

         Law Review Articles: Law review articles contain in-depth information or commentary on narrow areas of law. They are written by judges, law professors, practitioners, or students.

         Uniform Laws and Model Acts: Uniform Laws and Model Acts are legislation drafted by the Commission on Uniform Laws. If enacted by a state legislature, it is mandatory authority in that jurisdiction; if not enacted, it is only persuasive authority.

         Restatements: Restatements are summaries of the existing common law drafted by the American Law Institute.

§13.4   OTHER SECONDARY SOURCES

§13.4.1   Legal Dictionaries

Just as encyclopedias have their legal counterparts, so do dictionaries. As a student you will use legal dictionaries to learn the "language of the law"; as a practitioner you will use them to translate the Latin maxims that continue to haunt judicial opinions.

Although there are numerous legal dictionaries, the two major ones are *Black's Law Dictionary,* which is published by West, and *Ballentine's Law Dictionary,* which is published by Lawyers Co-operative. Both include definitions, guides to pronunciation, and, for many of the definitions, citations to authority. Another dictionary worth noting is *Bouvier's Law Dictionary & Concise Encyclopedia.* Although last published near the turn of the century, it is well respected and useful for looking up terms that are no longer widely used.

Dictionaries are frequently cited as persuasive authority.

§13.4.2   Words and Phrases

Another source of definitions is a set called *Words and Phrases,* which is published by West. In addition to including definitions for legal terms, *Words and Phrases* defines words that may be important in a legal dispute. For example, it defines "assemble," "movable," "acquiesce," and even "specially manufactured." Like a legal dictionary, it also includes citations to cases and can, therefore, be used both as persuasive authority and as a finding tool.

West also includes a words and phrases section in its digests. Usually located at the end of the Descriptive Word Index volumes, these sections include pinpoint citations to cases that have judicially defined particular words and phrases.

§13.4.3   Form Books

Form books are books of forms or clauses that can be inserted into forms.

There are a number of form books on the market. Some, such as Bender's *Federal Practice Forms,* include forms for a specific jurisdiction. Others, such as *Fletcher Corporation Forms Annotated* (Callaghan) have forms for a particular area of law. Still others, such as *West's Legal Forms* and *Am. Jur. Legal Forms,* include a wide range of forms that can be adapted to a number of different jurisdictions.

A particular form can be located using the form book's index or using cross-references contained in other publications by the same publisher.

Note

The forms contained in form books should be used only as a guide. The language that you use will be determined by the facts in your case and your jurisdiction's law. _____

Section Summary	*Other Secondary Sources*

Type: Persuasive authority

Sources: *Legal Dictionaries:* The two major law dictionaries are *Black's Law Dictionary* and *Ballentine's Law Dictionary.* Legal dictionaries define legal terms.

Words and Phrases: Words and Phrases defines both legal and nonlegal terms. It also contains citations to cases setting out definitions.

A words and phrases section is included in most West digests. Although definitions themselves are not set out, pinpoint cites to cases setting out the definitions are.

Form Books: Form books contain sample forms. Some sets contain forms for a particular jurisdiction, others for a particular area of law, and still others a wide range of nonjurisdiction-specific forms.

Chapter 14

Shepard's *Citators*

One of the most embarrassing things that can happen to an attorney is to learn, while standing in front of the court, that the case that he or she has relied on has been overruled. The conversation usually goes something like this.

Attorney: We have based our position on *State v. Smith,* a 1991 decision by the Court of Appeals. In that case, the State —

Judge: (interrupting the attorney) Counsel, are you aware that that decision was overruled by the Supreme Court earlier this month?

Attorney: (long pause) No, your Honor. I was not.

To make sure that you don't find yourself in this position, shepardize every statute and every case that you cite in your brief. In addition, shepardize every statute and case cited by your opponent. One of the easiest ways to win a case is to show that the case that the other side has relied on is no longer good law.

Because the shepardizing process is discussed in detail in section 5.5 and section 15.2.11 (pages 101-107 describe the process of shepardizing a statute; pages 121-127 describe the process of shepardizing cases; pages 463-464 describe *Shepard's* online), this chapter sets out only some general information about *Shepard's.*

§14.1   HOW CITATORS WORK

Citators serve two purposes: They tell you whether the original source is still good law, and they provide you with a list of authorities that have cited that source. For example, a case citator (1) tells you whether the case that you are relying on was reversed on appeal or overruled in a later case and (2) provides you with a list of cases, law review articles, and A.L.R. annotations that have cited the case.

439

Citators do this by listing the sources that have cited the original source. This list is then annotated. For example, in a case citator, the abbreviations before the history entries tell you whether the citation is to the same or a connected case, whether certiorari was granted or denied, and whether the higher court affirmed or reversed. The abbreviations before the treatment citations tell you whether the cite is to a case in which the court questioned or explained the decision in the cited case or followed or overruled the cited case's holding. (See the example on page 123.)

§14.2 SHEPARD'S CITATORS

Shepard's publishes a wide variety of citators. There are *Shepard's* citators for state and federal statutes, state and federal cases, and a variety of secondary sources (for example, law reviews, restatements, uniform laws). The following is a partial list of the *Shepard's* citators.

Shepard's Banking Law Citations
Shepard's Bankruptcy Citations
Shepard's Code of Federal Regulations Citations
Shepard's Corporation Law Citations
Shepard's Federal Occupational Safety and Health Citations
Shepard's Federal Rules Citations
Shepard's Federal Tax Citations
Shepard's Hawaii Citations
Shepard's Law Review Citations
Shepard's Military Justice Citations
Shepard's Professional and Judicial Conduct Citations
Shepard's Restatement of the Law Citations
Shepard's Southern Reporter Citations
Shepard's Uniform Commercial Code Citations
Shepard's United States Citations (cases)
Shepard's United States Citations (statutes, court rules)
Shepard's United States Patents and Trademarks Citations
Shepard's Wyoming Citations

§14.3 COVERAGE OF DIFFERENT CITATORS

Not all *Shepard's* citators have the same coverage. Consequently, what you get when you shepardize depends, at least in part, on which citator you use.

§14.3.1 Differences in Coverage of State and Regional Reporters

State cases can be shepardized in either the citator for that state or the appropriate regional citator.

When a state's decisions are published in both an official (state) reporter and regional reporter, the case can be shepardized under either citation. If you shepardize the case in the state citator using the citation to the state reporter, you obtain the following information.

- a parallel citation to the regional reporter
- citations to other decisions from the same state
- citations to federal cases
- citations to law review articles, A.L.R. annotations, annotations in L. Ed. 2d, and selected treatises

If you shepardize the same case in the same citator but under the regional reporter citation, you find the following.

- a parallel citation to the state reporter
- citations to other decisions from the same state
- citations to federal cases

You get still different entries if you shepardize the case in the regional citator using the citation to the regional reporter. You will find the following:

- a parallel citation to the state reporter
- citations to other decisions from the same state
- citations to decisions from other states
- citations to federal cases
- citations to A.L.R., L. Ed. 2d, and selected treatises

Exhibits 14.1 to 14.4 show the information that you would find if you shepardized the same case in both the state and regional citators and online.

§14.3.2 Differences in Coverage for Various Supreme Court Citators and Reporters

United States Supreme Court decisions can also be shepardized under more than one citation. The most comprehensive list of sources can be found under the official (U.S.) citation:

- parallel citations to S. Ct. and L. Ed.
- citations to other federal cases
- citations to state cases
- citations to administrative decisions, articles in the ABA journal, and selected treatises

EXHIBIT 14.1 Sample Page from *Shepard's New Mexico Citations**

NEW MEXICO REPORTS

Vol. 92

d599F2d¹⁶89	102NM¹¹393	—93—	—112—	14NML179	—181—	—217—	—261—
599F2d¹90	102NM407	(582P2d1306)	(583P2d476)	30A₄428n	(585P2d325)	(585P2d1098)	(586P2d1090)
716F2d⁶338	103NM153		95NM³485	30A₄442n	98NM¹546	97NM⁵241	1COA75§ 9
f716F2d¹¹339	4A₃1221s	—94—	f96NM²26		99NM224	102NM289	97A₃174n
f716F2d⁹339		(582P2d1307)	96NM⁵27	—147—	103NM³76	103NM²23	97A₃195n
649FS⁴116	—64—	97NM³234	96NM⁵380	(584P2d194)	23A₃932s	103NM⁵01	
649FS⁸117	(582P2d1277)	97NM⁴234	96NM²577	s92NM180			—264—
649FS¹⁶120	93NM⁴538	101NM⁸281	96NM³577	94NM¹224	Volume number of cited case	d42)
18A₃1376s	96NM⁴574	103NM⁸36	97NM⁵80	98NM486		25
23A₃932s	97NM²373	103NM⁵659	98NM³127	102NM³576			
84A₃1073s	97NM⁴572	10A₄217n	100NM³4		94NM⁴337	9NML367	—266—
22A₄23n	99NM¹²718	13A₄550n	101NM⁸802	—151—	j94NM338		(587P2d44)
	100NM100		102NM177	(584P2d198)	95NM⁹735	—230—	s92NM260
—44—	100NM²747	—98—		98NM¹803	96NM²276	(585P2d1352)	93NM¹213
(582P2d816)	101NM112	(583P2d462)	—116—	99NM¹583	96NM⁴638	s92NM260	93NM²213
s93NM761	102NM²43	99NM¹410	(583P2d480)		98NM⁴538	92NM⁶356	Cir. 9
100NM²72	102NM⁴43	101NM¹761	12NML296	—152—	99NM⁵334	f93NM¹²233	517FS²910
76A₂678s	102NM⁵44	9NML37		(584P2d199)	d99NM⁴335	93NM¹²479	9NML419
	102NM⁴401	1PST425§63	—118—	j96NM739	d99NM⁴345	f95NM¹²639	
—47—	102NM⁶405	16A₄934n	(584P2d165)	98NM²792	13NML287	j96NM490	—269—
(582P2d819)	102NM⁷405		92NM⁴271			96NM796	(587P2d47)
93NM⁷91	102NM⁴742	—100—	92NM⁴478	—155—	—192—	97NM¹¹539	US cert den
93NM⁴361	13NML284	(583P2d464)	96NM⁹15	(584P2d202)	(585P2d336)	97NM¹²540	in441US908
e94NM³166		s92NM109	98NM⁴457	d97NM¹733	96NM¹⁴635	98NM⁴434	s92NM260
e94NM⁴166	—70—	93NM210	j454US926	d97NM²733	96NM¹⁴636	99NM⁴712	92NM²689
d96NM¹¹3	(582P2d1283)	93NM⁷238	j102SC426	j97NM734	98NM⁴60	Cir. 10	e95NM⁶385
j96NM5	101NM¹495	f93NM480		100NM²304	98NM⁹164	614F2d1269	o95NM386
96NM¹68	103NM²333	94NM¹621	—121—	100NM¹550	98NM414		12NML291
96NM⁷385		95NM⁷126	(584P2d168)	103NM¹94	98NM¹²623	—236—	
97NM⁷615	—72—	95NM³727	97NM¹⁴241		98NM²627	(586P2d317)	—272—
f99NM²697	(582P2d1285)	97NM⁷609	98NM¹¹45	—158—	98NM²711	101NM⁵55	(587P2d50)
f99NM³697		100NM³154	98NM⁷326	(584P2d205)	98NM⁹731	103NM¹450	s92NM260
f99NM⁴697	—74—	f100NM¹¹54	99NM⁸716	s92NM180	99NM²433		101NM¹42
99NM¹⁰809	(582P2d1287)	100NM¹196		Cir. 10	99NM¹499	—237—	
101NM²108	92NM²358	102NM748	—127—	732F2d¹114	101NM¹²339	(586P2d318)	—274—
	93NM²232	13NML328	(584P2d174)	63MnL774	101NM¹415	US cert den	(587P2d52)
—52—	f93NM208	14NML93	s92NM180	4COA787§ 3	101NM¹688	in442US930	s92NM260
(582P2d824)	93NM²209	44A₃1078s	93NM¹343	77A₂215s	j101NM688	s92NM260	93NM²292
s90NM552							00NM³51
92NM357							
96NM¹743					Page number of	—275—
97NM¹29					cited case	(587P2d53)
98NM¹281			—89—			3NM⁵295
9NML167			(582P2d1302)	Parallel citation	9NM⁶52
94HLR153			96NM⁴87		102NM¹97
	Analysis note	j98NM668		A₄223n
—54—	("j" means the case is	Cir. 5	Headnote number	
(582P2d82(	cited in the dissenting	659F2d709	(the "4" means the	—278—
93NM³471	opinion)	Cir. 10	citing case; 96 NM 87	587P2d425)
e99NM³30		f693F2d²108	used the cited case for	
101NM²62		81McL1485	the proposition stated	—280—
12NML31⁵	Law review article	35A₈F461s	in headnote 4 of the	587P2d427)
14NML161			cited case)	9NM87
15NML27⁹				
14A₄708n	A.L.R. annotation		Citing cases	—283—
				587P2d430)
—57—				4NM³406
(582P2d12⁷				5NM⁵245
cc90NM12⁴				5NM584
cc90NM254	(582P2d1296)	7NM²167	(584P2d179)	(584P2d1310)	—210—	97NM⁵45	96NM⁸667
92NM¹¹288	f100NM¹71	97NM²180	s92NM180	Cir. 10	(585P2d1091)	97NM²192	j99NM595
93NM¹²488	100NM123	97NM⁴180		614FS981	97NM¹652	98NM²200	f103NM⁸768
94NM¹⁴723	100NM⁵51⁷	101NM¹211	—135—	10NML185	22A₄717n	102NM⁵132	f103NM⁸768
94NM²724		101NM⁴459	(584P2d182)	15NML446			Cir. 10
95NM481	—89—	102NM⁴449	94NM698	68Cor305	—211—	—256—	762F2d⁶864
j95NM483	(582P2d1302)		94NM774	RLPB§ 2.21	(585P2d1092)	(586P2d1085)	12NML149
j96NM5	96NM⁴87	—109—	95NM¹321	86A₃80s	29A₄914n	94NM288	
96NM²325	j98NM668	(583P2d473)	d97NM²725		29A₄946n	96NM¹586	—287—
96NM²768	Cir. 5	m92NM100	99NM¹687	—179—	29A₄976n	96NM605	(587P2d434)
e96NM⁸769	659F2d709	93NM⁴210	101NM⁶607	(585P2d323)		98NM⁵437	92NM765
97NM²226	Cir. 10	15NML238	f102NM¹99		—215—	100NM¹693	92NM¹807
j97NM421	f693F2d²108		f102NM299		(585P2d1096)	f100NM694	93NM¹82
98NM²625	81McL1485		Cir. 10		Cir. 10	102NM151	93NM84
99NM748	35A₈F461s		749F2d⁷613		39BRW¹503	102NM⁴352	93NM¹220
100NM2			17MJ959		100A₃103n		
101NM²158			12NML400		100A₃107n		*Continued*

PACIFIC REPORTER, 2d SERIES (New Mexico Cases)

Vol. 582

—1277—	726P2d⁶357	—480—	—198—	—336—	614F2d1269	e622P2d⁶290	—442—
(92NM64)		(92NM116)	(92NM151)	(92NM192)		o622P2d291	(92NM295)
602P2d⁴1025			653P2d¹179	633P2d¹⁴1233			s586P2d1089
632P2d⁴1212	**Vol. 583**		661P2d¹483	633P2d¹⁴1234	**Vol. 586**	—50—	h603P2d³302
640P2d²479		**Vol. 584**		644P2d⁴1049		(92NM272)	610P2d⁴216
642P2d⁴175	—462—		—199—	646P2d⁹591	—317—	s586P2d1089	e623P2d⁴1000
663P2d¹²377	(92NM98)	—165—	(92NM152)	649P2d⁴482	(92NM236)	677P2d¹1078	j623P2d1002
666P2d779	658P2d¹1137	(92NM118)	j634P2d1291	651P2d¹²1267	678P2d¹230		j625P2d1254
676P2d²824	688P2d¹1265	587P2d⁴49	653P2d²168	651P2d²1271	708P2d¹1051	—52—	633P2d⁴1243
678P2d1187	719P2d⁶821	590P2d⁴177		652P2d²733		(92NM274)	635P2d¹1326
690P2d²1037	728P2d¹464	627P2d³410	—202—	652P2d⁹753	—318—	s586P2d1089	635P2d²1326
690P2d²1037		649P2d⁴760	(92NM155)	659P2d²319	(92NM237)	599P2d²1089	j636P2d326
690P2d⁵1038	—464—	j454US926	d643P2d¹297	660P2d¹589	US cert den	665P2d³313	661P2d⁴505
696P2d⁴489	(92NM100)	j102SC426	d643P2d²297	681P2d¹²1116	in442US930		733P2d¹2
696P2d⁶493	s583P2d473		j643P2d298	683P2d¹970	s586P2d1089	—53—	o733P2d¹3
696P2d⁷493	598P2d1170	—168—	669P2d²1099	687P2d¹1039	cc559P2d398	(92NM275)	
700P2d⁴645	599P2d²391	(92NM121)	673P2d¹834	j687P2d1039	e607P2d²125	599P2d⁵1092	—444—
728P2d480	f601P2d450	638P2d¹⁴1086	703P2d¹191	721P2d¹⁴1311	617P2d¹⁴1315	653P2d⁸883	(92NM297)
	614P2d¹33	644P2d¹¹559			e635P2d¹²323	d691P2d¹890	597P2d⁷1198
—1283—	619P2d⁷571	648P2d⁷784	—205—	—342—	666P2d780		j623P2d1013
(92NM70)	625P2d³1244	653P2d⁷516	(92NM158)	(92NM198)	703P2d¹⁵914	—425—	636P2d²325
684P2d¹1160	642P2d⁷212		s585P2d324			(92NM278)	636P2d³325
706P2d²875	667P2d³461	—174—	Cir. 10	—647—	—717—	—427—	679P2d³276
	f667P2d¹461	(92NM127)	732F2d¹114	(92NM202)	(92NM246)	(92NM280)	704P2d⁶458
—1285—	668P2d¹312	s585P2d324		s586P2d1089	692P2d1318	654P2d540	733P2d²872
(92NM72)	700P2d651	600P2d¹289	—713—	d599P2d⁴1096	730P2d²4		Cir. 9
		601P2d¹72	(92NM162)			—430—	525FS¹⁰1039
—1287—	—468—	607P2d²1170	664P2d⁸1006	—649—	—1079—	(92NM283)	
(92NM74)	(92NM104)	d607P2d⁴1171	673P2d1342	(92NM204)	(92NM250)	611P2d³1100	—451—
588P2d²559	f632P2d¹755	611P2d224	d676P2d1333	711P2d¹912		620P2d⁵1270	(92NM304)
595P2d²1222	640P2d¹943	626P2d⁸304			—1083—	624P2d526	
f598P2d1168	666P2d¹228	626P2d¹¹1298	—1306—	—651—	(92NM254)	634P2d⁸689	—960—
598P2d²1169	d666P2d²230	632P2d³1205	(92NM166)	(92NM206)	636P2d²316	637P2d²1247	(92NM307)
619P2d²197	679P2d²271	642P2d²181	s582P2d1292	668P2d¹328	636P2d⁵316	f713P2d⁵1024	591P2d¹284
	680P2d¹621	645P2d¹453	614P2d17		637P2d²1247	f713P2d⁶1024	632P2d¹1165
—1289—	Cir. 10	665P2d286	617P2d²167	—1091—	647P2d²402	Cir. 10	682P2d¹199
(92NM76)	599FS¹387	665P2d¹287	665P2d³313	(92NM210)	692P2d⁵57	762F2d⁶864	709P2d²186
588P2d²566		668P2d¹319	679P2d1292	642P2d¹1111			
	—470—	f677P2d⁷1069	699P2d634		—1085—	—434—	—963—
—1293—	(9					(92NM287)	(92NM310)
(92NM80)	598					595P2d403	o619P2d¹1234
603P2d⁴1103	e59{	**—1302—**	Note that there are no law		595P2d⁵777	620P2d²885
605P2d³1167	603	**(92NM89)**	review citations, no A.L.R.		596P2d¹525	621P2d⁷510
617P2d³146	612	**628P2d⁴332**	annotations, and no citations		596P2d527	649P2d1386
617P2d³173	637	**j651P2d1312**	to decisions from states		598P2d¹1180	e671P2d²1138
666P2d1270	637	**Cir. 5**	outside of New Mexico.		600P2d¹1210	682P2d²203
673P2d¹147	637	**659F2d709**			601P2d¹719	686P2d988
692P2d³536	680	**Cir. 10**			608P2d528	727P2d¹75
713P2d²1014	684	**f693F2d²108**			610P2d¹1202	727P2d²76
	697				e623P2d¹994	
—1296—	730				j623P2d997	—966—
(92NM83)					f638P2d¹1074	(92NM313)
f665P2d¹1162	—473—	621P2d¹1133	s582P2d1292	723P2d250	638P2d¹1097	s586P2d1089
666P2d1270	(92NM109)	d643P2d²289	650P2d¹830	723P2d⁴251	650P2d¹851	c624P2d⁵540
673P2d⁵142	m583P2d464	662P2d¹1354	656P2d887	726P2d²1380	653P2d888	
723P2d²980	598P2d⁴1170	686P2d⁶949	703P2d³173	**Vol. 587**	d660P2d¹616	—973—
		f691P2d¹892			f696P2d481	(92NM320)
—1302—	—476—	f691P2d²892	—331—	—1105—	725P2d¹584	s588P2d554
(92NM89)	(92NM112)	721P2d¹410	(92NM187)	(92NM224)	—42—	612P2d³1339
628P2d⁴332	623P2d³999	Cir. 10	598P2d⁶648	703P2d181	(92NM264)	644P2d²1060
j651P2d1312	f627P2d²868	749F2d⁷613	610P2d⁴224		621P2d²1138	644P2d³1060
Cir. 5	627P2d⁸869	17MJ959	j610P2d225	—1352—	—435—	647P2d407
659F2d709	630P2d⁵1235		625P2d⁹1252	(92NM230)	(92NM288)	f657P2d1198
Cir. 10	633P2d²685	—194—	629P2d²352	s586P2d1089	j619P2d562	f670P2d³125
f693F2d²108	633P2d²685	(92NM147)	633P2d⁴1236	588P2d⁶557		f670P2d⁵125
	636P2d⁵899	s583P2d324	650P2d⁴822	f599P2d¹²386	—438—	e712P2d16
—1306—	645P2d³1383	608P2d¹536	657P2d⁵1183	601P2d²1449	(92NM291)	723P2d²981
(92NM93)	664P2d³1017	650P2d8	d657P2d⁴1184	f624P2d¹²	733P2d¹1324	
	689P2d⁵1273	698P2d³446	d657P2d⁴1194	[1036	Cir. 9	—1334—
—1307—	692P2d1326			j632P2d367	517FS²910	(92NM323)
(92NM94)	j727P2d573			635P2d999		d603P2d²293
638P2d³1079	j732P2d1388			641P2d¹¹1086	—47—	d603P2d³293
638P2d⁴1079				641P2d¹²1087	(92NM269)	d603P2d⁵293
681P2d⁶66				649P2d⁴502	US cert den	620P2d¹882
702P2d⁸356				663P2d⁴371	in441US908	
712P2d⁵5				Cir. 10	s586P2d1089	*Continued*
					594P2d²349	

410

EXHIBIT 14.3   **Sample Page from *Shepard's Pacific Reporter Citations***

Vol. 582   PACIFIC REPORTER, 2d SERIES

Ariz	681P2d⁶66	605P2d1192	– 4 –	– 37 –	– 73 –	159CaR²903	669P2d¹³7

Ariz
714P2d¹³391
714P2d¹³392
Utah
614P2d³¹1239
Wash
d694P2d¹³646
Wyo
677P2d⁶216

– 1283 –
(92NM70)
684P2d¹1160
706P2d²875

– 1285 –
(92NM72)

– 1287 –
(92NM74)
588P2d²559
595P2d²1222
f598P2d1168
598P2d²1169
619P2d²197
5A±258n

– 1289 –
(92NM76)
588P2d²566
95A±617s

– 1293 –
(92NM80)
603P2d⁴1103
605P2d³
617P2d³
617P2d³
666P2d1
673P2d¹
692P2d³
713P2d²
Wyo
642P2d³
642P2d³

– 129
(92NM
f665P2d¹
666P2d1
673P2d⁵
723P2d²
ND
319NW774
Wis
275NW173

– 1302 –
(92NM89)
628P2d⁴332
j651P2d1312
Cir. 5
659F2d709
Cir. 10
f693F2d²108
Mont
722P2d⁶1162
35A̅RF461s

– 1306 –
(92NM93)

– 1307 –
(92NM94)
638P2d³1079
638P2d⁴1079

681P2d⁶66
702P2d⁶356
712P2d⁵5
NC
339SE861
10A±217n
13A±550n

– 1311 –
d606P2d²564
Mich
324NW546
324NW547

– 1315 –
582P2d¹1322
AgD§3.11

– 1318 –
31LE861s
65A±1048s

– 1323 –
602P2d²220
611P2d⁹273
620P2d⁹418
620P2d²1327
632P2d²427
637P2d⁷901
651P2d1342
654P2d⁴637
655P2d⁴567
660P2d637
661P2d¹⁰904
693P2d⁷626

(283Or147)
s526P2d469
s536P2d517
s538P2d70
s429US363
s50LE550
s97SC582
cc439P2d575
589P2d717
611P2d698
625P2d²1332
639P2d¹133
674P2d94
684P2d⁸599
Cir. 9
672F2d¹796
563FS612
583FS⁸867
583FS¹⁰869

– 1365 –
(283Or201)
f600P2d²374
605P2d¹⁰699

605P2d1192
605P2d²1193
605P2d⁷1193
f607P2d²745
608P2d²1172
609P2d²851
611P2d²663
619P2d²921
630P2d²352
634P2d²1337
j634P2d1341
670P2d²165
f699P2d²202
700P2d²700
713P2d²647
714P2d²620
j719P2d860
Cir. 7
776F2d162
Cir. 10
794F2d⁶554
610P2d¹1337
164CaR¹846
172CaR⁶82
NM
612P2d⁴244
e612P2d²246
Utah
651P2d1342
Conn
464A2d55
464A2d60

651P2d²185

– 1384 –
(35OrA387)
583P2d⁶1160
588P2d⁶85
588P2d⁶643
601P2d907
621P2d¹66
650P2d1041
678P2d744
Mass
416NE943

Vol. 583

– 1 –
(35OrA711)
m587P2d1036
Idaho
710P2d³638

– 4 –
(35OrA763)
(36OrA173)

– 7 –
(35OrA779)
586P2d²394
601P2d¹857
601P2d²858
619P2d²251
45A±875s
2COA531§27

– 9 –
(35OrA799)
582P2d850
591P2d1205
599P2d467
601P2d⁶844
ND
368NW538
95A±1265s

– 12 –
(35OrA805)
s580P2d206
591P2d¹1197
595P2d1277
651P2d¹137

– 14 –
(35OrA809)
f596P2d¹1013
607P2d¹747
616P2d¹545

– 26 –
(35OrA843)

– 30 –
(36OrA19)
590P2d¹797
Mich
307NW429

– 31 –
(36OrA127)

– 34 –
Case 1
(36OrA161)

– 34 –
Case 2
(36OrA165)

– 34 –
Case 3
(36OrA167)

– 37 –
Case 3
(36OrA173)

– 38 –
Case 2
s603P2d363

– 40 –
(35OrA665)
s581P2d520

– 44 –
f586P2d⁵443
680P2d⁵750
717P2d⁶718
76A±262s

– 46 –
f611P2d²733

– 50 –
598P2d¹348
600P2d¹981
620P2d¹523
666P2d887
695P2d⁵105

– 53 –
674P2d⁴634

– 64 –
(1A±1263)
j616P2d602
649P2d41

Vt
499A2d28
98A±325s

– 69 –
f583P2d¹¹74
j586P2d439
601P2d⁵919
j601P2d921
602P2d704
602P2d³707
602P2d⁸708
604P2d⁴474
609P2d⁷942
641P2d⁷123
648P2d391
664P2d⁶449
665P2d⁷1315
668P2d⁷568
680P2d⁷1048
Cir. 10
531FS999
6A±65n

– 73 –
602P2d704
655P2d³692

– 82 –
624P2d⁴684
632P2d⁴869
699P2d⁴1210

– 85 –
608P2d629

– 87 –
cc612P2d357
619P2d¹1391

– 89 –
624P2d⁶691
635P2d53
656P2d⁶454

– 92 –
f600P2d¹518
f600P2d²518
c600P2d¹519
c600P2d²519
605P2d¹1233
613P2d²520
Cir. 10
595FS²290
CtCl
697F2d²1351
Tex
621SW646

– 105 –
635P2d86
642P2d²740
657P2d⁴274
668P2d1257
Cir. 10
e700F2d¹602
700F2d607
e700F2d¹610
758F2d¹1384
583FS1266
Mo
687SW886
So C
345SE745

– 109 –
(22C3d29)
(148CaR584)
s141CaR336
612P2d²882
633P2d²194
677P2d²851
154CaR²471

159CaR²903
164CaR²162
165CaR²792
176CaR²529
179CaR²376
187CaR²337
200CaR²445
204CaR654
216CaR²639
f217CaR²748
218CaR²775
224CaR²568
225CaR²642

– 113 –
(22C3d38)
(148CaR588)
f157CaR²182
157CaR³182
157CaR⁴182
f157CaR⁶182
d227CaR²782
d227CaR⁷783
228CaR⁶683
228CaR⁷683

– 121 –
(22C3d51)
(148CaR596)
cc175CaR307
155CaR¹547
165CaR²54
170CaR60
176CaR²323

417NE163
78A±460s
46A±240s
100A±194n
4COA89§5

– 130 –
(22C3d67)
(148CaR605)
583P2d¹3766
586P2d¹³923
j591P2d958
592P2d¹³316
594P2d³986
j594P2d990
601P2d206
f618P2d¹217
618P2d⁸219
618P2d⁹223
c618P2d⁶225
j618P2d226
628P2d880
f634P2d936
636P2d³29

669P2d¹³7
672P2d118
674P2d
[¹³¹317
700P2d³422
j700P2d431
715P2d671
d720P2d¹¹6
148CaR¹³907
150CaR¹³442
151CaR⁵235
f151CaR⁹237
f151CaR⁴238
j153CaR470
153CaR¹³829
154CaR161
154CaR666
154CaR⁴667
153CaR³561
j155CaR565
158CaR³91
158CaR¹291
159CaR190
160CaR³847
160CaR¹³882
162CaR¹²777
d162CaR
[¹³843
d162CaR⁴846
d162CaR⁵846
d162CaR⁶846
d162CaR
[¹²846
f162CaR847
162CaR848
j162CaR848
d162CaR⁴848
d162CaR
[¹²848
d162CaR
[¹³848
f163CaR⁶375
f164CaR¹503
164CaR⁶505
d164CaR
[¹³749
164CaR897
167CaR³756
168CaR377
f168CaR¹671
f168CaR⁸673
168CaR⁹677
c168CaR⁶679
j168CaR680
d169CaR⁶117
169CaR³573
f169CaR³842
170CaR³673
170CaR¹²699
171CaR¹³177
171CaR³179
171CaR⁴206
173CaR³192
173CaR⁶430
174CaR328
174CaR⁸605
174CaR¹719
176CaR¹513
176CaR³513
f177CaR585
178CaR³340
d179CaR642
179CaR³688
180CaR⁴7
180CaR⁷8
Continued

Note that an A.L.R. annotation is included but a law review citation is not.

– 1302 –
(92NM89)
628P2d⁴332
j651P2d1312
Cir. 5
659F2d709
Cir. 10
f693F2d²108
Mont
722P2d⁶1162——Citation from a state outside of New Mexico
35A̅RF461s

376

EXHIBIT 14.4   **Online *Shepard's* State Citation in State Citator***

```
            (c) 1992 McGraw-Hill, Inc. - DOCUMENT 1 (OF 1)

CITATIONS TO: 92 N.M. 89
SERIES: SHEPARD'S NEW MEXICO CITATIONS
DIVISION: NEW MEXICO REPORTS
COVERAGE: Shepard's 1987 Bound Volume Through 08/92 Supplement.

NUMBER  ANALYSIS            CITING REFERENCE                  PARA   NOTES
------  ----------------    ----------------------------      ----   ----------
   1    parallel citation   (582 P.2d 1302)
   2                         96 N.M.  87                        4
   3    dissenting opinion   98 N.M. 668
   4                        105 N.M. 577                        4
   5                        106 N.M. 570                        6
                            Cir. 5
   6                        659 F.2d 709
                            Cir. 10
   7    followed           693 F.2d 108                         2
   8                        81 Mich. LR 1485
   9                        35 A.L.R. Fed. 461                         annot supp
------------------------------------------------------------------------------
To see the text of a citing case, press the citing reference NUMBER and then
the TRANSMIT key.
For further explanation, press the H key (for HELP) and then the TRANSMIT key.
 Press Alt-H for Help or Alt-Q to Quit.
```

EXHIBIT 14.5   **Online *Shepard's* Regional Citation in Regional Citator***

```
            (c) 1992 McGraw-Hill, Inc. - DOCUMENT 1 (OF 2)

CITATIONS TO: 582 P.2d 1302
SERIES: SHEPARD'S PACIFIC REPORTER CITATIONS
DIVISION: PACIFIC REPORTER, 2d SERIES
COVERAGE: Shepard's 1987 Volume & Supplements Through 08/92 Supplement.

NUMBER  ANALYSIS            CITING REFERENCE                  PARA   NOTES
------  ----------------    ----------------------------      ----   -------
   1    parallel citation   (92 N.M.  89)
   2                        628 P.2d 332                        4
   3    dissenting opinion   651 P.2d 1312
   4                        734 P.2d 1260                       4
   5                        746 P.2d 1102                       6
   6                        819 P.2d 1351                       3
                            Cir. 5
   7                        659 F.2d 709
                            Cir. 10
   8    followed           693 F.2d 108                         2
--------------------------------------------------------------------------
To see the text of a citing case, press the citing reference NUMBER and then
the TRANSMIT key.
For further explanation, press the H key (for HELP) and then the TRANSMIT key

 Press Alt-H for Help or Alt-Q to Quit.
```

The following information is obtained when the same case is shepardized using the S. Ct. or L. Ed. citation.

- parallel citation to U.S.
- citations to other federal cases
- citations to state cases after 1984
- citations to A.L.R.

Citations to law reviews can be found using *Shepard's Federal Law Citations in Selected Law Reviews.*

§14.4 Tips on Using *Shepard's*

In using *Shepard's* citators, keep the following in mind.

1. *Shepard's* citators are not cumulative. Depending on how old the case is, you may need to look in a number of different volumes (hardbound volume, hardbound supplement, and one or more paper supplements). To determine what volumes you need, check the coverage notes printed on the cover of the most recent supplement.

2. You may obtain different information depending on which citator and citation you use.

3. If you are citing a case using its official (state reporter) citation, use the headnote numbers that appear in the official reporter; if you are using the regional reporter citation, use the headnote numbers that appear in the regional reporter.

4. You don't need to read every case cited in *Shepard's*. If the list of cites is long, check those cases whose citation is preceded by an "o" (overruled), an "r" (reversed), an "m" (modified), a "q" (questioned), or a "c" (criticized). If the list of citations is short, you may want to check each case listed.

Section Summary	**Shepard's *Citators***

Type: Finding tool

Sources: *Shepard's* citators are available for jurisdictions and subject areas. They are used to check the current status of statutes, cases, rules, and other sources of authority and to find additional authority on an issue of law.

           Shepard's citators are not cumulative, and the coverage varies from set to set.

Chapter 15

Computer-Assisted Legal Research

Few people have a neutral attitude about computers. Either they are high-tech demons that have depersonalized and dehumanized modern life, making it more alien, more Orwellian, or they are miracles of the twentieth century, the panacea for all problems, the scientific solution for the information explosion.

The same is true for people's attitudes about computer-assisted research. It is seen by some as an overrated, over-priced, glitzy shortcut that can lead to shoddy work and by others as an efficient, effective, modern approach to accessing information. In short, book researchers often consider computers anathema; computers researchers often consider books anachronistic. And never the twain shall meet.

Or will they? Effective researchers have always known when to use what. Long before the age of LEXIS and Westlaw, astute researchers knew the benefits and limitations of an annotated versus an unannotated code and when to and when not to use other finding tools such as the looseleaf services. Computer-assisted research is no different. It is a tool, and in this case, the tool includes a system, usually LEXIS or Westlaw.

Many of the resources discussed in the preceding six chapters are available via computer as well as in their original print form. The computer is merely an alternative means for assessing these resources. The question then is, when should one use the books and when should one use the machine?

This section will discuss not only how to use computers to do legal research but also when to use them. Much of the "when" information is integrated in the discussion that follows, but as a general rule, you may find the following advice helpful: Use computers when you cannot easily find the same information in a book.

It really is that simple.

§15.1   INDICES AND FULL-TEXT SEARCHING

The unique power of computer-assisted research is its ability to search documents "full-text." The ability to do full-text searching means that, with limited exceptions, every word in a document can be used as an access point. The practical benefit of full-text searching is that you no longer need to rely on an index as the sole means for obtaining references to authority.

For example, suppose you are looking for cases concerning a police officer stopping and frisking a person. If you had to rely on an index, you might look under "stop" or "frisk" or even "arrest" and find nothing. Suppose that in this particular index cases of this type are listed under "warrantless searches." If you are unfamiliar with this terminology or even if you know the term but have temporarily forgotten it, the index will be worthless to you in this instance. In fact, it could even be detrimental because you might assume there are no such cases because you were unable to locate them in the index.

Full-text searching allows you to bypass indices. If you want to look for cases using the word "frisk," the computer will retrieve all cases in which that word is used anywhere in the case.

Another problem with indices is that they require generalization. For example, cases concerning cars, regardless of model, will probably be indexed under either "car" or "automobile." But what if you want to find cases about a certain kind of car, such as a Pinto? An index will refer you to cases about cars, but then you have to locate those concerning Pintos by browsing through all the cases. Full-text searching, by contrast, allows you to search for cases with the word "Pinto."

Full-text searching ability, then, is one reason why computer-assisted research can be the more efficient way to do legal research. Used judiciously, it can overcome the what-is-the-right-search-term problem as well as focus the research in ways that are not yet possible when researching in books. Throughout this discussion, search terms and commands (that is, material you would actually type into the computer) appear in italic type.

§15.2   LEXIS AND WESTLAW

§15.2.1   Similarities and Differences in the Two Systems

When lawyers talk about computer-assisted research, they usually mean LEXIS and Westlaw, two separate services for accessing legal materials via computer. LEXIS and Westlaw are similar in that both have the same types of information available. Both services have the text of state and federal cases. Both have the United States Code, Code of Federal Regulations, Federal Register, decisions of many administrative agencies, and many law review articles. Both are also nearing the point where they have the statutes (codes) of all fifty states. Their dates of coverage differ for some materials, but both continue to add retrospectively.

LEXIS and Westlaw also have some important differences. LEXIS is associated with the publisher Lawyers Co-operative. Thus, A.L.R. annotations are available only on LEXIS. Additionally, LEXIS is part of LEXIS/NEXIS, a computer-assisted research service that comes with a LEXIS subscription and that includes national newspapers, financial information, and other nonlegal information.

Westlaw, by contrast, allows access to DIALOG, which is mostly nonlegal, scientific, technical, or business-related material. An even more important Westlaw feature, however, is that within Westlaw you can use the West Key Number System and other West-created enhancements for searching in its databases. This feature allows you to search the West synopses and headnotes. Furthermore, you can run a key number search online, either using the key number alone as a search term or using it in combination with keyword searching.

LEXIS and Westlaw also differ in many coverage dates and in their pricing structure. The two systems also use different terminology to describe similar entities. Despite what may seem like a litany of differences, though, the two systems are still far more alike than they are different. Consequently, it makes sense to learn about them together, noting the differences as they occur.

§15.2.2   Composition of LEXIS and Westlaw Services

The structure and mechanics of LEXIS and Westlaw, like much else in the systems, are similar. It is the terminology that each uses to describe its system that varies.

In LEXIS, you first choose a "library" from a menu screen. A "library" in this sense is a broad collection of documents. The GENFED library, for instance, contains federal documents such as the *United States Code,* the *Code of Federal Regulations,* and federal cases. See Exhibit 15.1.

Once you select a LEXIS library by typing in its name and transmitting it to the computer, you then must select a LEXIS "file."

A file is a subcategory of a library. Files vary in size. In the GENFED library, for instance, the DIST file contains all published cases (and some unpublished cases) from federal district courts. The COURTS file, by contrast, contains cases from all federal courts. See Exhibit 15.2.

In Westlaw, you select a "database" from the screen's menu before running a search. Unlike LEXIS, there is no subcategory. Databases, like libraries and files, vary in size. The ALLSTATES database, for example, contains published cases from all fifty states and the District of Columbia. The GA-ST database contains only the current statutes for the state of Georgia. See Exhibit 15.3.

EXHIBIT 15.1   **LEXIS Library Menu***

```
                         LIBRARIES -- PAGE 1 of 2
    Please TRANSMIT the NAME (only one) of the library you want to search.
    - For more information about a library, TRANSMIT its page (PG) number.
    - To see a list of additional libraries, press the NEXT PAGE key.
    NAME    PG NAME    PG NAME    PG NAME    PG NAME    PG NAME    PG NAME    PG

    - - - - - L E X I S - U S - - - - - - - - - PUBLIC       FINANCIAL  --NEXIS--
    GENFED  1 CODES   1 LEGIS   1 STATES  1 CITES   6 RECORDS      COMPNY 15 NEXIS  13
                                                      ASSETS   6 MERGER 15 BACKGR 13
    ADMRTY  2 FEDCOM  3 MILTRY  4 CORP    2 LAWREV  6 DOCKET   6 NAARS  15 BANKS  14
    BANKNG  2 FEDSEC  3 PATENT  4 EMPLOY  2 MARHUB  6 INCORP   6           CMPCOM 13
    BKRTCY  2 FEDTAX  3 PENBEN  4 HEALTH  3 LEXREF  6 LIENS    6 --INT'L-- CONSUM 13
    COPYRT  2 IMMIG   3 PUBCON  4 INSRLW  3 ABA     6 VERDCT   9 WORLD  16 ENRGY  14
    ENERGY  2 INTLAW  3 PUBHW   4 MEDMAL  3 BNA     6 --MEDIS-- ASIAPC 16 ENTERT 13
    ENVIRN  2 ITRADE  3 REALTY  4 PRLIAB  4 TAXRIA  6 GENMED  12 EUROPE 16 INSURE 13
    ESTATE  2 LABOR   3 TRADE   5 STENV   4 TAXANA  6 MEDEX   12 MDEAFR 16 LEGNEW 14
    ETHICS  2 LEXPAT  3 TRDMRK  5 STSEC   4 ALR     6 MEDLNE  12 NSAMER 16 MARKET 14
    FAMILY  2 M&A     4 TRANS   5 STTAX   4 -ASSISTS-           CANADA 16 PEOPLE 14
    FEDSEN  3 MSTORT  5 CAREER  6 UCC     5 PRACT   12 POLITICAL          SPORTS 13
                                  UTILTY  5 GUIDE   12 CMPGN   14          TRAN   14
                                                      EXEC    14

        AC for AUTO-CITE    LXE (LEXSEE) to retrieve a case/document by cite
        SHEP for SHEPARD'S  LXT (LEXSTAT) to retrieve a statute by cite
    Press Alt-H for Help or Alt-Q to Quit.
```

The documentation for the services contains a complete list of the available files and databases. Many users prefer to bypass these, however, because the systems are menu-driven. Once you have entered a valid

---

EXHIBIT 15.2   **LEXIS File Menu***

```
    Please TRANSMIT, separated by commas, the NAMES of the files you want to search.
    You may select as many files as you want, including files that do not appear
    below, but you must transmit them all at one time.  To see a description of a
    file, TRANSMIT its page (PG) number.
                    FILES - PAGE 1 of 8 (NEXT PAGE for additional files)

      NAME   PG DESCRIP            NAME   PG DESCRIP          NAME   PG DESCRIP

      ---COURT GROUP FILES--     ---LEGAL DEVELOPMENTS--     ----ADMINISTRATIVE-----
    OMNI     1 Fed Cases & ALR  USLIST 11 Sup.Ct Summaries ALLREG 16 FEDREG & CFR
    COURTS   1 Fed Cases        PRE-VU 12 Sup.Ct Preview   FEDREG 16 Fed. Register
    CURRNT   1 Cases aft 1990   USLW   12 US Law Week       CFR    16 Code of Fed.Reg
    NEWER    3 Cases aft 1944   USLWD  12 US Law Wk Daily  COMGEN 14 Comp.Gen.Decs.
    SUPCIR   1 US,USAPP & CAFC  APPSUM 13 Ct App Summaries  ------LEGISLATIVE------
      ---U.S. COURT FILES---    PUBS   37 Legal Pubs       RECORD 26 CongRec aft 1984
    US       1 US Supreme Ct    EXTRA  39 In the News ...  BILLS  27 All Bills Files
    USAPP    1 Cts of Appeal    --SUPREME COURT BRIEFS-    BLREC  26 CongRec & BLTEXT
    FED      8 FedCir&Spec Ct   BRIEFS 11 Argued aft 9/79  PUBLAW 15 US Public Laws
    DIST     1 District Courts  ---------RULES---------    USCODE 15 USCS & PUBLAW
    CLCT     2 Claims Court     RULES  31 Federal Rules      ------ANNOTATIONS------
                                CIRRUL 33 Circuit Ct Rules ALR    40 ALR & L.Ed.Annos
    To search by Circuits press NEXT PAGE.  NOTE:  Only court files can be combined.
    Press Alt-H for Help or Alt-Q to Quit.
```

```
_____WESTLAW DIRECTORY WELCOME SCREEN_____P1_____
_____GENERAL STATE DATABASES                                     P6_____

-------------------- STATE DATABASES: DOCUMENT INDEX ----------------------
Multistate ....... Next Page    Court Orders .... P15      Reg. Tracking ..P8
Admin. Law/Code .. P8           Court Rules ..... P16      Statutes-Anno. .P21
At. Gen. Op. ..... P10          Indices ......... P17      Statutes-Unanno.P22
Bill Tracking .... P11          Legis. Service .. P18      Uniform Laws ...P413
Case Law ......... P14          Regional Rptrs .. P20
-------------- STATE AND TERRITORY DATABASES: DIRECTORY LOCATIONS -----------
AL..P23   DC..P48   IA..P70   MN..P94    NM..P118   PA..P140   VT..P162
AK..P26   FL..P51   KS..P73   MS..P97    NY..P121   PR..P143   VI..P165
AZ..P29   GA..P54   KY..P76   MO..P100   NC..P124   RI..P144   VA. P166
AR..P32   GU..P57   LA..P79   MT..P103   ND..P127   SC..P147   WA. P169
CA..P35   HI..P58   ME..P82   NE..P106   MP..P130   SD..P150   WV. P172
CO..P39   ID..P61   MD..P85   NV..P109   OH..P131   TN..P153   WI. P175
CT..P42   IL..P64   MA..P88   NH..P112   OK..P134   TX..P156   WY. P178
DE..P45   IN..P67   MI..P91   NJ..P115   OR..P137   UT..P159
----------------------------------------------------------------------------
If you wish to:
    Select a database, type its IDENTIFIER, e.g., ALLSTATES and press ENTER
    View information about a database, type SCOPE followed by its IDENTIFIER
        and press ENTER
```

*Certain materials reproduced herein are reprinted with permission of West Publishing
Company.

password and identified the research (for billing purposes), the initial
screen that appears is a menu screen.

From the first menu screen, you can select other menu screens to
locate the appropriate library and file, or database, to be searched. After
entering the name of the library and file, or database, you enter the
search. If you know the identifier (for the library and file or for the
database), you can enter it at the initial menu screen, thereby bypassing
the other menu screens and saving time.

§15.2.3   Search Words

Because computers can search for nearly every word in a document, the basic search component in computer-assisted research is "the
word." A "word" for these purposes is defined as any string of characters
with a space on either side. Consequently, words in computer-assisted
research include not only standard words such as *contract* or *tort* but
also "words" like *WD-40* and *26.04.010.*

In fact, because unique words are more useful as search words than
common words, numbers like *26.04.010* are some of the best search
words. Strings of numbers in a legal document, like *26.04.010,* usually
refer to a citation, and a citation is often the perfect search word for
finding specific documents, such as cases or statutes.

In contrast, common words such as *will* and *service* are poor search words because they have many meanings other than as references to legal concepts. Unfortunately, because these words often appear in legal materials with these alternative meanings, using such words as search words can cause retrieval of irrelevant cases. Therefore, unique words, when they exist, are generally the best ones for full-text searching.

§15.2.4   Truncation and Root Expansion

One problem with language is that there are many ways to describe the same concept. More precisely, a root word may have many endings. For example, the concept of contributing negligence may be referred to in the following ways:

> contributory negligence
> contributorily negligent
> negligent contributorily
> contributed to the negligence
> contribution on the plaintiff's part

This list of choices does not even take into account the fact that some jurisdictions may refer to this concept as *comparative negligence* rather than *contributory negligence.*

Because it would be burdensome to enter all the alternative forms into the computer, both computer services allow truncation and root expansion. All you need to do is type the root word and use the truncation symbol at the end.

There are two symbols that can be used to truncate: the asterisk (*) and the exclamation point (!). The * is a universal character. It occupies one space and only one space. Thus, *contribut** would obtain documents with *contribute* but not *contributor* or *contribution.*

More than one * may be used to truncate. Adding additional asterisks will expand the root up to and including the number of asterisks. For example, *contribut**** would obtain *contribute, contributory,* and *contribution.* It would not obtain *contributorily.*

Usually, root expansion is best done with the !. A single ! gets all suffixes to the root regardless of the number of letters. Thus, *contribut!* would obtain *contribute, contribution, contributory,* and *contributorily.*

Why then would a researcher ever use an asterisk rather than an exclamation point for truncation? An example of a rare occasion when the * might be preferable in truncating would be *execut**** to obtain *executor, executive,* and *executrix* but eliminate *executioner.*

The * does, however, have a use that the ! does not. It can be used in the middle of a word. Thus, *dr*nk* would obtain *drink, drank,* and *drunk.*

Note too, though, that if the * is used in the middle of a word, some character must be in the * location for it to be retrieved. Thus, *judg*ment* does *not* obtain both forms of the word (*judgement* and *judgment*). It obtains only *judgement.*

Finally, neither the * nor the ! can be used at the beginning of a word. Thus, ****regulation* will obtain nothing.

Section Summary

- The basic search component in computer-assisted legal research is the word.
- If possible, search using unique words.
- Retrieve variations of a root word by truncating, using * or !.

§15.2.5   Hyphenation

Another feature in our language that complicates computer-assisted research is the hyphen. Unfortunately, LEXIS and Westlaw differ in their treatment of hyphens.

LEXIS treats hyphens as spaces. Thus, in LEXIS *pre-judgment* would obtain *pre judgment* and *pre-judgment* but not *prejudgment.*

Westlaw, by contrast, "normalizes" hyphenated words. "Normalizing" means a hyphenated query will retrieve both the hyphenated word and the word as a single word. Thus, in Westlaw *pre-judgment* would obtain *pre-judgment* and *prejudgment,* but not *pre judgment.* Note, however, that the hyphenation must be in the typed query for the normalization to occur. Thus, *prejudgment* will not obtain *pre-judgment* in either Westlaw or LEXIS.

Retrieval

Search Word	*LEXIS*	*Westlaw*
prejudgment	prejudgment	prejudgment
pre-judgment	pre-judgment	pre-judgment
	pre judgment	prejudgment
	but not	*but not*
	prejudgment	pre judgment

LEXIS: hyphen = space
Westlaw: hyphen = word with or without hyphen

§15.2.6   Plurals and Capitalization

Both systems are programmed to retrieve the plural form of a word if the singular is searched. This feature can be turned off on Westlaw by typing the pound sign (#) in front of the word. In LEXIS, a search of a plural form retrieves the singular form as well. In Westlaw, a search of the plural form only retrieves that form.

§15.2.7   Noise Words (Stop Words)

Neither system will search for certain words known as "noise words" or "stop words." These are words that are so commonly used in the language that searching for them would be of little value and would significantly burden the computer's abilities. Examples are words like *of, the,* and *very.*

There are approximately 100 noise or stop words. A complete list of each system's noise or stop words can be found in their respective documentation.

§15.2.8   Connectors

Although it is true that unique words are the best search terms, rarely does a single word or phrase retrieve relevant documents without also retrieving a large number of irrelevant documents.

A good search usually requires a combination of several words. The relationship between the words is expressed to LEXIS and Westlaw by the use of connectors. Four connectors are used in computer-assisted legal research: *or, and,* the proximity connector *w/* or */,* and *not.*

a.   OR

The connector *or* is used for synonymous terms. It means that either the word to the left of the *or* or the word to the right of the *or* must appear in the document for it to be retrieved. In LEXIS, the convention used for the *or* connector is merely typing *or* between the two words. Thus, in LEXIS, *car or automobile* retrieves all documents with either *car* or *automobile* anywhere in the document.

The same convention (adding *or*) also works in Westlaw. However, the preferred method of searching using the *or* connector in Westlaw is to leave a space between the words. In other words, in Westlaw, a space is treated as an *or* connector. Therefore, in Westlaw, *car automobile* will retrieve all documents with either *car* or *automobile* anywhere in the document.

To reiterate, typing the word *or* will work in both LEXIS and Westlaw. In addition, Westlaw treats a space as the connector *or.*

This difference is probably the single most important distinction in search logic between the two systems. Where it becomes problematic is in phrase searching. If, for example, you want to search for cases dealing with the writ of habeas corpus, the search is done on LEXIS as *habeas corpus.*

If the same string of characters is typed into Westlaw, however, that service will read it *habeas or corpus.* Thus, the lawyer would retrieve not only cases with *habeas corpus* in them, but also all cases with *corpus juris* or *corpus delicti.* Many an unwary or infrequent Westlaw user has fallen into this trap.

The way to do a phrase search in Westlaw is to put the phrase in quotation marks (" "). Thus, in Westlaw, *"habeas corpus"* would retrieve all cases with the phrase *habeas corpus* in them.

To review, then, the connector *or* is used for synonymous terms. It means that either the word on its left or the word on its right must appear in the document for it to be retrieved. The convention for entering this connector in a search is to type *or.* However, in Westlaw, a space is also treated as an *or.* Finally, to search for a phrase in Westlaw, quotation marks must surround the phrase. Quotation marks are not necessary for a phrase search in LEXIS.

Section Summary

CONNECTORS

OR — for synonymous terms

    LEXIS or Westlaw: *car or automobile*

    Westlaw: *car automobile*

Phrase search

    LEXIS: *habeas corpus*
    Westlaw: *"habeas corpus"*

b. AND

The second connector is *and.* It is narrower than *or* but still fairly broad. The *and* connector requires that both the word to the left of *and* and the word to the right of *and* appear in the same document. One can be the first word in the document, the other the last word, but as long as they both appear somewhere in the document, the document will be retrieved.

In both LEXIS and Westlaw, the convention for entering this connector is merely typing the word *and.* In Westlaw, the ampersand (&) may also be used. Thus, in both services, *slip and fall and snow* would retrieve all documents that have all three words — *slip, fall,* and *snow* — somewhere in the document.

And is used when the words that a lawyer wants to find may not be located close to each other. An example might be when a lawyer wants to find cases on the statute of limitations for negligent manufacture resulting in the explosion of a motor vehicle's gas tank. The words relating to the vehicle, the gas tank, and the explosion will probably be located near one another. They would likely be in the court's recitation of the facts. For these words, proximity connectors (discussed in the next section) would be better than *and.* However, it might be several pages before the court's analysis turned to issues of negligent manufacture or the statute of limitations. Therefore, the words used to search for those concepts should probably be connected to the exploding gas tank concept with *and.*

c.   Proximity Connectors

There are two types of proximity connectors. The first is the numerical connector (available on both LEXIS and Westlaw). The second is the grammatical connector (available only on Westlaw).

1.   Numerical Connectors

Numerical connectors specify that only a certain number of words can intervene between the connected words. The convention used in numerical connectors is *w/#* (# representing any number from 1 to 255). For numbers larger than 255, an *and* connector is appropriate. Westlaw's preferred numerical connector is */#.* The *w/#,* however, works in both systems.

Earlier, we discussed the different ways of referring to the concept of contributory negligence. Below are examples of a search for this concept under both systems.

> LEXIS: *contribut! w/4 negligen!*
> Westlaw: *contribut! /4 negligen!*

Recall that the ! is used to expand the roots of both words. The *w/4* or */4* requires that, at the most, four words can intervene between *contribut!* and *negligen!.* Therefore, the search would retrieve all of the following:

> *contributory negligence,*
> *contributorily negligent,*
> *negligent contributorily,* and
> *contributed to the negligence*

It will not retrieve *contribution on the plaintiff's part* because the search requires that the word *negligen!* be used within four words of *contribut!,* and it does not in this phrase.

Notice that *w/#* and */#* do not specify order. That is, it does not matter which word occurs first in the text. Order can be specified by using the connector *pre/#* in LEXIS and + # in Westlaw. The following are examples of these connectors:

>LEXIS: *John pre/1 Kennedy*
>Westlaw: *John +1 Kennedy*

The *pre/#* and + # are useful in searching for citations. In a case citation, the name of the case always precedes the volume number and the volume number always precedes the page number. When looking for cases citing *University Nat. Co. v. Gray's Harbor County,* 12 Wash. 2d 549, 122 P.2d 501, the following searches might be used:

>LEXIS: *University pre/10 12 pre/2 549*
>Westlaw: *University +10 12 +2 549*

This example raises two issues. The first issue is, why not specify *12 Wash. 2d 549* itself? The answer is that the reporter abbreviation may be a problem. The *Bluebook* says *Washington Reports, Second Series* is abbreviated Wash. 2d. The *Washington Reports Style Manual* (used by that state) says the correct abbreviation is Wn.2d.

In addition, problems often occur in reporter abbreviations because of punctuation (here, the period) and spacing. All the following can be found as abbreviations for Washington Reports, Second Series, in both LEXIS and Westlaw.

Wash.2d	Wn.2d
Wash. 2d	Wn. 2d
Wash2d	Wn2d
Wash 2d	Wn 2d

The point is that the volume and page numbers are the most important part of a citation. If they alone are not enough to limit the search to only those documents citing the case, then the name can be added. Using *pre/#* or + # eliminates the pitfalls that reporter abbreviations can create.

The second issue raised by the example is, why would anyone search for a case citation when the case can be shepardized? The answer is that many of the materials available online are available long before they appear in print. United States Supreme Court cases, for example, are available within hours of their release. Unfortunately, it is a matter of months before a case that cites another is available in *Shepard's.*

Consequently, because *Shepard's* is not useful for finding cases that are very recent, using the computer as a citator (using the citation as a search) is an effective way of updating *Shepard's.*

To recap, *w/#* and */#* allow you to specify the proximity of search words to each other. These connectors are narrower than the *and* connector. The *w/#* and */#* do not specify sequence. However, sequence can be specified with the *pre/#* and + #. When these connectors are used, the word to the left of the connector must occur in the text before the word to the right of the connector.

Finally, one difference between the two services is in what is considered a "word" for the purpose of counting intervening words. LEXIS does not count noise or stop words (see section 15.2.7) as intervening words; Westlaw does. The result is that *w/25* in LEXIS is different from */25* in Westlaw. The *w/25* of LEXIS is probably closer to */40* in Westlaw. The following sentence may be illustrative:

> Common law copyright is that right that an author has in his or her unpublished literary creations.

Suppose a researcher did the following searches:

LEXIS:	*copyright w/5 unpublished*
Westlaw:	*copyright /5 unpublished* OR
	copyright w/5 unpublished

LEXIS would retrieve a document with the illustrative sentence because it would not count the noise words: *is, that, that, an, has, his, or, her.* Thus, only three words intervene in the LEXIS search. Westlaw would count all intervening words, including stop words. Because eleven words intervene, the document would not be retrieved in Westlaw. This fact is important to remember when deciding what number to use in searches using a proximity connector.

> ### Section Summary

CONNECTORS

AND — requires both words around it to be present for retrieval.

| LEXIS: | *slip and fall* |
| Westlaw: | *slip and fall* or *slip & fall* |

Proximity connectors (*w/#*; */#*) — specify number of words that can intervene between words

LEXIS:	*slip w/5 fall*
Westlaw:	*slip /5 fall* or
	slip w/5 fall
	(does not specify order)

To specify order, use *pre/#*; *+ #*

| LEXIS: | *John pre/1 Kennedy* |
| Westlaw: | *John + 1 Kennedy* |

2. Grammatical Connectors

In addition to the numerical proximity connector, Westlaw also has grammatical connectors. The connectors are */s* for words in the same sentence and */p* for words in the same paragraph. Sequence can be specified by using *+s* and *+p* (for preceding words in the same sentence and preceding words in the same paragraph, respectively). With these connectors, the number of intervening words is irrelevant. As long as the connected words occur within the same grammatical component, the document will be retrieved.

This type of connector is useful because the English language is based on grammar rather than on word proximity. The latter can roughly estimate grammar, but the real thing is usually better. The following are examples of Westlaw grammatical connectors:

> *copyright /s unpublished*
> *libel! slander! defam! /p "public figure"*

d. NOT

The final connector is the *not* connector. LEXIS calls it "and not"; Westlaw calls it "but not." The *not* connector excludes terms to the right of the connector. Terms to the left are treated as they normally would be in a search request. The convention used in LEXIS is to type *and not.* Westlaw's convention is the percent sign (%). The following are examples of the *not* connector:

> LEXIS: *breach! w/5 warranty and not contract*
> Westlaw: *breach! /s warranty % contract*

The above searches might be used if a researcher is looking for breach of warranty as a cause of action in tort. This leads to a caution. Always remember that the computer itself is literal; it is not intelligent. In the above example, it is possible that a judge might write an opinion that says: "Breach of warranty is usually an issue in contract law. Here, however, we explore its effect in tort law." This is exactly the type of case that the researcher wants to find. It would not be retrieved, though, because the word *contract* appeared. The *not* connector may have utility (especially with the field searches, discussed shortly), but it should be used with some caution.

§15.2.9   Search Order of Connectors

Both LEXIS and Westlaw are programmed so that they search certain connectors first. The search order is as follows:

1. *or*
2. proximity connectors from smallest to largest (for example, *w/5* before *w/25*)

3. *and*
4. *not*

The computer's search order may seem like a small, technical point, but it is important practical knowledge for the legal researcher. You may have used the right words and connectors, but the computer may still not be running the search you think it is.

For example, if you want cases dealing with worker's compensation the following searches might be used:

> LEXIS: *industrial insurance or work! w/2 compensation*
> Westlaw: *"industrial insurance" work! /2 compensation*

The above searches will not retrieve the desired documents. The reason is the searching order of connectors. Because the computer is programmed to search *or* first, it will initially come up with the subset of documents with either the phrase *industrial insurance* or words with the root *work.* It will then take this subset and combine it with *compensation* (requiring that *industrial insurance or work!* precede *compensation* with two or fewer intervening words). The result is that the search retrieves all occurrences of *worker's compensation* or *workmen's compensation;* however, it gets only documents with the phrase *industrial insurance* if that phrase precedes *compensation* by two or fewer words (which is unlikely). Thus, the search will fail to retrieve most occurrences of *industrial insurance.*

Any search that doesn't do what you think it will is obviously a problem. The solution is to override the programmed search order. The convention used to override the programmed search order is to place the words that are to be searched together in parentheses. In the above example, the correct search would be the following:

> LEXIS: *industrial insurance or (work! w/2 compensation)*
> Westlaw: *"industrial insurance" (work! /2 compensation)*

You can use as many sets of parentheses as are necessary in a search. Indeed, because you may not recall the order of searching, the safest way of searching is to use parentheses.

§15.2.10   Segment/Field Searching

The computer's ability to do full-text searching is enhanced even further by the ability to limit the word search to certain portions of the document. These portions are called "segments" by LEXIS or "fields" by Westlaw.

As each document is entered into the computer, certain identifiable parts are labeled to allow for segment and field searching. Unfortunately, the two services use different labeling for these parts. For example, the following labels are for some of the parts of a case that can be searched:

LEXIS case segments	Westlaw case fields
name	title
counsel	attorney
opinionby	judge
headnote[1]	digest
date	date

The segments and fields available differ with the type of document. Those available in each file or database can be found in the documentation for each service or by entering the appropriate command while online. With rare exceptions, the convention for running a segment or field search is to type the name of the segment or field followed by the words to be found within it in parentheses.

The following are some uses of segment and field searches with cases. If the parties to a case are known, these searches could identify the case:

LEXIS: *name (talbot and fountain products)*
Westlaw: *title (talbot and "fountain products") OR*
            ti or (talbot and "fountain products")

In this search, *and* is used as a connector instead of looking for *talbot v. fountain products* because the case caption may actually read: *Talbot, et al. v. Fountain Products.* Remember, the computer looks for exact strings of characters and because these strings do not match, the case would not be retrieved.

Note

In both LEXIS and Westlaw, you may use upper or lower case; they are both read the same. In addition, when using Westlaw, you may abbreviate field names, as was done in the last example above.

A proximity connector is not used in the above example because *talbot* may the first name in a class action that includes hundreds of people. In other words, the word *talbot* may not be close to *fountain products.* Because the search is limited only to words in the name or

---

1. In LEXIS, the headnote includes only non-West produced headnotes. If the official state reporter has headnotes, they are searchable in LEXIS. Because the *Federal Reporter* and *Federal Supplement* (among other reporters) are published by West Publishing Company and the headnotes are created and copyrighted by it, there is no searchable headnote segment in LEXIS for cases reported in them. Westlaw, by contrast, has the headnotes from the regional reporter in its database.

title of the case, you need not worry about using the normally broad connector *and.*

As you undoubtedly remember, similar research can be done using conventional resources. Case names can be found using the Table of Cases or Defendant-Plaintiff Table in a digest (see section 12.3). The computer, however, allows you to go a step further. On the computer, a title or name search can be combined with other search terms. Thus, if you are preparing for litigation against Sears on a discrimination claim, the following searches could prove useful:

> LEXIS: *name (sears) and employ! w/5 discriminat!*
> Westlaw: *ti (sears) and employ! /s discriminat!*

Citing another suit against the same defendant as authority in current litigation can be quite persuasive. This type of research cannot easily be done using conventional resources.

Another example of a segment/field search that cannot be easily done by conventional means is looking for opinions by a certain judge. With computers, the search is as follows:

> LEXIS: *OPINIONBY (Byrd)* OR
>   *writtenby (Byrd)*
> Westlaw: *JU (Byrd)*

Note

In LEXIS, *opinionby* retrieves cases for which the judge wrote the opinion of the court; *writtenby* retrieves all of the judge's opinions (including concurrences and dissents).

Again, the search can also be tailored to allow searching for opinions on certain topics:

> LEXIS: *opinionby (byrd) and antitrust*
> Westlaw: *ju (byrd) and antitrust*

Sometimes students find it useful when preparing for job interviews to look at cases argued by potential employers. This search can be done with the *counsel* segment (LEXIS) or the *attorney* (or its abbreviation, *at*) field (Westlaw). Finally, sometimes a researcher wants cases only before or after a certain date — perhaps because of legislation changing the law. This can be done with the *date* segment or field.

All of the above are merely examples of what segments and fields are available and how they might be useful. To get more information on what is searchable in LEXIS and Westlaw, consult the documentation provided by the services.

§15.2.11　Cite-Checking Online

a.　Shepard's *Online*

In addition to the full-text searching capacity of documents and parts of documents, both LEXIS and Westlaw have citation services available. By merely typing the appropriate command, you can find in one place all of *Shepard's* entries for a particular case. This display has the advantage over the print version of *Shepard's* of including all the necessary *Shepard's* volumes.

Note

> Unlike *Shepard's* in print form, *Shepard's* online is cumulative.

Another advantage of *Shepard's* online is that the notations in the margins (concerning analysis and treatment) are spelled out in full, making it unnecessary to consult the prefatory material in the book to interpret the abbreviations.

A third advantage of *Shepard's* online is that a copy of a display can be made by merely entering the print command. Finally, from the online *Shepard's* display, you can look at any of the citing cases in the citation list by merely typing the number assigned to that case. The computer will then go to the place in the citing case where the shepardized case is cited. From this screen, you can continue with further research or return to the original *Shepard's* display by entering the appropriate command.

An important point to remember in using *Shepard's* online is that it is the same in content as the print version. It is not any more current. Because one of the oft-repeated advantages of computer-assisted legal research is that many materials are first available online, researchers may mistakenly assume that *Shepard's* is also more current online. This is not true.

b.　*AutoCite and InstaCite*

Both LEXIS and Westlaw do contain a citation service for cases that is more current than *Shepard's*. LEXIS calls its service AutoCite; Westlaw calls its service InstaCite. They are similar to each other, but slightly different from *Shepard's*.

Instead of giving cites to every case that has mentioned the case being researched, AutoCite and InstaCite give citations to only those cases that may affect the validity of the holding in the case being cite-checked. If a later case uses the earlier one as authority for a certain proposition, or if it follows the holding of the earlier decision, it will not appear in the AutoCite or InstaCite display. In other words, the only cases that appear are those that criticize, disagree with, or otherwise change the holding.

The AutoCite or InstaCite display also contains any additional published court proceedings in the same case whether they alter the holding or not. Thus, the services include lower court opinions and related subsequent actions concerning the parties to the suit. AutoCite (LEXIS) also includes any A.L.R. annotations citing the case.

The purpose of AutoCite and InstaCite is strictly citation verification. They exist to answer the question: "Is this case still good law?" Although *Shepard's* online can also be used for citation verification, AutoCite and InstaCite have the advantage of being more current than *Shepard's. Shepard's,* on the other hand, has its own advantage: Besides supplying information on whether an authority is still good, *Shepard's* gives other cases that may provide additional, more recent, or better authority.

Note

Many recently released cases have not been processed into the AutoCite, InstaCite, or *Shepard's* services. However, these cases can still be full-text searched using the techniques previously learned. By using some combination of the case name and cite as search terms, recent cases citing a known case can be found. If the case is a heavily cited authority, a date restriction can be added to limit the number of cases retrieved. For instance, to find recent cases citing the landmark libel case of *New York Times v. Sullivan,* 376 U.S. 254 (1964), the following searches might be used:

    LEXIS: *sullivan pre/5 376 pre/5 254 and date aft 1992*
    Westlaw: *sullivan +S 376 +s 254 and date (after 1992)*

Using LEXIS or Westlaw as a citator does not provide the additional analysis available in the cite-checking services. However, it is the way to find most current cases citing a given authority.

§15.2.12   Costs of Computer-Assisted Legal Research

The single greatest drawback to computer-assisted legal research is its cost, or rather its costs. The computer, printer, and other equipment cost money. A subscription to LEXIS or Westlaw costs money. The searching itself costs money. Depending on how it is done, printing may also cost money. Finally, long-distance phone charges may apply.

The following discussion addresses only those costs charged by LEXIS and Westlaw and not costs such as the purchase of equipment or long-distance charges.

The costs of the LEXIS and Westlaw services are always changing; furthermore, the services sometimes offer special deals. The following, however, are the basic costs:

a. Subscription

In 1992, a subscription to either LEXIS or Westlaw was approximately $125-$150 per month. The price may be reduced if the user guarantees a certain amount of online use each month. The subscription allows access to the services.

b. Search Costs

Once online, you incur additional charges. Typically, both LEXIS and Westlaw bill for the amount of time spent online. In 1992, the rate was approximately $180 per hour, or $3 per minute. Certain larger files or databases (such as those covering all state cases) cost substantially more (approximately 1.75 times the normal rate). All of these prices may be reduced for higher volumes of use.

LEXIS has an alternative method of billing. This second method has two components. The first component is the online charge (like that discussed above). The user is charged a flat rate from sign-on to sign-off. The rate, however, is much lower than that for the other billing method (about 55 cents per minute).

The second component of this billing method is a search charge. Each time you send a search request to the computer (including cite checks), you are charged a fee for the search. The price of a search depends on the size of the file. In 1992, prices ranged from $13 for small files (like those of most individual states) to $26 for larger files (like the one including all state decisions). Cite-checking is less expensive; in 1992, it cost approximately $2.50 per citation checked.

For some searches, the first method of billing is cheaper; for others, the second method is. The LEXIS user, however, cannot elect a method for each search. You choose a billing method and that method attaches to all searches.

c. Printing

There are no printing costs while you are online. However, if you choose to send material to the printer or download material in large portions after sign-off, costs attach. The reason is that if a user prints while online, the services make money through the online charges. If, however, a user signs off while the material is printed or downloaded, that money would be lost. To make up for this loss, in 1992, both LEXIS and Westlaw charged 3 cents per line of text for offline printing and downloading.

As you can see, the use of computers for legal research can be expensive. However, computer-assisted legal research can also save you time, which in turn may save money.

Furthermore, there are some research tasks that can be done on computers that cannot be done using conventional resources. All of these factors — cost, time, research capability — should be considered in choosing any approach to researching a legal problem.

§15.3   ONLINE SEARCH STRATEGIES

Now that we have touched on the various aspects of computer-assisted legal research, we can effectively discuss strategy. This discussion assumes you have decided to do a LEXIS or Westlaw search. (The next chapter will discuss how to choose which research tool is best for a particular issue.)

Step 1: Plan Your Search

The first rule in online searching is to think about the legal problem carefully before going online. Plan your search; know what you will do with the retrieved documents (for example, browse through them or print the cites). Also, have contingency plans in case the search doesn't retrieve what you thought it would. For example, one option is to print the screen that is retrieved and then sign off or enter a command (such as *db* in Westlaw) that stops the billing. You can then look at the printout to determine what went wrong without worrying about online costs accruing.

Step 2: Prepare Search Terms

In creating a computer search, focus on the words that would typically be used in a discussion of the issue. The words may refer to a thing (such as a weapon) a place (such as a store), or a person (such as a child). If any of the words are unique, all the better. And remember, citations are considered words by the computer.

Next, determine any synonyms for those words. They will be combined with each other by an *or* connector. Also, any words that have alternative forms of their root should be truncated.

Step 3: Prepare Connectors and Analyze Their Order

The next step is to identify how the words will be related to each other in a document discussing the issue. How would a judge (or legislator, or author) say this? Based on knowledge of the language and of the law, choose connectors that approximate where you think the words would appear in a relevant document. The ability to approximate effectively is more of an art than a science; you will get better with time and practice.

It is a good idea to write a search out before going online. That way, you can analyze whether connectors will be searched in the proper order. Verify any questionable spellings and check documentation so that you can enter the correct identifier for the file or database without relying on menu screens. You should look for that file or database that contains the potentially relevant documents at the least cost. For example, looking for Arizona cases in the OMNI file of the STATES library on LEXIS, or the ALLSTATES database on Westlaw, rather than in the particular file or database for Arizona, is a costly mistake.

§15.4   OTHER COMPUTERIZED RESEARCH SERVICES

Apart from LEXIS and Westlaw, other vendors offer computer-assisted research products. These online research services offer access to materials that are primarily nonlegal and that concern all aspects of life. They contain material such as scientific and technical publications, statistics, and current awareness information. Some of this information might be useful to you in a particular case.

Probably the most prominent of these services is called DIALOG. Although DIALOG is now available through Westlaw, it is also available independent of Westlaw.

In law, the only other noteworthy full-text online retrieval service is called View-Text. View-Text is like a scaled-down version of LEXIS. It accesses only A.L.R. annotations, but its costs are much lower than those of LEXIS and Westlaw.

Increasingly, legal publishers are publishing their materials in CD-ROM format. The information available through these services is obtained from the compact disc rather than from a mainframe computer via phone lines. It is not as current, then, as services such as LEXIS and Westlaw, but no phone charges are incurred.

CD-ROM services may include bibliographic citations and indexing or indexing only (for example, WILSONDISC's *Index to Legal Periodicals* or Infotrac's *Legaltrac*). They may include abstracts as well as bibliographic records (for example, Congressional Information Service's *CIS Abstracts*). They may also be full-text (for example, West Publishing's CD-ROM version of *Federal Practice and Procedure* or Matthew Bender's *Taxmaster*).

CD-ROM products can be expensive. The format, however, is ideal for printed matter that takes up large amounts of space or is difficult to access even with an index. The value of the ability to look for any terms in a document is hard to overestimate, especially in obscure subjects. Furthermore, it may be less expensive to spend a large amount of money once to purchase a CD-ROM product than to spend a smaller amount of money time and again over the years for a subscription or for search costs.

Each of these CD-ROM products and other available computerized resources uses different search conventions. Documentation or instruction is usually available from the vendors.

Section Summary	*Computer-Assisted Legal Research*

Type: Primary authority, secondary authority, finding aid

Sources: Computer-assisted legal research is an alternative means for accessing many sources. Statutes, cases, secondary sources and *Shepard's* are all available online.

In computer-assisted legal research the primary basic search is the word. By using words and connectors, you can bypass using indices. Many materials are available online before they are available in other formats. Some materials are only available online.

The key question concerning computer-assisted research is whether, in a given situation, it is time-efficient and cost-effective.

Chapter 16

How to Approach a Legal Research Problem: Sample Research Plans

Although each client's case is unique, the process of researching each legal question is not. Just as there are standard plans for organizing an objective memorandum, opinion letter, and brief, there are also standard research plans.

One of those plans, the plan for doing statutory research, is set out in Chapter 5. Section 5.4 describes the planning process, and section 5.5 shows how an attorney would do the research itself.

This chapter builds on this material and the material set out in Chapters 9 through 15, providing you with research plans for the most common types of research problems. Although these plans may need to be modified to fit your particular problem, they provide the basic framework for researching each type of problem.

In using these plans, begin by determining the type of research. Is the issue governed by statute? common law? administrative rule or regulation? international law? If you are unsure, consult a secondary source covering the subject area. Then go through the steps outlined in section 5.4: (1) draft a preliminary issue statement, (2) determine what law governs, (3) decide what sources to use, and (4) prepare a list of search terms. Also remember the value of doing background reading. The time spent obtaining an overview of the area of law almost always makes the subsequent research, analysis, and writing more efficient and more sophisticated.

The following is a list of the research plans presented in this chapter.

Plan 1   Statutory Research: When the Governing Statute Is Known
Plan 2   Statutory Research: When the Governing Statute Is Not Known
Plan 3   Statutory Research: Federal Legislative Histories
Plan 4   Federal Administrative Law
Plan 5   Common Law Research: When the Name of the Case Setting Out the Common Law Rule Is Known
Plan 6   Common Law Research: When the Name of the Case Setting Out the Common Law Rule Is Not Known
Plan 7   Procedural Issues
Plan 8   International Law

Research Plan 1
Statutory Research: When the Governing Statute Is Known

Legal Question: Whether a particular statute applies or how a particular statute should be interpreted or applied.

Jurisdiction: (Can be either federal or state)

Type of Law: Statutory

Search Terms: _____

Step 1:   Using the statute's section number, locate the text of the statute in the main volume of the annotated code. (If you know the title of the statute but not its number, use the Popular Name Table.)

Step 2:   Update the statute using the pocket part and other supplementation, *Shepard's,* and, if there is a possibility of recent legislative action, LEXIS or Westlaw.

Step 3:   Read and analyze the statute, applying the language of the statute to the facts of the client's case. Also locate and read (a) the official comments, if any, (b) any introductory sections (for example, sections setting out the purpose or effective date), and (c) any cross-references.

Step 4:   If it is clear that the elements are (or are not) met, stop. If it is not clear whether the elements are met, continue.

Step 5:   Locate cases interpreting and applying the statute using the Notes of Decision that follow the text of the statute in the annotated code. To locate recent cases, use the pocket part and *Shepard's.*

Step 6:   Analyze and shepardize those cases that appear useful.

Step 7:   If necessary, locate and analyze persuasive authority. Use LEXIS, Westlaw, the regional or decennial digests, *American Law Reports* (A.L.R.), or *Uniform Laws Annotated* (U.L.A.) to locate cases from other jurisdictions. Use the *Index to Legal Periodicals* (I.L.P.), *Current Law Index* (C.L.I.), *Current Index to Legal Periodicals* (C.I.L.P.), or LEXIS or Westlaw to locate law review articles.

Step 8:   If necessary, check the legislative history. (See Research Plan No. 3.)

Research Plan 2
Statutory Research: When the Governing Statute Is Not Known

Legal Question: Whether a particular statute applies or how a particular statute should be interpreted or applied.

Jurisdiction: (Can be either federal or state)

Type of Law: Statutory

Search Terms: _____

Step 1:   Use the subject or topic index to locate the numbers of the potentially relevant statutory sections. (Use the search terms listed above; as a general rule, move gradually from the narrowest to the broadest search term.) Look up those sections in the main volumes of the annotated code.

Step 2:   Update the relevant statutory sections using the pocket part and other supplementation, *Shepard's,* and, if there is a possibility of recent legislative action, LEXIS or Westlaw.

Step 3:   Read and analyze the statute, applying the language of the statute to the facts of the client's case. Also locate and read (a) the official comments, if any, (b) any introductory sections (for example, sections setting out the purpose or effective date), and (c) any cross-references.

Step 4:   If it is clear that the elements are (or are not) met, stop. If it is not clear whether the elements are met, continue.

Step 5:   Locate potentially applicable cases using the Notes of Decision following the statute, the pocket part, and *Shepard's.*

Step 6:   Analyze and shepardize those cases that appear useful.

Step 7: If necessary, locate and analyze persuasive authority. Use LEXIS, Westlaw, the regional or decennial digests, *American Law Reports* (A.L.R.), or *Uniform Laws Annotated* (U.L.A.) to locate cases from other jurisdictions. Use the *Index to Legal Periodicals* (I.L.P.), *Current Law Index* (C.L.I.), *Current Index to Legal Periodicals* (C.I.L.P.), or LEXIS or Westlaw to locate law review articles.

Step 8: If necessary, check the legislative history. (See Research Plan No. 3.)

Research Plan 3
Statutory Research: Federal Legislative Histories

Legal Question: Whether a particular statute applies or how a particular statute should be interpreted or applied.

Jurisdiction: Federal

Type of Law: Statutory

Search Terms:

Step 1: Using Nancy Johnson's *Compiled Sources of Legislative History,* determine whether there is a prepared legislative history. If there is, locate and use that history.

Step 2: If there is no prepared legislative history, use the historical information following the text of the statute to determine the date on which the statute was enacted.

Step 3: If the statute was enacted before 1941, use the Congressional Index Service (C.I.S.) indices (Serial Set Index, Committee Print Index, and Committee Hearing Index) to locate references to reports, hearings, prints, and other documents. The documents themselves are available on microfiche in most large or government depository libraries. Use the indices to the *Congressional Record* or *Congressional Globe* to locate references to the pages on which the floor debates appear.

If the statute was enacted between 1941 and 1969, use *United States Code, Congressional and Administrative News* (U.S.C.C.A.N.) to locate excerpts from House and Senate hearings and reports and the dates the act was considered in Congress. The dates of consideration can then be used to locate relevant material in the *Congressional Record.* The full text of House and Senate hearings and reports can often be found on microfiche in large libraries or in federal depositories.

If the statute was enacted after 1969, locate citations to House and Senate Hearings, House and Senate Reports, and the *Congressional Record* using the Abstracts (Volume 1) and Index (Volume 2) of Congressional Information Service (C.I.S.) for the year the statute was enacted. The full text of the hearings and reports can then be found on microfiche available in most large libraries or federal depositories. The relevant portions of the *Congressional Record* can be found using the dates of consideration.

Note: U.S.C.C.A.N. can also be used for statutes enacted after 1969. It is not, however, as comprehensive as C.I.S.

For more about the sources cited, see section 10.2.

Research Plan 4
Federal Administrative Law

Legal Question: Whether a particular federal regulation applies or how a particular federal regulation has been interpreted or applied.

Jurisdiction: Federal

Type of Law: Enacted

Search Terms: _____

Step 1: Determine whether there is a looseleaf or similar service that brings together the relevant statutes, regulations, administrative decisions, and commentary. If there is, read the "How to Use This Set" section at the beginning of the set to determine (a) what the set contains, (b) how the set is organized and indexed, and (c) when and how the material contained in the set is updated. Then use the set to research the question.

Step 2: If there is no looseleaf or similar service or if the looseleaf service does not contain all of the necessary information, use Research Plan 2 to locate the citation to the relevant United States Code section.

Step 3: Locate the citations to the relevant federal regulations using (a) the index to the *Code of Federal Regulations* (C.F.R.), (b) the cross-reference tables in the "Index and Finding Aids to the Code of Federal Regulations" volume to the *United States Code Service* (U.S.C.S.), or (c) a key word search in LEXIS or Westlaw.

Step 4:   Using the citations, locate and read the relevant regulations in the main volumes of the *Code of Federal Regulations* (C.F.R.).

Step 5:   Update the C.F.R. using the "List of Sections Affected" volumes of the C.F.R. Further update, using "C.F.R. Parts Affected During (Month)" tables located at the back of the most recent volumes of the *Federal Register* (check the volumes for the periods not covered by the "List of Sections Affected") or LEXIS or Westlaw.

Step 6:   Apply the regulation to the facts of the client's case. If the application is clear, stop. If the application is not clear, continue.

Step 7:   Use *Shepard's* to locate cases, law review articles, and other materials discussing the relevant regulations. Cases can also be found in looseleafs, online, or as separately published government publications. If you have difficulty locating cases, try calling the agency. For federal agencies, phone numbers can be located using the United States Government Manual.

Step 8:   Read and analyze the materials located. Remember to shepardize cases to determine (a) whether they are still good law and (b) whether there are more recent cases on point.

Research Plan 5
Common Law Research: When the Name of the Case Setting Out the Common Law Rule Is Known

Legal Question: Whether a particular common law rule applies or how a particular common law rule has been interpreted or applied.

Jurisdiction: (Can be either federal or state)

Type of Law: Common Law

Search Terms: _____

Step 1:   If appropriate, do background reading in a legal encyclopedia, hornbook, treatise, practice book, *American Law Reports* (A.L.R.), or law review to obtain an overview of the area of law.

Step 2:   If the citation to the case is known, locate the case in the official or regional reporter. (If possible, use a reporter published by West; this will allow you to use West's Key Number System to find additional cases.) If the citation is not known, locate the citation using the Plaintiff-Defendant or Defendant-Plaintiff tables in the digest or *Shepard's.*

Step 3: Read and analyze the case.

Step 4: If the case is on point, shepardize it using *Shepard's* and, for the most recent information, LEXIS or Westlaw.

Step 5: If the case answers the question, stop. If it does not, locate additional cases from the same jurisdiction by looking up (a) the cases cited by the court in its opinion, (b) the applicable key numbers in the digest for that jurisdiction, or (c) the relevant citations from *Shepard's.*

Step 6: Read, analyze, and shepardize cases found as a result of Step 5 and follow up on any additional leads (citations found in decisions or *Shepard's*).

Step 7: If necessary, locate and analyze persuasive authority. Use LEXIS, Westlaw, the regional or decennial digests, or A.L.R. to locate cases from other jurisdictions. Use the *Index to Legal Periodicals* (I.L.P.), *Current Law Index* (C.L.I.), *Current Index to Legal Periodicals* (C.I.L.P.), or LEXIS or Westlaw to locate law review articles.

Research Plan 6
Common Law Research: When the Name of the Case Setting Out the Common Law Rule Is Not Known

Legal Question: Whether a particular common law rule applies or how a particular common law rule has been interpreted or applied.

Jurisdiction: (Usually state)

Type of Law: Common Law

Search Terms:

Step 1: If appropriate, do background reading in a legal encyclopedia, hornbook, treatise, practice book, *American Law Reports* (A.L.R.), or a law review to obtain an overview of the area of law. If the name of a case is located, switch to Research Plan 5: When the Name of the Case Setting Out the Common Law Rule Is Known. If a case is not located, continue.

Step 2: Locate cases using either the applicable digest or LEXIS or Westlaw. If you use a digest, use the subject or topic index to locate the potentially applicable topic headings and, if it is a West publication, key numbers. (As a general rule, begin with your narrowest search term and then move gradually to the broadest.) If you use LEXIS or Westlaw, select the appropriate library and file (or database) and search, using terms that are likely to have been used by the courts.

Step 3:   Look up the applicable topic headings and key numbers. Read through the Notes of Decisions, identifying the five or six cases that appear most useful.

Step 4:   Locate, read, and analyze the cases identified as part of Step 3. If the cases appear useful, shepardize them (a) to determine whether they are still good law and (b) to locate additional cases.

Step 5:   If the cases answer the question, stop. If they do not, locate additional cases from the same jurisdiction by looking up (a) additional cases from the Notes of Decision, (b) cases cited by the courts in their opinions, or (c) cases listed in *Shepard's.*

Step 6:   Read, analyze, and shepardize the cases found as a result of Step 5 and follow up on any additional leads (citations found in decisions or *Shepard's*).

Step 7:   If necessary, locate and analyze persuasive authority. Use LEXIS, Westlaw, the regional or decennial digests, or A.L.R. to locate cases from other jurisdictions. Use the *Index to Legal Periodicals* (I.L.P.), *Current Law Index* (C.L.I.), *Current Index to Legal Periodicals* (C.I.L.P.), or LEXIS or Westlaw to locate law review articles.

Research Plan 7
Procedural Issues

Legal Question: Whether a particular procedural rule applies or how a particular procedural rule has been interpreted or applied.

Jurisdiction: (Can be state, federal, or local)

Type of Law: Procedural

Search Terms: _____

Step 1:   If necessary, do background reading to determine whether the issue is governed by a court rule or by statute or other authority. Practice books are usually the most helpful.

Step 2: Once you have determined the type of authority (for example, court rule or statute), use the index in the appropriate set to locate the applicable rule or rules. Check the pocket part or other supplementation to make sure that you have the current version of the rule.

Step 3: Read and analyze the rule and the official comments, if any. If the rule answers the question, stop. If it does not, continue.

Step 4: Use the Notes of Decision following the rule or *Shepard's* to locate cases interpreting or applying the rule. Update these sources using *Shepard's*.

Step 5: If necessary, locate secondary sources discussing the rule and its application. Treatises are often a good source. Note: Because many state rules are modeled on the federal rules, commentary on the federal rules may be relevant to state court interpretations.

Step 6: For some procedural issues, it may be necessary to locate the appropriate form. Look for references to forms in annotated codes, practice books, and specialized form books.

Research Plan 8
International Law

Although international law and research are beyond the scope of this book, we have included this research plan to assist those students competing in Jessup, the international law moot court competition.

There are two branches of international law: public international law and private international law. Public international law focuses on the relationships among nations (usually referred to as states). In contrast, private international law focuses on the relationships among individuals or entities in different states. Most Jessup questions involve questions of public international law.

In public international law, the four most important sources of law are (1) international conventions (treaties and other international agreements), (2) international custom, (3) general principles of law recognized by civilized nations, and (4) judicial decisions and teachings of the most highly qualified publicists (expert commentators) of the various nation states. See Article 38(1) of the Statutes of the International Court of Justice.

Step 1: Begin by doing background reading to familiarize yourself with the basic concepts and terminology. An excellent source is *An Introduction to International Law* by Mark W. Janis (Little, Brown, 1988).

Step 2: Use the *Index to Legal Periodicals* and the *Index to Foreign Legal Periodicals* to locate law review articles discussing, in either general or specific terms, the type of international dispute in question.

Step 3: Locate and read potentially applicable articles. Note the issues discussed and the authorities cited.

Step 4: Identify and locate the relevant treaties. If the United States is a probable signatory, use *Treaties in Force* or *A Guide to Treaties in Force.* If the United States is not a signatory, use *Multilateral Treaties: Index and Current Status.*

   The text of treaties to which the United States is a signatory can usually be found in *United States Treaties and Other International Agreements.* To find the text of treaties to which the United States is not a signatory check the *Consolidated Treaty Series,* the *United Nations Treaty Series,* and the *League of Nations Treaty Series.*

Step 5: Determine if the states involved in the dispute are currently signatories and thus bound by the treaty. (Even if a party is not a signatory, you may be able to use the treaty as evidence of international custom.)

Step 6: Analyze the text of the treaty.

Step 7: Look for additional authority: for example, look for evidence of custom, general principles of law, judicial decisions, and teachings of publicists. Useful sources for this research include the *Restatement of the Law, The Foreign Relations Law of the United States 3d, The Encyclopedia of Public International Law, Principles of Public International Law* by Ian Brownlie, and articles from law reviews and other legal periodicals.

   Note: Because the International Court of Justice and other international judicial tribunals decide so few cases, it is unlikely that you will find a case "on point." You may, however, be able to use the principles enunciated in those cases. Decisions of the International Court of Justice are published in its *Reports of Judgments, Advisory Opinions and Orders.* Recent decisions are also available online on LEXIS and Westlaw. The decisions of other tribunals (for example, the Court of Justice of the European Community or the European Court of Human Rights) can be located in major law libraries and are increasingly available online.

Step 8: Update the materials you have found. Although this updating is not easy, the following steps should be taken: (a) shepardize treaties and international agreements to which the United States is a signatory using *Shepard's United States Citations;* (b) use LEXIS or Westlaw to find recent law review articles and citations to pre-existing authorities; (c) use *International Legal Materials* to determine whether new documents have been published on the subject.

Another way of double-checking your research is to begin your research from a different starting point than your original one. If you end up with the same result, you are probably safe.

A reminder: International law is governed by different principles than the domestic law of the United States. Understanding those principles is the key component in doing effective research in international law.

Part IV

A Guide to Citation

Chapter 17

Legal Citation

An important part of legal writing is the citation to legal authority. In an effort to standardize legal citation form, a detailed set of citation rules has been developed. These rules are contained in *The Bluebook: A Uniform System of Citation,*[1] a publication of the Harvard Law Review Association. Unfortunately, many law students find the *Bluebook* overly complex and difficult to use. This chapter is an attempt to demystify the *Bluebook.* It is intended as a guide to the *Bluebook,* not a substitute for it.

The chapter is designed for use by first-year law students in their legal writing course. Thus, it includes only those citation rules that apply to the types of authority most commonly cited in legal writing papers. For citations to other types of authority, such as legislative and administrative materials, looseleaf services, and international materials, consult the *Bluebook* itself.

To properly form a citation, you must know what components it should contain and how to put them together. This can be learned from the rules that apply to each type of authority. But always keep in mind the basic common-sense rule: A citation should contain the information necessary for a reader to easily look up any reference that you have made.

§17.1   UNDERSTANDING THE *BLUEBOOK*

One of the keys to using the *Bluebook* effectively is to understand how it is organized. Start by perusing the table of contents on pages ix-xvii and the section entitled "Introduction" on pages 3-9.

---

1. All references in this chapter are to the 15th edition, published in 1991.

§17.1.1　Thumb Index

Notice the back cover of the *Bluebook*. The *Bluebook* is divided into eleven sections, easily accessible by using the thumb index.

§17.1.2　Examples

Examples of all basic citation forms are located on the inside front and back covers. Examples of basic citation forms for each type of authority are located at the beginning of the rule on that type of authority. See, for example, rules 10.1, 12.1, 13.1, 14.1, and 19.1.

§17.1.3　Tables

Section T contains tables illustrating specific citation forms and abbreviations for all courts, reporters, and statutory and administrative compilations, both federal and state. Similar tables for foreign jurisdictions are also found in section T.

§17.1.4　Rules 1-9

Rules 1-9 contain general rules of citation and style as opposed to the specific rules for citation to certain types of authority found in Rules 10-20. The general rules apply to all types of citations. They should be read carefully; they will be referred to throughout this chapter.

§17.1.5　Typeface Conventions

It is important to note that most of the examples in section R of the *Bluebook* are in the printer's typefaces required for law review footnotes. See Rule 2 for an explanation of typeface conventions for law review text and footnotes.

However, most law school students use word processors or typewriters. Therefore, they should follow the simpler typeface conventions set forth in Practitioners' Note P.1 and in all examples found in the Practitioners' Notes (section P). In other words, what is italicized in the *Bluebook* should be in italics or underlined; what is in large and small capitals or ordinary roman type should be in ordinary roman type. One exception to this rule is book titles (Rule 15), which should be italicized or underlined. Compare the examples on the inside back cover (Quick Reference: Court Documents and Legal Memoranda) with those on the inside front cover (Quick Reference: Law Review Footnotes).

§17.1.6   Index

When in doubt, consult the index (section X). It is detailed and quite helpful. Note that the page numbers in roman type lead to instructions or rules, while those in italic type refer to examples of citation forms.

§17.2   FORMING CITATIONS TO CASES

First-year law students studying legal writing and research generally cite more to cases than to any other type of legal authority. This reflects the "case analysis" style of legal education prevalent at most law schools.

The rules for citing cases, found in section R10 of the *Bluebook,* are somewhat more complex than those for statutes and most other types of authority. Rule 10.1 lists the components that a citation to a case should contain.

§17.2.1   Name

Read rules 10.2.1 and 10.2.2 carefully to understand how to modify the case name that appears at the beginning of the opinion. Do not rely on the version of the name used in the running head in the reporter; legal publishing companies do not always use *Bluebook* format.

If you are using the case name as part of a citation, abbreviate any words listed in Table T.6 and use the geographical abbreviations listed in Table T.10. If you are using the case name as part of a sentence in the text, only abbreviate the words in rule 10.2.1(c). Remember: Never abbreviate the first word of the name of a party or "United States."

§17.2.2   Reporter

Consult the tables in section T to determine what reporter(s) to cite and how to abbreviate them. Include in the citation a volume designation, the abbreviated name of the reporter, and the page on which the case report begins. Rule 10.3.2. The parallel citation to the official reporter is required in only two situations: (1) when you are writing a brief, and (2) when the case you are citing is a case from your own state. Do not give a parallel citation for United States Supreme Court cases. See page 165 of the *Bluebook.*

For all other legal documents, cite *only* to the appropriate West regional reporter. Rule 10.3.1(b).

Note

Because this chapter is aimed primarily at first-year law students, the examples reflect the 15th edition's elimination of parallel citations to official state reporters. However, if the legal writing or moot court program requires students to write briefs or other documents for submission to a moot court, the citations should include a citation to the official state reporter as well as the West regional reporter. See Practitioners' Note P.3; see also section 7.10.2(c) of this book for an example of this citation form.

_____

§17.2.3 Court and Date

The year the case was decided must appear in parentheses after the citation. Rule 10.5. In addition, that parenthetical phrase should contain a designation of the court (including its geographical jurisdiction) that decided the case. Rule 10.4.

a. State Cases

For state decisions, indicate the state (abbreviated according to Table T.10), the deciding court (abbreviated according to Table T.7), and the date of the decision in the parenthetical following the citation. For example:

Connelly v. Puget Sound Collections, 553 P.2d 1354 (Wash. Ct. App. 1976)

Do not include the name of the court if it is the highest court of the state (usually the state supreme court):

Hangman Ridge Training Stables, Inc. v. Safeco Title Ins. Co., 719 P.2d 531 (Wash. 1986)

b. Federal Cases

In citations to cases of the United States Court of Appeals, published in the *Federal Reporter,* give the number of the circuit in the parenthetical. There is no need to indicate what state the case came from:

Kuehner v. Schweiker, 717 F.2d 813 (3d Cir. 1983)

In citations to federal district court cases, published in the *Federal Supplement,* give the district in the parenthetical. Note that some states have more than one geographical district, while others have only one (for example, D. Mass. or D.D.C.) (Rule 10.4(a)):

Wilk v. American Medical Ass'n, 671 F. Supp. 1465 (N.D. Ill. 1987)

§17.2.4 Subsequent History

The subsequent history of a case is discovered through shepardizing. All subsequent history must be appended to the primary citation, with the exception of history on remand or any denial of a rehearing, the first time the case is cited. Rule 10.7. Use the explanatory phrases (underlined or italicized) listed in Table T.9. If the two opinions were decided in the same year, include the date only after the subsequent history. For example:

United States v. Neelly, 202 F.2d 221 (7th Cir.), *cert. denied,* 345 U.S. 997 (1953)

If they were decided in different years, include both dates (Rule 10.5(c)):

Quick Point Pencil Co. v. Aronson, 425 F. Supp. 600 (E.D. Mo. 1976), *rev'd,* 567 F.2d 757 (8th Cir. 1977)

§17.2.5 Other Parenthetical Information

Any other pertinent information can be supplied in another parenthetical following the citation. See the examples of the types of information that can be given parenthetically in Rule 10.6. It is important to indicate in a parenthetical the nature of the holding if it is not the single, clear holding of a majority of the court (for example, dictum, dissenting opinion, plurality opinion, and so on). It is also important to provide information regarding the weight of the authority (for example, 2-1 decision, per curiam, mem., en banc). See also Rule 1.5 on parenthetical information generally.

§17.2.6 Spacing

Consult Rule 6.1(a) for proper spacing of citations. Remember: Close up adjacent single capitals (numbers are treated as single capitals):

N.W.2d   F.2d   W.D.N.Y.   A.L.R.4th

Do not close up single capitals with longer abbreviations:

Wash. 2d   So. 2d   F. Supp.   U. Pa. L. Rev.

Notice that in the above examples, there is no period after an ordinal number indicating a series.

§17.3   FORMING CITATIONS TO STATUTES

Citations to statutes, as well as to constitutions and legislative, administrative, and executive materials, are governed by section R 11-14. All citations to statutes should contain the following components: (1) if necessary, the volume or title number; (2) the abbreviated name of the code; (3) the section, paragraph, or article number of the statute; and (4) the date of the code. (Use the year the code volume was published, not the year the statute was enacted.) Rule 12.3.

§17.3.1   Federal Codes

If possible, cite to the official code, which is the United States Code (U.S.C.). Rules 12.2.1, 12.3. Only cite to an unofficial code if the statute has not yet appeared in U.S.C. Note that if you cite to a code that is not published by the federal or state government, you must give the name of the publisher, editor, or compiler in the parenthetical phrase that contains the year of the code (Rule 12.3.1(d)):

36 U.S.C. § 1301 (1988)

36 U.S.C.A. § 1301 (West 1988)

36 U.S.C.S. § 1301 (Law. Co-op. 1981)

a. Supplements, Official Code

In general, cite to the latest version of U.S.C., which is published every six years. The latest edition is 1988. Every year after the main volumes are published, a yearly supplement is added.

If the complete statute is in the main volume, cite only to it:

18 U.S.C. § 474 (1988)

If the statute was enacted before 1988, but amended afterwards, cite to both the main volume and the supplement in which the amendment first appears:

25 U.S.C. § 1613 (1988 & Supp. I 1989)

If the statute was enacted after 1988, cite only to the supplement in which it first appears:

16 U.S.C. § 4301 (Supp. I 1989)

b.   Supplements, Unofficial Code

The supplements to the unofficial codes are generally cumulative; that is, each yearly supplement supersedes the supplement for the previous year. Thus, when citing statutes enacted after the main volumes were published, cite only to the latest supplement:

7 U.S.C.A. § 18 (West 1980 & Supp. 1990)

21 U.S.C.S. § 1301 (Law. Co-op. Supp. 1990)

See generally Rules 12.3.1(e), 3.2(c).

§17.3.2   State Codes

State codes vary widely in the format of their citations. Consult the tables in Table T.1 to determine what components the citation should contain and how to abbreviate them. The material is located under the heading "statutory compilations."

Some state codes are divided into titles or chapters, each separately sectioned. For example:

Ill. Ann. Stat. ch. 48, para. 138.2 (Smith-Hurd 1986)

In others, each section is differently numbered; there is no need to indicate the volume, chapter, or title number separately (Rule 12.3.1(b)):

Conn. Gen. Stat. Ann. § 16-230 (West 1988)

Some state codes are divided by subject-matter title, which must be included in the citation (Rule 12.3(c)):

N.Y. Dom. Rel. Law § 109 (McKinney 1988 & Supp. 1990)

§17.3.3   Parenthetical Information

Explanatory parenthetical phrases after a citation can be useful when citing statutes as well as cases. See Rule 12.7 for the types of information that can be conveyed this way. See also Rule 1.5 on parenthetical information generally.

§17.3.4   Symbols, Spacing, and Punctuation

Always use section symbols in citations; however, in text, the word "section" should be spelled out. Rule 6.2(b).

When citing multiple sections, use two section symbols. If citing consecutive sections, give inclusive numbers (Rule 3.4(b)):

42 U.S.C. §§ 1471-1490 (1988)

Identical numbers or letters preceding a punctuation mark may be omitted:

Wash. Rev. Code §§ 7.70.010-.090 (1989)

If a hyphen or dash would be confusing, use the word "to" to indicate consecutive sections:

Colo. Rev. Stat. Ann. §§ 34-60-101 to -123

When citing scattered sections, separate the sections with commas:

Cal. Veh. Code §§ 22349, 22364 (West Supp. 1990)

When citing multiple *subsections* within a section, use only one section symbol. Note that there is a space between the final section and the date, but not between the main section and the subsection. For example:

26 U.S.C. § 166(j)(1)-(6) (1988)

In general, use the original punctuation separating sections from subsections (Rule 3.4(a)):

N.D. Cent. Code § 25-03.1-21 (1978)

La. Rev. Stat. Ann. § 12:803 (West 1969)

§17.3.5   Special Statutory Citation Forms

Some types of enactments require special, usually simplified, citation forms.

a.   Procedural and Court Rules

Current federal and state court rules and procedural rules, such as rules of civil procedure, criminal procedure, or evidence are cited according to Rule 12.8.3. Use abbreviations from the list in T.7 and T.10

and the examples given in the *Bluebook* and below. No date is necessary. For example:

Fed. R. Evid. 802

Wash. Super. Ct. Civ. R. 56

b. Uniform Acts

Uniform acts can be cited as part of the code of a state that has adopted the uniform act, with or without the title of the act:

Unif. Child Custody Jurisdiction Act, Wash. Rev. Code § 26.27.030 (1990) *OR*

Wash. Rev. Code § 26.27.030 (1990)

If not citing to the law of a particular state, include a citation to *Uniform Laws Annotated.* Include the year in which the uniform act was last amended (Rule 12.8.4):

Unif. Child Custody Jurisdiction Act § 3, 9 U.L.A. 115 (1988)

c. Restatements

Cite to a restatement by section and include the date it was adopted or most recently amended (usually indicated on the title page) (Rule 12.8.5):

Restatement (Second) of Property § 2.2 (1977)

§17.4 FORMING CITATIONS TO SECONDARY SOURCES

The term "secondary source" is used to refer to authorities that discuss, analyze, or comment on the law but do not contain the law itself (as do cases and statutes). Books, treatises, periodicals, and annotations are all considered secondary sources and may be used as persuasive authority in your writing. The general rules for all books and periodicals are found in section R 15-17 of the *Bluebook.*

§17.4.1 Books

For purposes of this chapter, a "book" is defined as a single-volume monograph. Multivolume works are referred to as "treatises" and are discussed in section 17.4.2 below.

a.   Components of the Citation

A citation to a book should contain the following components: (1) the author's full name as it appears on the publication (Rule 15.1.1); (2) the full main title as it appears on the title page (Rule 15.2); (3) in parentheses, an indication of the edition, if there has been more than one, and the year of publication (Rule 15.4); and (4) if desired, an indication of the page or section number (or both) on which the cited material appears (Rule 3.3(a)).

Remember: The examples in section R of the *Bluebook* are given in the typeface for law review footnotes. In typewritten briefs and memoranda, the author's name should appear in ordinary roman type, and the title should be underlined or italicized. Practitioners' Note P.1(b).

Use an ampersand to connect multiple authors, but do not use any abbreviations in the book title (Rule 15.2):

Earl W. Kintner & Jack L. Lahr, *An Intellectual Property Law Primer* 207 (1982)

Laurence H. Tribe, *American Constitutional Law* § 3-20, at 147 (2d ed. 1988)

b.   Institutional Authors

If the author of the book is an institution, the citation must contain its complete name, abbreviated. Use the same abbreviations suggested for case names in Table T.6 and the geographical abbreviations in Table T.10. In addition, the words "United States" may be abbreviated. If necessary, include both the subdivision that prepared the work and the body of which the subdivision is a part (Rule 15.1.3(a)):

Office of Legal Policy, U.S. Dep't of Justice, *Wrong Turns on the Road to Judicial Activism: The Ninth Amendment and the Privileges and Immunities Clause* 72 (1988)

c.   Special Citation Forms

Some well-known books require special citation forms. Two examples are given below; see Rule 15.7 for others.

Black's Law Dictionary 1506 (6th ed. 1990)

The Federalist No. 37, at 231 (James Madison) (J. Cooke ed., 1982)

§17.4.2   Treatises

The term "treatise" is usually applied to multivolume reference works. Most federal and state practice guides are also cited as treatises. Citations to treatises must contain the same components as citations to books; additionally, they should contain a reference to the volume of the treatise (Rule 3.2(a)):

4 Charles Alan Wright & Arthur Raphael Miller, *Federal Practice and Procedure* § 1027 (2d ed. 1987)

IA Barbara Barker & Irene Scharf, *Washington Practice: Methods of Practice* § 37.6 (3d ed. 1989)

Many treatises are supplemented with pocket parts or separately bound pamphlets. If the cited material appears only in the supplement or is divided between the main volume and the supplement, that fact should be indicated in the citation (Rules 15.4(e) and 3.2(c)):

3A John Allen Appleman, *Insurance Law and Practice* § 1760 (1967 & Supp. 1990)

§17.4.3   Legal Encyclopedias

Citations to legal encyclopedias should contain the following components: (1) the volume number; (2) the abbreviated title; (3) the title of the subject article; (4) a reference to the section of the article being cited; and (5) in parentheses, the year of the volume and any indication of use of a supplement. For example:

27 Am. Jur. 2d *Eminent Domain* § 499 (1966)

70 C.J.S. *Physicians, Surgeons, and Other Health Care Providers* § 69 (1987 & Supp. 1990)

§17.4.4   Periodicals

The periodicals most often cited in law school papers are law reviews or law journals. Annotations and newspapers are, however, also treated as periodicals. See generally Rule 16.

a.   *Components of the Citation*

A citation to a legal periodical should contain the following components: (1) the author's full name; (2) the title of the article, italicized or underlined; (3) the volume number of the journal; (4) the name of the journal, abbreviated according to the lists in Tables T.13 and T.10.; (5) the beginning page number of the article; and (6) the year of publication in parentheses. For example:

> Frances Kahn Zemans, *Fee Shifting and the Implementation of Public Policy,* 47 Law & Contemp. Probs. 187 (1984)

If the journal has no volume number, use the year of publication as the volume and omit the date in parentheses (Rule 16.2):

> Robinson O. Everett, *The New Look in Military Justice,* 1973 Duke L.J. 649

b. Student-Written Articles

Law review pieces written by students are usually designated as notes, comments, casenotes, or projects. The citation should contain the student's full name as it appears at the beginning or end of the piece, followed by the designation, then the title. (If the piece is unsigned or signed with initials, include only the designation.) Rule 16.5.1.

> Jakob S. Harle, Comment, *Challenging Rent Control: Strategies for Attack,* 34 UCLA L. Rev. 149 (1986)

> Daniel W. Galvin, Note, *The Effect of Tax Foreclosure Sales on Servitudes: Olympia v. Palzer,* 11 U. Puget Sound L. Rev. 193 (1987)

c. Annotations

A citation to an article in *American Law Reports* (A.L.R.) is similar to a periodical citation. Give the author's full name, followed by the designation "Annotation." The citation should refer to the beginning page of the annotation, not the case being analyzed. Include the date of the volume, not the case. For example:

> Danny R. Veilleux, Annotation, *Medical Practitioner's Liability for Treatment Given Child Without Parent's Consent,* 67 A.L.R.4th 511 (1989)

d. Newspapers

Citations to newspaper articles are governed by Rule 16.4. The citation form for signed articles is similar to that for periodical articles, except that the complete date and a designation of the section should be included. Use Table T.13 as a guide for abbreviating the newspaper title. For example:

> Gail Diane Cox, *Right-to-Die Cases Raise Questions on Quality of Life,* Nat'l L.J., Dec. 17, 1990, at A3

§17.5   Using Citations

Although the *Bluebook* supplies all the information we need to form citations, it doesn't always make it clear how to use citations in your legal writing. The following discussion is meant to clarify the most important style rules found in section R 1-9 of the *Bluebook.*

§17.5.1   Generally

Provide a citation to authority whenever you state a rule, proposition, holding, or quotation from a case, statute, or other authority. Citations may be made in either of two ways: in citation clauses or in citation sentences. Rule 1.1.

A citation clause is formed by including a citation, set off by commas, as part of a sentence.

EXAMPLE

In *Benton v. Johncox,* 49 P. 495, 499 (Wash. 1897), the court referred to the "natural flow" variation of the riparian doctrine.

In a citation sentence, the citation or citations form a separate sentence, beginning with a capitalized letter and ending with a period.

EXAMPLE

However, it is well settled that the riparian doctrine's "reasonable use" variation now applies in this state. *Brown v. Chase,* 217 P. 23 (Wash. 1923).

As a general rule, use citation clauses sparingly. Stylistically, citation sentences are often preferable because they don't interrupt the flow of your writing as much as citation clauses. However, if an authority supports only part of a sentence, it must be cited in a clause immediately following the proposition it supports.

EXAMPLE

Unlike the common law rule, *e.g., Boyd v. Hutton,* 210 P. 33 (Wash. 1922), Washington's Uniform Partnership Act provides that an incoming partner is liable for partnership debts incurred prior to his or her admission to the partnership.

---

§17.5.2   Signals

The proper citation of any authority includes an indication of why the particular authority was cited and what relationship the authority bears to the proposition stated. This is done by using signals to introduce citation sentences or clauses. Rule 1.2. A signal should be underlined unless it is used as the verb of a longer sentence. Rule 1.2(e).

a.   Signals That Indicate Support

1. No signal.   A direct citation to a case or other authority without the use of an introductory signal is appropriate whenever the cited authority directly supports a statement made in the text, identifies the source of a quotation, or identifies an authority referred to in the text.

2. E.g.   The cited authority is one of several examples that could be given in support of the proposition. This signal can also be used in combination with other signals, such as *see, e.g.,* and it is the only signal that requires a comma after it.

3. Accord.   This signal is commonly used to introduce an authority or string of authorities that are on point but are not the direct source of the proposition or quotation. *Accord* is also used to introduce the law of another jurisdiction that is in agreement with the law of the jurisdiction previously cited.

4. See.   The cited authority supports the proposition for which it is cited. However, the statement is *not* made directly in the cited authority but logically follows from it. This signal is often incorrectly used when no signal should be used.

5. See also.   The cited authority constitutes additional source material that supports the proposition. This signal is commonly used to cite an authority supporting a proposition when authorities that state or directly support the proposition have already been cited or discussed. It is useful to include a parenthetical explanation of the source material's relevance (Rule 1.5) following a citation introduced by *see also.*

    6. *Cf.* This signal, meaning "compare," is used when the cited authority supports a different proposition from the one made in the text, but the different proposition is sufficiently analogous to lend support to the statement made in the text. A parenthetical explanation should accompany a citation introduced by *cf.* to show how the holding of the cited authority differs from the given proposition.

b. Signals That Indicate Contradiction

    1. *Contra.* This signal is used when the cited authority directly contradicts a statement made in the text. It is the equivalent of no signal in support of a statement.

    2. *But see.* This signal is used when the cited authority would suggest a conclusion contrary to that set forth. It is the equivalent of *see* used in support of a proposition.

    3. *But c.f.* The cited authority supports a proposition analogous to the *opposite* of the position stated in the text. The use of a parenthetical explanation, as with *cf.,* is strongly recommended.

c. Signal That Indicates Background Material

    See generally is used when the cited authority provides helpful background material related to the issue under discussion. This signal is often used to direct the reader to law review articles, treatises, annotations, and so on.

d. Parenthetical Explanations

    As noted above, some signals require the use of a parenthetical explaining the relevance of the case or other authority cited. However, such an explanation can be used with any citation, regardless of the signal. Usually they are used to summarize the holding of a case or the relevant portion of a statute, or to present a succinct quotation from the authority. Use a parenthetical if you want to cite to a case or statute and provide a brief explanation of what it is about without discussing it in detail in the text. See Rules 1.5, 10.6, and 12.7.

EXAMPLE

Several other Washington statutes protect consumers by proscribing unfair or deceptive acts or practices by certain types of businesses. *See, e.g.,* Wash. Rev. Code § 19.118 (1989) ("lemon law" providing dispute resolution procedures for buyers of defective cars); *id.* § 19.158 (limiting commercial telephone solicitation to daytime hours); *id.* § 19.16.440 (requiring collection agencies to be licensed); *id.* § 19.102.020 (prohibiting chain distributor schemes).

---

e.   Order of Signals

When more than one signal is used to introduce various authorities, the signals should be listed in the order shown above. Thus, signals showing positive support (together with the authorities they introduce) will be given before signals showing contradictory holdings, and signals introducing background material will always go last. If the citations used are introduced by signals of the same type (positive, negative, or background), they may be strung together within a single citation sentence, separated by semicolons. Signals of different types, however, must be grouped in different citation sentences. See the example following Rule 1.3.

f.   Order of Authorities Within Each Signal

When a given signal is used to introduce several authorities, these sources must be arranged in a precise order, based on the strength of the support offered. Read Rule 1.4 carefully to determine the correct order of authorities in a string citation.

§17.5.3   Pinpoint Cites

A pinpoint cite (or jump cite) refers the reader to a particular page on which a statement is found. Pinpoint citations are required for all quotations and should be used whenever a reference is made to a specific rule, proposition, or holding from a case or other authority. It is not necessary to give a pinpoint cite when you are referring to the case generally or when an entire case stands for a proposition. Be sure also to give a pinpoint citation in the parallel citation. If the page number is not available, use a blank. See generally Rule 3.3.

Rovinski v. Rowe, 131 F.2d 687, 689 (6th Cir. 1942)

State v. Stockton, 647 P.2d 21, 24 (Wash. 1982)

§17.5.4   Short Forms

Once the full citation to a case or other authority has been established, you may use an abbreviated form of citation in subsequent references to the authority. Different short forms are appropriate in different situations. Rule 4.

a. Id.

You may use *id.* to refer to the immediately preceding authority. In other words, if you have cited a case in full, and your next citation is to the same case, use *id.* Do not use *id.* if you mentioned other authorities between your first full citation and your subsequent reference. Rule 4.1.

> *Id.* at 689 (reference to the preceding case)

> *Id.* § 41.56.030(2) (reference to the preceding statute)

b. Short Case Citations

You may use a short form to cite to a case that has previously been cited in full in the same general discussion, but is not the immediately preceding authority. Use one of the parties' names for the short form, but do not use the name of a governmental litigant, such as "State" or "United States." If the name of the case has been mentioned in the text, you may use just a reference to the volume, reporter, and page number. Rule 10.9.

> *Rovinski,* 131 F.2d at 689 *OR* 131 F.2d at 689

c. Statutes

The first mention of a statute within each general discussion should give a full citation. Subsequent references in the same general discussion may use any short form that clearly identifies the statute. Depending on the context, the short form could consist of a shortened version of the citation, a popular name of the act with a section number, or merely a section number. Rule 12.9. *Id.* may also be used to refer to the immediately preceding citation. Rule 4.1. Remember: If you are referring to the section in text, rather than citing it, you must spell out the word "section." Rule 6.2(b).

EXAMPLE

First Reference

On the federal level, the Comprehensive Environmental Response, Compensation and Liability Act (CERCLA) imposes liability on owners for past hazardous waste disposal. 42 U.S.C. §§ 9601-9657 (1988).

Possible Subsequent References

42 U.S.C. § 9612

Id. § 9612

CERCLA § 9612

section 9612 (in text)

---

d. Supra *and "Hereinafter"*

Supra and "hereinafter" may be used to refer to legislative materials, administrative and executive materials, books, pamphlets, unpublished materials, periodicals, services, newspapers, and international materials. They should not be used to refer to cases, statutes, or constitutions. Also, do not use *supra* when *id.* would be appropriate. Rule 4.2.

1. Supra. Once you have cited an authority in full, subsequent references to the same authority may be made by the use of *supra* (if *id.* is not appropriate). Generally, the *supra* form consists of the author of the work followed by a comma and the word *supra* and a pinpoint cite. Rule 4.2(a) and Practitioners' Note P.4(d).

First reference: 3 Kenneth Davis, *Administrative Law Treatise* 371-98 (2d ed. 1980)

Subsequent reference: 3 Davis, *supra,* at 390

If no author is given, use the title.

Symposium, supra, at 289

S. Rep. No. 181, *supra* note 4, at 14, *reprinted in* 1977 U.S.C.C.A.N.

2. Hereinafter. For authority that would be cumbersome to cite with the simple *supra* form, a special shortened form may be established. After the first citation to the authority, place the word "hereinafter" and the special shortened form in brackets. Thereafter, use the shortened form followed by a comma and the word *supra.* The shortened form should appear in the same typeface as the full citation. Rule 4.2(b).

First reference (appears on page 6 of your memo): *Telecommunications for the Hearing Impaired and the Needy:*

Hearings on H.R. 2213 Before the Subcomm. on Telecommunications and Finance of the House Comm. on Energy and Commerce, 100th Cong., 1st Sess. 14 (1988) [hereinafter *Telecommunications Hearings*]

Subsequent reference: *Telecommunications Hearings, supra,* at 27

§17.6   QUOTATIONS

Direct quotations from authorities can be effective in legal writing; however, use them sparingly. It is usually better to paraphrase judicial language rather than to quote it at length. Quote only language that is particularly apt or well stated. It is often wise, however, to quote statutory language directly, because the exact wording is important when interpreting statutes.

§17.6.1   Formatting Quotations

Quotations of fifty or more words should be indented left and right, without quotation marks, and single-spaced. The citation should begin at the left margin on the line following the quotation. See the example in Rule 5.1(a). Quotations of forty-nine or fewer words should be enclosed in quotation marks, but not otherwise set off from the rest of the text. The citation should follow immediately. Don't forget to include a pinpoint cite to the page number on which the quotation appears. Rule 5.1(b).

§17.6.2   Editing Quotations

When you quote, you must be scrupulously accurate in reproducing the exact language used by the authority. If you edit the quote in order to isolate the relevant language, you must indicate to the reader that you have done so.

a.   Omissions

If, after deleting language at the *beginning* of a sentence, the remaining quoted language stands alone as a full sentence, capitalize the first letter and enclose it in brackets. Never use an ellipsis to begin a quotation. The fact that a lower case letter was changed to upper case indicates that words have been left out. Rule 5.3.

"[T]he right of the people to keep and bear arms, shall not be infringed."

If language has been omitted from the *middle* of a sentence, use an ellipsis to show where the language was deleted:

> "No person shall . . . be subject for the same offense to be twice put in jeopardy of life or limb."

To show an omission from the *end* of a sentence, use an ellipsis followed by a period or other final punctuation:

> "Congress shall make no law respecting an establishment of religion . . . ."

b. Alterations

Rule 5.2 governs the alteration of quotations. As just seen, use brackets to indicate when a letter has been changed from lower to upper case or vice versa. You can also use brackets to change or add a word for the sake of clarity.

EXAMPLES

"The [district] court correctly found that the conspirators were arrested after they had completed all of the acts they were required to perform to commit this crime."

"A jury could find beyond a reasonable doubt that the indictment fairly described [appellant's] brutal crime."

Brackets are also used to alter tense or number for grammatical consistency.

EXAMPLE

Further, the defendant violated section 9.41.050 when he "carr[ied] a pistol concealed on [his] person without a license to carry a concealed weapon."

Use "[sic]" to indicate significant mistakes, usually in spelling or grammar, in the original.

EXAMPLES

"Even questions that are usually routine must be proceeded [sic] by *Miranda* warnings if they are intended to produce answers that are incriminating."

"While a jury is not literally 'the hangman,' only they [sic] may supply the hangman's victims."

---

c. *Parentheticals*

Indicate in a parenthetical clause after the citation any change of emphasis or omission of citations or footnote numbers. Rule 5.2.

EXAMPLES

"The question now is whether the rule is to be limited to cases involving *intentional* infliction of injury or is also to be applied to *negligent* infliction of emotional distress." *Ver Hagen v. Gibbons,* 177 N.W.2d 83, 84 (Wis. 1970) (emphasis added).

"The development of constitutional law subsequent to the Supreme Court's unequivocal repudiation of the line of cases ending with *Bailey v. Richardson* and *Adler v. Board of Education* is more relevant than the preceding doctrine which is now 'universally rejected.'" *Illinois State Employees Union, Council 34 v. Lewis,* 473 F.2d 561, 568 (7th Cir. 1972) (citations omitted).

---

§17.6.3   Quotations Within Quotations

Whenever possible, a quotation within a quotation should be attributed to its original source. Rule 5.2. This is done by using an explanatory parenthetical.

EXAMPLE

"[W]henever an act of Congress contains unobjectionable provisions separable from those found to be unconstitutional, it is the duty of this court to so declare . . . ." *Regan v. Time, Inc.,* 468 U.S. 641, 658 (1984) (quoting *El Paso & Northeastern R.R. Co. v. Gutierrez,* 215 U.S. 87, 96 (1909)).

See also rule 1.6(d).

A Final Note

Many new legal writers fall into one of two traps: They undercite or overcite. Although you must support each statement of law with a citation to authority, it is seldom appropriate to string together (string cite) more than two or three authorities. When numerous authorities support the statement of law, pick the best one, two, or three, using a signal (*e.g.* or *accord*) to introduce them.

Part V

A Guide to
Effective Writing

Although we attempt in this part of the book to give legal writers general recommendations and rules of thumb about what makes some legal writing effective, it is important to remember at least three points about the notion of "effective legal writing."

First, effectiveness in legal writing is a relative thing. By this we mean that there are degrees of effectiveness and the same degree or level of effectiveness is not needed in every situation. The trick, of course, is to make the writing effective enough so that it accomplishes its goal without laboring over it to the point that it consumes all of the working day and night. In short, some balance is appropriate here.

Second, effectiveness in legal writing, and in all writing for that matter, always depends on the context. What will please and even delight one reader may irritate or anger another. An organizational scheme that is effective in one instance may be dead wrong in another. Even precision and conciseness, those most sought-after characteristics of effective legal writing, can be ineffective in some instances in which vagueness and verbosity accomplish the desired objective. In short, writing that most readers would consider competent, stylistically pleasing, and even eloquent in the abstract but that does not work in a given context is, in that context, ineffective.

Finally, effectiveness is a fairly subjective notion. Again, we can give you the standard advice and even some brilliant (!) insights of our own about what is and is not effective legal writing, but then you must filter all that through your own sense of whether you think something works. If, as you are writing a given piece, your instincts tell you it is working (or it is not working) and all the theory and advice tell you the opposite, we suggest that you look at it again. If your instincts and common sense still insist that the conventional wisdom about effective legal writing is not working here, then trust your instincts.

Chapter 18

Effective Writing — The Whole Paper

§18.1 THE PSYCHOLOGY OF WRITING

Writing is not for the faint-hearted. It takes courage, perseverance, creativity, and flexibility, not to mention intelligence and a solid foundation of writing skills. A fair number of lawyers and judges profess to like writing and even say that they find the process satisfying. If you are in this fortunate group, this section of this chapter is not addressed to you.

If you are among the less fortunate — those who have felt overwhelmed by the prospect of writing, who have struggled with writer's block, who have found writing to be a difficult, perhaps even painful process — there is hope. Writing, like most other skills, becomes more pleasurable with each successful experience. It also helps to know where the usual stumbling blocks are in the process and how to get past them.

Few legal writers have trouble getting started on the research phase of a writing project. Many encounter their first stumbling block when it is time to move from research to writing. A typical avoidance mechanism is to keep researching long past the point of need. Writers who have developed this pattern of approaching writing tasks usually postpone putting pen to paper or fingers to keyboard until the last possible moment. Then they write, almost out of desperation, and end up turning in a final product that is really a rough draft. By delaying the writing process, they make it virtually impossible to do any quality drafting, revising, editing, and proofreading. The result is yet another unsatisfying writing experience.

If this describes your typical writing process, you may be able to break out of this habit by developing a schedule for the completion of the entire document. In this schedule, allot a reasonable amount of time to complete the research but be firm about when you will begin writing.

Give yourself mini-deadlines for completing an outline, producing a first draft, revising, editing, and proofreading. Allow breathing room in this timetable for technical problems such as a broken printer ribbon or personal problems such as a flat tire. If at all possible, plan as though your deadline is one day sooner than the real deadline. To do this, you may find it easier to write the schedule backwards, starting with the final deadline and allowing time for proofreading, then editing, all the way back to research.

Sample Schedule for a Two-Week Writing Project

Week 1 research and organize research
Week 2 Day 1 brainstorm, create plan, outline
        Day 2 drafting
        Day 3 drafting
        Day 4 revising
        Day 5 editing, last-minute citation checks
        Day 6 proofreading
        Day 7 final product (ready a day early!)

For shorter time frames and quick turnarounds, a writing schedule is even more critical. In such cases, you will probably be working with half-day, quarter-day, or even hour units, but the principles are still the same. Figure out how much of the total time should be spent researching and how much should be spent writing. Create mini-deadlines for yourself. Start with your final deadline and work backwards as you plan.

Sample Schedule for a Two-Day Writing Project

Day 1 research and organize research
Day 2 by 10:00 a.m. brainstorm, plan outline
      by 2:00 p.m. drafting
      by 3:00 p.m. revising
      by 4:00 p.m. editing
      by 4:30 p.m. proofreading
      by 5:00 p.m. final product completed (and in the partner's
           hands!)

With practice, you may find that you don't need as much of your total available time for research and that you can begin to allow a larger percentage of your time for writing.

Schedules are invaluable, but many writers need more than a schedule to get them started writing. It is an enormous help if your research notes are organized in a way that will facilitate the writing process. Instead of organizing your research around cases, organize it around the law or the points you want to make. Under each point, list the statutes, cases, or authorities on which you will rely. (See section 5.5.8.)

You can then color code any photocopies you made of those authorities. For instance, for the exception-to-the-specially-manufactured-goods problem in Chapter 5, you might decide to use blue for anything related to "suitable for sale to others in the ordinary course of business," red for anything about the "nature of the goods," and so on. A numbering system can be used in the same way, but be sure that you don't subconsciously assume that the point that you have marked as a "3" must automatically precede whatever point you are making as "4."

Color coding or numbering helps during the drafting phase because it gives you a way to quickly gather up all the information you have collected on a given point (grab all the red) and then physically order those sheets. The same sheets may have other colors or numbers on them, but while you are writing about the "red point" — the nature of the goods — you can stay focused on the part of the notes and photocopied cases that concerns that point. When it comes time to do the "blue point," the same sheet gets picked up and ordered into the information about "suitable for sale to others in the ordinary course of business."

If color coding or numbering does not appeal to you, you may find that having separate file folders or a tabbed notebook does. The key is to develop files or sections of the notebook for the points you want to make in the whole document, not separate files or notebook sections for each analogous case. This means you may need two or more photocopies of the same page of a case so that it may be filed under each of the appropriate points.

§18.2   OUTLINES, WRITING PLANS, AND ORDERED LISTS

Unfortunately, student writers are taught to write outlines long before they ever·need one. Some time in junior high or high school most of us were first exposed to outlines, but the outlines were for relatively short, uncomplicated papers whose organization we were perfectly capable of keeping in our heads. The task wasn't large enough or complex enough to warrant an outline. As a result, many student writers discarded the concept of an outline or a written writing plan because it seemed relatively useless at the time it was introduced.

For professional writers (and lawyers are professional writers) who must organize extensive and complex material, spending time creating an outline or writing plan or even just an ordered list almost always saves time in the end. Done properly, an outline or plan will keep you from backtracking, repeating yourself, forgetting or missing a key point, or finally discovering what it is you want to say after you have written the whole thing the wrong way.

But creating order in extensive and complex material is a task worthy of more than just the writer's time; it is also worthy of the writer's complete attention. It deserves a distinct block of time for focusing on just that task. Trying to create order at the same time you are drafting sentences and paragraphs just means that you must keep track of several big tasks all at once. No wonder writing under such conditions is stressful.

Writing a good outline or plan may also mean that you have to change some of your preconceived ideas about outlines. First of all, the outline or plan is for you, the writer, not for a teacher. Roman numerals and capital A's and B's are not terribly important. Use them if they help; discard them if they hinder. Even if you discard the roman numerals, letters, and numbers, keep the indentations. They will help you distinguish among main points, subpoints, sub-subpoints, and supporting details.

As the writer, what you want and need from the outline is the big picture of how the pieces fit together. To make sure you can see everything at once, write your outline on one side of a page or pages. That way you can lay the whole outline out before you and see the entire structure at one time.

There are as many ways to go about creating an outline or writing plan as there are writers. Below are some time-tested techniques that you may find helpful. Use whichever ones work for you and any others that have been successful for you in previous writing projects.

§18.2.1   Read It All; Mull It Over

Before beginning to write the outline or plan, read through all of your research. Let your mind mull it over while you do some mindless task such as mowing the lawn or taking a bath. While you are engaged in the mindless task, your mind will almost certainly begin organizing the ideas.

§18.2.2   Don't Overlook the Obvious

One obvious way of beginning to organize is to determine how the court will approach the problem. Are there any threshold questions the court will consider first? If so, place them first in your outline. What will the court look at and decide second, third, and so on? Your organizational scheme should mirror the process the court will follow.

Furthermore, in creating an organization for your document, do not assume that you always have to create a brand-new, never-seen-before organizational scheme. Most documents fit comfortably in one of the common organizational plans. Borrow freely from the bank of common knowledge about how to organize an elements analysis, a balancing test, or a discussion of the development of a trend, to name but a few. Many discussion sections follow an IRAC (issue, rule, analysis, conclusion) plan or use mini-IRACs in some of the sections. (See Chapter 5.11.)

§18.2.3   Find Order Using a Three-Column Chart

The three-column chart can be an effective way to find order in a document, particularly when the document does not immediately appear to fall into any of the typical organizational patterns. In the first column, make one giant list of everything you think the final document should include. Be as comprehensive as possible. Dump everything you have in your brain about the case into this list. Do not worry about the order of the items.

COLUMN ONE: THE BRAIN DUMP

- Requirements for exception
  1. goods specially manufactured for buyer
  2. unsuitable for sale to others in ordinary course of seller's business
  3. manufacture commenced
- no written contract
- oral contracts should be the rule
- "specially manufactured" not defined
- "specially manufactured" refers to nature of goods
- manufacturer had to specially set looms
- *Flowers:* buyer's name/artwork on wrapping material
- wrapping material & carpet are personalized
- a family flower is not a name
- *Colorado Carpet:* carpeting available at outlets
- policy: goods themselves are evidence of contract
- seller of custom-made goods not exempt from Statute of Frauds
- if all goods custom, no written contract necessary
- seller of custom goods as likely to fabricate
     contract as seller of ready-made goods
- quote from *Wackenhut* court
- undue hardship for seller
- wholesaler easily sold rugs to a third party

Once this list is complete, use the second column to begin doing some preliminary ordering of that list. Column One probably already contains some natural groupings of ideas. If so, place them together in the Column Two at roughly the point in the document where you guess they will go.

For example, the writer knows the rule section will probably come early in the memo, so he or she moves the requirements for the exception close to the top of Column Two. Should anything precede or immediately follow the requirements? A quick glance down Column One yields at least one other point about rules: There is no written contract. This point should come before a discussion of the exception and its requirements.

After the list of requirements, it seems natural to move right to the first requirement and *Flowers,* the case that helps explain what constitutes "specially manufactured for the buyer." Because the writer knows he or she will make an argument for BCC based on *Flowers,* that argument is placed next on the list.

The writer proceeds down the list from Column One and finds roughly where each item will fit in Column Two. By the end, he or she may have some stray items, in this case, "goods themselves are evidence of the contract" and "undue hardship for seller." They may be worked in now or saved for Column Three.

COLUMN TWO: PRELIMINARY ORDERING OF IDEAS

- no written contract
- specially manufactured goods exception
- requirements for exception
    1. goods specially manufactured for buyer
    2. unsuitable for sale to others in ordinary course of seller's business
    3. manufacture commenced under circumstances . . . & prior to receipt of notice of repudiation
- First requirement: goods specially manufactured for buyer
- *Flowers:* buyer's name & artwork on wrapping material
- wrapping paper is personalized
- BCC's argument: like wrapping material, rugs are personalized
- Therefore, rugs specially manufactured for buyer . . .

Column Three is used to further refine the order of the list. This is the time to test out various places where the stray items may fit. In this case, because two of the items seem to be policy reasons for the specially manufactured goods exception, they might fit right before or after the list of requirements. The other two items — "'specially manufactured' not defined" and "'specially manufactured' refers to nature of goods" — belong in the rule section of the first requirement.

Doing Column Three is also the time to check to see if anything was forgotten. Look for all the standard features of legal analysis (burden of proof, plain language arguments, policy arguments, and so on) and all the standard "moves" a lawyer makes (argument, counterargument, rebuttal, countervailing policy argument, and so on).

In this case, who has the burden of proof? Does the other side have an argument based on the first requirement? based on *Flowers?* based on policy? Where will these counterarguments and rebuttals fit? Given the rough plan from Column Two, it is relatively easy to add in those pieces as needed. The added pieces are in boldface type in the following chart.

COLUMN THREE: REFINED ORDER

- no written contract
- specially manufactured goods exception
- requirements for exception
- **party seeking exception has burden of proof**
    1. goods specially manufactured for buyer
    2. unsuitable for sale to others in ordinary course of seller's business

   3.   manufacture commenced under circumstances . . . & prior to receipt of notice of repudiation

- **policy underlying exception**
  1. goods themselves are evidence of contract
  2. undue hardship for seller
- First requirement — goods specially manufactured for buyer
- **"specially manufactured" not defined**
- **"specially manufactured" refers to nature of goods**
- *Flowers:* buyer's name & artwork on wrapping material
- wrapping paper is personalized
- **contrast with *Colorado Carpet*: carpeting available at outlets, so not specially manufactured**
- **BCC's plain language argument**
- BCC's argument: like wrapping material, rugs are personalized
- **distinguish rugs from carpet in *Colorado Carpet***
- Therefore, rugs specially manufactured for buyer and so on.

Working in this way, you will find that the secret to the three-column chart is that you focus on one main task with each column, and as you move through the columns, you get more and more control over the material. When you are moving from Column Two to Column Three, for example, you may begin to see that this material does fit into one of the standard organizational plans after all. By the time you reach Column Three, voila! You have an outline.

§18.2.4   Talk to a Colleague

Whenever you are having trouble getting a large amount of material organized in your mind, try talking it over with a colleague. Use the approach that you are going to explain the issue(s) to your listener. As you are talking, notice how you are naturally organizing the material. Jot down key words and phrases that come to mind as you are speaking. Don't be afraid to talk through the parts with which you are having the most difficulty. It may free you to address these areas if you begin by saying something like "this is the part I'm having trouble with" or "this is the part that is still rough in my mind." Let your listener question you about any part of the material and provide his or her own insights.

If talking out the issue(s) seemed helpful, sit down immediately afterwards and write out the organization you discovered as you were speaking. If you find that talking-before-writing becomes a valuable organizing technique for you, you may even want to tape record the talk-before-write sessions.

§18.2.5   Try a New Analogy or Format

If you have an incurable phobia about outlines, relabel or redesign what it is you are doing when you develop the organization for a document. Some writers are more comfortable developing a "writing plan." Others like to think in terms of an "ordered list." You may need an entirely new analogy for what you are doing. Think instead of an architect creating a blueprint for a building or an engineer designing a new aircraft.

Some people prefer horizontal flow charts to vertical outlines. There is nothing magical about organizing ideas from top to bottom in an outline. If working from left to right in a flow chart feels more comfortable to you, do it.

Others can find and better visualize an organizational scheme by using a technique called clustering. To use clustering, simply begin by putting one main idea in a circle and then attach related subpoints.

Exhibit 18.1 is an example of clustering for the *Patterson* case in Chapter 7.

Begin a new circle for each main idea, each time attaching related subpoints. Eventually, you will end up with a map of your mind. See Exhibit 18.2.

Now look for clusters of ideas; these will usually become sections in the final document. You may even find that after doing the clustering diagram you can see that the material fits into one of the standard organizational plans. The final step is to translate the clustering diagram into a traditional outline.

Notice too that beginning with a clustering diagram has one distinct advantage over beginning with the format of a traditional outline. Traditional outlines develop a hierarchy that suggests that all the items have superordinate-subordinate relationships. Such a hierarchical framework may artificially limit your thinking. Clustering, on the other hand, lends itself to thinking about a variety of relationships, such as contrast, cause/effect, and possession.

EXHIBIT 18.1   **Basic Cluster for the *Patterson* Case**

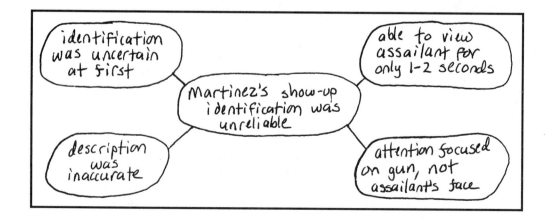

EXHIBIT 18.2   Finished Cluster for the *Patterson* Case

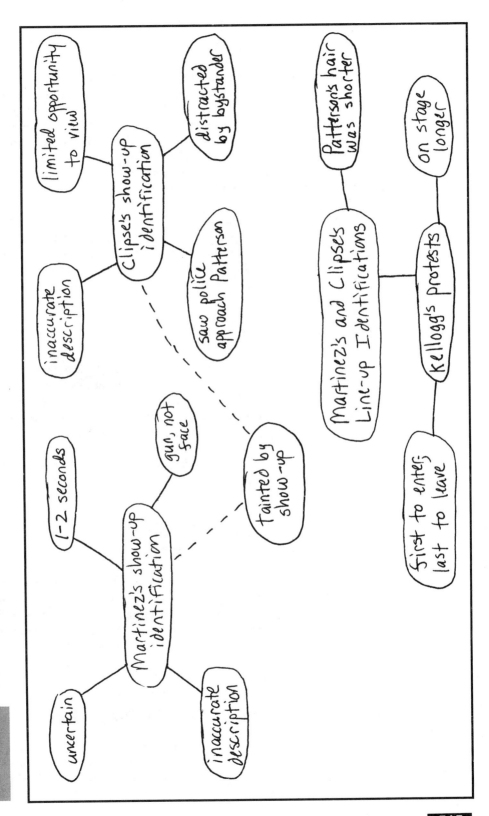

§18.2.6   Consider Your Reader, Purpose, and Theory of the Case

After spending hours in the library — in the trenches, so to speak — it is a good idea to review the basics before composing a battle plan. For whom are you writing this document? What are that reader's purposes? What are your purposes? What is your theory of the case? Is this a case about mistaken identity, inappropriate police procedures, self-defense, or freedom to assemble? Your theory of the case, your "theme," if you will, should be evident in every section of the outline, from the statement of facts or statement of the case to the rule, discussion, or argument sections.

One final note before leaving the subject of outlines: Like the blueprint for a building or the design for a new aircraft, outlines should be aids and not straitjackets for the writer. Don't be afraid to revise an outline that isn't working; don't be afraid to change an outline when you get a better idea.

§18.3   DRAFTING THE DOCUMENT

If creating an outline is the first stumbling block for most writers, the second comes when it is time to start drafting. Some people call it "writer's block"; others call it "the white page syndrome." Whatever the name, the experience is essentially the same. Faced with what seems to be an overwhelming task, the writer freezes. Nothing seems like the perfect beginning, so nothing gets written.

If you are one who tends to freeze when you must start writing, try some of the following techniques.

§18.3.1   Give Yourself Optimum Writing Conditions

Make writing as pleasant as possible. Start drafting at the time of day and in the place where you do your best thinking and writing. If you are a morning person, don't start drafting at 5 p.m. unless you absolutely must. If you prefer a legal pad to a computer, by all means use a legal pad. Treat yourself to a new fancy pen if that will make you feel better about writing.

§18.3.2   Trick Yourself into Getting Started

If you have written an outline or kept research notes in your own words, you have already started drafting. By expanding outline labels into phrases, then clauses, then sentences, you can gradually slip into the creation of the first draft. By fleshing out your research notes, you can gradually move into developing the language that will appear in your draft. For some writers, this gradual "drift" into drafting helps them avoid writer's block.

§18.3.3   Write What You Know Best First

For some reason, many writers seem to think that they must write a document in order — the first sentence first, then the second sentence, the first paragraph before the second paragraph, and so on. This notion about writing is not a problem as long as the writer knows how to begin.

However, when you are not quite sure how to begin, it's often a good idea to start writing a draft at the point in the material where you are the most confident. Get the writing rolling and let your subconscious work through how to begin the document.

The same is true when you are hopelessly stuck in the middle of a document. Try skipping over the problem area for a time and keep writing about another section. With a bit of luck, you may figure out what to do about the problem area without letting it bring the whole project to a halt.

One caution, though: If you start in the middle of a document or if you skip over a problem area for the time being, you will have to come back and make sure the sections are logically and stylistically connected.

§18.3.4   "Get the Juices Flowing"

Athletes who are preparing to perform do warm-up and stretching exercises. Some writers find that freewriting has similar benefits when done before drafting. Others find that they can "get the writing juices flowing" by reading other similar documents or rereading other documents that they themselves have written.

§18.3.5   Take It One Step at a Time

Many writers are overwhelmed by the prospect of drafting twenty pages or more. Writing a page or even just a paragraph, however, seems relatively easy. The trick then is to give yourself small parts of the whole document to do at any one time.

Your goal for the next hour, for example, may be to write the rule section. Before lunch you may want to complete a paragraph about the plaintiff's policy argument on the last element. By breaking the large task into several smaller tasks, you allow yourself to focus on one part at a time and direct all your energy toward writing that part well.

§18.3.6   Reward Yourself

As you complete small parts of the larger writing task and as you see yourself meeting deadlines in your personal timetable, reward yourself. Rewards can be something as small as a break for a cup of coffee or as large as an evening off for a movie. What matters is that writing needs to become a pleasurable task at which you feel successful. If rewards along the way help promote those feelings and attitudes, they are worth a try.

§18.4   REVISING

Revision, or re-vision, means "to see again." When you revise, you step back from the project and try to see it with fresh eyes. This is not an easy thing to do. Many writers have difficulty adopting a revisionist perspective. They have a tendency to avoid rethinking the whole document and prefer instead to limit themselves to tinkering with smaller editing issues such as sentence structure or word choice.

To help make the shift from drafter to reviser, you may find it helpful to try one of the following techniques.

§18.4.1   Develop a Revision Checklist

A revision checklist should focus on the large issues in writing. Below is a sample revision checklist that can be used for most documents.

Revision Checklist

- Will this document meet the reader's needs?
- Is the tone right for this document and this reader?
- Is the document well organized?
- Are all the ideas well developed?
- Is the analysis conclusory or superficial? What would make it more sophisticated?
- What else should be included?
  - A plain language argument?
  - An argument based on an analogous case?
  - A policy argument?
  - A countervailing policy argument?
  - A rebuttal to an argument?
- What can be omitted?
- Is the theory of the case, or theme, evident in all sections of the document?

On your own revision checklist, add any other characteristic writing problems that have been pointed out to you by your legal writing professor, classmates, colleagues, or other readers.

§18.4.2   Write an After-the-Fact Outline

Of all the areas to rethink when you are revising, the most challenging is often the organization. One simple way to check the paper's organization is to create an after-the-fact outline. An after-the-fact outline is an outline of what you actually wrote, not a plan that precedes the writing.

To create an after-the-fact outline, simply read each of your paragraphs and try to sum up the point in that paragraph in a phrase, clause, or, at most, a sentence. (If you can't do this summarizing, that alone suggests that the paragraph needs revision.) Record the summarizing phrase, clause, or sentence on the outline, using indentations to show what are main points, subpoints, and sub-subpoints. Keep the outline on one side of a page or pages so that you can lay the whole outline before you and see it all at once. (See section 5.20.2.)

Use after-the-fact outlines the way you would an aerial photograph of ground you just covered on a hike. Seen from this perspective, is the way you traveled through the material the most efficient one? Do you have any needless backtracking? Repetition? Did you miss anything along the way? If so, where can you easily add it?

Now that you have the "big picture" well in mind, are there ways you can prepare your reader for the twists and turns your path will take? For example, are there insights you should add to your roadmap paragraph that will help your reader? What kinds of signposts will help the reader stay on track? (See section 19.2.)

§18.4.3   Do a Self-Critique

Revision can be the most satisfying of all the stages in writing because it is a bit like having a good debate with yourself. The draft is your own initial thinking and organization. (It is recorded so you don't have to worry about losing or forgetting something as you test it.) Now, leave the role of the writer and become a critical reader. Step back and examine the quality of the work. Play the devil's advocate. Where can you punch holes in this thing? Where are its weaknesses? Where are its strengths? Using what you find, you can return to the role of the writer and improve the draft.

§18.4.4   Check for Unity and Coherence

For a draft to be well written, the entire document, as well as each paragraph and section, must have unity and coherence. Unity at the document level means that every part of the document contributes to the overall thesis. In a memo, the thesis is essentially the same as your conclusion. Thus, if a memo's thesis, or conclusion, is that *the specially manufactured goods exception will probably not apply because the carpet was suitable for resale in the ordinary course of the seller's business,* then every word, sentence, and paragraph in that memo should work toward explaining how you got to that thesis.

Many writers, though, do not have a clear idea in their own minds of what their thesis is until they have completed a draft. In the act of drafting, however, they discover what it is they are trying to say. This way of arriving at a thesis, or controlling idea, is perfectly fine. What it means, though, is that now that the writer has discovered the thesis he or she must go back through the draft with that thesis in mind, making sure that all the parts are working toward that one goal.

The same process may be true at the paragraph level. The writer may begin drafting the paragraph without a clear idea of what point he or she is trying to make. In the act of drafting the paragraph, however, the writer discovers what the point is and how it contributes to the larger whole. At this point, then, the writer should first add or revise the topic sentence and then go back through the paragraph making sure all the parts contribute to the paragraph's point. (See section 20.2.1 for more about unity.)

Like unity, coherence is also important at both the document and the paragraph level. Consequently, a good revision strategy is to check at both the document and the paragraph level to see if you are using the common devices for creating coherence.

- logical organization
  - chronological, spatial, topical
  - general to specific, specific to general
  - IRAC: issues → rules → application → conclusion
- roadmap paragraphs
- topic sentences
- signposts, dovetailing, and transitions
- repetition of key terms
- parallelism
- pronouns

(See section 20.2.2 for more about how these devices create coherence.)

Two final points about revising: First, drafting and revising are not always separate, distinct stages in the writing process; some revising inevitably occurs even as the first draft is being written. Second, if at all possible, do some of your revising on a hard copy. Seeing your writing on just a computer screen can be misleading. Because you can see only a small portion of a whole document at a time, you may overlook problems with some of the larger issues in writing.

§18.5   EDITING

Editing is an examination of the smaller issues in writing. As with revising, you must once again step out of the role of the drafter and look at the writing with a critical eye, but this time the critical eye is focused on smaller issues such as sentence structure and word choice.

When editing for sentence structure, all writers should pay particular attention to the subjects and verbs of their sentences. If the subject-verb combination is effective, many other writing problems will clear themselves up automatically. (See section 5.23.1 and Chapter 22.)

Legal writers should also make an extra effort to edit for precision and conciseness. (See sections 23.1 and 23.2.) Sloppy word choice and added verbiage may be overlooked in other types of writing, but they are unforgiveable in legal writing. In addition to editing for sentence structure and word choice, each writer should edit for his or her habitual problem areas.

If this seems like a lot to think about all at once, you are right. For this reason, many writers find it easier to edit for just one or two writing problems at a time. If, for example, you know that you have problems with spelling, do one reading in which you focus just on spelling every word correctly. If, on the other hand, your typical problem is wordiness, do one reading with the single goal of editing out all unnecessary words.

Editing Tips

1. Don't let yourself fall in love with a particular phrase or sentence. No matter how well crafted an individual phrase or sentence is, if it doesn't work with the whole paragraph, indeed the whole document, it is not an effective phrase or sentence.

2. Be selective about whom you ask for editing advice. Although you can sometimes get excellent editing advice from others, there are far too many examples of the blind leading the mildly nearsighted. What often works better is to notice the parts of the paper that your reader/editor pointed out as problems and figure out with that reader what threw him or her off track. This procedure is much less risky than the unquestioning use of an inexperienced editor's rewrites.

3. There are ways to get the editing information that you need. For example, if you are wondering whether to add a transition at a given point in the paper, ask a reader to read up to that point and then, without reading what follows, to predict what will be discussed next. If the reader can easily predict where the writing is headed, a transition is probably unnecessary. If the reader is unsure or wrong about where the writing is headed, a transition will signal the shift in thought. Such techniques are more "editor-proof" than asking the same person if a transition is needed at that point.

4. Read your writing aloud or, better yet, have a colleague read it aloud to you while you follow along on another copy. Mark any part of

the writing that the reader misreads or stumbles over or anything that just doesn't sound right to you when you hear it. This technique will not tell you how to fix something, but it will give you a good idea of what needs to be fixed.

5. Spend the majority of your editing time on the section or sections of the document that you found hardest to write. No need to keep massaging the opening sentence long after you know it reads smoothly. Force yourself to focus your editing energy on the rockiest parts of the paper.

6. As with revising, if at all possible, do some of your editing on hard copy. The same language looks slightly different on a page than it does on a computer screen, possibly because words are lights on a computer screen but marks of ink on a page. For some reason, that small change from screen to page allows you to see the writing with different, fresh eyes. Remember, too, that your readers will not be looking at a computer screen; they will be reading your writing from hard copy.

§18.6   PROOFREADING

Whether you or your secretary types your writing, you will be the one who is responsible for the final product. Any missed words, format problems, or typos are ultimately your missed words, format problems, or typos. Consequently, every lawyer, no matter how competent his or her support staff, needs to know a few simple proofreading strategies.

First of all, proofreading is a distinct skill. It is not the same as normal reading or editing or revising. It is reading for errors. Consequently, to proofread properly, you need to remember a few important things.

Slow down. Speed reading and proofreading are mutually exclusive terms. Proofreading should be done at your slowest reading rate. One technique for slowing yourself down is to cover up all but the line you are proofreading with another sheet of paper. This technique also helps you to focus on the individual words on the page, so you will see transposed letters in the middle of words and notice missing words rather than read them in where they should be.

Also, consider proofreading the last third of your document first. Chances are there are more errors in the last sections simply because you and your typist were probably more tired and rushed when those sections were done. If that's true, then it makes sense to use the time when you are freshest on the part of the document that needs it most.

If at all possible, do your proofreading at a completely separate time — ideally, a day or more after you have completed drafting and revising. Even a small break in time allows you to see the document anew and bring fresh eyes and thinking to the pages.

Proofread all parts of the document, including headings, charts, appendices, captions, and page numbers.

Double check all dates and monetary figures and the spelling of every name.

§18.7   MYTHS ABOUT WRITING

No one seems to know exactly where they come from, but over the years a number of myths have developed about writing. Many of these myths have been repeated and even taught to several generations so that now they have taken on an air of legitimacy. They seem to be part of the common knowledge about writing, although one never sees them repeated in reputable composition textbooks.

Grammar historians have uncovered the source of one or two of these myths, such as the so-called rule never to split an infinitive, but most of the myths seem to have developed from some short-cut methods used decades ago by elementary school teachers to prevent young children from writing sentence fragments or run-on sentences. For example, if a child is taught "never to start a sentence with *because*," perhaps the child will stop treating *because* dependent clauses as sentences.

The most unfortunate consequence of these myths about writing is the unnecessary and artificial constraints they place on sophisticated writers. In the office memorandum concerning the exception for specially manufactured goods (Chapter 5), for example, the memo writer needed to use the split infinitive "to specially set the looms." All the other options seem awkward or imprecise. The myth hovers over the writer's head, however, making him or her feel uneasy about using this construction.

What to do? Because at least some of the myths are treated as gospel by some readers, it is probably unwise to make split infinitives or any of the other myths a trademark of your writing style. When another, equally good construction is available, use it instead. But when the best thing to do is to start the sentence with "and" or "but" (as this sentence does) or to violate any of these other non-rules, do so — and do so without guilt.

Myth: Never Start a Sentence With "And," "But," or "Or"

Although there is no real rule that you cannot start a sentence with the conjunctions "and," "but," or "or," it is often a good idea to choose a more specific transition. If using one of these conjunctions is the hasty or lazy choice, it is probably the wrong choice.

Occasionally, however, one of these conjunctions is the perfect transition, especially because each is a one-syllable word that gets the next sentence started quickly. For this reason, it is usually not a good idea to start a sentence with "and," "but," or "or" and then follow the conjunction with a comma. When you do, you start the sentence up quickly only to immediately slow it down.

One final caveat about using "and," "but," or "or" at the beginnings of sentences: As transitions, these three words tend to sound relatively informal. In addition, because they pick up the pace of the writing, they can also make the writing sound a bit breezy.

Myth: Never Start a Sentence With "Because" or "However"

Legal writers often need to describe cause/effect relationships. In such cases, the best sentence structure is often "Because (fill in the cause), (fill in the effect)." This is a perfectly fine and exceedingly useful sentence structure. There is no rule prohibiting its use. (Unfortunately, in erroneously trying to avoid beginning a sentence with "because," some writers use "since" to begin sentences depicting a cause/effect relationship. See "as," "because," and "since" in the Glossary of Usage for preferred usage for these three words.)

Similarly, there is no rule prohibiting beginning a sentence with "however." Stylistically, however, it is often a better idea to move the transition "however" further into the sentence so that it immediately precedes the point of contrast, as is the case in this sentence.

Myth: Never End a Sentence With a Preposition

Winston Churchill did more than anyone else to debunk this writing myth. Churchill pointed out the idiocy of this non-rule when he wrote the following marginal comment on a state document: "This is the sort of English up with which I will not put."

Notwithstanding Churchill's remark, many readers profess to be offended by sentences that end with prepositions. For this reason, it is not a good practice to end sentences with prepositions when they can be easily revised.

EXAMPLE

Winfield may be able to get title to the entire triangle, not just the part which the bathhouse is built upon.

Revised:

Winfield may be able to get title to the entire triangle, not just the part upon which the bathhouse is built.

Notice that some sentences ending with a preposition are not easily revised using the technique above because the preposition works with the verb to create a meaning that is different from the meaning of the verb alone. For example, "to put up with" has a meaning far different from the meaning of "to put." Consequently, the best way to revise such verb + preposition combinations is to use a synonym ("to put up with" = "to tolerate").

Myth: Never Write a One-Sentence Paragraph

One-sentence paragraphs are not *per se* wrong, although they are often a sign of lack of development of the ideas in the writing. Numerous one-sentence paragraphs have the added drawback of making the writing seem unsophisticated.

For these reasons, use one-sentence paragraphs infrequently. Save them for occasions when the paragraph serves as a transition between two large sections of a document or when a shorter paragraph will give the reader a breather between two or more extremely long paragraphs. Notice too that a well-written one-sentence paragraph is usually made up of a fairly long sentence, although on rare occasions a one-sentence paragraph composed of a short sentence can be quite dramatic. (See section 20.4 for more about paragraph length.)

Myth: Never Split an Infinitive

Grammar historians tell us that we acquired this non-rule at the time grammarians attempted to force the English language into the Latin grammar system. In Latin, infinitives are one word; hence, infinitives are never split in Latin. Without regard to either the obvious fact that infinitives are two words in English (to see, to argue, to determine) or the obvious fact that speakers of English regularly split infinitives with a modifier, the non-rule was created so that English grammar could conform to Latin grammar.

This all seems terribly silly until you remember that at the time English was considered an inferior, upstart, unruly language and Latin was considered a superior, well-designed, systematic language. Moreover, devising a grammar that actually described the way English was used was unheard of at the time. The purpose of grammar, it was thought, was to bring order to a language raging out of control.

What should a legal writer do then about split infinitives? Because the split infinitive myth is so firmly entrenched in many educated readers' minds, it is not worth the possible negative reaction to a given split infinitive if there are reasonably good ways to change it. In fact, many split infinitives are redundant ("to completely comprehend," "to finally finish") and need the modifier removed.

However, when the split infinitive is the best, indeed the most precise, way to express a point, stand your ground and use it.

Note

Do not split infinitives with "not." Move the "not" before the infinitive.

EXAMPLE

The defendant explained that to not attend the meeting would have drawn undue attention to him.

Revised:

The defendant explained that not to attend the meeting would have drawn undue attention to him. *OR*

The defendant explained that not attending the meeting would have drawn undue attention to him.

Chapter 19

Connections Between Paragraphs

§19.1 HEADINGS

Headings serve two purposes for the reader: They signal the overall structure, and they help the reader locate where he or she is in a document. In other words, headings are useful indicators of the large-scale organization as well as finding devices.

As indicators of organization, headings work a bit like a table of contents. They give the reader the framework within which to fit the ideas. They are reminders of what is a large concept, what is a subpoint, and what is a supporting detail in this document.

As finding devices, headings are invaluable to readers. A reader who does not have the time to read the whole document can use the headings to find the exact section he or she must read. For readers who have previously read the whole document and later need to refer to a point, headings are a quick way to locate that point.

Like all other headings, argumentative headings in briefs must be both indicators of overall structure and finding devices. In addition, they have a third important function: They persuade. (See section 7.9 for more on writing argumentative headings.)

Even though headings in objective memos are somewhat less important to the overall document than argumentative headings are to a brief, they still must be well written. The best headings in memos are fairly short, not more than one typed line and usually less than half a line, and they capture the content in a nutshell. This is no small feat. The trick is to remember the reader and how that reader is likely to use the headings.

For headings to be helpful structural indicators, they must be written in parallel form (see section 25.7) and in a consistent format. If the document has headings and subheadings, the reader will be able to identify the different levels of headings if they use compatible but different formats. For example, the main headings may use roman numerals and boldface and the subheadings may use capital letters and underlining. (See section 27.2.2 for capitalization in headings.)

EXAMPLE

    I. **Main Heading**
         A. <u>Subheading</u>
         B. <u>Subheading</u>
    II. **Main Heading**
         A. <u>Subheading</u>
         B. <u>Subheading</u>

Note

The time-honored advice that "You can't have a 1 without a 2, and you can't have an A without a B" is still good advice. In other words, do not create a heading or a subheading unless there is at least one more heading or subheading at that same level.

Developing a good format for headings is generally quite simple. The bigger challenge is composing the content in the headings. To be useful finding devices, headings must capture the essence of the following section with enough specificity to be meaningful and enough generality to encompass the entire section.

Often the law itself will suggest the content of various sections of the document and hence the headings. An elements analysis or a list of factors, for example, lends itself nicely to a document with the elements or factors as the headings.

But don't automatically assume that each element or factor deserves its own heading. Undisputed elements will probably require minimal discussion. Consequently, the document will appear chopped up if the writer uses a separate heading for each one. More important, the reader is not likely to need a heading for each undisputed element. In such a case, it usually works better to group all the undisputed elements under one heading and the disputed elements under a second heading with separate subheadings for each disputed element.

EXAMPLE

    I. **Undisputed Elements**
    II. **Disputed Elements**
         A. <u>Open and Notorious</u>
         B. <u>Hostile</u>

The key to composing good headings, then, is finding the key words and phrases that sum up the following section. Sometimes the easiest way to write a heading is to reread the section and simply ask yourself, "In a nutshell, what is this section about?" The answer should be close to what would make a good heading. For example, if the answer is "the court's lack of jurisdiction in this matter," then omit what can be easily inferred and the heading becomes "Lack of Jurisdiction."

Another way to arrive at the right heading is to assume you are discussing the document with a colleague and need to refer to a given section. What would you call that section? If "the history of the statute" is the first thing that comes to mind, then that may very well be the best heading.

But what if you were writing an office memo for the *Patterson* case and the first thing that came to mind for a particular section was something like "whether or not the court will admit the eyewitnesses' line-up identifications"? Although this clause may accurately sum up the section, consider how it will look as a heading:

EXAMPLE

Whether or Not the Court Will Admit the Eyewitnesses' Line-up Identifications

---

The heading exceeds the one-line limit and includes some information that the reader can easily infer. Now consider these four substitute headings for the same section:

EXAMPLE

1. The Line-up
2. Line-up Identifications
3. Admissibility of Line-up Identifications
4. Admissibility of Eyewitnesses' Line-up Identifications

Option 1 is probably too general. It is unlikely the following section will include everything about the line-up. The reader will need more specific direction. Option 2 is better. Even so, if the focus of the following section is on the *admissibility* of the identifications, that key word in the heading will be helpful to the reader. Option 4 is also acceptable, but the word "eyewitnesses" can probably be inferred. Option 3 is the best. It sums up the section; it includes the key words and phrases; and it is short enough to be read at a glance.

One last thought about headings: Headings are for the reader, not the writer. The most common mistake legal writers make regarding headings is to use them as crutches for the writer rather than as aids for the reader. Headings should not be used as artificial bridges between two sections of the document. The connection between the sections should be made without the heading. If the headings in a document were removed, the sections should still naturally flow from one to the next.

§19.2   ROADMAPS AND SIGNPOSTS

§19.2.1   Roadmaps

Roadmaps are introductory paragraphs that give readers an overview of the entire document. They give readers the "big picture" perspective so that readers will be able to understand how numerous discrete bits of information fit together in the larger whole.

Like real roadmaps, roadmap paragraphs orient readers in several ways: They establish the parameters and overall structure of the discussion; they suggest what will be important and hence what deserves the readers' particular attention; and they create expectations for how the discussion will unfold and how it will conclude. (See section 5.22.1.)

Although not every objective memo needs a roadmap paragraph, those with several steps in the analysis are a great deal easier to read if the writer uses one to set the stage for what follows. For example, if the attorney requesting the Beaver Custom Carpet memo in Chapter 5 had asked a broader question, such as whether the contract was enforceable under the UCC Statute of Frauds, the memo would have required several more steps in the analysis. Consequently, a roadmap paragraph like the one that follows would have provided a helpful overview.

EXAMPLE

The McKibbins claim that because there was no written contract, the oral contract is unenforceable under this state's version of the UCC Statute of Frauds. The first thing the court will have to determine, then, is whether the UCC applies at all. If the court finds that the UCC does govern the contract, the court will then have to decide whether the Statute of Frauds bars BCC's claim. Because BCC did not comply with the formal requirements of the Statute of Frauds, the court will find that the contract is unenforceable unless one of the exceptions included in the Statute applies. The only exception likely to apply is the specially manufactured goods exception.

A good roadmap paragraph also tells readers where to focus their attention. For example, if the applicable law includes several elements or factors, the reader will find it helpful to be told in the roadmap paragraph which elements or factors are critical to a case. This relieves readers from worrying about all the elements or factors and allows them to concentrate on only the disputed elements or the pivotal factors.

EXAMPLE

To claim a prescriptive easement, the Oregon Wilderness Watchers will have to satisfy four elements by clear and convincing evidence: 1) that its use was open and notorious; 2) that its use was continuous and uninterrupted; 3) that its use was adverse to the right of the owner; and 4) that its use of the property met each of the other requirements for over ten years. *See Thompson v. Scott,* 528 P.2d 509, 510 (Or. 1974). Although OWW should have no difficulty satisfying the first and fourth elements, the second element and especially the third element will be difficult to satisfy.

Note

Roadmap paragraphs that use the "first, we will look at _____ ; then we will look at _____ ; and finally we will look at _____ " approach tend to sound unsophisticated. Substituting "I" or "this memorandum" is no better. A better approach is to use the court as the actor. "First, the court must determine _____ ; if the court finds _____ , it must then consider _____ ."

Compare the following roadmap paragraphs. Notice how much more sophisticated Examples 2 and 3 sound. Example 2 uses the court as the actor, so it is now clear to the reader that the memorandum is tracking the court's decisionmaking process. Example 3 uses the two parties as actors to get away from the "you-and-me, dear reader" approach and to set up a logical progression of sub-issues. Notice that "we" in Example 3 refers to the client and attorney, not to the writer and reader.

EXAMPLE 1   UNSOPHISTICATED ROADMAP PARAGRAPH

In this memorandum, we will examine three issues. First, we will look at whether the statute applies. If we find that it does not, then we will look at whether the Oregon Wilderness Watchers had an easement. If we find that an easement was created, then we will examine the scope of the easement.

| EXAMPLE 2 | BETTER ROADMAP |

In deciding this case, a court would consider three issues. A court would first determine whether the statute applies. If it does not, the court would then determine whether the Oregon Wilderness Watchers had an easement. If the court determines that an easement had been created, the court would then decide the scope of the easement.

| EXAMPLE 3 | BETTER ROADMAP |

Our client would like to prevent or limit the use of a path across his property by the Oregon Wilderness Watchers (OWW). An Oregon statute exists that provides for public recreational use, while protecting the owner's interest in his land, and we will argue that it applies to this case. OWW will contend that the statute does not apply and that a prescriptive easement exists. If a prescriptive easement does exist, our client wants to limit the scope of its use.

---

§19.2.2   Signposts

Signposts are those words and phrases that keep readers oriented as they progress through a piece of writing. They can be used as a connecting thread throughout a whole document or through a smaller section.

To be the most effective, a series of signposts needs to be signaled in advance. For example, a writer may signal a series of signposts when he or she opens a section by saying, "There are four exceptions to the Statute of Frauds." In the subsequent discussion, the writer can then use the words "first," "second," "third," "fourth" (or "final" or "last"), and "exception" to signal shifts to each new exception.

The following example is an excerpt from a memo for the broader question, whether the contract is enforceable under the UCC Statute of Frauds. The set-up for the signpost series and the signposts are in boldface type.

EXAMPLE

    There are four exceptions to the Statute of Frauds, but three of them are not applicable. The first of these inapplicable exceptions, § 4-2-201(2), applies only to transactions "between merchants." In an earlier section, § 4-2-201(1), a merchant is defined as "a person who deals in goods of the kind or otherwise holds himself out as having knowledge or skill peculiar to the practices or goods involved in the transaction or to whom such knowledge or skill may be attributed by his employment of an agent or broker or other intermediary who by his occupation holds himself out as having such knowledge or skill." Because the McKibbins presumably had little or no experience in the carpeting business and because they hired no intermediary to negotiate the transaction for them, the court will probably not find that they are merchants. This exception, then, does not apply.

    The second inapplicable exception, § 4-2-201(3)(b), provides that a contract that does not satisfy the requirements of subsection (1) is still enforceable if the party against whom enforcement is sought admits in his pleading, testimony, or otherwise in court that a contract for sale was made. Because we are not at the litigation stage of this case yet, this exception does not apply.

    The third inapplicable exception, § 4-2-201(3)(c), provides that a contract is enforceable with respect to goods for which payment has been made and accepted or which have been received and accepted. The McKibbins made no payment for the rugs, and they never received the rugs, so this exception also does not apply.

    The exception that may be applicable is the exception for specially manufactured goods . . . .

    Notice that most signpost series use the ordinal numbers (first, second, third, and so on) before a noun such as "element," "exception," "factor," "issue," "part," "prong," "reason," "requirement," "question," or "section."

EXAMPLES

three issues

the first issue, the second issue, the third issue

a two-part test

the first part of the test, the second part of the test

three questions to consider

the first question, the second question, the final question

Once a signpost series is set up, do not change terminology. If there were three questions in the introduction to the series, it will be confusing to readers if the second question is suddenly re-labeled "the second issue." (See section 23.1.4.)

Do not worry that legal readers will find such consistency boring. Legal readers are reading for information, not entertainment. Consistent terminology in signposts adds to the document's clarity. (See section 5.22.2.)

Chapter 20

Effective Paragraphs

§20.1 The Function of a Paragraph

Paragraphs exist for many reasons. First, they help writers organize what they are writing. Second, they help readers see and understand that organization. Third, they give readers a psychological, as well as a logical, break.

Writers need paragraphs as much as readers do. Paragraphs are like tidy boxes in which to sort information. They make writing a manageable task. When faced with the task of writing up all their research on a legal question, many writers feel overwhelmed. But when faced with the task of writing a paragraph to explain one small part of that research, most writers feel they can do it.

Readers need paragraphs so that they can absorb information in manageable bits. If the typical legal reader must comprehend twenty hours' worth of research in the roughly twenty minutes it takes to study an eight-page memo, he or she will need some way to see significant groupings of ideas. That way is the paragraph.

But paragraphing is more than a matter of logic and organization. It is also a matter of reader comfort and aesthetics. After all, those "boxes" into which the writer is fitting ideas can be huge containers that are too heavy to lift or small cartons with barely enough room for half an idea.

When paragraphs are too long, readers tend to become bewildered, even lost, or worse, lulled into inattention. Paragraphs that are too short, on the other hand, make the writing and the thinking seem skimpy and inconsequential. Readers need paragraphs that are the right size to comfortably follow what the writer is saying.

Paragraphs also change the look of a page. They create more white space, which can be a welcome relief. Anyone who has opened a book to see a solid mass of type on page one knows how intimidating overly long paragraphs can be. In contrast, the visual break at the beginning of a paragraph signals a brief mental breather. Ah, says the reader, I can see that this is broken up into reasonable segments.

Finally, to truly understand the function of a paragraph, one must also consider where it fits into the team of organizational elements within a whole piece of writing. The first significant organizational element is, of course, the sentence. Here, words are grouped for the first time. After that comes the paragraph. It is the first significant grouping of sentences. From there we have paragraphs blocks, sometimes sections with their own headings, and then the whole document.

As the first significant grouping of sentences, a paragraph becomes a kind of mini-composition all its own. It has a beginning, a middle, and an end. It makes a point — its topic — that is larger than the point of a sentence.

The following paragraph illustrates how a paragraph is a mini-composition. It is taken from the middle of an argument section of a memorandum of law in opposition to a motion to disclose the identity of a state informant.

EXAMPLE

Beginning

The fact that the informer is present at the alleged drug transaction is not determinative of whether the testimony of that informant is relevant or necessary. *Lewandowski v. State,* 389 N.E.2d 706 (Ind. 1979). In *Lewandowski,* the Indiana Supreme Court held that "[m]ere presence of the informer when marijuana was sold to a police officer has been held to be insufficient to overcome the privilege of nondisclosure." *Id.* at 710. The court made the same

Middle

ruling on nearly identical facts (informant introduced officer to defendant and was present during purchase of illegal drugs) in *Craig v. State,* 404 N.E.2d 580 (Ind. 1980).

Ending

In the instant case, the state's informant served mainly as a line of introduction and as such her testimony does not automatically become relevant or necessary to the defendant's case simply because she was present at the scene.

Paragraphs, then, function as mini-compositions within the larger composition, or document. They divide up the information and present it in neat little packages.

§20.2　Unity and Coherence in Paragraphs

§20.2.1　Paragraph Unity

To be a mini-composition, a paragraph must have its own topic, that is, its own point to make, and all the elements of the paragraph must work together to make that point. When they do, the paragraph has unity.

Look again at the paragraph about the state informant.

EXAMPLE

> The fact that the informer is present at the alleged drug transaction is not determinative of whether the testimony of that informant is relevant or necessary. *Lewandowski v. State,* 389 N.E.2d 706 (Ind. 1979). In *Lewandowski,* the Indiana Supreme Court held that "[m]ere presence of the informer when marijuana was sold to a police officer has been held to be insufficient to overcome the privilege of nondisclosure." *Id.* at 710. The court made the same ruling on nearly identical facts (informant introduced officer to defendant and was present during purchase of illegal drugs) in *Craig v. State,* 404 N.E.2d 580 (Ind. 1980). In the instant case, the state's informant served mainly as a line of introduction and as such her testimony does not automatically become relevant or necessary to the defendant's case simply because she was present at the scene.

All of the information in the paragraph is about one topic: the informant's testimony is not necessarily relevant or necessary simply because the informant was present at the drug transaction. This topic is introduced at the beginning of the paragraph by a topic sentence, developed and supported by two sentences in the middle of the paragraph, and then concluded by the last sentence.

What the paragraph does not do is stray from this topic. Even though the writer will need to refer to both *Lewandowski* and *Craig* later in the memo to support other points, he or she did not get sidetracked and try to do it here. The paragraph stays on course and makes its point. It has a clear focus; it has unity.

§20.2.2　Paragraph Coherence

When a paragraph is coherent, the various elements of the paragraph are connected in such a way that the reader can easily follow the writer's development of ideas. Coherence can be achieved in a number of ways: by following easily recognized organizational patterns, particularly those that are established patterns for legal writing; by establishing and then using key terms; and by using sentence structure and other coherence devices to reinforce the connections between ideas.

a.   Using Familiar Organizational Patterns

The most important way of achieving coherence is to arrange the ideas in a predictable, familiar pattern. All readers expect certain patterns — cause/effect, problem/solution, chronological order — and when writers meet those expectations, the ordering of the ideas is easy to follow. Legal readers have some additional patterns that they have come to expect in legal writing. For example, once a rule, standard, or definition has been laid out, legal readers naturally expect it to be applied. They expect a court's holding to be followed by its rationale. In office memos, arguments are almost always followed by counterarguments. In both office memos and briefs, the IRAC pattern (issue, rule, analysis/application, and conclusion) and all its variations are commonplace and expected.

Notice how the writer of the following paragraph uses the IRAC pattern to achieve coherence.

EXAMPLE

Issue	The second element, continuous, is in dispute. To satisfy this element, OWW does not need to establish that its use was con-
Rule	stant. *See Kondor v. Prose,* 622 P.2d 741 (Or. Ct. App. 1981). It need show only that its use of the path was consistent with its needs. *Id.* OWW will argue that its use was consistent with its needs. To do its research,
Application	OWW needed to use the path only two or three times per month, and it did so from 1967 to 1977. Although we could argue that use of the path two or three times per month is sporadic, this argument is not persuasive because of the rural quality of the land.
Conclusion	Therefore, the court will probably find that OWW satisfies this element.

Writers can also achieve coherence in paragraphs by creating reader expectations and then fulfilling them. For example, when a writer sets up a list of factors, elements, reasons, or issues, the reader naturally expects the writing to follow up on that list. In the following paragraph, the writer uses this technique to create a coherent discussion of how the statutory term "ways of this state" will be construed in a case in which an intoxicated driver was on the shoulder of the road.

EXAMPLE

> However, a narrow construction of the term "ways" is unlikely. In fact, there are two strong indications that Montana will favor a broad construction: 1) an extension stated in the statutory definition of "highway"; and 2) an interpretation of "ways" given in a Montana Supreme Court decision. By statutory definition, "[h]ighway means the entire width between the boundary lines of every publicly maintained way when any part thereof is open to the use of the public for purposes of vehicular travel, *except that for the purpose of chapter 8 the term also includes ways which have been or shall be dedicated to public use*" (emphasis added). Mont. Code Ann. § 61.1.201 (1983). Chapter 8 includes offenses committed while under the influence of alcohol. Because the legislature expanded the statutory definition for alcohol-related offenses, it follows that the legislature intended to broaden, not narrow, the term. Following the legislature's lead, the Montana Supreme Court stipulated that "ways" encompasses state and county right-of-ways, including borrow pits, which road maintenance crews use as sources of dirt and gravel. *State v. Taylor,* 661 P.2d 33, 35 (Mont. 1983). It is highly unlikely that the court would include borrow pits but exempt shoulders from the term "ways." Therefore, the court will probably conclude that Mr. Renko's truck was on the ways of the state open to the public.

---

b.   *Establishing and Using Key Terms*

Of the various methods a writer has at his or her disposal for creating coherence, repetition of key terms is certainly the easiest and one of the most important. In the following paragraph about the state informant, one or more of the key terms used — <u>informant</u>, **present** or **presence**, <u>testimony</u>, and RELEVANT OR NECESSARY — appear, in a different typeface, in every sentence. Together they are part of a network of connecting threads that create a coherent theme for the paragraph.

EXAMPLE   **EXAMPLE WITH KEY TERMS HIGHLIGHTED**

> The fact that the <u>informer</u> is **present** at the alleged drug transaction is not determinative of whether the <u>testimony</u> of that <u>informant</u> is RELEVANT OR NECESSARY. *Lewandowski v. State,* 389

N.E.2d 706 (Ind. 1979). In *Lewandowski,* the Indiana Supreme Court held that "[m]ere **presence** of the <u>informer</u> when marijuana was sold to a police officer has been held to be insufficient to overcome the privilege of nondisclosure." *Id.* at 710. The court made the same ruling on nearly identical facts (<u>informant</u> introduced officer to defendant and was **present** during purchase of illegal drugs) in *Craig v. State,* 404 N.E.2d 580 (Ind. 1980). In the instant case, the state's <u>informant</u> served mainly as a line of introduction and as such her <u>testimony</u> does not automatically become RELEVANT OR NECESSARY to the defendant's case simply because she was **present** at the scene.

The following paragraph from the memo concerning the intoxicated driver on the shoulder of the road also demonstrates the repetition of key terms. Notice how the writer makes logical connections between the key terms to show that **ways of the state open to the public** may not be construed to include SHOULDERS of the road.

EXAMPLE   **EXAMPLE WITH KEY TERMS HIGHLIGHTED**

Although the primary issue of the case focuses upon resolving questions pertaining to actual physical control, the issue of whether Mr. Renko's truck was on the **ways of the state open to the public** deserves brief analysis. The traffic code states that "**'ways of the state open to the public'** means any highway, road, alley lane, parking area, or other public or private place <u>adapted and fitted for public travel</u> that is in common use by the public." Mont. Code Ann. § 61.8.101(1) (1983). The language specifically states "<u>adapted and fitted for public travel</u>." Because Mr. Renko's truck was found on the SHOULDER, the court would have to determine whether the SHOULDER of a highway is <u>adapted and fitted for public travel</u>. In defining other statutory language, the Montana Supreme Court resorted to dictionary definitions. Webster defines SHOULDER as "either edge of a roadway: specifically: the part of the roadway *outside the <u>traveled</u> way*" (emphasis added). It is possible, then, that the court could interpret the statutory language narrowly and conclude that the term **"ways"** does not encompass SHOULDERS.

In short, this paragraph is itself an analysis of the key terms.

ways of the state open to the public = <u>adapted and fitted for public travel</u>

SHOULDER = *outside the traveled way*; therefore,
SHOULDER may not = **ways of the state open to the public**

c.　*Using Sentence Structure and Other Coherence Devices*

In addition to using familiar organizational patterns and repeating key terms, writers can create coherence through their sentence structure and through a number of other common coherence devices. Dovetails (beginning a sentence with a reference to the preceding sentence) and other transitions create connections by establishing links between sentences. (See Chapter 21.) Parallelism within a sentence or between sentences shows the reader which ideas should be considered together and which should be compared and contrasted. (See section 25.7.) Even pronouns in their own small way provide subtle links within the writing because they are a connection to the noun they replace.

EXAMPLE

The fact that the informer is present at the alleged drug transaction is not determinative of whether the testimony of that informant is relevant or necessary. LEWAN-DOWSKI V. STATE, 389 N.E.2d 706 (Ind. 1979). IN LEWANDOWSKI, the Indiana Supreme Court held that "[m]ere presence of the informer when marijuana was sold to a police officer has been held to be insufficient to overcome the privilege of nondisclosure." *Id.* at 710. The court made the same ruling on nearly identical facts (informant introduced officer to defendant and was present during purchase of illegal drugs) in *Craig v. State,* 404 N.E.2d 580 (Ind. 1980). In the instant case, **the state's informant** served mainly as a line of introduction and as such **her** testimony does not automatically become relevant or necessary to the defendant's case simply because **she** was present at the scene.

DOVETAILING

Parallelism

Parallelism

Pronouns

For the following paragraph, notice how the parallel phrases "on the defendant's ability to operate the vehicle" and "on the vehicle's condition" in the opening, topic sentence set up the organizational pattern. The writer then signals the beginning of each half of the discussion by using the parallel sentence openers "in focusing on the defendant's con-dition" and "in focusing on the vehicle's condition." Note too the dove-tailing between sentences 2 and 3 ("he would have been able to operate the vehicle" → "not only is it possible that he could have operated the truck") and between sentences 4 and 5 ("defined" → "by that defini-tion"). Once again, pronouns also subtly provide coherence ("defen-dant" → "he," "truck" → "it," "court" → "it").

EXAMPLE

If some form of operability is required, then the court must decide whether to focus on the defendant's ability to operate the vehicle or on the vehicle's condition. *See State v. Smelter,* 674 P.2d 690, 693 (Wash. App. 1983). In focusing on the defendant's condition, the court could find that because the defendant had the key and was in the cab of the truck, he would have been able to operate the vehicle had he been awakened. Not only is it possible that he could have operated the truck, it is evident that he did drive the truck from the tavern to the freeway before parking it on the shoulder. In focusing on the vehicle's condition, the Washington court used the trial court's "reasonably operable" standard and defined that term as any malfunction short of a cracked block or a similar problem that would render the vehicle totally inoperable. *Id.* at 693. By that definition, Mr. Renko's truck was reasonably operable regardless of whether it would start. Therefore, if the Montana court considers operability an issue, it would probably find that Mr. Renko was capable of operating the vehicle and that the vehicle was in reasonably operable condition.

To sum up, then, if a paragraph has unity, it has all the right pieces. If a paragraph is both unified and coherent, then all the right pieces are arranged and connected in such a way that the reader can easily follow them.

§20.3   PARAGRAPH PATTERNS

Every paragraph needs a focus, a topic, a point to make. In addition, every paragraph needs a shape, a way of moving through sentences to make that point. The example paragraph on page 541 about the rele-vance of the informant's testimony has one of the most common shapes or patterns: that of a fat hourglass.

An hourglass paragraph begins with a general statement about the topic. This statement may take up one or more sentences. The paragraph then narrows to the specific support or elaboration or explanation the writer has for that general statement. The paragraph concludes with a more general sentence or two about the topic.

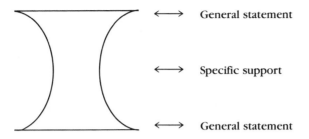

A variation of this pattern is the V-shaped paragraph. Like the hourglass paragraph, the V-shaped paragraph begins with a general discussion of the topic and then narrows to the specific support. The V-shaped paragraph ends with the specific support; it does not return to a general statement.

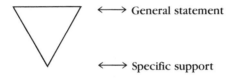

EXAMPLE   V-SHAPED PARAGRAPH

Kraft Savings, one of three savings and loans represented on Kraft Island, does a significant amount of the banking business on Kraft Island. As of 1986, Kraft Savings had 2.2 million dollars in deposits, 9.6 million dollars in outstanding loans, and a large volume of business with the Kraft City Council. In 1986, Kraft Savings handled 40 million dollars in transactions for almost 1900 customers in about 2400 accounts.	General statement Specific support

---

Both the hourglass and the V-shaped paragraph patterns work well in legal writing. Both use the opening sentence or sentences as an overview of what is to come and then proceed to support that generalization with specifics. In some senses, both patterns, but particularly the hourglass pattern, resemble deductive reasoning.

EXAMPLE	PARAGRAPH USING DEDUCTIVE REASONING

Major premise	The purpose of summary judgment is to eliminate useless trials on formal issues that cannot be factually supported or, if factually supported, cannot as a matter of law lead to a result favorable to the non-moving party. *Buris v. General Ins. Co.,* 553 P.2d 125 (Wash. 1976). A summary judgment motion permits the court to pierce formal allegations of fact in pleadings and grant relief to a plaintiff when it appears from uncontroverted facts that no genuine issue exists. *Preston v. Duncan,* 349 P.2d 605 (Wash.
Minor premise	1960). Here the facts regarding the accident are undisputed. Ms. Hawkins readily admits that her car collided with Eli Reisman's car. CP 27. Officer Sanchez's testimony establishes that Ms. Hawkins was negligent in failing to concentrate fully on the hazardous
Conclusion	road conditions. RP 59. Consequently, partial summary judgment is appropriate.

Less common, but also useful, is the inverted V paragraph. Here, the writer begins with the specifics and then concludes with a general statement. This pattern resembles inductive reasoning and, like inductive reasoning, has some risks. The reader may feel disoriented without an overview statement, or the reader may miss the relevance of some supporting evidence because he or she does not know where the writer is heading. Even so, the inverted V pattern can be effective, particularly in persuasive writing, if the writer is able to lay out the specific support in such a way that the reader reaches the desired conclusion even before it is stated. This technique has the effect of making the reader feel like he or she arrived at the conclusion independently, not after being told what to think. (See section 7.10.2.)

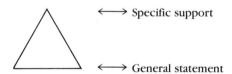

$\longleftrightarrow$ Specific support

$\longleftrightarrow$ General statement

§20.4   Paragraph Length

First, the truth. Not all paragraphs are three to five sentences long. Most are, but not all. In fact, quite a few well-written paragraphs are as short as two sentences and, yes, some well-written paragraphs contain only one sentence. One-sentence paragraphs are neither a goal to strive for nor a taboo to be feared. Writers simply need to know when they have finished what they set out to do in the paragraph.

Similarly, good paragraphs may run many sentences longer than five. It is not outrageous for a paragraph in legal writing to include seven or even eight sentences, as long as the writer needed that many to make the point. However, writers should keep in mind the reader's comfort and avoid seven- and eight-sentence paragraphs about complicated discussions of law. Remember too that an eight-sentence paragraph is likely to create a solid page of type, which, as we discussed in section 20.1, has a negative psychological impact.

The following five-paragraph example is from one section in an appellate brief. Notice the number of sentences in and the length of each paragraph. Also note that citation sentences are not counted as substantive sentences.

EXAMPLE

I. The Trial Court Erred in Holding That the Plaintiff Is a Public Figure as a Matter of Law

The states have a legitimate interest in compensating plaintiffs for damage to reputation inflicted through defamatory publications. *Gertz v. Robert Welch, Inc.,* 418 U.S. 323, 341 (1974). While recognizing that "[s]ome tension necessarily exists between the need for a vigorous and uninhibited press and the legitimate interest in redressing wrongful injury," the U.S. Supreme Court has stressed that the plaintiff's right to the protection of his reputation must not be sacrificed when the court balances these two competing interests. *Id.*

Two-sentence paragraph

In an attempt to balance the interests of the media against the interests of plaintiffs injured by defamatory statements, the Court developed three classes of plaintiffs: public officials, public figures, and private figures. *New York Times v. Sullivan,* 376 U.S. 254, 279 (1964); *Curtis Publishing Co. v. Butts,* 388 U.S. 130 (1966); *Gertz,* 418 U.S. at 343. Because public figure plaintiffs are held to a higher standard of proof in defamation suits, the Court has made it clear that the public figure standard is to be con-

Three-sentence paragraph

strued narrowly. *Gertz,* 418 U.S. at 341, 352. The Court will not lightly find a plaintiff to be a public figure. *Id.* at 352.

Three-sentence paragraph

The first class of public figure defined by the Court in *Gertz* is the limited purpose public figure. To become a limited purpose public figure, a plaintiff must voluntarily inject himself into a particular public controversy and attempt to influence its outcome. *Id.* at 351, 352. By doing so, the plaintiff invites public attention and comment on a limited range of issues relating to his involvement in the controversy. *Id.* at 351.

One-sentence paragraph

The Court described the second class of public figure, the all-purpose public figure, as having "assumed roles of especial prominence in the affairs of society," or as occupying "positions of such persuasive power and influence," or as "achieving such pervasive frame or notoriety that he becomes a public figure for all purposes and in all contexts." *Id.* at 345, 351.

Six-sentence paragraph

Under these narrow definitions laid down by the U.S. Supreme Court, Vashon Savings and Loan is neither a limited purpose public figure nor an all-purpose public figure. Therefore, the trial court erred in granting defendants' motion for partial summary judgment on the public figure issue. Furthermore, this error was prejudicial because it resulted in the plaintiff's being held to a higher standard of proof at trial. But because the standard of review is *de novo* when a partial summary judgment order is appealed, this court is not bound by the erroneous trial court decision below. *Herron v. Tribune Publishing Co.,* 108 Wash. 2d 162, 169, 736 P.2d 249, 255 (1987); *Noel v. King County,* 48 Wash. App. 227, 231, 738 P.2d 692, 695 (1987). Rather, the court must apply the *Gertz* public figure standard to the facts of this case and reach its own independent determination. Correct application of the standard will result in a holding that Vashon Savings and Loan is a private figure for purposes of this defamation suit.

First, a few comments about the above example. Notice that the length of each paragraph is primarily determined by content. The writer wrote as few or as many sentences as she needed to make each point. The length of each paragraph is further determined by reader comfort and interest. Some variety in paragraph length helps keep the writing interesting. Short, one- or two-sentence paragraphs tend to work in places where the reader needs a bit of a break before or after an unusually long paragraph. Too many short paragraphs, though, and the writing begins to seem choppy and superficial.

An occasional long paragraph allows the writer to go into depth on a point. Too many long paragraphs, though, and the writing slows down to a plod and seems heavy and ponderous.

Short paragraphs can also be effective when the writer is making a major shift, change, or connection between ideas. Consequently, short paragraphs frequently serve as transitions between major sections and as introductions or conclusions to major sections.

In the following example, the writer had just concluded his discussion of the first requirement of the statutory exception in the preceding paragraph. The one-sentence paragraph that follows introduced several paragraphs that dealt with the second requirement.

EXAMPLE   **EXAMPLE OF AN INTRODUCTION TO A SECTION**

The second requirement of the statutory exception — that the goods be unsuitable for sale in the ordinary course of the manufacturer's business — will probably be met.

Occasionally, extremely short paragraphs can be effective attention grabbers, particularly in persuasive writing. This technique will work only if the writer uses short paragraphs infrequently.

Long paragraphs work best in situations where the writer has been careful to lay out an organizational plan for the paragraph and then uses signposts (see section 19.2.2) to keep the reader oriented. In the following paragraph, the writer announces the paragraph's organizational plan in sentence one when she says there are three reasons. Then each reason is announced by the signposts, "first," "second," and "third."

EXAMPLE

In Arizona, the exclusion of religious beliefs or opinions elicited for the purpose of affecting the credibility of a witness is mandated for three reasons. *State v. Thomas,* 636 P.2d 1214 (Ariz. 1981) (citing 3 Jack B. Weinstein & Margaret A. Berger, *Evidence* ¶¶ 610 [01], 610-2 (1981). First, evidence of the religious beliefs of a witness often is irrelevant; injection of the religious beliefs of a witness into testimony can complicate issues, confuse the jury, and waste the court's time. *Id.* Second, admission into evidence of the religious beliefs of a witness can prejudice the jury; once a witness expresses a religious belief, jurors are inclined to attach weight to the testimony of the witness on the basis of whether they agree with that religious belief. *Id.* Third, the introduction of the religious belief of a witness can have constitutional implications; when a criminal defendant is confronted by a prosecuting witness whose testimony has been bolstered by evidence of the religiosity of that witness, the defendant's due process right to a fair trial is abrogated. *Id. See* U.S. Const. amend. XIV; Const. art. I, § 22. Both Arizona and Oregon appellate courts have found that when trial courts allow the prosecution to violate the constitutional and evidentiary rules against inquiring about the religious beliefs of a witness, the trial courts commit fundamental error of constitutional magnitude. *See Thomas,* 636 P.2d at 1217-18; *Estabrook,* 91 P.2d at 850.

In short, there is no magic or perfect length for a paragraph. When Abraham Lincoln was asked how tall a man should be, he said, tall enough so that his legs reach the ground. How long should a paragraph be? Long enough to make the writer's point. See Exercises 20.A and 20.B in the *Practice Book.*

§20.5   TOPIC AND CONCLUDING SENTENCES

Again, the truth. Not all paragraphs have topic and concluding sentences. In fact, many well-written paragraphs have neither.

However, and this is a big "however," many well-written paragraphs do have topic sentences, and those that don't, have an implied topic sentence that governs the paragraph as firmly as any written topic sentence. The same is true for concluding sentences. Well-written paragraphs that do not have an explicit concluding sentence have an implied concluding sentence. The writer may have chosen not to write out the concluding sentence because it is painfully obvious; nevertheless, the reader knows what the conclusion of that paragraph is.

The point then is to know what topic and concluding sentences do for a paragraph. Once you know how they work, then you can decide if a stated or an implied topic or concluding sentence is appropriate.

When in doubt, state your topic sentence. If you don't, your reader may also be in doubt.

§20.5.1   Stated Topic Sentences

The following examples demonstrate how the standard topic sentence works. Notice that the topic sentence has two functions: It introduces or names the topic and it asserts something about the topic.

EXAMPLE 1

Under a liberal reading of Fed. R. Civ. P. 4(d)(1), the courts have considered several other factors in evaluating if service was proper. First, the courts have recognized that "each decision proceeds on its own facts." *Karlsson,* 318 F.2d at 668. Second, the courts consider whether defendant will return to the place where service was left. *Id.* Third, the courts look at whether service was reasonably calculated to provide actual notice to the defendant. *Minnesota Mining & Mfg. Co. v. Kirkevold,* 87 F.R.D. 317, 323 (D. Minn. 1980).

EXAMPLE 2

Defendants have used the following articulated reasons to successfully rebut a plaintiff's prima facie case. In *Kelly,* the defendant testified that the plaintiff was terminated because he was the least effective salesman. *Kelly,* 640 F.2d at 977. Similarly, in *Sakellar,* the defendant alleged that the plaintiff lacked the skills and experience for the position. *Sakellar v. Lockheed Missiles,* 765 F.2d at 1456. And in *Sutton,* the defendant discharged the plaintiff for "intemperate and impolitic actions." *Sutton,* 646 F.2d at 410.

One common weakness of some novice legal writers is to write topic sentences that merely name the topic. These "topic sentences" fall under the category of "The next thing I'm going to talk about is . . . ."

Compare the following two topic sentences. Which will a reader find more helpful?

EXAMPLE 1

Another case that discussed actual malice is *Rosenbloom v. Metromedia, Inc.,* 403 U.S. 29 (1971).

EXAMPLE 2

The court extended these protections in *Rosenbloom,* holding that plaintiffs in a defamation action would have to prove actual malice if the statements published were of public or general interest. *Rosenbloom v. Metromedia,* 403 U.S. 29 (1971).

The topic sentence in Example 1 does little more than name a case. The topic sentence in Example 2 is far superior. It introduces the point the paragraph will make — that plaintiffs in a defamation action would have to prove actual malice if the statements published were of public or general interest. The topic sentence also includes a nice bridge, or transition, from the earlier discussion about *Sullivan.*

In addition, the topic sentence in Example 2 demonstrates an excellent method for writing topic sentences that introduce a new case. It begins with a transition that relates the point from the new case to the previous discussion and then follows with a paraphrase of the holding. Paraphrasing the holding at this point makes good sense. Invariably, the holding is the point a writer wants to get out of a case, so it works perfectly as the topic sentence.

EXAMPLE 1

The court extended these protections in *Rosenbloom,* holding that plaintiffs in a defamation action would have to prove actual malice if the statements published were of public or general interest. *Rosenbloom v. Metromedia,* 403 U.S. 29 (1971). The Court wrote, "If a matter is a subject of public or general interest, it cannot suddenly become less so merely because a private individual is involved, or because in some sense the individual did not 'voluntarily' choose to become involved." *Rosenbloom,* 403 U.S. at 43.

EXAMPLE 2

> **In *Messenger,* the court held that the trespassory slashing of trees was a permanent form of property damage.** *Messenger v. Frye,* 28 P.2d 1023 (Wash. 1934). However, the tree slashing in that case was extensive. It was the extent of the injury, not the type of injury, which made the damage irreparable and therefore permanent. Unlike the slashed trees, the damage to the four rosebushes in our case should not be considered extensive because only four out of twenty rosebushes were damaged. The rosebushes can probably be replaced, thus restoring the Archers' property to its original condition. Therefore, the damage to the rosebushes and buds is temporary, and the Archers will recover only for the restoration cost of the rosebuds and bushes, as well as the diminished use value of their property.

EXAMPLE 3

> **In an analogous Arizona case, *State v. Thomas,* the trial court was found to have committed an error of constitutional magnitude when it allowed the prosecution to do exactly as the prosecution did in the instant case.** *Thomas,* 636 P.2d at 1219. In *Thomas,* the only pertinent evidence was the testimony of the defendant, who stood accused of rape, and the testimony of the prosecuting witness. During the trial, the prosecution questioned the prosecuting witness about her religious beliefs and church-related activities, eliciting from the witness that she was a religious person. *Id.* at 1217. In closing argument, the prosecution told the jury that the ultimate issue was the credibility of the witnesses, and that before the jury could believe the defendant, it had to believe that the prosecuting witness, an "uprighteous, religious, moralistic type," was a liar. *Id.* The appellate court held that admission of the religious references was an error of constitutional magnitude. *Id.* 1219.

As we have seen, the first sentence of a paragraph is usually the topic sentence. After all, the best place to begin is usually with an introduction of what will follow.

Topic sentences may, however, appear later in a paragraph, particularly if the opening sentence or sentences are used to provide a transition to or background for the topic.

The following example is taken from the beginning of the second argument in the same memorandum in opposition to the defendants' motion for partial summary judgment. Notice how sentence 1 serves as a transition between the two arguments and sentence 2 provides background for sentence 3, the topic sentence.

EXAMPLE

Transition

Sullivan and *Gertz* dealt with individual citizens who had been libeled and who had sought redress in the courts. The case before the court today is different; the plaintiff is a state chartered savings and loan, a business entity. The significance of the different status of a business entity and its reputation, as compared to a private individual, has been recognized in several federal courts. The court in *Martin Marietta v. Evening Star Newspaper,* 417 F. Supp. 947, 955 (D.D.C. 1976) stated that "[t]he law of libel has long reflected the distinction between corporate and human plaintiffs" and that "a corporate libel action is not a basic [sic] of our constitutional system, and need not force the first amendment to yield as far as it would be in a private libel action." *Martin Marietta,* 417 F. Supp. at 955 (citations omitted). The *Marietta* court continued, "Corporations, which do not possess private lives to begin with, must similarly [to public figures] be denied full protection from libel." *Id.*

Background

Topic sentence

See Exercise 20.C in the *Practice Book.*

§20.5.2   Implied Topic Sentences

Many paragraphs with implied topic sentences occur in statements of fact. Although some statements of fact have paragraphs that are thematically organized and use traditional topic sentences, most have a chronological organization with implied topic sentences. Many use a mix of the two.

Practically all paragraphs in statements of fact depend on their narrative, or storytelling, quality to help keep the writing unified, or focused. The organizing principle, or topic, of such paragraphs may be what happened in a given time period, what happened to a given person, or what facts make up a given part of the situation.

The following paragraph appeared in the statement of facts from a case about whether service of process was valid when it was left at a spouse's home. The preceding paragraph explained that the defendant, Ms. Clay-Poole, has a job and residence in New York and that her husband has a job and residence in California. In this paragraph, no topic sentence is stated, but one is certainly implied.

EXAMPLE

Ms. Clay-Poole and Mr. Poole usually see each other about once a month for three or four days. They split the traveling about equally, although Ms. Clay-Poole travels to San Diego somewhat more frequently than Mr. Poole travels to Albany. They are happy with this arrangement; consequently, they do not intend to move in together permanently.

The implied topic sentence of this paragraph is that Ms. Clay-Poole and Mr. Poole have a commuter marriage. The writer could have stated the topic sentence, but in this case the topic may be sufficiently obvious to leave it implied.

§20.5.3   Concluding Sentences

To be worthwhile, concluding sentences need to do more than just restate the topic sentence. If they don't, then the paragraph will not seem to have advanced the line of reasoning in the paper. Look again at the paragraph about whether a drug informant's testimony is relevant. Notice how the topic and concluding sentences are not simply artful clones of each other.

EXAMPLE

The fact that the informer is present at   Topic sentence
the alleged drug transaction is not determi-
native that the testimony of that informant is
relevant or necessary. *Lewandowski v.
State,* 389 N.E.2d 706 (Ind. 1979). In *Lewandowski,* the Indiana Supreme Court
held that "[m]ere presence of the informer

Supporting
sentences

Conclusion

when marijuana was sold to a police officer has been held to be insufficient to overcome the privilege of nondisclosure." *Id.* at 710. The court made the same ruling on nearly identical facts (informant introduced officer to defendant and was present during purchase of illegal drugs) in *Craig v. State,* 404 N.E.2d 580 (Ind. 1980). The state's informant in the instant case served mainly as a line of introduction and does not as such automatically become relevant or necessary to the defendant's case simply because she was present at the scene.

The topic sentence introduces the topic and serves as a general statement of that point. The concluding sentence advances the line of reasoning in the memo by taking that topic, or that point, and applying it to the instant case. It rather neatly argues that the rationale in *Craig v. State* is applicable in the instant case because in both cases the informant "served mainly as a line of introduction." This concluding sentence is not just extra baggage, the obligatory "Now I'm going to tell you again what I told you before." It is a working sentence, a significant sentence, perhaps the most significant sentence in the paragraph.

In the following example, the writer of another memo uses the concluding sentence of a paragraph to extend the point made in the topic sentence. The topic sentence makes the point that the plaintiff has certain interests and rights; the concluding sentence furthers the discussion by saying that the plaintiff has been deprived of those rights.

EXAMPLE

The plaintiff will probably compare the facts of the instant case to the facts of *Moore* to show the court's recognition of an individual's proprietary interests in the tissue of her body. There as here, the defendant used tissue from the plaintiff's body to develop a commercially valuable product. There as here, the "owner" did not consent to the use of his tissue for the development of this product. Therefore, the defendant's action in *Moore* violated the plaintiff's rights under *Bouvia* to determine what should have been done with his body. Likewise, the women in our case had no knowledge of the use of fetal tissue for research. Therefore, the University's actions deprived the women of their right to determine what should have been done with the fetal tissue taken from their bodies.

The subsequent paragraph in the same memorandum demonstrates a slightly different and effective way to use topic and concluding sentences. In the following example, notice how the topic sentence introduces an argument and the concluding sentence extends the point by drawing the logical conclusion if that argument is accepted.

EXAMPLE

Conversely, the University will argue that fetal tissue does not meet the broad definition of property. The fetal tissue had no exchangeable value at the time of the abortion, or the plaintiff would not have had the abortion in the first place. The lack of value is demonstrated by the plaintiff's signing away of her rights to the fetal tissue before the abortion procedure. In fact, the fetal tissue by itself has no exchangeable value; it is the cell line developed from the tissue that carries value. If the fetal tissue has no exchangeable value, then the University cannot invade plaintiff's property rights by actionable wrong. No actionable wrong exists if no value is recognized in the fetal tissue.

Earlier we saw how a paraphrase of the holding often makes an excellent topic sentence. Paraphrasing the holding can also be an effective way to conclude a paragraph about an analogous case.

EXAMPLE

Recently, the Georgia appellate court addressed the issue of consent in relation to the disposal of a stillborn child. *See McCoy v. Georgia Baptist Hospital,* 306 S.E.2d 746 (Ga. Ct. App. 1983). In that case, the mother delivered a stillborn child in the defendant hospital. Both parents had signed a consent form authorizing the hospital to dispose of the body "in any manner they deem advisable." *Id.* at 747. Thereafter, the mother discovered that the body had been placed in a freezer and left there for approximately one month. The court held that the parents released their quasi-property interests in the child's body to the defendant hospital when they signed the consent form.

Another effective technique for writing concluding sentences is to use a particularly apt quotation. This technique allows the writer to introduce the point in the topic sentence with language of his or her own making and then finish with a colorful or memorable quotation from the court or another authority.

EXAMPLE

The California Appellate Court recently decided that an individual is entitled to full property rights in his organs and other bodily tissue. In *Moore v. Regents of UCLA,* 249 Cal. Rptr. 494 (Cal. Ct. App. 1988), the appellant's diseased spleen was removed by the appellee research hospital. Appellee subsequently discovered that Moore's spleen and other bodily tissue had unique characteristics that could be used to develop substances with potential commercial value. Moore was never told of appellee's discovery and continued to allow appellee to extract bodily tissue from him under the auspices of continuing treatment. The appellate court held that Moore had certain rights in his bodily tissue that should be recognized and protected. The court went on to say that "[t]he rights of dominion over one's own body, and the interests one has therein . . . are so akin to property interests that it would be a subterfuge to call them something else." *Id.* at 505.

One word of caution, though: Many legal writers overuse quotations. For the technique of concluding with a quotation to be effective, it should be used only occasionally and only when the quotation is unusually well stated.

Remember, too, that every paragraph does not absolutely have to have a stated concluding sentence. As with implied topic sentences, implied concluding sentences are permissible as long as the reader can easily surmise what the conclusion to that paragraph is.

As a writer, you must decide when a concluding sentence will help your reader and when it will seem like overkill. However, when in doubt, include a concluding sentence. What may seem obvious to you as the writer may not be so obvious to the reader.

Another possible rule of thumb for deciding when a concluding sentence can be left implied is to note when the concluding sentence simply restates the topic sentence and does not extend the line of reasoning being developed. Read the following paragraph, first with the concluding sentence and then without it.

EXAMPLE

Topic sentence   In our case, the plaintiff will argue that
                            fetal tissue is recognized as property under

the general definition set forth in *Washington Fruit* and *Labberton* because it has exchangeable value and because it is the subject of ownership. The exchangeable value of fetal tissue is evidenced by the agreement between the abortion clinics and the University to exchange the use of the tissue in research for the rendering of pathological services. The University must believe that the fetal tissue has value, or it would not be willing to provide medical services in exchange for the use of the fetal tissue. Additionally, fetal tissue is the subject of ownership because it was once part of the plaintiff's body, and an individual has certain property interests in the tissue of her body. Thus, the plaintiff will argue that because the fetal tissue has exchangeable value and because it is the subject of ownership, fetal tissue is property.

Supporting sentences

Concluding sentence

The writer of the memo from which this paragraph was taken decided that such a concluding sentence would be overkill. We agree. Rather than restate the obvious, he decided to open the next paragraph with a sentence that assumed the implied conclusion of the preceding paragraph.

EXAMPLE   NEXT PARAGRAPH

The plaintiff will further argue that the clinics recognize these property interests by obtaining a signed consent form relinquishing possession of the aborted fetus to the clinic for disposal.

Notice that the phrases "further argue" and "these property interests" signal to the reader that he or she should assume an implied conclusion to the preceding paragraph. See Exercise 20.D in the *Practice Book*.

§20.6   Paragraph Blocks

One reason why many paragraphs may not have topic sentences or concluding sentences yet function well in a piece of writing is that the paragraphs are part of a larger organizational element: a paragraph block. Like paragraphs, paragraph blocks are mini-compositions, only this time the beginning is likely to be a paragraph or two, the middle is usually several paragraphs, and the end is also a paragraph or more.

The beginning paragraph or paragraphs work like a topic sentence. It is a general statement that introduces the topic of the paragraph block and asserts something about that topic. Usually, the beginning paragraph will include a transition from the previous discussion.

The middle paragraphs contain the subpoints — the explanation, elaboration, or specifics that support the topic paragraph. Ideally, each of the middle paragraphs will be organized like a mini-composition with its own topic sentence, supporting sentences, and concluding sentences.

The concluding paragraph or paragraphs work in the block the same way a concluding sentence works in a paragraph. They bring the discussion back to the broad general topic, but in a way that advances the line of reasoning in the paper. Frequently this is done by pointing out the ultimate outcome of the discussion in the paragraph block or by applying the discussion in the paragraph block to the instant case.

The following example demonstrates how a fairly typical paragraph block works.

EXAMPLE   **PARAGRAPH BLOCK**

Topic paragraph

There is only one recent case in which a court has found a financial institution to be an all-purpose public figure. That case, *Coronado Credit Union v. KOAT Television, Inc.*, 656 P.2d 896 (N.M. Ct. App. 1982), was decided incorrectly. In holding that a credit union was an all-purpose public figure, the New Mexico Court of Appeals extended and broadened the *Gertz* standard in a way the Supreme Court never intended.

Supporting paragraph

By ignoring the Court's mandate to construe the all-purpose public figure standard narrowly, the *Coronado* court extended this standard to include all financial institutions. The court considered the following factors to reach this per se rule: 1) Financial institutions as corporations are chartered by the state; 2) Financial institutions are regulated by the state through statutes; and 3) Financial institutions deal in areas of general public concern. *Id.* at 904.

The fatal flaw in the court's analysis is best illustrated by applying these three factors to the fact pattern in *Gertz.* In *Gertz,* the Supreme Court held that the plaintiff attorney was not an all-purpose public figure. 418 U.S. at 352. But if the *Coronado* analysis is used, the opposite result would have been reached: 1) Attorneys must be licensed by the state to practice law and must meet certain state requirements to obtain that license; 2) Attorneys are subject to regulation by the state through Professional Codes of Conduct; and 3) Attorneys deal in areas of general public concern and interest. In fact, lawyers are officers of the court, and as such, must seek the public good in the administration of justice.

> Supporting paragraph

Thus, under the *Coronado* analysis, Mr. Gertz and indeed all attorneys would be classified as all-purpose public figures. Such a result is in direct opposition to the Court's holding in *Gertz.* Consequently, the rule applied in *Coronado* is far too broad and could not withstand constitutional scrutiny.

> Concluding paragraph

From the previous example, you can see that a carefully crafted paragraph block resembles a set of nesting blocks. The following example demonstrates how a large paragraph block may contain smaller paragraph blocks that in turn contain paragraphs that are mini-compositions. Labels for the larger paragraph block structure are boldfaced.

EXAMPLE

The second requirement of the statutory exception — that the goods be unsuitable for sale in the ordinary course of the manufacturer's business — will probably be met.

> **Topic paragraph**

First, because Rainbow's business consists of soliciting orders for custom-manufactured towels, attempts to market completed towels would not be within the ordinary course of its business. The company does not regularly deal with the marketing of goods already manufactured. The nature of Rainbow's business distinguishes

> Topic sentence

it from *Colorado Carpet*. There, the seller was in the business of purchasing carpet from wholesalers or manufacturers and re-selling it to retail purchasers. *Colorado Carpet,* 668 P.2d at 1391. The court found that Colorado Carpet regularly dealt with the marketing of carpets and could reasonably be expected to find a buyer in the regular course of its business. *Id.* Such is not the case with Rainbow. The company has neither the marketing personnel nor the contacts with customers interested in buying ready-made towels. Therefore, Rainbow would be unable to sell the towels within the ordinary course of its business operations.

Supporting paragraph

Concluding sentence

    Next, our client could argue that by definition, customized and unique towels are unsuitable for sale to others. The very qualities that qualify the towels as specially manufactured make it unlikely that other buyers would purchase them. This argument is supported by the *Wackenhut* court, which stated that there was a substantial possibility that the seller manufactured customized cameras suitable for sale to the original buyer only. *Wackenhut,* 669 F.2d at 1036. Similarly, each order that Rainbow fills is tailored specifically to the wants or needs of a certain buyer. No other buyer is likely to want or need beige towels with a "happy face" center and purple trim.

Topic sentence

Supporting paragraph

Concluding sentence

    Stover may claim that the towels would be suitable for sale if they were altered. The standard for alterations as stated in *Wackenhut* is that if, with slight alterations, the goods would be suitable for sale to others, the exception does apply. *Id.* at 1037. In this case, the logo was dyed into the towels and is not removable. Therefore, alteration to make the towels salable is not feasible.

Topic sentence

Supporting paragraph

Concluding sentence

    Finally, Stover may argue that these towels are certainly suitable for sale to someone if the price is low enough. But one of the policies underlying the statutory exception is that of fairness. It would be unfair to the seller to construe "suitable for sale to others" as meaning that it must sell the goods at any price. In *Walter Balfour & Co.*

Topic sentence

v. Lizza & Sons, Inc., 6 U.C.C. Rep. Serv. (Callaghan) 649, 651 (N.Y. Sup. Ct. 1969), the court found that the seller had made a reasonable effort to resell steel doors at a reasonable price. The plaintiff was not expected to sell the doors for mere scrap value. Rather, the doors were held to be unsuitable for sale to others. Thus, the court would probably not expect Rainbow to sell the towels at far below the contract price. They would be found unsuitable for sale to others in the ordinary course of business.

Supporting/ concluding paragraph

Concluding sentence

Conclusion

The following excerpt from a memo shows how two paragraph blocks work together to complete a section under the heading of "negligence." An elements of the law analysis lends itself nicely to paragraph block writing. In the example, notice how the paragraph that concludes one paragraph block also serves as the topic paragraph for the second block. Again, paragraph block labels are boldfaced.

EXAMPLE

Negligence

If Dennis's negligence created the emergency, then we cannot use the emergency doctrine. Negligence is defined as failing to act as a reasonable person. This general principle is best explained by way of illustration, and the courts provide numerous examples.

Topic paragraph

Speed excessive to conditions can be negligent. For example, when a defendant's logging truck rounded a curve and was unable to stop within three hundred seventy-five feet, his speed was found to be negligent. *Sandberg v. Spoelstra,* 285 P.2d 564 (Wash. 1955). When early morning visibility was restricted to seventy-five feet by a heavy rainfall, the court held that a speed of fifty miles per hour could be negligent. *Pidduck v. Henson,* 467 P.2d 322 (Wash. Ct. App. 1970). Finally, when daylight visibility exceeding one hundred feet was restricted to about three car lengths at night because

Topic sentence

Supporting paragraph

of the glare of a street light, the court held that a speed under the twenty-five miles per hour posted limit could be negligent. *Sonnenberg v. Remsing,* 398 P.2d 728 (Wash. 1965).

Topic sentence

Failure to heed road hazard warnings can also be negligent. Thus, when a driver confronted a multiple car accident on the freeway, where patrol cars were present with flashing lights and other cars were parked along the shoulder and median, the driver was negligent for not slowing down.

Supporting paragraph

Schlect v. Sorenson, 533 P.2d 1404 (Wash. Ct. App. 1975). Likewise, when a driver is warned of a fog hazard, drives into a deteriorating fog bank, and collides with a stopped vehicle, the driver is negligent. *Hinkel v. Weyerhaeuser Co.,* 494 P.2d 1008 (Wash. Ct. App. 1972).

Topic sentence

Finally, violations of the rules of the road can be negligent per se. When the driver of a semi-trailer observed a car stalled in the road ahead of it, slowed, switched lanes, and passed to the rear of the automobile where it struck one of the occupants on the highway, the driver was

Supporting paragraph

negligent. The driver was negligent as a matter of law for failing to obey several rules of the road: 1) reducing speed when confronted with hazards, 2) sounding horn to warn pedestrians of danger, 3) changing lanes only when safe to do so, and 4) signaling a lane change for one hundred feet before turning. *NeSmith v. Bowden,* 563 P.2d 1322 (Wash. Ct. App. 1977).

Topic sentence

Plaintiff is likely to employ all the above arguments. She will argue that Dennis was negligent because his speed was

Concluding paragraph/topic paragraph

excessive, because he failed to heed road hazards, and because he violated the rules of the road.

Topic sentence

Dennis's speed was not excessive for the conditions he faced. Although plaintiff may cite *Sandberg, Pidduck,* and *Sonnenberg,* we can distinguish the conditions in *Pidduck* and *Sonnenberg* from the conditions that Dennis faced. In both cases, visibility was restricted by unusual circumstances. Dennis faced no unusual circumstances. He was rounding a gradual curve under the speed limit, and there is no indication that the curve was so tortuous that it required a reduced speed limit. Nor is there any indication that there was a lower speed limit for night driving as opposed to day driving. In *Sandberg,* the driver had three hundred seventy-feet in which to stop, and there was no obstruction in his lane when the driver collided with a vehicle in the other lane. Although we do not have the exact distance, apparently Dennis had much less space in which to stop. Also, he faced an obstruction in his own lane.

Supporting paragraph

Dennis's situation is analogous to the facts in *Ryan v. Westgard,* 530 P.2d 687 (Wash. Ct. App. 1975), where the driver was found to be not negligent. There, the driver was following approximately one hundred feet behind another car. This car swerved into another lane, and the following driver confronted yet another car going extremely slowly. He attempted to stop, but collided with the slower vehicle. The court reasoned that the plaintiff was following the car in front of him at a proper speed until the moment that vehicle swerved out into the adjoining lane. Like the driver in *Ryan,* Dennis too was travelling at a proper speed until the moment his vehicle encountered the stalled bus. Therefore, Dennis's speed was not excessive.

Topic sentence

Supporting paragraph

Concluding sentence

Plaintiff will also argue that Dennis was negligent for failing to slow when confronted with a road hazard. Again, we can distinguish the warning that our client received from the warnings given in *Schlect* and *Hinkel.* Dennis was not warned several miles in advance of the obstruction as was the driver in *Hinkel.* Nor did he confront a multiple car accident with flashing patrol car lights and cars parked along the highway as did the driver in *Schlect.*

Pair of topic sentences

Supporting paragraph

Dennis rounded a curve and confronted a bus with flashers on that was stopped in the left lane of the freeway at 11:30 p.m. His situation is more analogous to the

Topic sentence

Supporting paragraph

cases in which drivers faced sudden and unexpected obstacles after little warning. *Haynes v. Moore,* 545 P.2d 28 (Wash. Ct. App. 1975); *Leach v. Weiss,* 467 P.2d 894 (Wash. Ct. App. 1970). In *Haynes,* the driver confronted a car, which he first saw when fifty feet away, stopped on a bridge. He braked, but collided with the car. He was found to be not negligent. Likewise, in *Leach,* the driver confronted a car stopped on a bridge, braked, crossed the center line, and collided with another vehicle. The driver

Concluding sentence

was not negligent. Neither is Dennis negligent.

Topic sentence

Finally, plaintiff will argue that our client was negligent for violating the rules of the road. Dennis was driving in the left hand lane and was not passing or turning. This conduct violates Wash. Rev. Code § 46.61.100, which requires that a driver stay in the rightmost lane except when passing or turning. Under *NeSmith,* 563 P.2d at 1326, this violation creates a prima facie case of negligence. However, we

Supporting paragraph

can argue that this conduct was not negligence because it did not endanger the class of persons that this rule was designed to protect. The purpose of Wash. Rev. Code § 46.61.100 is to protect vehicles traveling in the same direction by promoting safe passing. *Sadler v. Wagner,* 486 P.2d 330 (Wash. Ct. App. 1971). Edith was not passing Dennis, and Dennis was not

Concluding sentence

passing Edith. Thus, Edith does not fall within the class of persons this rule was designed to protect, and Dennis was not negligent.

Concluding paragraph

Dennis was not negligent because of excessive speed, he was not negligent for failing to heed road hazard warnings, and he was not negligent for failing to obey the rules of the road. His conduct did not create the emergency. We can submit substantial evidence in support of this second element, even though we can expect opposing counsel to make this a difficult issue.

Paragraph blocks that correspond to major divisions within a memo or brief are sometimes introduced by headings. (See section 19.1.) Used properly, headings can be a helpful aid to busy readers because they allow readers to quickly locate particular sections in a piece of writing. Make sure, however, that you don't begin to substitute headings for well-written transitions and topic sentences. Headings should be aids to readers, not crutches for writers.

Lest we leave you with the impression that all paragraph blocks exactly follow the models we have shown, let's look at a variation on the theme before leaving the subject of paragraph blocks.

Notice in the next example that one sentence at the beginning of the first paragraph in the block serves as the topic "paragraph" for the three-paragraph block. Each paragraph then has its own individual topic sentence and conclusion. The paragraph block, however, has no stated conclusion. The writer chose to use an implied conclusion to avoid conclusion overkill.

EXAMPLE

In addition, the University can distinguish this case from *Moore* on several grounds. First, in *Moore* the appellee and the appellant had a direct relationship with each other. The appellant entrusted his physical well-being and continuing medical treatment to the appellee, hoping to be cured of his disease. Therefore, the appellee had a higher duty of care to Moore while administering continuing treatment. In our case, the only connection between the University and the plaintiff is that the University conducts pathological tests on the fetal tissue to determine if there are any diseases or genetic disorders present. The clinical patients do not entrust the University with their care, nor do they depend on the University directly for treatment or medical advice. Therefore, the University's duty of care is limited to the proper administration of pathological testing and the timely relaying of the test results to the clinic.

Second, the tissue taken from Moore had unique qualities that allowed the appellee to develop products it could not have developed with another individual's tissue; therefore, the uniqueness of Moore's tissue

Topic "paragraph"

Topic sentence

Concluding sentence

Topic sentence

Concidentally

made it very valuable. In our case, the University can derive the same cell line from approximately one percent of the fetal cells it uses. Consequently, the fetal cells used for this product are not unique, nor can the traits of one fetal cell be distinguished from

Concluding sentence — the traits of another. Thus, the substantial value of fetal tissue is questionable.

Topic sentence — Finally, the decision in *Moore* was based largely on punitive measures rather than on the use of the appellant's tissue. The appellees in *Moore* continued to extract bodily tissue and fluids from appellant for many years after his splenectomy. Moore repeatedly travelled from Washington State to California at the request of the appellee with the impression that these trips were for continued care relating to Moore's disease. Instead, the sole purpose of the appellee's actions were to further its research. Here, the University makes no representations of continued care or treatment to the plaintiffs, nor does it repeatedly extract tissue from the plaintiffs for the purpose of furthering its research. Unlike the

Concluding sentence — defendant in *Moore,* the University does not deliberately deceive plaintiffs to obtain additional tissue; rather, the University obtains fetal tissue that would have normally been disposed of by the clinics.

See Exercises 20.E, 20.F, 20.G, 20.H, and 20.I in the *Practice Book.*

Chapter 21

Connections Between Sentences

Transitions are the primary connectors between sentences. When used properly, transitions state the relationship between the ideas in the sentences they serve to connect and signal how the ideas are moving in a line of reasoning.

Under the large umbrella term "transition," there are several types:

1. generic transitions,
2. orienting transitions, and
3. substantive transitions.

Still other transitions, headings and signposts, are used to make connections between paragraphs and over a longer piece of writing. (See Chapter 19.)

§21.1 GENERIC TRANSITIONS

Generic transitions include those words and phrases that are used in every kind of writing; consequently, they are familiar to all readers and writers.

Exhibit 21.1 lists the most common generic transitions grouped by function.

§21.1.1 Using Generic Transitions

The first question writers have about generic transitions is when to use them. In theory, that would seem simple. Because generic transitions signal those shifts or changes inherent in human thought and

EXHIBIT 21.1   **Generic Transitions**

For Contrast

however	nevertheless*	but
on the other hand	conversely	still
by (in) contrast	notwithstanding	yet
on the contrary	nonetheless*	instead
contrary to _____	alternatively	though
unlike _____	even so*	although
despite _____	rather	even though

For Comparison

similarly	analogously	in like manner
likewise	in the same way	
	for the same reason	

For Cause and Effect

therefore*	accordingly	hence
consequently*	thus*	since
as a result	because	so
		for

For Addition

also	moreover	besides
further	too	and
in addition	additionally	
furthermore		

For Examples

for example	to illustrate	specifically
for instance	namely	that is*

For Emphasis

in fact	certainly	still*
above all	indeed	clearly

For Evaluation

more important	surprisingly	unquestionably
unfortunately	allegedly	
fortunately	arguably	

*Generic transition that falls under more than one category.

EXHIBIT 21.1 *(continued)*

For Restatement

in other words	more simply	to put it differently
that is*	simply put	

For Concession

granted	of course	to be sure

For Resumption After a Concession

still*	nonetheless*	all the same
nevertheless*	even so*	

For Time

subsequently	later	earlier
recently	eventually	afterwards
meanwhile	shortly thereafter	until now
initially	simultaneously	since
formerly	at the time	by the time

For Place

adjacent to	here	nearby
next to	beyond	opposite to

For Sequence

first, second, third	next	then
former, latter	final	later
in the first place	finally*	primary, secondary

For Conclusion

in summary	in brief	thus*
in sum	in short	therefore*
to sum up	to conclude	consequently*
finally*	in conclusion	to (in) review

*Generic transition that falls under more than one category.

represented by the categories in the list above, it would seem that all writers should have to do is insert an appropriate transition to signal each time they make such a shift in their writing.

In practice, it is not so simple. For one thing, there are no transition rules or black and white laws about when a transition is required. In fact, even experienced, eloquent writers do not always agree about when a transition is appropriate and when it is cumbersome. For beginning law students and new associates in a firm, such differences in opinion can be confusing; one reader wants more transitions added, the next reader edits them out.

The thing to remember then is, to some extent, the number and placement of generic transitions is a matter of personal style and preference. On the other hand, there is a kind of general consensus about when to use generic transitions. You can find that consensus and develop your own sense about when to use generic transitions in one or more of the following ways. First, observe how other writers, particularly professional writers, use generic transitions. For example, notice how they rarely omit transitions that signal contrast and ones that show movement up or down the ladder of abstraction. Particularly observe the ways skilled legal writers use generic transitions to keep their readers on track.

Second, read your own writing aloud. Let your ear tell you when a new sentence starts with a jolt rather than a smooth connection.

Third, listen to someone else read your writing aloud. Try stopping that reader at several points along the way (particularly when there is no transition) and asking if he or she can guess what the next sentence will discuss. If the connections between the ideas are so obvious that the reader can anticipate where the writing is headed, probably no transition is needed. Conversely, if your reader needs more guidance through your points, add the appropriate generic transitions as needed.

Fourth, and most important, when writing, constantly ask yourself what will help your reader. Keeping the reader's perspective and needs in mind will help you decide when a generic transition is a helpful guide and when it is extra baggage.

§21.1.2 Problems with Generic Transitions

Some legal writers have a tendency to write as though others can read their minds. *They* know where they are headed in their writing, so they blithely assume their readers do too. These writers omit transitions because the connections between the ideas are obvious to them. They forget to consider whether these connections are obvious to the reader. For example, notice in the first pair of sentences that follow how jarring the second sentence seems without the transition for contrast, and then notice how in the revised second sentence the reader easily adjusts once the generic transition for contrast is added.

EXAMPLE

Mr. Wry, the owner of the Fitness Club, may claim that although Hillary's restaurant has lost several customers, the majority of the customers will return. Mr. Hillary may argue that the loss of several customers is significant to his business.

Revised:

Mr. Wry, the owner of the Fitness Club, may claim that although Hillary's restaurant has lost several customers, the majority of the customers will return. Mr. Hillary, *on the other hand,* may argue that the loss of several customers is significant to his business.

Other writers omit transitions in hopes of being more concise, forgetting that being concise, although important, is a relative luxury compared to being clear.

Legal writers should also take great care to select the precise transition that best describes the relationship between the two ideas or sentences. Selecting the wrong transition can be even more misleading than using no transition at all. In the following example, the writer mistakenly selected a transition for comparison rather than one for addition.

EXAMPLE

Because some overt physical activity and noise are normally generated by fitness and aerobics classes, the Fitness Club's classes are not unreasonably noisy or offensive. *Similarly,* bathing suits are not unusual or unanticipated sights in a waterfront area.

Revised:

Furthermore, bathing suits are not unusual or unanticipated sights in a waterfront area.

The need for precision in transitions also means that it is not enough simply to select the right category of generic transition. Generic transitions within the same category often have distinct meanings and connotations. For example, two transitions for conclusion — "to sum up" and "finally" — have entirely different meanings. "To sum up" should signal a brief overview or general statement about the entire piece of writing; "finally" should signal that the last point is about to be made.

In some instances, generic transitions are similar in meaning but quite different in tone. For example, two transitions for cause and effect — "therefore" and "hence" — mean almost the same thing, but "therefore" creates a matter-of-fact tone while "hence" carries with it a feeling of heavy solemnity and old wisdom.

A word of warning then: Use the list of generic transitions in Exhibit 21.1 with care. Do not automatically assume that transitions grouped in the same category are synonymous.

Of course, you will find that some generic transitions in the same category are virtually synonymous. In such instances, you may find that the list offers some variety that may free you from using the same generic transition ad nauseam.

Some final advice about transitional expressions: First, because transitions show the connection between two ideas, it is best to place the transition right at the point of connection. In the following example, the transition showing the cause/effect relationship comes too late to help the reader very much.

EXAMPLE

Hillary was made insecure in the use of his property when patrons threatened not to return. The Fitness Club and its activities constitute a nuisance as a result.

Revised:

As a result, the Fitness Club and its activities constitute a nuisance.

Second, the break between paragraphs can also serve as a kind of transition. The white space is a strong signal that the writing is moving to a new point. See Exercise 21.A in the *Practice Book.*

§21.2   ORIENTING TRANSITIONS

Orienting transitions provide a context for the information that follows. They serve to locate for the reader — physically, logically, or chronologically — the ideas or points in the rest of the sentence.

Two of the most common orienting transitions in legal writing are (1) those that include times and dates and (2) those that refer to cases.

EXAMPLES

On October 26, 1992, Leonard Thomas was admitted to Mountain View Rest Home and Retirement Village.

At 2:00 a.m. on January 1, 1993, David Wilson was arrested and charged with reckless driving and driving while intoxicated.

In *Bugger,* the court found that the position of the driver in the case was insignificant.

In the instant case, the son was not the executor of the will.

In the case at hand, there is no indication that the defendant intended to deceive the plaintiff about her rights under the contract.

Note

One commonly used orienting transition, the word "here," can be ambiguous when the previous sentence ends with a citation. Some readers may interpret "here" to refer to the previously cited case; others may interpret "here" to refer to the case at hand.

EXAMPLE

If some form of operability is required, then the court must decide whether to focus on the defendant's ability to operate the vehicle or on the vehicle's condition. *State v. Smelter,* 674 P.2d 690 (Wash. Ct. App. 1984). Here, the defendant had the key and was in the cab of the truck.

Revised:

In the case at bar, the defendant had the key and was in the cab of the truck. *OR*

In *Smelter,* the defendant had the key and was in the cab of the truck.

Other orienting transitions create a context by directing the reader to adopt a certain point of view, by supplying the source of the information that follows, or by locating the information historically or chronologically.

From the bank's perspective, granting a second loan would be ill-advised and risky.

According to Dallas Police Department Officer James Richardson's report, Officers Richardson and Loe entered the warehouse at 12:30 a.m.

Over the last twenty years, courts have realized that some exceptions to the general principle were necessary.

Orienting transitions frequently occur at the beginning of a section. In such positions, orienting transitions are not so much connections between points within the writing as they are connections between the writing and the mind of a reader first coming to the material.

Orienting transitions also occur at the beginning of paragraphs. From this position, they help readers adjust or "shift gears" as they mentally move along a line of reasoning within a larger idea. Of course orienting transitions can occur within a paragraph, and when they do, they work like all other transitions to bridge the gap between sentences and between ideas.

Here are several more examples of orienting transitions. Note the variety of ways orienting transitions provide a context for what follows.

To give a historical perspective:

In the 1970s, the court narrowed the scope of the "discretionary" category by emphasizing that the State must show that "a policy decision, consciously balancing the risks and advantages, took place . . . ."

In a recent decision, the court upheld a conviction when the driver was asleep or passed out and remained in a position to regulate the vehicle's movement.

To suggest a case's importance:

EXAMPLE

In an often cited case, the court overturned a conviction for "actual physical control" when the motorist's vehicle was parked on the shoulder of the highway.

To give a chronology:

EXAMPLE

In March of 1985, the Wilsons were advised that their fence encroached approximately 30 feet on the Anders' property. In response, the Wilsons claimed previous and current exclusive right, as well as title and interest to the disputed property.

To announce a shift in topic:

EXAMPLES

As for damages, the court will probably enjoin those activities that constitute a private nuisance.

In regard to the prosecution's allegation that Mr. Hayes's original attorney thwarted the discovery process, Mr. Hayes will point out that he was unaware that his original attorney shredded the requested documents.

Note

Some legal writers avoid the orienting transitions beginning with "as for," "as to," "in regard to," and "regarding" on the grounds that they are an abrupt, ineffective, or lazy way to make a significant shift in topic. These writers prefer that significant shifts in topics be introduced by full sentences.

EXAMPLE

Revised:

The question of damages will be more difficult to predict. The court will probably enjoin those activities that constitute a private nuisance, but awarding damages for Hillary's lost profits is less likely.

Revised:

The prosecution's second allegation, that Mr. Hayes's original attorney thwarted the discovery process, should be directed at Mr. Hayes' original attorney, not at Mr. Hayes. Mr. Hayes was unaware that his original attorney shredded the requested document. He cannot be held responsible for the unsanctioned actions of his lawyer.

As with generic transitions, the biggest problem writers have with orienting transitions is the question of when to use them. The answer is the same for all types of transitions: Use them when the reader needs them.

Achieving a reader's perspective, however, is not easy. One way writers can help themselves to develop a reader's perspective is to ask themselves after they have completed a draft if there is any background information underlying what they have written that they have neglected to include. If so, that information can often be inserted in one or more orienting transitions.

In the end, though, developing judgment about when to use orienting transitions is like most of the other individual skills that make up good legal writing; it will come with practice and with attention.

§21.3   Substantive Transitions

Thus far, we have looked at generic transitions, which are like glue between sentences, and at orienting transitions, which are backdrops for information or sometimes windows through which information can be seen.

The third type of transition, substantive transitions, can best be compared to the interlocking links of a chain. Like the links of a chain, substantive transitions serve two functions: they make a connection and they provide content. In short, they live up to their name — they are both substantive and transitional. The following two sentences include an example of a substantive transition.

EXAMPLE

Bugger and *Zavala* are the only cases in which a conviction was overturned when the motorist's vehicle was totally off the road. While these holdings could be helpful to our client, the Montana court will still probably interpret the statute to include the shoulder of the highway.

Here, the substantive transition is "while these holdings could be helpful to our client." It serves as a transition connecting the two sentences for two reasons: first, it is placed at or near the beginning of the following sentence, where it can help bridge the gap between the ideas; and second, it uses the phrase "these holdings" to refer back to the information in the previous sentence. In short, the transition looks both forward and back.

But, as we said before, a substantive transition does not serve merely as a transition; it also provides new content. It points out that "these holdings" "could be helpful to our client" before going on to the main point of the sentence, that the court still is likely to interpret the statute as including the shoulder of the highway.

§21.3.1   The Structure of Substantive Transitions

Substantive transitions often have a technique called dovetailing as the basis for their structure.

Dovetailing

A carpenter who wants a strong joint between two pieces of wood is likely to use the dovetail, a special joint characterized by the tight fit of interlocking pieces of wood. Similarly, a writer who wants a strong joint between two sentences uses a dovetail of words to connect the ideas. Through the dovetail, he or she interlocks ideas by creating an overlap of language. The overlap of language may be as simple as the repetition of terms from one sentence to the next or use of pronouns to refer back to an earlier noun.

Here is an example of a dovetail that uses repetition of terms.

EXAMPLE

In *Esser,* four people agreed to share costs and build a road. After the road was built, each person used the road under a claim of right.

Sentence 1	*Sentence 2*
. . . four people . . . build a road.	After the road was built, each person used the road . . .

Note that words may be repeated in their exact form or in a similar or related form.

A slightly more complicated dovetail than the one in the previous example requires the writer to find a word or phrase to use in the second sentence that sums up the idea of the previous sentence. Here is an example of a dovetail that uses a summarizing phrase.

EXAMPLE

Search and seizures are governed by the Fourth Amendment to the U.S. Constitution and Article I, Section 7 of the Washington Constitution. Both of these provisions have been interpreted as requiring that search warrants be valid and that searches and seizures be reasonable.

Sentence 1	*Sentence 2*
Fourth Amendment . . . and Article I	Both of these provisions . . .

Note that in both cases the words in the dovetail tend to be toward the end of the first sentence and toward the beginning of the second.

Often the summarizing noun or phrase will be preceded by a hook word such as "this," "that," "these," "those," or "such."

The following example includes a dovetail using a hook word and a summarizing noun phrase.

Realizing that she would not be able to stop in time to avoid hitting the bus, Mrs. Long swerved her vehicle around the bus and into the parallel lane of traffic. This evasive action resulted in her sideswiping another vehicle in the oncoming lane.

Connecting idea	*Connecting idea*
swerved . . . into . . . traffic	This evasive action
	hook *summarizing*
	word *noun phrase*

To form an effective dovetail, then, a legal writer can use one or more of the following techniques:

1. move the connecting idea to the end of the first sentence and to the beginning of the second sentence;
2. repeat key words from the first sentence in the second sentence;
3. use pronouns in the second sentence to refer back to nouns in the first sentence;
4. state the connecting idea in a specific form in the first sentence and then restate it in a summarizing noun or phrase in the second sentence;
5. use hook words such as "this," "that," "these," "those," and "such" before a repeated key word or summarizing noun or phrase.

Another way to think about dovetailing is to remember that most sentences are made up of two parts: old information and new information. The old information is what has already been named or discussed. It usually appears near the beginning of a sentence. The new information is the point the writer wants to add. It usually appears near the end of a sentence.

Sentence	
old information	new information

A dovetail takes the new information from the end of one sentence and restates it as the now old information at the beginning of the subsequent sentence.

Sentence 1		*Sentence 2*	
A	B ⟶ B	old	C
old	new	information	new
information	information		information

Obviously, though, it is unrealistic to assume that all sentences should follow a strict A + B, B + C, C + D pattern. In reality and in good legal writing, the pattern is not followed rigidly. Quite often, for example, sentence three will start with old information B.

Sentence 1		*Sentence 2*		*Sentence 3*	
A	B	B	C	B	D
old	new	old	new	old	new

EXAMPLE

In 1983, the Montana legislature adopted new and stricter laws to deal with drunk drivers. This legislation extended law enforcement jurisdiction and generally provided for faster and stiffer penalties. Brendon J. Rohan, *Montana's Legislative Attempt to Deal with the Drinking Driver: The 1983 DUI Statutes,* 46 Mont. L. Rev. 309, 310 (1985). This legislation also demonstrates a definite trend in Montana towards greater liability for the individual and a preference toward upholding drunk driving convictions regardless of mitigating circumstances.

Another useful variation of the pattern is to begin a sentence with a combination of two earlier pieces of old information.

Sentence 1		*Sentence 2*		*Sentence 3*	
A	B	B	C	B + C	D
old	new	old	new	old + old	new

EXAMPLE

When the defendant entered his hotel room, he was surprised to find two men rummaging through his suitcase. One of the men turned toward him, drew his gun, and aimed it at the defendant. Under these circumstances, the defendant had every reason to believe that he was being robbed and that his life was in danger.

This pattern works well when the writer wants to point out the similarity in two or more cases just cited.

EXAMPLES

Courts in both Arizona and Utah did not uphold convictions when the vehicle's motor was off. *State v. Zavlo,* 666 P.2d 456 (Ariz. 1983); *State v. Bugger,* 483 P.2d 442 (Utah 1971). These cases are significant because in both instances the engine was off and the vehicle was completely off the highway.

In *Rogers,* the city was held responsible when a building inspector erroneously told a builder that certain property was zoned for apartments. *Id.* at 1098. In a similar case, the court held that common sense would dictate that reliance on a building permit was justified; otherwise there would be no purpose in requiring a permit. *J & B Dev. Co. v. King County,* 669 P.2d at 472. These building permit cases may be distinguished from the present situation because the purpose of providing some measure of increased safety would be served whether or not the parents relied on the report.

Some writers unconsciously reverse the old → new pattern. They begin a sentence with new information and tack on the old, connecting information at the end. The result is a halting, disjointed style. If you examine your own writing, you may find that you can quickly improve the flow simply by revising with the old → new pattern in mind.

EXAMPLE

The defendant need not insure the plaintiff's safety; he need exercise only reasonable care. *Potter v. Madison Tavern,* 446 P.2d at 322. He has breached his duty to the plaintiff if he has not exercised reasonable care.

Revised:

If he has not exercised reasonable care, he has breached his duty.

Occasionally, however, it is awkward, if not impossible, to move the old information to the very beginning of a sentence and the new information to the very end. In such cases, remember that the old →

new pattern is a general principle, not an absolute rule. In the following sentence, for example, it would be awkward to move the first half of the dovetail — whether the secretary's actions were capricious and arbitrary — to the end of the first sentence.

EXAMPLE

The issue is whether the Secretary's actions were capricious and arbitrary when he failed to hire the required number of inspectors. If his actions were of such a nature, then the court would find the State liable.

In the following example, the second half of the dovetail — "these policy concerns" — works better at the end of the second sentence.

EXAMPLE

The discovery rules were formulated to prevent unfairness and to allow the parties to narrow issues, avoid surprises, and prepare adequately for cross-examination. *Ruiz v. Hamburg-American Line,* 478 F.2d 29, 32 (9th Cir. 1973). Disclosure of the expert's name does not further any of these policy concerns.

Two final bits of advice about dovetailing:

1. Avoid using hook words without repeating a key term or using a summarizing noun or phrase. (See section 25.5.2 on broad pronoun reference.)

EXAMPLE

In common law, a duty is established when the defendant stands in a special relationship to the plaintiff. This can exist between a special defendant and a specific defendant.

Revised:

This special relationship can exist . . . .

---

2. Consider using dovetailing to break up overly long sentences.

EXAMPLE

This holding by the *Knoll* court is considered the "ratified intent" approach to analyzing searches, which suggests that when evidence is taken to aid the government and when the government uses the evidence, the taint of the illegal action is transferred to the government, which makes the use unlawful.

Revised:

This holding by the *Knoll* court is considered the "ratified intent" approach to analyzing searches. This approach suggests that when evidence is taken to aid the government and when the government uses the evidence, the taint of the illegal action is transferred to the government. The transfer of the taint of the illegal action makes the use unlawful.

The following example shows how dovetailing ($\longrightarrow$) works in a longer piece of writing, a fact section for a client letter. Note that generic transitions (GT), orienting transitions (OT), and substantive transitions (ST) work together to create flow.

EXAMPLE

Your husband Don had been suffering from lung cancer for the past six months and was placed on the respirator machine. During that time, he spoke frequently about committing suicide in order to end the pain. To understand the pain your husband was going through, you attended several Euthanasia Society meetings.

"past six months" → "during that time"

"to end the pain" → "To understand the pain" (ST)

On July 15, 1990, you were with your husband in the hospital all day. Again, your husband told you about his pain and thoughts of committing suicide. Afterwards he fell asleep. Later, on the same day, you watched your husband awake from his sleep and attempt unsuccessfully to flip the switch on the respirator machine. After his

OT: "On July 15, 1990 . . . all day" → "again"

GT: "afterwards"
GT: "later"
"On the same day" dovetails back to "July 15, 1990"

unsuccessful attempts, you helped your husband flip the switch off and then walked out of the room. When you realized that your husband might die because of your assistance in flipping off the switch, you ran back to the room and flipped the switch back on. By that time, your husband was dead.

"Attempt unsuccessfully" → summarizing noun phrase "his unsuccessful attempts"

ST: "When you realized . . . your assistance"; note summarizing noun phrase "your assistance"

GT: "by that time"

See Exercises 21.B, 21.C, 21.D, and 21.E in the *Practice Book.*

§21.3.2   The Content of Substantive Transitions

The discussion at the beginning of this section suggested that the new content in substantive transitions could often be compared to half steps in a line of reasoning. These half steps are sometimes articulated inferences that one can reasonably draw from the previous sentence or idea.

EXAMPLE

The owners of the factory could agree to release the fumes only after certain hours at night or only under certain weather conditions. While these steps may ameliorate the situation, the question remains whether any emission of toxic fumes is reasonable.

In the preceding example, a thoughtful reader would surely be able to infer the content of the substantive transition — "while these steps may ameliorate the situation" — after reading the first sentence. Consequently, some may argue that it would be better to replace the substantive transition with a more concise generic transition like "even so" or "still." Obviously, writers must exercise judgment and weigh the relative merit of completeness versus conciseness.

In the following two examples, notice how the generic transition, although more concise, is less persuasive for the Bells than the substantive transition.

Generic Transition:

The Bells' doctor, Peter Williams, advised them that future pregnancies had a seventy-five percent chance of ending in a stillbirth. Consequently, the Bells decided that Mr. Bell would have a vasectomy.

Substantive Transition:

The Bells' doctor, Peter Williams, advised them that future pregnancies had a seventy-five percent chance of ending in a stillbirth. Relying on Dr. Williams's advice, the Bells decided that Mr. Bell would have a vasectomy.

Notice how the generic transition "consequently" seems fairly neutral. It suggests that the Bells' decision to have Mr. Bell undergo a vasectomy was the expected consequence of an unfavorable statistical probability. The substantive transition "relying on Dr. Williams's advice," on the other hand, stresses the Bells' dependence on their doctor's professional opinion. Mentioning the doctor again by name not only reminds the reader that the doctor was the source of the information but also emphasizes the role he played in the Bells' decision.

Although it would be impossible to enumerate the many ways substantive transitions are used in legal writing, there are a few common situations in which they are particularly effective.

a.   Bridging the Gap Between Law and Application

Perhaps the most common use of substantive transitions in legal writing occurs at junctures between law and application. Again, because it is a given in legal writing that the law will be applied, some may argue that substantive transitions at those points merely state the obvious. Most readers, however, seem to prefer a smooth "shifting of gears" to leaping into the application "cold."

Compare the following two examples and note how the substantive transition "under the rule announced in *Parnell*" draws the rule and its application together better than a generic transition can.

EXAMPLE

Generic Transition:

When a juror could have been excused for cause, reversible error occurs when the accused is forced to exercise all his peremptory challenges before the jury is finally selected. *State v. Parnell,* 463 P.2d 134 (Wash. 1969). *See also State v. Gilchrist,* 590 P.2d 809 (Wash. 1979). In the case at hand, Chapman accepted the jury with one peremptory challenge unexercised. Thus, he was not forced to use all his peremptory challenges before the final selection of the jury. Therefore, the Court of Appeals' decision in finding harmless error is sustainable.

Substantive Transition:

This court has previously held that reversible error occurs in a situation when the accused is forced to exercise all his peremptory challenges before the jury is finally selected. *State v. Parnell,* 463 P.2d 134 (Wash. 1969). *See also State v. Gilchrist,* 590 P.2d 809 (Wash. 1979). In the case at hand, Chapman accepted the jury with one peremptory challenge unexercised. Thus, he was not forced to use all his peremptory challenges before the final selection of the jury. Under the rule announced in *Parnell,* the Court of Appeals' decision in finding harmless error is sustainable.

Frequently the factors or elements in the law are mentioned well before the point where they are applied. When there is intervening information, the substantive transition becomes even more important in helping the reader follow the discussion.

In the following example, the five factors that the Tenth Circuit listed for determining an expert's status were first named on page four of a memo. The first opportunity the writer had for showing how the court would apply these factors occurred two pages later. In such a situation, the substantive transition is critical.

EXAMPLE

Applying the factors listed in *Ager,* 622 F.2d at 501, the court will first find that the consultation was initiated as custom dictated.

---

b. Applying Another Court's Rationale

Similarly, substantive transitions are often used when the reasoning of one court has been laid out in detail and this reasoning will now be applied to the case at hand. Note that in the following example, as in the previous example, the substantive transition begins with that important signal word "applying."

EXAMPLE

Recent Washington court decisions have developed a more liberal definition of inadvertent. *State v. Henry,* 676 P.2d 521 (Wash. Ct. App. 1984). In *Henry,* officers had learned from an informant that the defendant was heavily armed, and one officer testified during the trial that he was looking for guns as well as cocaine, which was specified in the warrant; yet, the court held that the guns were found inadvertently. *Id.* at 533. In doing so, the court relied on the definition of "inadvertent" provided in *State v. Callahan,* 644 P.2d 735, 736 (Wash. Ct. App. 1982): "[T]he term 'inadvertent' in the context of the plain view doctrine, simply means that the officer discovered the evidence while in a position that does not infringe upon any reasonable expectation of privacy, and did not take any further unreasonable steps to find the evidence from that position." The *Henry* court concluded that the officers were looking in places that were likely to contain drugs, that a person can harbor no reasonable expectation of privacy concerning a place that is likely to contain drugs, and that the officers took no further, unreasonable steps to find the guns. Therefore, the discovery was inadvertent by the Washington definition. *Henry,* 676 P.2d at 523. The court added that there was no evidence that the drug search was a pretext for a gun search. *Id.*

The state's position in the instant case is stronger. At the time they received the search warrant for marijuana, the officers neither had knowledge nor expected that they might find incriminating photographic evidence of another crime. When he looked in the envelope, Morrison had no reason to believe that the photographs would be evidence of any crime.

Thus, applying the *Henry* rationale to the *Ehrlich* case, the court would probably find that Morrison was looking in a place that was likely to conceal drugs (the envelope might have contained drugs as well as photographs), so Ehrlich had no reasonable expectation of privacy. After looking in the envelope, Morrison took no further unreasonable steps to find the photographs. Therefore, the discovery was inadvertent.

---

c.   *Gathering Together Several Facts*

Another juncture where substantive transitions can be used effectively occurs between a list of numerous individual facts and a statement about their significance as a group.

In the following example, the substantive transition "based on these admissions" is essential. It is the one place where the point is made that three facts taken together were the basis for the court's action.

EXAMPLE

In his deposition, Edwards acknowledged that the railroad tie had appeared wet and slippery before he stepped on it. He also stated that he had regularly delivered mail to the Bates's residence for two years and that he was familiar with the premises, including the railroad tie. Finally, Edwards acknowledged that he attended weekly postal safety meetings and knew about the hazards posed by wet surfaces.

Based on these admissions, the trial court granted summary judgment in favor of Bates and dismissed Edwards's negligence action.

In the next example, the substantive transition "when faced with all these facts" is not so much essential as it is persuasive.

EXAMPLE

Ms. Jones admits that the weather on the morning of the accident was cold and overcast. Ms. Jones further admits that there was still snow on the ground and that she had considered putting chains on her tires before leaving for work. The other two drivers, Mr. Smith and Ms. Block, both state that the traffic was traveling slower than usual because of hazardous icy conditions. The police officer who arrived on the scene shortly after the accident also reports that the weather was cold and the roads were icy. When faced with all these facts, Ms. Jones had to know of the danger of ice on the road that morning.

---

d. Gathering Together Several Ideas

Substantive transitions can also be used to pull together two or more large ideas that have been developed over several paragraphs or even several sections of a memo or brief.

The following example appeared toward the end of an appellate court memorandum that affirmed the trial court's decision to grant the petition for modification of child support. Earlier in the memo, the appellate court reviewed the trial court's findings (1) that the child support modification would not inflict a financial hardship on the supporting parent and (2) that the factual circumstances (the child's age and propensity for higher education) had changed substantially, thereby allowing the court to modify the support order. The Court of Appeals added a third point, a policy consideration. The court observed that because children of parents who are still married often continue to receive support after majority for higher education, it would be a special disadvantage of children of divorced parents if one of their parents were not expected to provide advanced education. Each of these three points was fully developed in one or more paragraphs.

Now notice how the substantive transition brings all three points together as the basis for the court's decision and how it allows the writer to move smoothly to the last section of the memo.

EXAMPLE

Absent any financial hardship to the father and given the change in circumstances, the father should, as a matter of policy, be required to contribute to his daughter's higher education.

---

e.   Bridging the Gap Between Sections of a Document

Substantive transitions are undoubtedly more effective than generic transitions at junctures between large sections of a paper. Even when headings are used for larger sections, substantive transitions are still needed to show the similarities or differences between the sections.

In the following example, the writer has just completed a long section on the Ninth Circuit's comments on the inappropriateness of bonuses for services rendered to a bankrupt estate. The following sentence begins the section under the heading Contingency Fees. The substantive transition — "unlike a bonus fee arrangement" — shows the connection between the sections.

EXAMPLE

Contingency Fees

Unlike a bonus fee arrangement, there is nothing that prevents a contingency fee agreement from being enforced in bankruptcy. *In re Yermahov,* 718 F.2d 1465, 1470 (9th Cir. 1983).

To sum up then, substantive transitions are those special points in writing where the writer pulls two or more thoughts together and, in doing so, creates a powerful bond between ideas. By overlapping the language and merging the ideas, the writer does more than just connect the points; he or she weaves them together.

Some final thoughts about transitions: Although the artificial system of dividing transitions into separate categories makes it easier to understand their separate functions, it also masks the ways in which generic, orienting, and substantive transitions are similar. One can argue, for example, that all transitions, including generic transitions, provide some content or that all transitions orient the reader. Consequently, how you categorize a particular transition is not really important; what is important is that you be able to use all three categories of transitions to create connections in your own writing.

Chapter 22

Effective Sentences

Effective sentence writing begins with the subject-verb unit. Those two key sentence positions should contain the crux of the sentence's message. If these two parts of the sentence are written well, then many of the other parts of the sentence will fall into place.

Consequently, our discussion of effective sentence writing begins with four points about the subject-verb unit: the use of active and passive voice, the use of concrete subjects, the use of action verbs, and the distance between subjects and verbs. The remainder of the chapter will include points that concern the whole sentence: sentence length and emphasis.

§22.1 ACTIVE AND PASSIVE VOICE

The term "voice," when it is applied to the subject-verb unit, refers to the relationship of the subject to the action expressed in the verb. This rather vague concept is easier to understand in terms of the difference between active and passive voice.

§22.1.1 Identifying Active and Passive Voice

In the active voice, the subject of the sentence is doing the action described by the verb.

The judge overruled the objection.
   (subject)   *(verb)*   *(direct object)*

In the sentence above, the subject "judge" is doing the verb "overruled." Another way to look at it is to remember that in the active voice the subject is "active," or acting.

In the passive voice, the subject of the sentence is having the action of the verb done to it.

The objection was overruled by the judge.
   (subject)   *(verb)*

In this sentence, the subject "objection" is not doing the overruling; rather, the verb "overruled" is being done to the subject. Another way to look at it is to remember that in the passive voice the subject is "passive." It is not acting; it is acted upon.

Notice that in the passive voice the person or thing doing the verb is either mentioned in a prepositional phrase ("by the judge," as in previous example) or omitted, as in the example below.

The objection was overruled.
   (subject)   *(verb)*

In a nutshell, then, the following is the distinction between active and passive voice:

ACTIVE VOICE	PASSIVE VOICE
the subject acts	the subject is acted upon

Note

Passive voice is different from past tense. Even though both concern the verb, past tense refers to the time of an action and passive voice refers to the relationship of an action to the subject of the sentence.

See Exercise 22.A in the *Practice Book.*

§22.1.2   Effective Use of Active Voice

Generally, the active voice is preferred over the passive voice for several reasons:
   1. It is more concise.

EXAMPLES

The marshal left the summons.

(active voice — 5 words)

The summons was left by the marshal.

(passive voice — 7 words)

---

2. It uses a more vigorous verb.

EXAMPLES

The plaintiffs filed a complaint in the superior court of Chavez County, New Mexico.

(active voice — verb "filed" is crisp and vigorous)

A complaint was filed by the plaintiffs in the superior court of Chavez County, New Mexico.

(passive voice — verb "was filed" loses much of its vigor; the auxillary verb "was" and the preposition "by" dilute the energy of "filed")

---

3. It allows information to be processed more readily.

EXAMPLE

The defendant's attorney must offer the deposition into evidence.

This active voice sentence is easy to process mentally. The reader can visualize the subject "defendant's attorney" doing the verb "must offer" to the object "deposition" as quickly as the words are read. The sentence suggests a mini-drama that readers can visualize in their minds.

EXAMPLE

The deposition must be offered into evidence by the defendant's attorney.

Although the information in this passive voice sentence is not difficult to process, readers must read the entire sentence before they will be able to visualize the sentence in their minds. By the midpoint in the sentence, "The deposition must be introduced into evidence," the action has begun, but it being done by unseen hands. The "actor" in the mini-drama does not come in until the end of the sentence.

In both objective and persuasive legal writing, active voice is usually preferred when you want to make a point that someone or something performed a particular action. Active voice emphasizes who or what is responsible for committing an act. See Exercise 22.B in the *Practice Book.*

EXAMPLES

The defendant embezzled over $1,000,000.

(active voice — emphasizes that the defendant is responsible for the act)

Over $1,000,000 was embezzled by the defendant.

(passive voice — it is still clear that the defendant performed the act, but now the amount of money is the point of emphasis)

Over $1,000,000 was embezzled.

(passive voice — doer of the action is either unknown or left unsaid; emphasis is on the amount of money)

---

§22.1.3   Effective Use of Passive Voice

Although it is true that active voice is generally preferable over passive voice, there are several situations in which passive voice is more effective.

1. Use passive voice when the person or thing performing the action is unknown or relatively unimportant.

EXAMPLES

A portion of the tape was erased.

The safe's hinges must be examined before the manufacturer's liability can be determined.

---

2. Use passive voice when it is undesirable to disclose the identity of the person or thing performing the action.

EXAMPLES

The plaintiff's retirement benefits were discontinued.

Toxic fumes were ventilated out of the plant between 2:00 and 3:00 a.m.

---

3. Use passive voice when the deed, rather than the doer, should be emphasized.

EXAMPLES

A cure for Alzheimer's disease has been found.

All four defendants were convicted of first degree murder.

---

4. Use passive voice when the passive voice allows the writer to keep the focus of the writing where it belongs, as in the following example from a paragraph about mistake in a contract.

EXAMPLE

A mistake can also be attributed to Lakeland Elementary School for believing the price of the playground equipment included installation.

---

5. Use passive voice when it provides a stronger link between preceding and subsequent sentences or clauses. (See section 21.3 on dovetailing.) This link is enhanced by moving the connecting ideas to the end of the first sentence (or clause) and then picking up on that point at the beginning of the second sentence (or clause).

Sentence 1	*Sentence 2*
connecting idea	connecting idea

EXAMPLE

Under the Revised Code of Washington, Title 62A, contracts for the sale of goods are regulated by the Uniform Commercial Code. The UCC outlines the requirements for a valid contract for the sale of goods and the various steps necessary to the contract's performance.

The first sentence uses passive voice so that "Uniform Commercial Code" will be at the end of the sentence. The second sentence begins with "The UCC" to provide a strong link between the sentences.

Sentence 1	*Sentence 2*
by the Uniform Commercial Code	The UCC

EXAMPLE

Big Yard Toys, Inc. bid on the manufacture of the playground equipment, and the bid was accepted by Lakeland Elementary School.

The second main clause uses passive voice. It begins with "the bid" as a strong link to the preceding main clause.

Clause 1	*Clause 2*
bid on the manufacture	and the bid was accepted

Note

Avoid mixing active and passive verbs when writing a compound verb. (Reminder: Both parts of a compound verb have the same subject.)

EXAMPLES

Example: Ms. Meyers left her motel room and was followed by
        (subject)(active)   *(passive)*
        the defendant.

Revised: After leaving her motel room, Ms. Meyers was followed by the defendant.

Example: <u>Roger Harrison</u> <u>sent</u> in his 1991 tax form and <u>was</u> lat-
          (subject)   *(active)*
        er <u>audited</u> by the I.R.S.
        (passive)

Revised: Roger Harrison sent in his 1991 tax form, which was later audited by the I.R.S.

For legal writing, you will need passive voice for both objective and persuasive writing. In objective writing, you will often have instances when the person or thing performing the action is unknown; when the deed, rather than the doer of the deed, should be emphasized; when the passive voice allows the writer to keep the focus of the writing where it belongs; and when the passive voice provides a stronger link between preceding and subsequent sentences or clauses.

In persuasive writing, you will find that the passive voice allows you to downplay who performed certain actions. For example, counsel for the defense may want to use the passive voice when admitting wrongdoing by the defendant.

EXAMPLE

A purse was taken from the plaintiff by the defendant.

(passive voice used to downplay defendant's action)

Counsel for the plaintiff will use active voice to emphasize that it was the defendant who took the purse.

EXAMPLE

The defendant took the plaintiff's purse.

See Exercises 22.C and 22.D in the *Practice Book.*

§22.2   CONCRETE SUBJECTS

Effective subjects of sentences are concrete rather than abstract. They are real people and real things that readers can mentally visualize.

Unfortunately, in legal writing we are often forced to use abstractions as subjects of our sentences. The law and its application often require that we focus on ideas and concepts, so many times we end up placing them in the subject position. Consequently, legal readers appreciate having as many concrete subjects as possible to help bring the writing back down to earth.

To find the most effective concrete subject of a sentence, ask yourself, "Who (or what) is doing something in this sentence?" Then place that real person or thing in the subject position of the sentence.

EXAMPLE

Example: A <u>decision</u> <u>was made</u> by the district manager to elim-
           (subject)   *(verb)*
           inate all level four positions.

Revised: The <u>district manager</u> <u>decided</u> to eliminate all level four
             (subject)   *(verb)*
             positions.

Note

The preceding example illustrates a common problem in legal writing known as nominalization. Nominalization is the process of converting verbs into nouns (for example, "decide" → "decision"). The effect in the sentence is twofold: (1) the real action of the sentence is buried in a noun, making the sentence more ponderous and turgid, and (2) the verb becomes either a passive voice substitute or a *to be* verb substitute, making the sentence less energetic.

In many sentences, the real person or thing acting in the sentence has been buried in an abstraction or omitted altogether.

EXAMPLES

Example: The <u>awarding</u> of damages <u>will be left</u> to judicial dis-
           (subject)   *(verb)*
           cretion.

Revised: The judge will decide whether to award damages.
                  (subject)   (verb)

Example: Determination of legislative intent requires reading
                  legislative history.

Revised: An attorney must read legislative history to determine
                  legislative intent.

Often the subject position in the sentence is taken up by an almost meaningless abstraction such as "nature of," "kind of," "type of," "aspect of," "factor of," or "area of." Notice how the sentence improves when these meaningless abstractions are omitted and real people and real things are placed in the subject position.

EXAMPLE

Example: The nature of the defendant's argument was that he
                  (subject)   (verb)
                  was "temporarily insane."

Revised: The defendant argued that he was "temporarily in-
                  (subject)   (verb)
                  sane."

Both the subject position and verb position are often taken up by the many weak subject-verb combinations that use the "it is _____ that" pattern.

It is important to note that
It is likely (unlikely) that
It is obvious (clear) that
It is essential that

To revise sentences with this weakness, look after the "that" for the real subject and verb. See Exercise 22.E in the *Practice Book.*

EXAMPLES

Example: <u>It</u> <u>is</u> obvious that the defendant was not read his
       (subject/verb)
       rights.

Revised: The <u>defendant</u> <u>was not read</u> his rights.
       (subject)   *(verb)*

Example: <u>It</u> <u>is</u> unlikely that the defendant will plead guilty.
       (subject/verb)

Revised: The <u>defendant</u> probably <u>will not plead</u> guilty.
       (subject)   *(verb)*

---

§22.3   ACTION VERBS

Effective verbs show real action rather than vague action or state of being. To find the most effective verb for a sentence, ask yourself, "What is someone or something actually doing in the sentence?" Then place that action in the verb position.

Common Pitfalls to Avoid When Selecting a Verb

1. Avoid overusing forms of the verb "to be" (am, are, is, was, were) as a main verb. Use forms of the verb "to be" only when the point of the sentence is that something exists.

EXAMPLES

Example: The <u>owner</u> of the land <u>is</u> East Coast Properties, Inc.
       (subject)   *(verb)*

Revised: <u>East Coast Properties, Inc.</u> <u>owns</u> the land.
       (subject)   *(verb)*

Example: There <u>are</u> four <u>elements</u> that must be proved to re-
       (verb)   *(subject)*
       cover damages under the family car or purpose doc-
       trine.

Revised: Four <u>elements</u> <u>must be proved</u> to recover damages
           (subject)   *(verb)*
           under the family car or purpose doctrine.

Note

The sentence openers "There is" or "There are" or "There was" or "There were" are weak unless the point of the sentence is that something exists. With these four sentence openers, the subject comes after the verb.

----

2. Avoid using vague verbs. Verbs such as "concerns," "involves," "deals (with)," and "reveals" tells the reader little about the real action in the sentence.

EXAMPLES

Example: <u>Swanson</u> <u>dealt</u> with a sales contract that contained
           (subject) *(verb)*
           an open item and that was signed by a homebuilder
           and a couple who were prospective buyers of a home.

Revised: In *Swanson,* a <u>homebuilder</u> and a <u>couple</u> who were
                       (subject)   *(subject)*
           prospective buyers of a home <u>signed</u> a contract that
                                        (verb)
           contained an open item.

---

3. Avoid nominalization, that is, burying the real action in a noun, and avoid burying the action in an adjective. See Exercise 22.F in the *Practice Book.*

EXAMPLES

Example: The <u>corporate officers</u> <u>had</u> an informal meeting at an
               (subject)   *(verb)*
           undisclosed location.

Revised: The <u>corporate officers</u> <u>met</u> informally at an undis-
                  (subject)   *(verb)*
closed location.

Example: Rhode Island <u>courts</u> <u>have not</u> yet <u>made</u> a decision
                   (subject) (verb)
about whether public schools can refuse admission to
a student with acquired immune deficiency syndrome
(AIDS).

Revised: Rhode Island <u>courts</u> <u>have not</u> yet <u>decided</u> whether
                   (subject) (verb)
public schools can refuse admission to a student with
acquired immune deficiency syndrome (AIDS).

Example: The <u>policy</u> underlying the doctrine of adverse posses-
             (subject)
sion <u>is</u> favorable to the Morgans.
     (verb)

Revised: The <u>policy</u> underlying the doctrine of adverse posses-
             (subject)
sion <u>favors</u> the Morgans.
     (verb)

---

§22.4   Distance Between Subjects and Verbs

An effective sentence has its subject and verb close together. When
they are close together, the reader can identify the subject-verb unit
quickly and comprehend the entire sentence more easily. When they are
far apart and separated by many intervening words, the reader will find
it much more difficult to understand the sentence.

EXAMPLE

Example: <u>Information</u> about Mutual Trust Bank's standard op-
            (subject)
erating procedures and about how the contractor
drew up his loan application <u>will be required</u> by the
                                (verb)
court.

Revised: The <u>court</u> <u>will require</u> information about Mutual Trust
             (subject)   (verb)
             Bank's standard operating procedure and about how
             the contractor drew up his loan application.

In some cases, the writer will have to rewrite one sentence as two
sentences to keep the subjects and verbs close together.

EXAMPLE

Example: A <u>case</u> in which a section 11-902 charge was dropped
             (subject)
             because the driver was found lying in the highway
             near his truck <u>shows</u> that a driver's presence in the vehicle
                            (verb)
             is a prerequisite for finding him guilty.

Revised: In one case, the <u>court</u> <u>dismissed</u> a section 11-902
                              (subject) (verb)
             charge because the driver was found lying in the high-
             way near his truck. The <u>court</u> <u>reasoned</u> that a driver's
                                     (subject) (verb)
             presence in a vehicle is a prerequisite to finding the
             defendant guilty.

Note

Another reason for keeping subjects and verbs close together is to
reduce the chance that they will not agree in number. (See section
25.4). In the following example, the writer has mistakenly made the
verb agree with the singular noun "script" when the plural subject "quality and mutilation" requires the plural verb "are."

EXAMPLE

Inferior <u>quality and mutilation</u> of the musical play *Not Enough*
         (subject)

Lovin' as a result of Skylark Productions' revisions of the script
<u>is</u> hard to establish.
(verb)

Occasionally a writer must separate the subject and verb with
quite a bit of information. In such cases, if the intervening information
can be set off by punctuation, the reader will still be able to identify the
subject-verb unit fairly easily.

EXAMPLE

The <u>Lanham Trademark Act</u>, a law primarily designed to prevent
          (subject)
deceptive packaging of goods in interstate commerce, <u>has been</u>
                                                        (verb)
<u>interpreted</u> to include false attribution and distortion of literary and
artistic works.

Remember too that keeping subjects and verbs close together is
desirable but not absolutely required. There will be times in legal writing when it is all but impossible to keep subjects and verbs close together. See Exercises 22.G and 22.H in the *Practice Book.*

§22.5   SENTENCE LENGTH

Whenever a legal writer asks "how long should my sentences be?"
the only possible answer is "it depends." Obviously sentence length is
primarily governed by what you are trying to say. Some ideas take more
words to convey than others. Even given that constraint, though, a writer still has quite a bit of flexibility regarding the length of each sentence.
Decisions on sentence length, then, should also be made based on two
other factors: the reader and the context.

§22.5.1   The Reader

Effective sentence length is that which the reader can handle comfortably. Educated readers — judges, attorneys, some clients — can comfortably read somewhat longer sentences than the general public.
Consequently, legal writers can usually write sentences for their readers

that average about twenty-two words per sentence with only a rare sentence exceeding a thirty-five word limit. For readers with less education, shorter sentences are usually more effective.

Notice how the overly long sentence in the following example creates a feeling in the reader of a mental overload. Several overly long sentences written one after another only compound this feeling.

EXAMPLE

The post-trial motion was supported by an affidavit by a juror that stated that a fellow juror discussed the case with a professional truck driver who was familiar with the accident scene and who told the juror that the accident could not have occurred as the plaintiff stated. (48 words)

There are several ways to revise overly long sentences such as the one in the example above so that they become more readable. The first way is to break up an overly long sentence into two or more separate sentences.

EXAMPLE

Revised:

The post-trial motion was supported by an affidavit by a juror. In his affidavit, the juror stated that a fellow juror discussed the case with a professional truck driver who was familiar with the accident scene. The truck driver told the juror that the accident could not have occurred as the plaintiff stated.

The second way to revise an overly long sentence is to create manageable units of meaning within the sentence. A writer can do this by identifying structural components within the sentence, especially phrases and clauses, and setting them off with appropriate punctuation.

Obviously, the writer must still comply with the rules of punctuation and not assume he or she can punctuate randomly. One rule of punctuation that can be used in such situations is comma rule 2 for setting off introductory phrases and clauses. (See section 26.1.) Notice how much more readable the following example becomes when, in Revision 1, the "if" clause is moved to the front of the sentence where it can be set off from the rest of the sentence by a comma.

EXAMPLE

The Reynoldses will be responsible for both the attacks on the Halversons' chickens and Mr. Halverson's medical bills resulting from the dog bite if the plaintiff can show that the Reynoldses should have known of their dog's viciousness. (38 words)

Revision 1:

If the plaintiff can show that the Reynoldses should have known of their dog's viciousness, (15 words) then they will be responsible for both the attacks on the Halversons' chickens and Mr. Halverson's medical bills resulting from the dog bite. (23 words)

Other punctuation marks, such as the colon, can sometimes be added to create a break within a sentence.

EXAMPLE

Revision 2:

If the plaintiff can show that the Reynoldses should have known of their dog's viciousness, (15 words) then they will be responsible for the following: (8 words) the attacks on the Halversons' chickens and Mr. Halverson's medical bills resulting from the dog bite. (16 words)

This technique of arranging phrases and clauses so that they can be set off by punctuation is particularly helpful when writing questions presented. In the following example, the reader is expected to absorb the information in fifty-six words straight without a punctuation break.

EXAMPLE

Under New Hampshire law did the trial court create prejudicial error by refusing plaintiffs' motion for a new trial because of jury misconduct when the motion was supported by a juror affidavit stating that another juror discussed the case with an alleged expert outside the trial context and then related the information to the entire jury?

In Revision 1, the writer has broken up this same information into more readable units by using a comma to set off the introductory phrase and a conjunction between two main clauses. (See section 26.1, Rules 1 and 2.)

EXAMPLE

Revision 1:

Under New Hampshire law, did the trial court cause prejudicial error by refusing plaintiffs' motion for a new trial because of jury misconduct when the motion was supported by a juror affidavit, (32 words) and that affidavit stated that another juror discussed the case with an alleged expert outside the trial context and then related the information to the entire jury? (27 words)

In Revision 2, the writer has used commas between a series of parallel clauses (here, "when" clauses) to help break up the information into manageable units. (See section 25.7.) Even though the revised sentence is longer than the original, it is more readable because the reader gets the information in smaller, more manageable units.

EXAMPLE

Revision 2:

Under New Hampshire law, did the trial court create prejudicial error when it refused plaintiffs' motion for a new trial because of jury misconduct, (24 words) when the motion was supported by a juror affidavit, (9 words) and when that affidavit stated that another juror discussed the case with an alleged expert outside the trial context and then related information to the entire jury? (27 words)

The third way to solve sentence length problems is to eliminate wordiness. (See section 23.2.)

EXAMPLE

Proceeding on the assumption that all lawyers have a basic understanding of the more traditional torts, the speaker outlined and presented the following synopsis and review of what are considered to be the most prominent contemporary types of legal actions for which a general business attorney should prepare and in which he or she should reasonably expect to participate at some point in his or her career. (67 words)

Revised:

Assuming lawyers understand traditional torts, the speaker described the main types of tort cases that a business attorney should be prepared to handle. (23 words)

See Exercises 22.I and 22.J in the *Practice Book.*

§22.5.2   The Context

Earlier we said that decisions about sentence length should be based on both the reader and the context. Readers rarely see a sentence in isolation. Most sentences occur in a context; they are preceded by other sentences and followed by other sentences. Consequently, how readers respond to the length of any given sentence depends, in part, on the sentences that surround it.

For example, a forty-word sentence that is unwieldy in one context may work in another. A short, snappy sentence that drives a point home in one paragraph may seem trite and unsophisticated in another. Even a steady diet of medium-length sentences is unappetizing. Such writing tends to be monotonous and bland.

When it comes to sentence length, then, consistency is not a virtue. Effective sentences, that is, sentences that convey the desired information and keep the reader interested, vary in length.

The following example from a statement of facts shows how lack of variety in sentence length makes the writing less interesting to read. In the eleven sentences that follow, the range in sentence length is only from nine words in the shortest sentence to nineteen words in the longest sentence.

EXAMPLE

On December 15, 1992, Officers Jack Morrison and Wayne Fiscis of the Phoenix police department searched Victor Ehrlich's apartment. (17 words) They had in their possession a valid search warrant for marijuana. (11 words) Marijuana was found in both the living room and the kitchen. (11 words) While searching the bedroom, Officer Morrison found a large manila envelope in one of the dresser drawers. (17 words) Photographs were protruding from the top of the envelope. (9 words) Morrison looked inside and found photographs of Ehrlich with three young girls sitting on his lap. (16 words) Ehrlich was wearing only boxer shorts, and the girls were nude from the waist up. (15 words) Considering the photographs to be perverse, Morrison showed them to Fiscis, who agreed that they looked suspicious. (17 words) They seized the photographs as well as the marijuana. (9 words) The defendant, Victor Ehrlich, has now contested this seizure. (9 words) He has made a motion to suppress the photographic evidence as the result of an unconstitutional seizure. (17 words)

The following revised version is more interesting to read because sentence length now ranges from six words in the shortest sentence to twenty-nine words in the longest.

EXAMPLE

Revised:

On December 15, 1985, Officers Jack Morrison and Wayne Fiscis of the Phoenix Police Department searched Victor Ehrlich's apartment. (17 words) They had in their possession a valid search warrant for marijuana. (11 words) After finding marijuana in both the living room and the kitchen, they searched the bedroom, where Officer Morrison found a large manila envelope in one of the dresser drawers. (29 words) Seeing photographs protruding from the top of the envelope, Morrison looked inside and found photographs of Ehrlich with three young girls sitting on his lap. (25 words) Ehrlich was wearing only boxer shorts. (6 words) The girls were nude from the waist up. (8 words) Considering the photographs to be perverse, Morrison showed them to Fiscis, who agreed that they looked suspicious. (17 words) They seized the photographs as well as the marijuana. (9 words) The defendant, Victor Ehrlich, has now contested this seizure and has made a motion to suppress the photographic evidence as the result of an unconstitutional seizure. (26 words)

Note

Part of what makes the revised version effective is its use of short sentences. The four short sentences were all used to highlight particularly significant facts.

In the next section we will discuss how to use short sentences to best effect.

§22.5.3 The Power of the Short Sentence

Used sparingly, short sentences can energize writing. Not only can they provide relief to readers who have just labored through several long sentences, they also tend to highlight the information they contain.

Note how in the following example the short sentence serves both as a welcome break after two fairly long sentences and as a way to emphasize the significant point that individuals in both cases were possibly motivated by a reward.

EXAMPLE

In two recent decisions, *United States v. Snowadzki,* 723 F.2d 1427 (9th Cir. 1984), and *United States v. Black,* 767 F.2d 1334 (9th Cir. 1985), individuals conducting unlawful searches were considered to have acted as private parties, not as government agents. In both cases, the individuals obtained the documents unlawfully and then turned them over to the government, which later submitted them as evidence at trial. In each instance, a reward was offered.

In the following example, the writer has remembered how readers welcome a short sentence after several long sentences, but has forgotten that a short sentence also highlights the information it contains.

EXAMPLE

At about 2:00 a.m. on Saturday, February 22, 1993, our client, Mr. David Lendl, left a local restaurant where he had been drinking and began driving south on Interstate 10 to his sister's home in El Paso. After driving for approximately ten minutes, Mr. Lendl realized that he was becoming sleepy and somewhat nauseous, so he decided to change destinations and head back to his own apartment in Las Cruces. Feeling increasingly tired and ill, he pulled off the freeway and onto the shoulder of an exit ramp where he stopped and got out of the car. There he threw up. He then attempted to restart the car's engine but was unable to do so because the carburetor was flooded.

Unless the writer believes that the client's act of throwing up is significant, it does not deserve the emphasis that comes with a short sentence. See Exercises 22.K and 22.L in the *Practice Book.*

§22.6 EMPHASIS

Creating emphasis is important in both objective and persuasive legal writing. In objective writing, the writer needs to let the reader know where to focus his or her attention. By using emphasis properly, the writer signals to the reader the main point or thrust of an objective discussion or explanation.

In persuasive writing, emphasis becomes one of the advocate's most effective tools. Emphasis allows the advocate to spotlight those points that favor the client and downplay those that hurt the client. It also allows the advocate to hammer home his or her theory of the case so that the reader begins to see the case as the writer does.

Emphasis, then, is a natural part of all writing. In fact, you will probably find that you are already using some of the strategies for emphasis that will be discussed in this section. In the previous section, for example, we saw how short sentences can be used to emphasize key points. Notice again how the revision of the following sentence demonstrates the startling effect a short sentence can have.

EXAMPLE

Original:

The defendant lied when she testified that she was in St. Paul, Minnesota, at the time of the robbery.

Revised:

The defendant testified that she was in St. Paul, Minnesota, at the time of the robbery. She lied.

Besides short sentences, emphasis can be achieved in several other ways:

A. telling the reader what is important
B. underlining (or italics or boldface)
C. using positions of emphasis
D. using punctuation to highlight a point
E. using single-word emphasizers
F. changing the normal order in a sentence
G. repeating key words
H. setting up a pattern (and sometimes breaking it)

Of all these strategies, the most common and least sophisticated are the first two: (A) simply telling the reader what is important and (B) underlining. Some writers consider these first two strategies too obvious and overused to be effective. Others feel that they can be effective if used selectively. Regardless of which point of view you agree with, be sure not to overuse these two strategies or, for that matter, any of the eight strategies, because overuse dilutes the impact they have on readers.

§22.6.1   Telling the Reader What Is Important

Sentence openers such as "it is important to note that," "it is note-worthy that," "most important," or "above all" serve only one pur-pose — to alert the reader to the importance of the point that follows. Used rarely, these sentence openers can help the reader identify which points deserve heightened emphasis. Used frequently, these same sen-tence openers bog down the writing and make it wordy. The following examples from persuasive and objective writing show how these sen-tence openers may be used.

EXAMPLES

Above all, the court should consider the defendant's past record as a good husband, model father, and leader in the community.

It is important to note that the check was postdated.

Note

That last example may be even more emphatic when revised into a short sentence: The check was postdated.

You may also tell the reader what is important in mid-sentence. Expressions such as "especially," "particularly," and "most important" can be used in this way when they are inserted right before the point to be emphasized.

EXAMPLES

The court should consider the defendant's past record as a good husband, model father, and, most important, leader in the com-munity.

Lying, particularly lying in court, is not the mark of an innocent man.

§22.6.2 Underlining

Underlining is undoubtedly the simplest and least sophisticated strategy for emphasis. It requires no restructuring of the sentence and little, if any, planning. The writer simply underlines the word or words to signal emphasis. If you do decide to use underlining for emphasis, be extremely selective. The following examples show how underlining may be used for emphasis.

EXAMPLES

The contract <u>permits</u> but does not <u>require</u> the tenant to add land-scaping and similar outdoor improvements.

Lionel Porter's uncle promised to pay for his college education <u>if</u> he majored in business.

Note

It is sometimes tempting to assume that readers will not detect subtle emphasis and must be told which words are crucial. Many writers would consider the underlining in the previous two examples unnecessary and possibly even condescending. The remaining strategies for emphasis are significantly more subtle and therefore more suitable for sophisticated readers.

---

§22.6.3 Using Positions of Emphasis

When it comes to emphasis, all parts of the sentence are not created equal. That is, the beginning, middle, and end of a sentence are not equally emphatic.

In most sentences, writers place new information at the end of a sentence. Also, the end of the sentence is the point of climax. Everything in the sentence builds toward the words at the end. Consequently, in most sentences, the most emphatic position is at the end.

The next most emphatic position is usually at the beginning. Here the writer typically sets the stage for the rest of the sentence. The reader expects the beginning of the sentence to demonstrate how the new information in this sentence is connected with what has already been discussed.

The middle of the sentence is usually the least emphatic. Skillful advocates know that in this part of the sentence they can place unfavorable information and points they do not wish to highlight.

The following grid illustrates the positions in a sentence and their degree of emphasis.

SENTENCE

beginning	middle	end
somewhat emphatic	least emphatic	most emphatic

Examine the following two examples, either of which could appear in an objective memo. Example 1 places "are not attractive nuisances" in the end position, so this version should occur in a memo that emphasizes the point that natural streams are usually not attractive nuisances.

EXAMPLE 1

Unless they are concealing some dangerous condition, natural streams that flow through the hatchery are not attractive nuisances.

Example 2 places "unless they are concealing some dangerous condition" in the end position, so this version is likely to occur in a memo that emphasizes that a concealed dangerous condition made a natural stream an attractive nuisance.

EXAMPLE 2

Natural streams that flow through the hatchery are not attractive nuisances, unless they are concealing some dangerous condition.

Now in the following example from a persuasive brief, note how the end position emphasizes that the error was harmless.

EXAMPLE

Even if the trial court mischaracterized the property, the entire division was fair; thus, the error was harmless.

To emphasize that the entire division of property was fair, the same sentence can be revised.

EXAMPLE

Revised:

Even if the trial court mischaracterized the property, the error was harmless because the entire division was fair.

The following revision places undue emphasis on the court's possible mischaracterization of the property. Consequently, it is the least persuasive and least effective version.

EXAMPLE

Weak Revision:

The entire division was fair, and the error was harmless, even if the trial court mischaracterized the property.

The following example shows how the beginning position, as well as the end position, can be used to highlight points.

EXAMPLE

Despite his earlier attempts at plea bargaining, the defendant now claims not only that he is innocent but also that he has been framed.

As ethical members of the legal profession, legal writers must often include information that is unfavorable to their client. Rather than concede a point in a short sentence, which will highlight the unfavorable point, it is often better to include it with favorable point and arrange the material so the reader ends with the point favorable to your client. Consequently, the middle or the beginning of the sentence is a better position for unfavorable information.

EXAMPLE

Although Mr. Brown admits that he raised his voice during the altercation with Mrs. Smith, he never threatened Mrs. Smith, as Mrs. Smith claims, but rather reminded her of his rights as a property owner.

Combining the End Position with Other Strategies for Emphasis

By using the emphatic end position in combination with another strategy for emphasis, legal writers can achieve even more emphasis.

Here the end position, combined with punctuation, is used for dramatic effect.

EXAMPLE

The courtroom fell silent in anticipation of the jury's verdict: guilty.

In the next example, the end position, combined with use of a phrase telling the reader what is important, is used to suggest a climax.

EXAMPLE

Before awarding custody, the court must consider the mental and physical health of all individuals involved, the child's adjustment to home and school, the relationship of the child with his parents and siblings, the wishes of the parents, and, most important, the wishes of the child.

In the next example, the end position, combined with the technique of setting up a pattern and breaking it, is used to startle the reader.

EXAMPLE

Daniel Klein was loyal to his parents, loyal to his wife, loyal to his friends, and disloyal to the company that had employed him for thirty years.

Note

The characterization of most emphatic, somewhat emphatic, and least emphatic for the end, beginning, and middle of sentences is a general, not an absolute, principle. In the following subsections we will see how punctuation, single-word emphasizers, and changing normal word order can make the beginning and even the middle of sentences strong points of emphasis.

Note

The positions of emphasis can also be applied at the paragraph and document levels.

§22.6.4   Using Punctuation for Emphasis

Commas, colons, and dashes can all be used to set up a point in an appositive at the end of a sentence. An appositive is a restatement of an earlier word or group of words. It is often a more detailed substitute for the earlier word or group of words. In the following examples "expert witness" is an appositive for "one term," "bribe" is an appositive for "exchange of money," and "greed and more greed" is an appositive for "two things."

EXAMPLES

All of the prosecution's arguments depend on the definition of one term, "expert witness."

Throughout the United States, such an exchange of money is known by one name: bribe.

The defendant was motivated by only two things — greed and more greed.

Notice, however, that all three marks of punctuation cast a slightly different light on the words that follow them. The comma, as a rather commonplace punctuation mark, suggests in the following example that there is nothing too surprising about the silent partner being his brother.

EXAMPLE

This construction contract included a silent partner, his brother.

The colon requires a longer pause; consequently the phrase "his brother" receives more emphasis in the example that follows. Colons also have an aura of formality that somehow suggests the seriousness of what follows them.

EXAMPLE

This construction contract included a silent partner: his brother.

The longer pause from the dash gives even more emphasis to "his brother." Also, the dash suggests that it is rather surprising that the brother is the silent partner.

EXAMPLE

This construction contract included a silent partner — his brother.

Note

Some writers feel the dash also conveys a sense of informality. Consequently, many legal writers avoid the dash in legal prose.

Pairs of commas or pairs of dashes can also be used to set off appositives and parenthetical expressions in the middle of sentences. Because pairs of commas are the standard punctuation in such cases, they give the enclosed information less emphasis than a pair of dashes. See Exercise 22.M in the *Practice Book.*

EXAMPLES

The defense counsel's final argument, that the accident was unavoidable, will fail because the defendant's earlier statement shows that she considered the possibility of an injury during a high wind storm.

The defense counsel's final argument — that the accident was unavoidable — will fail because the defendant's earlier statement shows that she considered the possibility of an injury during a high wind storm.

§22.6.5   Using Single-Word Emphasizers

Certain words in our language carry natural emphasis. Such words ("no," "not," "never," "only," "any," "still," "all," "every," "none") convey natural emphasis because they either dramatically change or intensify the meaning of the words they modify.

EXAMPLE

A change made to the contract must be approved by both parties.

Revision 1:

Any change made to the contract must be approved by both parties.

Revision 2:

A change may be made to the contract only if approved by both parties.

Note that the most effective way to use *not* for emphasis is to place a comma before it and use it as a contrasting element.

EXAMPLES

It is the taxpayer, not the tax preparer, who is responsible for the accuracy of all information on the form.

Mrs. Field's express wish was for the jewelry to go to her niece, not her daughter.

Three other single-word emphasizers ("clearly," "obviously," and "very") are so overused by legal writers and, in the case of "very," by the general public that they have lost much of their ability to emphasize. Ironically, then, sentences that contain "clearly," "obviously," and "very" seem to have more impact when these words are omitted.

EXAMPLE

Weak:

Clearly, the defendant knew she was committing a crime.

Revised:

The defendant knew she was committing a crime.

Notice that in the example, "clearly" would be stressed. In the revision, "knew" gets the natural stress.

EXAMPLE

Weak:

Many residents complained about the very loud noise coming from the factory.

Revised:

Many residents complained about the loud noise coming from the factory.

"Very" is often an unnecessary prop for a word. Usually, a word such as "loud" conveys the right level of meaning by itself. If, however, "loud" is too weak a term for your purpose, it is better to choose a stronger term rather than to rely on "very" to bolster meaning. See Exercise 22.N in the *Practice Book.*

EXAMPLE

Revised:

Many residents complained about the ear-splitting noise coming from the factory.

§22.6.6 Changing the Normal Word Order

Readers expect the traditional subject-verb-object order in sentences. When a writer changes this expected order, the change draws attention to itself and emphasizes whatever words are out of the traditional order.

The most common change is from active voice to passive voice (see sections 22.1.1 to 22.1.3). Another fairly common change is to insert the words to be emphasized between either the subject and the verb or between the verb and its object.

EXAMPLES

Martin Fuller, blinded by grief, lost his grip on reality and opened fire on the parking lot.

(subject and verb separated by "blinded by grief")

He shot — apparently at close range — both of the parents of Tim O'Connell.

(verb and object separated by "apparently at close range")

Another, less frequent change is to delay the subject and verb and open the sentence with a part of the sentence that would normally come at the end.

EXAMPLE

Mrs. Taylor rewrote her will only one week before she died.

Revised:

Only one week before she died, Mrs. Taylor rewrote her will.

An even more radical change is to begin an active voice sentence with its object.

EXAMPLE

The jury did not believe her testimony.

Revised:

Her testimony the jury did not believe.

Note

Some of the examples seem to contradict the earlier advice about keeping subjects and verbs close together and using the end position in sentences to achieve emphasis. None of the strategies for emphasis work as an absolute rule. The writer should use his or her judgment in selecting which strategy is effective in each instance.

As a strategy for emphasis, changing the normal word order should be used carefully and rarely. Frequent use, particularly of delaying the normal word order and beginning active voice sentences with the object, will make that writing sound awkward and contrived. See Exercise 22.O in the *Practice Book.*

§22.6.7   Repeating Key Words

Many writers mistakenly assume that repetition is a sign of incompetence. This assumption leads them to search desperately for synonyms of words that recur frequently in a given office memo or brief.

While it is true that needless repetition is ineffective, it is also true that deliberate repetition can be a powerful strategy for emphasis. Key terms and key points should reverberate throughout a piece of legal writing. Like the dominant color in a beautiful tapestry, key words and phrases should be woven throughout to create an overall impression that *this* is what the case is about.

Consider the following excerpt from the respondent's brief in a case where the appellant, a church, wants to operate a grade school without the special use permit required by the city's zoning ordinance for all schools in residential areas. Throughout the excerpt, three different words — "code," "use," and "school" — are deliberately repeated for emphasis. We have boldfaced these three words so you can see how frequently they appear.

EXAMPLE

ARGUMENT

I. THE TRIAL COURT PROPERLY CONSTRUED AND APPLIED BOTH THE ZONING AND BUILDING **CODES** BECAUSE THE CHURCH HAS CHANGED THE **USE** OF ITS BUILDING BY OPERATING A FULLTIME GRADE **SCHOOL.**

The church must comply with the requirements of the zoning and building **codes** before it may legally operate its **school.** Each of these **codes** makes accommodation for **uses** that legally existed prior to enactment of the **code.** However, the church never operated a **school** prior to the **codes'** enactment, so full compliance with the **codes** is required for the new **use** involved in operating a **school.**

§22.6.8   Setting up a Pattern

The earlier strategy of repeating key words is closely tied to another strategy for emphasis: setting up a pattern. In such cases a pattern is set up and key words are repeated within that pattern. This kind of deliberate repetition can be used effectively within one sentence or in a sequence of sentences.

EXAMPLES

The prosecution's case depends on solid evidence, solid reasoning, and solid authority.

Lieutenant Harris has been described by his superiors as an "exemplary officer" — exemplary in his demeanor and professionalism, exemplary in his management of subordinates, exemplary in his performance of duty, and exemplary in his loyalty to the service.

Both women were abducted in the same locale. Both women were abducted at night. Both women were abducted while alone. Both women were abducted by the same man: Edward Smith.

Note that to achieve a climactic effect, the writer usually used parallel structure (see section 25.7) to create the pattern and then arranged the material in an order of increasing importance. Thus, emphasis was achieved by the pattern, the repetition of key words, and the end position. Notice too that this strategy for emphasis is best suited for persuasive writing.

Variation: Deliberately Breaking a Pattern

A rather dramatic variation of the pattern strategy is to set up the pattern and deliberately break it. This variation depends on the pattern and repetition of key words to create a certain expectation in the reader. The reader's surprise when the pattern is broken creates heightened emphasis. See Exercise 22.P in the *Practice Book*.

EXAMPLES

The defendant acted under a common scheme, for a common motive, but with uncommon results.

It is true that, in New York, many activities engaged in by a church are held to be an integral part of that church, *see, e.g., Unitarian Universalist Church of Central Nassau v. Shorten,* 63 Misc. 2d 978, 314 N.Y.S.2d 66 (1970). It is also true, however, that each case rests on its own facts. *Community Synagogue v. Bates,* 1 N.Y.2d 445, 453, 154 N.Y.S.2d 15, 22, 136 N.E.2d 488, 493 (1956).

---

§22.6.9   Strategies for Emphasis in Context

Up until now we have examined and practiced the strategies for emphasis in mostly isolated sentences or short sequences of sentences. To understand how these strategies are used in context, read the following excerpt from a respondent's brief. Note which strategies are used extensively and which are used less frequently. The boldface type indicates repetition of key words. Pattern sentences are <u>underscored.</u>

EXAMPLE

C. The trial court properly found that the church had to comply with the minimum safety standards set out in the building **code** because operation of the **school** is a changed **use** of the building rather than a prior, legal **use.**

The Sumner Church has changed the way it **uses** its building. It first **used** its building only for church services; now it **uses** the building for church services and as a **school.**

Before 1985, the church building was used for weekly church services and for occasional meetings. The only **"school"** was the one-hour Sunday **school** offered on Sunday mornings and the vacation bible school offered for two weeks each summer. Neither of these **"schools"** was a **school** in the traditional sense. <u>The only instruction</u> given was religious instruction. <u>The only teachers</u> were ministers and unpaid volunteers from the congregation.

In contrast, the **school** that the Church is now operating in the building is a traditional **school.** Instead of operating for one hour a week or for two weeks each summer, the school operates all day long, five days a week, nine months a year. Furthermore, the curriculum is similar to that offered in public grade **schools.** Although the children receive some religious instruction, most of their time is spent on reading, spelling, arithmetic, social studies, and science. Their teachers are full-time, paid faculty members who are certified by the State, not ministers or volunteers. Consequently, despite any church involvement with the **school,** the First Christian Academy is an "educational **use**" of the building as defined by the **code.**

The Michigan Court of Appeals has recognized that even **schools** operated as part of churches are subject to building codes applicable to **schools.** *Hough v. North Star Baptist Church,* 312 N.W.2d 158 (Mich. Ct. App. 1981). The church in *Hough* sought to operate a fulltime **school** without meeting the fire **code.** Even though the court recognized that the **school** was an integral part of the church program, the court held that it was also a **school** under the **code.** As a **school,** the building had to comply with fire regulations for **schools.**

<u>Contrary to the Sumner Church's contention,</u> the **school** does not qualify under

---

Short sentence

"only" as emphasizer
End position

"only" as emphasizer /
Two short sentences / Two "only"s as emphasizers /
<u>Pattern sentences</u>

End position /
Change in normal order in sentence

End position

"not" as emphasizer /
End position

End position

"even" as emphasizer

End position

End position
End position
<u>Setting up a pattern</u>

End position /
Telling
what is
important /
Underlining

the **code's** grandfather clause as a prior, legal **use** because it was opened after the building **code** was adopted. It is important to note that[1] Section 306 of the **code** specifies that if there is <u>any</u> change in the **use** of the building, Section 502 applies. Section 502 specifies that if the changed **use** of the building would fall within a category of occupancy different from that of the original **use,** a new certificate of occupancy is required. Furthermore, the grandfather clause indicates that the drafters intended to accommodate prior **uses,** not changes or extensions of a **use.** Clearly,[2] a fulltime grade **school** is not the same **use** as a two-week bible school.

"not" as
emphasizer /
"not" as
emphasizer
<u>Repeating
earlier pattern</u>

<u>Also contrary to the church's contention,</u> *Westbury* is not controlling in the present case on the issue of whether the Sumner Church has changed the **use** of its building. *Westbury Hebrew Congregation v. Downer,* 59 Misc. 2d 387, 302 N.Y.S.2d 923 (1971). *Westbury* is a zoning ordinance case. This is a building **code** case. In *Westbury,* the court held that it was unreasonable for the city to require a church to buy an additional 34½ acres of land merely because the church had opened a **school** in its building. The *Westbury* court also held that the city had no important interest in requiring a church to occupy fifty acres of land if it wanted to operate a **school.** In fact, in a previous proceeding, the ordinance at issue had already been declared arbitrary and unreasonable. Furthermore, the ordinance at issue applied only to parochial **schools,** not public **schools.** Based on that discrimination, the statute was held to be unconstitutional on its face.

Short sentence
Short sentence

"no" as
emphasizer

"only" as
emphasizer /
"not" as
emphasizer /
End position /
<u>Sets up a
pattern</u>

In contrast to *Westbury,* <u>the City of Sumner Building **Code**</u> does not discriminate between church educational **uses** and public educational **uses.** The **code** requires

---

1. Many legal writers would consider "it is important to note that" a wordy construction and simply begin the sentence with "Section 306."

2. Many legal writers avoid "clearly" as an emphasizer because it is often overused.

that any building that is **used** for educational purposes for more than four hours per day or twelve hours per week meet Group C occupancy requirements. The Church's **use** subjects it to the **code's** requirement. Unlike *Westbury,* there is no unconstitutional discrimination against churches on the face of the law.

 Furthermore, the City of Sumner's building **code** requirements are not arbitrary and unreasonable. In contrast to *Westbury,* the city has an important interest in assuring that fire regulations are met: public **safety.** Nowhere in *Westbury* does that court indicate that had a fire **safety** regulation been at issue, the church would be excused from compliance. The zoning ordinance in *Westbury* was unreasonable because no important state interest was shown in the case. The building **code's** regulation is reasonable because of a demonstrated importance to public **safety.**

"any" as emphasizer

Short sentence

"no" as emphasizer

Pattern repeated

End position / Punctuation / "Nowhere" as emphasizer / Change in normal word order / Sets up a pattern / "no" as emphasizer / Pattern repeated / End position

See Exercises 22.Q and 22.R in the *Practice Book.*

Chapter 23

Effective Words

A powerful agent is the right word. Whenever we
come upon one of those intensely right words in a
book or a newspaper the resulting effect is physical
as well as spiritual, and electrically prompt.

— Mark Twain,
Essay on William Dean Howells

§23.1 DICTION AND PRECISION

Such a seemingly simple thing. Use the right word, Twain tells us,
and the effect is physical, spiritual, electric, prompt. But right is a relative
thing, isn't it? Some words are more right than others. Some words approach the desired meaning; others capture it, embody it, nail it to the
wall in a way that leaves both the writer and reader satisfied, almost
breathless.

Take the word "right," for example. Twain chose "right" to describe the kind of word he meant, even though the thesaurus suggests
that he might have chosen any number of so-called synonyms. How
about the "noble" word, the "proper" word, the "suitable" word, the
"exact" word, the "accurate" word, the "correct" word, or even the
"precise" word?

What is it about "right" that makes it the right choice?

First of all, denotation — that is, the word's definition. "Noble" is
the wrong choice because it has the wrong denotation. Webster tells us
that "noble" means "possessing outstanding qualities." The definition of
"noble" also includes a tie to some kind of superiority. Something is
"noble" because it has a "superiority of mind or character or ideals or
morals." The kind of words Twain talks about do something different
than possess outstanding qualities or superiority.

"Proper" seems to have the right denotation. "Proper" is defined
as "marked by suitability, rightness, or appropriateness." Later in the def-

inition we find "strictly accurate" and "correct." These meanings seem closer to Twain's intention. But wait a minute. Further still in the definition we see "respectable," "strictly decorous," and "genteel." But do we have to include all of the possible definitions of a word when we use it? Obviously not, but in the case of "proper," these later definitions are clues about the connotations, or associations, that the word carries.

The word "proper" has close ties with the word "propriety," which means "the quality or state of being proper." "Propriety" also means "the standard of what is socially acceptable." If "the proper thing to do" has overtones of decorum and civility, then "the proper word" might also suggest a bit of politeness in its selection. It's doubtful that Twain meant that a "polite word" is a powerful agent.

"Suitable" has similar denotation and connotation problems. Part of the definition of "suitable" is "adapted to the use or purpose." If "suitable words" are those that are adapted to a certain use or purpose, then it is unlikely anything with such a chameleon-like quality can ever be physical, spiritual, electric, or prompt.

"Exact" has the virtue of meaning in "strict, particular, and complete accordance with fact" and the minor flaw of connoting a kind of mathematical or scientific measurement. Still, it is a far better choice than "noble," "proper," or "suitable."

In fact, "exact," "accurate," "correct," "precise," and "right" all have what dictionaries call "the shared meaning element." They all mean "conforming to fact, truth, or a standard."

What is it then about the word "right" that makes it preferable to the other four words, that makes it just right? It has the right denotation and the right connotation, and it has the right sound.

Go back to the quotation at the beginning of the chapter. Try reading the first sentence aloud as it is. Now, one at a time, substitute the words "exact," "accurate," "correct," and "precise" for "right." Read each of these versions aloud. Notice how much harder it is to get the desired emphasis with the three-syllable *accurate.* Even the two-syllable words dilute, albeit just a bit, the punch that we hear in the one syllable *right.* Furthermore, *right* has a kind of honesty and simplicity that captures the spirit of Twain's insight.

Now what does all of this mean for a writer of legal briefs and memos? The same thing it means for any good writer. Finding the right word to express one's meaning is critical to clear communication. With anything other than the right word, you have sacrificed precision; you have sacrificed exact meaning.

In cases like Twain's in which several words can express the intended meaning, the writer can then go beyond precision to eloquence to find the word with just the right sound. (See Chapter 24: Eloquence.) For now, though, we will focus just on diction and precision and the word choice problems that frequently occur in legal writing. (Three categories of word choice problems, legalese, nonsexist language, and bias-free language, deserve special attention and are discussed in sections 23.3, 23.4, and 23.5 respectively.)

Note

As is true of so many other aspects of writing, there are "errors" in word choice that matter a little and errors that matter a lot. Some are outright mistakes that suggest a lack of sophistication; others are a matter of observing convention, and others are more a matter of judgment. Some errors suggest sloppiness on the part of the writer, and still others can have significant legal consequences.

---

§23.1.1   Colloquial Language

Word choice, like every other choice in legal writing, is governed by the document's purpose, the reader's expectations, and the writer's role. Because legal writing is done for serious reasons and in a professional context, legal writers should select words that reflect seriousness and professionalism. Slang, colloquialisms, or informal expressions that are acceptable in everyday spoken language are usually out of place in legal writing.

EXAMPLES

Poor:

The defendant's sister is into stained glass windows.

Revised:

The defendant's sister makes stained glass windows as a hobby.

Poor:

The prosecutor noted that Mr. Webb is hung up about how clean his car is, what gas is used in it, and how it is driven.

Revised:

The prosecutor noted that Mr. Webb feels strongly about how clean his car is, what gas is used in it, and how it is driven.

There is only one exception to the general ban on using slang, colloquialisms, and informal language in legal writing — when the writer is quoting. While a writer of a trial brief would be ill-advised to call the defendant "a bad dude," he or she may effectively use that expression if it appeared in the record.

§23.1.2 Reader Expectations and Idioms

A writer's choice among synonyms should also be affected by the reader's expectations. Legal readers, for example, expect to hear about "analogous" cases or "similar" cases, not "comparable" cases or "matching" cases or "kindred" cases.

Read the following example and see if any word is jarring for legal readers.

EXAMPLE

Beaver Custom Carpets will probably argue that there are significant parallelisms between its case and *Flowers.*

Revised:

Beaver Custom Carpets will probably argue that there are significant similarities between its case and *Flowers.*

Similarly, some synonyms have the correct denotation and connotation, but their use is jarring because the reader expects certain idiomatic combinations.

Consider the following example. Which word doesn't seem quite right?

EXAMPLE

Corporations can elude liability by dissolution.

Although the thesaurus may list "elude" as a synonym for "avoid" and "escape," readers expect either the idiom "avoid liability" or the idiom "escape liability."

EXAMPLE   **REVISED**

Corporations can avoid liability by dissolution.

Numerous verbs have certain prepositions with which they commonly combine. In common usage, for example, one always "infers *from*" something. A client may "agree *to*" sign a contract, but she may not "agree *with*" the way you are handling her case.

When in doubt about which idiom or preposition is appropriate, consult one of the better dictionaries or a usage guidebook. Another strategy to try is to read the sentence aloud. Native speakers of English can usually "hear" which preposition is correct. Try reading the following example aloud to determine which preposition needs to be changed.

EXAMPLE

Publishers must be able to publish matters of public concern without fear for a lawsuit.

Although one can fear *for* one's life, one can live in fear *of* a lawsuit.

EXAMPLE   **REVISED**

Publishers must be able to publish matters of public concern without fear of a lawsuit.

---

§23.1.3   Not-Really-Synonymous Synonyms

Of the many types of imprecision, the most common is the simple substitution of a not-really-synonymous "synonym." In the following example, the writer knew that there were several things he had to prove under the doctrine of adverse possession, but he forgot what to call those "things."

EXAMPLE

The *condition* of hostility must also be proved.

"Condition" is not completely wrong; the reader can probably figure out what the writer intended. But "condition" is not precise. By using the precise term "element," the writer conveys the exact intended meaning, and he makes it clear that he is doing an elements analysis of the problem.

EXAMPLE   **REVISED**

The element of hostility must also be proved.

Sometimes writers try to dress up a simple idea in a fancy vocabulary word and end up instead with a word choice that misses the mark.

EXAMPLE

The McKibbins may argue that rugs are totally diverse from closed circuit television camera security systems because few consumers have a need for such elaborate security systems.

Revised:

The McKibbins may argue that rugs differ from closed circuit television camera security systems because few consumers have a need for such elaborate security systems.

The most serious type of "not-really-synonymous synonym" problem occurs when writers attempt to use words they are not quite sure of. Needless to say, it can be embarrassing to find that you have used a word that only sounds like the word you intended.

EXAMPLE

Mrs. Harris's most saline point is that Mr. Harris intends to move the children over 250 miles away.

Undoubtedly, the writer intended the point to be "salient," not salty.

See Exercise 23.A in the *Practice Book.*

§23.1.4 Same Term for the Same Idea

Another common precision problem in legal writing is the misuse of elegant variation. In other words, legal writers sometimes try to use synonyms for key terms in their writing in the mistaken belief that using the same term over and over again bores their readers.

What they have forgotten, though, is that their legal readers have been carefully trained to read statutes and, according to the rules of statutory construction, a different term signals a different idea.

Many legal readers carry this rule over into their memo and brief reading. A change in a key term starts them wondering: "Does the writer mean the same thing as before, or is this really something new?" In short, in legal writing, using an elegant variation of a key term probably will not make the writing more interesting, but it may make the writing confusing.

Read the following example and note how the writer uses the term "stability" and its variations consistently but floats back and forth among the terms "factor," "principle," and "element."

EXAMPLE

Under the applicable case law, the relevant **factors** used by the courts in deciding custody disputes are the stability of the parent and the role of the primary caretaker. *In re Maddox*, 641 P.2d 665 (Or. Ct. App. 1982). Stability seems to be the overriding **principle** that the Oregon courts use to decide custody disputes. It seems that if the court can determine that one parent is more stable than the other, custody is usually granted to the more stable parent. Another **element** appears, as in *Maddox*, where the father argued that he devoted a significant amount of time to the children, even though the mother was the primary caretaker during the marriage. *Id.* at 667. Both of these **factors** relate back to the first part of the statute, which deals with the emotional ties and interest and attitudes.

In cases like the example above, the reader does not know whether to accuse the writer of sloppy writing or to try to make some fine distinction between "factor," "principle," and "element." In many cases, there is a legal distinction between "factor" and "element" or between "factor" and "principle." In those cases, substituting the terms for each other would be more than confusing; it would be legally inaccurate.

In short, then, legal readers appreciate appropriate variety, but they do not appreciate variety at the expense of clarity.

Sometimes legal writers inadvertently use different terms for the same idea. This inadvertent use seems to occur most frequently when the writer was the one to label an idea. For example, after reading numerous cases on a given issue, the writer may realize that courts typically go through three steps in their analysis. The writer may then refer to a three-step analysis or a three-part analysis or a three-pronged analysis, depending on which best describes what courts have done.

Once a writer has decided which label to use, though, he or she must be consistent. A reader who was introduced to a "three-pronged" analysis will be confused if later in the writing the "second prong" is called the "second step" or the "third prong" is called the "third part" or, worse yet, the "third test." See Exercise 23.B in the *Practice Book*.

§23.1.5   Apples and Rutabagas

In the preceding sections, we saw how disconcerting it can be for readers when writers aren't careful about what they call something. Equally disconcerting for readers are situations in which writers are sloppy about the comparisons they make.

EXAMPLE

The facts of *Turner* are similar to our case.

Because a case includes more than just the facts, it is incongruous to compare just the facts of one case to another entire case.

EXAMPLE   **REVISED**

The facts of *Turner* are similar to the facts in our case.

See Exercise 23.C in the *Practice Book*.

§23.1.6   Subject-Verb-Object Mismatch

Not all problems of precision are a matter of just one poorly chosen word. All too frequently, the problem is a poorly chosen combination of words. Read the following example from a case about a custody dispute and see if the subject, verb, and object go together.

EXAMPLE

Dr. Davis's <u>occupation</u> as an obstetrician <u>has shown</u> a <u>diminished</u>
   (subject)   *(verb)* *(object)*
<u>ability</u> to provide consistent care and guidance for her children.

Can an occupation show a diminished ability to do anything? Obviously not. What has happened to this writer is that she has gotten tangled in her own verbiage and written something nonsensical. What she wants to say is that Dr. Davis is an obstetrician and that people who are obstetricians often have demanding, irregular schedules and therefore less time and energy to give consistent care and guidance to their own children.

Consider the following possible revision.

EXAMPLE   POSSIBLE REVISION

As an obstetrician, Dr. Davis may be unable to provide consistent care and guidance for her children.

Of course, the revision's meaning is somewhat different from the meaning in the original sentence. Dr. Davis, rather than the profession of being an obstetrician, has become the subject. In the earlier sentence, she merely had a "diminished ability" to provide consistent care and guidance for her children; in the revision, she is "unable" to do these things.

Consider the following compromise revision.

EXAMPLE   POSSIBLE REVISION

Dr. Davis's occupation, obstetrician, may impair her ability to provide consistent care and guidance for her children.

To determine whether this or any other subject-verb-object combination is mismatched, lift those three parts out of the sentence and see if they make sense as a unit.

    occupation may impair ability
    (subject)   *(verb)* *(object)*

Does "occupation may impair ability" make sense? Most readers would say that it does; some, however, would argue against the personification of "occupation" and suggest that occupations cannot "impair" anything. Precision, as we said earlier, is a relative thing.

One common personification used in law that many readers consider imprecise is the use of a case in the subject position when the writer actually means the court that presided over that case.

EXAMPLE

The case *In re Miller,* 670 P.2d 819 (Colo. Ct. App. 1983), reversed the trial court's decision because of the trial court's undue emphasis towards "motherly instincts."

Using the "lift-out" strategy, we get the following combination:

case	reversed	decision
(subject)	*(verb)*	*(object)*

To be more precise, place the real actor, the appellate court, in the subject position.

EXAMPLE

Revised:

In *In re Miller,* 670 P.2d 819 (Colo. Ct. App. 1983), the appellate court reversed the trial court because of the trial court's undue emphasis towards "motherly instincts."

---

appellate court	reversed	trial court
(subject)	*(verb)*	*(object)*

Occasionally, legal writers mistakenly end up with a combination that essentially means "X equals X"; that is, the subject or beginning of the sentence and object or end of the sentence are the same.

EXAMPLE

The purpose of the legislation is compensatory intent.

---

purpose	is	intent
(subject)	*(verb)*	*(predicate nominative)*[1]

There is virtually no difference between "the purpose of the legislation" and "the intent of the legislation." More than likely, the writer intended to say that the purpose of the legislation was to compensate someone.

EXAMPLE   **REVISED**

The purpose of the legislation is to compensate victims of such crimes.

Part of matching the right subject with the right verb is understanding how the legal system works. Knowing exactly what courts, juries, parties to litigation, legislatures, and agencies do and don't do makes it easier to select appropriate verbs.

For example, "the court finds" is the right combination for describing the action a court takes in a finding of fact. "The court held" is the right combination for describing the actions of a court in a particular case. "The court ruled" is the right combination for describing the actions a court takes on a particular issue, such as a motion or an objection, in a particular case. Courts can also "deny motions" or "grant injunctions"; they can "take something under advisement."

Courts can "apply the law," they can "apply a standard," and they can "apply a test"; they never "apply the facts." In other words, courts apply law to fact, not fact to law.

EXAMPLE

Incorrect:

Applying the facts of this case to the law, the court held that the defendant was negligent.

Correct:

Applying the law to the facts of this case, the court held that the defendant was negligent.

---

1. The term "predicate nominative" is used instead of "object" with linking verbs. (See section 25.1.)

EXHIBIT 23.1   **Typical Subject-Verb-Object Combinations**

TYPICAL SUBJECT-VERB-OBJECT COMBINATIONS

the court found (findings of fact)
the court ruled (ruling on an objection or a motion)
the court held (law applied to facts of a specific case)
the court determined (or must determine)
the court granted an injunction
the court granted the motion
the court denied the motion
the court applied the law (the test, the rule, the standard)
the court adopted the test
the court ordered (psychological testing, discovery)

the court relied on
the court followed
the court concluded
the court examined
the court reasoned

the appellate court affirmed the trial court's decision
the appellate court modified the trial court's decision
the appellate court reversed the trial court's decision
the appellate court upheld the trial court's decision
the appellate court remanded the case

In *Smith,* the court criticized the court's holding in *Jones.*
In *Smith,* the court explained the court's holding in *Jones.*
In *Smith,* the court followed the court's holding in *Jones.*
In *Smith,* the court limited the court's holding in *Jones.*
In *Smith,* the court questioned the court's holding in *Jones.*
In *Smith,* the court expanded upon the court's holding in *Jones.*
In *Smith,* the court overruled *Jones.*

the jury found the defendant (guilty or not guilty)
the jury determined that the defendant was (was not) liable
the jury awarded damages

the defendant (or plaintiff) argued, stated, maintained, asked, claimed, al-
    leged, asserted, responded, rebutted, countered, moved

the legislature passed, enacted, amended
the legislature intended to (promote, encourage, prevent, protect)
the legislature wanted to (promote, encourage, prevent, protect)

EXHIBIT 23.1   *(continued)*

> the agency determined, decided
> the agency ruled
> the agency promulgated, investigated, proposed, mediated

In cases in which the court is both the decider of law and the trier of fact, courts perform an additional set of duties. When no jury is present, the court will "find" the criminal defendant guilty or innocent, and the court will "award" civil damages.

As both the decider of law and the trier of fact, the court may "make determinations" or simply "determine" something about the law or the facts. Even so, "determine" is more commonly used for findings of fact.

For cases up on appeal, appellate courts have a variety of actions they can perform. They can "affirm," "modify," "reverse," or "remand" a case; they can also "criticize," "distinguish," "explain," "follow," "limit," "overrule," or "question" the decisions in another case.

The court never takes on the role of one of the parties to litigation. Consequently, as a general rule, the court does not "claim," "allege," "assert," or "argue." The court is in a position to "say," not to "claim."

Even though it is technically incorrect to say "the court claimed," "the court asserted," or "the court argued," there are a few times when these combinations may be strategic word choices. In instances in which the writer is disagreeing with another court, for example, a writer may deliberately use "the court claimed" as a pejorative attack on another court's reasoning. The effect, of course, is the subtle undermining of the court's authority.

Another instance in which it is appropriate to use a combination like "the court argued" occurs when members of the same court differ. Consequently, a law professor or the author of a law review article may say "Justice X argued" to describe a position that justice took when trying to persuade the other members of the same court.

Juries, on the other hand, are charged with different tasks from judges. They "find" that a defendant is guilty or innocent, they "determine liability," and they "award damages," but they do not "rule" on the law. Consequently, "a jury found," "a jury determined," and "a jury awarded" are appropriate combinations. In a jury trial, the jury, not the judge, "renders a verdict," and the judge, not the jury, "enters a judgment" based on that verdict. In a bench trial, the judge "renders a verdict."

Defendants and plaintiffs perform certain acts as well. They "argue," "state," "ask," "claim," "contend," "allege," "assert," "respond," "rebut," and "counter," but they do not "apply" the law. That is for the court to do.

Incorrect:

Applying the majority rule, the defendant will argue that the benefit of having a healthy baby outweighs the burden.

Correct:

The defendant will argue that the court should apply the majority rule and hold that having a healthy baby outweighs the burden.

Either party to litigation can make a preliminary motion. Although you often hear, for example, that "the plaintiff made a motion for summary judgment," it is more concise to say "the plaintiff moved for summary judgment."

Legislatures, of course, perform entirely different functions from judges, juries, and litigants. The legislature may "enact a statute," it may "amend a statute," and it may "pass a law." It does not "hold" or "find." When it comes to policy, it is appropriate to say that the legislature "intended," "wanted to promote," "wanted to encourage," "wanted to prevent," or "wanted to protect."

Like judges, agencies "make determinations" (or just "determine"), and they "decide" things. Rarely does an agency "hold"; save "hold" for the few times when an agency issues an opinion. Even then, it is more likely to "rule." And of course, agencies perform many other functions such as "promulgate," "investigate," "propose," and "decide."

Criminal Cases	*Civil Cases*
accused	sued
charged	action filed against
guilty	liable
innocent	not liable

Perhaps the most glaring errors in word choice made by novice legal writers are those that stem from confusion over criminal and civil cases. Use "accused," "prosecuted," and "charged" for criminal cases. The defendant in a civil suit may be "sued" or "an action may be filed" against him or her; a civil suit defendant is not "accused," "prosecuted," or "charged."

Similarly, defendants in civil suits are not "found guilty or inno-cent"; they are "found liable" or "not liable."

The outcome of a trial is a "judgment," not a "settlement." Use "settlement" for those agreements reached by parties through negotia-tion, not litigation. Parties may "settle out of court." See Exercise 23.D in the *Practice Book.*

§23.1.7   Grammatical Ambiguities

Before leaving the topic of precision, we must consider those times when writing becomes ambiguous and imprecise because the writer has not paid close attention to the grammar of the sentence. Modifiers, in particular, can create unintended meanings because modifiers seem to be free-floating spirits that can find a home in many different spots in a sentence.

Consider, for example, that all-purpose and significant modifier "only." In the following nine-word sentence, "only" can find a home in no fewer than four places, but each time "only" moves, the meaning of the sentence changes.

EXAMPLE

The defendant talked to the plaintiff on July 1.

Only the defendant talked to the plaintiff on July 1. *(No one but the defendant talked to him.)*

The defendant **only** talked to the plaintiff on July 1. *(He did not write to him, threaten him, whatever; they only talked.)*

The defendant talked **only** to the plaintiff on July 1. *(The defen-dant did not talk to anyone else, just the plaintiff.)*

The defendant talked to the plaintiff **only** on July 1. *(The talk oc-curred only on one day, July 1.)*

"Only" is not the only modifier legal writers have to keep close tabs on; other single-word modifiers such as "almost," "even," "hardly," "just," "merely," "nearly," "scarcely," and "simply" can also float around in a sentence, radically changing meaning with each move.

The rule for "only" and other single-word modifiers is to place them immediately before the word(s) they modify. (See section 25.6 for more on misplaced modifiers.)

Other modifiers create ambiguity or uncertainty because they are "dangling"; that is, they don't have a noun in the sentence to modi-fy.

EXAMPLE

By calling attention to the defendant's post-arrest silence, the jury was allowed to make prejudicial and false inferences.

Who, or for that matter what, called attention to the defendant's post-arrest silence? Grammatically, it appears that it was the jury because "jury" is the noun closest to that modifying phrase. Logically, though, we know that that meaning is unlikely. Who did it, then? The prosecutor? The defendant's counsel? The judge? We can only guess because the writer left that modifier dangling with no stated noun to modify.

EXAMPLE   POSSIBLE REVISION

By calling attention to the defendant's post-arrest silence, the prosecutor allowed the jury to make prejudicial and false inferences.

(For a more detailed explanation of dangling modifiers, see section 25.6.2.)

Finally, a third type of modifier problem can also make legal writing ambiguous. Although known in grammar books as squinting modifiers, these modifiers are misnamed because they do not really squint; rather, they appear to be looking both forward and back.

EXAMPLE

Taxpayers who file their returns promptly receive their refunds.

What does "promptly" modify? Does the filing occur promptly, or does the receipt of refunds occur promptly? It cannot be both because a modifier can modify only one grammatical element in a sentence.

EXAMPLE   POSSIBLE REVISIONS

Taxpayers who promptly file their returns receive their refunds.

Taxpayers who file their returns receive their refunds promptly.

Taxpayers who promptly file their returns receive their refunds promptly.

In addition to modifiers, there are a few clauses that can sometimes be ambiguous. Be particularly careful with clauses that begin with "because." They can appear to be modifying either the main verb or a preceding clause.

EXAMPLE

Our client will not be able to assert that it is in his daughter's best interest to live with him because she is better adjusted to her home in Colorado.

Does the writer mean that the client won't be able to make this assertion because the daughter is better adjusted to the Colorado home, or does the writer mean that because she is better adjusted to the Colorado home, it is in her best interest to live with the client? (See Exercise 23.E in the *Practice Book.*)

EXAMPLE   **POSSIBLE REVISIONS**

Because his daughter is better adjusted to her Colorado home, our client will not be able to assert that it is in her best interest to live with him.

Our client will not be able to assert that, because his daughter is better adjusted to her Colorado home, it is in her best interest to live with him.

---

§23.2   CONCISENESS

Wordy writing is fat writing. It is burdened by extra words, extraneous ideas, and sometimes too much of a good thing.

Concise writing is lean writing. It is clear, focused, and efficient. Like a trim athlete, concise writing has muscle and strength where it is needed. It gets the job done with grace and ease because the working parts of the sentences are well built.

The question for most legal writers is how to transform overweight, sluggish writing into writing that is both strong and slender. The first and most important way to achieve this kind of strong efficiency is for the writer to keep the context of the writing uppermost in mind. Context here includes at least three considerations:

1. who the reader is;
2. what the reader wants to get out of the writing; and
3. what the writer wants the reader to get out of the writing.

Remembering the context in which a piece of writing occurs will do more than anything else to keep the writing focused and therefore concise. Forgetting the context will lead to many wordiness problems, including the first three discussed in this chapter.

§23.2.1   Don't State the Obvious

Judges, lawyers, and most clients are well-informed, busy people. They appreciate legal writers who recognize their intelligence and value their time. They don't want to spend time reading the legal equivalent of "the sky is blue" or "people breathe air," unless, of course, you have something new to say about what is obvious.

Wasting time with sentences in a memo or a brief like "Now I am going to discuss the cases that are relevant to this issue" or "The appellate court will not reconsider factual issues" annoys legal readers. It is a given that an office memo will discuss cases that are relevant to the issue; it is old news unworthy of both the writer's and reader's time to say that appellate courts don't retry a case on its facts.

Novice legal writers often state the obvious because it reminds them of the steps they must go through in legal analysis. For example, a writer who begins the discussion section of a memo with "To determine the answer to this question, we must first look at the rule that ..." has not recognized that a legal reader would be shocked to find something other than the rule at this point in the memo.

Consider the following excerpt from a draft of a memo.

EXAMPLE

Our client bears the burden of establishing that the action meets the federal removal requirements. Some of these requirements are more important than others, but all are required before removal may occur. To understand these requirements, it is easiest to break down 28 U.S.C. § 1441(a) (1988) into its component parts and discuss each part separately.

Besides the wordiness that comes from the redundancy in the first two sentences — requirements are required — the last sentence is no more than an announcement that one should do the obvious: analyze the requirements. Such a statement to a legal reader is a bit like a restaurant adding to its menu that silverware will be provided. While such reminders to self are natural in an early draft, they should be edited out before the writing is submitted to the reader.

Novice and experienced legal writers often fall into the "stating the obvious" trap when they are trying to compose topic and transitional sentences within a discussion or argument section.

Suppose, for example, that a writer has just completed a paragraph about the holding, rationale, and facts of an analogous case. The writer now wants to compare the facts of the analogous case with those of the instant case. At first the writer may be tempted to begin with something like "*Moore* and our client's case are factually similar." This announcement should be quickly obvious, however, and unworthy of mention. What the writer needs to discuss in this topic sentence is the nature of these similarities or why those similarities suggest a certain outcome. A topic sentence more like "Similarly, in our case, the defendant also used tissue from the plaintiff's body to produce a commercially valuable product" not only moves the discussion along more quickly, it also helps the reader to see how the upcoming information should be used.

§23.2.2   Don't Start Too Far Back

Some novice legal writers fall prey to a cousin of the "stating the obvious" problem — starting too far back. They forget that there is common knowledge among legal readers and that these same readers don't need to be taken all the way back to the United States Constitution for every issue any more than they need to be reminded that we are a society governed by laws. In short, the writing problem often is one of determining where to begin and what not to say.

Consider the following example of starting too far back from a draft of a memo about a case in which criminal charges had been filed against the client who had photocopied a dollar bill and, after a friendly bet, had tried it in a change machine.

EXAMPLE

Counterfeiting has been classified as an offense affecting the administration of governmental functions because the power to coin money was expressly granted to Congress and denied to the states by the terms of the Constitution. Hence, counterfeiting is a federal crime and the penalty for passing counterfeit money is found in the United States Code. Congress has enacted statutes making counterfeiting a federal offense; the various counterfeiting crimes are defined by these statutes, and these statutes determine the essential elements of the respective crimes.

The background information in the preceding example is unnecessary. The writer of this excerpt seems to have forgotten who the reader is and what that reader is likely to know.

Writers who have a tendency to start too far back often fill their writing with background information that *they* needed in order to focus their ideas or to clarify a point. Even if they needed the information to analyze the problem, that does not automatically mean that their reader will need it too.

For example, because of a lack of experience, the writer may have had to do a fair amount of spade work to fill in a skimpy background in a given area of law. Unless the writer believes the reader needs the same kind of review or preliminary discussion, it should be omitted from the reader's version.

Furthermore, writers are obliged to save their readers from at least some of the blind alleys they explored. Legal writers who were successful writers as undergraduates often have a difficult time realizing this. In law there is no extra credit for arguments that don't work. Legal writing is not an account of all the work that the writer did; it is an account of what the reader needs to know.

Another way this tendency to write for oneself rather than for the reader manifests itself is in the narrative style some legal writers adopt. Rather than give the reader a carefully crafted explanation of the issue at hand, some writers tend to describe their own process of discovery. At worst, this narrative-of-their-discovery sounds like this: "First, I looked at _____ ; then I realized _____ , which reminded me that _____ , so I looked at _____ and found _____ ."

Happily, few legal writers err to that degree. More common, however, is an occasional intrusive phrase like "when researching our client's case, I proceeded under the assumption that . . . ," which can easily become "presumably."

Thus far, we have primarily discussed legal writing that starts too far back analytically. Occasionally legal writers start too far back historically. They give long, careful explanations of how a particular area of law has evolved when all the reader wants is a discussion of how the end result of that evolutionary process applies to the facts of a case at hand.

This is not to say that tracing the history of a statute or a judicial trend is never appropriate. The point is to consider your specific reader and that reader's purposes, and then ask yourself if it is appropriate in the document you are writing. Put another way, don't write a law review article when the senior partner has assigned you an office memo.

§23.2.3   Don't Overuse Quotations

When to quote and how much to quote — these are two questions that all legal writers wrestle with. Like many other issues in legal writing, there is a range of opinion about when quoting is appropriate, even required, and when the writer should merely paraphrase and cite to authority.

Most legal readers agree that relevant portions of statutes should be quoted. The trick, of course, is to pare the quotation down to that which is relevant.

In the following example, the writer has mistakenly quoted more of the statute than her reader needs. The case she is working on does not have anything to do with obstruction of a highway or the closing of a channel, but rather with whether a noisy aerobics club with patrons in skimpy attire is a private nuisance.

EXAMPLE

> In determining whether there is a cause of action for private nuisance, the court is guided by Washington Revised Code § 7.48.010 (1992), which provides the following:
>
>> The obstruction of any highway or closing the channel of any stream used for boating or rafting logs, lumber or timber, or whatever is injurious to health or indecent or offensive to the senses, or an obstruction to the free use of property, so as to essentially interfere with the comfortable enjoyment of the life and property, is a .ıuisance and the subject of an action for damages and other and further relief.

First, edit out all of the statute that is extraneous to the case:

> [t]he obstruction of any highway or closing the channel of any stream used for boating or rafting logs, lumber or timber, or whatever is injurious to health or indecent or offensive to the senses, or an obstruction to the free use of property, so as to essentially interfere with the comfortable enjoyment of the life and property, is a nuisance and the subject of an action for damages and other and further relief.

Appropriately pared down then, the quotation looks like this:

> [W]hatever is . . . indecent or offensive to the senses, or an obstruction to the free use of property, so as to essentially interfere with the comfortable enjoyment of the life and property, is a nuisance . . . .

Note the use of ellipses to indicate words omitted in the middle and at the end of the quotation. The brackets, which are used to show that the "w" was not capitalized in the original, also show that the original did not begin at the word "whatever." (See section 26.5 for more on the use of ellipses and brackets in quotations.)

Although there is a great deal of agreement about quoting relevant portions of statutes, there is some disagreement about whether common law should be set out verbatim. One rule of thumb is that if a specific phrase reappears in the cases, then that phrase has become the standard or familiar "rule" and should therefore be quoted.

Generally, it is best to paraphrase the holding and rationale and cite to authority. Occasionally, however, the particular language of the holding or court's reasoning is so apt or well stated that a quotation is effective. This tactic works best when used rarely.

Never quote facts of a case, although you may want to quote the exact words of a person in a fact statement when those words suggest the person's attitude, motive, or intention.

It may also be helpful to know what your reader prefers. Some readers like to see the original language; many would rather read a paraphrase that more directly addresses the issue at hand.

Remember, too, that many readers skim or even skip over quotations. If the only place a given point is made is in a quotation, then that point won't reach the quotation "skimmers" and "skippers."

When deciding how much to quote, consider as well what your purpose is. In persuasive writing, you will probably use fairly extensive quoting from the record to make points about errors and conflicting testimony. You might also use a few more quotations from analogous cases because they allow you to create emphasis and effective repetition. A well-written lead-in to a quotation, which makes your point, followed by a carefully selected quotation, which makes your point, allows you to make that point twice without being tedious. The same tactic used in objective writing, however, would be tedious.

The cardinal rule of quotations can be summed up as follows: *Quote **only** when the language itself is worth attention.* The language of statutes is always worth our attention; the specific language of common law is sometimes worth our attention; and, occasionally, the language of a court stating its holding or expressing its rationale is so memorable that it should not escape our attention. In all three instances, quote; otherwise, don't.

§23.2.4   Create a Strong Subject-Verb Unit

The quickest way to achieve an energetic yet lean style is to make sure that the subject-verb unit carries the core of meaning in the sentence. In other words, put the real action of the sentence in the verb; put the doer of that action in the subject.

All too frequently in ineffective legal writing, the real action of the sentence (what should be the verb) is buried in a noun. This practice of changing verbs to nouns, known as nominalization, tends to make sentences wordy and lifeless (see sections 22.2-22.3). Because the real action in the sentence is somewhere other than the verb, the writer must find a substitute to fill the verb slot in the sentence, usually either a form of the verb "to be" or some other filler verb that expresses no real action. Such substitutes rob the sentence of its energy and crispness.

EXAMPLE

Our case is an illustration of this point.
　　　(verb)

Revised:

Our case illustrates this point.
　　　　(verb)

The following examples are but a few of the many ways legal writers can make their writing more concise by finding the real action in the sentence. The trick is to ask yourself "what are the people really doing?" Are they "reaching" or are they "agreeing"? Is the court "making" something or "stating" something?

reached an agreement ⟶ agreed
made a statement ⟶ stated
perform a review ⟶ review
made a recommendation ⟶ recommended
supports an inference ⟶ infers
made the assumption ⟶ assumed

If the real doer of the action is somewhere other than in the subject, then the subject of the sentence is also inevitably wordy because the writer has had to manufacture some language to fill that slot in the sentence.

Sometimes writers fill the subject slot with wordy expletives like "there is," "there are," "there was," "there were," "it is," or "it was." Avoid these expletive constructions unless the point of the sentence is that something exists.

EXAMPLE

It was his intention to return to Maryland.

Revised:

He intended to return to Maryland.

When writers inadvertently slip into the passive voice (see section 22.1), they inevitably create a wordy sentence with a weak subject.

EXAMPLE

Authorization for the contract was given by the district manager.

Revised:

The district manager authorized the contract.

If the doer of the action is not in the sentence at all, then the sentence is not just wordy; it may be vague, imprecise, overly abstract, and wordy.

EXAMPLE

These are the facts that were used to make an assessment of your situation.

Revised:

I used these facts to assess your situation.

---

§23.2.5   Avoid Throat-Clearing Expressions

Frequently legal writers create wordy sentences because they fill both the subject and verb slots with throat-clearing expressions that add little, if any, meaning to the sentence. These expressions seem to have more to do with getting the writer warmed up to the task of articulating his or her point than with content.

EXAMPLE

It must be remembered that the statute requires that service be made at the dwelling house or usual place of abode.

Revised:

The statute requires that service be made at the dwelling house or usual place of abode.

Most but not all of these throat clearing expressions fall into the pattern "It is _____ that":

> It is expected that
> It is generally recognized that
> It is significant that
> It is a known fact that
> It is obvious that
> It is believed that
> It is felt that
> It is essential that
> It is crucial that
> It is conceivable that

Some add a bit more content by using a verb other than "is," but waste the subject and verb slots on something other than the real actor and action.

EXAMPLE

It would appear that we can draw many parallels between *Walter*
(s)   (v)
and the instant case.

Revised:

Apparently, we can draw many parallels between *Walter* and the
     (s)   (v)
instant case.

The writer who revises out the throat-clearing "it would appear that" may then realize that even "apparently" is filler in this sentence.

> **EXAMPLE**

Revised:

We can draw many parallels between *Walter* and the instant case.

Notice how the following throat-clearing expressions may be reduced to one word or completely edited out.

It seems more likely than not that ⟶ probably
It can be presumed that ⟶ presumably
It may be argued that ⟶ arguably *or* say who may
argue

A fair number of the throat-clearing expressions spend time saying
that someone should take note of something.

It should also be noted that
It is interesting to note that
It is worth noting that
It is crucial to note that
It is important to note that

If the writer can presume that the reader is already taking special
note of all that is written, then such expressions are superfluous.

To sum up, then, a writer can create a strong, concise subject-verb
unit in four ways:

1. making the doer of the action the subject;
2. making the real action the verb;
3. avoiding expletive constructions; and
4. avoiding throat-clearing expressions.

(For an extended discussion on writing strong subject-verb units,
see sections 22.2 and 22.3.)

One commonsense reminder: Do not edit out every conceivable
bit of wordiness from your writing. If you do, your writing will become
sparse and lifeless. Even Olympic athletes need some fat to be healthy
and vigorous. The key is to develop judgment for when a given expression fleshes out a point and when it merely pads or weighs it down.

After attending to these first two considerations — focus and subject-verb units — legal writers should then look for other kinds of wordiness that can be revised and edited out. Note that the previous sentence
said "revised and edited out." Being concerned about wordiness in the

early stages of drafting is premature. First efforts and early drafts are, by nature, wordy and over-written.

In fact, at the beginning of the writing process, it may even be healthy for a writer to have an excess of words to work with. Thus, all the suggested strategies for conciseness in this section (with the important exception of considering the reader, the reader's goal, and the writer's goal) should be applied late in the drafting stage or in the revising or editing stages. See Exercise 23.F in the *Practice Book.*

§23.2.6   Don't Use Pompous Language

A traveling geological formation acquires little vegetative growth. Translation: A rolling stone gathers no moss.

If only that were true. All too often, legal writers who are really "rolling" through an analysis begin gathering all kinds of moss in the form of stilted, stuffy, overly formal words. Instead of valuing their ideas for their clarity and simplicity, legal writers sometimes feel that they have to "dress them up" so that they look lawyerly and sound erudite. They may have forgotten that their readers want to understand what they are saying, not be impressed by their vocabulary.

The following are but a few of the many words and expressions that legal writers use to dress up an otherwise simple point. Resist the temptation. Keep it simple. Your readers will love you for it.

allocate ⟶ give or divide
ascertain ⟶ make sure
cease ⟶ stop
commenced ⟶ began
constitute ⟶ make up
emulate ⟶ copy
endeavor ⟶ try
finalize ⟶ complete, finish, end
implement ⟶ carry out or put put into effect
initiated ⟶ began
objective ⟶ goal or aim
originate ⟶ start
preclude ⟶ shut out or prevent
prior to ⟶ before
promulgate ⟶ issue or publish
pursuant to ⟶ under
render ⟶ make or give
secure ⟶ get, take, obtain
subsequent ⟶ after
terminated ⟶ ended or finished
utilize ⟶ use
verification ⟶ proof

§23.2.7   Don't Repeat Yourself Needlessly

Language seems to be inherently redundant. Start trying to string a few words together and fairly soon some of those words will start making the same point. No matter how hard we try, words just keep coming out at a faster rate than the ideas, so naturally some words double up and say the same thing.

Some of this doubling up seems to come from a lack of faith in words. Somehow we don't quite trust them to mean what they say. For example, why does anyone ever say or write "close proximity"? Isn't proximity always close? How about "mutual cooperation"? When is cooperation not mutual?

What logic is there in the expression "sworn affidavit"? If an affidavit is a "sworn statement in writing," then is a "sworn affidavit" a "sworn sworn statement in writing"?

The following are a sampling of many common redundancies adapted from a list called "Dog Puppies" compiled by writer and editor Yvonne Lewis Day.[2] A few extra redundant phrases have been added by the authors. The word or words in parentheses should be omitted.

(a distance of) twenty feet	descend (down)
(a period of) six months	(different) kinds
(absolute) guarantee	(direct) confrontation
(absolutely) clear	during (the course of)
(actual) experience	during (the year of) 1957
(advance) planning	each (and every)
(advance) warning	each (separate) incident
alongside (of)	(empty) space
(and) moreover	(end) result
appreciate (in value)	eradicate (completely)
(as) for example	(essential) element
ascend (up)	estimated (roughly) at
ask (a question)	(false) pretenses
(as to) whether	few (in number)
(at a) later (date)	(foreign) imports
at (the) present (time)	(future) plans
(basic) fundamentals	(general) public
(but) (however)	(important) essentials
(but) nevertheless	indicted (on a charge)
(close) scrutiny	(integral) part
combine (together)	is (now) pending
(complete) monopoly	join (together)
(completely) destroyed	(local) residents
consensus (of opinion)	(major) breakthrough
(current) trend	(many) (different) ways
depreciate (in value)	(mass) media

---

2. Adapted from "The Economics of Writing" by Yvonne Lewis Day, reprinted with permission from the August 1982 issue of *The Toastmaster.*

merged (together)
my (own) opinion
my (personal) opinion
never (at any time)
never (before)
off (of)
(over) exaggerate
(past) experience
(past) history
(past) records
permeate (throughout)
(personal) friendship
(plan) ahead
postponed (until later)
(pre-) planned
probed (into)
protest (against)
(rate of) speed

recur (again)
refer (back)
reflect (back)
reiterate (again)
repeat (again)
reported (to the effect) that
revert (back)
(separate) entities
(specific) example
(State's) prosecutor
(suddenly) exploded
(temporary) reprieve
(thorough) investigation
3 a.m. (in the morning)
(underlying) (basic) assumption
(unexpected) surprise
(usual) custom

Many redundancies and wordy expressions have an "of" in them. Some legal writers find that they can spot many wordy constructions simply by looking for "of's" and editing out about half of them.

The preceding list of redundancies includes those expressions that are common to writers in all disciplines. The language of law is much worse; it has made redundancy an art. In fact, to the average reader, the lawyer's motto seems to be: "When in doubt, say it twice."

One source of these redundancies, according to David Mellinkoff,[3] has been the law's tendency to draw on more than one language at a time to describe a single idea. Consequently, we get tautologies such as "null and void" when either "null" or "void" alone would be sufficient.

buy (Old English) or purchase (French)
own (Old English) or possess (French)
minor (Latin) or child (Old English) or infant (French)
will (Old English) or testament (Latin)
property or chattels (French) or goods (Old English)
pardon (French) or forgive (Old English)
constable (French) or sheriff (Old English)
larceny (French) or theft or stealing (Old English)
attorney (French) or lawyer (Old English)

Mellinkoff adds that other redundancies such as "aid and abet," "part and parcel," and "safe and sound" come from law's early oral

---

3. David Mellinkoff, *The Language of the Law* 58 (1963).

tradition when the rhythm and sound of the words made them not only more memorable but also more powerful in the minds of the people.[4]

The question for modern legal writers, then, is whether doubling phrases serve any purpose for their readers. Is there some important distinction between "perform" and "discharge"? Is "cease and desist" more memorable or more emphatic than just "cease" or "desist"?

If the answer to these questions is no, then what the writer has done by using doubling phrases is to double the words the reader must read. No new content, just more words — not exactly the way to win over a busy reader.

The last-ditch argument usually raised by the defenders of doubling phrases is that these phrases are "terms of art" and therefore precise, untouchable descriptions of legal concepts. According to Mellinkoff, however, a legal term of art is "a technical word with a specific meaning."[5] He points out that most of the doubling phrases do not qualify as terms of art because they are either "not technical or have no specific meaning."[6]

If, in fact, a doubling phrase comes from an applicable statute or case law, then it may be a good idea for a legal writer to use it in the same form. It *may* be. The point is to choose words based on reasons, not on habit.

(Admittedly, some repetition in legal writing is done for effect. Used properly, repetition can be persuasive and even eloquent. Obviously, the discussion in this section refers to mindless, not deliberate, repetition.)

§23.2.8   Clean Out the Clutter

Some legal writers are word pack rats. They love words and collect them for their own sake. And like most pack rats, they are not particularly discriminating. They have extra words, often meaningless words, stashed in every nook and cranny of their writing.

Real pack rats have a right to the clutter they collect. After all, they are the only ones who live in it. Unfortunately, legal writers who are word pack rats force their readers to live in their clutter as well. Most readers would rather not.

Clutter in writing takes several forms. One of the most common is the extraneous prepositional phrase. Notice how easily prepositional phrases can begin to grow and multiply.

---

4. David Mellinkoff, *supra,* 42-44.
5. David Mellinkoff, *Legal Writing: Sense & Nonsense* 7 (1981).
6. *Id.*

EXAMPLE

We are filing a motion for summary judgment.

Clutter:

We are in the process of filing a motion for summary judgment.

More Clutter:

At this point in time, we are in the process of filing a motion for summary judgment.

Still More Clutter:

At this point in time, we are in the process of filing a motion for summary judgment with the court.

Eight words have quickly grown to twenty, with no real gain in content.

Again, as we saw in the earlier list of redundancies, the "of" preposition tends to be a frequent offender. Although we cannot write without any "of" phrases, in most people's writing about half of them can be eliminated or tidied up.

EXAMPLE

Persons with emphysema who voluntarily move to the city of Los Angeles have contributed to their own illness.

Revised:

Persons with emphysema who voluntarily move to Los Angeles have contributed to their own illness.

EXAMPLE

In the absence of any evidence of drugs on the premises, the police officers' actions can be given the interpretation of an invasion of privacy.

Revised:

Without evidence of drugs on the premises, the police officers' actions were an invasion of privacy.

Notice that the "of the" can be eliminated from some phrases and made into possessives in others.

all of the defendants ⟶ all defendants
some of the evidence ⟶ some evidence
none of the witnesses ⟶ no witness

the family of the victim ⟶ the victim's family
the position of the employees ⟶ the employees' position
the reasoning of the court ⟶ the court's reasoning

Before leaving the topic of extraneous "of" phrases, we should discuss their frequent companion: empty nouns. Nouns like "area," "aspect," "basis," "character," "circumstances," "field," "kind," "manner," "matter," "nature," "situation," and "type" rarely add any real content to writing. Most should be edited out.

the basis of your testimony ⟶ your testimony
the field of chemical engineering ⟶ chemical engineering
the nature of your argument ⟶ your argument

Other modifiers besides prepositional phrases like to clutter up sentences. Adverbs, in particular, like to creep in legal writing sentences, often in the disguise of precision. You can usually (there's one!) spot adverbs by their *-ly* ending, but look out for "quite," "rather," "somewhat," and "very" too.

EXAMPLE   ADVERB CLUTTER

Basically, the witness seemed quite relaxed as she carefully outlined the rather long list of extremely technical calculations she had made.

Revised:

The witness seemed relaxed as she outlined the long list of technical calculations she had made.

Frequently, adverbs do add a shade of meaning that the writer intends. "The witness spoke softly" is not the same as "the witness spoke."

The question for the careful legal writer, then, is (1) whether the adverb adds important content, and, (2) if so, whether the adverb is the best way to express that content. "Spoke softly" may be more precisely and more concisely written as "whispered," "murmured," or "mumbled."

One adverb that deserves special mention is "clearly." It is so overused in legal writing that one has to wonder if it has any meaning left. **Clearly,** it is time to think of a more sophisticated way to begin sentences. Legal writers **clearly** need to be more imaginative in their choice of modifiers for verbs. See Exercise 23.G in the *Practice Book.*

§23.2.9   Focus and Combine

Combining sentences and distilling ideas is an art. It does not come easily or quickly, but when it happens it is satisfying. If there is one magic formula for seeing what to cut and how to cut it, it is contained in the idea of focus, the first fundamental discussed in this section. Knowing exactly what your point is allows you to concentrate on that point and eliminate everything else.

Consider the following draft of a paragraph in a memo.

EXAMPLE

The fact that Acme is a lawful business will probably not be an issue in this case. Acme has satisfied all the necessary zoning and licensing requirements. Both parties will agree that Acme is a lawful business. **The probable issue, then, will be whether Acme's use of the property is reasonable.** Standard will argue that Acme's property use is unreasonable and therefore constitutes a nuisance; Acme will argue that the property use is reasonable and not a nuisance.

Once the writer realizes that the sentence in boldface is the focus of this paragraph, then he or she can begin combining and editing.

EXAMPLE   **REVISED**

Acme is a lawful business; it has satisfied all the necessary zoning and licensing requirements. The issue, then, will be whether Acme's use of the property is reasonable.

A clear focus will also help you decide which sentences can be combined and, when combining, which parts to keep as the main subject and verb and which parts to subordinate. For example, two sentences can often be combined into one by changing one of the sentences into a relative clause beginning with "which," "who," "whom," "whose," or "that."

EXAMPLE

Lewis appealed his sentence to Division II of the Court of Appeals. Division II of the Court of Appeals reversed and remanded for re-sentencing.

Combined:

Lewis appealed his sentence to Division II of the Court of Appeals, which reversed and remanded for resentencing.

EXAMPLE

The State's main witness was Arthur Hedges. Arthur Hedges agreed to testify after reaching a favorable plea bargain.

Combined:

The State's main witness was Arthur Hedges, who agreed to testify after reaching a favorable plea bargain.

Note

Use "who" for persons and the nominative case; use "whom" for the objective case; use "whose" when you need the possessive. Use "that" and "which" for things, but use "that" for restrictive clauses and "which" for nonrestrictive clauses.

In some cases, these same relative clauses can be reduced to phrases by deleting unnecessary who's, which's, and that's.

EXAMPLE

Her father, who is the president of the company, was indicted by a grand jury.

Revised:

Her father, the president of the company, was indicted by a grand jury.

Revised Again:

Her father, the company's president, was indicted by a grand jury.

The defendant lived in a room that was over the garage.

Revised:

The defendant lived in a room over the garage.

Frequently, two sentences can be combined when one of them defines or identifies part of the other.

For purposes of Georgia's wrongful death statute, a fetus is a child when the fetus is "quick." "Quick" is defined as having been perceived as moving in the mother's womb.

Combined:

For purposes of Georgia's wrongful death statute, a fetus is a child when the fetus is "quick," that is, having been perceived as moving in the mother's womb.

Upon entering the house, the police smelled phenyl-2-propanone. Phenyl-2-propanone is an organic chemical that is a necessary precursor ingredient of amphetamine.

Combined:

Upon entering the house, the police smelled phenyl-2-propanone, an organic chemical that is a necessary precursor ingredient of amphetamine.

A colon can sometimes be used to combine two sentences when the first sentence introduces a list or an explanation that will be given in full in the second sentence.

EXAMPLE

To assert the emergency doctrine, the defendant must be able to satisfy four elements. The four elements are (1) that he was suddenly confronted by an emergency; (2) that he did not cause the emergency by any negligence on his part; (3) that he was compelled to decide a course of action instantly; and (4) that he made such a choice as a reasonably careful person placed in such a position might have made.

Combined:

To assert the emergency doctrine, the defendant must satisfy the following four elements: (1) he was suddenly confronted by an emergency; (2) he did not cause the emergency by any negligence on his part; (3) he was compelled to decide a course of action instantly; and (4) he made such a choice as a reasonably careful person placed in such a position might have made.

EXAMPLE

Immediately after the assault, the plaintiff gave a description of his attacker to the police. He described his attacker as being a white female who was 5′10″, blonde, with blue eyes and a fair complexion.

Combined:

Immediately after the assault, the plaintiff gave the following description of his attacker to the police: a white female who was 5′10″, blonde, with blue eyes and a fair complexion.

Occasionally, two or more sentences that have the same subject can be combined by using compound verbs or by changing one set of verbs into participles.

EXAMPLE

The police officers discovered the laboratory used to make the amphetamine. The officers found a propane burner.

Combined (compound verbs):

The police officers discovered the laboratory used to make the amphetamine and found a propane burner.

EXAMPLE

Deascon asks this court to review the lower court's decision. He argues that the reasons given by the trial court for imposing an exceptional sentence are not supported by the record.

Combined (participle):

Deascon asks this court to review the lower court's decision, arguing that the reasons given by the trial court for imposing an exceptional sentence are not supported by the record.

To reduce phrases to words, be on the lookout for wordy constructions like "the fact that," most phrases built around "regard," "of" prepositional phrases, and phrases that end in "that."

because of the fact that	→ because
despite the fact that	→ although, even though
due to the fact that	→ because
except for the fact that	→ except for
in spite of the fact that	→ although, even though
in view of the fact that	→ because, considering that
owing to the fact that	→ because
the fact that he asked	→ his question
in regard(s) to	→ about, concerning
with regard to	→ about, concerning

by means of	→ by
by virtue of	→ by, under
for the purpose of	→ to
has the option of	→ may
in compliance with your request of	→ as requested, as you requested
in favor of	→ for
in the absence of	→ without
in the neighborhood of	→ about, approximately
on the basis of	→ from
over the signature of	→ signed by
in the event that	→ if
for the reason that	→ because

Legal writers are divided over whether (or not) to omit the "or not" in the expression "whether or not." Notice, for example, that the "or not" can be deleted from the preceding sentence with no loss in meaning. In such cases, it is better to delete it. Sometimes, however, the sentence becomes nonsensical if the "or not" is omitted.

EXAMPLE

Mr. Smith intends to pay for his daughter's college education whether or not the court awards him full custody.

Usually, the "or not" can be omitted when the word "if" can substitute for "whether." Retain "or not" if the substitution of "if" for "whether" changes the meaning, as it does in the example above. Some phrases are deadwood and can be omitted or replaced with one word. See Exercises 23.H, 23.I, and 23.J in the *Practice Book*.

at this point in time	→ omit or use "now"
at that point in time	→ omit or use "then"
in this day and age	→ omit or use "now," "nowadays"
in the case of	→ omit or use "in"
in reality	→ omit
in terms of	→ omit
in a very real sense	→ omit

§23.2.10   Avoid Excessive Conciseness

The question, of course, with the reducing and combining advocated in this section, is how much is too much? When does editing for conciseness improve the writing, and at what point does it hinder the readability of sentences?

Properly done, reducing and combining can make writing more focused and concise. Overdone, it can ruin writing by packing it too tightly and by creating overly long and overly complicated sentences.

One result of overdone combining is compound noun phrases, also known as noun strings. Like those Russian dolls that have a seemingly endless progression of smaller and smaller dolls inside each doll, compound noun phrases have modifier modifying modifier modifying modifier to the point that the reader forgets where the whole thing began. Such overpacking in a sentence strains even the most cooperative reader.

The prize for compound noun phrases goes to an insurance service that offers the following policy:

LIMITED PRACTICE LAWYERS PROFESSIONAL INDEMNITY INSURANCE
DISCIPLINARY PROCEEDINGS DEFENSE COVERAGE

One cannot help but wonder if the title is any indication of how readable the policy itself is.

Here is an example from a brief to the Supreme Court.

EXAMPLE

Alabama's silent prayer statute's failure to satisfy "the purpose" prong of the *Lemon* test renders it unconstitutional.

Revised:

Alabama's silent prayer statute fails to satisfy "the purpose" prong of the *Lemon* test; therefore, it is unconstitutional. *OR*

Alabama's statute on silent prayer fails . . . .

Notice that in the preceding example a nominalization, "failure," became the verb and the revision eliminated one of the possessives, "statute's." Because multiple possessives are always awkward, avoid them whenever possible.

Also remember that some nominalizations can be unpacked and improved by changing the noun into the participle, or adjective form, as is done with "exclusion" in the following example.

EXAMPLE

a broad prior conviction evidence exclusion rule

Revised:

a broad rule excluding evidence of prior convictions

Notice too from the preceding revision that not all "of" prepositional phrases should be eliminated.

Like all tricks of the trade, then, editing for conciseness must be used with discretion and an eye toward what the reader will find easier to read and understand.

§23.3   PLAIN ENGLISH V. LEGALESE

> Early in law school there seems to be an almost irresistible urge to clothe everything in the diction and style of the most incomprehensible insurance policy.
>
> — Norman Brand and John O. White[7]

> To communicate upon matters of technicality and complexity . . . is impossible with (and for) the nontechnical and simple person; and to use the language of simplicity in addressing a learned profession is to insult that profession.
>
> — Ray J. Aiken[8]
> "Let's Not Oversimplify Legal Language"

Above are but samplings of the heated, ongoing debate over legalese. Proponents of the traditional style of legal writing argue that legalese is part of the specialized discourse of lawyers and that it serves worthwhile purposes for lawyers and their readers. Proponents of "plain English," on the other hand, argue that legalese is responsible for many of the ills that plague legal writing, not the least of which is that lay readers cannot readily comprehend what their attorneys are writing.

If you read the law journals, you may get the impression that the advocates for simplified, plain English are winning the debate. Article after article decries the use of such mainstays of legal writing as Latin phrases and legal argot. Perhaps a more significant indication that legalese is on the way out is that several state legislatures have passed

---

7. *Legal Writing: The Strategy of Persuasion* 107 (1988).
8. *Let's Not Oversimplify Legal Language,* 32 Rocky Mtn. L. Rev. 364 (1960).

legislation requiring "simple," "clear," "understandable" language that uses "words with common and everyday meanings" in consumer contracts and insurance policies.[9]

If you read the writing of most practicing attorneys, however, you might get the impression that the advocates for the traditional style of legal writing have won the day. Corporate lawyers rely heavily on boilerplate, and most practitioners seem to have absorbed the language of their law school casebooks. They may have heard that legalese is dead, but they don't write like they believe it.

And so the debate rages on, and although the plain English v. legalese issue has been before the collective "court" of legal professionals and their clients for some time now, we have yet to reach a verdict. The trend seems to be toward plain English, but the resistance is strong. In short, in the matter of Plain English v. Legalese, the jury is still out.

So what is a legal writer to do? While the profession continues to wrestle with this issue, we would like to offer a simple test for determining whether any given bit of legalese should be used or relegated to the dustbin.

The Test

Given the document's reader, writer, purpose, and surrounding circumstances, does the legalese increase or decrease communication between writer and reader?

Under this test, if both reader and writer understand the phrase *res ipsa loquitur* and find it a concise way of expressing a concept, then the phrase is effective legal writing. If, on the other hand, the same phrase sends a client reader scurrying to a dictionary, then the virtue of its conciseness is outweighed by its lack of clarity for that reader. Thus, in the second context, the same phrase is ineffective legal writing.

With the test as a backdrop, let's examine legalese and its characteristics.

First of all, there is no agreed-upon definition of "legalese." One law review author has defined a legalism as "a word or phrase that a lawyer might use in drafting a contract or a pleading but would not use in conversation with his wife." George R. Smith, *A Primer of Opinion Writing, for Four New Judges,* 21 Ark. L. Rev. 197 (1967).

With a bit of editing, we can modify the definition to omit the sexism and to describe legalese: Legalese is language a lawyer might use in drafting a contract or a pleading but would not use in ordinary conversation. In short, legalese is distinct from human talk; it is law talk.

What then are the characteristics that distinguish law talk from ordinary human talk?

---

9. *See, for example,* Minn. Stat. § 325G.30.3, N.Y. Gen. Oblig. Law § 5-702, N.J. Rev. Stat. § 56:12-1, Conn. Gen. Stat. §§ 38-68s-x.

Group 1

- long sentences, especially those with excessive modification and qualification
- abstractions as subjects — the real "doers" or actors are often omitted or relegated to a prepositional phrase
- weak verbs — passive voice and nominalizations both sap the sentences of their natural energy

Group 2

- archaic word choice
- foreign phrases
- terms of art and argot
- use of "said" and "such" as articles
- omission of articles, especially "the"
- use of "same" as a noun
- avoidance of the first and second person (I, we, you)
- doubling phrases

The first group of characteristics primarily involve syntax, that is, the sentence structure. Traditionally, legal writing has been known for its overly long sentences (see section 22.5), with multiple intrusive phrases that added extensive modification and qualification. Frequently, readers had a hard time comprehending these sentences because either the subject or verb of these sentences was delayed by numerous details and exceptions. Furthermore, the subject and its verb were so far apart that the reader had difficulty finding the actor and action on which to hang all this modification and elaboration (see section 22.4).

Adding to the confusion were other characteristics, such as nominalizations (see sections 22.2 and 22.3) and passive voice (see section 22.1), that disguised the real actor and action in the sentence. Nominalizations (creating the noun form of a verb by adding a noun ending such as -tion) and passive voice teamed up to give the sentences a static quality: Nobody was home in traditional legal sentences, or if they were, they weren't doing anything.

The second group of characteristics occurs at the word level, and they are more a question of vocabulary: Is it better to use a formal word, an unfamiliar word, a foreign word, or a simple word? When is a word or phrase an unnecessary legalism, and when is it a term of art? When is one word enough, and when should it be bolstered by one or more synonyms to cover every possible contingency?

These characteristics of legalese are the focus of this section.

§23.3.1 Archaic Word Choice

In his article *The End of Legalese: The Game Is Over,* Robert W. Benson described legalese as "the medieval armor of lawyers." Robert

W. Benson, *The End of Legalese: The Game Is Over,* XIII Rev. of Law & Soc. Change 519, 522 (1984-85). His phrase is apt for a number of reasons, not the least of which is that the some of the language of law is straight out of the Middle Ages.

When, for example, have you heard a person on the street say "herein" or "witnesseth"? What then is achieved by retaining Old or Middle English words? A legal ring to the words? If so, at what cost? If clarity is the price the writer and reader pay, then the price is too high. If, on the other hand, the archaic language somehow gives the document the formality it needs without sacrificing clarity, then perhaps the language is suitable for the occasion.

Consider, for example, a story told by an attorney who was an advocate of plain English. Her client wanted her to draft a will. She drafted two versions: a plain English version and a traditional version. Although the attorney recommended the plain English version, the client selected the traditional version because it "sounded like a will." For this document and its purpose, the formality of "I hereby give, devise, and bequeath" was appropriate. It created the tone, the solemnity, and the timeless quality that the client wanted.

But what about client letters, office memoranda, and briefs to the court? Although these documents are formal in nature, do they require archaic language? Most authorities on legal language agree that they don't. In fact, we have some research that shows that appellate judges, who are the readers of the most formal of these documents, appellate briefs, strongly prefer plain English.[10]

The standard argument that "if I don't sound like a lawyer, I won't be believable" was strongly refuted in this research. In fact, the research showed that the judges were more likely to categorize writing in legalese as "poorly worded, unconvincing, vague, not concise, unpersuasive, uncreative, unscholarly, from a non-prestigious firm or an ineffective appellate advocate, unpowerful, incomprehensible and ambiguous."[11]

The legalese-ridden documents that the judges read included Old and Middle English words like "thereby" and "herein." Below is a fairly comprehensive list of other Old and Middle English words and phrases that should be avoided in client letters, office memoranda, and briefs. In some cases, a more appropriate substitute word or phrase follows in italics.

Compound words that begin with *here-, there-,* and *where-*

hereafter	thereabout	whereas[12]
herebefore	thereafter	whereat

---

10. Robert W. Benson & Joan B. Kessler, *Legalese v. Plain English: An Empirical Study of Persuasion and Credibility in Appellate Brief Writing,* 20 Loyola of Los Angeles L. Rev. 301-319 (1987).

11. *Id.* p. 315.

12. "Whereas" can often be eliminated or replaced with "because," "considering that," "while on the contrary," or "inasmuch as." At other times, it can be used

hereby	therefrom	whereby
herein	therein	wherefore
hereinabove → *above*	thereof	wheresoever
hereinafter	thereon	wherein → *there*
hereinunder → *below*	thereto	whereof
hereof	thereunto	whereon
heretofore → *before,*	therewith	whereupon
up to		
this		
time		

hereunder

herewith (enclosed herewith → *enclosed*)

aforementioned (omit or substitute *previously mentioned*)

aforesaid (omit or substitute *above*)

behoove → *to be necessary, to be proper*

comes now the plaintiff

foregoing (for the foregoing reasons) → *for these reasons*

forthwith → *immediately*

henceforth[13]

hitherto → *until this time, up to now*

pursuant to → *under* or *according to*[14]

thence → *from there, from that place, time* or *source, for that reason*

thenceforth → *from that time on, after that*

thereafter → *from that time on*

to wit → *namely, that is to say*

whence → *from where*

whensoever → *whenever*

§23.3.2   Foreign Phrases

Many of the Latin phrases that appear in legal writing create a barrier between writer and reader. Only a student on the way home from Latin class (or possibly a lawyer specializing in property) will be comfortable with a phrase like *Cujus est solum ejus est usque ad coelum et usque ad infero.* The rest of us would do one of two things: use the context to try to figure out what the writer meant or reach for the *Unabridged Black's Law Dictionary.* In either case, the Latin has not aided communication. Even the conscientious consulter of the dictionary will

---

but with care. Frequently, writers use it without seeming to know what it means. At times, "whereas" is the best choice; for example, using "whereas" is certainly better than the wordy "in view of the fact that."

13. Many would not object strenuously to "henceforth," but rather find it a bit dated. "From now on" is a satisfactory plain English substitute.

14. Sometimes "pursuant to" is a useful legalism that lawyers and judges find acceptable. Avoid, however, with nonlawyers.

understand the writer's meaning only by looking up the explanation the writer should have given the reader in the first place.

More often, the Latin is not so much confusing as it is unnecessary. Why say "supra" when "above" works just as well? Unnecessary Latin phrases make the writing appear stuffy and pretentious. When a simple English equivalent can be used without loss of meaning, use it.

Latin Words or Phrases to Avoid

arguendo → *for the sake of argument*

et al. → *and others*

infra → *below*

inter alia → *among other things*

per curiam → *by the court*

res gestae → use modern rules of evidence to characterize state-
          ments

seriatum → *in turn, serially, one after another*

sui generis → *unique*

supra → *above*

viz. (abbreviation for "videlicet") → *namely* or *that is to say*

Not all Latin should be replaced, however. Some Latin phrases ("gratis," "per diem") are sufficiently familiar to educated readers that their use does not impair communication. In fact, these phrases are often accepted as English.

Other Latin phrases ("amicus curiae," "per se") are equally familiar to lawyers and judges and can be used for these readers without a second thought. They are the "shop talk" of law. The same phrases, though, may need substitutes or explanation for client readers.

A final group of Latin phrases are so useful that few are willing to discard them. "Respondeat superior," for example, sums up a whole doctrine in tort law; "res judicata" is a fundamental rule of Civil Procedure. While these phrases will probably need clarification for readers who are not lawyers, the average legal reader would find them not only familiar but indispensable.

Latin Words or Phrases to Keep for Readers Who Are Lawyers

ad hoc	ex parte
ad litem	ex post facto
amicus curiae	gratis
bona fide	habeas corpus
caveat emptor	*id.* (abbreviation for *idem*)
certiorari	in limine
consortium	in personam
corpus delecti	ipso facto
de facto, de jure	mens rea
de novo	mandamus
dicta, dictum	modus operandi

nexus	quorum
nolo contendere	quid pro quo
non sequitur	res ipsa loquitur
penumbra	res judicata
per diem	respondeat superior
per se	scintilla
post mortem	stare decisis
prima facie	supersedeas
pro bono	

Of course, Latin is not the only foreign language that appears frequently in legal writing. Thanks to the Norman Conquest and its subsequent effect on the language of England, French plays an important role in the language of law.

The vast majority of the words derived from French are common terms that are already fully incorporated into English and as such pose few if any problems for readers ("assault," "defendant," "heir," "larceny," "mortgage," "plaintiff," "pleadings," "tort," "reprieve," and "verdict," to name just a few).

More likely as troublemakers are those words and phrases that are Old French. For the following French terms, use the suggested plain English substitutes.

alien or aliene (used as a verb) → to convey or to transfer
cestui que trust → beneficiary
cy-pres → as near as possible
en ventre sa mere → in its mother's womb
en vie → alive
feme covert → married woman
feme sole → single woman
save → except
seisin → possession or ownership

As we saw with Latin, though, there are French words and phrases that are terms of art for which we have no satisfactory plain English substitute. Although they will almost certainly require explanation for readers who are not lawyers, they are indispensable vocabulary for a lawyer.

French Words and Phrases to Keep

estoppel   laches   voir dire

Unfortunately, not all authorities on legal language agree about what is and is not a legal term of art. *De son tort,* for example, from the phrases *executor de son tort* and *trustee de son tort,* is sometimes replaced by the English equivalent *of his own wrong* and at other times treated as an indispensable phrase.

§23.3.3   Use of Terms of Art and Argot

In the preceding discussion on foreign words and phrases, we suggested that some Latin and French terms simply muddied the water for legal readers while others were indispensable. The difference between the dispensable and indispensable Latin and French was whether there was a satisfactory plain English substitute.

Terms of art, by definition, do not have satisfactory substitutes. Even though one might be able to give a short explanation of a term of art's meaning, complete understanding would take an extensive explanation.

A term of art, according to David Mellinkoff, is "a technical word with a specific meaning."[15] In *The Dictionary of Modern Legal Usage*, "terms of art" are defined as "words having specific, precise significations in a given specialty."[16]

Given these requirements, it should not be surprising that there are relatively few terms of art in law. Still, many lawyers seem to think that just about any word or phrase frequently used by lawyers or written into cases is a term of art. This misperception leads to a far more serious misperception that all these false terms of art are somehow precise and therefore good legal writing.

In fact, what we see here is mistaken cause/effect reasoning. If a term is specific and precise, then it may be a term of art, not the reverse: It sounds like a term of art; therefore, it must be specific and precise.

"Certiorari" is an excellent example of a true term of art. Perhaps a satisfactory short explanation is that it refers to the order written by a superior court to an inferior court requiring the inferior court to produce a certified record of a certain case.

For a full understanding of "certiorari," however, one would have to lay out a much larger context: how discretionary review and the appellate process work in general and specifically how the Supreme Court of the United States chooses cases it wishes to hear.

Argot, by contrast, is legal jargon or lawyers' shop talk. It is the shorthand of law, the quick-and-easy term or phrase that lawyers use among themselves. For this reason, argot is inappropriate when communicating with nonlawyers. Used with discretion, it can be effective communication among lawyers.

"Case on all fours" is a classic example of argot. Other common examples include "adhesion contract," "attractive nuisance," "Blackacre," "case at bar," "case-in-chief," "clean hands," "cloud on title," "court below," "four corners of the document," "horse case," "instant case," "off the record," "pierce the corporate veil," "reasonable man," "res ipsa loquitur," "sidebar," and "Whiteacre."

---

15. David Mellinkoff, *The Language of the Law* 16 (1963) (quoting *Webster's New International Dictionary* (2d ed. 1934)).

16. Bryan A. Garner, *The Dictionary of Modern Legal Usage* 539 (1987).

In writing, avoid argot that has degenerated into slang. "Cert denied" or "resipsey case" sounds cute rather than professional.

§23.3.4 Use of "Said" and "Such" as Adjectives

If you were a stand-up comic trying to make fun of the way lawyers write, all you would have to do is put "said" or "such" before almost every noun.

EXAMPLE

It was snowing and icy on January 9, 1991, when Mr. Smith, the plaintiff, was driving home from work along a deserted highway in his 1990 Honda Accord with chains on said vehicle's tires. Suddenly said plaintiff felt said vehicle jerk violently, and then said plaintiff heard a loud clanging of metal. Such clanging continued until such time as said plaintiff was able to pull said vehicle over to the shoulder of said highway. Upon inspection of said vehicle, said plaintiff realized that such clanging was caused when said chains had broken and then wrapped around the axle of said plaintiff's said vehicle. "Oh, *!?/*!" said said plaintiff.

In client letters, office memos, and briefs, rigorously avoid all use of "said" as an adjective. Replace with "the," "that," "this," or an appropriate, unambiguous pronoun.

"Such" can be used as an adjective with categories of persons, things, or concepts. For example, "such instances of neglect," "such witnesses as these," and "such an example of compassion" is not legalese. These phrases are good writing.

Do not, however, use "such" with singular nouns that are not categories of persons, things, or concepts but rather specific references to the same, previously mentioned singular noun. For example, "such payment" should be revised to "this payment"; "such stock certificate" should be changed to "the stock certificate."

§23.3.5 Omission of the Article "The"

Occasionally, one sees legal writing that has the sound of a police report.

EXAMPLE

Defendant denies that she hit plaintiff.

This rather terse style is achieved by omitting the article "the." The reason for omitting "unnecessary" articles in police reports may be that information needs to be recorded on forms. Happily, lawyers do not have such requirements, so they do not have to sacrifice a fluid writing style.

EXAMPLE　　**REVISED**

The defendant denies that she hit the plaintiff.

§23.3.6　Use of "Same" as a Pronoun

The phrase "acknowledging same" smacks of legalese. Replace "same" with "it," "them," or the noun "same" is replacing. These substitutes can be used whenever "same" is used as a pronoun.

EXAMPLE

The defendant first threatened Ms. Tyler with the tire wrench and then used same to smash her windshield.

Revised:

The defendant first threatened Ms. Tyler with the tire wrench and then used it to smash her windshield.

§23.3.7　Absence of First- and Second-person Pronouns

By convention, legal writers use the pronouns "I," "me," "we," "us," "you" and "your" rarely. Occasionally, in a client letter, a lawyer might write "I recommend" or, more commonly, "in my opinion." Much less frequent would be the phrase "I think" or (horrors!) "I feel" (the common explanation for the horrified reaction being that lawyers are paid to think, not to feel) in an office memorandum. Pity the naive attorney, though, who writes in a brief "you should rule" or "you must determine."

To get around the I's and you's in legal writing, because after all it is *I,* the writer, who is recommending and thinking, and it is *you,* the judge and reader, who is ruling and determining, legal writers resort to all sorts of linguistic gymnastics. Before discussing which of these gymnastic moves work and which lead to new problems, let's examine why the first- and second-person pronouns are *persona non grata* in legal writing.

First of all, remember the longstanding tradition of avoiding first and second person in any formal writing. While the recommendations about this issue have relaxed considerably for undergraduate research papers and the like, the original rationale applies to most legal writing. The facts and the application of law to those facts are the focus of attention for both writer and reader. As such, they should occupy center stage.

Second, the use of "I" and "you" often creates an inappropriately informal tone. While a bit of informality and familiarity may be appropriate in some client letters and an occasional office memo, generally these documents should be formal and professional in tone. (Remember, though, formal does not mean stilted.)

Third, indiscreet use of "you" in client letters and especially in briefs may make the writer appear arrogant, pushy, and disrespectful. Readers rarely like to be ordered around. Not surprisingly, "you must" or "you should" language often backfires. Rather than encouraging the reader to act as the writer wants, such language sets the stage for resistance to the writer's recommendations and arguments.

In the following example, the inclusion of "my," "I," and "you" is both distracting and inappropriate. The first-person references incorrectly place the emphasis on the writer, and the second-person references may even anger the judge.

EXAMPLE

In my research, I found that you must apply Washington Rule of Evidence 609(a) to the issue of the admissibility of evidence of a criminal defendant's prior convictions.

Revised:

In Washington, the issue of the admissibility of evidence of a criminal defendant's prior convictions is governed by Washington Rule of Evidence 609(a). *OR*

Washington Rule of Evidence 609(a) governs the issue of the admissibility of evidence of a criminal defendant's prior convictions.

The first revision of the example illustrates one of the common gymnastic moves that legal writers use to avoid the first- and second-person pronouns: use of the passive voice. While the passive voice is a good choice in some instances (see section 22.1.3), it can easily lead to dull, lifeless writing. Use with care.

Some legal writers use the pronoun "one" to get around using "you." This tactic works reasonably well as long as the writer does not use "one" several times and then shift — incorrectly — from "one" to the third-person pronoun "he," "she," "him," "her," "it," "they," or "them."

EXAMPLE

Incorrect:

One should avoid first-person pronouns in his or her legal writing.

Revised:

One should avoid first-person pronouns in one's legal writing.

Better:

One should avoid first-person pronouns in legal writing.

In office memos, some writers slip into a *we-they* style as they describe the various arguments the two sides can make. While this practice is accepted in some firms, it can easily be avoided by simply naming the parties.

Thus, instead of "they will argue . . . and we will rebut this argument by showing . . . ," legal writers can easily say "Smith will argue . . . and Jones will rebut this argument."

Frequently, a writer of an office memo is tempted to use "we" in the following situation. The writer has just explained the law or just described an analogous case to the reader. Now the writer wants the reader to follow along as he or she applies that law or case.

The writer might begin by saying "If we apply the plain meaning of statute X to our facts, we can see that the photocopy is a similitude" or "If we compare the actions of the defendant in *Smith v. Jones* to the actions of Brown, we can see that Brown, unlike Jones, knew he was lying to the F.B.I." This is not a serious writing sin, of course, but it is one that can be easily avoided.

Unfortunately, some writers try to write around the "we" in such instances and end up with a dangling modifier. (See section 25.6.2.)

EXAMPLES   **INCORRECT**

Applying the plain meaning of statute X to our facts, the photo-copy is a similitude.

Comparing the actions of the defendant in *Smith v. Jones* to the actions of Brown, Brown, unlike Jones, knew he was lying to the F.B.I.

There is a better way. The writer does want the reader to follow along as he or she makes the next logical connection, but the writer also wants to suggest that the *court* must see the same logical connection. Therefore, it makes good sense, both in terms of writing style and strategy, to say "If the court applies the plain meaning of statute X to our facts, it will find . . ." or "Applying the plain meaning of statute X to our facts, the court will find . . . ."

One final note about first- and second-person pronouns: Because these pronouns have gained acceptance in some other types of formal writing, they are likely to gain increasing acceptance in all but the most formal documents in legal writing. Watch the trend, and you will be able to adjust accordingly, especially if you keep in mind the test of always considering your reader, purpose, and the document's surrounding circumstances when making decisions about writing.

§23.3.8   Some Final Words About Legalese

In short, like most questions concerning law, the question "is legalese good or bad?" is best answered "it depends." It depends on the reader; it depends on the writer; it depends on the purpose of the document; it depends on the circumstances surrounding the document.

The thinking lawyer does not adopt the style of his or her predecessors without examining whether that style aids or hinders communication. Nor does the thinking lawyer automatically edit out all legalese simply because a few law review articles suggest it is passé or worse.

Different situations may require different choices. All will require a deliberate choice. See Exercise 23.K in the *Practice Book.*

§23.4   NONSEXIST LANGUAGE

Contrary to what many legal writers believe, the jury is in on the issue of nonsexist language. Authorities as diverse as *The New York Times Manual of Style and Usage,* the United States Department of Labor's *Dictionary of Occupational Titles,* and the United Church of Christ agree that gender-neutral language is here to stay.

The language of law, while a bit slower to change than the language of journalism, government, and even religion, has also begun to move in the direction of nonsexist word choices. Numerous states now require gender-neutral language in their legislation. Increasingly, legislators, practitioners, and jurists are realizing that some language they previously considered to be inclusive has just the opposite effect: It excludes.

Exclusion stemming from sexist language is not a new issue. For years feminists have argued against the subtle conditioning and preconceptions sexist language promotes. For example, if the members of a hiring committee agree that they should get "the best man for the job," are they as likely to select a woman to fill the position? What if these same members of the hiring committee simply refer to the person they want to hire as "he?" "*He* must be willing to work long hours." "If *his* previous experience includes a judicial clerkship, *he* will know the courts." "Can *he* bring in *his* fair share of clients?" Many are arguing that such uses of the masculine pronouns to refer supposedly to both sexes subtly, or not so subtly, suggest that the new hire will be male.

And how about language closer to law? If "judge" is defined as "an officer so named in *his* commission, who presides in some court . . . ,"[17] does that definition encourage women to aspire to the bench? If the law itself refers to "a landowner" by the masculine pronoun "he," does this reference somehow suggest that women do not own land?

Sexist language in law hurts women. There is no doubt about that. But it hurts men too. If we unconsciously refer to perpetrators of aggressive acts with masculine nouns and pronouns, even when the sex of the attacker is unknown, then we have begun to prejudice ourselves. If men are referred to by their last names and women are referred to by their first names, the reader is being encouraged to think of men objectively and women sympathetically.

Aside from the significant issues of fairness and prejudice, legal writers should also avoid sexist language because it is often ambiguous and imprecise. Does the sentence "Lieutenant Perkins is the woman pilot who was the first to challenge the Air Force's minimum height requirement for pilots" mean that Lieutenant Perkins was the first of all pilots to challenge this requirement, or does it mean that she was the first of that group of pilots who are women to challenge it? If a corporation's policy on sexual harassment reads, "Any man who sexually har-

---

17. *Black's Law Dictionary* 435 (5th ed. abridged 1979).

asses a fellow employee will be fired immediately," does this policy mean that women employed by the corporation are free to harass "fellow employees"? Does it mean that men and women may harass employees that are not "fellows"?

Perhaps the most immediate and pressing reason for using nonsexist language is the very real possibility that you may offend some readers if you don't.

In short, we have at least four good reasons for making the effort to use nonsexist language: fairness, clarity, precision, and reader reaction. These reasons more than justify the effort it takes to master the five problem areas legal writers face when trying to use gender-neutral language.

§23.4.1   Generic Use of "Man"

Avoid using the term "man" to mean all people or all of humanity. Similarly, avoid using expressions and other derivatives built on this broad use of the term *man.*

Sexist Terms	*Gender-neutral Substitutes*
man (noun) or mankind	people, humanity, human race, human beings, human population, *homo sapiens*
man (verb) as in "man the office"	staff, operate, run, work
a man who . . .	an individual who . . . , a person who . . . , one who . . . , someone who . . .
the common man, the average man, the man in the street	the common individual, the average citizen, the person in the street, ordinary people
man-made	hand-crafted, handmade, manufactured, machine-made, fabricated, synthetic, created
manpower	human energy, human resources, work force, personnel, staff
man-sized job	big job, enormous job
man-to-man	face-to-face, person-to-person

§23.4.2   Generic Use of "He"

It used to be standard practice for grammar and writing texts to advise writers to use masculine pronouns when the gender of the antecedent noun or pronoun could be either male or female. Now most grammar and writing texts advise writers to avoid the generic use of "he." Unfortunately, though, we have been unable to agree on a gender-neutral singular pronoun as a substitute. Until we do, we will need to use one or more of several approaches for avoiding the generic use of the masculine pronouns.

a. Revise the Sentence So That the Antecedent and Its Pronoun Are Plural

EXAMPLE

The holding suggests that a defendant waives his constitutional rights only through an affirmative or overt act.

Revision:

The holding suggests that defendants waive their constitutional rights only through affirmative or overt acts.

b. Revise the Sentence So That a Pronoun Is Not Needed

EXAMPLE

As a general rule, an employer is not liable for the work performed by his independent contractors.

Revision:

As a general rule, an employer is not liable for the work performed by independent contractors.

c. Replace the Masculine Noun and Pronoun With "One," "Your," or "He" or "She," as Appropriate

EXAMPLE

Every man has a right to defend his home.

Revisions:

One has a right to defend one's home.

You have a right to defend your home.

Everyone has a right to defend his or her home.

d. Alternate Male and Female Examples and Expressions

EXAMPLE

If a student enrolls at a university with the promise that he will receive an athletic scholarship and he later finds out that his scholarship has been revoked, he can sue the university for breach of contract. If, on the other hand, a student enrolls at a university with the promise that he will receive an athletic scholarship and he later refuses to play the sport, the university can sue him for breach of contract.

Revision:

If a student enrolls at a university with the promise that she will receive an athletic scholarship and she later finds out that her scholarship has been revoked, she can sue the university for breach of contract. If, on the other hand, a student enrolls at a university with the promise that he will receive an athletic scholarship and he later refuses to play the sport, the university can sue him for breach of contract.

e. Repeat the Noun Rather Than Use an Inappropriate Masculine Pronoun

EXAMPLE

Joinder of counts should not be used to embarrass or prejudice a defendant or to deny him a substantial right.

Revised:

Joinder of counts should not be used to embarrass or prejudice a defendant or to deny a defendant a substantial right.

One approach that is occasionally recommended for avoiding the generic "he" is to use the plural pronouns "they" and "their" for singular nouns and indefinite pronouns, such as "everyone" or "anybody." While using this approach may arguably solve the sexism problem, it still leaves the writer with an error in pronoun agreement (see section 25.4.2) as well as with more than a few logical inconsistencies, for example, "Everyone is entitled to their opinion." Rather than trade one problem for another, use one of the other five strategies outlined above for avoiding the generic "he."

§23.4.3   Gender-neutral Job Titles

Avoid job titles that suggest it is nonstandard for women to hold the position.

Sexist Terms	*Gender-neutral Substitutes*
businessman	business executive, manager
chairman	coordinator, presiding officer, head, chair
Congressman	Representative, member of Congress, congressional representative, Senator
councilman	council member
deliveryman	delivery clerk, courier
draftsman	drafter
doorman	doorkeeper
fireman	firefighter
foreman (as the head of a group of workers)	supervisor, head worker, section chief
insuranceman	insurance agent
juryman	juror
landlord	owner, manager, lessor
mailman, postman	postal carrier, postal worker, mail carrier
middleman	negotiator, liaison, intermediary
newspaperman	reporter, editor
paperboy	newspaper carrier
policeman	police officer
salesman	sales agent, sales representative
spokesman	representative, spokesperson
steward, stewardess	flight attendant
watchman	guard

§23.4.4 Sexist Modifiers

Unconsciously, writers sometimes assign needless sexist modifiers to words. Avoid modifiers that suggest that it is unusual for either a woman or a man to occupy a certain position.

Sexist Modifier	Revised
female judge	judge
lady lawyer	lawyer
male nurse	nurse
woman attorney	attorney

§23.4.5 Other Sexist Language

Avoid feminizing a word with a suffix, for example, "actress," "executrix," "testatrix." Such endings suggest that it is nonstandard for women to fill certain roles.

Avoid terms with connotations of youth (girl), decorum (lady), or informality (gal) unless the comparable term for males (boy, gentleman, guy) is also appropriate.

When using titles (Miss, Mrs., Ms.) before women's names, follow the particular woman's preference, if known, or, if unknown, use no title. In professional contexts, professional titles take precedence over social titles for both women and men, for example, Justice Sandra Day O'Connor, not Mrs. O'Connor. In salutations in letters, avoid using the outdated "Dear Sir" or "Gentlemen" when the sex of the receiver is unknown. Acceptable substitutes include "Dear Sir or Madam," "Ladies and Gentlemen," or the title of the receiver(s), as in "Dear Members of the Board." Some writers omit the salutation and use a reference line such as "To the Director of Operations" or "Re: Credit Department."

Sexist Term	Gender-neutral Substitutes
coed	student
divorcee	divorced person
forefathers	ancestors, forerunners, forebears
girl or girls (when applied to adult females)	woman or women
lady or ladies	woman or women (unless the equivalent "gentleman" or "gentlemen" is also used for men)
househusband, housewife	homemaker
man and wife	man and woman, husband and wife
old wives' tale	superstitious belief or idea

See Exercises 23.L, 23.M, and 23.N in the *Practice Book*.

§23.5 BIAS-FREE LANGUAGE

In addition to the concern that legal writers use nonsexist language in their documents, there are related concerns that the language of law be free of bias against other groups, such as racial, religious, and ethnic minorities, homosexuals, the elderly, the poor, and the disabled.

Making bias-free language choices is not always easy, though, particularly when one realizes that the preferred terms are constantly changing and not all members of any given group have the same preferences. These challenges tempt some to ignore or just give up on the issue of bias-free language in law. The argument seems to go something like this: "Why should I bother when *they* can't even decide what they want to be called?"

The temptation to avoid the issue is easier to resist, however, when one considers the power of language and its ability to shape perception. How we label something affects how we see it. Thus, language can serve to perpetuate stereotypes, or it can bring new insight and perspective. Choices in language can suggest that members of a group are inherently inferior or that they are valued members of society.

In short, what we call ourselves or someone else matters. Naming, or labeling, is both an enormous power and an enormous responsibility.

The following four general recommendations outline some advice for legal writers concerning the issue of bias-free language. Many of the specific recommendations and examples for commonly encountered terms are taken from McGraw-Hill's *Guidelines for Bias-Free Publishing.*

§23.5.1 Stay Abreast of the Preferred Terminology

All language changes over time. Some parts of language tend to change more rapidly, however, because of rapid changes in sensibilities and society's collective thinking about certain issues.

Notice, for example, the changes in terminology for these groups of people.

Colored People → Negro → Black → Black-American → African-American or Afro-American

Indian → American Indian → Native American

Oriental → Asian-American

Mexican-American → Chicano/Chicana or Hispanic or Latino

Handicapped → Disabled → Physically Challenged or Persons of Differing Abilities or Persons with Exceptionalities or Exceptional Persons

Elderly → Senior Citizens

Notice too that several of these progressions end with two or more choices, indicating a lack of consensus among the members of the group about the current preferred term.

Indeed, the lack of consensus may extend beyond different preferences among current terms. It is not uncommon, for instance, for older members of a group to prefer earlier, more traditional terms. Younger members of the black community may prefer to be called African-Americans while their parents or grandparents may prefer to be called blacks.

Does this mean that legal writers are faced with the impossible task of choosing among competing terms, each of which will inevitably make someone unhappy? Possibly.

In making the choice, though, legal writers are not without direction. Indeed, at least five factors can serve as guides. First, which term is preferred by this group of people at this time? Second, do the specific individuals involved, especially the clients, have a preference? Third, does the reader of this document have a preference? Fourth, does the law itself use a term for this group of people? Fifth, does the writer have a preference?

In other words, as with so many other tough questions in writing, the astute legal writer will use the overall context of the document, including reader, writer, and purpose, when making choices that concern bias-free language.

Question

Assume that you are representing a gay male who has been the victim of a hate crime. He has expressed a preference for the term "gay," rather than "homosexual." You strongly suspect, however, that the judge in the case prefers the term "homosexual." What do you do? Which term do you use when writing to the court?

_____

§23.5.2 Avoid Irrelevant Minority References

Perhaps the most subtle and possibly the most insidious prejudice that appears in some legal writing is unnecessary references to race, ethnic origin, or other minority categories.

Consider, for example, the case described in section 7.3, *State v. Patterson.* In that case, the race of the person who committed the assault is significant because the victim, Martinez, and the other eyewitness, Clipse, gave a description of the assailant and then picked Patterson out at both a show-up and a line-up. In such instances, race is appropriately included in legal writing.

In the same case, however, the victim, Martinez, happened to be Hispanic. Because there is no evidence that the assault was racially motivated, it is probably irrelevant that Martinez was Hispanic. Therefore, references to her race should not be included.

§23.5.3   Use Racial, Ethnic, and Religious Terms Precisely

Citizens from countries in both North and South America have from time to time expressed irritation and resentment over the use of the term "American" to refer to persons and things that are limited to the United States. America, they are quick to point out, includes more than just the United States of America. Indeed, it is imprecise to refer to the American economy or American law when one means the United States economy or United States law. Similarly, avoid the use of "we" or "our" to refer to the United States.

Notice too that the term "Jew" is not synonymous with the term "Israeli." Not all Israelis are Jews and not all Jews are Israelis. Similarly, the term "Arab" is not interchangeable with the term "Muslim." The term "Hebrew" refers to a language. Do not use it to refer to a person or a religion, except in references to ancient Israel.

§23.5.4   Choose the More Specific Term

Although there are exceptions, in most cases choose a more specific term over a more general term when using descriptive labels for groups of people.

For example, although "Asian" is acceptable, "Chinese," "Japanese," or other specific Asian nationalities are preferred when known. Names of specific tribes, such as Mohawk or Navaho, are preferred over the more general "Native American," but do not use the redundant "Navaho Indian."

Note

A relatively new term, "people of color," has gained considerable acceptance within the United States as an encompassing term for African-Americans, Native Americans, Mexican-Americans, and Asian-Americans. Although the term is more general than specific (contrary to the advice above), the term is increasingly preferred when describing lack of diversity or discriminatory practices that affect all these groups.

Chapter 24

Eloquence

Is it unrealistic for legal writing to be eloquent? After all, lawyers write under enormous time pressure. Who has the time to massage language to the point at which someone would call it "eloquent"?

Further, is it appropriate for legal writing to be eloquent? Should an office memo sound like it was written by Shakespeare? What client is willing to pay for a client letter that waxes poetic? Are judges more impressed by arguments or by the language they are wrapped in?

All these good questions really boil down to one question: Should a lawyer strive to write eloquently?

Yes, at least sometimes.

While it wouldn't hurt if every office memo and client letter were written eloquently, the one area in which eloquence undoubtedly pays off is briefs. An eloquent brief is a more persuasive brief. Of course the arguments must be sound and persuasive in and of themselves, but one cannot divorce the content of the argument from the form in which it is written. What one says and the way one says it are inextricably linked.

One striking bit of evidence that eloquent briefs are persuasive is the frequency with which well-articulated arguments from briefs reappear in judicial opinions. If imitation is the highest form of flattery, there can be nothing more flattering to a brief writer than to have a judge "lift" a phrase or more from the brief and incorporate it into the opinion.

But as we suggested before, eloquence is not something legal writers can add as a kind of finishing touch. Eloquence is not a tuxedo or an evening gown. A writer cannot "put on" eloquence any more than an artist can put on originality.

Eloquence in legal writing and originality in art are there throughout the creative process, often at the point of conception, again through the drafting and revising, and yet again in the final polishing.

§24.1   Purple Prose

Like artists who try to force themselves to be original, legal writers who try to force themselves to be eloquent will probably end up creating something that is either absurd or monstrous.

The following excerpt is from the Statement of Facts in a case about whether racial slurs create a cause of action for tort of outrage.

> Our client, Mr. Silvino Gomez, is a twenty-year-old of Mexican-American descent. Mr. Gomez's prowess as a basketball player brought him to the delighted attention of enthusiastic recruiters from several private colleges. He ultimately accepted an athletic scholarship from the University of Newton, where he matriculated and began playing his chosen sport in September 1990. His maiden voyage into the waters of college life was off to a promising start: Barely out of the starting gate, he showed himself to be as talented in the classroom as on the court, and his grades reflected his academic acumen. His interests that fall also included the very beautiful Elizabeth Jaynes, former steady of the team's star guard, Michael Wilson.

Some call writing like the example above "purple prose." Like the color purple, it is just too much. Instead of focusing the reader's attention on the point being made, it calls attention to itself. What's worse, the effort shows. Here's more purple prose from the same office memorandum.

> Silvino's freshman year was not to be without troubles, however. Storm clouds gathered on the horizon as the season got underway. Gomez, playing well, sensed that Wilson considered him a threat, and tension between the two stirred the air as Wilson harassed Gomez on the court. Although there was no "name-calling" during October, the dust flew in November when Wilson thundered at Gomez, "You fucking spic!" At first, the insults were made only when the coaches were absent, but in late November Wilson hurled them like lightning bolts during several practices in the presence of the coaches. In December, even the fans at several games were listening as Wilson's insults fell like hailstones on Gomez.

How to prevent the "purple prose syndrome"? The best safeguard is the axiom "when in doubt, don't." If you think the writing may be "too much," it probably is. Err on the side of subtlety.

Or if you are fortunate enough to have a candid colleague, get a second opinion. If you fear that something you have written may be overdone, ask that colleague to read the writing and let you know if you have stepped over the invisible line and into the realm of purple prose.

You might also try watching out for some of the common features of purple prose, many of which appear in the example above.

- excessive use of adjectives and adverbs: *delighted* attention, *enthusiastic* recruiters, *the very beautiful* Elizabeth Jaynes

- cliche-ridden phrases and images: *the dust flew, hurled them like lightning bolts*
- mixed metaphors: *maiden voyage* mixed with *out of the starting gate*
- overdeveloped metaphors: the weather metaphor in the second half of the example
- pretentious vocabulary: academic *acumen*

Other common features of purple prose not demonstrated in the previous example include the following:

- too much of any one of the poetic devices (for example, excessive alliteration, or the Peter Piper effect)
- heavy-handed use of stylistic devices
- excessive use of underlining and italics for emphasis

§24.2   Common Features of Eloquent Writing

Before writing can be considered eloquent, it must be clear, competent, and readable. Eloquent writing, however, goes a step beyond competence. The language is more than clear and energetic: It is memorable, striking, even poetic because the writer has paid attention to the sound, rhythm, and imagery of language.

Features of language that one may not have thought about since that last class in poetry — alliteration, assonance, cadence, stressed and unstressed syllables, onomatopoeia, simile, and metaphor — may be used, but they do not overwhelm eloquent legal writing. Rhetorical features that one may have noticed in aphorisms — parallelism, balance, antithesis — may also be used, particularly at key points.

Other features, such as electric verbs (see section 22.3), occasional short sentences (see section 22.5), variety in sentence length and sentence openers, and subtle devices for creating emphasis (see section 22.6), are fairly common.

Best of all, all this occurs naturally, apparently effortlessly, even though we know better. Like a pair of dancers who move as one body or a well-executed double play, eloquent writing is the perfect, harmonious matching of form and content. The reader feels satisfied, perhaps even uplifted, by the writing.

§24.2.1   Alliteration and Assonance

Eloquent writing begs to be read aloud. One wants to savor the language. Every word and phrase seems to be just the right choice. Quite simply, the writing sings.

Of the numerous features that affect the sound of a piece of writing, alliteration and assonance are probably the easiest to identify. Alliteration, or the repetition of consonant sounds, must be subtle or the writing will begin to sound like "Peter Piper picked a peck of pickled peppers." One way accomplished writers work in alliteration without overpowering the prose is to use it in the middle of words as well as at the beginning.

The following example demonstrates a subtle use of alliteration. The example is taken from the amicus brief for the United States in the landmark Supreme Court case *Wallace v. Jaffree,* which concerned the constitutionality of a state statute authorizing public school teachers to allow a moment of silence at the beginning of the school day for "prayer or meditation."

> Moment of silence statutes are libertarian in the precise spirit of the Bill of Rights: they accommodate those who believe that prayer should be an integral part of life's activities (including school), and do so in the most neutral and noncoercive spirit possible. The student may pray, but is equally free to meditate or daydream or doze. No one can even know what the other chooses to do: silence is precious because it creates the possibility of privacy within public occasions. To hold that the moment of silence is unconstitutional is to insist that any opportunity for religious practice, even in the unspoken thoughts of schoolchildren, be extirpated from the public sphere. It is to be censorial where the Religion Clauses are libertarian; it would make the very concept of religious accommodation constitutionally suspect.

The alliteration in this example is unobtrusive. In fact, most of us can read this passage and never consciously notice that it includes alliteration. Look again at these phrases:

> the most neutral and noncoercive spirit possible
> daydream or doze

The brief writer could have said "the most impartial and noncoercive spirit possible" or "the most objective and noncoercive spirit possible" or even "the most equitable and noncoercive spirit possible," but didn't. "Neutral," when coupled with "noncoercive," has both the right meaning and the right sound.

The same is true of "daydream and doze." Rather than select "doze," the writer could have easily said "nap," "rest," "sleep," or "snooze." All have similar meanings, but try substituting any one of the four in the original sentence to see what is gained by the alliterative "doze."

The brief writer saves the most subtle and arguably the most powerful alliteration for the clause "silence is precious because it creates the possibility of privacy within public occasions." This clause has two layers of alliteration. The more obvious is the repetition of the p sounds: "silence is precious because it creates the possibility of privacy within public occasions." The second layer is the repetition of s sounds, which is done by both the letters <u>s</u> and <u>c</u>: "<u>s</u>ilence is pre<u>c</u>ious because it create<u>s</u> the po<u>ss</u>ibility of priva<u>c</u>y within public oc<u>c</u>asions."

The soft "s" and "sh" sounds work perfectly in this context. They underscore the writer's meaning by gently, almost imperceptibly reminding the reader of the kind of quiet the writer wants the schoolchildren to have.

Assonance, or the repetition of vowel sounds, is similar to alliteration. In the following example, the brief writer repeated the *a* sound.

EXAMPLE

The absurdity of this implicit assumption is apparent when applied to the motivations of those responsible for the First Amendment itself.

Is the assonance overdone in the example above? Read it aloud to determine if it works.

§24.2.2 Cadence

Cadence is the rhythmic flow of the writing, what musicians might call "the beat." Unlike music, though, writing has no apparent time signature and few overt signals for where to place the emphasis. Even so, good writers control the pace and emphasis in their sentences by artful use of sentence structure, sentence length, punctuation, and stressed and unstressed syllables. Like good musicians, they "hear" what they are creating. They have developed an ear for language.

Read aloud the following selection from Supreme Court Justice Louis Brandeis.

In a government of laws, existence of the government will be imperiled if it fails to observe the law scrupulously. Our Government is the potent, the omnipresent teacher. For good or for ill, it teaches the whole people by its example. Crime is contagious. If the Government becomes a law-breaker, it breeds contempt for law; it invites every man to become a law unto himself; it invites anarchy. To declare that in the administration of the criminal law the end justifies the means — to declare that the Government may commit crimes in order to secure the conviction of a private criminal — would bring terrible retribution. Against that pernicious doctrine this Court should resolutely set its face.

This excerpt is rich with the features of eloquent prose, but for now let's look just at the rhythm in the language. Consider, for example, the phrase "the potent, the omnipresent teacher." The more common way to write two adjectives before a noun is "the potent, omnipresent teacher," without the extra "the." Why the extra "the" in the Brandeis version? Try scanning the phrase as you would a piece of poetry.

$$\smile \ / \ \smile \ \ / \ \smile \ / \ \smile \ / \ \smile$$
the po-tent, om-ni-pres-ent teach-er

The unvarying unstressed, stressed, unstressed, stressed syllable pattern is flat and lifeless, particularly when it comes in two-syllable, sing-song units. It does not give "omnipresent" enough emphasis. Add the extra "the," however, and the rhythm is more interesting and, more important, more compatible with the desired emphasis.

Now look at the last sentence of this selection.

... this Court should resolutely set its face.

This clause is easy to read aloud. It is a grand, solemn conclusion. Why? Scan the last four words.

$$/ \ \smile \ / \ \smile \ / \ \smile \ /$$
res-o-lute-ly set its face

The three one-syllable words "set its face" break up any sing-song effect. Further, notice where the stress falls — on "set" and "face." Thus, by ending the selection on a stressed syllable, a strong note, Justice Brandeis creates the sound of finality and conviction. Had Brandeis arranged the last clause so that it ended on "resolutely" (as he had the earlier one, "to observe the law scrupulously"), the unstressed syllable at the end of "resolutely" would have fought against the decisive closure he wanted.

$$/ \ \smile \ / \ \ / \ \smile \ / \ \smile$$
set its face res-o-lute-ly

Does this mean Justice Brandeis scanned his prose for stressed and unstressed syllables as he was writing it? That's highly unlikely. What is likely is that he *heard* the sound he was creating and, perhaps through trial and error, manipulated the words until he achieved the aural effect he wanted.

The preceding examples show that an extra syllable here or there or changing a stressed to an unstressed syllable or vice versa can make a difference in how writing sounds. Adding or deleting an extra word or syllable also makes a difference in the pace of the writing. Such a change in pace is particularly obvious when the word added or omitted is a conjunction in a series.

A typical series reads like "one, two, and three" or "red, white, and blue." Asyndeton, or the deliberate omissions of conjunctions in a series, quickens the pace. The same series without the conjunction — "red, white, blue" — sounds slightly rushed.

Polysyndeton, or the deliberate use of many conjunctions in a series, slows the pace and drags out the prose. Now the series takes more time: "red and white and blue."

Compare the following examples from a child custody case, in which the court looks at which of the parties was the child's primary caretaker. In an objective, neutral discussion of the father's care of the child, the following series may appear.

EXAMPLE

Mr. Lundquist had certain responsibilities regarding his daughter Anna's care: he drove her to school, checked her homework, and took her to medical appointments.

The attorney for Lundquist's former wife may use asyndeton to create the impression that Mr. Lundquist's care of his daughter was minimal.

EXAMPLE

Mr. Lundquist had few responsibilities regarding his daughter Anna's care: he drove her to school, checked her homework, took her to medical appointments.

Mr. Lundquist, on the other hand, will probably want to create the impression that he was an involved parent who spent a great deal of time with his daughter. Notice how the use of polysyndeton, in combination with other persuasive devices such as characterizing the facts and adding detail, creates the desired effect.

EXAMPLE

Mr. Lundquist had several significant responsibilities regarding his daughter Anna's care: he drove her to school each day and checked her homework every evening and took her to all regularly scheduled and emergency medical appointments.

To stretch out the series a bit further, the writer can even use both the conjunctions and the commas.

EXAMPLE

Mr. Lundquist had several significant responsibilities regarding his daughter Anna's care: he drove her to school each day, and checked her homework every evening, and took her to all regularly scheduled and emergency medical appointments.

Compare the following.

EXAMPLE   **A TYPICAL SERIES**

First-year law students take Contracts, Torts, Civil Procedure, Legal Writing, and Criminal Law.

Dropping the conjunction makes the writing sound clipped and a bit breezy.

EXAMPLE   **ASYNDETON**

First-year law students take Contracts, Torts, Civil Procedure, Legal Writing, Criminal Law.

Adding in all the conjunctions, on the other hand, suggests that the coursework for a first-year law student is overwhelming.

EXAMPLE   **POLYSYNDETON**

First-year law students take Contracts and Torts and Civil Procedure and Legal Writing and Criminal Law.

---

§24.2.3   Variety in Sentence Length

In section 22.5, we said that legal readers can comfortably read sentences that average around twenty-two words in length. We also suggested that long sentences, thirty-five words or more, are difficult to read unless they are broken into manageable units of meaning. Finally, we briefly touched on the power of the short sentence. All of these points apply to eloquent writing.

Let's look again at the earlier excerpt from Justice Brandeis.

> In a government of laws, existence of the government will be imperiled if it fails to observe the law scrupulously. Our Government is the potent, the omnipresent teacher. For good or for ill, it teaches the whole people by its example. Crime is contagious. If the Government becomes a law-breaker, it breeds contempt for law; it invites every man to become a law unto himself; it invites anarchy. To declare that in the administration of the criminal law the end justifies the means — to declare that the Government may commit crimes in order to secure the conviction of a private criminal — would bring terrible retribution. Against that pernicious doctrine this Court should resolutely set its face.

A reader's sense of how long a sentence is depends partly on the number of words in the sentence but also on the number of syllables in the sentence. Here's how the sentences in the Brandeis excerpt break down, both in the number of words they contain and in the number of syllables.

sentence 1	20 words	32 syllables
sentence 2	8 words	15 syllables
sentence 3	13 words	17 syllables
sentence 4	3 words	5 syllables
sentence 5	24 words	38 syllables
sentence 6	37 words	62 syllables
sentence 7	11 words	18 syllables

The variety in sentence length in this selection is remarkable — from 3 words to 37 words. Having variety, though, is not an end in itself. Notice how Brandeis uses sentence length. The one extremely short sentence, "Crime is contagious," is startling in its brevity. It hits the reader like a slap in the face. Its terseness creates the emphasis this point deserves.

The longest sentence in the selection has to be longer just to get across its points, but it also needs more words to create the effect of building to a climax. This sentence needs time to gather momentum. And even though it is fairly long, 37 words or 62 syllables, this sentence is easy to read because it comes in manageable units of meaning: 15 words, 18 words, and 4 words.

Such variety in sentence length helps create an interesting and varied pace. Deliberately breaking the "rules" can be another effective way to create reader interest. In the following excerpt from *Edwards v. Aguillard,* Justice Scalia uses a marathon sentence to help make a point.

> But the difficulty of knowing what vitiating purpose one is looking for is as nothing compared with the difficulty of knowing how or where

to find it. For while it is possible to discern the objective "purpose" of a statute (*i.e.,* the public good at which its provisions appear to be directed), or even the formal motivation for a statute where that is explicitly set forth (as it was, to no avail, here), discerning the subjective motivation of those enacting the statute is, to be honest, almost always an impossible task. The number of possible motivations, to begin with, is not binary, or indeed even finite. In the present case, for example, a particular legislator need not have voted for the Act either because he wanted to foster religion or because he wanted to improve education. He may have thought the bill would provide jobs for his district, or may have wanted to make amends with a faction of his party he had alienated on another vote, or he may have been a close friend of the bill's sponsor, or he may have been repaying a favor he owed the Majority Leader, or he may have hoped the Governor would appreciate his vote and make a fundraising appearance for him, or he may have been pressured to vote for a bill he disliked by a wealthy contributor or by a flood of constituent mail, or he may have been seeking favorable publicity, or he may have been reluctant to hurt the feelings of a loyal staff member who worked on the bill, or he may have been settling an old score with a legislator who opposed the bill, or he may have been mad at his wife who opposed the bill, or he may have been intoxicated and utterly *un*motivated when the vote was called, or he may have accidentally voted "yes" instead of "no," or, of course, he may have had (and very likely did have) a combination of some of the above and many other motivations. To look for *the sole purpose* of even a single legislator is probably to look for something that does not exist.

Sentence 5 is a linguistic tour de force. At 202 words, it must set some kind of record for sentence length, yet the sentence is quite readable because it is broken up into manageable units that vary between 8 and 24 words.

But no one thinks Justice Scalia wrote this sentence to demonstrate that he can write a long sentence that is readable. Rather, in this rare instance, an extremely long sentence dramatically made his point that there is an extremely long list of reasons why any single legislator may vote for a bill.

The selection also demonstrates our earlier point about variety in sentence length. Here the range is from 15 words to 202 words.

sentence 1	27 words
sentence 2	64 words
sentence 3	15 words
sentence 4	30 words
sentence 5	202 words
sentence 6	22 words

Notice what points Justice Scalia makes in his two shorter sentences.

§24.2.4   Variety in Sentence Openers

It is risky to suggest that legal writers should occasionally vary the openings of their sentences. In the hands of the wrong writer, this advice can lead to some clumsy prose.

For the most part, writers should follow the more traditional advice and begin the majority of their sentences with the subject. Writers who use all sorts of sentence openers other than the subject tend to write prose that sounds jumpy and disjointed. But writers who oversubscribe to the idea of starting sentences with the subject write incredibly boring prose.

The question then is when should a writer use something other than the subject to begin a sentence? Even in garden-variety prose, subjects are frequently preceded by phrases or clauses that establish a context or pick up on a previously established theme. (See sections 21.2 and 21.3 on orienting transitions and dovetailing.)

What is far more unusual and, when done well, more striking, is the inverted word order of some sentences. Such an inversion, known in classical rhetoric as anastrophe, focuses particular attention on whatever words are out of their normal or expected order. The Brandeis excerpt ended with an example of inverted word order.

> Against that pernicious doctrine this Court should resolutely set its face.

As always, to understand the drama and power this arrangement creates, all one has to do is read the sentence in the normal, expected word order.

> This Court should resolutely set its face against that pernicious doctrine.

Here are some more excerpts from the briefs in *Wallace v. Jaffree.* From the brief of the appellees:

> With great difficulty the state attempts to argue that this case creates tension between the Establishment and Free Exercise clauses.

From the amicus brief from the American Jewish Congress:

> The public schools serve as vehicles for "inculcating fundamental values," including "social, moral, or political" ones. *Bd. of Educ. v. Pico,* 102 S. Ct. 2799, 2806 (1982). Pointedly absent from this list are religious values. Education in those values is not, under the Constitution, the responsibility of the public schools; it is that of family and church.

The expected word order of the second sentence in the second example is "Religious values are pointedly absent from this list." Notice that by inverting the order, the brief writer not only places emphasis on what is out of order, "pointedly absent," but also strengthens the emphasis on "religious values" by moving it to the end of the sentence.

§24.2.5   Parallelism

Parallelism, or the use of similar grammatical structures in a pair or series of related words, phrases, or clauses, is required in some contexts. (See section 25.7.) Accomplished writers, however, treat parallelism not just as a grammatical requirement but as a stylistic opportunity. They use parallelism and its related forms to create special effects, emphasis, and euphony.

Here's an excerpt from the appellants' brief in *Wallace v. Jaffree*:

> This development is a tribute not only to the good sense of the American people, but also to the genius of the Framers of the body of the Constitution.

| *not only* | *to the good sense of the American people,* |
| *but also* | *to the genius of the Framers of the body of the Constitution* |

Look again at the Scalia excerpt. Justice Scalia uses a specialized version of parallelism called isocolon when he matches both the structure and the length of the parallel elements in the following sentence.

> In the present case, for example, a particular legislator need not have voted for the Act either because he wanted to foster religion or because he wanted to improve education.

| *either* | *because he wanted to foster religion* |
| *or* | *because he wanted to improve education* |

Some examples of isocolon go beyond matching the number of words and even match the number of syllables.

The same excerpt from Justice Scalia includes examples of another specialized form of parallelism: balance. In the sentence below, notice how the first half of the sentence is balanced against the second half.

> To look for the sole purpose of even a single legislator is probably to look for something that does not exist.

To look for	*is*	*to look for*
the sole purpose	*probably*	*something that*
of even a		*does not exist.*
single legislator		

The amicus brief of the United States in *Wallace v. Jaffree* also includes an excellent example of balance.

> To hold that the moment of silence is unconstitutional is to insist that any opportunity for religious practice, even in the unspoken thoughts of school children, be extirpated from the public sphere.

> > *To hold that . . .*   *is*   *to insist that . . . .*

Balance can also be created in a number of other ways. Here's an excerpt from Cardozo's opinion in *Hynes v. New York:*

> The approximate and relative become the definite and absolute.

> > | | | |
> > |---|---|---|
> > | *approximate* | *become* | *definite* |
> > | *and* | | *and* |
> > | *relative* | | *absolute* |

From the brief of the appellees in *Wallace:*

> The First Amendment is as simple in its language as it is majestic in its purpose.

> > | | |
> > |---|---|
> > | *as simple* | *as* (it is) *majestic* |
> > | *in its language* | *in its purpose* |

Also fairly common in eloquent legal writing is a related form of parallelism known as antithesis. Like balance, antithesis repeats similar parallel structures on both sides of the equation, but unlike balance, the ideas are in contrast. In other words, balance says X equals X, and antithesis says X does not equal X.

The structure of antithesis is usually quite simple and falls into one of two patterns:

> *not* _____ *but* _____
>
> _____ *, not* _____

Examples from the amicus brief of the United States in *Wallace:*

> The touchstone is not secularism, but pluralism.
> We believe that provision for a moment of silence in the public schools is not an establishment of religion, but rather a legitimate way for the government to provide an opportunity for both religious and nonreligious introspection in a setting where, experience has shown, many desire it. It is an instrument of toleration and pluralism, not of coercion or indoctrination.

Yet another variation of parallelism is the use of parallel openers. Parallel openers can start sentences, clauses, or phrases, and they often have the effect of building to a climax or suggesting that a point is well established. From the Brandeis excerpt:

> If the Government becomes a lawbreaker, it breeds contempt for law; **it invites** every may to become a law unto himself; **it invites** anarchy. **To declare that** in the administration of the criminal law the end justifies the means — **to declare that** the Government may commit crimes in order to secure the conviction of a private criminal — would bring terrible retribution.

From the Scalia excerpt:

> **He may have** thought the bill would provide jobs for his district, or **may have** wanted to make amends with a faction of his party he had alienated on another vote, or **he may have** been a close friend of the bill's sponsor, or **he may have** been repaying a favor he owed the Majority Leader, or **he may have** hoped the Governor would appreciate his vote and make a fundraising appearance for him, or **he may have** been pressured to vote for a bill he disliked by a wealthy contributor or by a flood of constituent mail, or **he may have** been seeking favorable publicity, or **he may have** been reluctant to hurt the feelings of a loyal staff member who worked on the bill, or **he may have** been settling an old score with a legislator who opposed the bill, or **he may have** been mad at his wife who opposed the bill, or **he may have** been intoxicated and utterly *un*motivated when the vote was called, or **he may have** accidentally voted "yes" instead of "no," or, of course, **he may have** had (and very likely did have) a combination of some of the above and many other motivations.

In the following excerpt from the EEOC brief in *Hishon v. King & Spaulding*, the brief writer combined parallel openers with antithesis.

> But the two Senators did not obliquely approach, let alone confront, even the "employment" of lawyers at law firms. They did not mention lawyers; they spoke of doctors instead. They did not discuss law partnerships; they spoke of hospitals instead.

§24.2.6 Onomatopoeia

"Snap," "crackle," and "pop" — these words are examples of onomatopoeia; that is, they sound like what they mean. So do "sizzle," "plop," "hiss," "click," "twang," "crinkle," and a host of others. These words sound like the natural sounds they represent.

Other words have an onomatopoeic quality even though the words don't represent a sound. Consider the word "weird." Not only does it sound weird, it is even spelled weird. The word "bizarre" works the same way; it looks and sounds bizarre. The list goes on. There is something grotesque in the look and sound of "grotesque," and it is hard to imagine a word that looks and sounds more unattractive than "ugly."

Consider the sound of words like "sensual," "lascivious," and "licentious." Notice how the rolling "s" and "l" sounds combine in various ways to give the words a lazy, even erotic sound. "Sultry" works the same way.

The "slippery slope" one hears so much about in law puts the "s" and "l" together as a consonant blend and achieves a different effect. The words seem to *slide* off the tongue with slow ease. Like a judicial system that has started down that slippery slope, there are no natural brakes to stop these words once they are formed on the lips. Notice too that "slick," "slime," "slink," "slither," "slush," and "sludge" all somehow share this same slippery, even oily quality.

Should legal writers use onomatopoeia in their writing? Consider the following versions of essentially the same point.

EXAMPLES

Harris suddenly took the keys and ran out the door.

Harris snatched the keys and ran out the door.

"Snatched" says in one word — even one syllable — what the first of the examples takes two words and four syllables to say. Its quickness mirrors the quickness in the action. It *sounds* like a quick grab at those keys.

Earlier we looked at an example of alliteration, "daydream or doze," and commented that all the synonyms for "doze" — "sleep," "nap," "rest," or "snooze" — were less effective because they lacked the alliteration. Notice too that "doze" has an onomatopoetic quality. The "z" sound in it reminds us of sleep. That is also why "snooze" is the best choice among the runners-up.

§24.2.7　Simile and Metaphor

Similes are indirect comparisons.

EXAMPLE

Lowell's mental irresponsibility defense is like the toy gun he used in the robbery — spurious.

Metaphors are direct comparisons.

EXAMPLE

Our Government is the potent, the omnipresent teacher.

To be effective, similes and metaphors need to be fresh and insightful. Unfortunately, all too many metaphors used in legal writing are cliche-ridden. How often must we hear that something or other is "woven into the fabric of our society"? When was the last time you actually thought about wolves and sheep when something or someone was described as a "wolf in sheep's clothing"?

Timeworn similes and metaphors suggest that the writer's thought processes are on autopilot, and no more than that will be expected of the reader. We can all mentally coast.

A fresh simile or metaphor makes demands of the reader. It asks the reader to bring to the new subject matter all the associations it has with the other half of the metaphor.

So powerful is metaphor that metaphors have become issues themselves. Consider, for example, the same landmark Supreme Court case from which we drew earlier excerpts, *Wallace v. Jaffree,* which involved the Alabama "silent meditation or prayer" in public schools statute. Throughout that case's history, both sides argued whether there was "an absolute wall of separation" between federal government and religion.

Reminder

Take particular care not to mix metaphors. The result is a confusing, sometimes ludicrous image, as in the example below.

EXAMPLE

Ms. Martinez will never forget the image of her assailant, which was forever imprinted on and burned into the pages of her memory.

---

§24.2.8   Personification

Like so many of the suggestions in this chapter, personification, or giving human traits or abilities to abstractions or inanimate objects, must be used with a light hand if it is to be used at all in legal writing.

In the brief of the appellees in *Wallace v. Jaffree,* the writer used personification to make a point about the intent of the Alabama legislature.

In 1982, in order to breathe religious life into its silent meditation statute, the Alabama legislature amended § 16-1-20 to expressly include "prayer" as the preferred activity in which the students and teachers may engage during the reverent moment of silence.

In his dissenting opinion in *Hoffa v. United States,* Chief Justice Warren uses personification to make a point about the government's actions and its witness.

Here the Government reaches into the jailhouse to employ a man who was himself facing indictments far more serious (and later including one for perjury) than the one confronting the man against whom he offered to inform.

Eloquent language does one of two things. It creates a satisfying sound or, as in the Warren excerpt above, it creates a memorable image. The best of the best does both. Such writing is memorable, even unforgettable. It grabs the reader's attention long enough to make the reader see something new or see something old in a new way.

It takes on a life of its own.

Part VI

A Guide to Correct Writing

This section of the *Handbook* was written as a review of grammar, punctuation, and mechanics. While most law students come to law school with a good command of these aspects of writing, some students complain that they have always had problems with spelling, or that they never really understood how to use a semicolon, or that they have heard about dangling modifiers but what in the world are they, anyway?

This section is designed to be a quick refresher and explanation for those students who have forgotten some of the basic rules or who, for some reason, never learned some of them. Even students who have strong backgrounds in grammar, punctuation, and mechanics may find it helpful to review some of the chapters in this section simply because legal writing puts more demands on the writer than do most other types of writing. Consequently, it may make your writing more efficient and more effective if you have all the rules, and hence all the options, at your fingertips.

Finally, although this section is entitled "A Guide to Correct Writing," the term "correct" is a slightly troubling one because it may suggest that the choices outlined in these chapters are absolutely the "right" ones in all circumstances. This is not true. In informal language, for example, certain other usage choices are not only acceptable but preferred. In legal writing, however, standard English is the norm and therefore the "correct" choice.

Chapter 25

Grammar

§25.1 Basic Sentence Grammar

Grammar, like law, is a system. Once you understand the basic workings of the system, you can begin to use the system effectively and efficiently.

Much of Part V, A Guide to Effective Writing, and Part VI, A Guide to Effective Writing, depends on understanding the grammar of an English sentence. This section is a quick review of basic sentence structure and the various components of most English sentences.[1]

§25.1.1 Sentence Patterns

In law, as in most other writing, most sentences are statements. These statements name someone or something (the subject) and then describe an action that that someone or something is performing (the predicate).

Smith	hit Jones.
(subject)	*(predicate)*

Smith's car	smashed into the railing.
(subject)	*(predicate)*

---

1. Although modern grammarians have persuasively argued that structural and transformational grammars more accurately describe the English sentence, the authors have elected to use traditional grammar, partly because it is more familiar to most readers and partly because it is sufficient for our purposes.

Occasionally, the predicate describes the state in which the subject exists, or the subject's state of being.

<u>Smith's car</u>   <u>is a total loss.</u>
   (subject)   *(predicate)*

At the heart of every subject is a noun or a pronoun. Nouns name persons (Supreme Court Justice David Souter), places (Austin, Texas), things (savings bond), and concepts (negligence). Because pronouns are substitutes for nouns, they too can serve as subjects.

At the heart of every predicate is a verb. Some verbs express an action (sue, plead, argue, allege); others show a state of being (forms of the verb to be, to become, to seem). Frequently, the main verb is preceded by other verbs known as auxiliary, or helping, verbs (might have been assaulted), which express time relationships and shades of meaning.

Pattern 1: Subject + Verb

To write a sentence, you will need at least one noun or pronoun for a subject and at least one verb for a predicate. This is the simplest sentence pattern.

subject	**predicate**
Lawyers	argue.
(noun)	*(verb)*

Pattern 2: Subject + Verb + Direct Object

Many verbs, however, cannot stand alone. They require a noun that will receive the action of the verb. We cannot, for example, simply say "lawyers make" and call that a sentence. "Make" what? To make sense, the verb needs a direct object. Notice that the direct object is part of the predicate.

subject	**predicate**	
Lawyers	make	arguments.
(noun)	*(verb)*	*(noun)*
		(direct object)

Direct objects "receive" the action of the verb.

Lawyers	make	arguments.
Judges	deny	motions.

Another way of thinking about this point is to say that the subject performs the action of the verb, and the verb "is done to" the direct object.

You can often find the direct object in a sentence by simply asking the question "what?" after the verb. Make what? Make *arguments.* Deny what? Deny *motions.*

Pattern 3: Subject + Linking Verb + Subject Complement

Similarly, state of being, or linking verbs, need nouns (or sometimes adjectives) to complete the idea. Because these words do not directly receive the action of the verb in the same way as a direct object, they are not called direct objects. Instead, they are called subject complements because they complement the subject by renaming or describing it.

subject	predicate	
Lawyers	are	advocates.
(noun)	*(linking verb)*	*(noun)* **(subject complement)**

subject	predicate	
Lawyers	are	aggressive.
(noun)	*(linking verb)*	*(adjective)* **(subject complement)**

Another way of thinking about how linking verbs work is to think of them as an equals sign (=) in the sentence. Unlike action verbs, linking verbs do not describe an action; they simply say that the subject is "equal to" the subject complement.

Lawyers = advocates
Lawyers = aggressive

Note

Some of the same words (am, is, are, was, were) function as linking verbs in some sentences and as auxiliary, or helping, verbs in other sentences. You can always tell whether one of these words is a linking verb or a helping verb by checking to see whether it is the only main verb in the sentence (then it is a linking verb) or whether it is followed by another main verb (then it is an auxiliary, or helping, verb).

EXAMPLE

The judge is the trier of fact.

In the preceding example, "is" is the only main verb; therefore, it is a linking verb.

EXAMPLE

The judge is speaking to the jury.

In the preceding example, "is" is followed by another main verb, "speaking"; therefore, "is" is an auxiliary, or helping, verb in this example. Notice that the combination "is speaking" is an action verb.

Pattern 4: Subject + Verb + Indirect Object + Direct Object

In another common pattern, the verb is followed by two nouns. The second noun after the verb, the direct object, receives the action of the verb. The first noun after the verb, the indirect object, identifies to whom or for whom (or what) the action is performed.

subject	**predicate**		
Lawyers	tell	clients	their options.
	(verb)	*(noun)*	*(noun)*
		(indirect object)	*(direct object)*

Pattern 5: Subject + Verb + Direct Object + Object Complement

In the last pattern, we also have two nouns following the verb, but in this pattern, the first noun is the direct object and the second noun is an objective complement. An objective complement renames or describes the direct object.

subject	predicate		
Smith	called	Jones	a liar.
	(verb)	*(noun)*	*(noun)*
		(direct object)	*(objective complement)*

Using these basic sentence patterns, we can now begin adding all those extras that make sentences interesting and complex.

§25.1.2   Single-Word Modifiers

Modifiers change, limit, describe, or add detail. Words that modify nouns or pronouns are, by definition, adjectives (*illogical* argument, *nervous* witness, *bearded* suspect).

Words that modify verbs, adjectives, or adverbs are adverbs (*quickly* responded, finished *soon, extremely* angry, *very* recently). Notice that adverbs often end in "-ly."

Any of our basic sentences can be expanded by using adjectives and adverbs as modifiers.

EXAMPLES

Thoughtful lawyers make very persuasive arguments.
  adjective   *adverb adjective*

Too many lawyers are overly aggressive.
adv. adj.   *adverb   adjective*

---

§25.1.3   Phrases

When expanding the basic sentence patterns, we are not limited to single-word modifiers. Groups of related words, or phrases, can also serve as modifiers. A phrase is easily distinguished from other groups of related words because a phrase always lacks a subject or a verb or both.

Probably the most common type of modifying phrase is the prepositional phrase. Prepositional phrases are made up of a preposition (words that show relationships between other words, such as "about," "at," "by," "for," "in," "of," "on," "to"), its object, and any modifiers.

Preposition	Modifiers	Object
at	the same	time
by	an	affidavit
for	a new	trial
in	the	verdict
under	this	section

Prepositional phrases can modify nouns, verbs, adjectives, or adverbs.

EXAMPLE

At 10:00 p.m. on April 5, 1990, a two truck collision occurred in Delaware between a truck driven by Constance Ruiz and a truck driven by Fred Miller.

Basic sentence patterns can also be expanded with verbals. Verbals are made from verbs, but they cannot serve as the main verb of a sentence. Instead, verbals are ways of using verb forms in other roles in a sentence. The three types of verbals — gerunds, infinitives, and participles — are described below. Notice that each can be expanded into a phrase.

a.   Gerunds

Gerunds always act as nouns, so they are found in slots in the sentence that require nouns (subject, objects). They are formed by adding "-ing" to the base form of a verb.

EXAMPLES

Impeaching his testimony will be difficult.
   (gerund)

Forgery includes writing a bad check.
      (gerund)

---

b. Participles

Participles act as adjectives. Present participles are formed by adding "-ing" to the base form of the verb; past participles usually add "-d" or "-ed." Irregular verbs have a special past participle form (for example, brought, drunk, stolen).

EXAMPLES

A television set <u>wrapped</u> in a blanket was found in the defendant's
             (participle)
trunk.

<u>Applying</u> this rule, the New York Supreme Court held that the ap-
(participle)
pellant's constitutional rights were not violated.

<u>Given</u> that forgery is not a crime of dishonesty, the court found
(participle)
that evidence of the prior conviction is inadmissible.

Notice that the only way to distinguish between a gerund and a present participle is to determine the role they perform in a sentence.

c. Infinitives

Infinitives can act as nouns, adjectives, or adverbs. The infinitive form is always "to" plus the base form of the verb.

EXAMPLE

<u>To extend</u> the all-purpose public figure standard <u>to include</u> all financial institutions ignores the Supreme Court's mandate <u>to construe</u> the standard narrowly.

---

d. Absolutes

One additional type of phrase, the absolute phrase, can also be used to expand the basic sentence patterns. Absolute phrases do not modify any one word or phrase in a sentence; instead, they are whole sentence modifiers. Absolute phrases are made up of a noun (or pronoun), a participle, and their modifiers.

attention   diverted

noun   +   *participle*

EXAMPLE

His attention diverted by the fire, the witness is unlikely to have viewed the fleeing arsonist for more than a second.

---

§25.1.4   Clauses

A group of related words that has both a subject and a verb is a clause. There are two types of clauses: main (or independent) clauses and subordinate (or dependent) clauses. A main clause can stand alone as a sentence. A subordinate clause cannot stand alone as a sentence because a subordinate clause is introduced by a subordinating conjunction or relative pronoun.

Common subordinating conjunctions

after	if	though
although	if only	till
as	in order that	unless
as if	now that	until
as long as	once	when
as though	rather than	whenever
because	since	where
before	so that	whereas
even if	than	wherever
even though	that	while

Relative pronouns

that	which	whom
what	who	whomever
whatever	whoever	whose

Notice that in subordinate clauses introduced by a relative pronoun, the subject of the clause is often the relative pronoun (Defendants *who do not take the stand* risk having jurors infer that they are guilty).

EXAMPLES

Main Clauses:

Martin retained full possession of the stock.

The trial court abused its discretion.

It failed to consider the statutory factors.

Subordinate Clauses:

although Martin retained full possession of the stock

that the trial court abused its discretion

when it failed to consider the statutory factors

Subordinate Clauses Attached to Main Clauses:

Although Martin retained full possession of the stock, the trial court awarded the stock to Judith.

The appellate court found that the trial court abused its discretion when it failed to consider the statutory factors.

---

§25.1.5   Appositives

Appositives are words or groups of words that follow a noun and rename it. They may also further describe or identify the noun.

EXAMPLES

Former White House aide <u>Oliver L. North</u> was the first key figure
                              (appositive)
to be prosecuted in the Iran-contra affair.

Jim Bakker, <u>television evangelist</u>, was convicted of twenty-four
                (appositive)
counts of fraud and conspiracy.

In *Texas v. Johnson,* <u>a case about a state criminal statute forbidding "the desecration of a venerated object,"</u> the Supreme Court ruled that burning the American flag as an expression of political discontent is protected by the First Amendment.

Appositives are frequently introduced by phrases (that is, such as, for example).

EXAMPLE

Evidence of some crimes, <u>such as fraud, embezzlement, and false pretense</u>, may be probative of a defendant's credibility as a witness.

---

§25.1.6   Connecting Words

Throughout this section, we have discussed how to expand the five basic sentence patterns by adding single-word modifiers, phrases, and clauses. We can also expand these basic sentence patterns by using connecting words that allow us to combine words or word groups of equal rank. For example, we can add one or more nouns to a subject to create a compound subject (Smith and Wilson hit Jones), or we can add one or more verbs to the predicate to create a compound predicate (Smith hit and kicked Jones).

In fact, with proper use of the various types of connecting words, just about any word, phrase, or clause can be compounded.

a. *Coordinating Conjunctions*

The most common connecting words are the seven coordinating conjunctions.

and	nor	yet
but	for	so
or		

"And," "but," "or," and "nor" can connect any two (or more) of the same kind of word or word group. "For" and "so" connect main clauses.

EXAMPLES

Connecting Two Nouns:

Crimes of dishonesty involve **fraud** <u>or</u> **deceit.**

Connecting Two Verbs:

The complaint stated that Defendants had **published** <u>but</u> not **retracted** a defamatory article about Vashon Savings and Loan.

Connecting Three Phrases:

Copies of the article were distributed **to subscribers, to newsstands,** <u>and</u> **to at least three civic groups.**

Connecting Two Subordinate Clauses:

Because there are only two witnesses <u>and</u> **because each witness has a different version of the facts,** the jury will have to choose which one to believe.

Connecting Two Main Clauses:

Vashon Savings and Loan has not assumed a role of especial prominence in the affairs of society, <u>nor</u> **does it occupy a position of pervasive power or influence.**

---

b.　Correlative Conjunctions

Correlative conjunctions come in pairs.

both . . . and	either . . . or	whether . . . or
not . . . but	neither . . . nor	as . . . as
not only . . . but also		

EXAMPLES

Plaintiff's contact with the community is <u>both</u> **conservative** <u>and</u> **low-key.**

The jury <u>either</u> **will not hear the defendant's testimony** <u>or</u> **will completely disregard it** if his prior convictions are admitted.

---

c.　Conjunctive Adverbs

Even though conjunctive adverbs do not connect parts of the sentence grammatically, they are useful because they show the relationship between two or more ideas.

The Most Common Conjunctive Adverbs

accordingly	further	likewise	similarly
also	furthermore	meanwhile	still
anyway	hence	moreover	then
besides	however	nevertheless	thereafter
certainly	incidentally	next	therefore
consequently	indeed	nonetheless	thus
finally	instead	otherwise	undoubtedly

EXAMPLES

Mrs. Davis admits that her physician told her that she has a drinking problem. She refuses, <u>nevertheless</u>, to attend Alcoholics Anonymous. <u>Instead</u>, she claims that she drinks only an occasional glass of wine.

Mrs. Davis will have $33,872 a year to spend as she sees fit; <u>therefore</u>, she has no need for the dividend income from the stock.

Mr. Davis has no means from his present income to repurchase the stock; <u>consequently</u>, the option to repurchase is worthless.

Notice too that because they do not connect parts of the sentence grammatically, conjunctive adverbs can often move in the sentence.

EXAMPLES

Tom Davis owned his own business; <u>however</u>, his son did not participate in the business because the two did not get along.

Tom Davis owned his own business; his son did not participate in the business, <u>however</u>, because the two did not get along.

§25.2 Fragments

Although there are a few exceptions, fragments are generally taboo in legal writing. In fact, of the kinds of errors a writer can make, fragments are considered one of the most egregious. In the minds of some readers, they are the mark of the barely literate.

Given the strong bias against this writing error, then, legal writers who are prone to writing sentence fragments should make it a priority to learn what sentence fragments are and how to avoid them.

Simply defined, a sentence fragment is an incomplete sentence. Theoretically, it may be missing its subject,[2] but more than likely it is missing a main verb, or it is a subordinate clause trying to pose as a sentence.

§25.2.1   Missing Main Verb

All verbals — gerunds, participles, and infinitives — are formed from verbs, but they cannot fill verb slots in a sentence. Consequently, they cannot serve as the main verb of a sentence. Some legal writers who are prone to writing fragments mistake verbals for main verbs. (See section 25.1 for definitions and explanations of verbals.)

EXAMPLE   **FRAGMENT**

The attorney objecting to the line of questioning.

In the example above, "objecting" is not a verb; it is a participle modifying "attorney." Because the example has no main verb, it is a fragment, not a sentence. To make it a sentence, either add a main verb or change "objecting" from a participle to a main verb.

EXAMPLE   **POSSIBLE REVISIONS**

The attorney objecting to the line of questioning <u>rose</u> to her feet.

The attorney <u>objects</u> to the line of questioning.

The attorney <u>was</u> objecting to the line of questioning.

Notice that the same word, "objecting," can be a participle or, with an auxiliary verb added, a main verb.

---

2. Imperative, or command, sentences such as "Sit down" or "Hang your coat in the cloakroom" may appear to have a missing subject, but the subject is always understood to be "you." Therefore, imperative sentences are not fragments even if they are only one word long, like "Run!"

§25.2.2 Subordinate Clauses Trying to Pose as Sentences

Take any main, or independent, clause and add a word like "although," "because," "if," "until," or "when" in front of it and it automatically becomes a subordinate, or dependent, clause.

until + main clause = subordinate clause

As a main clause, it is a sentence; as a subordinate clause standing alone, it is a fragment.

EXAMPLE

Main Clause:

The attorney objects to the line of questioning.

Subordinate Clause:

Until the attorney objects to the line of questioning

Subordinate clauses must be attached to a main, or independent, clause.

EXAMPLE

Until the attorney objects to the line of questioning, the judge will
                      (subordinate clause)   *(main clause)*
not rule.

"Although," "because," "if," "until," and "when" are not the only words, or subordinating conjunctions, that can change a main clause into a subordinate clause. Below is a fairly complete list of the most common subordinating conjunctions used in legal writing. Remember: If one of these words or phrases introduces a clause, that clause will be subordinate. It cannot stand alone.

Subordinating conjunctions

after	before	now that	till
although	even if	once	unless
as	even though	provided	until
as if	if	rather than	when
as long as	if only	since	whenever
as soon as	in order that	so that	where
as though	in that	than	whereas
because	no matter how	that	wherever
		though	while

Notice, too, that subordinate clauses may follow a main clause. In fact, many fragments are written because the writer should have attached a subordinate clause to the preceding main clause.

EXAMPLE

Fragment:

Kaiser's statement acknowledging our client's ownership of the land may have no effect on the hostility of his claim. Because he never acted in subordination to the true owner.

Corrected:

Kaiser's statement acknowledging our client's ownership of the land may have no effect on the hostility of his claim because Kaiser never acted in subordination to the true owner.

The relative pronouns — "who," "whoever," "whom," "whomever," "whose," "what," "whatever," "which," and "that" — also lure some writers into writing fragments.

EXAMPLE

Fragment:

The admission of a defendant's prior convictions may affect that defendant's decision to take the stand. Which would interfere with his right to testify freely on his own behalf.

Corrected:

The admission of a defendant's prior convictions may affect that defendant's decision to take the stand. Therefore, admission of his prior convictions would interfere with his right to testify freely on his own behalf.

Note

"Who," "which," and "what" are also interrogative pronouns that introduce questions. Questions introduced by "who," "which," and "what" are not fragments. ─────────

EXAMPLE

Which witness will corroborate the defendant's alibi?

In short, to determine if you have written a sentence and not a fragment, (1) make sure you have a verb, (2) make sure you have a subject, and (3) make sure your subject and verb are not preceded by a subordinating conjunction or a relative pronoun. See Exercises 25.A and 25.B in the *Practice Book*.

§25.2.3   Permissible Uses of Incomplete Sentences

There are a handful of permissible uses for incomplete sentences in legal writing.

    a.   in issue statements beginning with "whether"
    b.   as answers to questions
    c.   in exclamations
    d.   for stylistic effect
    e.   as transitions

a. In Issue Statements Beginning with "Whether"

Many issue statements, or questions presented, begin with the word "whether."

EXAMPLE

Whether, under Washington tort law on wrongful death or conversion, the Hoffelmeirs may collect punitive damages for the destruction of their pet cat when the cat was impounded and when, after Mr. Janske of the Humane Society tried unsuccessfully to contact the Hoffelmeirs, the animal was destroyed before the time required by the Sequim City Ordinance.

Although a grammarian would not consider the example above to be a complete sentence, most attorneys and judges find this format acceptable in legal writing. It is as though legal readers read in an elliptical "The issue is" before the "whether."

b. As Answers to Questions

Many office memos contain a brief answer section. Typically, a brief answer will begin with an incomplete sentence that is a short response to the legal question. This is an acceptable use of a fragment.

EXAMPLE

Probably not. In Washington, there is a strong policy against the award of punitive damages and, unless there is a statutory provision allowing for punitive damages, the courts will not award them. In this instance, there is no statutory provision allowing for punitive damages.

---

c. In Exclamations

Exclamations rarely occur in legal writing because they make the tone of the writing appear inflammatory, effusive, or sarcastic. The one place exclamations do appear in legal writing is in quoted dialogue. On such occasions, quote exactly what the speaker said and how he or she said it, including fragments.

d. For Stylistic Effect

Sophisticated writers who are well schooled in the rules of grammar can occasionally use an intentional fragment for stylistic effect. Most writers, however, should avoid writing any fragments.

EXAMPLE

It may have been unavoidable, but it still took courage. More courage than most of us would have had.

---

e.   As Transitions

As with fragments for stylistic effect, intentional fragments as transitions are a risk. Use them only if you are secure about and in complete control of your writing.

If you have already read sections 20.4 and 20.5 of this book, you may have noticed that the authors used two incomplete sentences as transitions to begin those sections.

EXAMPLES

First, the truth.

Again, the truth.

See Exercise 25.C in the *Practice Book.*

§25.3   VERB TENSE AND MOOD

§25.3.1   Tense

Verb tense does not pose problems for most legal writers who are native speakers of English. Native speakers tend to "hear" when the verb is right or wrong. Consequently, verb tense is one of those areas of writing that is best left alone, unless a writer is having problems.

For those native and non-native speakers of English who are having problems with verb tense in legal writing, the following is a quick review of the basic verb tense structure.

Throughout this review of verb tense, we will use a capital "X" to indicate the present on all time lines.

The term "tense" refers to the time in which the verb's action occurs in relation to the time when the writer is writing. For example, present tense is used for actions that occur in the present, that is, at the time the writer is writing.

EXAMPLE   **PRESENT TENSE**

The defendant <u>pleads</u> not guilty.

Time line: _____ X _____
the present
(the action is occurring
at the same time
the writer is writing)

Notice, however, that the "X" on the time line that represents "the present" may be as short as a fraction of a second or as long as several centuries, depending on what time frame the writer sets up.

Past tense refers to actions that occurred before the writer is writing.

EXAMPLE   **PAST TENSE**

Two years ago, this same prosecutor <u>charged</u> the defendant with aggravated assault.

Time line: _____ X _____
⟵ **the past** ⟶

Legal writers usually use the past tense when describing analogous cases.

EXAMPLE

In *Colorado Carpet,* the court <u>rejected</u> the argument for the specially manufactured goods <u>exception</u> because the carpet <u>was</u> not <u>cut</u> to a room size.

Future tense refers to actions that will occur after the writer is writing.

EXAMPLE   **FUTURE TENSE**

The plaintiff <u>will call</u> an expert witness.

Time line: _____ X _____
                                        ←—— **the future** ——→

The simple tenses — present, past, and future — are just that: simple and easy to use. Only the present tense offers a few noteworthy wrinkles.

In addition to its common use for actions that occur in the present, present tense is also used to express general truths and to show habitual actions.

EXAMPLES

Appellate courts <u>do</u> not <u>retry</u> a case on its facts.

The defendant <u>drinks</u> a six-pack or more of beer every Friday night before leaving the poker game.

Present tense can also be used to indicate the future when the sentence contains other words and phrases to signal a future time.

EXAMPLE

The court <u>hears</u> oral arguments later this afternoon.

The perfect tenses are a bit more complicated. Perfect tenses are designed to show that an action is completed before a certain time.

For example, the present perfect tense usually shows that an action is completed at the time of the statement. It is formed by using "have" or "has" before the past participle. In the sentence below, the present perfect "have tried" occurred before the present.

EXAMPLE   **PRESENT PERFECT TENSE**

The plaintiffs <u>have tried</u> this strategy before, but it is not working this time.

Time line: _____ X _____

                    ———————→

(action begun in past
and completed before
the present)

The present perfect tense is also used when the action was begun in the past and it continues on into the present.

EXAMPLES

The prosecutor <u>has lowered</u> his voice to a whisper in an attempt to rattle the witness.

The United States Supreme Court <u>has held</u> that the "consent of one who possesses common authority over premises or effects is valid as against the absent, nonconsenting person with whom that authority is shared." *United States v. Matlock,* 415 U.S. 164, 170 (1974).

Time line: _____ X _____

                    ———————→

(action begun in
past and continues
on into present)

The past perfect tense is used when one past action was completed before another past action. For example, a legal writer may find it useful to use the past perfect to distinguish the time sequence of the facts of the case from the time sequence of a court's actions, both of which occurred in the past.

Note that the past perfect tense is formed by adding "had" before the past participle.

EXAMPLE   PAST PERFECT TENSE

The court noted that the defendant <u>had known</u> about the defective brakes for three months.

Time line: _____ x _____ x _____ X _____
              had   *noted*   (present)
              known   (past)
              (past
              perfect)

The past perfect tense is also useful when discussing court proceedings at different levels. For example, a writer may use the simple past tense to describe the decisions of an appellate court and the past perfect to describe the decisions of the trial court.

EXAMPLE

The Court of Appeals <u>affirmed</u> the trial court, which <u>had ruled</u> that
                    (simple past)   *(past perfect)*
the statute did not apply.

The future perfect tense is used when an action that started in the past ends at a certain time in the future. It is formed by adding "will have" before the past participle.

EXAMPLE

By the time you finish dinner tonight, drunk drivers <u>will have claimed</u> five more victims on United States highways.

Time line: _____ X _____ x _____
                                          will have
                                          claimed

Every verb can also be progressive, that is, it can show continuing action by adding "-ing."

Present progressive: is claiming
Past progressive: was claiming
Future progressive: will be claiming
Present perfect progressive: has been claiming
Past perfect progressive: had been claiming
Future perfect progressive: will have been claiming

One last word about verb tense: One common myth is that writers have to maintain a consistent verb tense. Although writers should avoid needless shifts in verb tense, shifts in verb tense are required when there is a shift in time. Such a shift in time may even occur within the same sentence. See Exercises 25.D and 25.E in the *Practice Book.*

EXAMPLES

Her landlord <u>knows</u> that she <u>will be</u> unable to pay her rent.
　　　　　(present)　　　　　*(future)*

Although Mr. Henderson <u>built</u> the shed on the northwest corner of
　　　　　　　　　　　　(past)
the property in 1992, he <u>admits</u> that Ms. Kyte <u>has owned</u> that
　　　　　　　　　　　　(present)　　　　　　*(present perfect)*
corner since 1989.

Smith <u>will argue</u> that he <u>did</u> not knowingly or willingly <u>consent</u> to
　　(future)　　　　*(past)*　　　　　　　　　*(past)*
a search of his wallet.

---

§25.3.2　Mood

In grammar, the term "mood" refers to the approach the writer gives the verb. English has three moods: indicative, imperative, and subjunctive. The indicative mood is used for statements of facts or questions.

EXAMPLE　　**INDICATIVE MOOD**

The defendant <u>pleaded</u> "not guilty."

The imperative mood is used for sentences that are orders or commands. The subject of a sentence in the imperative mood is understood to be "you," the reader or listener.

EXAMPLE   IMPERATIVE MOOD

<u>Plead</u> "not guilty."

The subjunctive mood is the only mood that is a bit tricky. Although grammarians are constantly discussing its demise, the subjunctive mood is still used in a variety of situations.

1. The subjunctive is used to express ideas contrary to fact.

EXAMPLE

If I <u>were</u> the defendant, I would plead "not guilty."

---

2. The subjunctive is used to express a requirement.

EXAMPLE

The law requires that contracts <u>be</u> signed willingly, not under duress.

---

3. The subjunctive is used to express a suggestion or recommendation.

EXAMPLE

His attorney recommended that he <u>be</u> allowed to give his own closing argument.

---

4. The subjunctive is used to express a wish.

EXAMPLE

The clerk asked that the check <u>be</u> post-dated.

Note that the contrary-to-fact clauses begin with "if" and the requirement, suggestion, recommendation, or wish clauses all begin with an expressed or elliptical "that."

In addition, there are a few idioms such as "far be it from me" and "suffice it to say" that use the subjunctive mood.

The subjunctive mood is formed slightly differently depending on how it is used. For present conditions that are contrary to fact, it is formed from the past tense of the verb. For the verb "to be," it uses "<u>were</u>."

EXAMPLES

If I <u>took</u> a reading on the toxic particles being emitted right now, it would show that the factory has completely disregarded EPA guidelines.

If she <u>were</u> to testify, the defendant's sister would corroborate his story.

For past conditions that are contrary to fact, the subjunctive mood is formed from the past perfect.

EXAMPLE

<u>Had</u> the contract been signed, there would be no question that it is valid.

For requirements, recommendations, and suggestions, the subjunctive mood is formed from the infinitive form of the verb without the "to."

EXAMPLES

The law requires that the adverse possessor <u>prove</u> that the possession was open and notorious.

Mr. Hughes suggested that the store manager <u>notify</u> him of any discrepancies.

For wishes and desires, the subjunctive mood is formed from the past tense of the verb. For the verb "to be," "were" is used.

EXAMPLE

My client wishes that you <u>were</u> her attorney.

---

§25.4 AGREEMENT

Simply put, agreement is matching the form of one word to another. In legal writing, agreement can be a problem in two areas: (1) the agreement in number between a subject and verb and (2) the agreement in number between a pronoun and its antecedent.

§25.4.1 Subject-Verb Agreement

Singular subjects take singular verbs, and plural subjects take plural verbs.

For most native speakers of English, this kind of subject-verb agreement comes almost as naturally as breathing, as long as the sentence is short and simple.

EXAMPLES

The law requires that all drivers wear seat belts.

> singular subject = law
> singular verb = requires

The immigration laws require that all workers provide proof of citizenship before starting a job.

> plural subject = laws
> plural verb = require

Note

In English, we often think that adding "s" makes the plural form of words. This is true for nouns but not for verbs. We add an "s" to the singular form of present tense verbs (except the verb "to be") when they are matched with a singular noun or the pronouns "he," "she," or "it." For example, we say "a client maintain*s*," "he reject*s*," "she allege*s*," or "it confirm*s*."

In simple sentences, a writer can usually make subjects and verbs agree by listening to the way the sentences sound. The writer's ear tells him or her what matches and what doesn't. In longer, more complicated sentences, like those that often occur in legal writing, the ear is more likely to be misled. The following rules cover those situations.

Rule 1	**A Subject and Its Verb Must Agree Even When They Are Separated by Other Words**

When other words, particularly nouns, come between a subject and its verb, the writer may inadvertently match the verb to a word other than the subject. The following example demonstrates this error in agreement.

EXAMPLE   **INCORRECT**

Custom-made <u>towels</u> imprinted with the hotel's logo <u>satisfies</u> the
               (subject)   *(verb)*
requirement that the goods be specially manufactured.

The writer has mistakenly chosen the singular verb "satisfies" to match with the intervening noun "logo" when the verb should be the plural form "satisfy" to agree with the plural subject "towels." One way writers can check for this kind of agreement error is to read their subjects and verbs together without the intervening words. "Towels satisfy" will sound right to native speakers.

Note

The number of the subject is not changed by adding intervening words that begin with expressions such as "accompanied by," "as well as," "in addition to," "with," "together with," or "along with." These expressions are considered prepositions and not coordinating conjunctions (see section 25.1), so they modify the subject. They do not change its number.

In the following example, the verb "suggests" correctly agrees with the subject "statement."

EXAMPLE

The defendant's statement to the police, as well as her testimony at trial, suggests that her actions were premeditated.

Rule 2   Two or More Subjects Joined by "And" Usually Take a Plural Verb

Subjects joined by "and" are plural. This rule does not change even if one or all of the subjects are singular.

EXAMPLE

North Star Cinema and Highland Heights Theater question the validity of the admissions tax.

Unfortunately, writers sometimes hear only the second half of the subject with the verb and mistakenly select a singular verb ("Highland Heights Theater questions"). To correct this agreement error, you may find it easier to mentally substitute the word "they" for plural subjects when trying to use your ear to find the correct form of the verb ("they question").

Exception A

Occasionally two or more parts of the subject make up one idea or refer to one person or thing. In such cases, use a singular verb.

EXAMPLE

His wife and beneficiary was the only person mentioned in the will.

Exception B

Occasionally the words "each" or "every" precedes one or more of the parts of a plural subject. In such cases, use a singular verb.

EXAMPLE

Every juror and spectator in the courtroom expects the defendant to testify.

Rule 3	**Subjects Joined by "Or" or "Nor" Take Verbs That Agree With the Part of the Subject Closest to the Verb**

To check subject-verb agreement in sentences with subjects joined by "or" or "nor," simply read only the second half of the subject with the verb and let your ear help you select the correct verb form. In the following examples, read "Lazar Television is" and "her older sisters have."

EXAMPLES

Neither Horizon Telecommunications nor Lazar Television is the type of enterprise that the bulk sales statutes seek to regulate.

The child's mother or her older sisters have been caring for her after school.

Note

In a verb phrase like "have been caring" the helping, or auxiliary, verbs are the ones that change.

singular:	has been caring
plural:	have been caring

Rule 4	**Most Indefinite Pronouns Take Singular Verbs**

Indefinite pronouns are ones that do not refer to any definite person or thing, or they do not specify definite limits. The following is a list of the most common indefinite pronouns:

all	each	everything	none
any	either	neither	somebody
anyone	everyone	nobody	someone
anybody	everybody	no one	something

Usually these pronouns refer to a single, indefinite person or thing, so they take singular verbs.

EXAMPLE

Everyone who takes the stand swears to tell the truth.

A few indefinite pronouns — "none," "all," "most," "some," "any," and "half" — may take either a singular or a plural verb depending on the noun to which they refer.

EXAMPLES

All of the jewelry was recovered.

All of the rings were recovered.

| **Rule 5** | **Collective Nouns Take Singular Verbs When the Group Acts as One Unit; Collective Nouns Take Plural Verbs When the Members of the Group Act Separately** |

The following is a list of the most common collective nouns in legal writing:

jury	committee	board
audience	team	majority
family	crowd	number
Supreme Court	appellate court	fractions (when
names of com-		used as
panies/cor-		nouns)
porations		

The following examples all use collective nouns that are acting as one unit, so the verbs are singular.

EXAMPLES

The jury has reached its verdict.

The appellate court affirms the conviction.

Two thirds of the board is absent.

The following example uses a collective noun whose members are acting separately, so the verb is plural.

EXAMPLE

The jury have all had an opportunity to state whether they believe in capital punishment.

Note

Even though it is correct to use a plural verb with a collective noun when the members are acting separately, it usually sounds awkward. Consequently, many writers prefer to revise their sentences so that they don't have collective nouns that require plural verbs.

EXAMPLE   **REVISED**

The jurors have all had an opportunity to state whether they believe in capital punishment.

Note

An easy way to tell if the collective noun "number" is singular or plural is to check whether "number" is preceded by "a" or "the." "A number" requires a plural verb; "the number" requires a singular verb.

EXAMPLES

A number of witnesses are willing to testify that they saw the defendant drive out of the parking lot.

The number of union members who are seeking early retirement is growing.

| Rule 6 | **Nouns Ending in "s" That Are Singular in Meaning Take Singular Verbs** |

Despite their "s" ending, words like "aesthetics," "athletics," "economics," "mathematics," "news," "physics," "politics," "statistics," and "tactics" are usually considered singular because they describe a whole concept or body of knowledge.

EXAMPLE

Politics is inappropriate in a court of law.

Note

When "statistics" refers to individual facts, it takes a plural verb.

EXAMPLE

The enrollment statistics show that the university has consistently discriminated against Asian students.

| Rule 7 | **Linking Verbs Agree With Their Subjects, Not Their Subject Complements** |

In the following example, the linking verb "was" agrees with "testimony," not the subject complement "contradictory and intentionally misleading":

EXAMPLE

The defendant's testimony was contradictory and intentionally misleading.

In the next example, the linking verb "is" agrees with "part," not "arguments."

EXAMPLE

The best part of any trial is the closing arguments.

See section 25.1 for more on subject complements.

| **Rule 8** | **Verbs Agree With Their Subjects Even When the Subjects Come After the Verb** |

Subjects follow verbs after expletive constructions such as "there is" and "there are."

EXAMPLE

There is a possibility that the defendant will plead "temporary insanity."

There are several options for ensuring that your loan is repaid.

Subjects may also follow verbs when normal word order is changed for emphasis.

EXAMPLE

At no time was Brown aware that his conversations were being tape recorded.

At no time were Brown and Smith aware that their conversations were being tape recorded.

Rule 9	The Title of a Work or a Word Used as a Word Takes a Singular Verb

EXAMPLE

Tactics in Legal Reasoning is an excellent resource for both law students and practitioners.

When a word is used as a word, it is often enclosed in quotation marks or preceded by "the word."

EXAMPLES

"Premises" has at least two different meanings: (1) the introductory propositions to a syllogism or (2) the area of land surrounding a building.

The word "premises" has two different meanings.

Compare the previous examples, both of which used the singular verb "has," with the following example, which requires the plural verb form "have."

EXAMPLE

The premises have been searched by the police.

Rule 10	**When Used as Subjects of Relative Clauses, the Relative Pronouns "That," "Which," and "Who" Agree in Number With Their Noun Antecedents; Consequently, Their Verbs Must Also Agree in Number With Their Noun Antecedents**

In the following example, "who" refers back to the plural "attorneys"; consequently, the verb "are" agrees in number with "attorneys."

EXAMPLE

The attorneys who are representing the plaintiff are Linda Rhodes-Lines and Malcolm S. Hanover.

Note

The phrase "one of the _____" can cause confusing agreement problems when it is followed by a relative pronoun. Decide whether the relative pronoun refers to "one" or to the noun in the blank before selecting the verb for the relative clause. One test for determining the relative pronoun's antecedent is to try omitting "of the _____." If the meaning of the sentence does not change, then the relative pronoun refers back to "one."

EXAMPLE

Our client is one of the several board members who are accused of price fixing.

In the preceding example, the writer intends to say that several board members are accused of price fixing and that the client is one of this group. Consequently, "who" refers to "several board members," so the verb "are accused" must be plural.

EXAMPLE

Our client is the only one of several board members who is accused of price fixing.

In the preceding example, the writer intends to say that the client is one of several board members, but he or she is the only one accused of price fixing. Consequently, "who" refers to "one," so the verb "is accused" must be singular.

| **Rule 11** | **Money, Distance, and Measurement Subjects Usually Take Singular Verbs** |

EXAMPLE

Twenty thousand dollars is a reasonable fee for a case of this complexity.

See Exercise 25.F in the *Practice Book.*

§25.4.2   Pronoun-Antecedent Agreement

A pronoun must agree with its antecedent. The noun a pronoun refers to is known as its antecedent.

Pronouns are substitutes for nouns. They have no independent meanings. Consequently, they must refer to a noun and be consistent with that noun in gender, person, and number.

Legal writers usually do not have problems making their pronouns and antecedents agree in gender or person. Agreement in number, however, can be a bit more difficult.

Rule 1	**Singular Antecedents Require Singular Pronouns; Plural Antecedents Require Plural Pronouns**

EXAMPLES

<u>William MacDonald</u> may claim that <u>his</u> constitutional rights were
    (antecedent)   *(pronoun)*
violated.

<u>William MacDonald</u> and <u>Grace Yessler</u> may claim that <u>their</u> con-
    (antecedent)   *(antecedent)*   *(pronoun)*
stitutional rights were violated.

This rule, although simple on the surface, becomes a little trickier when the pronoun substitutes for a generic noun that is singular. Because English does not have a singular generic pronoun to fit these situations, writers are left with less-than-ideal choices.

For example, in informal writing and oral language, you may frequently see or hear a plural pronoun used as a substitute for a singular generic noun, as in the ungrammatical example below. In formal writing, such as legal writing, this practice is unacceptable.

EXAMPLE   **UNGRAMMATICAL**

The <u>defendant</u> may claim that <u>their</u> constitutional rights were
    (antecedent)   *(pronoun)*
violated.

Some writers try to solve the problem by resorting to the traditional masculine pronoun for all generic nouns. This practice is unacceptable to many modern writers who believe that language should be nonsexist. (See section 23.4.)

EXAMPLE   **MASCULINE PRONOUN**

The <u>defendant</u> may claim that <u>his</u> constitutional rights were
    (antecedent)   *(pronoun)*
violated.

Occasionally, the problem can be solved by making the generic noun plural. Unfortunately, not all sentences will allow this quick fix.

EXAMPLE   **PLURAL NOUN**

<u>Defendants</u> may claim that <u>their</u> constitutional rights were vio-
(antecedent)   *(pronoun)*
lated.

Even fewer sentences will allow a writer to remove the pronoun altogether without substantial revision or loss in meaning.

EXAMPLE   **REMOVED PRONOUN**

The defendant may claim that the constitutional rights were violated.

The example above avoids the grammatical problem but with a significant loss in meaning: The belief that one actually possesses constitutional rights is no longer included in the sentence's meaning.

What is left, then, is the option of using the slightly awkward "he or she," "his or her," "himself or herself."

EXAMPLE

The <u>defendant</u> may claim that <u>his or her</u> constitutional rights were
    (antecedent)   *(pronouns)*
violated.

While not perfect, this option seems to be the best choice, provided the writer doesn't put more than one "he or she," "his or her," or "himself or herself" in a sentence.

Exception to Rule 1:

Occasionally the word "each" or "every" precedes one or more of the parts of a plural antecedent. In such cases, use a singular pronoun.

> **EXAMPLE**
>
> Every girl and woman in the community feared for her safety.

Rule 2	**When a Pronoun Refers to Two or More Antecedents Joined by "Or" or "Nor," the Pronoun Agrees With the Nearer Antecedent**

> **EXAMPLE**
>
> Either <u>David Wilson</u> or <u>Donald Wilson</u> left <u>his</u> keys in the car.
>   *(antecedent)*   *(antecedent)*   *(pronoun)*

Notice that this rule for pronoun agreement is similar to Rule 3 for subject-verb agreement.

Note

When a singular and a plural antecedent are joined by "or" or "nor," place the plural antecedent last so that the pronoun can be plural.

> **EXAMPLE**
>
> Neither the <u>defendant</u> nor his <u>brothers</u> admit knowing where <u>their</u> neighbors keep items of value.

Rule 3	**When an Indefinite Pronoun Is the Antecedent, Use the Singular Pronoun**

Indefinite pronouns are ones that do not refer to any definite person or thing, or they do not specify definite limits. The most common indefinite pronouns are "all," "any," "anyone," "anybody," "each," "either," "everyone," "everybody," "everything," "neither," "nobody," "no one," "none," "somebody," "someone," and "something."

EXAMPLE

Anyone would have noticed that his or her license plate was removed.

Notice that this rule for pronoun agreement is similar to rule 4 for subject-verb agreement (see page 740).

As with Rule 1, writers must take care not to use the informal and ungrammatical plural pronoun or the traditional generic "he" as a pronoun substitute for an indefinite pronoun.

EXAMPLES

Ungrammatical:

Somebody must have used their phone to call the police.

Masculine pronoun:

Somebody must have used his phone to call the police.

Corrected:

Somebody must have used his or her phone to call the police. *OR*

Somebody must have used the phone to call the police.

Rule 4   **When a Collective Noun Is the Antecedent, Use a Singular Pronoun If You Are Referring to the Group as One Unit and a Plural Pronoun If You Are Referring to the Individual Members of the Group**

Some common collective nouns are "jury," "committee," "appellate court," "Supreme Court," "majority," "board," "team," "family," "audience," "crowd," "number," and the names of companies and corporations. See Exercise 25.G in the *Practice Book*.

The jury must not be misled about Jason Richardson's credibility when it is considering his testimony.

Shopping Haven discriminated against John Adams when it failed to issue him a new credit card for an existing account.

§25.5   PRONOUN REFERENCE

Pronouns are substitutes for nouns. Consequently, pronouns usually[3] refer back to a noun, and that noun is known as the antecedent.

Marino moved for reconsideration, but her motion was denied.
(antecedent)   *(pronoun)*

Legal writers tend to have two kinds of problems with pronouns and their antecedents: (1) they use plural pronouns to refer back to singular antecedents; and (2) they use pronouns that have unclear or ambiguous antecedents. The first problem is one of grammatical agreement, and it is discussed in the second half of section 25.4 on agreement. The second problem is the focus of this section.

§25.5.1   Each Pronoun Should Clearly Refer Back to Its Antecedent

Consider the following sentence:

Officer Robert O'Malley, who arrested Howard Davis, said that he was drunk at the time.

---

3. Indefinite pronouns such as "someone," "anybody," "everything," and "neither" do not refer back to nouns. Also, some pronouns that are parts of idioms ("it is likely that . . . ," "it is clear that . . . ," "it is raining") do not have antecedents.

As it stands, the sentence has two possible readings because the pronoun "he" has two possible antecedents: Officer Robert O'Malley and Howard Davis. To clear up the ambiguity, do one of two things:

1. repeat the noun rather than use a pronoun, or
2. revise so that the pronoun is no longer ambiguous.

EXAMPLE   **POSSIBLE REVISIONS**

Officer Robert O'Malley, who arrested Howard Davis, said that Davis was drunk at the time.

Howard Davis was drunk when he was arrested by Officer O'Malley.

Officer O'Malley was drunk when he arrested Howard Davis.

According to the arresting officer, Robert O'Malley, Howard Davis was drunk at the time of the arrest.

Officer Robert O'Malley, who arrested Howard Davis, admitted being drunk at the time of the arrest.

See Exercise 25.H in the *Practice Book.*

§25.5.2   Avoid the Use of "It," "This," "That," "Such," and "Which" to Refer Broadly to a General Idea in a Preceding Sentence.

Consider the following sentences:

EXAMPLE

Even if Mr. Smith's testimony about possible embarrassment caused by Acme is adequate to justify a damage award, emotional harm is difficult to quantify. This makes it unlikely that Mr. Smith will receive any substantial recovery.

To what does "this" in the second sentence refer? Because it does not seem to refer back to any specific noun in the preceding sentence, the reader is left to guess exactly how much or how little of the preceding discussion "this" is supposed to encompass.

The solution to many broad pronoun reference problems is often a rather simple one: Add a summarizing noun after the pronoun to show the limits of the reference.

EXAMPLE   **CORRECTED**

This <u>difficulty</u> makes it unlikely that Mr. Smith will receive any substantial recovery.

The same technique often works well with "that" and "such."

EXAMPLE

Mrs. Marquette has testified that Mr. Marquette has beaten her and their children on at least three occasions, that he has locked them out of their home twice, and that he has threatened to "cut their throats" if they told anyone. According to Mr. Marquette, that is a lie.

Corrected:

Mrs. Marquette has testified that Mr. Marquette has beaten her and their children on at least three occasions, that he has locked them out of their home twice, and that he has threatened to "cut their throats" if they told anyone. According to Mr. Marquette, that testimony is a lie.

Sometimes it is better to omit "that" and "such" and use only a summarizing noun.

EXAMPLE

A court will consider modifying child custody arrangements if both parents request a modification or if there has been a substantial change in the circumstances. Such has occurred in this case.

Corrected:

A court will consider modifying child custody arrangements if both parents request a modification or if there has been a substantial change in the circumstances. A substantial change in the circumstances has occurred in this case.

The use of the pronoun "which" to refer broadly to a preceding idea is a trickier problem to correct. Look at the following example and see if you can determine what the "which" stands for. Keep in mind the basic rule that a pronoun is a substitute for a noun.

EXAMPLE

In *Boone v. Mullendore,* Dr. Mullendore failed to remove Mrs. Boone's fallopian tube, which resulted in the birth of a baby.

The only nouns that "which" could possibly refer to are the case name, "Dr. Mullendore," and "fallopian tube." Obviously none of these nouns resulted in the birth of a baby. Instead, the writer seems to suggest that "which" is a substitute for the following idea: Dr. Mullendore's failure to remove Mrs. Boone's fallopian tube. Notice that in expressing what the "which" referred to, we had to use the noun "failure" rather than the verb "failed." To correct the error, then, we must add the noun "failure" to the sentence.

EXAMPLE   **CORRECTED**

In *Boone v. Mullendore,* Dr. Mullendore's failure to remove Mrs. Boone's fallopian tube resulted in the birth of a baby.

Notice that in correcting the broad pronoun "which," the writer often omits the word "which."

Sometimes the pronoun "which" appears to refer broadly to a preceding idea but, on closer examination, refers to a noun that appears much earlier in the sentence. To clear up any potential confusion about the "which," the writer can often repeat the previous noun and change the "which" to "that." See Exercise 25.I in the *Practice Book.*

> **EXAMPLE**
>
> Admission of Moore's prior conviction will adversely affect his con-
> stitutional right to testify in his own defense, which is central to
> this case.
>
> ***Corrected:***
>
> Admission of Moore's prior conviction will adversely affect his con-
> stitutional right to testify in his own defense, a right that is central
> to this case.

Note

Be sure to distinguish between the incorrect use of "which" to
refer broadly to a previously stated idea and the correct use of "which"
to introduce nonrestrictive clauses.

§25.5.3   Pronouns Should Refer Back to Nouns, Not Adjectives

Occasionally a word that appears to be a noun is actually an adjective because it modifies a noun.

> **EXAMPLE**
>
> the Rheams building
> *(adjective) (noun)*

Often the possessive form of a noun is used as an adjective in a
sentence.

> **EXAMPLE**
>
> the defendant's alibi
> *(adjective) (noun)*

But because a pronoun must always refer to a noun, adjectives that are noun look-alikes cannot serve as a antecedents for pronouns.

EXAMPLES

Incorrect:

The Rheams building has undergone as many facelifts as he has.

Corrected:

The Rheams building has undergone as many facelifts as Rheams himself has.

Incorrect:

After hearing the defendant's alibi, the jurors seemed to change their opinion of him.

Corrected:

The jurors seemed to change their opinion of the defendant after they heard his alibi.

Admittedly, this rule is a grammatical technicality. Infractions rarely create ambiguity. Even so, because correctness and precision are required in legal writing, it is best to heed the rule. See Exercises 25.J and 25.K in the *Practice Book*.

§25.6   MODIFIERS

Using modifiers correctly is simple. All one has to do is (1) remember to keep modifiers close to the word or words they modify, and (2) make sure the words they modify are in the same sentence as the modifiers.

§25.6.1   Misplaced Modifiers

Forgetting to keep modifiers close to the word or words they modify leads to misplaced modifiers. Some words — "almost," "also," "even," "ever," "exactly," "hardly," "just," "merely," "nearly," "not," "only," "scarcely," "simply" — are particularly prone to being misplaced. Place these words immediately before the words they modify.

Notice, for example, how the placement of "only" changes the meaning in the following sentences.

EXAMPLES

Only the defendant thought that the car was rented.
No one but the defendant thought that.

The defendant only thought that the car was rented.
He did not know for sure.

The defendant thought only that the car was rented.
He thought one thing, nothing else.

The defendant thought that the only car was rented.
Only one car was available, and it was rented.

The defendant thought that the car was only rented.
He did not think it was leased or sold.

Note

In speech, such single-word modifiers are often put before the verb even when the speaker does not intend them to modify the verb. Some authorities accept placing "only" immediately before the verb if it modifies the whole sentence.

Speech:	He only drove ten miles.
Writing:	He drove only ten miles.

Phrases, particularly prepositional phrases, can also be easily misplaced in sentences. The result can be imprecise writing, an awkward construction, and unintentional humor.

The writer of the following example was surprised to find out that because of a misplaced modifier he had inaccurately placed the brother instead of the cabin in New Hampshire.

EXAMPLE

The defendant owned a cabin with his brother in New Hampshire.

Revised:

The defendant and his brother owned a cabin in New Hampshire.

In the following example, the phrase "contrary to the wishes of his wife" is both awkward and misleading; it seems to be modifying "form."

EXAMPLE

Mr. Barry mailed the form contrary to the wishes of his wife to the home office in Toronto.

The sentence can be made a bit clearer by treating the phrase "contrary to the wishes of his wife" as an interruptor and setting it off from the rest of the sentence with commas. Now the phrase does not appear to modify "form." Better still, to improve the sentence construction and to show that the phrase modifies the entire clause "Mr. Barry mailed the form to the home office in Toronto," revise the sentence as follows.

EXAMPLE   REVISED

Contrary to the wishes of his wife, Mr. Barry mailed the form to the home office in Toronto.

The misplaced modifier in the following example gave the writer a meaning she never intended.

EXAMPLE

The witness to the events may be unavailable after the accident.

Although there are contexts in which this sentence is correctly written, the writer intended to say, "The witness to the events after the accident may be unavailable." Her version made it sound like an intentional "accident" was being planned for the specific purpose of making the witness "unavailable"!

Take care to place clauses that begin with "who," "which," and "that" immediately after the noun they modify.

EXAMPLE

The victim described her attacker as having a tattoo on his right buttock, which was shaped like a peace sign.

This sentence suggests that the attacker's right buttock, not his tattoo, was shaped like a peace sign.

EXAMPLE   **REVISED**

The victim described her attacker as having a tattoo that was shaped like a peace sign on his right buttock.

See Examples 25.L, 25.M, and 25.N in the *Practice Book.*

§25.6.2   Dangling Modifiers

Dangling modifiers are those modifiers that do not have a noun in the sentence that they can modify; hence, they are "dangling," or unattached to an appropriate noun. Legal writers tend to write dangling modifiers for one of two reasons: (1) the noun or pronoun the modifier is intended to modify is in the mind of the writer but inadvertently omitted from the sentence; or (2) the writer wanted to avoid the first person pronouns "I" or "we"[4] and, in doing so, left a modifier dangling.

EXAMPLE

By calling attention to the defendant's post-arrest silence, the jury was allowed to make prejudicial and false inferences.

In the example above, the modifier "by calling attention to the defendant's post-arrest silence" should modify the noun "the prosecutor," which does not appear in the sentence. Unfortunately, it seems to be modifying the noun closest to it: "the jury."

---

4. Many authorities on legal writing still advise legal writers to avoid using first-person references.

EXAMPLE   **REVISED**

By calling attention to the defendant's post-arrest silence, the prosecutor encouraged the jury to make prejudicial and false inferences.

Notice how in the following example the dangling modifier can be corrected by including the pronoun it modifies, "we," or by revising the sentence so that the dangling modifier is no longer a modifier.

EXAMPLE

In deciding whether to attempt to quash service, more than the technical merits of the case have to be considered.

Revised:

In deciding whether to attempt to quash service, we must consider more than the technical merits of the case. *OR*

A decision about whether to attempt to quash service must be based on more than the technical merits of the case.

You can see that the majority of dangling modifiers occur at the beginnings of sentences. One way to avoid writing this type of dangling modifier is to remember to place the noun the modifier modifies right after the comma separating the modifier from the main clause.

Modifier,	Main Clause
(noun)	

By calling attention . . . silence, the prosecutor. . . .

If you are having difficulty deciding what noun the modifier should modify, ask yourself who or what is doing the action described in that modifier. Then place the answer to that question right after the comma separating the modifier from the main clause.

In deciding . . . service, we must consider . . . .

Notice too that when the real actor in a sentence is in the subject position, the problem of dangling modifiers is usually solved. (See section 22.2 for more on using effective subjects in sentences.)

Note

Many kinds of grammatical structures can be dangling. The most common are participles (marked by the "-ing," "-ed," or past endings), infinitives (to + verb, "to show"), and prepositional phrases.

Some dangling modifiers can also be corrected by adding a subject to the modifier.

EXAMPLE

While petitioning for a permit, zoning regulations in the area were changed.

Revised:

While the mental institution was petitioning for a permit, zoning regulations in the area were changed.

Note

Subordinate clauses, like the one in the revision above, are not dangling modifiers.

Dangling modifiers can also occur at the ends of sentences. Again, the problem is that the noun the modifier modifies does not appear in the sentence.

EXAMPLE

This motion was denied in the interest of judicial economy, reasoning that there was evidence that raised a question regarding Anderson's knowledge of the relationship.

Who or what is doing the reasoning that there is evidence? Most certainly the court, but the noun "court" does not appear in the sentence.

EXAMPLE   **REVISED**

Reasoning that there was evidence that raised a question regarding Anderson's knowledge of the relationship, the court denied this motion in the interest of judicial economy.

It is also permissible to leave the modifier at the end of the sentence, as long as it modifies the subject of the sentence.

EXAMPLE   **REVISED**

The court denied this motion in the interest of judicial economy, reasoning that there was evidence that raised a question regarding Anderson's knowledge of the relationship.

The example could also be correctly revised by changing the modifier to a subordinate clause. See Exercise 25.O in the *Practice Book.*

EXAMPLE   **REVISED**

The court denied this motion in the interest of judicial economy because there was evidence that raised a question regarding Anderson's knowledge of the relationship.

§25.6.3   Squinting Modifiers

Squinting modifiers are labeled as such because they appear to be looking both backward and forward in a sentence; that is, they appear to be modifying both the word that precedes them and the word that follows them.

EXAMPLE

The bridge inspection that was done frequently suggested that the drawbridge electrical system was beginning to fail.

This sentence has two possible interpretations: Are the inspections themselves done frequently, or are there frequent suggestions throughout the inspection report?

EXAMPLE   **REVISED**

The bridge inspection that was frequently done suggested that the drawbridge electrical system was beginning to fail. *OR*

The bridge inspection that was done suggested frequently that the drawbridge electrical system was beginning to fail.

---

§25.7   PARALLELISM

Consider the following pairs of sentences. What is it about version B of each pair that makes it easier to read?

EXAMPLE

1A. The defendant claims that on the day of the murder he was at home alone washing his car, he mowed his lawn, and his dog needed a bath so he gave him one.

1B. The defendant claims that on the day of the murder he was at home alone washing his car, mowing his lawn, and bathing his dog.

2A. Dr. Stewart is a competent surgeon with over twenty years of experience and who is respected in the local medical community.

2B. Dr. Stewart is a competent surgeon who has over twenty years of experience and who is respected in the local medical community.

3A. The defendant claimed the evidence was prejudicial and that it lacked relevance.

3B. The defendant claimed the evidence was prejudicial and irrelevant.

In all the preceding pairs, the version A sentences lack parallelism and, as a result, are grammatically incorrect, as well as clumsy and unsophisticated. The version B sentences do not change the content significantly; they simply use the structure of the sentence to make that content more apparent and more accessible. Specifically, they use parallelism.

In grammar, parallelism is defined as "the use of similar grammatical form for coordinated elements." This definition may seem overly abstract or vague until it is broken into its components.

"Coordinated elements" are parts of a sentence joined by conjunctions, such as "and," "but," "or," "nor," and "yet." Sometimes they are pairs, but often they are a series or a list.

"Similar grammatical form" simply means that a noun is matched with other nouns, verbs are matched with other verbs, prepositional phrases are matched with other prepositional phrases, and so on.

For example, look at the poorly coordinated elements in sentence 1A above.

> washing his car,
> he mowed his lawn, and
> his dog needed a bath so he gave him one

Even without analyzing exactly what kind of phrase or clause each one of these elements is, we can see that they do not have similar grammatical form. Now look at the coordinated elements of sentence 1B. Note how the "-ing" endings make the items parallel.

> washing his car
> mowing his lawn, and
> bathing his dog

Matching endings of the first key word in each of the elements is one way to make elements parallel.

Now compare the coordinated elements in 2A and 2B.

> 2A.   with over twenty years of experience and
>   who is respected in the local medical community

> 2B.   who has over twenty years of experience and
>   who is respected in the local medical community

Again, without doing an analysis of the grammar of each element, we can see, or perhaps hear, that 2B is parallel, but this time the parallelism is signaled by using the same word, "who," to introduce each element.

In some cases, however, you will not be able to rely on matching endings to key words or matching introductory words; you will have to find the same grammatical form in order to make the elements parallel.

In 3A, for example, the writer has tried to match an adjective, "prejudicial," with a relative clause, "that it lacked relevance." The writer could have used the second tip — matching introductory words — and created the following parallel elements:

> that the evidence was prejudicial and
> that it lacked relevance

The more concise and better choice is to find the appropriate adjective to match "prejudicial."

> prejudicial and
> irrelevant

Because many sentences in legal writing are long and complicated, parallelism is critical for keeping the content and its presentation manageable. In the following sentence, for example, the defendant's two concessions are easier for the reader to see because they are set out in parallel construction.

EXAMPLE

Counsel for the defendant conceded that she did assault Coachman and that a trial would determine only the degree of the assault.

---

conceded $\Bigg<$ that she did assault Coachman

that a trial would determine only the degree of the assault

Notice too in both the preceding and subsequent examples that by repeating the introductory word "that," the writer has made the parallelism more obvious, which, in turn, makes the sentence easier to read.

EXAMPLE

When questioned at the parole hearing, Robinson claimed that it was wrong to tell only one side of the story, that he had not received permission but felt he had a right to write what he wanted, and that people had a right to hear the other side of the story.

---

claimed
- that it was wrong to tell only one side of the story,
- that he had not received permission but felt he had a right to write what he wanted, and
- that people had a right to hear the other side of the story.

Note

Writing parallel elements is required for grammatical sentences; repeating an introductory word to heighten the parallelism is not required, but rather recommended for making the parallelism more obvious to the reader.

Issue statements can also become much more manageable when the legally significant facts are laid out using parallel construction. The following example uses "when" as the introductory word to each element. Notice too how the legally significant facts are not only written using parallel construction but also grouped according to those that favor the defendant and those that favor the plaintiff. The conjunction "but" helps the reader see the two groupings.

EXAMPLE

Under Federal Rule of Civil Procedure 4(d)(1), is service of process valid when process was left with defendant's husband at his home in California, when defendant and her husband maintain separate residences, when defendant intends to maintain a separate residence from her husband, but when the defendant regularly visits her husband in California, when the defendant keeps some personal belongings in the California house, when defendant receives some mail in California, and when defendant received actual notice when her husband mailed the summons and complaint to her?

---

when process was left with defendant's husband at his home in California

when defendant and her husband maintain separate residences

when defendant intends to maintain separate residence from her husband, BUT

when defendant regularly visits her husband in California

when the defendant keeps some personal belongings in the California house

when defendant receives some mail in California

when defendant received actual notice when her husband mailed the summons and complaint to her

Parallelism is also critical, indeed required, when setting out lists.

EXAMPLE

Wilson challenges the admission of three photographs, which he claims are gruesome: (1) the photograph of Melissa Reed as she appeared when discovered at the crime scene; (2) the photograph of Melinda Reed as she appeared when discovered at the crime scene; and (3) a photograph of Wilson wearing dental retractors to hold his lips back while exposing his teeth.

Lists require parallelism when they are incorporated into the writer's text, as in the example above, and when they are indented and tabulated, as in the example below.

EXAMPLE

The school district will probably be liable for the following:

1. the cost of restoring the Archers' rose bushes, as well as the lost use value of their property during restoration;
2. the cost of replacing Mr. Baker's windows and the market value of his vase; and
3. compensation to the Carlisles for the annoyance and inconvenience they have experienced.

Note

To create parallelism, match the *key* words in each element; the parallelism is not destroyed if all the modifying words and phrases do not match exactly.

In the following examples, the key words "received" and "released" match, and the key words "for . . . harm" and "for . . . expenses" match.

EXAMPLES

In *Pepper,* the injured plaintiff <u>received</u> medical treatment and <u>released</u> the defendant from liability.

The Bells are seeking damages <u>for severe emotional and financial harm</u> and <u>for substantial medical expenses</u> related to the pregnancy.

To summarize, then, writers can correct problems in parallelism in one of three ways:

1. match the endings of key words,
2. match introductory words, or
3. use the same grammatical form.

See Exercise 25.P in the *Practice Book.*

Earlier we said that parallelism is required for coordinated elements joined by "and," "but," "or," "nor," and "yet." Parallelism is also required for elements joined by correlative conjunctions.

The most common correlative conjunctions are "either ... or," "neither ... nor," "not only ... but also," "both ... and," "whether ... or," and "as ... as."

To make the elements joined by one of these pairs parallel, simply match what follows the first half with what follows the second half.

either _____	either <u>similar</u>
or _____	or <u>identical</u>

EXAMPLE

Campbell's prior convictions are either similar or identical.

---

neither _____	neither <u>the photographs</u>
nor _____	nor <u>the testimony</u>

EXAMPLE

Neither the photographs nor the testimony can prove who actually committed the alieged assault.

---

not only _____   not only <u>verbally</u>
but also _____   but also <u>physically</u>

EXAMPLE

The defendant admits that she not only verbally but also physically abused her children.

Take care when using these pairs. All too frequently legal writers lose the parallelism in their sentences by misplacing one of the words in these pairs.

EXAMPLE

The purpose of the rule is to ensure that actual notice is provided either by personal or constructive service.

---

either _____   either <u>by personal</u>
or _____   or <u>constructive</u>

"By personal" is not parallel with "constructive."

EXAMPLES   REVISED

The purpose of the rule is to ensure that actual notice is provided either by personal or by constructive service. *OR*

The purpose of the rule is to ensure that actual notice is provided by either personal or constructive service.

Parallelism is also required when elements are compared or contrasted. Many of the comparing and contrasting expressions use "than."

more than   less than   rather than

EXAMPLES

Wilson's attention was centered more on the assailant's gun than on his face.

The court applied the "clearly erroneous" standard rather than the arbitrary and capricious standard.

See Exercise 25.Q in the *Practice Book.*

Chapter 26

Punctuation

§26.1 THE COMMA

Commas are everywhere. They are the most frequently used punctuation mark and, unfortunately, the most frequently misused punctuation mark. They give most legal writers fits. Few writers seem to be able to control the little buzzards, and most seem to be more than a bit controlled by them. Many fairly good legal writers admit that they punctuate by feel, especially when it comes to commas. They rely on the "rule" that one should use a comma whenever the reader should pause — advice that works about 70 percent of the time and fails about 30 percent of the time.

It is no wonder that few legal writers know and apply all the rules for commas. There are too many of them. In this section, we will have no fewer than twenty rules, all designed to govern one little punctuation mark. Even so, these twenty rules don't cover every conceivable use of the comma, just the high spots.

The good news, however, is that not all of these rules are equally important. Some are critical; misapplication of these rules will either miscue the reader or change the meaning of a sentence as significantly as a misplaced decimal can change the meaning of a number. The critical rules are listed under the heading "Critical Commas: Those That Affect Meaning and Clarity."

The next section, "Basic Commas: Those That Educated Readers Expect," includes all the commonly known comma rules. Using these rules incorrectly probably will not affect meaning, but it may distract the reader and even cause him or her to wonder about the writer's professionalism.

There are other comma rules, though, that the average reader will not know, and he or she will not notice whether they are applied correctly. Still, these rules are helpful to writers who not only care about writing correctly but also recognize that knowing the more esoteric

EXHIBIT 26.1   Overview of the Comma Rules

OVERVIEW OF THE COMMA RULES

CRITICAL COMMAS: Those That Affect Meaning and Clarity

Rule 1.   Use a comma before a coordinating conjunction joining two main clauses.

The prosecutor spoke about the defendant's motive, and the jury listened carefully.

Rule 2.   Use a comma to set off long introductory phrases or clauses from the main clause.

Using their overhead lights and sirens, the police followed the defendant out of the area.

Rule 3.   Use a comma to prevent a possible misreading.

At the time, the prosecution informed Jones that it would recommend a sentence of eighteen months.

Rule 4.   Use a comma to set off nonrestrictive phrases or clauses.

Officer Bates, acting as a decoy, remained outside on the sidewalk.

BASIC COMMAS: Those That Educated Readers Expect

Rule 5.   Set off nonrestrictive appositives with commas.

A corrections officer called Diane Cummins, the defendant's girlfriend.

Rule 6.   Set off nonrestrictive participial phrases with a comma or commas.

The trial court denied the motion, finding that the seizure fell under the plain view doctrine.

EXHIBIT 26.1   *(continued)*

Rule 7. **Use a comma or commas to set off transitional or interrupting words and phrases.**

The trial court, however, imposed an exceptional sentence of thirty months.

Rule 8. **Use commas according to convention with quotation marks.**

Corbin said, "I never saw the other car."

Rule 9. **Use a comma or commas to set off phrases of contrast.**

Adams initially indicated that he, not Wilson, was involved in the robbery.

Rule 10. **Use commas between items in a series.**

Wong had no money, identification, or jewelry.

Rule 11. **Use a comma between coordinate adjectives not joined by a conjunction.**

The contract was written in concise, precise language.

Rule 12. **Use commas according to convention with dates, addresses, and names of geographical locations.**

The land in Roswell, New Mexico, was surveyed on October 4, 1991, and purchased less than a month later.

ESOTERIC COMMAS: Those That Are Required in Sophisticated Sentence Structures

Rule 13. **Use commas to set off absolutes.**

His career destroyed, Williams lapsed into a state of depression.

EXHIBIT 26.1 *(continued)*

Rule 14. **Use a comma to indicate an omission of a word or words that can be understood from the context.**

The first witness said the attacker was "hairy"; the second, bald.

Rule 15. **Use commas to set off expressions that introduce examples or explanations.**

Collins testified that Adams had participated in the robbery and had fenced some of the items, namely, a camera, stereo, and silver.

UNNECESSARY COMMAS: Those That Should Be Omitted

Rule 16. **Do not use a comma to set off restrictive adverbial clauses that follow the main clause.**

Complicity may be found if a defendant participates in the early stages of an activity that results in the attack on the victim.

Rule 17. **Do not use a comma to separate a subject from its verb or a verb from its object.**

The idea that an individual can obtain another person's property through adverse possession is difficult for many people to accept.

Rule 18. **Do not use a comma to separate correlative pairs unless the correlatives introduce main clauses.**

Neither the United States Supreme Court nor this court has ever ruled that a defendant has a due process right to an instruction on lesser included offenses.

*Rule 19. **Do not use a comma between a conjunction and introductory modifiers or clauses.**

The fire had completely destroyed the trailer, and according to the fire chief, there was some concern that the overhead structure of the barn would collapse.

EXHIBIT 26.1   *(continued)*

***Rule 20.   Do not use a comma between "that" and introductory modi-
fiers or clauses.**

He testified that when they returned to his hotel room, Wells demanded
a $150 fee.

*Some authorities disagree on these comma rules.

---

comma rules allows them to add to their repertoire those sentence
structures that require using these rules.

Finally, the last group of comma rules includes those situations in
which commas are inserted unnecessarily. Please notice, too, that some
of the last rules are marked with an asterisk (*). The asterisk indicates
those few comma rules about which some authorities disagree. See Exhibit 26.1.

One final comment before launching into this comma extravagan-
za: More and more editors and writers favor what has come to be called
"open punctuation." Open punctuation means using only as much punctuation as is necessary to make the meaning clear. "Close punctuation"
is just the opposite; using as much punctuation as the rules will allow.
Given the current preference for open punctuation, then, you may want
to omit the comma when the rules and context make it optional simply
because every unnecessary pause breaks up the flow of the writing.

§26.1.1   Critical Commas: Those That Affect Meaning and Clarity

---

| **Rule 1** | **Use a Comma Before a Coordinating Conjunction Joining Two Main, or Independent, Clauses** |

Reminder

There are seven coordinating conjunctions: "and," "but," "or,"
"for," "nor," "yet," and "so."[1]

---

1. Some writers prefer to use a semicolon before "yet" and "so." The semicolon signals a longer pause.

Reminder

A main, or independent, clause has its own subject and verb, and it can stand alone as a sentence.

Brackets mark the main clauses in the following examples.

$$
\underset{[\textit{main clause}]}{\underline{\qquad\qquad}} , \quad \overset{\text{coordinating}}{\underset{}{\text{conjunction}}} \quad \underset{[\textit{main clause}]}{\underline{\qquad\qquad}}
$$

EXAMPLES

[The prosecutor spoke about the defendant's motive], and [the jury listened carefully.]

[The corrections officer contacted several other persons], but [none knew of Wilson's disappearance.]

When applying Rule 1, be sure that you are not mistakenly assuming that a comma must precede every coordinating conjunction. It precedes those coordinating conjunctions that join two main clauses.

In the example below, "but" is preceded by a comma because it joins two main clauses. "And," on the other hand, joins two noun phrases ("the motion to sever" and "the motion for a new trial"), not two main clauses, so it is not preceded by a comma.

EXAMPLE

[The trial court did not err in denying the motion to sever and the motion for a new trial], but [it did err in giving the accomplice liability instruction.]

In addition, be sure to distinguish between sentences with two main clauses (subject-verb, and subject-verb), which require a comma before the conjunction, and sentences with compound verbs (subject-verb and verb), which do not require a comma before the conjunction.

EXAMPLES

Two Main Clauses:

The defendant's girlfriend denied that she knew where he was, and she refused to answer any more questions.

Compound Verbs:

The defendant's girlfriend denied that she knew where he was and refused to answer any more questions.

Writers who omit the comma before a coordinating conjunction joining two main clauses miscue their readers. No comma before a coordinating conjunction signals the second half of a pair of structures other than main clauses. This error is often labeled a fused sentence or run-on sentence. When the main clauses are short and closely related, the comma before the coordinating conjunction may be omitted.

EXAMPLE

The prosecutor spoke and the jury listened.

Exception to Rule 1

When the main clauses are long or when they have internal punctuation, use a semicolon before the coordinating conjunction.

EXAMPLE

After analyzing the defendant's claim under ER 401, the court rejected it, explaining that the evidence at issue was relevant to the question of falsity; and because falsity was an element to be proved by the plaintiff, the evidence met the ER 401 requirements of probative value and materiality.

See Exercise 26.A in the *Practice Book.*

Rule 2	Use a Comma to Set Off Long Introductory Clauses or Phrases From the Main, or Independent, Clause

If a main, or independent, clause is preceded by introductory material, the reader will need a comma to signal where the introductory material ends and where the independent clause begins.

```
_____ , _____
[long introductory            [main clause]
clause or phrase]
```

Long introductory clauses that must be set off with a comma are easy to spot. Because they are clauses, they will have a subject and a verb. Because they are subordinate, not main, clauses, they will also begin with a subordinating conjunction such as "after," "although," "as," "because," "before," "if," "unless," "until," "when," or "where." (See section 25.1 for more on subordinate clauses and subordinating conjunctions.)

EXAMPLES

As the Court of Appeals noted, delivery would require actual or constructive possession by the accused.

If the accident was unavoidable, Smith's intoxication was not "a cause . . . without which the death would not have occurred."

When Abbott failed to return to the work release facility, a corrections officer called his mother's home.

Of the many kinds of introductory phrases used in legal writing, the most common are prepositional phrases, infinitive phrases, and participial phrases. (Section 25.1 defines and explains prepositions, infinitives, and participles. It is not critical, however, to be able to identify the types of introductory phrases to punctuate them correctly.)

EXAMPLES

Introductory Prepositional Phrase:

In the present case, the record shows that Thompson initially assaulted Blevins.

Introductory Infinitive Phrase:

To support a finding that the trial court abused its discretion, a defendant must point to specific prejudice.

Introductory Participial Phrase:

Using their overhead lights and sirens, the police followed the defendant out of the area.

Note

Be sure to distinguish between introductory participial phrases, which modify the subject, and gerunds that are the subject. (See section 25.1 for more on gerunds.) A gerund subject should not be followed by a comma. To do so would separate a subject from its verb. (See Rule 17 in this section.) Compare the use of the phrase "using their overhead lights and sirens" in the preceding and subsequent examples. Both are punctuated correctly.

EXAMPLE   **GERUND SUBJECT**

Using their overhead lights and sirens was routine procedure.

Notice that long introductory phrases are often made up of several prepositional phrases or a combination of prepositional, infinitive, and participial phrases.

EXAMPLES

Two Introductory Prepositional Phrases:

[On the evening] [of August 13, 1990], Larry Utter was robbed at gunpoint while making a deposit at a local bank.

Introductory Prepositional and Infinitive Phrases:

[At the hearing] [on McDonald's motion] [to dismiss], the parties stipulated to the admission of an incident report prepared by McDonald's probation officer.

Furthermore, there is no specific rule for what constitutes a "long" phrase or clause. An introductory phrase or clause of four or more words is usually set off with a comma, but writers have some discretion, particularly with introductory phrases.

Short prepositional phrases, for example, are often set off by a comma, especially when the writer wants to emphasize the information in the phrase, as with dates or case names.

EXAMPLES

In 1988, the Oltmans removed the fence separating their property from the farm.

In *Harris,* the defendant was charged with first degree robbery.

Short, introductory transitional expressions, such as "consequently," "for example," "however," "nevertheless," "therefore," and "on the other hand," are almost always set off by a comma.

EXAMPLES

Consequently, unlawful restraint is invariably an element of the greater offense of attempted kidnapping.

Nevertheless, the defendant maintains that he was in Boston when the robbery occurred.

See Exercise 26.B in the *Practice Book.*

Rule 3   **Use a Comma to Prevent a Possible Misreading**

A reader should be able to read your sentences correctly the first time. If a comma can prevent a possible misreading, it should be included.

EXAMPLES

Confusing:

People who can usually hire their own lawyer.

Revised:

People who can, usually hire their own lawyer.

Although under Rule 2 you have the discretion to omit a comma after a short introductory material, you must use the comma if a reader might at first mistakenly assume that part of the main clause is part of the introductory material.

EXAMPLES

Confusing:

At the time the prosecution informed Jones that it would recommend a sentence of 18 months.

Revised:

At the time, the prosecution informed Jones that it would recommend a sentence of 18 months.

See Exercise 26.C in the *Practice Book.*

| **Rule 4** | **Use a Comma to Set Off Nonrestrictive Phrases or Clauses** |

Nonrestrictive phrases or clauses do not restrict or limit the words they modify. They give additional information.

Restrictive phrases or clauses restrict or limit the words they modify. They add essential information.

EXAMPLES

Nonrestrictive Phrase:

Officer Bates, <u>acting as a decoy</u>, remained outside on the sidewalk.

Nonrestrictive Clause:

Officer Bates, <u>who acted as a decoy,</u> remained outside on the sidewalk.

In both of the examples above, "Officer Bates" is completely identified by her name. "Acting as a decoy" or "who acted as a decoy" does not give restricting or limiting information, so both are set off by commas.

If the name of the officer were unknown, the writer may need to use the phrase or clause as a way to identify the officer. The phrase or clause would then be restrictive because it would limit the meaning of "officer." When used as a restrictive phrase or clause, the same words are not set off by commas.

EXAMPLES

Restrictive Phrase:

An officer <u>acting as a decoy</u> remained outside on the sidewalk.

Restrictive Clause:

An officer <u>who acted as a decoy</u> remained outside on the sidewalk.

A few more examples may be helpful in learning to distinguish which phrases and clauses are nonrestrictive and therefore set off by commas.

EXAMPLE   **NONRESTRICTIVE CLAUSE**

The child's father, who is six months behind in his child support payments, has fled the state.

"The child's father" clearly identifies the individual in question; "who is six months behind in his child support payments" does not restrict or limit the meaning of "the child's father," even though it is important information for understanding the sentence.

EXAMPLE **RESTRICTIVE CLAUSE**

The uncle who lives in Oklahoma has agreed to care for the child until an appropriate foster home is found.

This sentence suggests that the child has more than one uncle. "Who lives in Oklahoma" restricts or limits the meaning of "the uncle." It is the uncle in Oklahoma, not the one in Arkansas, who has agreed to care for the child.

Notice that whether a phrase or clause is punctuated as restrictive or nonrestrictive can significantly change the meaning of a sentence.

EXAMPLE

Attorneys who intentionally prolong litigation for personal gain misuse the legal system.

The preceding sentence says that there is a restricted or limited group of attorneys — those who intentionally prolong litigation for personal gain — who misuse the legal system.

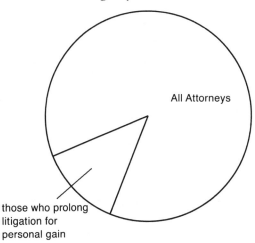

All Attorneys

those who prolong litigation for personal gain

EXAMPLE

Attorneys, who intentionally prolong litigation for personal gain, misuse the legal system.

The preceding sentence does not refer to a restricted or limited group of attorneys. It says that all attorneys misuse the legal system and that all attorneys intentionally prolong litigation for personal gain.

All attorneys
prolong litigation
for personal gain.

Note

Restrictive and nonrestrictive clauses that modify people begin with "who" or "whom." Careful writers still observe the usage rule that restrictive clauses that modify things or objects use "that" and nonrestrictive clauses that modify things or objects use "which." (See the Glossary of Usage for an extended explanation and more examples of the distinction between "that" and "which.")

EXAMPLES

Incorrect Usage:

The instruction which is unchallenged is an accomplice instruction that includes the "ready to assist" language.

Revised:

The instruction that is unchallenged is an accomplice instruction that includes the "ready to assist" language. *OR*

Instruction 21, which is unchallenged, is an accomplice instruction that includes the "ready to assist" language.

The following chart sums up the key points in Rule 4.

Restrictive	restricts the word it modifies	no commas	who/whom that
Nonrestrictive	does not restrict the word it modifies	commas	who/whom which

See Exercises 26.D and 26.E in the *Practice Book*.

§26.1.2   Basic Commas: Those That Educated Readers Expect

Rule 5   Set Off Nonrestrictive Appositives With Commas

Reminder

Appositives are nouns or noun substitutes that follow another noun to identify it or further describe it.

EXAMPLE

A corrections officer called <u>Diane Cummins</u>, <u>the defendant's girl-</u>
                                    (noun)   *(appositive)*
<u>friend</u>.

Because most appositives are nonrestrictive, they need to be set off with commas. However, restrictive appositives, like the restrictive phrases and clauses in Rule 4, add essential information that restricts or limits the preceding noun; therefore, restrictive appositives are not set off with commas.

EXAMPLE   NONRESTRICTIVE APPOSITIVE

The court sentenced the defendant, a juvenile, to a term outside the standard range.

There is only one defendant; "a juvenile" adds additional, not restricting or limiting, information about the defendant.

EXAMPLE   RESTRICTIVE APPOSITIVE

The defendant's brother Joseph contradicted the story another brother Daniel told to the police.

The defendant has more than one brother, so the noun phrases "defendant's brother" and "another brother" must be restricted or limited by the brothers' names.

Some appositives are introduced by the word "or." Be sure to distinguish between the oppositional "or," which is a restatement of or explanation for the preceding noun, and the disjunctive "or," which introduces an alternative to the preceding noun.

EXAMPLES

Appositional "Or":

You may designate an attorney-in-fact, or agent, to make your health care decisions in the event you are unable to do so. ("Attorney-in-fact" and "agent" are the same thing.)

Disjunctive "Or":

The girl's father or uncle always accompanied her on dates. ("Father" and "uncle" are alternatives.)

Rule 6	**Set Off Nonrestrictive Participial Phrases With a Comma or Commas**

Reminder

Participles, which are formed from verbs, can serve as adjectives. Present participles have an "-ing" ending; past participles have a variety of endings, depending on whether the verb is regular or irregular. Common past participle endings include "-d," "-ed," "-t," "-n," and "-en."

verb	*present participle*	*past participle*
reason	reasoning	reasoned
find	finding	found

Many sentences in legal writing use a beginning or an ending participial phrase to describe the rationale for the action expressed in the main verb. Such participial phrases are not dangling or misplaced (see section 25.6.2) if, as in the following examples, they modify the subject of the sentence.

EXAMPLES

Reasoning that the sentence imposed was disproportionate to the gravity of the offense, the State Supreme Court reversed and remanded for resentencing.

The State Supreme Court reversed and remanded for resentencing, reasoning that the sentence imposed was disproportionate to the gravity of the offense.

Finding that the seizure fell under the plain view doctrine, the trial court denied the motion.

The trial court denied the motion, finding that the seizure fell under the plain view doctrine.

Restrictive participial phrases should not be set off with commas. In the following example, "washing his hands" restricts or limits the meaning of "the man." See Exercise 26.F in the *Practice Book.*

EXAMPLE

The attendant noticed blood on the shirt of the man washing his hands.

Rule 7	Use a Comma or Commas to Set Off Transitional or Interrupting Words and Phrases

Legal writers frequently break the flow of a sentence intentionally by inserting a word or phrase in the middle of a main clause. Readers have no trouble understanding what the main clause is and what the transitional or interrupting word or phrase is as long as those transitions or interrupters are set off with commas.

$$\underline{\hspace{3cm}} , \; \underline{\text{interrupter}} , \; \underline{\hspace{3cm}}$$
(main)   *(clause)*

EXAMPLES

The trial court, however, imposed an exceptional sentence of thirty months.

The Court of Appeals held that Wells, through her own fault and connivance, caused the delay between the time the State filed the information and the time of Wells's arraignment.

Note, however, that many of the same transitional words and phrases (for example, "however," "therefore," "on the other hand," "for example") that interrupt a main clause can also be used between two main clauses. Be sure to distinguish between the two and punctuate accordingly.

EXAMPLES

Interrupter:

His vision, therefore, was blurred.

Transition between two main clauses:

The driver lost his contact lenses; therefore, his vision was blurred.

Rule 8	**Use Commas According to Convention With Quotation Marks**

Commas are frequently used to separate short or informal quotations from words in the same sentence that introduce, interrupt, or follow the quotation.

EXAMPLES

Corbin said, "I never saw the other car."

"I never saw the other car," Corbin said, "until it was right on top of me."

"I never saw the other car," said Corbin.

Note

Commas are placed inside closing quotation marks,[2] but outside closing parentheses or brackets.

EXAMPLES

Inside Closing Quotation Marks:

Identification searches are valid if limited to wallets or other "common repositories of identification papers," and the examination is confined to locating a driver's license or similar document. 3 W. LaFave, *Search and Seizure* § 9.4(g), at 545-46 (1987).

A 24-month sentence does not appear to be "clearly excessive," especially when the presumptive range of 12-14 months could have been increased by 12 months under Wash. Rev. Code § 9.94A.310 (1989).

Outside Closing Parentheses:

Both of the defendants are young (19 and 20), and both of them are first-time offenders.

---

2. In Great Britain a comma is placed inside closing quotation marks only if it is part of the quotation.

Quotations that are immediately preceded by "that" do not have a comma between the quotation and "that."

EXAMPLE

In *Herron v. King,* the court stated that "actual malice can be inferred from circumstantial evidence including . . . the reporter's knowledge that his sources are hostile to the plaintiff . . . ." 109 Wash. 2d at 524, 746 P.2d at 302.

See Exercise 26.G in the *Practice Book.*

Rule 9	**Use a Comma or Commas to Set Off Phrases of Contrast**

Phrases of contrast usually begin with "not," "but," or "yet."

EXAMPLES

Adams initially indicated that he, not Wilson, was involved in the robbery.

The court of appeals affirmed the trial court, but on different grounds.

Note

Some writers occasionally omit commas with phrases of contrast that begin with "but." These writers would omit the comma before the "but" in the preceding example. Either way is correct. In addition, commas are usually omitted between elements joined by the paired conjunctions "not only . . . but also . . . ."

EXAMPLES

The trial court not only overruled defense counsel's repeated objections but also accused the defendant's attorney of intentionally delaying the proceedings.

The memorandum suggested that interviewers not only look more favorably at applicants who are 35 or under but also disregard applicants who are 50 or over.

Rule 10	**Use Commas Between Items in a Series**

Reminder

A series is three or more items that are grouped together and that are in the same grammatical form. Each item may be as short as one word or as long as a clause.

EXAMPLES

Series of Single Words:

Wong had no money, identification, or jewelry.

Series of Verb Phrases:

Mason moved at least twice during the period of his escape, changed his name and his appearance, and held four or five jobs.

Series of Clauses:

Jones could not remember who he was, where he lived, what he did for a living, or what he had done during the last two weeks.

Even a series composed of short main clauses can use commas to separate the items.

EXAMPLE

Matthews pulled a knife on O'Hara, she screamed, and he turned and ran away.

Note

Although the comma before the final "and" in a series is sometimes described as "optional," legal writers should make it a habit to include it because some sentences become ambiguous when that comma is omitted.

EXAMPLE

Mrs. Corsini wants her property divided equally among the following relatives: Michael Corsini, Glenda Corsini, Ralph Meyers, Joanna Mitchem, Louis Mitchem, Donna Mitchem and Donald Mitchem.

Should the property be divided six or seven ways? Assume Donna Mitchem and Donald Mitchem are married. Did Grandmother Corsini intend for the couple to get one-sixth of her property, or did she intend for each of them to receive one-seventh?

Adding a comma before the final "and" tells the reader that the property should be divided seven ways. Adding another "and" before "Donna Mitchem" says that it should be divided six ways and that Donna and Donald should, as a couple, receive a one-sixth share.

Ordinarily, commas are not used to separate pairs of words, phrases, or clauses that are joined by coordinating conjunctions.

EXAMPLES

Pair of Words:

Lundquist was <u>arrested</u> and <u>charged</u> with negligent homicide.

Pair of Phrases:

The Supreme Court is remarkably free <u>to emphasize certain issues of the case over others</u> or <u>to stress completely new issues.</u>

Pair of Clauses:

The trial court asked the defendant <u>whether he understood his right to a jury trial</u> and <u>whether he received any promises of better treatment if he waived that right.</u>

When a writer does use a comma before a coordinating conjunction joining a pair, the comma forces an unusual pause. Writers should use such a forced pause only when trying to suggest a bit of drama.

EXAMPLE

The gunman smiled at Kellogg, and then shot him.

Commas are not used between items in a series when all the items are joined by coordinating conjunctions. As a stylistic technique, joining all the items in a series with conjunctions has the effect of slowing down a series, which may be desirable on rare occasions when the writer wants the reader to focus special attention on each of the individual items in the series. (See pages 696-698 of the *Handbook* and Exercise 26.H in the *Practice Book.*)

EXAMPLE

There is no indication that the delay was negligent or deliberate or unusual.

Rule 11   **Use a Comma Between Coordinate Adjectives Not Joined by a Conjunction**

Coordinate adjectives are two or more adjectives that independently modify the same noun.

concise, precise language

(adjective) (adjective) (noun)

The test for whether adjectives are coordinate is simple: (1) reverse the order of the adjectives; or (2) add an "and" between the adjectives. If the adjectives are modifying the noun independently, then changing their order or adding an "and" will not change the meaning.

1. precise, concise language
2. concise, precise language
3. precise and concise language

The following example does not contain coordinate adjectives. Instead, "black" modifies "leather" and "leather" modifies "briefcase." Notice that you can tell that the adjectives are not coordinate by applying either part of the test. Both create awkward constructions.

EXAMPLE

black leather briefcase

Reverse Order:

leather, black briefcase

Add "and":

black and leather briefcase

Rule 12   Use Commas According to Convention With Dates, Addresses, and Names of Geographical Locations

When a full date is written out in the month-day-year order, use a comma after the day so that a reader can easily see the correct groupings of the digits.

July 4, 1776

Dates in this order also require a comma (or other punctuation) after the year when the sentence continues after the date.

EXAMPLE

The land was surveyed on October 4, 1986, and purchased less than a month later.

If the day is omitted or if the full date has the month and date reversed, omit commas because there are no adjacent groupings of digits.

July 1776   4 July 1776

EXAMPLE

Martin and Hughes were arrested on 21 December 1988 and charged with first-degree assault.

Use commas to set off individual elements in addresses and geographical names. Note that the state and zip code are considered one element and therefore not separated by a comma. When addresses or geographical names are followed by the remainder of a sentence, they should be followed by a comma.

Chicago, Illinois   Ontario, Canada

EXAMPLES

Send the bill to Mr. and Mrs. Arthur Meiering, 3000 La Jolla Lane, Roswell, New Mexico 88201, before Tuesday.

The string of robberies began in San Diego, California, and ended in Oakland, California, after the police arrested the defendant.

When possible, rephrase a date or geographical name used as a modifier when the date or geographical name will have to be followed by a comma.

EXAMPLES

Awkward:

the June 21, 1988, meeting

Revised:

the meeting on June 21, 1988

Awkward:

the Atlanta, Georgia, public health official

Revised:

the public health official from Atlanta, Georgia

See Exercise 26.I in the *Practice Book.*

§26.1.3   Esoteric Commas

Rule 13   **Use Commas to Set Off Absolutes**

Reminder

Absolutes are made up of either a noun or pronoun followed by a participle. They modify an entire sentence or main clause and can appear at the beginning, at the end, or within a sentence.

his <u>career</u> <u>destroyed</u>   their <u>lights</u> <u>flashing</u>
    (noun) (participle)   *(noun) (participle)*

his <u>gun</u> <u>drawn and loaded</u>   the <u>last</u> <u>being</u> a year ago
    (noun)   *(participles)*   *(noun) (participle)*

EXAMPLES

His career destroyed, Williams lapsed into a state of depression.

The police followed the defendant for less than one mile, their lights flashing.

The defendant reentered the tavern, his gun drawn and loaded, and proceeded to order the tavern's patrons to line up against the wall.

She testified that on four or five occasions, the last being a year ago, he demanded that she rewrite her will.

Rule 14	**Use a Comma to Indicate an Omission of a Word or Words That Can Be Understood From the Context**

EXAMPLE

The first witness said the attacker was "hairy"; the second, bald.

In Texas there are five elements to the crime; in Delaware, four.

Rule 15	**Use Commas to Set Off Expressions That Introduce Examples or Explanations**

"For example," "for instance," "that is," "namely," "*i.e.*," "*e.g.*," and "*viz.*" are usually followed by a comma. A comma can also be used before these expressions if the break in the flow of the sentence is slight. Dashes or semicolons are used before these expressions if the break is substantial. See Exercise 26.J in the *Practice Book.*

EXAMPLES

Collins testified that Adams had participated in the robbery and had fenced some of the items, namely, a camera, stereo, and silver.

The State must prove that the defendant acted by color or aid of deception — that is, that he operated to bring about the acquisition of the property or services by either creating or confirming another's false impression, which he knew to be false, or by failing to correct another's impression, which he had previously created.

Our company will accept all standard forms of identification, *e.g.,* birth certificate, driver's license, or military identification.

Note

Some authorities suggest that writers avoid the abbreviations "*i.e.,*" "*e.g.,*" and "*viz.*" in the text of their writing and use their English equivalents instead ("that is," "for example," and "namely" respectively). The rationale for this suggestion is that many readers misunderstand the abbreviations. If you decide to use the abbreviations, remember to italicize or underline them.

___

§26.1.4   Unnecessary Commas

Rule 16	Do Not Use a Comma to Set Off Restrictive Adverbial Clauses That Follow the Main Clause

Reminder

Adverbial clauses have their own subject and verb, and they are introduced by an adverb such as "although," "because," "before," "when," and "while."

Reminder

A restrictive adverbial clause restricts or limits the action of the verb to a time, manner, or circumstance. Nonrestrictive adverbial clauses give additional information.

Clauses introduced by the adverb "if" are always restrictive, so they are not set off by commas.

EXAMPLE

Complicity may be found if a defendant participates in the early stages of an activity that results in the attack on the victim.

Clauses introduced by the adverbs "because" and "unless" are usually restrictive, although they can be nonrestrictive.

EXAMPLES

Summary judgment was granted because the plaintiff failed to establish the prima facie elements.

Special damages may not be presumed without proof unless actual malice is proved.

When clauses beginning with "after," "as," "before," "since," "when," and "while" restrict the time of the main verb, they should not be set off with commas.

EXAMPLES

The tractor trailer entered the parking lot as the game was ending and the crowd was beginning to leave the stadium.

Morton was drinking beer while he was driving the boat.

When adverbial clauses beginning with "as," "since," or "while" do not restrict the time of the verb but rather express cause or condition, they are nonrestrictive and should be set off by commas. (But see the Glossary of Usage on use of "as" and "since" for causation.)

EXAMPLES

Southworth returned to the scene of the assault, as he feared that he had lost his neck chain in the scuffle.

Vereen was unable to read the contract, since she had had eye surgery only two days earlier.

Note

Clauses introduced by the adverbs "although" and "though" are always nonrestrictive, so they must be set off with commas.

EXAMPLES

Del Barker admits that he received his 1972 tax statement, although he claims that the only notice he received of the filing requirements was from general news articles in the newspaper.

Each physician received compensation and paid expenses in direct proportion to his production of the gross income of the partnership, even though the partnership was an equal partnership.

See Exercise 26.K in the *Practice Book.*

Rule 17	**Do Not Use a Comma to Separate a Subject From Its Verb or a Verb From Its Object**

Legal writers are often inclined to write long subjects. When they do, it is tempting to insert a comma after the subject and before the verb because the reader will need a pause. The comma is the wrong solution; instead, the writer should revise the sentence.

In the following example, the subject is enclosed in brackets.

EXAMPLES

Incorrect:

[The idea that an individual can obtain another person's property through adverse possession], is difficult for many people to accept.

Revised:

Many people find it difficult to accept the idea that an individual can obtain another person's property through adverse possession.

In the following example, the verb "received" is incorrectly separated from its object, "the note," by a comma.

Incorrect:

Bloomquist had received from a fellow employee at Landover Mills, a note describing where the "crack house" was located.

Revised:

A fellow employee at Landover Mills sent Bloomquist a note describing where the "crack house" was located.

Exception

Nonrestrictive modifiers and interrupters that separate a subject from its verb should be preceded and followed by commas, even though the commas separate the subject from its verb. (See Rules 4, 5, and 7 in this section.)

Rule 18	Do Not Use a Comma to Separate Correlative Pairs Unless the Correlatives Introduce Main Clauses

Reminder

Correlative pairs include "either . . . or," "neither . . . nor," "both . . . and," and "not only . . . but also."

Incorrect:

Neither the United States Supreme Court, nor this court has ever ruled that a defendant has a due process right to an instruction on lesser included offenses.

Revised:

Neither the United States Supreme Court nor this court has ever ruled that a defendant has a due process right to an instruction on lesser included offenses.

Main Clauses:

Either the manager will have to describe the damage done to the apartment, or he will have to return your deposit.

Note

The correlative pair "not only . . . but also" connects two elements, so a separating comma is inappropriate. Some authorities, however, do recommend a comma to separate the "not . . . but" pair because it is used to contrast elements.

| *Rule 19 | Do Not Use a Comma Between a Conjunction and Introductory Modifiers or Clauses |

When a coordinating conjunction joins two main clauses, the second main clause frequently begins with introductory modifiers or its own subordinate clause. Although some writers add a comma after the conjunction and before the introductory modifier or clause, this extra comma is needless; it merely slows the sentence down.

————————— , and ————————————————————
[*main clause*]   [*introductory*   [*main clause*]
                       modifiers/clause]

EXAMPLES

Incorrect:

The fire had completely destroyed the trailer, and, according to the fire chief, there was some concern that the overhead structure of the barn would collapse.

Revised:

The fire had completely destroyed the trailer, and according to the fire chief, there was some concern that the overhead structure of the barn would collapse.

Incorrect:

The woman demanded that Thomas hand over his wallet, but, when Thomas replied that he did not have his wallet, the woman shot him in the chest.

Revised:

The woman demanded that Thomas hand over his wallet, but when Thomas replied that he did not have his wallet, the woman shot him in the chest.

---

*Rule 20	**Do Not Use a Comma Between "That" and Introductory Modifiers or Clauses**

EXAMPLES

Incorrect:

He testified that, when they returned to his hotel room, Wells demanded a $150 fee.

Revised:

He testified that when they returned to his hotel room, Wells demanded a $150 fee.

See Exercises 26.L, 26.M, and 26.N in the *Practice Book.*

§26.2   THE SEMICOLON

The semicolon is one of the easiest punctuation marks to learn how to use. Unfortunately, some legal writers avoid using semicolons because they believe semicolons are quite complicated and will require learning numerous rules. Exactly the opposite is true. There are only two general rules for using semicolons; all other uses are variations or exceptions to these two rules.

Rule 1	Use a Semicolon to Separate Main, or Independent, Clauses Not Joined by a Coordinating Conjunction

---

main clause; main clause
_____

Reminders

Main clauses contain a subject and verb. They can stand alone as a sentence.

There are only seven coordinating conjunctions: "and," "but," "or," "for," "nor," "yet," and "so."

EXAMPLES

Officer Thompson administered the breathalyzer test; the results showed that the defendant's blood alcohol level was over the maximum allowed by the state.

The plaintiff is a Nevada resident; the defendant is a California resident.

If you use a comma or no punctuation between main clauses, you will produce a comma splice or run-on sentence. (See section 26.6.)

Note on Effective Use

Main clauses joined by a semicolon should be closely related in meaning. Often the semicolon suggests that the ideas in the connected main clauses work together as a larger idea. (See the first example above.) The semicolon can also be used to balance one idea against another. (See the second example above.) In all cases, the semicolon signals to the reader to pause slightly longer than a comma but shorter than a period. This length of pause helps the reader to see the ideas in the main clauses as more closely related to each other than the ideas would be in two separate sentences.

Variation on Rule 1

To show the relationship between the main clauses, a conjunctive adverb frequently follows the semicolon separating main clauses. The conjunctive adverb is usually followed by a comma. The most commonly used conjunctive adverbs are "accordingly," "also," "besides," "consequently," "furthermore," "hence," "however," "indeed," "instead," "likewise," "meanwhile," "moreover," "nevertheless," "still," "then," "therefore," and "thus." (See section 25.1.)

main clause; *therefore,* main clause

EXAMPLES

The summons was not delivered to his usual place of abode; therefore, service was not effected in the manner prescribed by law.

The elements of the test have not been completely defined; however, the court has clarified the policies underlying the rule.

Conjunctive adverbs may also occur in the middle of main clauses. In such cases, they are usually preceded and followed by a comma.

main, *therefore,* clause

EXAMPLE

The motor was not running, however, because of a problem with the distributor cap.

Compare the preceding example and the following example.

EXAMPLE

The motor was not running because of a problem with the distributor cap; however, the inoperability of the vehicle was irrelevant.

See Exercises 20.O and 20.P in the *Practice Book.*

Rule 2	Use Semicolons to Separate Items in a Series If the Items Are Long or If One or More of the Items Has Internal Commas

Reminder

A series is three or more items of equal importance. If the items in a series are relatively short or if they do not have internal commas, then the items can be separated by commas.

item 1, item 2, and item 3

Typical series with items separated by commas

item 1; item 2; and item 3

long items separated by semicolons

item 1; , item 2 , ; and item 3

internal commas in one or more items separated by semicolons

EXAMPLES

Long Items:

The Montana court has applied these definitions to cases with the following fact patterns: the driver was asleep and intoxicated; the driver was positioned behind the steering wheel; the vehicle's motor was running; and the vehicle was parked.

Long Items:

The court must determine the following issues to resolve your claim:

1. whether your ex-landlord sent you a written statement within thirty days of termination;
2. whether your ex-landlord withheld your deposit in bad faith; and
3. whether the court wishes to include attorneys' fees as part of a possible damage award.

Internal Commas:

The prosecutor called the following witnesses: Linda Hastings, an advertising executive; Samuel Hedges, an accountant; and Timothy Lessor, president of the company.

Internal Commas:

The defendant claims to reside in Maryland, even though (1) his car is registered in California; (2) he is registered to vote in California; and (3) all of his financial assets, including stocks, bonds, and a savings and checking account, are in a California bank.

See Exercise 26.Q in the *Practice Book.*

§26.2.1   Use of the Semicolon With "Yet" or "So"

Some writers prefer to use a semicolon rather than a comma before the conjunctions "yet" and "so" when they join two main clauses. Either the comma or the semicolon is correct in the following examples, but note that the longer pause suggested by the semicolon adds a bit more emphasis to the conjunction and to the words that immediately follow the semicolon.

EXAMPLES

Our client was legally intoxicated at the time of the arrest, so being asleep or unconscious is not a defense.

Our client was legally intoxicated at the time of the arrest; so being asleep or unconscious is not a defense.

---

§26.2.2   Use of the Semicolon With Coordinating Conjunctions

Usually main clauses joined by a coordinating conjunction require only a comma before the conjunction. (See section 26.1, Rule 1.) However, when the main clauses are long and grammatically complicated or when they have internal commas, it is helpful for the reader if a semicolon rather than a comma precedes the coordinating conjunction. The semicolon makes it easier to spot the break between the main clauses.

_____ ; but   ,   ,   _____

main clause   *main clause*

EXAMPLE

Your landlord can withhold a reasonable amount to cover the cost of repairing the window; but if he failed to send you a check for the remainder of the deposit, or if he failed to state why he withheld the deposit, or if he failed to do both within thirty days of termination of the lease, then he forfeited his right to withhold any part of the deposit.

§26.2.3   Use of the Semicolon With Citations

Because citations are either sentences or clauses, they should be treated as main clauses. Consequently, multiple citations are separated with semicolons. See Exercises 26.R and 26.S in the *Practice Book.*

EXAMPLE

Oklahoma courts have consistently held that if an intoxicated driver is in his or her vehicle and is capable of exercising actual physical control over it, then the driver has satisfied all elements required for a section 11-902 conviction: *Houston v. State,* 615 P.2d 305 (Okla. Crim. App. 1980); *Mason v. State,* 603 P.2d 1146; *Hughes v. State,* 535 P.2d 1023 (Okla. Crim. App. 1975).

§26.3   THE COLON

Colons are useful to legal writers for a number of reasons. They are regularly used to introduce quotations or lists, and they are often the best way to set up explanations or elaborations.

EXAMPLES

Quotation:

In support of this result, the court noted that the limitation on the use of the corpus delicti rule is based on the "suspect nature" of out-of-court confessions: "Corroboration of the confession is required as a safeguard against the conviction of the innocent persons through the use of a false confession of guilt." *Id.* at 419.

List:

There are three ways to measure a plaintiff's recovery for personal property damage: 1) if the destroyed personal property has a market value, the measure is that market value; 2) if the destroyed property has no market value but can be replaced, then the measure is the replacement cost; or 3) if the destroyed property has no market value and cannot be replaced, then the measure is the property's intrinsic value.

Explanation/Elaboration:

The periodic polygraph examinations are arguably connected logically to the ultimate goal of Nyles's rehabilitation: to deter him from molesting children.

Mr. Baker has sustained personal property damage: his picture windows and valuable vase were smashed.

The main function of a colon is to introduce what will follow. For this reason, a colon requires a lead-in main clause that is grammatically complete.

grammatically complete main clause:

In the example that follows, "the subsections that do not apply are" is not grammatically complete; therefore, the colon is used incorrectly.

EXAMPLE   INCORRECT

The subsections that do not apply are: 201-1, 201-1(3)(b), and 201-1(3)(c).

One way to correct the example is to omit the colon.

EXAMPLE   REVISED

The subsections that do not apply are 201-1, 201-1(3)(b), and 201-1(3)(c).

Another option is to add filler expressions, such as "the following" or "as follows," to make the lead-in main clause grammatically complete.

EXAMPLE   **REVISED**

The subsections that do not apply are the following: 201-1, 201-1(3)(b), and 201-1(3)(c).

Note

What follows the colon may or may not be a main clause. If a complete sentence follows a colon, the writer has the option of capitalizing the first word of that sentence.

Quotations that are integrated into the writer's own sentences are not introduced by a colon.

EXAMPLES

The first letter the Bakers received stated that "permits are issued subject to existing water rights."

Fair market value is "the amount of money a purchaser willing, but not obligated, to buy the property would pay an owner willing, but not obligated, to sell it, taking into consideration all uses to which the property is adapted and might in reason be applied." *Dillon v. O'Connor,* 412 P.2d 126, 128 (Wash. 1966).

Because colons set up the endings of sentences, they can be used effectively and stylistically to create emphasis. (See section 22.6.4.) Notice how the writers of the following sentences used colons to highlight a point.

EXAMPLES

Orlando's trial was originally scheduled for May 15, 1985: ninety-three days after his arraignment.

The legislature has already determined the standard range for Norris's offense: fourteen to eighteen months.

Gibson claimed that his intent was to do a lawful act: administer parental discipline.

Remember to doublespace after a colon. See Exercise 26.T in the *Practice Book.*

§26.4   THE APOSTROPHE

Apostrophes determine possession — who owns what. If you and your clients care about who owns what and about whether ownership is clearly stated, then apostrophes are worth the few minutes it takes to learn how to use them correctly.

All the apostrophe rules are important, but take special note of Rules 5 and 6. Misusing these two rules can create either ambiguity or the appearance of incompetence.

Rule 1	**Use "'s" to Form the Possessive of Singular or Plural Nouns or Indefinite Pronouns Not Ending in "-s"**

defendant's alibi   expert's testimony
family's income   children's guardian
a day's wages   a year's revenue
anybody's guess   everyone's concern

Rule 2	**Use "'s" to Form the Possessive of Singular Nouns Ending in "-s"[3] as Long as the Resulting Word Is Not Difficult to Pronounce**

James's contract   Congress's authority
business's license   witness's testimony

---

3. A few recognized authorities, including *The Associated Press Stylebook and Libel Manual,* recommend using only an apostrophe with singular proper names.

Note

Three or more "s" sounds together are difficult to pronounce. When necessary, avoid three "s" sounds together by dropping the "s" after the apostrophe.

In the examples above, the double "s" ending in "business" or "witness" makes only one "s" sound, so when the "'s" is added, as in "business's" and "witness's," only two "s" sounds are required. However, when these same words are followed by words that begin with "s," then the "s" after the apostrophe is dropped for ease in pronunciation.

business' sales   witness' signature

For the same reason, many idioms that include the word "sake" drop the "s" after the apostrophe.

for goodness' sake   for righteousness' sake
for appearance' sake   for conscience' sake

Although almost all singular proper names follow the standard rule and form their possessive by adding "'s," those few proper names with internal and ending "s" sounds also drop the "s" after the apostrophe for ease in pronunciation. Note that the "s" sound may be made by a "z" or an "x" as well as an "s."

Jesus' teaching   Moses' laws
Velasquez' hearing   Alexis' prior conviction
Kansas' case law

But   Arkansas's case law (because the final *s*
in Arkansas is silent)

Exception

When forming the possessive of ancient classical names, add only the apostrophe.

Achilles' heel   Hercules' labors

Rule 3	**Use Only an Apostrophe to Form the Possessive of Plural Nouns Ending in "-s"**

framers' intent   workers' rights
four cities' plan   two agencies' concern
ten dollars' worth   thirty days' notice

Plural proper nouns follow the same rule.

Smiths' attorney   Thomases' dog

It is easier to form plural possessives correctly if you form the plural first and then apply the rules for possessives.

Singular   Plural   Plural Possessive
day ⟶ two days ⟶ two days' labor
family ⟶ families ⟶ families' petition
Jones ⟶ Joneses ⟶ Joneses' pre-marital agreement

Note

Occasionally a singular idea is expressed in words that are technically plural, for example, "United States," "General Motors," or "Olson Brothers." In such cases, apply the rule for forming plural possessives and add just an apostrophe.

United States' commitment   General Motors' lobbyists

Rule 4	**Use "'s" After the Last Word to Form the Possessive of a Compound Word or Word Group**

mother-in-law's statement   district manager's idea
attorney general's office   somebody else's problem
the Governor of Florida's
     recommendation

Don't use "'s" to form the possessive of a long word group, such as "The American Association of Lovers of Dogs and Cats." Use "of" or "for" instead: attorney of (or for) The American Association of Lovers of Dogs and Cats.

Rule 5	To Show Joint Possession, Use "'s" Only After the Last Noun in a Group of Two or More Nouns; to Show Individual Possession, Use "'s" After Each of the Nouns in a Group of Two or More Nouns

John and Mary's stocks ⟶ stocks are jointly owned

John's and Mary's stocks ⟶ some stocks are owned by John; some are owned by Mary

the governor and legislature's report ⟶ one report from both

the governor and legislature's reports ⟶ more than one report but still from both

the governor's and legislature's reports ⟶ one or more reports from the governor; one or more reports from the legislature

Rule 6	To Form the Possessive of Personal Pronouns, Do Not Use the Apostrophe

hers   its   ours   theirs   whose   yours

Many writers confuse the contractions "it's," "they're," and "who's" with the possessive of the personal pronouns "its," "their," and "whose."

it's = it is	its = possessive of "it"
they're = they are	their = possessive of "they"
who's = who is	whose = possessive of "who"

Besides showing possession, the apostrophe has a few other uses, including the formation of contractions and some plurals.

Rule 7	**To Form Contractions, Use the Apostrophe to Substitute for One or More Omitted Letters or Numbers**

it's = it is   ma'am = madam
they're = they are   class of '68 = class of 1968
who's = who is

Note

Contractions are used rarely in formal writing, including most legal writing.

Rule 8	**To Form the Plural of Numbers, Letters, or Words Referred to as Words, Add "'s"**

seven 0's   cross all the t's
1950's   and dot all the i's
two Boeing 767's   replace all the
                         and's with or's

Note

Some authorities recommend adding just "s" to make numbers plural: 1950s, two Boeing 767s.

See Exercises 26.U, 26.V, and 26.W in the *Practice Book.*

§26.5   OTHER MARKS OF PUNCTUATION

§26.5.1   Quotation Marks

a.   *Identification of Another's Written or Spoken Words*

There is nothing mysterious about quotation marks; they do just what their name suggests: They mark where something is quoted.

Although many legal writers have a problem with excessive quoting (see section 23.2.3), there are still several occasions, most notably statutes and memorable phrasing, where quoting is necessary or appropriate. For these occasions, use quotation marks around those words that are not your own and that you have taken from the cited source.

EXAMPLE 1

The relationship between Southwestern Insurors and each of its agents is governed by an agreement that includes the following statement: "The location of the agent's office cannot unduly interfere with the business established by another agent."

EXAMPLE 2

In the *Ryan* case, the Court of Appeals ruled that the plaintiff's choice in not swerving was "prudent under the circumstances." *Id.* at 508.

EXAMPLE 3

The bartender testified that he overheard the defendant say he would "permanently get even" with Meyers.

Take care to quote the source's words exactly; use the ellipsis (see section 26.5.2) to indicate any omissions you have made to the wording and brackets (see section 26.5.3) to indicate changes in capitalization and additions for clarity and readability.

EXAMPLE 4

In his *Roviaro* dissent, Justice Clark observed that "[e]xperience teaches that once this policy [of confidentiality] is relaxed . . . its effectiveness is destroyed. Once an informant is known, the drug traffickers are quick to retaliate." *Id.* at 67.

Notice that in Examples 2, 3, and 4 the quotation is integrated into the writer's own sentence. When you integrate a quotation into one of your own sentences, be sure that the parts fit. The grammar of your sentence must be compatible with the grammar of the quotation.

EXAMPLE

Incorrect:

An actionable nuisance is "an obstruction to the free use of property, so as to essentially interfere with the comfortable enjoyment of life and property, is a nuisance and the subject of an action for damages and other further relief." Wash. Rev. Code § 7.48.010 (1992).

Revised:

An actionable nuisance is "an obstruction to the free use of property, so as to essentially interfere with the comfortable enjoyment of life and property . . . ." Wash. Rev. Code § 7.48.010 (1992).

---

b. Block Quotations

According to Rule 5.1(a) in the *Bluebook,* writers should not use quotation marks around quotations of fifty words or more. A quotation of this length should be set up as a block quotation, that is, single-spaced, indented left and right, and without quotation marks.

The University of Chicago Manual of Legal Citation (also known as the *Maroon Book*) recommends that writers use their discretion about whether to incorporate quotations into the text or set them up as block quotations. This source notes that most quotations that run more than six lines should be set out in block form.

To further complicate the issue, some court rules require quotation marks for block quotations. As a writer, then, determine which method your reader prefers and then apply it. Know too that the trend seems to be toward using block quotations for long quotations that are not quite fifty words. The rationale seems to be that it is easier for the reader to see where the quotation begins and ends.

EXAMPLE 5

Davis argues that the trial court erred in giving instruction 19, which read as follows:

> Evidence has been introduced in this case regarding the fact that stop signs were installed in the neighborhood of Ohio and Texas

Streets approximately one and one-half years after the accident of
December 24, 1989. You are not to consider this evidence as proof
of negligence nor as an admission of negligence on the part of the
City.

EXAMPLE 6

The *Sholund* court held that no contract arose between the in-
sured and the insurance company:

> [W]here the agent represents two or more companies, no one of
> them can be bound until the agent allocates the risk, or some por-
> tion thereof, to it by some word or act. Until that is done, there is
> no contract, because of failure of parties . . . . In the present case,
> the record is totally devoid of any act or word on the part of the
> agent to designate the appellant as the company to take the risk
> until after the property was destroyed by fire. He merely thought
> the appellant would take it. Thoughts can become binding as con-
> tracts only when transformed into acts or words.

Id. at 113-15.

Block quotations also tend to highlight the quoted material; consequently, some writers use them for persuasive reasons even when the
quotation is fairly short.

c.   *Effective Lead-ins for Quotations*

In Examples 1, 4, and 5, the quotations are not integrated into the
writer's own sentences; instead, they are formally introduced and set up
as separate statements.

Notice how the lead-ins to these formally introduced quotations
are written. The language in the lead-ins prepares the reader for the
quotation, sometimes by summarizing or paraphrasing the quotation,
sometimes by explaining in advance why the quotation is significant.

Compare the lead-ins in the following pairs. Notice how the ineffective lead-ins do little more than indicate that a quotation will follow.
In contrast, the effective lead-ins guide the reader into the quotation
and suggest what the reader should look for in the quotation.

EXAMPLE

Ineffective Lead-in:

The court found the following:

> The juvenile has an extensive record of adjudications and diver-
> sions for a variety of criminal offenses . . . . The court concludes
> that a sentence within the standard range would constitute a man-
> ifest injustice . . . . [C]ommitment . . . for a period of fifty-two (52)
> weeks is a more appropriate and reasonable sentence, taking into
> consideration the age of the defendant, his level of criminal sophis-
> tication and lack of success in rehabilitation . . . .

Effective Lead-in:

The court found a "manifest injustice" and increased Boyd's sentence because of his criminal history:

> The juvenile has an extensive record of adjudications and diver-
> sions for a variety of criminal offenses . . . . The court concludes
> that a sentence within the standard range would constitute a man-
> ifest injustice . . . . [C]ommitment . . . for a period of fifty-two (52)
> weeks is a more appropriate and reasonable sentence, taking into
> consideration the age of the defendant, his level of criminal sophis-
> tication and lack of success in rehabilitation . . . .

Ineffective Lead-in:

In *Curtis v. Blacklaw,* the court said the following:

Effective Lead-in:

In *Curtis v. Blacklaw,* the court explained the relationship between
the standard of ordinary care and the emergency doctrine:

> [T]he existence of a legally defined emergency does not alter or
> diminish the standards of care imposed by law upon the actors . . . .
> With or without an emergency instruction, the jury must determine
> what choice a reasonably prudent and careful person would have
> made in the same situation.

Id. at 363.

Ineffective Lead-in:

In the present case, the trial court made the following finding:

Effective Lead-in:

In the present case, the trial court found that the community had
not sustained its burden: "Although there is evidence of miscellaneous improvements made to the property, there is a failure of

evidence that it was these improvements that enhanced and caused the property to appreciate." CP 72.

Notice too that when a quotation is formally introduced and preceded by a colon, the portion of the sentence before the colon — the lead-in — must be grammatically complete. (See section 26.3.)

EXAMPLES

Incorrect:

It is a cardinal rule of statutory construction that a court must: "ascertain and give effect to legislative intent and purpose, as expressed in the act."

Correct:

It is a cardinal rule of statutory construction that a court must do the following: "ascertain and give effect to legislative intent and purpose, as expressed in the act."

Also Correct:

It is a cardinal rule of statutory construction that a court must "ascertain and give effect to legislative intent and purpose, as expressed in the act."

---

d.   Quotations Within Quotations

Occasionally, something you want to quote will already have quotation marks in it, either because your source quoted someone else or because your source used a term in a special way. For a quotation within a quotation, use single quotation marks (an apostrophe on most keyboards).

EXAMPLES

Baxter argues that the trial court erred when it included the following in an instruction on accomplice liability: "The word 'aid' means all assistance whether given by words, acts of encouragement, support, or presence."

"Police must discover incriminating evidence 'inadvertently,' which is to say, they may not 'know in advance the location of [certain] evidence and intend to seize it,' relying on the plain view doctrine as a pretext." *Texas v. Brown,* 460 U.S. 730, 743 (1983) (quoting *Coolidge,* 403 U.S. at 370).

---

e. Quotation Marks with Other Marks of Punctuation

Periods and commas go inside closing quotation marks; semicolons and colons go outside closing quotation marks. Dashes, question marks, and exclamation points go inside closing quotation marks when they are part of the quotation and outside closing quotation marks when they are part of the larger sentence.

EXAMPLES

Davis's employer described him as a "street-smart youngster who knew what not to get involved with."

The jury below could have arguably considered Wilson's insulting remarks to Harris as "unlawful," thereby depriving Harris of her self-defense claim.

Parole is a "variation on imprisonment"; therefore, parole and its possible revocation are a continuing form of custody relating back to the criminal act.

---

f. Other Uses for Quotation Marks

Quotation marks may also indicate that a word is being used in some special way.

EXAMPLES

Mrs. Hartley claims that her husband played "mind games" with her to get her to sign the agreement.

Taylor approached Zimp about the possibility of obtaining an "umbrella" policy that would provide coverage in excess of his underlying automobile and homeowner's policies.

The Court of Appeals held that the attorney's phrasing was calculated to imply that Morris was a "hired gun" for insurance carriers.

Special terms are often introduced by phrases like "the word" or "the term." Put the words that follow these phrases in quotation marks, but do not use quotation marks around words that follow "so-called."

EXAMPLE

The words "beyond a reasonable doubt" in the constitutional error test created confusion in the Arizona courts for some time.

Quotation marks should also be used around words that follow the terms "signed," "endorsed," or "entitled."

EXAMPLE

The contract was signed "Miss Cathryn Smith," not "Ms. Kathryn Smith."

Do not use quotation marks around the single words *yes* and *no;* do not use quotation marks around a paraphrase.

EXAMPLE

When the officer asked her if she needed a ride home, she said yes.

---

§26.5.2   Ellipses

Use the ellipsis (three spaced periods) to indicate an omission in a quotation. The ellipsis allows you to trim quotations down and focus the reader on the parts of the quotation that are relevant to your case.

EXAMPLE

Helen signed a quitclaim deed to Richard, disclaiming "an interest in the . . . property."

Space before the first period and after the last period in an ellipsis. When the omission occurs in the middle of a quoted sentence, retain any necessary punctuation. Notice, for example, that the comma after "union" is retained in the following quotation because it is necessary punctuation for the sentence as it is quoted.

EXAMPLE

"We the people of the United States, in order to form a more perfect union, . . . do ordain and establish this Constitution for the United States of America."

When the omission occurs at the end of quoted sentence, use the ellipsis (three spaced periods) to indicate that omission and then space and add a fourth period for the punctuation to end the sentence.

EXAMPLE

"We the people of the United States, in order to form a more perfect union, . . . do ordain and establish this Constitution . . . ."

When the omission occurs after the end of a quoted sentence, punctuate the quoted sentence and then insert the ellipsis. In such a case, the sentence period is closed up to the last word in the sentence. This is demonstrated in the next two examples, both of which are quotations from the following original material.

EXAMPLE

Original Material:

The hostility/claim of right element of adverse possession requires only that the claimant treat the land as his own as against the world throughout the statutory period. The nature of his possession will be determined solely on the basis of the manner in which he treats the property. His subjective belief regarding his true interest in the land and his intent to dispossess or not dispossess another is irrelevant to this determination.

Quotation from the Preceding Material:

The hostility/claim of right element of adverse possession requires only that the claimant treat the land as his own as against the world throughout the statutory period. . . . His subjective belief regarding his true interest in the land and his intent to dispossess or not dispossess another is irrelevant to this determination.

Id. at 860-61.

Another Quotation from the Same Original:

"The hostility/claim of right element of adverse possession requires only that the claimant treat the land as his own as against the world throughout the statutory period. . . . [H]is intent to dispossess or not dispossess another is irrelevant to this determination." *Id.* at 860-61.

When the omission occurs at the beginning of the quotation, do not use an ellipsis. The reader will be able to tell that the original quotation did not begin at that point because the quotation begins with a lower case letter.

EXAMPLE

Incorrect:

In 1970, King granted to the State a ". . . permanent easement assignable in whole or in part" over King's property. CP 106.

Correct:

In 1970, King granted to the State a "permanent easement assignable in whole or in part" over King's property. CP 106.

When the quoted material is just a phrase or clause, no ellipsis is needed before or after the quoted material.

An omission, to be actionable, must show "tacit authorization" or "deliberate indifference." *Wellington v. Daniels,* 717 F.2d 932, 936 (4th Cir. 1983).

When a paragraph or more is omitted, indent and use the ellipsis plus the fourth period for the end punctuation.

The Safe Drivers' Insurance policy contains the following relevant provisions:

Definitions

. . . .

A car is a 4-wheel motor vehicle licensed for use on public roads. It includes any motor home that is not used for business purposes and any utility trailer.

. . . .

A motor vehicle is a land motor vehicle designed for use on public roads. It includes cars and trailers. It also includes any other land motor vehicle while used on public roads.

Like all good things, ellipsis marks can be misused. Never use the ellipsis to change the original intent in the quotation. Also, take care not to overuse the ellipsis in any one quotation. Too many omissions make the quotation difficult to read.

§26.5.3　Brackets

Brackets are used to show changes in quotations. The most common are additions of clarifying material and changes in capitalization and verb tense.

EXAMPLES

Addition of Clarifying Material:

"The privilege [of nondisclosure] recognizes the obligation of citizens to communicate their knowledge of the commission of crimes to law enforcement officials and, by preserving their anonymity, encourages them to perform that obligation." *Lewandowski v. State,* 389 N.E.2d 706, 708 (Ind. 1979) (quoting *Roviaro v. United States,* 353 U.S. 53, 62 (1957)).

Capitalization Change:

"[A] municipality may be held liable under 1983 for the intentional conduct of its governing body, . . . [b]ut we have held city police chiefs *not* to be such officials, . . . as they are almost uniformly subordinate to the city's governing body." *Languirand,* 717 F.2d at 227 (emphasis in original).

Change in Verb Tense:

The Council authorized the construction of a twelve-story tower, finding that reducing the tower to this height "substantially mitigate[s] adverse impacts on the land use pattern in the vicinity."

Use empty brackets [ ] to indicate where a single letter is omitted.

In some cases, a pronoun in a quotation may be ambiguous in the new context, so for clarity the writer substitutes the appropriate noun in brackets. In such cases, the omission of the pronoun does not need to be indicated.

EXAMPLE

At the time of her medical release, Wainwright made the following admission: "I did continue to have some pain and discomfort in my back, neck, and arms, but [Dr. Rodgers] felt this was normal pain and discomfort and that it would go away."

Occasionally, something that you want to quote has a significant error in it. In such cases, use a bracketed *sic* immediately after the error to indicate that the error was in the original and not inadvertently added.

EXAMPLE

On the day after the union vote was held, the shop foreman issued a memo to all machinists stating that how they voted "would not effect [*sic*] their performance reviews."

§26.5.4   Parentheses

In everyday writing, parentheses are used to add additional information to sentences. They are one way to signal that that information is of lesser importance.

EXAMPLE

Newcombe wrested a half a gram of marijuana (worth $10) from Tyson's pocket.

Because conciseness is a cardinal virtue in legal writing, legal writers usually edit out any information that is of lesser importance. As a natural consequence, you will rarely encounter parenthetical inserts in legal writing.

This does not mean that parentheses themselves do not appear anywhere in legal documents. They are frequently used in the following ways.

a.   *To Enclose Short Explanations of Cases Within Citations*

EXAMPLE

Washington courts have held the emergency doctrine inapplicable when only a sudden increase in degree of an already existing condition has placed the actor in a position of peril. *Mills v. Park,* 409 P.2d 646 (Wash. 1966) (where the defendant's vision in a snowstorm was further obscured by a snowplow throwing snow on defendant's car). *See also Hinkel v. Weyerhaeuser Co.,* 494 P.2d 1008 (Wash. Ct. App. 1972) (where the defendant was warned of a cloud of dense smoke ahead).

b.   To Refer Readers to Attached or Appended Documents

> **EXAMPLE**
>
> Before signing the agreement, Jones crossed out the language "at time of closing" in paragraph 12 and inserted the language "pro ratio as received by sellers" in paragraph 24. (See appendix 1.)

Note

When a parenthetical reference is set up as a separate sentence, as in the example above, the period goes inside the closing parentheses. When the parenthetical reference is inserted in the middle of a sentence, place any punctuation required for the sentence outside the closing parenthesis.

> **EXAMPLE**
>
> Before signing the agreement, Jones crossed out the language "at time of closing" (paragraph 12, appendix 1), and Smith inserted the language "pro ratio as received by sellers" (paragraph 24, appendix 2).

c.   To Confirm Numbers

> **EXAMPLE**
>
> In 1989, Patrick and Rose Milton borrowed five thousand dollars ($5,000) from Southern Security Company.

d. To Enclose Numerals That Introduce the Individual Items in a List

EXAMPLES

To decide whether the same claim for relief is involved in both cases, a court must determine (1) whether the same primary right is involved in both cases and (2) whether the evidence needed to support the second action would have sustained the first action.

The company's regulations list seven circumstances under which an employee may be separated from his or her job: (1) resignation, (2) release, (3) death, (4) retirement, (5) failure to return from a leave of absence, (6) failure to return from a layoff, and (7) discharge or suspension for cause.

e. To Announce Changes to a Quotation That Cannot Be Shown by Ellipses or Brackets

EXAMPLE

"[I]solated incidents are normally insufficient to establish supervisory inaction upon which to predicate § 1983 liability." *Wellington,* 717 F.2d at 936 (footnote omitted).

The court held that "[a]n instruction, *when requested,* defining intent is required when intent is an element of the crime charged." *Id.* (emphasis added).

f. To Introduce Abbreviations after a Full Name Is Given

EXAMPLE

Beaver Custom Carpets (BCC) has been in business for one year.

See Exercise 26.X in the *Practice Book.*

§26.5.5   The Hyphen

The two principal uses of hyphens are to divide words at line breaks and to combine words to form compound modifiers or compound nouns.

a.   Word Division

Use a hyphen to divide a word at the end of a line only under the following circumstances:

a. The break occurs between syllables (one-syllable words must not be divided);
b. Enough of the word appears on both of the lines for the reader to identify the word easily (do not leave one letter at the end of a line or fewer than three letters at the beginning of a line, such as "a-part" or "abrupt-ly"); and
c. Both parts of the word appear on the same page.

b.   Compound Modifiers and Compound Nouns

Somewhat more problematic for legal writers is deciding when a pair or grouping of modifiers or nouns should be joined by hyphens to show that they are acting as one unit.

The first step is a simple one: If the modifiers do not precede the noun they modify, then they are not hyphenated.

EXAMPLES

Owens's argument ignores other rules of statutory construction that are <u>well established.</u>

Owens's argument ignores other <u>well-established</u> rules of statutory construction.

This case has set precedents that are <u>far reaching.</u>

The case has set <u>far-reaching</u> precedents.

Notice that legal writers use many compound modifiers that begin with "well." As long as these modifiers precede the noun they modify, they will be hyphenated.

a well-reasoned opinion	a well-defined test
a well-known fact	a well-founded argument

Obviously, though, not all compound modifiers begin with "well," and unfortunately, often the only way to know whether to hyphenate is to consult a good dictionary with a recent publication date. The recent publication date is important because our language changes: What was once two or more separate words may later be hyphenated and eventually combined into one word.

air plane ⟶ air-plane ⟶ airplane

Still separate

trier of fact	sudden emergency doctrine
stop payment order	pyramid sales scheme
profit and loss statement	prima facie case
leave of absence	lame duck session
hit and run accident	family car doctrine

Hyphenated

price-fixing contract	take-home pay
out-of-pocket expenses	stop-limit order
out-of-date certificate	court-martial
cross-examination	

Combined

wraparound mortgage	quitclaim deed
counterclaim	

Our changing language also gives us new hyphenated nouns.

frame-up   split-off   squeeze-out

Many words are in transition. For example, you may notice that "line-up" is spelled with a hyphen in some cases and as the combined word "lineup" in others. The same is true for "pre-trial" and "pretrial." In such instances, consult your most recent authority and try to be consistent within the document you are writing. (Be sure to use all variations of a word when doing computer-assisted research.)

In addition to using the dictionary as a guide to hyphen use, there are a few general rules about when to use hyphens.

1. Always hyphenate modifiers and nouns that begin with the prefixes "all," "ex," and "self."

all-American	all-purpose
ex-partner	ex-judge
self-defense	self-incrimination

2. Other prefixes, including "anti," "co," "de," "inter," "intra," "multi," "non," "para," "pro," "re," "semi," and "super," generally should not be used with a hyphen.

antibiotic	multinational
antitrust	noncommissioned
codefendant	nonpayment
coheir	paralegal
degenerate	prorate
dehydrate	reactionary
interagency	reallocate
interbank	reassert
interstate	semiannual
intrastate	supersede

Unfortunately, however, there are enough exceptions to this general rule that you may often have to look up the word you need. The following exceptions apply to larger categories of words:

   a.   Use the hyphen when it is needed for clarity ("re-create" and not "recreate");
   b.   Use the hyphen when it is needed to prevent a doubled vowel ("re-enact," "de-emphasize") or a tripled consonant;
   c.   Use the hyphen when it is needed because the second element is capitalized ("post-World War II," "un-American," or "anti-Semitic").

3. "Elect" is the one suffix that usually requires a hyphen.

governor-elect   president-elect

4. Hyphens are used to form compound numbers from twenty-one to ninety-nine. Hyphens are also used with fractions functioning as adjectives, but not with fractions functioning as nouns.

the twenty-fourth amendment
the seventy-second Congress
one-half acre *but*
   one half of the employees
two-thirds majority *but*
   two thirds of the board

5. Hyphens are often used to join a number and a noun to make a compound modifier.

twenty-year-old appellant	ten-year lease
three-mile limit	three-judge court
thirty-day letter	ten-acre tract
nine-year-old conviction	first-year student

6. Do not use a hyphen in the following instances:

1. when the first word in a two-word modifier is an adverb ending in "-ly" ("previously taxed income," "clearly erroneous view," "jointly acquired property");
2. when the compound modifier contains a foreign phrase ("bona fide purchaser," "per se violation");
3. when a civil or military title denotes one office ("justice of the peace" but "secretary-treasurer").

Sometimes two or more compound modifiers share the same second element. In such cases, use hyphens after each first element and do not use the second element twice.

high- and low-test gasoline
nine- and ten-acre parcels

7. Hyphens are also frequently used to combine two parties into one modifier.

      attorney-client privilege   husband-wife tort actions

8. Writers have the option of using hyphens when the hyphen will prevent a misreading.

"re-cover the sofa" as opposed to "recover the sofa"

See Exercises 26.Y and 26.Z in the *Practice Book*.

§26.5.6   The Dash

Dashes are rarely used in legal writing. The consensus seems to be that dashes are too breezy and informal for the serious work of law.

Still, there are few occasions when the dash is useful. For example, in sentences in which a list is an appositive, a pair of dashes can be used to signal the beginning and end of the list.

EXAMPLES

By 1988, the defendant had opened up bank accounts in several foreign countries — Switzerland, Brazil, South Africa, and Spain — all under different names.

The new conservative bloc — Rehnquist, O'Connor, Scalia, and Kennedy — controlled the major cases of the 1988-1989 term.

Similarly, a dash is needed to set off an introductory list containing commas.

EXAMPLE

Name-calling, threats, and repeated beatings — these were the ways Wilson gave attention to his son.

When used with discretion, dashes can also be an effective way to create emphasis (see section 22.6.4). Notice how in the following pair of sentences, the dashes do more than the commas to highlight what they enclose.

EXAMPLES

Commas:

The prosecution's questions, over repeated objections, about Ms. Patten's religious beliefs cannot be deemed inadvertent.

Dashes:

The prosecution's questions — over repeated objections — about Ms. Patten's religious beliefs cannot be deemed inadvertent.

Commas:

The victim's age, 18 months, made him particularly vulnerable.

Dashes:

The victim's age — 18 months — made him particularly vulnerable.

Dashes can also be used to show abrupt shifts or to cue the reader that the words that follow are shocking or surprising.

EXAMPLE

Several witnesses — including the defendant's mother — testified that they believed Willie was capable of committing such a
heinous crime.

Note

On most keyboards, the dash is formed by hitting the hyphen key
twice. There is no space before or after the dash.

§26.6   COMMA SPLICES AND FUSED SENTENCES

§26.6.1   Comma Splices

Perhaps the most common punctuation error in all writing, not just
legal writing, is the comma splice. Simply put, a comma splice is the
joining of two main, or independent, clauses with just a comma. This is
the pattern for a comma splice:

     main clause,   main clause

Reminder

A main clause has both a subject and verb and can stand alone as
a sentence.

EXAMPLES   **COMMA SPLICES**

The prosecutor spoke about the defendant's motive, the jury listened carefully.

The corrections officer contacted several other persons, none
knew of Wilson's disappearance.

Mr. Baker sustained personal property damage, his picture windows and valuable vase were smashed.

There are five simple methods for correcting a comma splice. When correcting a comma splice, use the method that best suits the context.

1. Make each main clause a separate sentence.

EXAMPLE

The prosecutor spoke about the defendant's motive. The jury listened carefully.

---

2. Add a coordinating conjunction ("and," "but," "or," "for," "nor," "yet," "so") after the comma separating the two main clauses. (See Rule 1 in section 26.1.)

EXAMPLE

The corrections officer contacted several other persons, but none knew of Wilson's disappearance.

---

3. Change the comma separating the two main clauses to a semicolon. (See section 26.2.)

EXAMPLE

The corrections officer contacted several other persons; none knew of Wilson's disappearance.

---

4. Change one of the main clauses to a subordinate clause.

EXAMPLES

While the prosecutor spoke about the defendant's motive, the jury listened carefully.

Although the corrections officer contacted several other persons, none knew of Wilson's disappearance.

---

5. If the second main clause is an explanation or illustration of the first main clause, use a colon to separate the two main clauses. (See section 26.3.)

EXAMPLE

Mr. Baker sustained personal property damage: His picture windows and valuable vase were smashed.

Comma splices often occur in sentences that have two main clauses and a conjunctive adverb introducing the second main clause. This is incorrect:

main clause,   therefore,   main clause

Reminder

The most commonly used conjunctive adverbs are "accordingly," "also," "besides," "consequently," "furthermore," "hence," "however," "indeed," "instead," "likewise," "meanwhile," "moreover," "nevertheless," "still," "then," "therefore," and "thus."

EXAMPLE   **INCORRECT**

The summons was not delivered to his usual place of abode, therefore, service was not effected in the manner prescribed by law.

Such comma splices are usually best corrected by using the third method, changing the comma to a semicolon.

EXAMPLE   **CORRECTED**

The summons was not delivered to his usual place of abode; therefore, service was not effected in the manner prescribed by law.

They can also be corrected by changing the comma to a period.

EXAMPLE   **CORRECTED**

The summons was not delivered to his usual place of abode. Therefore, service was not effected in the manner prescribed by law.

Conjunctive adverbs can also interrupt a main clause. In such cases, the conjunctive adverb is correctly preceded and followed by commas.

    main,   therefore,   clause

EXAMPLE

The defendant, therefore, was not judged by a jury of his peers.

---

§26.6.2   Fused Sentences

Fused sentences, also known as run-on sentences, are a less frequent but even more serious writing error than comma splices. A fused sentence has no punctuation or coordinating conjunction between two main clauses. This is the pattern for a fused sentence:

    Main Clause   Main Clause

| EXAMPLE | **FUSED SENTENCE** |

The prosecutor spoke about the defendant's motive the jury listened carefully.

Fused sentences can be corrected using the same methods for correcting comma splices.

Note

Occasionally, one hears an overly long, rambling sentence described as a "run-on sentence." This is an incorrect use of the term. A
run-on sentence is the same thing as a fused sentence: Either the punctuation or the coordinating conjunction is omitted between two main
clauses.

See Exercises 26.AA and 26.BB in the *Practice Book.*

Chapter 27

Mechanics

§27.1   Spelling

Correct spelling. That's a given in legal writing. Unfortunately, though, it is not a given for each individual legal writer. We have not all been blessed with the same rigorous training, the same interest, and the same aptitude for any of the areas related to writing. Nowhere is this more evident than in spelling.

So, what does a law student, a practitioner, a paralegal, a clerk, or even a Supreme Court Justice do if he or she is a terrible speller? Certainly not resign oneself to a lifetime of poor spelling. Such a defeatist attitude is unworthy of a legal professional. But changing, indeed reversing, a lifelong habit or trend is never easy. Such a change almost always requires that we first change what we think or believe.

If we think spelling doesn't really matter, then we will never give it the sustained effort it requires. If we think we don't have the time to work at it, then we certainly won't find the time it takes to improve. (Fortunately, a few minutes a day is all it takes.) And if we are firmly convinced that "once a poor speller, always a poor speller," then we will undoubtedly fall victim to that self-fulfilling prophesy.

In short, the right attitude is a critical prerequisite to becoming a good speller. Once you decide that spelling is important and that you can be good at it, then you are ready to try some of the approaches discussed later in the section. But first you have to begin with your own attitude about spelling. And that is where we will begin.

§27.1.1   Getting Motivated

Most of us realize that spelling correctly is no great intellectual achievement. The ability to create and develop a good argument is certainly more significant than knowing how to spell the word "argument." Consequently, many of us neglect spelling, believing that our time should be spent on "more important things." This is a mistake. For in neglecting to learn how to spell "argument," we may in fact be hampering our ability to make an argument. Why? Poor spelling, even an occasional misspelling, is a distraction for readers.

Take the sentence you just read. Suppose you had read: "Por speling, even an occassionall mispeling, is a detraction for reders." What happened to you as you read that sentence? Did you think about the point the sentence was making, or was your attention on how the words were spelled?

Most readers, particularly ones who are good spellers, cannot help but mentally correct misspelled words as they read. Their attention is drawn away from what the writer is saying and, ironically, toward the very thing the writer least wants to emphasize: his or her ability to spell.

Some readers are particularly annoyed by spelling errors. These are the people who tend to equate good spelling with a virtue and poor spelling with a character flaw. Rightly or wrongly, this group of readers seems to assume that poor spelling is indicative of other, less apparent weaknesses. The inference seems to be that "if this writer can't or didn't bother to spell correctly, he or she is probably lax about other matters as well."

Whether or not you agree with this view, the fact remains that legal writers who are poor spellers are at a disadvantage. Their readers — whether friend or foe, self-righteous or forgiving — have a needless obstacle to communication: misspelled words. So, unless you are willing to accept working with a self-imposed disadvantage, improving your spelling is a goal worthy of every legal writer.

Of course, there is no one best way to improve your spelling. Everyone learns differently, so you should be the one to decide which of the methods discussed below will work best for you. Some people find it helpful to use two or more methods together. The important point is to decide what you are going to do and stick with it.

§27.1.2   Spelling Crutches

It is possible to improve the spelling in the end product of your writing without actually learning how to spell a single new word. The methods discussed in this section all require that you rely on someone or something besides yourself for checking your spelling. These spelling crutches get the job done, but they do have drawbacks.

a.   Dictionaries

The time-honored method of checking spelling has always been to "look it up in the dictionary." Even the best speller needs to double-check spelling in the dictionary from time to time.

Dictionaries are undoubtedly valuable resources for spelling, but they do have drawbacks. One needs to have a fairly good idea of how a word is spelled before it can be double-checked in the dictionary. Even then, the writer may have to scan numerous pages before locating the word. If the same word has to be looked up frequently, using the dictionary can become a time-consuming process.

A more efficient way of using the dictionary for spelling is to look up a word once and then use one of the other spelling methods to reinforce learning.

b. Legal Spellers

Rather than scan numerous pages in a standard dictionary, some legal writers find that it is faster to check spelling in a legal speller. These handy, pocket-sized books contain alphabetical lists (without definitions) of legal words and words that frequently occur in legal contexts. They also show correct word divisions. The disadvantage of legal spellers is that there are occasions (law school exams, the bar exam) when they, as well as dictionaries, cannot be used.

c. Computer Software

More and more software companies are offering programs that will correct spelling. If you always have access to a computer for writing, these spelling programs can be a godsend. Their disadvantage is obvious, though. Computer spelling programs check spelling by making a blind match between the words you have typed and the words in the program's memory. The program does not consider context. Consequently, it will read "torte" as spelled correctly without knowing whether the writer intended a wrongful act or a cake with rich frosting.

d. Secretaries and Typists

Many legal professionals who are poor spellers rely on their secretaries or typists to correct spelling errors. If you can find an individual who is 100 percent reliable as a speller and who understands the content of what you are writing, then you may have found the best spelling crutch of all. Even so, the perfect secretary or typist has many of the same drawbacks as dictionaries and legal spellers (they cannot be used in law school exams or for the bar), and they have one disadvantage that is unique — they can be hired away!

§27.1.3 Spelling Strategies

Without a doubt, all the best methods for improving your spelling have you learning to spell the words yourself. This may seem like a formidable task, especially if you truly are a terrible speller, but it can be done in just a few minutes a day. In fact, learning to spell the words you use frequently will save you time in the long run because you won't have to keep checking how those words are spelled.

Before applying the spelling strategies discussed below, begin by analyzing the spelling errors you tend to make. For a designated period of time, perhaps one week, keep track of the words you have to look up.

The chart below was designed to help you categorize your misspellings. From the chart, you can determine whether there is a pattern to your misspellings; if so, you can focus your attention on that specific type of spelling problem and choose a spelling strategy that specifically addresses that problem. Notice too that in the second column you are asked to write the word with the trouble spot circled or enlarged. This simple technique in itself reinforces visual memory of the part of the word that is difficult to remember. Use the category numbers in the following list in the last column. One is done for you.

Categories of Spelling Errors

1. when to use "ei" and when to use "ie" (receive, achieve, seize, their, thief)
2. when to and when not to drop the silent "e" (admire, admiration; judge, judgment; admissible, admissibility)
3. when to and when not to change the "y" to "i" (try, tries, tried; defy, defiance; delay, delays; pay, paid; deputy, deputize)
4. when to and when not to double the final consonant (occur, occurred, occurrence; commit, commitment, committed)
5. getting the middle right (accommodate, rescind, rescission, injunction)
6. guessing the schwa (the vowel sound in unaccented syllables) (separate, independence, severance, benefit)
7. pronunciation — omitting letters in pronunciation often leads to omitting letters in spelling (quantity, probably), and the same is true if you add letters in pronunciation (athletic, disastrous)
8. sound-alikes — learning the difference in meaning between the sound-alikes (its, it's; too, to, two; then, than; pendant, pendent; hale, hail; principal, principle)
9. other — any other misspelling that doesn't fall into the first eight groups

Word (spelled correctly)	Word (spelled correctly with trouble spot circled or enlarged)	Category of error
receive	reCEIve	1

a.   Spelling Rules

Using "ei" or "ie" (category 1)

There are two rules that you can use to distinguish between the "ei" and "ie" words.

1. Use "i" before "e," except after "c" when the two vowels are pronounced as "ē" (as in "see").

believe	receive
niece	perceive
brief	deceive
field	conceive
relief	deceit
grievance	receipt

2. Use "ei" if pronounced as "ā" (as in "day").

e<u>i</u>ght	v<u>ei</u>n	n<u>ei</u>ghbor
fr<u>ei</u>ght	w<u>ei</u>gh	h<u>ei</u>nous

There are several exceptions. Note that most of the exceptions do not pronounce "ie" or "ei" as either "ē" or "ā." If you have trouble spelling any of the exceptions, use the mnemonic strategy (memory trigger) that is discussed later in this section. Here are some examples of mnemonics to help you remember these exceptions.

neither	not difficult to remember if you can spell "either"
weird	this word is weird and an exception to the rule
foreign	another one foreign to the system
sheik	yet another one foreign to the system
their	"their" is the possessive form of "they," so keep the "e" where it belongs and change "y" to "i"
height	because of the "-ight" ending, it is like "right," "night," and "light"
conscience, science	because of the "-ence" ending, it is like "independence" and "convenience"
forfeit	with this one you forfeit the rule
seize, seizure, leisure	remember to "seize your leisure" or have a "leisure seizure"
financier	easy to remember this exception because another rule (add "-er" to mean "one who") takes precedence; plus, "A financi<u>er</u> is fanci<u>er</u> than a banker."

This poem is an easy way to remember the "ei/ie" rule and some of its exceptions:

Use <u>i</u> before <u>e</u> except after <u>c</u>
Or when sounded as <u>a</u>
As in n<u>ei</u>ghbor and w<u>ei</u>gh;
But th<u>ei</u>r, w<u>ei</u>rd, and <u>ei</u>ther,
For<u>ei</u>gn, s<u>ei</u>ze, n<u>ei</u>ther,
L<u>ei</u>sure, forf<u>ei</u>t, and h<u>ei</u>ght,
Are exceptions spelled right.

The following sentence is another way to remember the exceptions:

> At his height, the financier for the weird foreign sheik
> neither seizes nor forfeits his leisure.

Dropping the Silent "e" (category 2)

Adding suffixes to words is usually not a problem unless the word ends in a silent "e." When the silent "e" occurs, here are the rules to apply.

1. Does the suffix begin with a vowel? If so, drop the "e."

kindle + ed = kindled   nerve + ous = nervous
admire + ation = admiration   blue + ish = bluish
abide + ing = abiding   imagine + able = imaginable

2. However, if the silent "e" is preceded by a soft "c" or "g" and the suffix begins with a vowel, the "e" is not usually dropped.

manage + able = manageable
notice + able = noticeable
courage + ous = courageous
advantage + ous = advantageous

3. If the suffix begins with a consonant, the final "e" is usually kept.

extreme + ly = extremely   retire + ment = retirement
force + ful = forceful   safe + ty = safety
one + self = oneself   use + less = useless

The exceptions to the dropping-the-silent-"e" rule include some words commonly used in legal writing. These five exceptions retain the silent "e."

foresee + able = foreseeable
dye + ing = dyeing (to distinguish it from "dying")
singe + ing = singeing (to distinguish it from "singing")
shoe + ing = shoeing (to prevent mispronunciation)
mile + age = mileage (to prevent mispronunciation)

These five exceptions drop the final "e" even though the suffix begins with a consonant.

argue + ment = argument   true + ly = truly
judge + ment = judgment   due + ly = duly
acknowledge + ment = acknowledgment

Changing "y" to "i" (category 3)

One rather consistent rule of English spelling is to change the "y" to an "i" before adding a suffix. However, there are a few additional criteria to consider if you want that rule to work properly.

1. Does the word end in a consonant + y? If so, then change the "y" to "i" and add the suffix <u>unless</u> the suffix is "-<u>ing</u>."

rely + ance = reliance	try + ed = tried
rely + ing = relying	try + ing = trying

2. If a vowel precedes the "y," there is no change.

delay + ed = delayed   employ + ment = employment

There are a few exceptions to this rule — five of them have a vowel before the "y" and still change it to "i," and one has a consonant before the "y" and does not change it to "i":

pay, paid   shy + ness = shyness
say, said
lay, laid
day, daily
slay, slain

If you have changed the "y" to "i" and want to form the plural, add "es" instead of just "s."

duty + es = duties

Doubling the Final Consonant (category 4)

When adding a suffix to a word, you double the final consonant *only if* the following conditions exist.

1. The suffix begins with a vowel.
2. The root word contains only one syllable, or
3. the root word contains more than one syllable and its primary accent is on the last syllable of the root word once the suffix is added.
4. Only one vowel precedes the final consonant (the final consonant cannot be preceded by another consonant).

plan + ing = planning	drop + ed = dropped
run + ing = running	omit + ed = omitted
occur + ed = occurred	admit + ing = admitting
occur + ence = occurrence	submit + ed = submitted
defer + ed = deferred	forgot + en = forgotten

In the following examples, the final consonant is not doubled because one of the required conditions does not exist.

1. The suffix does not begin with a vowel.

commit + <u>m</u>ent = commitment

Note that when "commit" takes a suffix that begins with a vowel,
the final "t" is doubled: committed, committing.

2. A consonant, rather than one vowel, precedes the final consonant.

rele<u>n</u>t + ed = relented

3. Two vowels, rather than the required one vowel, precede the
final consonant.

f<u>ea</u>r + ing = fearing
discl<u>ai</u>m + er = disclaimer

4. The accent is not on the final syllable of the root word once the
suffix is added.

benefit + ed = benefited
differ + ed = differed
refer + ence = reference

Note that when "refer" takes other suffixes, the accent is on the
final syllable of the root word; consequently the final consonant is doubled: refe<u>r</u>red, refe<u>r</u>ring, refe<u>r</u>ral.

Using Flash Cards and Personal Spelling Lists to
Get the Middle Right (category 5)

Most people, particularly fast readers, rarely focus on the middles
of words. Consequently, when these people write, they don't have a
strong mental image of how the middle of a given word looks.

To solve this kind of spelling problem, then, we need a spelling
strategy that highlights that part of each word.

In the second column of the chart earlier in this section, the trouble spot in a word was enlarged or circled. This same highlighting technique can be used when making a set of flash cards or a personal spelling
list.

Suppose, for example, that you have difficulty remembering how
to spell "foreseeable." If the problem is with the first "e," your highlighted area should make that "e" dominant. Of course, there are several ways

to do this, so you should choose whichever way makes you "see" the word in your mind.

> forEseeable
> FOREseeable
> foRESeeable

This highlighting technique works particularly well with flash cards that have only one word printed on each card. By isolating the word and then highlighting the trouble spot, you can be sure that your attention is on not only that word but the part of that word that causes you problems.

Flash cards have other simple but invaluable advantages. Law students can keep a dozen or so index cards in each law textbook for quickly jotting down key words or terms of art that they predict they will have difficulty spelling. These flash cards, which can double as bookmarks, can be quickly reviewed in spare moments before or after class. Once a word is memorized, it can be filed away and pulled out again only if the word becomes a problem in the future. The beauty of the flash card method, then, is that it involves a bare minimum of time invested.

Personal spelling lists that use the highlighting technique work reasonably well, but they have a few noteworthy disadvantages. First of all, the person reviewing the list has to work at focusing on individual words; the list format tends to encourage the eye to move down the list too quickly. Second, lists tend to be somewhere else when you need them. If it becomes inconvenient to write down a word, the odds increase that it won't be recorded. The list may also be elsewhere when you have that spare minute to review spelling.

Using Mnemonics (categories 5, 6, and 9, in particular, but useful for all categories)

Mnemonics, or memory triggers, are useful gimmicks for remembering almost anything. In the section on the "ei/ie" spelling rule, several mnemonics were suggested for remembering the exceptions to that rule. Here are some other examples of mnemonics that can be used for spelling.

> For the word "believe": Never be<u>lie</u>ve a <u>lie</u>.
> For the word "separate": Remember "sep<u>ar</u>ate" is <u>par</u> for the course. Also, "sepa<u>rate</u>" also has <u>a rat</u> in it.
> For the word "defendant": All defend<u>ants</u> are <u>ants</u>.

A good mnemonic, then, is memorable, not necessarily true. Obviously all defendants are not ants; the point is to remember the "-ant" ending.

Often the more absurd the connection you create between the word and its spelling, the easier it will be to remember. You may also find that the mnemonics that you make up yourself stick with you best.

Sometimes mnemonics can be combined with flash cards or personal spelling lists so that the highlighted area corresponds with the memory gimmick. For example, to remember the "n" in "environment" try making a flash card that highlights the "on me" in "environment": envirONMEnt.

Emphasizing and Overemphasizing Pronunciation (categories 6 and 7)

If you tend to pronounce "privilege" with a "d" sound in the last syllable, you are likely to spell it with a "d." If you say "athletic" with four syllables rather than the correct three, you are apt to add an extra vowel after the "th." Consequently, some spelling problems can be corrected simply by checking a dictionary for the correct pronunciation and learning to say the word properly.

Schwa sounds (the vowel sound in an unaccented syllable) present a slightly different problem. By definition, schwa sounds are indistinguishable; when they are pronounced correctly, you can't tell whether they represent an "a," "e," "i," "o," or "u." For purposes of spelling, not speaking, then, you can overemphasize pronunciation in words that contain difficult-to-spell schwa sounds. "Permissible" becomes "permiss-IBle"; "existence" becomes "exisTENce"; and "warrant" becomes "war-RANT."

Distinguishing Between Sound-Alikes (category 8)

Unfortunately, the English language is full of pairs and trios of words that have similar pronunciation but distinct meanings. If you have trouble with affect/effect, principle/principal, discrete/discreet, all together/altogether, ensure/insure, counsel/council, compliment/complement, farther/further, lose/loose, it's/its, their/there/they're, to/too/two, cite/sight/site, elicit/illicit, or any of the other sound-alikes, refer to the Glossary of Usage at the end of this book.

Additional Strategies for Spelling (category 9)

Prefixes. Prefixes do not change the spelling of a word when they are added. Do not drop a letter from or add a letter to the prefix or the original word.

    dis + satisfied = dissatisfied
    mis + spell = misspell
    ir + revocable = irrevocable
    un + necessary = unnecessary
    im + moral = immoral

Remember too that knowing what a prefix means can be a clue to correct spelling. For example, if you have trouble remembering whether a word begins with "pre" or "per," consider whether the word's definition includes the notion of "before," which is the meaning of "pre."

precedent — something done or said before
precede — to go before
premeditate — to think about before

Plurals.   Most nouns form their plural by adding just "s."

case ⟶ cases
statute ⟶ statutes

Some nouns ending in "f" or "fe" change the ending to "ve" before adding the "s" for the plural.

wife ⟶ wives
shelf ⟶ shelves

Nouns ending in "s," "sh," "ch," or "x" add "es" to form the plural.

loss ⟶ losses
bush ⟶ bushes
switch ⟶ switches
tax ⟶ taxes

Note that the "es" ending, unlike the "s" ending, usually adds an extra syllable to these words. Also note that verbs ending in "s," "sh," "ch," or "x" form the third-person singular in the same way.

clutch ⟶ clutches
kiss ⟶ kisses

Nouns ending in "o" preceded by a vowel usually add just "s" to form the plural.

folio ⟶ folios

But nouns ending in "o" preceded by a consonant usually add "es" to form the plural.

zero ⟶ zeroes

Nouns that have changed the "y" to "i" add "es" to form the plural.

copy ⟶ copies
reply ⟶ replies

The formation of some plurals is borrowed from another language.

crisis $\longrightarrow$ crises	datum $\longrightarrow$ data
analysis $\longrightarrow$ analyses	stratum $\longrightarrow$ strata
hypothesis $\longrightarrow$ hypotheses	phenomenon $\longrightarrow$ phenomena
basis $\longrightarrow$ bases	medium $\longrightarrow$ media
alumna (feminine) $\longrightarrow$ alumnae	criterion $\longrightarrow$ criteria
alumnus (masculine) $\longrightarrow$ alumni	

Notice the tendency to give such words anglicized plurals. For words that have two plural forms, either is correct, but the older forms (the second column) are more commonly seen in law. In fact, most legal readers would consider "memorandums" or "dictums" an error.

Singular	*Older Plural*	*Anglicized Plural*
memorandum	memoranda	memorandums
dictum	dicta	dictums
appendix	appendices	appendixes
index	indices	indexes
focus	foci	focuses

Compound nouns form plurals by adding "s" to the last word if all the words of the compound noun are equally significant.

booby trap $\longrightarrow$ booby traps

If one word is more significant than the others, the "s" is added to that word.

brother-in-law $\longrightarrow$ brothers-in-law
passerby $\longrightarrow$ passersby
mile-per-hour $\longrightarrow$ miles-per-hour

(See section 26.5.5 for more information on the use of hyphens.)
To form the plural of dates, figures, or symbols, you can add either "s" or "'s."

the 1940s *or* the 1940's

To form the plural of letters, abbreviations, numbers, and words used as words, add "'s."

The i's must be dotted and the t's crossed.
M.D.'s
One of the 5's was omitted.
The disjunctive or's in that law make it ambiguous.

Note that the letters, numbers, and words used as words are italicized (or underlined), but the "'s" is not.

Possessives.   See section 26.4 on the apostrophe for a complete discussion of how the possessive forms of words are spelled.

Variant Spellings.   Many dictionaries show more than one spelling for a given word. The first spelling shown will be the preferred spelling and the one you should use.

Unless you are practicing law in Great Britain, use American and not British spellings.

British	*American*
judgement	judgment
acknowledgement	acknowledgment
theatre	theater
criticise	criticize
realise	realize
humour	humor
colour	color
jewellery	jewelry
cancelled	canceled
travelled	traveled

b.   Spelling Lists

Many handbooks and books about writing offer lists of commonly misspelled words. When using such a list, study only a few words at a time.

The following chart contains some commonly misspelled words that occur frequently in legal writing. You should supplement this list with a study of the sound-alike words in the Glossary of Usage and the formation of the possessive.

1. paid
   forty
   their

2. coming
   writing
   across

3. receive
   believe
   achieve

4. judgment
   argument
   separate

5. appellate
   appellant
   appellee

6. statute
   statutory
   statutorily

7. omitting
   omission
   omitted

8. committed
   committing
   committee
   commitment

9. occurred
   occurring
   occurrence

10. referred
    referral
    reference

11. analyze
    criticize
    recognize

12. allege
    allegation
    acknowledge
    privilege

13. consistent
    pertinent
    convenient
    efficient

14. apparent
    independent
    analogous
    unnecessary

15. permissible
    reversible
    admissibility

16. occasional
    accommodate
    foreseeable
    among

17. government
    environment
    harassment
    fundamental

18. warrant
    hearsay
    injunction
    subpoena

19. carefully
    accidentally
    basically

20. physically
    undoubtedly
    entirely

21. liaison
    rescission
    recision

22. supersede
    succeed
    aggravate
    exaggerate

23. evidentiary
    contributorily
    nuisance
    negligence

24. existence
    absence
    license

25. defendant
    appearance
    attendance
    descendant

26. benefited
    beneficial
    recommend

27. category
    bureaucracy
    probably
    representative

28. develop_
    certain
    against

29. condemn
    guaranteed
    mortgage
    illiterate

30. definite
    maneuver
    possession
    unanimous

31. perform
    precede
    prejudice

32. proceed
    procedure
    seize

33. similar
    familiar
    sincerely
    truly

34. eighth
    height_
    paroled
    questionnaire

35. irrelevant
    respondent

One Final Note About Spelling

Always spell people's names correctly. Make a point of checking whether it is Stephen with a "ph" or Steven with a "v," Schmitt with a "t" or Schmidt with a "d." There is no quicker way to annoy or even alienate a reader than to misspell his or her name.

§27.2   Capitalization

§27.2.1   General Rules

In English, there are two general rules for capitalization: (1) to mark the beginning of a sentence, and (2) to signal a proper name or adjective.

a. Beginning of a Sentence

The first word of a sentence is always capitalized. Even sentence fragments such as those that begin brief answers in legal memoranda have their first word capitalized.

A complete sentence enclosed in parentheses starts with a capital letter, unless the parenthetical sentence occurs within another sentence.

EXAMPLE

The Wilsons extended their garden beyond the property line and onto the disputed strip. (See Attachment A.) *but*

The Wilsons extended their garden beyond the property line (see Attachment A) and onto the disputed strip.

---

1.   Quotations

Capitalize the first word of a direct quotation when the quotation is formally introduced and set up as a separate sentence.

EXAMPLE

The Supreme Court unanimously struck down a policy banning women of child-bearing age from hazardous but top-paying jobs: "Decisions about the welfare of future children must be left to the parents who conceive, bear, support and raise them rather than to the employers who hire those parents."

Do not capitalize the first word of a direct quotation when the quotation is integrated into the writer's sentence. (See section 26.5.3 for discussion of the use of brackets when making a change to a quotation.)

EXAMPLE

The Supreme Court unanimously struck down a policy banning women of child-bearing age from hazardous but top-paying jobs, stating that "[d]ecisions about the welfare of future children must be left to the parents who conceive, bear, support and raise them rather than to the employers who hire those parents."

Do not capitalize the beginning of the second segment of a split direct quotation.

EXAMPLE

"Concern for a woman's existing or potential offspring," wrote Justice Blackmun for the majority, "historically has been the excuse for denying women equal employment opportunities."

---

2. Sentence Following a Colon

When a full sentence follows a colon, the writer has the option to capitalize the first word of the sentence following the colon.

EXAMPLES

Correct:

The company has evidence that Mrs. McKibbin accepted the written proposal: She made a telephone call to place the order for the rugs.

Also Correct:

The company has evidence that Mrs. McKibbin accepted the written proposal: she made a telephone call to place the order for the rugs.

Do not capitalize the first word after the colon if what follows the colon is less than a complete sentence.

> **EXAMPLE**

In *Traweek,* the court found that the appearance of the defendants differed from the witness's description in just one detail: the color of the shirts worn by the defendants.

If the items in a series following a colon are not complete sentences, do not capitalize the first word in each item.

> **EXAMPLE**

The parties will dispute whether three of the four elements of the sudden emergency doctrine are met: (1) whether Mr. Short was confronted by a sudden and unexpected emergency, (2) whether his own negligence created or contributed to that emergency, and (3) whether he made a choice such as a reasonable person placed in the same situation might make.

---

b. Proper Nouns and Adjectives

As a general rule, capitalize a word used to name someone or something specific; use lowercase when the same word is used as a general reference.

the President of Shell Oil
a president of a company

Stanford Law School
a law school

Environmental Protection Agency
an agency of the federal government

Note

Unfortunately, there is disagreement about whether to apply this rule to the words "defendant" and "plaintiff" (and similar terms such as "appellant," "appellee," "respondent," and "petitioner"). Some authorities apply this rule and capitalize these words when they refer to the parties in the matter that is the subject of the document.[1] Others simply

---

1. See the *Bluebook* (15th ed.), *Practitioners' Notes.*

say not to capitalize the terms at all[2] or not to capitalize them when they appear before a name[3] as in the example "defendant Smith." All agree that these words should be capitalized on cover sheets for briefs.

Even with this general rule as a guide, legal writers often find it difficult to determine when certain words that commonly occur in legal writing ("act," "amendment," "bill," "circuit," "code," "constitution," "court," "federal," "national," "statute," and "the") should be capitalized. Use the following list as a quick reference.

"Act"

Capitalize the word "act" when it is part of a full title.

the Clean Air Act
the Controlled Substance Act of 1970, *but*
an act passed by the legislature

"Act" is also capitalized when it is used as the short form of a proper name.

the Clean Air Act ⟶ the Act

"Amendment"

Despite the general rule to capitalize names of specific nouns, several authorities[4] insist that the word "amendment" is not capitalized when it is used to designate one of the specific amendments to the Constitution. Perhaps because this practice defies logic, other authorities[5] insist that it should be. Whichever course a writer selects, it is important to be consistent throughout the same document.

fifth amendment　　　*or*　　　Fifth Amendment

All agree that a general reference to an amendment should not be capitalized.

an amendment to the tax laws

---

2. See *The Texas Law Review Manual on Style* (4th ed.).
3. See *The Chicago Manual of Style* (13th ed.).
4. See *Webster's Legal Speller,* the *Bluebook* (15th ed.), and *The Texas Law Review Manual on Style* (4th ed.).
5. See *Webster's Legal Secretaries Handbook, The New York Times Manual on Style and Usage* and *The Chicago Manual of Style* (13th ed.).

Notice that when referring to one of the amendments to the Constitution, most writers spell out ordinals through nine and use figures for 10 and above.

fifth amendment   14th amendment

When two or more amendments are mentioned together, use figures if either is for 10 or above.

the 5th amendment and the 14th amendment

"Bill"

With the exception of the Bill of Rights, "bill" should be written in lowercase. This practice does seem to be an exception to the general rule of capitalizing words that are part of a full title.

Senate bill 47   House bill 11

"Circuit"

Capitalize "circuit" when it is used as part of a full title. Use lowercase when "circuit" is part of a general reference.

United States Court of Appeals for the Second Circuit, *but*
circuit courts

"Code"

Capitalize "code" when it is part of a full title. Use lowercase for all general references.

The United States Internal Revenue Code
United States Code, *but*
the tax code
state codes
unofficial code

"Constitution"

Capitalize "constitution" when used as part of the full title of any constitution or when used as a short form reference to the United States Constitution.

the United States Constitution
the Constitution (short for United States Constitution), *but*
a new state constitution

"Court"

Probably the most common capitalization question in legal writing is when should "court" be capitalized.

1. The official and full names of all international and higher courts are capitalized.

International Court of Justice
United States Court of Appeals for the Third Circuit
Texas Court of Appeals
Arizona Supreme Court

2. Always capitalize "court" when referring to the United States Supreme Court. Note that even the short forms for referring to the United States Supreme Court are capitalized.

the Supreme Court of the United States
the United States Supreme Court
the Supreme Court
the Court (short form for Supreme Court)

3. Do not capitalize "court" if part of the name of a city or county court.

the Phoenix night court
Hampton municipal court
juvenile court

Note

Despite the agreement among the authorities about not capitalizing "court" if it is part of the name of a city of county court, most practitioners seem to ignore the rule and capitalize "court" in such instances.

———————

4. Capitalize "court" in a document when referring to the very court that will receive that document.
5. Capitalize "court" when the term specifically refers to the judge or presiding officer.

It is the opinion of this Court . . . .

Other personifications such as "Your Honor" and "the Bench" are also capitalized.

"Federal"

The word "federal" is capitalized only when it is part of a specific name.

Federal Bureau of Investigation
Federal Deposit Insurance Corporation
Federal Energy Regulatory Commission, *but*
federal government
federal agents
federal court

"National"

The word "national" is capitalized only when it is part of a specific name.

National Security Council, *but*
national security interests

Note

Another test for whether to capitalize "federal" or "national" is whether the word following those terms is capitalized. If it is, then capitalize "federal" or "national" because it is part of a specific name.

"Statute"

Use lowercase for "statute," unless it is part of a title.

federal statutes
state statutes
statute of limitations, *but*
Statute of Frauds

"The"

In names and titles, capitalize "the" only if it is part of an official name.

The Hague, *but*
the *Bluebook*
the United States Supreme Court
the American Bar Association

§27.2.2   Headings

The most important thing to remember about capitalization in headings is consistency. If local rules or convention dictates that certain types of headings require all capital letters, be consistent with that rule or convention. If there are no rules governing capitalization in the type of headings you are writing, develop a system that can be used consistently throughout the document.

Elaine C. Maier, in her book *How to Prepare a Legal Citation,* outlines the following suggested scheme "in descending order of subordination":

1. All letters of all words in the heading are capitalized.
2. All initial letters of all words in the heading are capitalized.
3. All initial letters of all words in the heading except articles, conjunctions, and prepositions of four letters or fewer are capitalized.
4. The sentence style of capitalization is used; that is, only the first letter of the first word and proper nouns are capitalized.[6]

Use the same capitalization level to indicate comparable levels in your text. (Boldface, underlining, and other typefaces may also be used to create levels in text.)

In situations where you are developing your own scheme of capitalization in headings, remember that having more than five words typed in all capitals slows your reader down. For this reason, it may be best to use all capitals at a level where you have only relatively short headings.

§27.2.3   Miscellaneous Rules for Capitalization

Academic Degrees

Academic degrees are capitalized, but some have lowercase internal letters.

J.D.   LL.M.   M.D.   Ph.D.

Acronyms

Most acronyms are written in all capitals (OPEC, NASA, CERCLA). Abbreviations of government agencies, corporations, and military organizations are also in all capital letters (EEOC, FCC, IBM, USMC).

---

6. Elaine C. Maier, *How to Prepare a Legal Citation,* Barron's Educational Series, Inc. 1986, p. 158.

Compass Points and Geographical Names

Compass points are capitalized when they refer to a geographical region; adjectives derived from compass points are also capitalized.

the Middle West
the Northeast
Southern hospitality
Southwestern cuisine, *but*
the car was heading west
the fence runs along the northern boundary

Topographical Names

Capitalize topographical names when they are part of a proper name.

Lake Superior	a lake
the Mississippi River	the river
the Rocky Mountains	those mountains

In legal documents, words such as "state," "county," or "city" are capitalized when they are part of a specific name.

Washington State
Chaves County
the City of Spokane
the State of Florida
Commonwealth of Virginia

Similarly, capitalize words such as "bridge," "square," "building," "park," and "hotel" when they are part of a place name.

Brooklyn Bridge	Central Park
Transamerica Building	Tiananmen Square

Judges' Names

The Supreme Court has a tradition of spelling judges' names in all capitals when the names are referred to in opinions.

Rules of Law

Despite efforts at uniformity, several rules of law are known by several versions of their name, all with differing capitalization. The common issue is whether a certain phrase is part of the title of the rule. The general guideline is to capitalize the words that are essential to the rule's name. Another reasonable guideline is to use the most common form of the rule's name.

Is it, for example, "the rule in Shelley's case," "the Rule in Shelley's case," "the Rule in Shelley's Case," or "The Rule in Shelley's Case"? Using the guideline of capitalizing those words that are essential to the rule's name, "rule in" and "case" should be capitalized because they are commonly treated as part of the name. "The," on the other hand, should probably be lowercase to avoid making the phrase look like a book title.

Is it the "rule against perpetuities," the "Rule against Perpetuities," or the "Rule Against Perpetuities"? Professor Dukeminier asked this question in his article *Perpetuities: Contagious Capitalization*[7] and determined that "Rule against Perpetuities" and "rule against perpetuities" were both commonly used and therefore acceptable. "Rule against Perpetuities" is preferable, according to Dukeminier, for historical reasons.

What should a legal writer do, then, when faced with a similar question? Consider the following factors:

1. What words are essential to the rule's name?
2. What capitalization is most common?
3. Is there a historical reason for preferring one version over another?

The most important consideration of all, though, is consistency. Once you have determined which version you will use, use it consistently throughout the document.

Titles

Capitalize titles of court documents. Use all capitals for titles on the documents themselves.

Trademarks

Use all capitals to distinguish a trademark from the name of a company or corporation.

XEROX	(trademark)	Xerox	(corporation)
EXXON	(trademark)	Exxon	(corporation)

---

7. Jesse Dukeminier, *Perpetuities: Contagious Capitalization,* 20 J. Legal Educ. 341 (1968).

Vessels

Although one occasionally sees all capitals used for the name of a vessel, capitalizing only the first letter is preferred.

Titanic   Valdez

§27.3   ABBREVIATIONS AND SYMBOLS

§27.3.1   General Rules for Abbreviations

Abbreviations, or shortened forms, should be used primarily for the convenience of the reader. Properly used, an abbreviation saves *reader* time and energy. It gets across the same message in less space.

The temptation for writers, of course, is to use abbreviations that are convenient for them. A writer who fails to adopt the reader's perspective may use an abbreviation to save writer time and energy only to find that the reader is unsure, confused, or even frustrated by the abbreviation.

One source of abbreviation confusion is the sheer number of specialized abbreviations used in some legal documents.[8] The result of such overuse is obvious: a harried reader who has to keep turning back in the document to keep the abbreviations straight. The solution to the problem is equally obvious: Avoid using numerous specialized abbreviations in the same document.

Note

All of the abbreviation rules that follow apply to abbreviations in textual sentences, not in citations. (See Chapter 17 for a discussion of abbreviations in citations.)

Rule 1.   Abbreviate only when the abbreviation will be clear for the reader.

Rule 2.   If an abbreviation will be initially unfamiliar to the reader, use the full form first and then follow with the abbreviation in parentheses.

---

8. Writing about a case in which no fewer than seven different groups of initials were used, Justice Rehnquist complained that "the 'alphabet soup' of the New Deal era was, by comparison, a clear broth." *Chrysler Corp. v. Brown,* 441 U.S. 281, 284, 286-87 (1979).

Mrs. Kearney telephoned Beaver Custom Carpets (BCC) and asked if it manufactured custom-made carpets. BCC's representative took down a description of the carpets she wanted made.

Mr. Washburn wants to know whether the Oregon Wilderness Watchers (OWW) can create a prescriptive easement across his land. OWW has been using a path across Washburn's property to reach its property.

Note

Abbreviations created for a specific document, such as BCC and OWW in the examples above, are usually written in all capitals. Notice that common abbreviations that are acronyms (ERIC, SARA, ERISTA) are also written in all capitals, unless they have been fully incorporated into the language (radar, sonar, scuba, and zip code).

§27.3.2   Miscellaneous Rules for Abbreviation

Geographical Names

U.S. Postal Service abbreviations are acceptable when used on envelopes and in other situations when an address is written in block form. Note that state abbreviations are all capitalized without end periods.

Professor Mary Brown
8990 6th Ave. NE
Tacoma, WA 98498

The same words (avenue, street, northeast, Washington) should be spelled out when they appear in text. Note that all compass points (northeast, southwest) are also lower case, unless they are used as the name of a region (the Pacific Northwest, the South).

"Saint" may be abbreviated when it is part of a name of a city (St. Louis); follow the bearer's preference when it is part of a person's name (David Saint-Johns, Ruth St. Denis).

Foreign Phrases

Some Latin words commonly used in legal texts and citations are abbreviations, so they should be followed by periods *(id., i.e., e.g.)*. Others are complete words (the *ex* in *ex parte* or *re*), so a period should not be used.

Names of Laws

The first time a law is mentioned in text, its title should be typed out in full; thereafter, abbreviations can be used. (See the *Bluebook* for how to write the names of laws in citations.)

> first mention: Article II, Section 3
> later references: Art. II, Sec. 3

Academic Degrees

Academic degrees are abbreviated. Note too that capitalization should be checked with a dictionary.

> Ph.D.   LL.D.   M.B.A.   C.P.A.
> J.D.   LL.B.   LL.M.   M.D.

Time

The abbreviations for *ante meridiem* and *post meridiem* are most commonly written as unspaced, lowercase letters with periods.

> 9:00 a.m.   *or*   9:00 A.M.

Measures and Weights

When the numeral is written out,[9] the unit must also be written out. When the figure is used, the unit may be abbreviated.

> one hundred square miles   *or*   100 sq. mi.
> one hundred eighty pounds   *or*   180 lbs.

---

9. According to the *Bluebook* Rule 6.2(a), numbers from zero to ninety-nine are written out and larger numbers use numerals, unless the number begins a sentence. Numbers used at the beginning of a sentence must be written out.

Double Punctuation

Occasionally, an abbreviation will be the last word in a sentence. In such cases, do not add an additional period after the period for the abbreviation.

> The officer had checked in at 8:00 p.m.
>
> Clark claimed she had a Ph.D.

A period for an abbreviation can be used with a question mark or an exclamation point.

> Did the officer check in at 8:00 p.m.?

§27.3.3   Inappropriate Abbreviations

Informal abbreviations

Avoid informal abbreviations such as "ad," "cite," "exam," "memo," "phone," "quote" (as a noun), and "&" in formal legal writing. Use the more formal, full name: "advertisement," "citation," "examination," "memorandum," "telephone," and "quotation," and "and."

Dates

Do not abbreviate dates. Write them out in full.

> Monday, February 11, 1991, *not*
> Mon. Feb. 11, '91

Abbreviations Between Lines or Pages

Do not separate parts of an abbreviation. The full abbreviation should be on one line on one page.

Beginnings of Sentences

Avoid beginning a sentence with an abbreviation unless the abbreviation is a courtesy title (Mr., Mrs., Ms., Dr., Messrs.).

Titles

Most titles other than Mr., Mrs., Ms., Dr., and Messrs. are not abbreviated.

> Professor John Q. LaFond
> Dean James E. Bond
> General Colin Powell

When "Honorable" and "Reverend" are preceded by "the," then "honorable" and "reverend" are spelled out; when used without "the," they can be abbreviated.

| The Reverend James P. Coyne | *but* | Rev. James P. Coyne |
| The Honorable Walter Jackson | *but* | Hon. Walter Jackson |

§27.3.4   General Rules for Symbols

Rule 1.   Do not begin a sentence with a symbol.

"Section" and "paragraph" are always spelled out at the beginning of a sentence.

> Section 289 was amended in 1989, *not*
> § 289 was amended in 1989.

The symbol for "section," §, or §§ for "sections," must be used in footnotes or citations as long as it does not begin a sentence. Be sure to separate the symbol from the number following it with a space.

Rule 2.   Use the symbol for dollar ($) and percent (%) with numerals. Spell out the words if the numbers are spelled out.

fifteen dollars	*or*	$15.00
sixty percent	*or*	60%

There is no space between $ or % and their accompanying numerals.

§27.4   ITALICS

In legal writing, italics are most commonly used for case names, titles of publications, foreign phrases, introductory signals, and, occasionally, emphasis. When a particular typewriter or computer does not have italics, underlining is an acceptable substitute.

Rule 1. All case names, including the *v.*,[10] should be in italics.

Smith v. Jones
United States v. Foster

If underlining is used, underline the blank spaces between the words.

Smith v. Jones
United States v. Foster

Rule 2. Italicize all introductory signals, phrases introducing related authority, and explanatory phrases in citations. (See the *Bluebook* for a complete list.)

Accord	*See also*	*Cf.*	*E.g.,*
aff'd	*cert. denied*	*rev'd*	*withdrawn*
cited with		*construed in*	
approval in			

Note

"See" is not italicized when it is used in text, rather than as part of the citation, to introduce an authority.

Rule 3. Italicize all titles of publications when they appear in text. (See the *Bluebook* for titles in citations.)

Titles of books, reports, periodicals, newspapers, and plays are all italicized when they appear in textual sentences. Even titles of nonprint media such as television and radio programs, musical works, and works of visual art are italicized.

Handbook of Federal Indian Law
Index to Legal Periodicals
Yale Law Review
New York Times
Presumed Innocent
L.A. Law

The Bible, however, is not italicized.

---

10. Some attorneys do not italicize the *v.*, presumably because the Supreme Court of the United States does not. *Bluebook* rules, however, require that the *v.* be italicized.

Rule 4. Italicize names of aircraft, ships, and trains.

Hindenburg *Nimitz* *Orient Express*

Rule 5. Italicize foreign words that are not incorporated into the English language.

carpe diem
qua
infra
supra

Rule 6. Italics can be used to indicate that a word is being used as a word.

Article 6 is silent about what constitutes *service* as opposed to *merchandise.*

Rule 7. If used sparingly, italics can be used for emphasis.

Fremont's coach insists that he *asked* all of his players to participate in the drug-testing program.

Use of italics or underlining for emphasis occurs most commonly in long quotations. In such cases, the writer must indicate whether the emphasis was added or whether it was part of the original quotation.

EXAMPLE

The Soldiers' and Sailors' Civil Relief Act does not operate to extend the time period during which the defendant must be served:

> The period of military service shall not be included in computing any period now or hereafter to be limited by any law, regulation, or order for the bringing of any action or proceeding in any court, board, bureau, commission, department, or other agency of government by or against any person in military service or by or against his heirs, executors, administrators, or assigns, whether such cause of action or the right or privileges to institute such action or proceeding shall have accrued *prior to or during* the period of such service . . . .

50 U.S.C. § 525 (1976) (emphasis added).

---

§27.5   Conventions of Formal Writing

The conventions of formal writing apply to legal writing, particularly briefs and memoranda. Consequently, some practices that are acceptable in informal writing or oral language are generally considered inappropriate in formal legal documents.

§27.5.1   Use of First-Person Pronouns

Although in recent years there has been a bit more acceptance of first-person pronouns (I, me, my, we, our, us) in legal writing, most legal writers still use only third person in legal memoranda and briefs.

"Our" is fairly well accepted when used in office memos to refer to the client's case ("in our case"), although purists still prefer that the client's name be used ("in Brown's case"). "My" is well accepted in client letters ("in my opinion"), and many attorneys use other first-person pronouns throughout client letters ("I received your letter," "please call me if you have any questions").

§27.5.2   Use of Contractions

Contractions are closely associated with the informality of most oral language. For this reason, there has been strong resistance to the use of contractions in legal writing. Occasionally, you will see a contraction used in a client letter, but these instances are not the norm. As a general rule, avoid contractions in all legal writing.

§27.5.3   Numbers

The *Bluebook,* also known as *A Uniform System of Citation,* sets the standard for what is the acceptable way to write numbers in legal writing. In a nutshell, the rule is to spell out numbers from zero to ninety-nine in text and from zero to nine in footnotes. For larger numbers, use numerals unless the number begins a sentence or the number is a round number (hundred, thousand).

If a series of numbers includes one or more numbers that should be written with numerals, then numerals should be used for the entire series.

> The dispatch operator received 104 calls on Friday, 72 calls on Saturday, and 11 calls on Sunday.

Numerals should be used with numbers that contain a decimal point, with numbers used for sections or subdivisions, and in contexts in which numbers are used frequently to refer to percentages and dollar amounts.

§27.5.4   Use of Questions and Exclamations

As a general rule, avoid questions in legal writing. With the exception of the question presented, or issue statement, sentences in legal writing are almost always statements, not questions or exclamations.

When you want to use a question, revise the question into a statement that says, in effect, this question exists.

EXAMPLE

Question:

Which test will the court apply?

Revised:

The court will determine which test to apply.

When you are tempted to use a rhetorical question, revise that point into a positive assertion or statement.

EXAMPLE

Question:

How can the police do their job if they are not allowed to stop suspects who match an eyewitness's description?

Revised:

The police will be unable to do their job if they are not allowed to stop suspects who match an eyewitness's description.

Exclamatory statements may appear to be forceful and therefore persuasive, but they often achieve the opposite effect. Instead of strengthening a position, exclamatory statements may weaken it because they make the writer appear unsophisticated, immature, or inflammatory. As a general rule, then, unless you are quoting another person, do not use exclamatory sentences.

Glossary of Usage

In grammar, "usage" simply means what word or phrase a native speaker of the language would use in certain situations. In legal writing, appropriate usage will typically be that of the educated professional. Choices will usually reflect a conservative, more traditional view of language.

Even in law, though, usage is not static. The language of law may be traditional and formal, but it is still living and changing. As a consequence, "correct" usage varies from time to time. What was once unacceptable may, in a decade, become the appropriate choice. For this reason, astute legal writers should consider the date of publication for any authority they consult about usage and, as always, they should consider the reader and purposes of the document they are producing.

In addition, all usage errors are not created equal. Some are egregious errors; others, more forgiveable. While it is certainly best to master all the usage questions in the following glossary, those marked with an asterisk (*) are important to learn first either because they appear frequently in legal writing or because they represent an error that would distract most readers.

*A/An.   Use "a" before words that begin with a consonant sound, and use "an" before words that begin with a vowel sound. Notice that some words begin with a vowel but still use "a" because the initial sound in the word is a consonant sound. This situation occurs when the word begins with a long "u" or "eu" and before the word "one" (a university, a one-hour delay). A few words (usually silent "h" words) begin with a consonant but still use "an" because the initial sound in the word is a vowel sound (an honor, an heir).

*A lot.   "A lot" as in the expression "a lot of time" is always spelled as two words. "Alot" as one word is never correct. Notice, however, that "a lot" tends to sound rather informal and may also be imprecise. For these reasons, "a lot" is often not the best choice in legal writing ("a lot of time" → "a great deal of time"; "a lot of prior convictions" → "numerous prior convictions"; "a lot of experience" → "considerable experience").

*Adverse/Averse. "Adverse" means "unfavorable," "opposed," or "hostile." One can get an "adverse verdict" or "adverse criticism." "Averse" means "disinclined" or "reluctant." Use "averse" to show a distaste for something or a tendency to avoid something. One may be averse to representing certain types of clients.

*Advice/Advise. "Advice" is the noun; "advise" is the verb. One can advise a client, or one can give advice to a client.

*Affect/Effect. Generally, "affect" is used as a verb meaning "to influence, impress, or sway": "The jury did not seem to be affected by the defendant's emotional appeal for mercy." "Affect" may also be used as a verb meaning "to pretend or feign": "The witness affected surprise when she was told that the signature was forged." Less common is "affect" used as a noun in psychology meaning "emotion."

The most common use of "effect" is as a noun meaning "the result, consequence, or outcome." "Effect" is also used to mean "goods," as in "one's personal effects," and "impression" as in "done for effect."

"Effect" is used as a verb meaning "to bring about or accomplish": "The mediator successfully effected an agreement between labor and management." Had the preceding example been "the mediator affected an agreement between labor and management" the meaning would have been significantly different. "Effected an agreement" means the agreement was reached; "affected an agreement" means the mediator had some influence on the agreement.

Study Aid

Part of what seems to confuse writers about "affect" and "effect" is that "affect" as a verb means "to have an effect on." For this reason, it may be helpful to analyze the grammar of a sentence in which "affect" or "effect" would appear. If the sentence needs a verb and you cannot substitute "to bring about," then use "affect." If the choice requires a noun, use "effect."

*Among/Between. Use "among" when discussing three or more objects or people; use "between" when discussing two objects or people: "The members of the Board of Directors could not agree among themselves." "Attorney-client privilege refers to those confidential communications that occur between a client and her attorney."

Amount/Number. Use "amount" with nouns that cannot be counted and "number" with nouns that can be counted: "The amount of grief this mother has suffered cannot be measured by the number of dollars a jury awards her."

And/or. Many authorities consider this usage cumbersome; others point out that it can be ambiguous, unless you use "and/or" to show that three possibilities exist (for example, husband and/or wife can mean (1) husband, (2) wife, or (3) both). Consequently, because the reader has to stop and sort through the three possibilities, it is easier on the reader to present each of the three possibilities separately (for example, "husband or wife or both").

Anxious/Eager.   "Anxious" comes from the root word "anxiety." Consequently, if one is "anxious," one is "concerned or worried": "I feel anxious about the interview." "Eager," on the other hand, means "looking forward to": "When asked what happened, the defendant was eager to talk to the police."

Study Aid

Use "anxious about," but "eager to." A defendant may be "anxious about" (worried about) testifying or "eager to" (looking forward to) testify.

As/Because/Since.   Because "since" has at least two meanings —"from some time in the past" and "because" — some sentences that begin with "since" may be ambiguous: "Since you have made these improvements, you have used the property almost daily during the summer months." The example sentence may mean that you have used the property almost daily since the time when you made the improvements, or it may mean that you have used the property almost daily because you made the improvements. For this reason, it is better to use "since" only for time references and "because" for cause-and-effect references. Similarly, avoid using "as" in cause-and-effect sentences because it may also be ambiguous and misunderstood to mean "while."

As/Like.   "Like" can be used as a preposition, not just as a conjunction. Consequently, if a full clause follows, use "as" or "as if": The defendant looked as if she were lying.

A While/Awhile.   "A while" is an article plus a noun; "awhile" is an adverb. Use awhile only when it modifies a verb, not as an object of a preposition: "The shopkeeper waited awhile before answering the officer's question; then he paused for a while before showing the officer the safe."

Bad/Badly.   "Bad" is an adjective; "badly" is an adverb. When the verb "feel" is used as a linking verb (a state of being, a state of mind), it must be followed by an adjective. Consequently, one "feels bad": "Olsen claims that he felt bad when he fired Baxter."

But however, But yet.   These phrases are redundant; avoid them. Use just "but" or just "however" or just "yet" alone.

Compare to/Compare with/Contrast.   Use "compare to" when pointing out only similarities; use "compare with" when pointing out similarities and differences; use "contrast" when pointing out only differences.

Complement/Compliment. A complement completes something: "Ajax, Inc. considered Smith to be the perfect complement to its sales department." A compliment is a flattering remark.

Comprise/Compose/Include. "Comprise" means "to contain": The panel comprises three judges. Notice that "is composed of" can substitute for "comprise." For precision's sake, do not substitute "include" for "comprise." "Comprise" denotes a complete listing; "include" may mean a partial listing.

Study Aid

The whole comprises all the parts. The whole is composed of all the parts. The whole includes some or all of the parts.

Contact. In informal English, "contact" is frequently used as a verb to mean to telephone, write, or talk face-to-face. In formal writing, it is better to use the precise choice.

Continual/Continuous. "Continual" means "frequently repeated"; "continuous" means "unceasing": "His clients' continual complaint was that he never returned telephone calls." "Continuous water flow cools the reactor."

Convince/Persuade. To convince someone means to change that person's mind; to persuade someone means to move that person to action: "Ms. O'Brien's goal was to convince Mr. Taylor that she was hardworking and then persuade him to give her a raise."

Study Aid

Use "convince of" or "convince that" but "persuade to."

Criteria/Criterion. "Criteria" is the plural form; "criterion" is the singular form. "Acme published the following criteria for the new position: a four-year college degree, experience in sales, and willingness to travel. It waived the first criterion for applicants who had completed Acme's own in-house training program."

Different from/Different than. Use "different from" unless the resulting sentence would be awkward.

Disinterested/Uninterested. "Disinterested" means "neutral, unbiased"; "uninterested" means "bored": "We want judges to be disinterested, not uninterested, in the cases before them."

Due to/Because of. Purists use "due" only as a noun or adjective, not as a preposition. Consequently, "due to" can be used in those sentence slots that call for an adjective, such as the subject complement, and as modifiers of nouns: "The damage was due to faulty wiring" (subject complement). "The deterioration due to severe weather conditions makes the bridge unsafe" (modifier of a noun). Although some authorities on usage point to the wide acceptance of "due to" as a preposition, most recommend that "because of" be used instead in preposition slots: "Because of his poor health, Justice Brennan resigned his position on the Supreme Court."

Study Aid

Because "due to" is always acceptable as a subject complement, look for a form of the verb "to be" as the main verb to determine whether "due to" can be used. Also, one test of whether "due to" is being used as an adjective is to substitute the phrase "attributed to."

e.g./i.e.   In textual sentences, the English equivalents for "e.g." (for example) and "i.e." (that is, or namely) are generally preferable to the Latin abbreviations, although "i.e." and "e.g." are appropriate in footnotes and parenthetical matter. When the Latin abbreviations are used, they should be italicized and followed by a comma.

Some writers mistakenly use "i.e." to mean "for example."

In citations, use the signal "e.g." according to Rule 1.2(a) in the *Bluebook.*

Etc.   Avoid using "etc." in legal writing. Whenever possible, replace "etc." with specifics, or use the appropriate English equivalent ("and so forth" or "and others") instead. Never use "and etc." This phrase is redundant; it means "and and so forth."

Farther/Further.   Use "farther" for geographical distances and "further" for showing other additions: "The placement of the fence suggested that the property line was farther north." "We can discuss this matter further after we have more facts."

Fewer/Less.   Use "fewer" for objects that can be counted; use "less" for generalized quantities or sums that cannot be counted: "Elaine used fewer sick days than any other employee. She also had less work."

*Good/Well.   Use "good" as an adjective and "well" as an adverb, except when referring to health: "The prosecutor is a good lawyer who prepares well for trial. Will the witness be well enough to testify in court?"

Hanged/Hung.   Use "hung" as the past tense for "hang" in all situations except executions: "The counterfeit bill was framed and hung in the lobby." "The whistleblower was hanged by the members as a warning to others."

*Have/Of.   "Have," not "of," should be used after the auxiliary verbs "could," "should," and "would": "The plaintiff could have offered a compromise before initiating the lawsuit."

Hopefully.   In the last decade, "hopefully" has been widely used to mean "I hope" or "we hope" as in the sentence "Hopefully, we will win this case." Several purists launched a highly publicized campaign to point out that "hopefully" originally meant "to be filled with hope"; therefore, the "correct" way to use "hopefully" was in sentences like this: "Hopefully, the client began reading the opinion letter from his attorney." This sentence meant the client was "filled with hope" as he read the attorney's opinion about his case, not that anyone was hoping the client would begin reading the letter. Perhaps the best solution to the "hopefully" problem for legal writers is to use alternate phrasing: "We hope we will win this case." "The client was hopeful as he began reading the opinion letter from his attorney."

*Imply/Infer.   "To imply" means "to indicate, suggest, or express indirectly": "At the show-up, the police officer implied that the defendant was the assailant when he said, 'Don't you think that's him?'" "To infer" means "to deduce, conclude, or gather": "The jury may infer that the defendant is guilty if it hears about her prior convictions."

Study Aid

Use "infer" when the actors in the sentence are drawing inferences *from* something.

Is when/Is where.   Do not use these constructions in sentences that are definitions. A well-crafted definition should have a noun following "is": "An endowment is the transfer of money or property to an institution." Not: "An endowment is when someone transfers money or property to an institution."

*Its/It's.   "Its" is the possessive form of "it." Like many other pronouns, "it" forms the possessive by simply adding "s," not "'s" (hers, yours, ours). "It's" is a contraction for "it is" or sometimes "it has."

Because contractions are generally avoided in legal writing, "its" or spelling out the words "it is" will be the correct choice in most legal writing.

Lay/Lie.   "Lay" is a transitive verb, which means it must have an object. "Lay" means to "put, place, or set down": "Just lay the file on my desk." "Lie" is an intransitive verb, which means it does not have an object. "To lie" means "to recline or remain": "The file will lie unopened on my desk until the bill is paid."

Study Aid

The confusion over "lay/lie" stems from the conjugation of these verbs. "Lay" is a regular verb (lay, laid, laid), but "lie" is an irregular verb (lie, lay, lain) with a past tense that matches the present tense of "lay." The simplest way to determine which word to use is to (1) decide which verb you need ("lay" or "lie") and (2) decide which tense is required.

Literally.   "Literally" is not an all-purpose intensifier. It has a specific meaning: "exactly what the words say." The sentence "The defendant was literally on pins and needles waiting to hear the verdict" means that somehow the defendant was positioned atop pins and needles.

*Lose/Loose.   "Lose" is the opposite of "win": "I am afraid you will lose in court." It can also mean "to mislay." "Loose" is the opposite of "tight": "The victim described his attacker as wearing loose clothing."

On/Upon.   In almost every instance, "upon" is just a more stilted way of saying "on." Some writers still prefer "upon" when they want to convey an upward motion, but in most other circumstances, "on" is preferable.

*Principal/Principle.   "Principle" is a noun meaning a "rule, truth, or doctrine": "The principle of negligence per se may make the plaintiff's evidentiary burden easier." "Principal" can be a noun meaning "the head person or official." In finance, "principal" also means "the capital sum," as distinguished from interest: "The principal of Lincoln High School authorized an investment that earned less than one percent on the principal." In criminal law, a principal is the chief actor or perpetrator or aider and abettor present at the commission of the crime. In real estate, a principal is a person who empowers another to act as his or her representative: "The broker owes his principal, the seller, loyalty and good faith."

"Principal" as an adjective means "main" or "chief": "The principal question before the jury is whether the eyewitness is credible."

Proved/Proven.   Use "proved" as the past participle of the verb and "proven" as an adjective. "The defendant has proved that he was at work at the time of the murder."

The reason is because.   Do not use this construction. Replace with "the reason is that."

Supposed to/Used to.   Be sure to include the final "d" in both expressions.

Sure and/Sure to.   Always use "be sure to."

Try and/Try to.   Always use "try to."

*Than/Then.   Use "than" for comparisons, such as "taller than," "greater than," "more than," and "rather than." Use "then" to denote a time.

That (When it cannot be omitted).   Do not omit the subordinate conjunction "that" when it will prevent a possible misreading. This problem occurs when a noun clause is used as the direct object. In such cases, the subject of the noun clause alone can be misread as the direct object. *Incorrect:* "Florida courts found a woman who had attempted three suicides and had been committed to a state mental hospital was an unfit and improper person." *Corrected:* "Florida courts found that a woman who had attempted three suicides and had been committed to a state mental hospital was an unfit and improper person."

That/Which/Who.   Use "that" and "which" for things; use "who" for people. Use "that" for restrictive clauses and "which" for nonrestrictive clauses: "The defendant's truck, which does not have oversized tires, was identified by the victim as the vehicle that hit him." The clause "which does not have oversized tires" is nonrestrictive because it does not restrict or limit the meaning of "defendant's truck." Unless the defendant has more than one truck and the reader needs the clause to determine which truck is meant, the phrase "defendant's truck" is already clearly identified. The clause "that hit him," on the other hand, restricts or limits the meaning of the noun "vehicle."

    Exception: "Which" is used in restrictive clauses that use the constructions "that which," "of which," or "in which."

*Their/There/They're.   "Their" is the possessive form of "they." "There" denotes a place ("stay there"), or it can be used as an expletive ("There is one last point I want to make"). "They're" is a contraction for "they are."

Through/Thru.   Always use "through."

Thus/Thusly.   Always use "thus."

*To/Too/Two.   "To" is a preposition with a great number of functional and idiomatic uses: "The defendant drove back to the city. To his surprise, the police had set up a roadblock. Ultimately, he was sentenced to death." "Too" is an adverb meaning "also," "very," or "excessively": "His story was too implausible." "Two" is the number.

Toward/Towards.   Both are acceptable; "toward" is preferred in the United States because it is shorter.

Use/Utilize.   Whenever possible, use "use."

When/Where.   "When" denotes a time; "where" denotes a place. When indicating a particular situation, choose "when" or "in which," not "where." Avoid the expression "a case where . . . ." A case is not a place. Replace with "a case in which . . . ." Common practice, however, seems to be to use "where" in parentheticals after citations.

Which/Who.   "Which" should not be used to refer to people.

Who/Whom.   Use "who" in most subject positions and "whom" in most object positions. (See below for the exception.)

    This rule of thumb means, however, that you will have to analyze a sentence before you can determine whether "who" or "whom" is correct. One easy way to analyze question sentences is to answer the question. If in the answer you use the subjective form ("I," "we," "he," "she," or "they"), then use *who* in the question. If in the answer you use the objective form ("me," "us," "him," "her," or "them"), then use *whom* in the question.

> <u>Who</u> is calling? (He is calling.)
> *(subject)*

> To <u>whom</u> does the clerk report? (The clerk reports to her.)
> *(object)*

For some questions, you may find it easier to determine whether to use "who" or "whom" if you recast the sentence in normal subject/verb/object order.

> <u>Whom</u> should I pay?
> *(object)*

> I should pay <u>whom</u>? (I should pay them.)

The greatest confusion concerning "who/whom" occurs in sentences in which the same pronoun appears to be the object of one part of the sentence and the subject of another part of the sentence.

> The police questioned a woman who they thought matched the victim's description.

The sentence above is correct. Although "who" may appear to be the object of "they thought," it is actually the subject of "matched the victim's description." A simple way to determine which form of the pronoun is correct in such situations is to mentally delete the subject/verb immediately after the "who" or "whom." If the sentence still makes sense, use "who"; if not, use "whom."

> The police questioned a woman who ~~they thought~~ matched the victim's description.

Use the same method to determine that "whom" is the correct choice in the following example.

> The man whom the police questioned matched the victim's description of her assailant.

> The man whom ~~the police questioned~~ matched the victim's description of her assailant.

When the subject and verb following the "who/whom" slot are

deleted, the sentence no longer makes sense. Notice too that you can isolate the clause "whom the police questioned," put it in normal order, "the police questioned whom," and answer the question ("the police questioned him") to determine that "whom" is the correct form.

Exception: The one exception to the rule is that "whom" is used for subjects of infinitives.

Whom does our client want to represent him?

Our client wants whom to represent him? (normal word order)

Our client wants her to represent him. (Answer the question or substitute another pronoun.)

Your/You're.   "Your" is the possessive form of "you." "You're" is the contraction for "you are."

Glossary of Terms

Active voice. Active voice is the quality of a transitive verb in which the action of the verb is performed by the subject: "Judges decide cases."

Advance Sheets. Advance sheets contain the most recent court decisions. Advance sheets are provided for most reporters, for example, for *United States Reports,* West's regional reporters, and official state reporters. Advance sheets are usually published bimonthly in soft bound pamphlets.

Alliteration. Alliteration is the repetition of consonant sounds as in "Peter Piper picked a peck of pickled peppers."

Analogous case. An analogous case is a case that is factually similar to the client's case. An argument based on an analogous case is an argument in which the attorney compares or contrasts the facts in a factually similar case with the facts in the client's case.

Analysis. When you analyze something, you examine it closely, identifying each part and determining how the parts are related. In law, there are two types of analysis: statutory analysis, which involves the close examination of a statute, and case analysis, which involves the close examination of a case.

Assonance. Assonance is the repetition of vowel sounds.

Bias-free language. Bias-free language is language that suggests that persons from minority racial, religious, and ethnic groups are valued members of society. The term is also used to refer to language that is sensitive to perceptions about the poor, the elderly, the disabled, and homosexuals.

Case law. Although the term "case law" is often used to refer to common law, in fact its meaning is broader. It refers to all court decisions including those interpreting or applying enacted law.

Case briefing. Case briefing is a technique used to analyze a court's written opinion. A case brief usually contains a summary of the facts, a statement of the issue(s), the court's holding, and the court's rationale.

Common law. The common law is a system of law created by the judicial branch. For example, much of tort law is common law; the causes of action and rules were created by the courts rather than by the legislature.

Concluding sentence. A concluding sentence in a paragraph is the sentence that sums up the main point of the paragraph. Although not every paragraph will have a concluding sentence, in those that do the concluding sentence is invariably the last sentence in the paragraph.

Connotation. The connotation of a word is all the associations the word carries with it. For example, the word "lawyer" may have positive connotations for individuals who respect lawyers or who aspire to be lawyers, but it may have negative connotations for people who have had bad experiences with lawyers. (Compare with **Denotation.**)

Denotation. The denotation of a word is its dictionary definition. (Compare with **Connotation.**)

Dicta. Comments made by a court that are not directly related to the issue before it or that are not necessary to its holding are dicta. Such comments are often preceded by the word "if": "If the evidence had established ...." Although in some cases dicta are easily identifiable, in other cases they may not be. If the issue is broadly defined, the statement may be part of the court's holding; if the issue is narrowly defined, the statement is dicta. Compare with **Holding.**

Dovetailing. Dovetailing is the overlap of language between two sentences that creates a bridge between those two sentences. Dovetails are often created by moving the connecting idea to the end of the first sentence and the beginning of the second sentence, repeating key words, using pronouns to refer back to nouns an earlier sentence, and using "hook words" (this, that, these, such) and a summarizing noun.

Elements analysis. When you do an elements analysis, you systematically analyze a set of requirements set out either in a statute or as part of a common law doctrine by determining whether, given a particular set of facts, each requirement is met.

Emotionally significant fact. An emotionally significant fact is one that, while not legally significant, may affect the way the judge or jury decides the case.

Enacted law. Enacted law is law created by the legislative or executive branches. Statutes and regulations are enacted law.

Finding. A finding is a decision on a question of fact. For example, a trial court judge may find a defendant incompetent to stand trial, or a jury may find that a police officer acted in good faith. Compare with **Holding.**

Generic transition.   Generic transitions are those transitions that are commonly used in writing to describe standard mental moves, such as "consequently" to show cause/effect or "however" to show contrast.

Headnote.   A headnote is a one-sentence summary of a rule of law found at the beginning of a court's opinion. Because headnotes are written by an attorney employed by the company publishing the reporter in which the opinion appears and not the court, they cannot be cited as authority.

Holding.   A holding is the court's decision in a particular case. "When the court applied the rule to the facts of the case, it held that . . . ." Thus, a holding has two components: a reference to the applicable rule of law and a reference to the specific facts to which that rule was applied. Because the holding is the answer to the legal question, it can be formulated by turning the issue (a question) into a statement. Compare with **Dicta.**

Integrated format.   The phrase "integrated format" refers to a method of organizing the discussion section of an objective memorandum. Instead of using the script format, in which the discussion section is organized around the arguments that each side makes, the writer organizes the discussion around legal principles or points.

Legalese.   Legalese is a broad term used to describe several common features of legal writing such as the use of archaic language, Latin terms, boilerplate language, and long and convoluted sentences. "Legalese" is usually a pejorative term.

Legally significant fact.   A legally significant fact is a fact that a court would consider significant either in deciding that a statute or rule is applicable or in applying that statute or rule.

Mandatory authority.   Mandatory authority is law that a court must apply in deciding the case before it.

Metaphor.   Metaphor is a direct comparison. For example, a journey is often a metaphor for life.

Nominalization.   Nominalization is the process of converting verbs into nouns (determine → determination).

Nonsexist language.   Nonsexist language is language that treats males and females as having equal value. It does not assume being male is the norm or that certain jobs or positions are primarily filled by males or females.

Onomatopoeia.   Onomatopoeia is the quality some words have when they sound like what they mean. For example, "plop" and "slap" both tend to sound like what they mean.

Orienting transitions.   Orienting transitions are transitions that provide a context for the information that follows. They locate the reader physically, logically, or chronologically.

Paragraph block. A paragraph block is a group of two or more paragraphs that together develop a point within a larger document.

Paragraph coherence. A paragraph has coherence when the various points raised in the paragraph are connected to each other. Common connecting devices include repetition of key words, transitional phrases, parallelism, and pronouns.

Paragraph unity. A paragraph has unity when all the points raised in the paragraph are related to one larger point, the paragraph's topic.

Passive voice. Passive voice is the quality of a transitive verb in which the subject receives rather than performs the action of the verb: "Cases are decided by judges."

Personification. Personification is the attribution of human qualities or characteristics to abstractions or inanimate objects.

Persuasive authority. Persuasive authority is law or commentary that a court may consider in deciding the case before it.

Plain English. Plain English is the term used to describe a movement to encourage the use of simple, straightforward language (in professions such as law) that is readily understandable by lay people. In other countries, the same movement is referred to as the "Plain Language Movement."

Policy argument. A policy argument is one in which the attorney argues that a particular interpretation of a statute, regulation, or common law rule is (or is not) consistent with current public policy, that is, the objective underlying a particular law. For example, child custody laws usually seek to provide stability for children; environmental laws usually try to balance the interests of developers and preservationists.

Purple prose. Purple prose is the overuse of flowery language that draws attention to itself.

Raise and dismiss. You can raise and dismiss issues, elements, and arguments. In each case, both sides will agree on the point; therefore, extensive analysis is not necessary. However, a writer goes through the raise-and-dismiss process to assure the reader that the point was considered.

Roadmap. Roadmaps are introductory paragraphs that give readers an overview of an entire document or a section of a document.

Rule. The rule is the legal standard that the court applies in deciding the issue before it. In some cases, the rule will be enacted law (a constitutional provision, statute, or regulation); in other cases, it will be a court rule (one of the Federal Rules of Civil Procedure); and in still other cases, it will be a common law rule or doctrine. Although in the latter case the rule may be announced in the context of a particular case, rules are not case-specific. They are the general standards that are applied in all cases. Compare with **Test**.

***Shepard's* citators.** *Shepard's* citators are books containing the information needed to update various authorities and to locate authorities that have cited particular sources. There are *Shepard's* citators for most state and regional reporters, state and federal statutes, law reviews, uniform laws, restatements, and a number of other sources.

Shepardizing. Shepardizing is the process used to determine the current status of an authority and to locate sources that have cited that authority. For example, an attorney would shepardize a court's opinion to determine whether it had been reversed, overruled, questioned, or followed and to locate other, more recent authorities that have cited the case as authority.

Signposts. Signposts are words and phrases that keep readers oriented as they move through a document. Transitional phrases, particularly ones like "first," "second," and "third," are the most common signposts. Topic sentences can also be considered a type of signpost.

Simile. Similes are indirect comparisons that use "like" or "as," such as "his mind is like a steel trap."

Slip opinion. A slip opinion is a court's written opinion in the form originally released by the court. For example, many state courts originally release their opinions in typed form. Slip opinions are not generally available to researchers.

Standard of review. "Standard of review" refers to the level of scrutiny an appellate court will use to review a trial court's decision. For example, in *de novo* review the appellate court does not give any deference to the decision of the trial court; it decides the issue independently. In contrast, when the standard of review is abuse of discretion, the appellate court defers to the trial court, reversing its decision only when there is not evidence to support it.

Substantive transitions. Substantive transitions are connecting words and phrases that also add content. Unlike generic transitions, which signal standard mental moves, substantive transitions tend to be document-specific. (See also **Dovetailing.**)

Synthesis. When you do synthesis, you bring the pieces together into a coherent whole. For example, when you synthesize a series of cases, you identify the unifying principle or principles.

Term of art. Although sometimes used to describe any word or phrase that has a "legal ring" to it, "term of art" means a technical word or phrase with a specific meaning. "Certiorari" is a true term of art; "reasonable person" is not.

Test. Although the words "rule" and "test" are sometimes used interchangeably, they are not the same. A test is used to determine whether a rule is met. Compare with **Rule.**

Topic sentence. A topic sentence is the sentence in a paragraph that introduces the key point in the paragraph or that states the topic of the paragraph. Topic sentences are often the first sentence in a paragraph.

Voice. Voice is the active or passive quality of a transitive verb.

Index